Weapons of the Weak

Weapons of the Weak

EVERYDAY FORMS OF PEASANT RESISTANCE

James C. Scott

YALE UNIVERSITY PRESS   NEW HAVEN AND LONDON

Designed by Nancy Ovedovitz and set in Garamond
No. 3 type by Brevis Press, Bethany, Connecticut.
Printed in the United States of America by
Courier Companies, Inc.

Library of Congress Catalog Card Number: 85–51779
International Standard Book Number: 0-300-03641-8 (pbk.)

The paper in this book meets the guidelines for
permanence and durability of the Committee on
Production Guidelines for Book Longevity of the
Council on Library Resources.

20   19   18   17   16   15   14   13   12

For Skip, Bernice, and Elinore
and with gratitude to Z and other friends in "Sedaka"

It is clear that no Herostratus among them has dared to go into the remote countryside to study the permanent conspiracy of those whom we still call "the weak" against those who believe themselves "strong"—of the peasantry against the rich. . . . is it not critical to portray at last this peasant who thwarts the [legal] Code by reducing private property into something that simultaneously exists and does not exist? You shall see this tireless sapper, this nibbler, gnawing the land into little bits, carving an acre into a hundred pieces, and invited always to this feast by a petite bourgeoisie which finds in him, at the same time, its ally and its prey. . . . Out of the reach of the law by virtue of his insignificance, this Robespierre, with a single head and twenty million hands, works ceaselessly, crouching in every commune . . . bearing arms in the National Guard in every district of France, since by 1830, France does not recall that Napoleon preferred to run the risk of his misfortunes rather than to arm the masses.

Honoré de Balzac
Letter to P. S. B. Gavault
introducing *Les Paysans*

Do not imagine that Tonsard, or his old mother or his wife and children ever said in so many words, "we steal for a living and do our stealing cleverly." These habits had grown slowly. The family began by mixing a few green boughs with the dead wood; then, emboldened by habit and by a calculated impunity (part of the scheme to be developed in this story), after twenty years the family had gotten to the point of taking the wood as if it were *their own* and making a living almost entirely by theft. The rights of pasturing their cows, the abuse of gleaning grain, of gleaning grapes, had gotten established little by little in this fashion. By the time the Tonsards and the other lazy peasants of the valley had tasted the benefits of these four rights acquired by the poor in the countryside, rights pushed to the point of pillage, one can imagine that they were unlikely to renounce them unless compelled by a force stronger than their audacity.

Balzac, *Les Paysans*

. . . the binary division between resistance and non-resistance is an unreal one. The existence of those who seem not to rebel is a warren of minute, individual, autonomous tactics and strategies which counter and inflect the visible facts of overall domination, and whose purposes and calculations, desires and choices resist any simple division into the political and the apolitical. The schema of a strategy of resistance as a vanguard of politicisation needs to be subjected to re-examination, and account must be taken of resistances whose strategy is one of evasion or defence—the Schweijks as well as the Solzhenitsyns. There are no good subjects of resistance.

Colin Gordon on Michel Foucault, *Power/Knowledge*

Contents

Maps

Tables

Appendix Tables

Preface

The limitations of any field of study are most strikingly revealed in its shared definitions of what counts as relevant. A great deal of the recent work on the peasantry—my own as well as that of others—concerns rebellions and revolutions. Excepting always the standard ethnographic accounts of kinship, ritual, cultivation, and language—it is fair to say that much attention has been devoted to organized, large-scale, protest movements that appear, if only momentarily, to pose a threat to the state. I can think of a host of mutually reinforcing reasons why this shared understanding of relevance should prevail. On the left, it is apparent that the inordinate attention devoted to peasant insurrections was stimulated by the Vietnam war and by a now fading left-wing, academic romance with wars of national liberation. The historical record and the archives—both resolutely centered on the state's interests—abetted this romance by not mentioning peasants except when their activities were menacing. Otherwise the peasantry appeared only as anonymous contributors to statistics on conscription, crop production, taxes, and so forth. There was something for everyone in this perspective. For some, it emphasized willy-nilly the role of outsiders—prophets, radical intelligentsia, political parties—in mobilizing an otherwise supine, disorganized peasantry. For others, it focused on just the kinds of movements with which social scientists in the West were most familiar—those with names, banners, tables of organization, and formal leadership. For still others, it had the merit of examining precisely those movements that seemed to promise large-scale, structural change at the level of the state.

What is missing from this perspective, I believe, is the simple fact that most subordinate classes throughout most of history have rarely been afforded the luxury of open, organized, political activity. Or, better stated, such activity was dangerous, if not suicidal. Even when the option did exist, it is not clear that the same objectives might not also be pursued by other stratagems. Most subordinate classes are, after all, far less interested in changing the larger structures of the state and the law than in what Hobsbawm has appropriately called "working the system . . . to their minimum disadvantage."[1] Formal, organized political activity, even if clandestine and revolutionary, is typically the preserve of the middle class and the intelligentsia; to look for peasant politics in this realm is to look largely in vain. It is also—not incidentally—the first step toward concluding that the peasantry is a political nullity unless organized and led by outsiders.

And for all their importance when they do occur, peasant rebellions—let alone

1. Eric Hobsbawm, "Peasants and Politics," *Journal of Peasant Studies* 1, no. 1 (1973): 3–22.

revolutions—are few and far between. The vast majority are crushed unceremoniously. When, more rarely, they do succeed, it is a melancholy fact that the consequences are seldom what the peasantry had in mind. Whatever else revolutions may achieve—and I have no desire to gainsay these achievements—they also typically bring into being a vaster and more dominant state apparatus that is capable of battening itself on its peasant subjects even more effectively than its predecessors.

For these reasons it seemed to me more important to understand what we might call *everyday* forms of peasant resistance—the prosaic but constant struggle between the peasantry and those who seek to extract labor, food, taxes, rents, and interest from them. Most forms of this struggle stop well short of outright collective defiance. Here I have in mind the ordinary weapons of relatively powerless groups: foot dragging, dissimulation, desertion, false compliance, pilfering, feigned ignorance, slander, arson, sabotage, and so on. These Brechtian— or Schweikian—forms of class struggle have certain features in common. They require little or no coordination or planning; they make use of implicit understandings and informal networks; they often represent a form of individual self-help; they typically avoid any direct, symbolic confrontation with authority. To understand these commonplace forms of resistance is to understand much of what the peasantry has historically done to defend its interests against both conservative and progressive orders. It is my guess that just such kinds of resistance are often the most significant and the most effective over the long run. Thus, Marc Bloch, the historian of feudalism, has noted that the great millenial movements were "flashes in the pan" compared to the "patient, silent struggles stubbornly carried on by rural communities" to avoid claims on their surplus and to assert their rights to the means of production—for example, arable, woodland, pastures.[2] Much the same view is surely appropriate to the study of slavery in the New World. The rare, heroic, and foredoomed gestures of a Nat Turner or a John Brown are simply not the places to look for the struggle between slaves and their owners. One must look rather at the constant, grinding conflict over work, food, autonomy, ritual—at everyday forms of resistance. In the Third World it is rare for peasants to risk an outright confrontation with the authorities over taxes, cropping patterns, development policies, or onerous new laws; instead they are likely to nibble away at such policies by noncompliance, foot dragging, deception. In place of a land invasion, they prefer piecemeal squatting; in place of open mutiny, they prefer desertion; in place of attacks on public or private grain stores, they prefer pilfering. When such stratagems are abandoned in favor of more quixotic action, it is usually a sign of great desperation.

Such low-profile techniques are admirably suited to the social structure of the

2. Marc Bloch, *French Rural History,* trans. Janet Sondheimer (Berkeley: Univ. of California Press, 1970), 170.

peasantry—a class scattered across the countryside, lacking formal organization, and best equipped for extended, guerrilla-style, defensive campaigns of attrition. Their individual acts of foot dragging and evasion, reinforced by a venerable popular culture of resistance and multiplied many thousand-fold, may, in the end, make an utter shambles of the policies dreamed up by their would-be superiors in the capital. Everyday forms of resistance make no headlines. But just as millions of anthozoan polyps create, willy-nilly, a coral reef, so do the multiple acts of peasant insubordination and evasion create political and economic barrier reefs of their own. It is largely in this fashion that the peasantry makes its political presence felt. And whenever, to pursue the simile, the ship of state runs aground on such reefs, attention is usually directed to the shipwreck itself and not to the vast aggregation of petty acts that made it possible. For these reasons alone, it seems important to understand this quiet and anonymous welter of peasant action.

To this end, I spent two years (1978–80) in a Malaysian village. The village, which I call Sedaka, not its real name, was a small (seventy-household), rice-farming community in the main paddy-growing area of Kedah, which had begun double-cropping in 1972. As in so many other "green revolutions" the rich have gotten richer and the poor have remained poor or grown poorer. The introduction of huge combine-harvesters in 1976 was perhaps the coup de grace, as it eliminated two-thirds of the wage-earning opportunities for smallholders and landless laborers. In the course of two years I managed to collect an enormous amount of relevant material. My attention was directed as much to the ideological struggle in the village—which underwrites resistance—as to the practice of resistance itself. Throughout the book I try to raise the larger issues of resistance, class struggle, and ideological domination that give these issues their practical and theoretical significance.

The struggle between rich and poor in Sedaka is not merely a struggle over work, property rights, grain, and cash. It is also a struggle over the appropriation of symbols, a struggle over how the past and present shall be understood and labeled, a struggle to identify causes and assess blame, a contentious effort to give partisan meaning to local history. The details of this struggle are not pretty, as they entail backbiting, gossip, character assassination, rude nicknames, gestures, and silences of contempt which, for the most part, are confined to the backstage of village life. In public life—that is to say, in power-laden settings—a carefully calculated conformity prevails for the most part. What is remarkable about this aspect of class conflict is the extent to which it requires a shared worldview. Neither gossip nor character assassination, for example, makes much sense unless there are shared standards of what is deviant, unworthy, impolite. In one sense, the ferociousness of the argument *depends* on the fact that it appeals to shared values that have been, it is claimed, betrayed. What is in dispute is not values but the facts to which those values might apply: who is rich, who is poor, how rich, how poor, is so-and-so stingy, does so-and-so shirk work? Apart from the sanctioning power of mobilized social opinion, much of this struggle can also be read as an effort by the poor to resist the economic and ritual marginalization they now suffer and to insist on the minimal cultural decencies of citizenship in this small community. The perspective adopted amounts to an implicit plea for the value of a "meaning-centered" account of class relations. In the final chapter I try to spell out the implications of the account for broader issues of ideological domination and hegemony.

The fourteen months I spent in Sedaka were filled with the mixture of elation, depression, missteps, and drudgery that any anthropologist will recognize. As I was not a card-carrying anthropologist, the whole experience was entirely new to me. I do not know what I would have done without the very practical lectures on fieldwork sent to me by F. G. Bailey. Even with this wise advice, I was not prepared for the elementary fact that an anthropologist is at work from the moment he opens his eyes in the morning until he closes them at night. In the first few months, perhaps half my trips to the outhouse were for no purpose other than to find a moment of solitude. I found the need for a judicious neutrality—that is, biting my tongue—to be well-advised and, at the same time, an enormous psychological burden. The growth of my own "hidden transcript" (see chapter 7) made me appreciate for the first time the truth of Jean Duvignaud's comment: "For the most part, the village yields itself to the investigator and often he is the one to take refuge in concealment."[3] I also found neighbors who were forgiving of my inevitable mistakes, who were tolerant—to a point—of my curiosity, who overlooked my incompetence and allowed me to work beside them, who had the rare ability to laugh at me and with me at the same time, who had the dignity and courage to draw boundaries, whose sense of sociability included talking literally all night if the talk was animated and it was not harvest season, and whose kindness meant that they adapted better to me than I to them. What my time among them meant for my life and my work, the word gratitude cannot begin to cover.

Despite a determined effort to trim the manuscript, it remains long. The main reason for this is that a certain amount of storytelling seems absolutely essential to convey the texture and conduct of class relations. Since each story has at least two sides, it becomes necessary to allow also for the "Roshomon effect" that social conflict creates. Another reason for including some narrative has to do with the effort, toward the end, to move from a close-to-the-ground study of class relations to a fairly high altitude. These larger considerations require, I think, the flesh and blood of detailed instances to take on substance. An example is not only the most successful way of embodying a generalization, but also has the advantage of always being richer and more complex than the principles that are drawn from it.

3. Jean Duvignaud, *Change at Shebika: Report From a North African Village* (New York: Pantheon, 1970), 217.

Wherever the translation from Malay was not straightforward, or where the Malay itself was of interest, I have included it in the text or footnotes. As I never used a tape recorder, except for formal speeches given by outsiders, I worked from fragmentary notes made while talking or immediately afterward. The result is that the Malay has something of a telegraphic quality, since only the more memorable fragments of many sentences were recoverable. Early in my stay, as well, when the rural Kedah dialect was strange to my ears, quite a few villagers spoke to me in the simpler Malay they might use at the market. A glossary of specific Kedah dialect terms that appear in the text and notes will be found in appendix D.

This book is for a special reason, I suspect, more the product of its subjects than most village studies. When I began research, my idea was to develop my analysis, write the study, and then return to the village to collect the reactions, opinions, and criticisms of villagers to a short oral version of my findings. These reactions would then comprise the final chapter—a kind of "villagers talk back" section or, if you like, "reviews" of the book by those who should know. I did in fact spend the better part of the last two months in Sedaka collecting such opinions from most villagers. Amidst a variety of comments—often reflecting the speaker's class—were a host of insightful criticisms, corrections, and suggestions of issues I had missed. All of this changed the analysis but presented a problem. Should I subject the reader to the earlier and stupider version of my analysis and only at the end spring the insights the villagers had brought forward? This was my first thought, but as I wrote I found it impossible to write as if I did not know what I now knew, so I gradually smuggled all those insights into my own analysis. The result is to understate the extent to which the villagers of Sedaka were responsible for the analysis as well as raw material of the study and to make what was a complex conversation seem more like a soliloquy.

Finally, I should emphasize that this is, quite self-consciously, a study of local class relations. This means that peasant-state relations, which might easily justify a volume on resistance, are conspicuously absent except as they impinge on local class relations. It means that issues of ethnic conflict or religious movements or protest, which would almost certainly become important in any political crisis, are also largely bracketed. It means that economic origins of the petty class relations examined here, which might easily be traced all the way to the board rooms of New York City and Tokyo, are not analyzed. It means that formal party politics at the provincial or national level is neglected. From one point of view all these omissions are regrettable. From another perspective the effort here is to show how important, rich, and complex local class relations can be and what we can potentially learn from an analysis that is *not* centered on the state, on formal organizations, on open protest, on national issues.

The unseemly length of the acknowledgments that follow is indicative of how much I had to learn and of the patience and generosity of those who taught me.

To the families of "Sedaka," whose names are disguised for obvious reasons, I owe a great personal debt—a debt that is the heavier because more than one would feel their hospitality abused by what I have written. That is, of course, the human dilemma of the professional outsider, and I can only hope that they will find what follows an honest effort, by my own dim lights, to do justice to what I saw and heard.

My institutional affiliation while in Malaysia was with the School of Comparative Social Sciences at the Universiti Sains Malaysia in Penang. I could not have been more fortunate as a guest or scholar. At the School, I want particularly to thank Mansor Marican, Chandra Muzaffar, Mohd Shadli Abdullah, Cheah Boon Kheng, Khoo Kay Jin, Colin Abraham, the Deputy Vice-Chancellor—then Dean—Kamal Salih, and Assistant Dean Amir Hussin Baharuddin for their advice and kindness. Nafisah bte. Mohamed was an exceptional tutor of the Kedah dialect who helped me prepare for the fieldwork. The Centre for Policy Research at USM has conducted much of the finest research on the Muda Scheme in Kedah and, for that matter, on agrarian policy anywhere. Lim Teck Ghee and David Gibbons of the Centre not only helped me plan the research but became valued friends and critics whose efforts are evident throughout the book—even when I decided to go my own way. Thanks are also due Sukur Kasim, Harun Din, Ikmal Said, George Elliston, and, of course, the Director of the Centre, K. J. Ratnam. Officials of the Muda Agricultural Development Authority's headquarters in Teluk Chengai near Alor Setar were unfailingly generous with their time, their statistics, and above all their great experience. One would look long and hard in any development project to find officials whose learning, rigor, and candor would match that of Affifuddin Haji Omar and S. Jegatheesan. Datuk Tamin Yeop, then General Manager of MADA, was also very helpful.

Members of the "invisible college" working and writing on rural Malaysian society whose paths crossed my own contributed enormously to my understanding. They are numerous and I shall undoubtedly overlook a few. Some might well prefer not to be implicated at all. But I should mention Syed Husin Ali, Wan Zawawi Ibrahim, Shaharil Talib, Jomo Sundaram, Wan Hashim, Rosemary Barnard, Aihwa Ong, Shamsul Amri Baharuddin, Diana Wong, Donald Nonini, William Roff, Judith and Shuichi Nagata, Lim Mah Hui, Marie-André Couillard, Rodolfe de Koninck, Lorraine Corner, and Akira Takahashi. Two staff members from Universiti Sains who came to Yale for graduate work, Mansor Haji Othman and S. Ahmad Hussein, were important sources of advice and criticism. Finally, I should single out the generosity of Kenzo Horii of the Institute of Developing Economies in Tokyo, who conducted a study of land tenure in Sedaka in 1968 and made the results available to me so that I could establish what a decade of change had meant.

The final manuscript was much changed thanks to the detailed criticism of colleagues. I made painful cuts; I dropped arguments they thought ludicrous or irrelevant—or both; I added historical and analytical material they thought necessary. Even when I spurned their wisdom, I was often driven to strengthen or shift my position to make it less vulnerable to a direct hit. Enough is enough, however; if they had had their way completely, I would still be at work revising and trying to reconcile the confusion they unwittingly sowed. I cannot wait to return the favor. Thanks to Ben Anderson, Michael Adas, Clive Kessler, Sam Popkin (yes, that's right), Mansor Haji Othman, Lim Teck Ghee, David Gibbons, Georg Elwert, Edward Friedman, Frances Fox Piven, Jan Gross, Jonathan Rieder, Diana Wong, Ben Kerkvliet, Bill Kelly, Vivienne Shue, Gerald Jaynes, and Bob Harms. There are unnamed others who agreed to read the manuscript— or even solicited it—and who, perhaps on seeing its bulk, had second thoughts. They know who they are. Shame!

A good many institutions helped keep me and this enterprise afloat since 1978. In particular, I should like to thank the John Simon Guggenheim Memorial Foundation, the National Science Foundation (Grant No. SOC 78-02756), and Yale University for support while in Malaysia. Most recently a postdoctoral Exxon Fellowship awarded by the Science, Technology, and Society Program of Massachusetts Institute of Technology made it possible to complete the final draft and most of the revisions. Carl Kaysen was tolerant of my preoccupation with the manuscript and, together with Martin Kreiger, Kenneth Kenniston, Charles Weiner, Peter Buck, Loren Graham, Carla Kirmani, Leo Marx, and Emma Rothschild, helped make my stay intellectually rewarding. A symposium on "History and Peasant Consciousness in Southeast Asia" sponsored by the National Museum of Ethnology in Osaka, Japan, and arranged by Shigeharu Tanabe and Andrew Turton helped sharpen my perspective. Another and more contentious workshop organized with the help of the Social Science Research Council and held at the Institute of Social Studies in The Hague was responsible for the analysis of resistance in chapter 7. I doubt if any of the participants of either exchange would want to subscribe fully to the argument I advance, but they should at least know how valuable their own writing and criticism have been for this work.

Thanks are due the following publications in which small portions of an earlier draft have appeared: *International Political Science Review* (October 1973); *History and Peasant Consciousness in Southeast Asia,* edited by Andrew Turton and Shigeharo Tanabe, Senri Ethnological Studies, No. 13 (Osaka: National Museum of Ethnology, 1984); *Political Anthropology* (1982); and, in Malay, *Kajian Malaysia* 1:1 (June 1983).

There are a good many typists, processors of words, and editors who are delighted that this manuscript is now out of their hands. Among the most delighted are Beverly Apothaker, Kay Mansfield, and Ruth Muessig; I do want to thank them for their fine work.

The relationship between this book and my family life is complex enough to rule out any of the banalities that usually appear in this space. Suffice it to say that, try though I may, I have never remotely persuaded Louise and our children that their function is to help me write books.

1 • Small Arms Fire
in the Class War

This is, exactly, *not* to argue that "morality" is some "autonomous region" of human choice and will, arising independently of the historical process. Such a view of morality has never been materialist enough, and hence it has often reduced that formidable inertia—and sometimes formidable revolutionary force—into a wishful idealist fiction. It is to say, on the contrary, that every contradiction is a conflict of value as well as a conflict of interest; that inside every "need" there is an affect, or "want," on its way to becoming an "ought" (and *vice versa*); that every class struggle is at the same time a struggle over values.

E. P. Thompson, *The Poverty of Theory*

RAZAK

The narrow path that serves as the thoroughfare of this small rice-farming village was busier than usual that morning. Groups of women were on their way to transplant the irrigated crop and men were bicycling their children to the early session of school in the nearby town of Kepala Batas. My children were all gathered, as usual, at the windows to watch as each passerby gazed our way from the moment the house came into view until it passed from view. This scene had become, in the space of a few weeks, a daily ritual. The villagers of Sedaka were satisfying their curiosity about the strange family in their midst. My children, on the other hand, were satisfying a more malevolent curiosity. They had come to resent mildly their status of goldfish in a bowl and were convinced that sooner or later someone would forget himself while craning his neck and walk or bicycle straight into the ditch alongside the path. The comic possibility had caught their imagination and, when it inevitably happened, they wanted to be there.

But something was amiss. A small, quiet knot of people had formed in front of the house next door and some passersby had paused to talk with them. Hamzah and his older brother, Razak, were there, as was Razak's wife, Azizah, and the village midwife, Tok Sah Bidan.[1] The tone was too subdued and grave to be casual and Azizah, along with other women from poor families, would normally have already left for work with her transplanting group. Before I could

---

1. A list of dramatis personae for this study, together with a map of the village and its environs, may be found in chapter 4.

leave the house, Haji Kadir, the well-to-do landlord with whose family we shared the house, walked in and told me what had happened. "Razak's little child is dead, the one born two seasons ago." "It's her fate; her luck wasn't good."[2]

The details were straightforward. Two days ago the child had come down with a fever. It was the end of the dry season in Kedah when fevers are expected, but this seemed to be more than the ordinary fever, perhaps measles, someone suggested. Yesterday she had been taken to Lebai Sabrani, a highly venerated religious teacher and traditional healer in the adjoining village of Sungai Tongkang. He recited verses of the Koran over her and suggested a poultice for her forehead. I am implicated in this too, Razak told me later. Had I not been visiting another village, he would have asked me to drive the child to a clinic or to the hospital in the state capital, Alor Setar. As it was, he did ask Shamsul, the only other automobile owner in the village, and was told that it would cost M$15 for gas. Razak did not have any money or, I suspect, enough confidence in hospitals to press the matter, and his daughter died shortly before dawn the next day.

Instinctively, I started for Razak's place, behind Hamzah's house, where the body would customarily be on view. Razak stopped me and said, "No, not there. We put her in Hamzah's house; it's nicer here." His embarrassment was evident from the way he avoided meeting my eyes.

Razak is the "down-and-out"[3] of the village, and his house was not only an embarrassment to him; it was a collective humiliation for much of Sedaka. When I had arrived in the village, Razak and his family were living *under* the house, not in it. Two walls of attap[4] and bamboo had fallen away and much of the roof had collapsed. "They live like chickens in a henhouse, a lean-to, not like Malays," villagers said with derision. Not long after that, the local leader of the ruling party, Basir, mindful of the fact that Razak had joined his party and embarrassed that any Malays in his village should live on the ground like the beasts of the field, got the subdistrict chief to provide a modest sum from his discretionary funds for lumber to repair the house. A small voluntary work party, all members of the ruling party, then repaired three walls, leaving the last wall and the roof for Razak to finish. After all, Razak and Azizah made attap roofing for a living. The roof remains as it was, however, and the boards to repair the last wall are gone. Razak sold them *twice*—once to Rokiah and once to Kamil,

---

2. *Habuan dia, nasib tak baik.* Here and elsewhere in the text, when it seems important or where reasonable people might differ on the translation, I have included the original Malay in the footnotes. A brief glossary of local Kedah dialect terms that may be unfamiliar to speakers of standard, urban Malay is also provided in appendix D.

3. *Papa-kedana.*

4. Long, rectangular "shingles" stitched together from the stems and leaves of the nipah palm, which constitute the roofs and occasionally the walls of poor houses.

but only Kamil got the lumber; Rokiah calls Razak an "old liar" and says he would sell his own children. She swears she will never buy anything from him again unless she takes delivery first.

As we mounted the ladder to Hamzah's house, I realized that this was the first time I had actually entered his family's one-room living and sleeping quarters. I never did enter Razak's house or the houses of six of the other poorest families in the village. They chose instead always to receive me outside, where we squatted or sat on simple benches. We remained outside because they were embarrassed about the condition of their houses and because actually entering the house would imply a level of hospitality (coffee, biscuits) that would strain their meager resources. When possible, I made an effort to meet on neutral grounds—in the rice fields, on the path—or perhaps in one of the two small shops in the village or at the twice-weekly nearby market, where I could legitimately play host. For the rich people of the village the problem never arose; they never went to the homes of the poor. Visiting, except between equals, was always done *up* the status ladder in the village, and particularly so during the ritual visits following the end of the Moslem fasting month.[5] In fact, the pattern of visits served to define the village status hierarchy. This pattern was broken significantly only in the case of grave illness or death in a poor household, when the normal rules of hospitality were suspended out of respect for a more universal human drama.

Thus it was that the death of Maznah (Razak's daughter) had opened Hamzah's house to me and to many others. She was lying on a tiny mattress surrounded by mosquito netting strung from the rafters. Her body was wrapped in a new white cloth, and her face was barely visible beneath a lace shawl of the kind women wear for prayer. Beside the netting was incense and a tin plate. Each new visitor would, after lifting the netting to look at the child, place money on the plate: as little as 50¢, or as much as M$2. The contributions to funeral expenses, known as "lightening" or "instant donations,"[6] were especially necessary in this case since neither Razak nor many of the other very poor villagers subscribed to a death benefit society that "insures" for funeral expenses. The money on the plate at the end of the day would provide for at least the minimal decencies.

There were perhaps twenty-five villagers, mostly women, sitting on the floor of the bare room talking quietly in small groups. A few men remained to talk among themselves, but most left quickly to join the other men outside. Razak, sitting by the door, was ignored, but his isolation was not a collective act of respect for his private grief. At feasts, at other funerals, at the village shops, and even at market stalls, the other men always sat somewhat apart from Razak. He did not intrude himself. His daughter's death was no exception; the men

5. Called *Hari Raya Puasa* or simply *Hari Raya*.
6. *Derma kilat*.

who left shuffled around him as if he were a piece of furniture. On the rare occasions when he was addressed, the tone was unmistakable. A group of men sitting in one of the village stores having ice drinks and smoking would hail his arrival with "Here comes Tun Razak" followed by knowing smiles all around. "Tun Razak" was the aristocratic title of Malaysia's second prime minister, and its application to this ragtag, frail, obsequious village pariah was intended to put him in his place. Whoever was treating that day would pay for his drink, and Razak would help himself to the tobacco and cut nipah leaves used to make peasant cigarettes. He was extended the minimal courtesies but otherwise ignored, just as today the village was burying his daughter but he himself might as well have been invisible.

Directly across the path, outside the combination village hall, religious school (*madrasah*),[7] and prayer house, a few young men had begun measuring the spare boards they had rounded up for a coffin. Yaakub thought the boards were far too long and Daud, the son of the village headman, was sent back to Hamzah's house with string to measure. Meanwhile Basir arrived with hot tea and the special canvas used for the bottom of the casket. The talk turned, as it often did in the coffee shops, to an exchange of stories about Razak's many capers, most of which were established staples of village gossip. Amin shared the most recent installment having to do with the subsidies given by the government for house improvement and permanent outdoor toilets.[8] Razak, along with other members of the ruling party—and only them—was the recipient of a porcelain toilet bowl. Despite explicit warnings against selling such material, Razak had exchanged his for Amin's plastic bowl and cash and in turn sold the plastic toilet to Nor for M$15. Yaakub, to the general merriment, asked why Razak should build a toilet anyway, when he did not even have a house.[9]

Yaakub then wondered whether anyone else had seen Razak dig into the curry at the wedding feast for Rokiah's daughter two days before, a feast to which he had not been invited. Shahnon added that only yesterday, when Razak turned up at the coffee stall in the town market, he invited him to have some coffee, it being understood that Shahnon would pay. The next thing he noticed, Razak had left after having not only drunk coffee but taken three cakes and two cigarettes. Others recalled, partly for my benefit, how Razak took payment for

---

7. The two-story building built with government help some fifteen years ago is generally referred to as the *madrasah,* since the ground floor is used regularly for religious classes as well as for village meetings. The upper floor is used exclusively as a prayer house (*surau*), especially during the fasting month. See in photo section following p. 162.

8. Called the *Ranchangan Pemulihan Kampung* (Village Improvement Scheme), the program made grants available to selected villages throughout the country. In this village, the assistance was distributed along strictly partisan lines. An account of this episode may be found in chapter 6.

9. *Apa pasal bikin jamban, rumah pun tak ada.*

attap roofing from Kamil and never delivered it and how Kamil gave him cash for special paddy seed that Razak said he could get from a friend in a nearby village. Accosted a week later, he claimed his friend with the seed had not been at home. Accosted again the following week, he claimed his friend had already sold the seed. The money was never returned. On various occasions, they claimed, Razak had begged seed paddy for planting or rice for his family. In each case, the gift had been sold for cash, not planted or eaten. Ghazali accused him of helping himself to nipah fronds from behind his house for roofing without ever asking permission and of having begged for a religious gift of paddy (*zakat*) even before the harvest was in. "I lost my temper," he added as many shook their heads.

When the well-to-do villagers lament, as they increasingly do, the growing laziness and independence of those they hire for work in the fields, the example of Razak is always close at hand. They have other illustrations, but Razak is by far the most serviceable. Any number of times, they claim, he has taken advance wages in cash or rice and then failed to show up for work. As for his poverty, they are skeptical. He has, after all, half a *relong* (.35 acre), which he rents out like a landlord rather than farming himself.[10] The general verdict is that he is simply not capable of getting ahead.[11] When the subdistrict chief (*penghulu*), Abdul Majid, confides to me that the poor are reluctant to work anymore and now insist on unrealistic wages, he seizes the example of Razak. "He has made himself hard up, it's his own doing."[12]

By now the simple coffin was nearly finished and Amin, the best carpenter in the village, began to add some small decorative touches at the ends. "No need to add decorations," put in Ariffin, and Amin left off. As they carried the coffin across to Hamzah's house, where Maznah lay, someone sized up the work and said, "shabby."[13]

Returning to my house I encountered a small group of Pak Haji Kadir's wife's friends talking about the child's death. They all seemed to agree that Razak and Azizah were largely to blame. After all, they took their sick daughter to Rokiah's feast the day before yesterday, fed her food she should not have had, and kept her up to all hours. "They don't eat at all well," said Tok Kasim's

10. Razak claims, with some justice, that he is too weak and ill to cultivate and that, in any case, he does not have the money for tractor charges, fertilizer, or seed.

11. *Tak pandai pusing.* The implication of this phrase is that Razak does not take pains, does not hustle.

12. *Dia buat susah.* Abdul Majid went on to describe many local Chinese families who had begun with nothing and were now rich. One might possibly translate this phrase as: "He is pretending to be hard up," since the verb for "shamming" (*membuat-buat*) is occasionally abbreviated.

13. *Lekeh.* This word in Kedah carries the meaning of "vulgar, common, shabby, not refined," and is much like the use of *kasar* in standard Malay. It is variously applied to people, feasts, commodities, music, cloth, personal behavior, and so forth.

wife, "they have to tag along at other people's feasts."[14] At my urging, the details of the family's scant cuisine emerged. For breakfast, if there was any money in the house, coffee and perhaps cassava or a bit of cold rice left over from the day before. Otherwise, only water. And Razak's family, someone added, drank water from the same ditch used for bathing. Rarely any porridge, never any milk, and almost never any sugar unless Azizah brought some back from her relatives in Dulang. By contrast, the village headman, Haji Jaafar, usually took his morning meal in the town coffee shop, where he had porridge or fried flat bread with sugar or curry, assorted cakes and sweets made with sticky rice, and coffee with sweetened condensed milk. The midday meal, the main one in the village, for Razak's family would typically include rice, vegetables that could be gathered free in the village,[15] and, if finances permitted, some dried fish or the cheapest fish from the market. No one had ever seen Razak buy vegetables. Fresh fish, when they had it, was normally cooked over an open fire, for it was rare that they could afford the 30¢ minimum purchase of the cheapest cooking oil. Haji Jaafar's midday meal, on the other hand, reflected both his wealth and his rather sumptuous tastes: a tasty curry made from the most expensive fish and market vegetables and, at least twice a week, a luxury that Razak never bought—meat.

Razak's household, like its food, was distinguished less by what it had than by what it lacked. The couple had no mosquito netting, which helped explain why their children's arms and legs were often covered with the scabs of old bites. Maybe once a year they bought a bar of the cheapest soap. They had to share three tin plates and two cups when they ate. They lacked even the traditional mats to sleep on, using instead an old cast-off plastic sheet Razak found at the market. As for clothes, Azizah had not bought a sarong since her wedding, making do instead with worn-out cloth given her by Basir's wife. Razak's one pair of pants and shirt were bought three years ago when there was a sale of secondhand clothing that had not been redeemed at the pawnbrokers. As Cik Puteh pointed out, the responsibility for this deplorable situation rested squarely with Razak. "He has land but he doesn't want to plant it." "He's always looking for short cuts."[16] "He takes the money first but doesn't want to come thresh paddy." "Now, those who are hardup are getting cleverer; there's more cheating these days."

14. *Makanan tak jenuh, kena tumpang kenduri orang.*

15. The generic term for such vegetables, which can be eaten raw with rice, is *ulam.* Some of the locally available *ulam* include *kangkong, daun cemamak, daun pegaga, bebuas, daun putat,* and the banana *spadix.* Both Razak and his wife would also occasionally catch rice-paddy fish with line and hook. Since the beginning of double-cropping and the increased used of pesticides, however, such fish have become less plentiful and may in fact have serious long-run health consequences for the poor who continue to eat them.

16. *Selalu cari jalan pendek.*

The sound of motorcycle engines next door told us that the body had been prepared for burial and the funeral procession was about to begin. Normally, in the case of an adult, the coffin would have been carried the two miles to the mosque with a cortege of men following on foot, on bicycle, and on motorcycle. Since Maznah was so small and light, Hamzah, her uncle, carried her wrapped in a new batik cloth slung over his shoulder like a bandolier as he rode pillion behind Basir on his Honda 70. The plain coffin was carried athwart Amin's motorcycle by Ghani Lebai Mat. Counting Razak and myself, there were only eleven men, and it was the first entirely motorcycle-born cortege I had ever seen. The villagers and later the Chinese shopkeepers in Kepala Batas paused briefly to watch us pass.

In the graveyard next to the mosque, Tok Siak (caretaker of the mosque) and his assistant were still digging the grave. Maznah, covered with a cotton winding sheet, was taken gently from the batik cloth and placed in the coffin on her side so that she would be facing Mecca. A large clod of clay from the grave was lodged against her back to prevent her position from shifting. Tok Siak was now bailing water from the grave with an old biscuit tin; the burial plot was on reclaimed paddy land and the seasonal rains had begun. The prayers, led by Lebai Sabrani, took less than ten minutes and it was over. Most of the men then entered the mosque to pray for Maznah's soul. When they emerged, Basir handed them envelopes containing a dollar, as is the custom.[17] The six men who had prayed returned the envelopes. Villagers believe that these prayers help lighten the burden of sin and speed the soul on its way to heaven; the more who pray, the more rapid the soul's progress. On the way back to the village, I asked Amin why there were so few people at the burial. He replied that, since Maznah was so young, her sins were few, and thus it was not so important that many people pray on her behalf. But it was a sensitive question, for we both remembered the burial of Tok Sah's infant granddaughter a month earlier when two or three times that number had come to the graveyard.

That night, again at Hamzah's house, there was a small funeral feast.[18] Not more than fifteen men came, and Haji Kadir led the brief Islamic prayers and chants. The expenses, for coffee, flat bread with sugar, and the makings of

17. These prayers after burial are called *Doa Talkin,* and the gift to those who pray varies, depending on the status of the deceased. This traditional practice is under attack by Islamic fundamentalists, who wish to purify Malay religious practice by banning pre-Islamic practices. In the adjacent state of Perlis, *Doa Talkin* are officially forbidden.

18. *Kenduri arwah* are normally celebrated on the first, second, third, seventh, fourteenth, fortieth, and hundredth days after a death in the family. *Kenduri arwah* may be celebrated at other times as well (often after harvest) and are sometimes combined with feasts of thanksgiving as well. The *kenduri,* much like the *selametan* in Indonesia, is clearly a pre-Islamic custom that has been thoroughly integrated with Islam.

peasant cigarettes came to less than M$12 and were partly defrayed by minute donations of coins. Razak, as usual, was ignored, invisible. Later, as Yaakub and I walked back home along the village path, he asked if I had noticed how the tobacco had run short because Razak had pocketed some for later use. "Shabby," was his summary.

Early in the morning, three or four days later, Razak appeared at the foot of my steps waiting to be asked up. Whenever he came to see me it was always early enough so that no one else was about; if someone else did happen by, he would fall silent and take the first opportunity to leave. Despite the fact that the gossip about him had long aroused my curiosity, I had already found myself avoiding much talk with him in public, having sensed that it could only set village tongues wagging. Was he taking advantage of me? What tales and slanders would he put in my ear? Did I actually approve of this good-for-nothing?

Razak had come to thank me for my large contribution to the funeral expenses. I had made a discreet donation directly into Razak's hands the day his daughter died, knowing that if I had put M$20 directly on the plate near the body, I would have received no end of scolding. [19]

Before long we passed on to the topic I had been raising recently in conversations with villagers: the enormous changes that have come to Sedaka since the beginning of double-cropping eight years ago. It was clear to Razak that things were generally worse now than before irrigation. "Before it was easy to get work, now there's no work in the village and the estates (rubber and oil palm) don't want anyone." "The poor are poorer and the rich are richer." [20] The trouble, he added, is mostly because of the combine-harvesters that now cut and thresh paddy in a single operation. Before, his wife could earn over M$200 a season cutting paddy and he could earn M$150 threshing, but this last season they only managed M$150 between them. [21] "People weren't happy when the ma-

19. I should add that much of this was conscience money in the sense that I felt guilty for having been out of the village the day before, when I might have driven the child to the hospital. Another reason for discretion was that such a large sum, given openly, would, I felt, have demeaned the smaller contributions on the plate, which represented a more than comparable sacrifice for others, and would have *publicly* placed Razak in my permanent debt.

20. *Orang susah, lagi susah; orang kaya, lagi kaya.* The fact that he should use the term *susah,* which might be translated as "hard up," for his class rather than the term *miskin* (poor) and the term *kaya* (rich) for those who are well-to-do rather than the term *senang* (comfortable), which would make a logical pair with *susah,* is significant. For further discussion, see chapter 5.

21. Figures on the loss of wages due to combine-harvesters may be found in chapters 3 and 4. Razak, however, is frail—many would say lazy too—and can thresh paddy for piece-work wages only half as fast as his younger brother, Hamzah.

chines came." "You can't even glean anymore."[22] What distressed him about the machine as well was how it removed money from the village and gave it to outsiders. Money that might have gone to paddy reapers and threshers from the village and in turn been used partly for local feasts within Sedeka was now paid directly to the owners of these expensive machines. As Razak put it, "They carry it away for their own feasts."[23]

Not only was wage work harder and harder to come by, but it was almost impossible now to find land to rent. In the old days, he said, landlords wanted you to take land and hardly bothered about the rent. Today, they farm all the land themselves or else rent out large plots under long-term leases to wealthy Chinese contractors with machinery. "They won't give (land) to their own people." "They won't even give five cents to someone who is hard up."[24]

Razak has begun to warm up to one of his favorite laments, one he shares with many of the other village poor: the growing arrogance and stinginess of the rich. It is reflected in what he sees as their attitude toward charity. Little wonder that Razak—with a tiny patch of rice land, four (now three) young children, and a frail physique (and many would say a reluctance to work)—should be concerned about charity. The official *poverty-level* income for a family of Razak's size would be M$2,400.[25] Their actual income, not counting charity, last year was less than M$800, by far the lowest in the village. It would be misleading to say they get by, for Maznah's death may be evidence that they do not. Without the small amount of charity they receive, without Azizah's frequent flights with the children back to her parents' village of Dulang when the food gives out, and perhaps without Razak's capers, which offend the village, it would be hard to imagine the rest of them surviving at all.

If others blamed Razak's situation on his own moral failings, he hurled the charge back at them. "There are lots of Malays who are not honest."[26] "Now, Malays who get wages of even three or four hundred dollars have become arro-

22. *La 'ni, katok pun tak boleh buat.* Gleaning was a traditional means for those with little or no land (rented or owned) to thresh paddy a second time for the grains left on the stalk from the first threshing. The machines now cut up the stalks and scatter them all over the field, eliminating the piles of paddy stalks that used to be left beside the threshing tubs when harvesting was done by hand.

23. *Bawa balik kenduri depa.*

24. *Lima duit pun tak bagi sama orang susah.*

25. Defined as "an income sufficient to purchase a minimum food basket to maintain a household in good nutritional health and the minimum needs for clothing, household management, transport, and communication." Cited in International Bank for Reconstruction and Development, *Malaysia: Selected Issues in Rural Poverty*, World Bank Report 2685-MA, vol. 2 (Washington, D.C.: World Bank, 1980), 4.

26. The words Razak used were *tak betul,* which is hard to render exactly in this context. A person who is *betul* would be honest and good-hearted.

gant."[27] "They don't help others out. In the village, they don't even give you a single cup of coffee." The charge is not strictly true. As nearly as I could calculate over a year, Razak's family received enough gifts of paddy and rice (milled paddy) to feed them for perhaps three months. At the end of Ramadan it is the duty of each Moslem to make a religious gift of rice, called *fitrah*. In addition to the customary gifts to the mosque, the *imam*, and the village prayer house, rice is often given, one gallon at a time, to poor relatives and neighbors, particularly those who have worked during the season for the farmer making the gift. Razak was given nearly ten gallons of rice as *fitrah*, although not without a residue of bitterness. Rather than waiting politely to be summoned to collect his *fitrah* as is customary, Razak went from house to house asking for it. Only a few refused;[28] after all, a family ought to be able to eat rice on the major Islamic feast day, and such gifts are seen as a way of cleansing one's own possessions. Razak collected smaller gifts, in the same fashion, on the second major Islamic feast day a month later.[29] The third occasion for religious gifts is at harvest time, when all Muslims are enjoined to tithe 10 percent of their harvest (the *zakat*). Despite the fact that official responsibility for *zakat* collection has recently been taken over by the provincial authorities, informal *zakat* payments along traditional lines persist. It is given in paddy, not rice, and is an important supplement to the income of poor, landless families. Razak received a gunny sack of paddy from his eldest brother in Yan, for whom he had threshed, and four or five gallons from within the village, by using his usual aggressive methods. From time to time, Razak also asks for small gifts of rice from likely prospects. Usually, he puts it in terms of advance wages, using language that masks the nature of the transaction, but the fiction is paper thin. Those who are importuned say he is "begging for alms."[30]

Being pushy has its rewards. Razak receives a good deal more food than many

27. *Sombong.* Along with the charge of being stingy, this is probably the most serious personal charge that is commonly heard in village society. People who are *sombong* have, in effect, removed themselves from the community by acting superior to their fellows. The opposite of *sombong* is *merendahkan diri*, "to act modestly" or "to lower oneself."

28. One wonders how much Razak would have gotten had he behaved less aggressively. I suspect much less, but I have no way of knowing.

29. *Hari Raya Haji,* when pilgrims leave for Mecca. Donations of rice on this occasion are normally given by the quarter gallon (*cupak*).

30. *Minta sedekah.* The social definition of what Razak is doing is important. As Simmel understands: "no one is socially poor until he has been assisted. . . . And this has general validity: sociologically speaking, poverty does not come first and then assistance . . . but a person is called poor who receives assistance." *Georg Simmel on Individuality and Social Forms,* ed. Donald N. Levine (Chicago: Univ. of Chicago Press, 1971), 175. In the same sense no one is a beggar in Sedaka until he is perceived to have asked for alms.

of the other poor in the village—more than Mansur, Dullah, Mat "halus" ("Skinny" Mat), Pak Yah, or Taib. The additional cost to his reputation is minimal; his standing is already virtually the definition of rock bottom.[31] On the other hand, he does not do nearly so well as his younger brother, Hamzah, who is often held up as an example of the deserving poor. Hamzah is an acknowledged hard worker, as is his wife; he serves as caretaker 'of the *madrasah* and he unfailingly appears to help with the cooking at feasts, to assist in house moving,[32] and to help repair the village path. After last season's harvest, and partly out of sympathy for a month-long illness that prevented him from working as usual, he received eight gunny sacks of paddy from villagers and relatives. Basir calls him the *"zakat* champ,"[33] contrasting the results with the meager return from Razak's more aggressive style. "We don't want to give alms to Razak, he's a liar—only to honest poor like Hamzah."[34] Fadzil, another influential villager, echoed these sentiments. "There are lots of poor who lie, cheat, and are lazy." "They look for a shady tree to perch on." "They want to gobble up the well-to-do."[35] In a reflective moment, however, he noticed the potential for a vicious cycle here. "If we don't give them alms because they steal, then maybe they have to keep stealing." This was as close as anyone I spoke with ever came to recognizing explicitly the importance of charity for the social control of the village poor.

On the political front, Razak has done what a prudent poor man might do to safeguard his and his family's interests. Four or five years ago he paid the M$1 subscription to join the village branch of the ruling party, which dominates politics and the division of whatever loaves and fishes filter down to the village level. "If you go with the crowd, there's a lot to be had. With the minority, it would be difficult. I used my head. I want to be on the side of the majority."[36]

---

31. Erving Goffman has captured the strange power that those without shame can exercise. "Too little perceptiveness, too little savoir-faire, too little *pride* and considerateness, and the person ceases to be someone who can be trusted to take a hint about himself or give a hint that will save others embarrassment. . . . Such a person comes to be a real threat to society; there is nothing much that can be done with him, and often he gets his way." *Ritual Interaction: Essays in Face-to-Face Behavior* (Garden City: Anchor Books, Doubleday, 1967), 40, emphasis added.

32. *Usung rumah* is meant literally here. The entire house is detached from its pillars and moved to a new location by a crowd sometimes approaching 120 men.

33. *Johan zakat.*

34. *Kita ta' mau bagi sedekah sama Razak, dia bohong, mau bagi saja sama orang miskin yang betul, macham Hamzah.*

35. *Mau makan orang yang ada.* The verb means literally "to eat" but is used here, as it often is, in the sense of "to exploit," to "live off of."

36. *Sebelah orang ramai, banyak. Sebelah sikit, lagi susah. Kita punya fikir otak, kita mau sebelah orang banyak. Kita,* literally "we," is often used in the sense of "I" or "my family" in the local dialect.

Razak's logic, shared by some but by no means all of the village poor, has paid the expected dividends. When a drought, a year earlier, forced the cancellation of the irrigated paddy season, the government created a work-relief program. Politics weighed heavily in the selection of workers and Razak was a winner. The local Farmer's Association office hired him to take care of their poultry for forty days at M$4.50 a day, and he was paid M$50 to help clear weeds from a section of the irrigation canal. None of the poor villagers who were on the wrong side of the political fence did nearly as well. The wood with which his house was partly repaired came through the political influence of Basir. More free wood and the toilet bowl that Razak sold were part of a subsidy scheme that, in Sedaka at least, was available only to followers of the ruling party. If the figure of speech were not so inappropriate to the Malay diet, one might say that Razak knew which side his bread was buttered on.

As a beneficiary of local patronage and charity, however reluctantly given, one might expect Razak to entertain a favorable opinion of his "social betters" in the village. He did not. He also sensed what they said behind his back. "I don't go to the houses of rich people; they don't ask me in. They think poor people are shabby (vulgar) people. They think we are going to ask for money as alms. They say we're lazy, that we don't want to work; they slander us."[37] What offended Razak as much as anything was that these same rich people were not above calling on the poor when they needed help. But when it came to reciprocity, there was none. "They call us to catch their (runaway) water buffalo or to help move their houses, but they don't call us for their feasts."

It has not escaped his notice either that he and many others like him are *invisible men*. "The rich are arrogant. We greet them and they don't greet us back. They don't talk with us; they don't even look at us! If the rich could hear us talking like this, they'd be angry."[38] Razak is special in some respects, but he is not unique. Compare what he has to say with this couplet from the agricultural laborers of Andalusia:

37. The word Razak used for "shabby," "vulgar," is *lekeh,* the same word used to describe Maznah's coffin and Razak's behavior. The word used here for slander is *mengumpat*.

38. *Orang kaya sombong. Kita tabik, depa tak tabik balik. Tak chakap, tak tengok pun. Kalau orang senang dengar kita sembang, depa marah* (I find it impossible to determine whether Razak's use of *kita* here means "I" or whether he wishes to include other poor people like himself in the statement). Just how deeply humiliating it is to be beneath notice, to be invisible, not to have one's greeting returned is at the core of Hegel's notion of the dialectic of self-consciousness. It is in an act as banal as a greeting that it becomes clear that one's own self-esteem is dependent on being accorded recognition by another, even if this greeting, as in Hegel's famous example of the duel, must come at the cost of life. See, for example, Hans Georg Gadamer, *Hegel's Dialectic: Five Hermeneutical Studies,* trans. Christopher Smith (New Haven: Yale Univ. Press, 1972), chap. 3.

I was a rich man and I became poor
to see what the world gave them.
And now I see that nobody
looks at the face of a poor man.[39]

A week after the funeral, I returned to my house from the market to find a
land-rover on the path in front of Hamzah's house. The emblem on the door
said "Ministry of Health." Presently, two nurses emerged from behind Hamzah's
house where Razak lived. They had instructions, they said, to make an inquiry
whenever a young child's death was reported and to try to help the family with
nutritional advice. They had left some powdered milk, but they seemed profoundly discouraged by what they had seen and learned. "What can you do with
people like that?" they asked no one in particular as they climbed into the land-
rover for the trip back to the capital.

HAJI "BROOM"

Before considering the significance of Razak for class relations in Sedaka, it is
instructive to introduce his symbolic, mirror-image twin, his fellow outcast from
the opposite end of the social pyramid, Haji Broom. My stories about him are
all secondhand, for he died some five or six years before I arrived in the village,
but they are plentiful.

Not long after I moved to Sedaka, Lebai Hussein invited me to attend a
wedding feast for his son Taha, who was marrying a woman from a village near
the town of Yan Keçhil, six miles to the south. To accommodate the large
number of guests, the bride's family had built a covered pavilion outside their
house where the male guests sat. Talk centered on the prospects for the current
main-season crop and on how the cancellation of the previous irrigated-season
crop due to the drought had postponed many marriages until the main-season
crop could be harvested.

Noticing what seemed to be a huge new warehouse on the horizon, I idly
asked my neighbor what it was. He told me that it was a rice mill being built
by Haji Rasid and his brother Haji Ani. At the mention of these two names
most of the other conversations in the pavilion stopped. I had somehow, it was
clear, stumbled on a subject of lively interest. For the next hour or so the men
regaled one another with stories about the two brothers and especially about
their father, Haji Ayub. In fact, as I quickly learned, the name of Haji Ayub
was a sure-fire conversational gambit in any company, sufficient to set off a small
avalanche of tales.

39. From Juan Martinez Alier, *Labourers and Landowners in Southern Spain*,
St. Anthony's College, Oxford, Publications, No. 4 (London: Allen & Unwin,
1971), 206.

There is little doubt that Haji Ayub became in his lifetime the largest owner of paddy land that the state of Kedah (and perhaps the whole country) had ever known. At the time of his death, he was reputed to have owned more than 600 relong (426 acres) of paddy fields in addition to his other holdings of rubber and orchard land. The magnitude of his feat must be viewed against an agrarian setting in which the median holding is less than three relong and a farmer who owns twenty relong is considered to be quite rich. Alarmed at the astonishing speed with which Kedah's rice land was passing into the hands of Haji Ayub, the State Assembly at one point actually forbade him to acquire more.

The stories that swirl around the career and exploits of Kedah's rice-land baron, however, touch less on his fabulous holdings per se than on his style of life and the manner in which he built his empire. What makes Haji Ayub such a conversational staple is his legendary cheapness. To judge from the popular accounts I was introduced to that afternoon, Kedah's richest landowner maintained, by choice, a style of life that was hardly distinguishable from Razak's. Like Razak, he lived in a broken-down house that had never been repaired or rebuilt.[40] Rather than buy manufactured cigarettes, he continued till the end of his life to roll his own peasant cigarettes, using the cheapest tobacco and *nipah* wrappers he cut from his own plants.[41] Like the poorest of the poor, Haji Ayub bought only a single sarong cloth a year and, if you passed him, you would have thought he was the village beggar. Surpassing even Razak, he was said to have eaten nothing but dried fish, except on feast days. Although he could have afforded a luxurious car, and a surfaced road passed near his house, he traveled by foot or on bicycle. Haji Kadir, at this point, brought down the house with a pantomime of Haji Ayub on his ancient Raleigh, weaving back and forth, accompanied by an approximation of the loud squeaking noises only the rustiest bicycles could possibly have made. It was in this fashion that Kedah's rice baron issued forth to collect rents from scores of tenants who had not already come of their own accord. The spirit of self-denial touched all aspects of his life save one: he had allowed himself three wives.[42]

The humor of Haji Ayub's tight-fisted ways depended of course on their contrast with his fabulous wealth. He had clearly become a legend because he represented the apotheosis of the rich miser, the unapproachable standard by

40. The condition of his house is often the first remark about Haji Ayub. In contrast, one of the very first investments that even modest peasants made with the first proceeds of double-cropping in 1971 was to repair or make additions to their houses.

41. It is a poor peasant indeed in Sedaka who does not buy (for 10¢) a bundle of *nipah* cigarette wrappers in the market.

42. The miser is the symbol of pure accumulation in the sense that he acquires money and property as an end in itself, not as a means to the pleasures they may provide. In this respect, Haji Ayub's three wives, one short of the maximum allowed by the Koran, may have represented simply another aspect of accumulation. On this subject, see Simmel's essay "Miser and Spendthrift," in *Georg Simmel,* 179–86.

which all other rich misers might be judged. In this respect, he was Razak's precise opposite number. But while Razak's fame was purely local, Haji Ayub was the pacesetter for the district if not the state of Kedah.

When it came to describing how Haji Ayub acquired all this land, the conversation was just as animated but not nearly so jovial. The whole process is perhaps best captured in the nickname by which he is widely known: Haji "Broom." Peasants prefer the English word in this case because, I suspect, its sound suggests a single, vigorous sweeping motion. Quite literally, Haji Broom swept up all the land in his path. The force of the word also connotes something akin to what is meant by saying that one has "cleaned up" at poker (that is, swept up all the chips on the table) or "cleaned out" one's opponents.[43] The image is more powerful precisely because it is joined with "Haji," a term of respect for those who have made the pilgrimage to Mecca. Thus the nickname "Haji Broom" accomplished for Haji Ayub more or less what the nickname "Tun Razak" accomplished for Razak.

Haji Broom's name came up not long afterward when I was asking a few villagers gathered under Pak Yah's house about moneylending and credit practices before double-cropping. Nor was explaining to me the notorious *padi kunca* system of credit and began his account with, "This is the way Haji Broom would do it." It involved an advance of cash roughly six months before harvest, repayable by a fixed quantity (a *kunca*) of paddy at harvest time, which typically amounted to an effective annual rate of interest approaching 150 percent. For at least half a century, until 1960, it was the standard form of seasonal credit extended by shopkeepers, rice millers, moneylenders, and not a few wealthy landlords. Virtually all observers of rice farming cited it both as a major reason for persistent poverty in the paddy sector and as the cause of defaults that further concentrated land ownership.[44] It was clear, moreover, that in this area Haji Broom and *padi kunca* were nearly synonymous.

43. The Malay verb "to sweep" (*sapu, menyapu*) carries the same metaphorical force. Thus when someone wished to describe how a rich man had rented up all the available land in the area, he would say, *Dia sapu semua* (He swept it all up).

44. See, for example, Unfederated Malay States, *Annual Report of the Advisor to the Kedah Government,* December 11, 1912, to November 30, 1913, W. George Maxwell (Alor Setar: Government Printer, 1914), 23; *Annual Report of the Advisor to the Kedah Government,* 1914, L. E. D. Wolferston (Alor Setar: Government Printer, 1915), 14; and Government of Malaysia, *Report of the Rice Production Committee, 1953* (Kuala Lumpur: 1954), vol. 1, p. 82. The Rice Production Committee describes the system as follows: "a man borrows, say M$50 for the purpose of obtaining credit over the planting season and promises to pay a kunca (160 gallons) of padi at harvest worth $102 at current government guaranteed minimum price, but $140 at the market average." It is worth noting here there is no necessary symmetry between the gain of the moneylender and the distress of the borrower. High interest rates in rural Southeast Asia have often reflected the actual cost of money and the high risk of debtor default. Thus, while these interest terms may have been punishing to small-holders, they do not imply a fabulous return to the lender.

If the practice of *padi kunca* skirts perilously close to the strong Islamic injunction against interest, it appears that Haji Broom also became a money-lender pure and simple. Mat "halus" said that Haji Broom regularly lent money, usually in M$100 amounts, for six months, requiring repayment of M$130 or M$140. "His sons, Haji Rasid and Haji Ani, do the same thing. It's sinful.[45] They've been doing it for seven generations. They only care about this world." Part of this lending, they said, was secondhand. That is, Haji Broom would take money from large Chinese moneylenders at 40 percent interest and relend it to peasants at 80 percent interest, pocketing the difference. In the eyes of these villagers, the fact that he worked hand-in-glove with the Chinese creditors in town made for an even worse transgression than if he had operated alone. The Chinese practice of lending cash at interest, on the other hand, occasions virtually no commentary; it is expected. After all, it is their normal business practice and nothing in their religion forbids it. For a Malay—a member of their own community, their own religion, and in this case a Haji—to practice usury despite its explicit denunciation in the Koran is to call forth the most profound censure.[46]

But the keystone of Haji Broom's fortune, the means by which most land fell into his hands, was the practice of *jual janji* (literally, promised sale).[47] Nor, Pak Yah, and Mat "halus" can each tick off easily the names of families in the area who lost land to Haji Broom in this fashion. The practice worked as follows: Haji Broom would lend a man a substantial sum in return for which the title to all or a part of the borrower's land would be transferred to Haji Broom. The written contract of sale provided that if, by a specified date, the borrower repaid the initial sum (nearly always less than the market value of the land), he could recover his land.[48] For the borrower, the loss of the land was, in principle at least, not irrevocable. In practice, of course, it often was, and most of the large landholdings in Kedah were acquired in this fashion. Haji Broom and a few

45. *Haram* here means "forbidden by Islamic law," but the force of the word as it is actually used conveys the deep sinfulness of taking interest; *makan bunga* (literally to "eat" interest).

46. One of the many relevant passages in the Koran reads as follows: "They who swallow down usury, shall arise in the resurrection only as he ariseth whom Satan hath infected by his touch. This, for that they say, Selling is only the like of usury, and yet God hath allowed selling, and forbidden usury. He then who when this warning shall come to him from his Lord, abstaineth, shall have pardon for the past, and his lot shall be with God. But they who return [to usury], shall be given over to the fire; therein shall they abide forever." Surah II:275. *The Koran,* trans. J. M. Rodwell (London: Everyman's Library, 1977), 369.

47. Analogous practices could be found throughout colonial Southeast Asia, for example in the Philippines, Vietnam, and Burma.

48. There are variants in the actual timing of the formal transfer of property and in the use rights to the land while it is thus "mortgaged," but the basic arrangements remain the same.

others, Nor adds, devised a new wrinkle to the procedure. A few days before the final date, he would go into hiding so that a peasant who was lucky enough to have amassed the cash to redeem his land could not find him. Once the date had passed, he would then immediately ask the court to award him the land of the defaulting borrower.[49] By such stratagems, Haji Broom turned nearly all his *jual janji* loans into land sales. As if to dramatize the finality of a loan from Haji Broom, Pak Yah noted that a visitor to the land baron's house would have found him seated in front of a large cupboard filled from top to bottom with land titles.

Something of a lighthearted competition had developed among the three men to tell the most outrageous stories about Haji Broom. Nor provided the finale by describing how the man treated his own sons. He would come to visit his son Haji Ani, Nor said, bearing a sack of one hundred sapodilla fruits (an inexpensive brownish fruit from the same tropical evergreen that produces chicle), ostensibly as a gift. Before leaving, he would ask Haji Ani to give him one hundred duck eggs in return. "Which is more expensive?" Nor asked me rhetorically. This is not just another story of Haji Broom's sharp dealing. Here he had violated the spirit of a gift to make a profit, he had actually *asked* for a return, and he had, above all, exploited his own family for his private gain. Mat "halus" summarized it all by describing his behavior as "the politics of getting ahead."[50]

When I remarked that I had never heard of a man so "stingy," Pak Yah corrected me, "Not stingy but greedy,"[51] thereby emphasizing that Haji Broom was not so much husbanding what he already had as plundering others. "He is without shame." In a sense, this last is the ultimate accusation, one that I have heard applied to Razak as well. For it is shame, that concern for the good opinion of one's neighbors and friends, which circumscribes behavior within the moral boundaries created by shared values. A man without shame is, by definition, capable of anything.[52]

49. While in theory a borrower could have deposited the required amount in an escrow account and informed the court, thereby saving his land, it was a rare peasant indeed who knew about, let alone exercised, this option.

50. *Politik hidup*. The term is not easy to translate; it also implies that Haji Broom is concerned solely with getting ahead in this world at the expense of his immortal soul.

51. *Bukan lokek, haloba*.

52. As Moroccan peasants put it succinctly: "Those who have no shame do as they please." Paul Rabinow, *Reflections on Fieldwork in Morocco* (Berkeley: Univ. of California Press, 1977), 158. This folk wisdom makes its tortuous way back to social science in the following guise: "to ostracize a man is to remove him from social controls. . . . He has nothing to lose by conformity and perhaps even something to gain by vexing them." George C. Homans, "Status, Conformity, and Innovation," in *The Logic of Social Hierarchies*, ed. Edward O. Lauman et al. (Chicago: Markham, 1970), 599.

Nor finally makes it clear that it is not Haji Broom's wealth per se that is offensive but rather the way in which he came by it and subsequently deployed it. "No matter if a person is rich, if he is a good man, the villagers will help him. If he had a feast, villagers would bring gifts of rice, even if he had a hundred gunny sacks in his granary already. But if he is not good-hearted, we don't want to help him at all."[53] Neither the fortune of Haji Broom nor the poverty of Razak would have become so notorious were it not for the shamelessness of their behavior, a shamelessness that breaks all the rules and makes of them virtual outcasts: the one becoming the symbol for the greedy rich, the other the symbol of the grasping poor.

Only in Haji Broom's case, however, does the condemnation take on a somewhat mythical, religious dimension. More than once I was told that, when Haji Broom fell ill, his body was so hot that he had to be moved beneath the house, where it was cooler. And when he was borne to the cemetery, they said, smoke (some say fire) was already rising from the freshly dug grave. When I once asked Ghazali, with deliberate naïveté, whether this had really happened, he replied, "Maybe, but it could be a fairy tale too."[54] The point of course does not depend on the actual truth value of such reports, but rather on the social fact that villagers should conjure up the fires of hell waiting to consume Haji Broom even before he was finally laid to rest.

Most of that class of wealthy landowners of which Haji Broom is simply the most blatant and therefore serviceable example are also Hajis. That is, they are also men who have fulfilled the fifth "pillar" of Islam by making the pilgrimage to Mecca. Some have in fact made more than a single pilgrimage. The pattern of association between religious status and landowning wealth evidently has its origins in the late nineteenth century when much of the Kedah rice plain was settled by migrants led by respected religious teachers. Land grants, voluntary gifts, and the Islamic tithe allowed much of this class to become something of a landed gentry, while strategic marriage alliances with officials and the lower aristocracy solidified their position.[55] By 1916, the Acting British Advisor was

53. Compare this with the comment made by Emmanuel Le Roy Ladurie in the course of his portrait of a thirteenth-century Albigensian village in southern France: "Wealth in itself was not the real object of attack. What the people of Montaillou hated was the unhealthy fat of the undeserving rich, clerics, and mendicants who exploited the village without giving in return any spiritual aid or even those services of help and protection habitually provided by a well-to-do domus or by wealthy local nobles." *Montaillou: Promised Land of Error,* trans. Barbara Bray (New York: Braziller, 1978), 341.

54. *Dongeng* could be variously translated as "legend," "fairy tale," "myth," all of which call into question its truth value.

55. See Afifuddin Haji Omar, *Peasants, Institutions, and Development in Malaysia: The Political Economy of Development in the Muda Region,* MADA Monograph No. 36 (Alor Setar: MADA, 1978), 50–56.

complaining about fraud on the part of the larger landholders who had applied for several smaller land grants, using bogus names in order to avoid the risks of applying openly to the State Council for a large grant.[56] Class barriers have, however, remained quite permeable, as Haji Ayub's case illustrates, and a good many wealthy Hajis in the region are comparative newcomers.

The fact that most of the larger Malay landowners, paddy traders, rice millers, and owners of agricultural machinery are also Hajis,[57] having amassed sufficient capital to make the pilgrimage, lends the title a highly ambiguous status. On the one hand, there is a genuine veneration for the act of pilgrimage itself and for the religious charisma that pilgrims thereby acquire. On the other hand, not a few of these pilgrims have accumulated the necessary capital for the Haji only by decades of sharp practices (for example, moneylending, taking *jual janji* land mortgages, renting land at the highest possible rates, being tightfisted with relatives and neighbors, minimizing ceremonial obligations), which most of the community judges abhorrent. Small wonder that villagers should be less than completely worshipful of a returning Haji whose trip to Mecca was financed by their land, their labor, and their rents.

Perhaps this is why the term *Haji* is often joined in popular parlance to adjectives that are anything but complimentary. *Haji Sangkut*[58] refers literally to a man who wears the cap and robe of a Haji without having made the pilgrimage, but it is also used to describe, behind their backs, actual pilgrims whose subsequent behavior continues to violate what the community would expect of a religious man. *Haji Merduk* and *Haji Karut*[59] refer to "false" or "fake" Hajis who have made the voyage to Mecca but whose conduct is anything but saintly. Since one of the main purposes of the Haj in village terms is to cleanse oneself of sin and prepare for Allah's judgment, it is an especially grave transgression—a sign of bad faith—to persist in sinful ways. As Basir says, "God will not accept Hajis like that. They have just wasted their money. There's no benefit. It's useless." The sins of such a Haji are worse than those of ordinary Muslims, Fazil adds, because "He knows it's wrong but he does it anyway. A false Haji is the very worst.[60] He goes to Mecca to wash his sins clean but . . . God doesn't like signs like that."

56. Unfederated Malay States, *Annual Report of the Acting Advisor to the Kedah Government, 1916,* G. A. Hall (Alor Setar: Government Printer, 1917), 2.
57. The reverse is not necessarily the case. That is, a good many Hajis are men of fairly modest financial means who have made considerable sacrifices, including the sale of land, to make the pilgrimage. Some never recover financially.
58. From the verb *sangkut* meaning "to hang something up on a peg," hence "to drape clothes on oneself." It is also possible that *sangkut* is a corruption of *songkok,* the Malay cap, thereby implying an imposter who wears the small skullcap of a Haji without having made the pilgrimage.
59. *Merduk* means "a thing or possession of no value" and *karut* means "false or untrue."
60. *Haji karut yang teruk sekali.*

Once, as a few of us sat around Samat's small village store, I asked Tok Kasim whether Haji Ani was like his father. We had just been discussing a well-known minister who had been dismissed, ostensibly for corruption, and Tok Kasim chose to draw the parallel. "A Haji who cheats and steals is just like a minister who does the same. Muslim punishment is more severe (than civil punishment).[61] It's worse because the rich are enjoined to help the poor. Those who don't are not afraid of God, they only want to take (not give). When a Muslim does this, it's the worst possible."

The title *Haji* is often heard in conjunction with other adjectives as well, most of them having to do with miserliness. Much as the Eskimos are said to have a great wealth of words to describe varieties of snow that would pass unnoticed in other cultures, the Malay tongue offers a sumptuous linguistic feast of terms to describe every possible degree and variety of tightfistedness.[62] Nearly all of them I have heard used at one time or another to modify the noun *Haji*. The terms most in vogue are *Haji Kedekut* and *Haji Bakhil,* each of which means stingy or miserly Haji. One Malay author remembers a chant with which she and her childhood friends used to bait a tightfisted Haji:

Haji Kedekut gets up at night
To count his money on the sly
He eats his rice with only salt
Sleeps on the floor without a mattress.[63]

It was some time before I realized that Haji Kadir, the well-to-do landlord in whose house I was staying, was the butt of similar jokes and fell into the same folk category. I was visiting a nearby village with Sedaka's ragtag soccer team,[64] and after the game some of our hosts asked where I was staying. When I replied that we stayed in the front of "Pak" Haji Kadir's house, I was greeted by blank stares of nonrecognition. I tried to describe the location of the house,

61. *Hukuman melayu lagi teruk.* Here the literal translation is "Malay punishment," but the reference is to religion, since the two are synonymous. Thus the phrase *masuk melayu,* which means literally "to become a Malay" and is used to describe people of other races who marry a Malay, is more appropriately translated as "to become a Muslim."

62. A by no means exhaustive list would include the following: *kedekut, kikir, bakhil, berkira, lokek, tamak, tangkai jering* (noun), *keras hati* (also means "stubborn").

63. Haji Kedekut, bangun malam
Kira duit, diam-diam
Makan nasi, lauk garam
Tidur lantai, tak ada tilam

Sri Delima, *As I Was Passing,* vol. 2 (Kuala Lumpur: Berita Publishing, 1978).

64. Team record for dry season of 1979: two wins, five losses, and one draw—a performance attributable only in part to the author's goal keeping.

thinking that he must surely be well known in these parts. The confusion continued until someone said, "Oh, that must be Kadir *Ceti*" and the smiles around then reflected both recognition and some embarrassment. *Ceti* refers to the notorious southern Indian Chettiar moneylending caste which, in Malaya and elsewhere in Southeast Asia, provided much of the finance capital for agrarian production from 1900 until the Second World War. As a caste specialized entirely to a profession forbidden by the Koran, they became, and remain, a symbol of usurious exploitation and debt bondage.

Although Haji Kadir was the only man with the nickname Pak Ceti in Sedaka, other villages in the vicinity had their own—Haji Lah Ceti and Pak Ali Ceti to name just two.[65] Once it became known that I had learned my landlord's nickname, the ice was broken and the stories came thick and fast. Much of the nearly twenty relong of paddy fields that he owned locally were acquired by default on money he had lent out, that is by *jual janji*. Abu Hassan's father had lost three relong to Pak Haji Kadir in this fashion, which explained why he occasionally, and to no avail, asked to rent back this plot of land. Villagers said that, like Haji Broom, Haji Kadir had re-lent money borrowed from one of the wealthy Chinese shopkeepers in Kepala Batas. Hamzah, his poor neighbor, complained that he would charge 20¢ for a coconut from his yard rather than simply make a gift of it as others would. Hamzah had another complaint. Last season he had worked as a laborer more often for Haji Kadir than for anyone else in the village and thus expected a gift of paddy (*zakat*) after the harvest. He got absolutely nothing, although far poorer farmers for whom he had worked had been quite generous.

The diet of *Kadir Ceti,* like that of the Haji Kedekut in the ditty, was the object of popular derision. Rather than buying fish from the market, he would, by choice, eat the same tiny, bony fish from the paddy fields that the poorest villagers ate of necessity. Even his brother-in-law, Pak Kasim, did not think he had changed since making the pilgrimage. "Even the Chinese in town call him *Ceti*. He always sits in the same chair. How could he change?"

Although Haji Broom and Kadir Ceti dominated the conversational landscape of miserly Hajis in Sedaka, there was no shortage of stories about other Hajis, living and dead, in the district. The torrent of abusive accounts was such that I eventually tired of them, although the villagers never did. There were Hajis who stole water buffalo; Hajis who boldly took things from stores without paying; Hajis who harvested crops planted in good faith by their tenants; Hajis who rented all their land to Chinese rather than to their own people; Hajis who

---

65. It appears that the term is widespread, at least in northeast Malaysia. On Mokhzani's list of Malay moneylenders in Perlis (the state immediately to the north of Kedah and forming part of the same rice (plain), half the entries bear the nickname *Ceti*. Mokhzani bin Abdul Rahim, *Credit in a Malay Peasant Society* (Ph.D. diss., University of London, 1973), 393–94.

insisted that tenants pay *them* a *zakat* tithe (reversing the usual direction of charity); and at least one Haji who was said to have kicked a woman while she was praying. And, of course, there were many good, pious, modest Hajis (perhaps a majority) whose pilgrimage and conduct were a great credit to Islam. The fact remains, however, that a vast majority of the rich landlords who had earned the animosity of the community were also Hajis. It was impossible to tell whether the cascade of stories was due simply to the inherent richness of the source material or to its social value as a cautionary tale for the rich and would-be rich who had not yet gone astray. Both, I suspect.

Two things were clear, though. First, nearly everyone thought that the problem of the shameless, greedy rich in general, and of shameless, greedy, rich Hajis in particular, was worse now than in the past. Even rich Hajis concurred, while excepting themselves from the charge. Sukur spoke for most when he said: "The old Hajis were real Hajis. These days, they aren't real Hajis. They only wear the robes. They just took a trip to Mecca (not a real pilgrimage). When they came back from Mecca they should be true, but they even practice *padi kunca*. They just want more money; the sky's the limit."[66] Second, it is clear that, when such Hajis die, their transgressions will earn them the most exquisite punishment their God can prepare. What that punishment will be precisely is a matter for conjecture. But Abdul Rahman captured the flavor of this speculation by concluding: "When they enter hell, they will swim in blood."

THE SYMBOLIC BALANCE OF POWER

The tales about Razak and Haji Broom—suitably embroidered, elaborated, and retold—have far more than mere entertainment value. They amount to an exchange of small arms fire, a small skirmish, in a cold war of symbols between the rich and poor of Sedaka. Hostilities, in this war as in most, are conducted over a shifting terrain in which there are many neutrals, bystanders, and reluctant combatants with divided loyalties. For the time being, at least, it remains a *cold* war both because many of the potential participants have important shared interests that would be jeopardized in an all-out confrontation and because one side, the poor, is under no illusions about the outcome of a direct assault. Thus, the "war news" consists almost entirely of words, feints, and counterfeints, threats, a skirmish or two, and, above all, propaganda.

The stories that circulate about Razak and Haji Broom are perhaps understood in this sense as propaganda. Like effective propaganda, they signify—they embody—an entire argument about what is happening in this small place. The mere mention of Razak's name by rich villagers conjures up a vision of the

66. The last phrase in Malay, *Banyak mana pun tak boleh cukup,* is difficult to render in English, and I have translated it rather freely. A more literal translation would be, "No matter how much, it wouldn't be enough."

grasping, dishonest poor, who violate the accepted standards of village decorum. In their view Razak is the negative model toward which the poor in general are, alas, heading. The mere mention of Haji Broom's name by poor villagers conjures up a vision of the greedy, penny-pinching rich, who likewise violate the accepted standards of village conduct. In their view, Haji Broom is the negative model toward which the rich in general are heading.

Haji Broom and Razak gain much of their power as symbols by virtue of their reality as concrete human examples of the behavior they have come to signify. Everyone in the village can observe Razak as he adds daily to his own legend. For Haji Broom, the experience is only slightly less direct. Nearly everyone has seen or met him and every adult has heard firsthand stories about his land grabbing and moneylending. Given the availability of palpable, local legends that villagers can check against their own experience, this kind of propaganda does not have to rely much on mere credulity to state its case. What one chooses to make of these living legends—precisely what they signify—is of course another matter. But they originate in social facts.

The value of Razak and Haji Broom as social banners, however, stems as much from the extravagance of their conduct as from their palpability. It is this extravagance that not only makes the tales engrossing[67] but makes them effective vehicles of propaganda. Even the poor of Sedaka agree that Razak's capers place him beyond the pale. Even Kadir Ceti will agree that Haji Broom's fortune was gotten by breaking the commands of Allah and of village society. The rich and the poor have each availed themselves of precisely the extreme examples that will best serve their case, examples that will have to be conceded by the "other side."

The stories that swirl around these two men must also be recognized as cornerstones of an ideological edifice under construction. They embody, as ideology, a critique of things as they are as well as a vision of things as they should be. They are attempts to create and maintain a certain view of what decent, acceptable human behavior ought to be. As negative examples of totally unacceptable behavior, they accomplish their purpose in the same way that any socially sanctioned account of deviance helps to define what is normal, correct, preferred behavior. Such stories can thus be read as a kind of social text on the subject of human decency. They are necessary precisely because the maintenance of a given symbolic order is always as problematic as its change. The ideological work of repair and renovation is never-ending.

The implicit purpose of these competing ideologies is not just to convince but to control; better stated, they aim to control by convincing. To the extent that they succeeded in shaping behavior, they achieve a class purpose as well.

---

67. In conversation as in literature the bizarre and the evil are always more gripping than the commonplace and the saintly. How else to explain the content of popular newspapers? Caliban is always more interesting than Ariel, Mephistopheles more interesting than the Angel of Light.

Should the rich be chastened by the tales about Haji Broom, they would not lend money at high interest, they would not make designs on the land of others, they would be generous with religious charity and feasts, and they would take on more tenants and workers. The benefits for the poor of such an arrangement are obvious. Should the poor, on the other hand, take the infamous example of Razak to heart, they would not importune the rich for gifts, they would not come to feasts uninvited, they would be faithful workers, and they would be as good as their word. The advantages for the rich of such an arrangement are equally obvious. There is a kind of symbolic equilibrium here. The message to the rich is: If you behave like Haji Broom, you can count on being villified as he is. To the poor, the message is: If you behave like Razak, you will be despised as he is. And if wishes became deeds, if ideology became practice, Sedaka would be a small utopia peopled by generous, sympathetic landlords and honest, hard-working tenants and laborers.

Alas, the equilibrium is only symbolic. These cautionary tales, after all, adjure the rich and the poor to forgo their immediate material interest in order to protect their reputation. But how important is a good name? Or, to put it the other way around, what is the cost of a bad name? The answer unfortunately depends a great deal on who you are, for the cost of a bad name hinges directly on the social and economic sanctions that can be brought into play to punish its bearer. In class terms, one must ask how dependent the poor are on the good opinion of the rich and vice versa. The politics of reputation is, in this respect, something of a one-sided affair.[68] It amounts to this: The rich have the social power generally to impose their vision of seemly behavior on the poor, while the poor are rarely in a position to impose their vision on the rich. A good name is something like a social insurance policy for the poor against the thousand contingencies of agrarian life. It is built by a record of deferential behavior, service at feasts and house movings, a willingness to work without quibbling too much about wages, and tacit support for the village leadership. It brings tangible rewards in terms of employment, charity, help at times of death or illness, and access to whatever subsidies the ruling party in the village has to distribute. It brings intangible rewards in terms of inclusion both in the informal pleasantries and in the ritual of village life. Razak, having forfeited his good name, thereby acquires a certain freedom to breach the etiquette of village life.[69] But he pays heavily for that freedom in work and public scorn. His only concession to form is his calculated membership in the ruling party. Hamzah, by contrast, has established and maintained a good name. It costs him the time

68. For an analysis of "the politics of reputation" and empirical studies, see F. G. Bailey, *Gifts and Poison: The Politics of Reputation* (New York: Schocken, 1971).

69. "Freedom's just another word for nothing left to lose" is quite apt in this instance. See also A. Solzhenitsyn, *The First Circle*, trans. Thomas P. Whitney (New York: Bantam, 1968), 96.

and labor he devotes to village projects, cooking at feasts, and taking care of the village prayerhouse (*surau*) and assembly hall (*balai*). It also costs him a certain amount of swallowed up bile, as we shall see, to feign a respect for his social betters that he does not always feel. But his reputation pays dividends in employment, *zakat* gifts, help when he is ill, and a public show of respect and consideration. Such rewards are significant; they are sufficient to ensure that all but three or four of the poor in Sedaka choose to conform in most respects to the standard of seemly behavior that is defined and imposed by the village elite.

The Haji Brooms and Kadir Cetis of this small world are heavily insulated from the effects of a bad name. They need little or nothing from the poor. It is ironic that their insulation—land and the income and power it provides—was acquired only by violating precisely those rules of generosity and consideration[70] that might have given them a good name. Now they are virtually beyond sanction.

There is one exception, however. The rich, while they may be relatively immune to material sanctions, cannot escape symbolic sanctions: slander, gossip, character assassination. But even on this small terrain, the contest is an unequal one. Nowhere is this more evident than in the fact that Razak is demeaned *to his face*, while Haji Broom and Kadir Ceti are invariably demeaned *behind their backs*. Thus Kadir Ceti is always addressed "Pak Haji" to his face, and I would be surprised if he was even aware of his popular nickname. The scorn in which he is held need never reach his ears nor trouble his sleep.

Of course, much of the public deference shown to Haji Kadir is "false" deference.[71] Poor villagers, and not only they, choose to dissemble, knowing full well the penalties of any other course. Thus when an old villager, Ishak, ventures to talk disparagingly about Haji Broom, he ends by asking me not to breathe a word of it to anyone in Yan or Mengkuang for fear of retaliation. What we have here is a difference between "onstage" and "offstage" behavior; to the extent that the deference expressed in public, power-laden situations is negated in the comparative safety of offstage privacy, we can speak unambiguously of false deference.

But even false deference is an unmistakable exhibition of the social power of the well-to-do. It is no small matter that the village elite continues to control the public stage. The public symbolic order is maintained through outward deference, to which there is no open challenge. On this largely symbolic plane, as well as in the sphere of material exchange, then, the social imbalance of power

70. The equivalent for "consideration" in Malay is *timbang rasa,* which means literally "to weigh feelings" (of others).

71. This brief analysis of "deference" benefits from the analyses of Howard Newby, "The Deferential Dialectic," *Comparative Studies in Society and History* 17, no. 2 (April 1975): 139–64, and Erving Goffman, "The Nature of Deference and Demeanor," *American Anthropologist* 58 (June 1956): 473–503.

allows public insults of Razak but prevents public insults of Haji Kadir or Haji Broom.

Those with power in the village are not, however, in total control of the stage. They may write the basic script for the play but, within its confines, truculent or disaffected actors find sufficient room for maneuver to suggest subtly their disdain for the proceedings. The necessary lines may be spoken, the gesture made, but it is clear that many of the actors are just going through the motions and do not have their hearts in the performance. A banal example, familiar to any motorist or pedestrian, will illustrate the kind of behavior involved. The traffic light changes when a pedestrian is halfway across the intersection. As long as the pedestrian is not in imminent danger from the oncoming traffic, a small dramatization is likely to ensue. He lifts his knees a bit higher for a step or two, simulating haste, thereby implicitly recognizing the motorist's right-of-way. In fact, in nearly all cases, if my impression is correct, the *actual* progress of the pedestrian across the intersection is no faster than it would have been if he had simply proceeded at his original pace. What is conveyed is the *impression* of compliance without its substance. But the symbolic order, the right of the motorist to the road, is not directly challenged; indeed, it is confirmed by the appearance of haste.[72] It is almost as if symbolic compliance is maximized *precisely* in order to minimize compliance at the level of actual behavior.

It is with analogous forms of minimal compliance that poor villagers are able to insinuate the insincerity of their performance. They may come to the feast of a rich villager but stay only long enough to eat quickly and leave. They have compiled with the custom of accepting the invitation, but their compliance skirts the edge of impropriety. They may also bring a gift in cash or kind that is less than what might be expected but not so little as to constitute a direct insult. They may, as "required," greet a big landowner on the village path, but their greeting is abbreviated and not as warm as it might be. All these and other forms of reluctant compliance stop short of overt defiance and at least conform to the minimal standards of politeness and deference that the rich are normally in a position to require. And yet they also signal an intrusion, however slight, of "offstage" attitudes into the performance itself, an intrusion sufficient to convey its meaning to the directors but not so egregious as to risk a confrontation.[73]

72. The opposite case, in which the pedestrian openly reufses to make even an appearance of haste (or actually slows down) also occurs. Here there is a direct defiance of the motorist's right to the road, an open breach of the symbolic order. The community of pedestrians in effect announces its prior right to the road. Such an open dare invites a game of "chicken" in which the motorist, alas, is usually best equipped to prevail.

73. A good deal of attention, as one might expect, has been devoted to such forms of "protest within compliance" under slavery. For two fine examples, see Eugene Genovese, *Roll, Jordan, Roll: The World the Slaves Made* (New York: Pantheon, 1974), and Lawrence W. Levine, *Black Culture and Black Consciousness* (New York: Oxford Univ. Press, 1977).

The kind of conflict with which we are dealing here is singularly undramatic. At one level it is a contest over the definition of justice, a struggle to control the concepts and symbols by which current experience is evaluated. At another level it is a struggle over the appropriateness of a given definition of justice to a particular case, a particular set of facts, a particular behavior. Assuming the rich ought to be generous, for example, is a certain landowner's refusal to make a gift a violation of that principle or is it a legitimate rebuff to a man who is only feigning poverty or who has, by his comportment, forfeited his right to charity? Finally, at a third level, of course, it is a struggle over land, work, income, and power in the midst of the massive changes brought about by an agricultural revolution.

The resources the different contestants bring to this contest hardly bear comparison. The local elite nearly always has its own way in the economic life of the village. Given its sway over resources, it can also largely control public ritual life—that is, the "onstage" conduct of most of the poor in the community. Only "backstage," where gossip, tales, slander, and anonymous sabotage mocks and negates the public ritual order, does elite control fall away. To return to the military metaphor, it is only here that the terrain is *relatively* favorable to the meager arsenal of the disadvantaged.

One might well ask: Why are we here, in a village of no particular significance, examining the struggle of a handful of history's losers? For there is little doubt on this last score. The poor of Sedaka are almost certainly, to use Barrington Moore's phrase, members of "a class over whom the wave of progress is about to roll."[74] And the big battalions of the state, of capitalist relations in agriculture, and of demography itself are arrayed against them. There is little reason to believe that they can materially improve their prospects in the village and every reason to believe they will, in the short run at least, lose out, as have millions of peasants before them.

The justification for such an enterprise must lie precisely in its banality—in the fact that these circumstances are the *normal* context in which class conflict has historically occurred. By examining these circumstances closely, it may be possible to say something meaningful about normal class consciousness, about everyday resistance, about commonplace class relations where, as is most often the case, neither outright collective defiance nor rebellion is likely or possible.

---

74. Barrington Moore, Jr., *Social Origins of Dictatorship and Democracy* (Boston: Beacon, 1966), 505.

2 • Normal Exploitation, Normal Resistance

Almost invariably doomed to defeat and eventual massacre, the great insurrections were altogether too disorganized to achieve any lasting result. The patient, silent struggles stubbornly carried on by rural communities over the years would accomplish more than these flashes in the pan.

Marc Bloch, *French Rural History*

As the editor of *Field and Garden* once wrote, great men are always unpopular with the common people. The masses don't understand them, they think all those things are unnecessary, even heroism. The little man doesn't give a shit about a great era. All he wants is to drop into a bar now and then and eat goulash for supper. Naturally a statesman gets riled at bums like that, when it's his job to get his people into the schoolbooks, the poor bastard. To a great man the common people are a ball and chain. It's like offering Baloun here, with his appetite, a small Hungarian sausage for supper, what good is that. I wouldn't want to listen in when the big shots get together and start griping about us.

Schweyk, in Bertolt Brecht, *Schweyk in the Second World War,* Scene I

THE UNWRITTEN HISTORY OF RESISTANCE

The idea for this study, its concerns and its methods, originated in a growing dissatisfaction with much recent work—my own as well as that of others—on the subject of peasant rebellions and revolution.[1] It is only too apparent that the inordinate attention accorded to large-scale peasant insurrection was, in North America at least, stimulated by the Vietnam war and something of a left-wing academic romance with wars of national liberation. In this case interest and source material were mutually reinforcing. For the historical and archival records were richest at precisely those moments when the peasantry came to pose a threat to the state and to the existing international order. At other times, which is to

1. See, for example, Barrington Moore, Jr., *Social Origins of Dictatorship and Democracy* (Boston: Beacon, 1966); Jeffrey M. Paige, *Agrarian Revolution: Social Movements and Export Agriculture in the Underdeveloped World* (New York: Free Press, 1975); Eric R. Wolf, *Peasant Wars of the Twentieth Century* (New York: Harper & Row, 1969); James C. Scott, *The Moral Economy of the Peasant* (New Haven: Yale Univ. Press, 1976); Samuel L. Popkin, *The Rational Peasant* (Berkeley: Univ. of California Press, 1979).

say most of the time, the peasantry appeared in the historical record not so much as historical actors but as more or less anonymous contributors to statistics on conscription, taxes, labor migration, land holdings, and crop production.

The fact is that, for all their importance when they do occur, peasant rebellions, let alone peasant "revolutions," are few and far between. Not only are the circumstances that favor large-scale peasant uprisings comparatively rare, but when they do appear the revolts that develop are nearly always crushed unceremoniously. To be sure, even a failed revolt may achieve something: a few concessions from the state or landlords, a brief respite from new and painful relations of production[2] and, not least, a memory of resistance and courage that may lie in wait for the future. Such gains, however, are uncertain, while the carnage, the repression, and the demoralization of defeat are all too certain and real. It is worth recalling as well that even at those extraordinary historical moments when a peasant-backed revolution actually succeeds in taking power, the results are, at the very best, a mixed blessing for the peasantry. Whatever else the revolution may achieve, it almost always creates a more coercive and hegemonic state apparatus—one that is often able to batten itself on the rural population like no other before it. All too frequently the peasantry finds itself in the ironic position of having helped to power a ruling group whose plans for industrialization, taxation, and collectivization are very much at odds with the goals for which peasants had imagined they were fighting.[3]

For all these reasons it occurred to me that the emphasis on peasant rebellion was misplaced. Instead, it seemed far more important to understand what we might call *everyday* forms of peasant resistance—the prosaic but constant struggle between the peasantry and those who seek to extract labor, food, taxes, rents, and interest from them. Most of the forms this struggle takes stop well short of collective outright defiance. Here I have in mind the ordinary weapons of relatively powerless groups: foot dragging, dissimulation, false compliance, pilfering, feigned ignorance, slander, arson, sabotage, and so forth. These Brechtian forms of class struggle have certain features in common. They require little or no coordination or planning; they often represent a form of individual self-help; and they typically avoid any direct symbolic confrontation with authority or with elite norms. To understand these commonplace forms of resistance is to understand what much of the peasantry does "between revolts" to defend its interests as best it can.

It would be a grave mistake, as it is with peasant rebellions, to overly romanticize the "weapons of the weak." They are unlikely to do more than mar-

2. For an example of such temporary gains, see the fine study by E. J. Hobsbawm and George Rude, *Captain Swing* (New York: Pantheon, 1968), 281–99.

3. Some of these issues are examined in James C. Scott, "Revolution in the Revolution: Peasants and Commissars," *Theory and Society* 7, nos. 1–2 (1979): 97–134.

ginally affect the various forms of exploitation that peasants confront. Furthermore, the peasantry has no monopoly on these weapons, as anyone can easily attest who has observed officials and landlords resisting and disrupting state policies that are to their disadvantage.

On the other hand, such Brechtian modes of resistance are not trivial. Desertion and evasion of conscription and of corvée labor have undoubtedly limited the imperial aspirations of many a monarch in Southeast Asia[4] or, for that matter, in Europe. The process and its potential impact are nowhere better captured than in R. C. Cobb's account of draft resistance and desertion in postrevolutionary France and under the early Empire:

> From the year V to the year VII, there are increasingly frequent reports, from a variety of Departments . . . of every conscript from a given canton having returned home and living there unmolested. Better still, many of them did not return home; they had never left it in the first place. . . . In the year VII too the severed fingers of right hands—the commonest form of self-mutilation—begin to witness statistically to the strength of what might be described as a vast movement of collective complicity, involving the family, the parish, the local authorities, whole cantons.
>
> Even the Empire, with a vastly more numerous and reliable rural police, did not succeed in more than temporarily slowing down the speed of the hemorrhage which . . . from 1812, once more reached catastrophic proportions. There could have been no more eloquent referendum on the universal unpopularity of an oppressive regime; and there is no more encouraging spectacle for a historian than a people that has decided it will no longer fight and that, without fuss, returns home . . . the common people, at least, in this respect, had their fair share in bringing down France's most appalling regime.[5]

The collapse of the Confederate army and economy in the course of the Civil War in the United States is a further example of the decisive role of silent and undeclared defections. Nearly 250,000 eligible whites are estimated to have deserted or to have avoided conscription altogether.[6] The reasons appear to have

---

4. See the fine account and analysis by Michael Adas, "From Avoidance to Confrontation: Peasant Protest in Precolonial and Colonial Southeast Asia," *Comparative Studies in Society and History* 23, no. 2 (April 1981): 217–47.

5. R. C. Cobb, *The Police and the People: French Popular Protest, 1789–1820* (Oxford: Clarendon, 1970), 96–97. For a gripping account of self-mutilation to avoid conscription, see Emile Zola, *The Earth,* trans. Douglas Parmee (Harmondsworth: Penguin, 1980).

6. See the excellent study by Armstead L. Robinson, "Bitter Fruits of Bondage: Slavery's Demise and the Collapse of the Confederacy, 1861–65" (New Haven: Yale Univ. Press, forthcoming), chaps. 5, 6.

been both moral and material, as one might expect. Poor whites, especially those from the nonslaveholding hill country, were deeply resentful of fighting for an institution whose principal beneficiaries were often excluded from service by law.[7] Military reverses and what was called the "subsistence crisis of 1862" prompted many to desert and return to their hard-pressed families. On the plantations themselves, the shortage of white overseers and the slaves' natural affinity with the North's objective, gave rise to shirking and flight on a massive scale. As in France, one could claim here too that the Confederacy was undone by a social avalanche of petty acts of insubordination carried out by an unlikely coalition of slaves and yeomen—a coalition with no name, no organization, no leadership, and certainly no Leninist conspiracy behind it.

In a similar fashion, flight and evasion of taxes have classically curbed the ambition and reach of Third World states—whether precolonial, colonial, or independent. As we shall learn, for example, the official collection of the Islamic tithe in paddy is, in Sedaka, only a small fraction of what is legally due, thanks to a network of complicity and misrepresentation that eviscerates its impact. Small wonder that a large share of the tax receipts of Third World states is collected in the form of levies on imports and exports; the pattern is in no small measure a tribute to the tax resistance capacities of their subjects. Even a casual reading of the literature on rural "development" yields a rich harvest of unpopular government schemes and programs nibbled to extinction by the passive resistance of the peasantry. The author of a rare account detailing how peasants—in this case in East Africa—have managed over several decades to undo or evade threatening state policy concludes in the following tone:

> In this situation, it is understandable if the development equation is often reduced to a zero-sum game. As this study has shown, the winners of those games are by no means always the rulers. The African peasant is hardly a hero in the light of current development thinking, but by using his deceptive skills he has often defeated the authorities.[8]

On some occasions this resistance has become active, even violent. More often, however, it takes the form of passive noncompliance, subtle sabotage, evasion, and deception. The persistent efforts of the colonial government in Malaya to discourage the peasantry from growing and selling rubber that would compete

7. This issue centered on the much resented "Twenty-Nigger Law," as it was known, which provided that a white man of draft age could be excused from military service if he was needed to supervise twenty or more slaves. This law, coupled with the hiring of substitutes by wealthy families, encouraged the widespread belief that this was "a rich man's war, but a poor man's fight." Ibid., chap. 5.

8. Goran Hyden, *Beyond Ujamaa in Tanzania* (London: Heinemann, 1980), 231.

with the plantation sector for land and markets is a case in point.[9] Various restriction schemes and land use laws were tried from 1922 until 1928 and again in the 1930s with only modest results because of massive peasant resistance. The efforts of peasants in self-styled socialist states to prevent and then to mitigate or even undo unpopular forms of collective agriculture represent a striking example of the defensive techniques available to a beleaguered peasantry. Again the struggle is marked less by massive and defiant confrontations than by a quiet evasion that is equally massive and often far more effective.[10]

The style of resistance in question is perhaps best described by contrasting, paired forms of resistance, each aimed more or less at the same objective. The first of each pair is "everyday" resistance, in our meaning of the term; the second represents the open defiance that dominates the study of peasant and working-class politics. In one sphere, for example, lies the quiet, piecemeal process by which peasant squatters have often encroached on plantation and state forest lands; in the other a public invasion of land that openly challenges property relations. In terms of actual occupation and use, the encroachments by squatting may accomplish more than an openly defiant land invasion, though the de jure distribution of property rights is never publicly challenged. Turning to another example, in one sphere lies a rash of military desertions that incapacitates an army and, in the other, an open mutiny aiming at eliminating or replacing officers. Desertions may, as we have noted, achieve something where mutiny may fail, precisely because it aims at self-help and withdrawal rather than institutional confrontation. And yet, the massive withdrawal of compliance is in a sense more radical in its implications for the army as an institution than the replacement of officers. As a final example, in one sphere lies the pilfering of public or private grain stores; in the other an open attack on markets or granaries aiming at an open redistribution of the food supply.

What everyday forms of resistance share with the more dramatic public confrontations is of course that they are intended to mitigate or deny claims made by superordinate classes or to advance claims vis-à-vis those superordinate classes. Such claims have ordinarily to do with the material nexus of class struggle—

9. The best, most complete account of this may be found in Lim Teck Ghee, *Peasants and Their Agricultural Economy in Colonial Malaya, 1874–1941* (Kuala Lumpur: Oxford Univ. Press, 1977). See also the persuasive argument in Donald M. Nonini, Paul Diener, and Eugene E. Robkin, "Ecology and Evolution: Population, Primitive Accumulation, and the Malay Peasantry" (Typescript, 1979).

10. For a careful and fascinating account of the ways in which China's production teams and brigades could, until the changes in 1978, have some influence on the definition of "surplus" grain that had to be sold to the state, see Jean C. Oi, *State and Peasant in Contemporary China: The Politics of Grain Procurement* (Ph.D. diss., Univ. of Michigan, 1983). Nearly all of this resistance was called "soft opposition" by those who practiced it and who made it clear that it was successful only if an "outward manifestation" of compliance was maintained. Ibid., 238.

the appropriation of land, labor, taxes, rents, and so forth. Where everyday resistance most strikingly departs from other forms of resistance is in its implicit disavowal of public and symbolic goals. Where institutionalized politics is formal, overt, concerned with systematic, de jure change, everyday resistance is informal, often covert, and concerned largely with immediate, de facto gains.[11]

It is reasonably clear that the success of de facto resistance is often directly proportional to the symbolic conformity with which it is masked. Open insubordination in almost any context will provoke a more rapid and ferocious response than an insubordination that may be as pervasive but never ventures to contest the formal definitions of hierarchy and power. For most subordinate classes, which, as a matter of sheer history, have had little prospect of improving their status, this form of resistance has been the only option. What may be accomplished *within* this symbolic straitjacket is nonetheless something of a testament to human persistence and inventiveness, as this account of lower-caste resistance in India illustrates:

> Lifelong indentured servants most characteristically expressed discontent about their relationship with their master by performing their work carelessly and inefficiently. They could intentionally or unconsciously feign illness, ignorance, or incompetence, driving their masters to distraction. Even though the master could retaliate by refusing to give his servant the extra fringe benefits, he was still obliged to maintain him at a subsistence level if he did not want to lose his investment completely. *This method of passive resistance, provided it was not expressed as open defiance, was nearly unbeatable,* it reinforced the Haviks' stereotype concerning the character of low caste persons, but gave them little recourse to action.[12]

Such forms of stubborn resistance are especially well documented in the vast literature on American slavery, where open defiance was normally foolhardy. The

---

11. There is an interesting parallel here with some of the feminist literature on peasant society. In many, but not all, peasant societies, men are likely to dominate every formal, overt exercise of power. Women, it is occasionally argued, can exercise considerable power to the extent that they do not openly challenge the formal myth of male dominance. "Real" gains are possible, in other words, so long as the larger symbolic order is not questioned. In much the same fashion one might contend that the peasantry often finds it both tactically convenient as well as necessary to leave the formal order intact while directing its attention to political ends that may never be accorded formal recognition. For a feminist argument along those lines, see Susan Carol Rogers, "Female Forms of Power and the Myth of Male Dominance," *American Ethnologist* 2, no. 4 (November 1975): 727–56.

12. Edward B. Harper, "Social Consequences of an Unsuccessful Low Caste Movement," *Social Mobility in the Caste System in India: An Interdisciplinary Symposium,* ed. James Silverberg, Supplement No. 3, *Comparative Studies in Society and History* (The Hague: Mouton, 1968): 48–49, emphasis added.

history of resistance to slavery in the antebellum U.S. South is largely a history of foot dragging, false compliance, flight, feigned ignorance, sabotage, theft, and, not least, cultural resistance. These practices, which rarely if ever called into question the system of slavery *as such,* nevertheless achieved far more in their unannounced, limited, and truculent way than the few heroic and brief armed uprisings about which so much has been written. The slaves themselves appear to have realized that in most circumstances their resistance could succeed only to the extent that it hid behind the mask of public compliance. One imagines parents giving their children advice not unlike advice contemporary wage laborers on plantations in Indonesia apparently hear from their own parents:

> I tell them [the youngsters] remember, you're selling your labor and the one who buys it wants to *see* that he gets something for it, so work when he's around, then you can relax when he goes away, but make sure you always *look like* you're working when the inspectors are there.[13]

Two specific observations emerge from this perspective. First, the nature of resistance is greatly influenced by the existing forms of labor control and by beliefs about the probability and severity of retaliation. Where the consequences of an open strike are likely to be catastrophic in terms of permanent dismissal or jail, the work force may resort to a slowdown or to shoddy work on the job. The often undeclared and anonymous nature of such action makes it particularly difficult for the antagonist to assess blame or apply sanctions. In industry, the slowdown has come to be called an "Italian" strike; it is used particularly when repression is feared, as in Poland under martial law in 1983.[14] Piece-work has of course often been used as a means of circumventing forms of resistance open to workers who are paid by the hour or day. Where piece-work prevails, as it did in silk and cotton weaving in nineteenth-century Germany, resistance is likely to find expression not in slowdowns, which are self-defeating, but in such forms as the "shortweighting of finished cloth, defective workmanship, and the purloining of materials."[15] Each form of labor control or payment is thus likely, other things equal, to generate its own distinctive forms of quiet resistance and "counterappropriation."

13. Ann Laura Stoler, *Capitalism and Confrontation in Sumatra's Plantation Belt, 1870–1979* (New Haven: Yale Univ. Press, 1985), 184.

14. See, for example, *New York Times,* Aug. 18, 1983, p. A6, "Polish Underground Backs Call for Slowdown," in which it is noted that "The tactic of a slowdown, known in Poland as an Italian Strike, has been used in the past by workers because it reduces the risk of reprisal."

15. Peter Linebaugh, "Karl Marx, the Theft of Wood, and Working-Class Composition: A Contribution to the Current Debate," *Crime and Social Justice* (Fall-Winter, 1976): 10. See also the brilliant analysis of piece-work by the Hungarian poet-worker Miklós Haraszti, *A Worker in a Worker's State,* trans. Michael Wright (New York: Universe, 1978).

The second observation is that resistance is not necessarily directed at the immediate source of appropriation. Inasmuch as the objective of the resisters is typically to meet such pressing needs as physical safety, food, land, or income, and to do so in relative safety, they may simply follow the line of least resistance. Prussian peasants and proletarians in the 1830s, beleaguered by dwarf holdings and wages below subsistance, responded by emigration or by poaching wood, fodder, and game on a large scale. The pace of "forest crime" rose as wages declined, as provisions became more expensive, and where emigration was more difficult; in 1836 there were 207,000 prosecutions in Prussia, 150,000 of which were for forest offenses.[16] They were supported by a mood of popular complicity that originated in earlier traditions of free access to forests, but the poachers cared little whether the rabbits or firewood they took came from the land of their particular employer or landlord. Thus, the reaction to an appropriation in one sphere may lead its victims to exploit small openings available elsewhere that are perhaps more accessible and less dangerous.[17]

Such techniques of resistance are well adapted to the particular characteristics of the peasantry. Being a diverse class of "low classness," scattered across the countryside, often lacking the discipline and leadership that would encourage opposition of a more organized sort, the peasantry is best suited to extended guerrilla-style campaigns of attrition that require little or no coordination. Their individual acts of foot dragging and evasion are often reinforced by a venerable popular culture of resistance. Seen in the light of a supportive subculture and the knowledge that the risk to any single resister is generally reduced to the extent that the whole community is involved, it becomes plausible to speak of a social movement. Curiously, however, this is a social movement with no formal organization, no formal leaders, no manifestoes, no dues, no name, and no banner. By virtue of their institutional invisibility, activities on anything less than a massive scale are, if they are noticed at all, rarely accorded any social significance.

Multiplied many thousandfold, such petty acts of resistance by peasants may in the end make an utter shambles of the policies dreamed up by their would-

16. Ibid., 13. In 1842, for Baden, there was one such conviction for every four inhabitants. For three centuries poaching was perhaps the most common rural crime in England and the subject of much repressive legislation. See, for example, the selections by Douglas Hay and E. P. Thompson in *Albion's Fatal Tree: Crime and Society in Eighteenth-Century England* by Douglas Hay, Peter Linebaugh, John G. Rule, E. P. Thompson, and Cal Winslow (New York: Pantheon, 1975).

17. Apparently the theft of wood in Germany in this period rarely touched communal forests. It goes without saying that, when a poor man survives by taking from others in the same situation, we can no longer speak of resistance. One central question to ask about any subordinate class is the extent to which it can, by internal sanctions, prevent the dog-eat-dog competition among themselves that can only serve the interests of appropriating classes.

be superiors in the capital. The state may respond in a variety of ways. Policies may be recast in line with more realistic expectations. They may be retained but reinforced with positive incentives aimed at encouraging voluntary compliance. And, of course, the state may simply choose to employ more coercion. Whatever the response, we must not miss the fact that the action of the peasantry has thus changed or narrowed the policy options available to the state. It is in this fashion, and not through revolts, let alone legal political pressure, that the peasantry has classically made its political presence felt. Thus any history or theory of peasant politics that attempts to do justice to the peasantry as a historical actor must necessarily come to grips with what I have chosen to call *everyday forms of resistance*. For this reason alone it is important to both document and bring some conceptual order to this seeming welter of human activity.

Everyday forms of resistance make no headlines.[18] Just as millions of anthozoan polyps create, willy-nilly, a coral reef, so do thousands upon thousands of individual acts of insubordination and evasion create a political or economic barrier reef of their own. There is rarely any dramatic confrontation, any moment that is particularly newsworthy. And whenever, to pursue the simile, the ship of state runs aground on such a reef, attention is typically directed to the shipwreck itself and not to the vast aggregation of petty acts that made it possible. It is only rarely that the perpetrators of these petty acts seek to call attention to themselves. Their safety lies in their anonymity. It is also extremely rarely that officials of the state wish to publicize the insubordination. To do so would be to admit that their policy is unpopular, and, above all, to expose the tenuousness of their authority in the countryside—neither of which the sovereign state finds in its interest.[19] The nature of the acts themselves and the self-interested muteness of the antagonists thus conspire to create a kind of complicitous silence that all but expunges everyday forms of resistance from the historical record.

History and social science, because they are written by an intelligentsia using written records that are also created largely by literate officials, is simply not well equipped to uncover the silent and anonymous forms of class struggle that

18. As Hobsbawn and Rude point out, it is not only conservative elites who have overlooked this form of resistance, but also the urban left: "The historians of social movements seem to have reacted very much like the rest of the urban left—to which most of them have traditionally belonged—i.e. they have tended to be unaware of it unless and until it appeared in sufficiently dramatic form or on a sufficiently large scale for the city newspapers to take notice."

19. But not entirely. District-level records are likely to prove rewarding in this respect, as district officials attempt to explain the shortfall in, say, tax receipts or conscription figures to their superiors in the capital. One imagines also that the informal, oral record is abundant, for example informal cabinet or ministerial meetings called to deal with policy failures caused by rural insubordination.

typify the peasantry.[20] Its practitioners implicitly join the conspiracy of the participants, who are themselves, as it were, sworn to secrecy. Collectively, this unlikely cabal contributes to a stereotype of the peasantry, enshrined in both literature and in history, as a class that alternates between long periods of abject passivity and brief, violent, and futile explosions of rage.

> He had centuries of fear and submission behind him, his shoulders had become hardened to blows, his soul so crushed that he did not recognise his own degradation. You could beat him and starve him and rob him of everything, year in, year out, before he would abandon his caution and stupidity, his mind filled with all sorts of muddled ideas which he could not properly understand; and this went on until a culmination of injustice and suffering flung him at his master's throat like some infuriated domestic animal who had been subjected to too many thrashings.[21]

There is a grain of truth in Zola's view, but only a grain. It is true that the "onstage" behavior of peasants during times of quiescence yields a picture of submission, fear, and caution. By contrast, peasant insurrections seem like visceral reactions of blind fury. What is missing from the account of "normal" passivity is the slow, grinding, quiet struggle over rents, crops, labor, and taxes in which submission and stupidity are often no more than a pose—a necessary tactic. What is missing from the picture of the periodic explosions is the underlying vision of justice that informs them and their specific goals and targets, which are often quite rational indeed.[22] The explosions themselves are frequently a sign that the normal and largely covert forms of class struggle are failing or have reached a crisis point. Such declarations of open war, with their mortal risks, normally come only after a protracted struggle on different terrain.

RESISTANCE AS THOUGHT AND SYMBOL

Thus far, I have treated everyday forms of peasant resistance as if they were not much more than a collection of individual acts or behaviors. To confine the analysis to behavior alone, however, is to miss much of the point. It reduces the

---

20. The partial exceptions that come to mind are anthropology, because of its insistence on close observation in the field, and the history of slavery and Soviet collectivization.

21. Zola, *The Earth*, 91.

22. I do not by any means wish to suggest that violence born of revenge, hatred, and fury play no role—only that they do not exhaust the subject, as Zola and others imply. It is certainly true, as Cobb (*Police and the People*, 89–90) claims, that George Rudé (*The Crowd in History, 1730–1848* [New York: Wiley, 1964]) has gone too far into turning rioters into sober, domesticated, bourgeois political actors.

explanation of human action to the level one might use to explain how the water buffalo resists its driver to establish a tolerable pace of work or why the dog steals scraps from the table. But inasmuch as I seek to understand the resistance of thinking, social beings, I can hardly fail to ignore their consciousness—the meaning they give to their acts. The symbols, the norms, the ideological forms they create constitute the indispensable background to their behavior. However partial or imperfect their understanding of the situation, they are gifted with intentions and values and purposefulness that condition their acts. This is so evident that it would hardly merit restating were it not for the lamentable tendency in behavioral science to read mass behavior directly from the statistical abstracts on income, caloric intake, newspaper circulation, or radio ownership. I seek, then, not only to uncover and describe the patterns of everyday resistance as a distinctive behavior with far-reaching implications, but to ground that description in an analysis of the conflicts of meaning and value in which these patterns arise and to which they contribute.

The relationship between thought and action is, to put it very mildly, a complicated issue. Here I wish to emphasize only two fairly straightforward points. First, neither intentions nor acts are "unmoved movers." Acts born of intentions circle back, as it were, to influence consciousness and hence subsequent intentions and acts. Thus acts of resistance and thoughts about (or the meaning of) resistance are in *constant* communication—in constant dialogue. Second, intentions and consciousness are not tied in quite the same way to the material world as behavior is. It is possible and common for human actors to conceive of a line of action that is, at the moment, either impractical or impossible. Thus a person may dream of a revenge or a millennial kingdom of justice that may never occur. On the other hand, as circumstances change, it may become possible to act on those dreams. The realm of consciousness gives us a kind of privileged access to lines of action that may—just may—become plausible at some future date. How, for example, can we give an adequate account of any peasant rebellion without some knowledge of the shared values, the "offstage" talk, the consciousness of the peasantry prior to rebellion?[23] How, finally, can we understand everyday forms of resistance without reference to the intentions, ideas, and language of those human beings who practice it?

The study of the social consciousness of subordinate classes is important for yet another reason. It may allow us to clarify a major debate in both the Marxist and non-Marxist literature—a debate that centers on the extent to which elites

---

23. Lest this seem implicitly and one-sidedly to treat consciousness as prior to and in some sense causing behavior, one could just as easily recoil one step and inquire about the construction of this consciousness. Such an inquiry would necessarily begin with the social givens of the actor's position in society. Social being conditions social consciousness.

are able to impose their own image of a just social order, not simply on the behavior of non-elites, but on their consciousness as well.

The problem can be stated simply. Let us assume that we can *establish* that a given group is exploited and that, further, this exploitation takes place in a context in which the coercive force at the disposal of the elites and/or the state makes any open expression of discontent virtually impossible. Assuming, for the sake of argument, that the only behavior observable is apparently acquiescent, at least two divergent interpretations of this state of affairs are possible. One may claim that the exploited group, because of a hegemonic religious or social ideology, actually accepts its situation as a normal, even justifiable part of the social order. This explanation of passivity assumes at least a fatalistic acceptance of that social order and perhaps even an active complicity—both of which Marxists might call "mystification" or "false-consciousness." [24] It typically rests on the assumption that elites dominate not only the physical means of production but the symbolic means of production as well[25]—and that this symbolic hegemony allows them to control the very standards by which their rule is evaluated. [26] As Gramsci argued, elites control the "ideological sectors" of society—culture, religion, education, and media—and can thereby engineer consent for their rule. By creating and disseminating a universe of discourse and the concepts to go with it, by defining the standards of what is true, beautiful, moral, fair, and legitimate, they build a symbolic climate that prevents subordinate classes from thinking their way free. In fact, for Gramsci, the proletariat is more enslaved at the level of ideas than at the level of behavior. The historic task of "the party" is therefore less to lead a revolution than to break the symbolic miasma that blocks revolutionary thought. Such interpretations have been invoked to account for lower-class quiescence, particularly in rural societies such as India, where a

24. See the argument along these lines by Richard Hoggart, *The Uses of Literacy* (London: Chatto & Windus, 1954): 77–78.

25. In the Marxist tradition one might cite especially Antonio Gramsci, *Selections from the Prison Notebooks,* ed. and trans. Quinten Hoare and Geoffrey Nowell Smith (London: Lawrence & Wishart, 1971), 123–209, and Georg Lukacs, *History and Class Consciousness: Studies in Marxist Dialectics,* trans. Rodney Livingston (Cambridge, Mass.: MIT Press, 1971). Marx, to my knowledge, *never* used the term "false-consciousness," although "the fetishism of commodities" may be read this way. But the fetishism of commodities mystifies especially the bourgeoisie, not merely subordinate classes. For a critical view of "hegemony" as it might apply to the peasantry, see James C. Scott, "Hegemony and the Peasantry," *Politics and Society* 7, no. 3 (1977): 267–96, and chap. 7 below.

26. For other explanations of the same phenomenon, see, for example, Frank Parkin, "Class Inequality and Meaning Systems," in his *Class Inequality and Political Order* (New York: Praeger, 1971), 79–102, and Louis Dumont, *Homo Hierarchicus* (London: Weidenfeld & Nicholson, 1970).

venerable system of rigid caste stratification is reinforced by religious sanctions. Lower castes are said to accept their fate in the Hindu hierarchy in the hope of being rewarded in the next life.[27]

An alternative interpretation of such quiescence might be that it is to be explained by the relationships of force in the countryside and not by peasant values and beliefs.[28] Agrarian peace, in this view, may well be the peace of repression (remembered and/or anticipated) rather than the peace of consent or complicity.

The issues posed by these divergent interpretations are central to the analysis of peasant politics and, beyond that, to the study of class relationships in general. Much of the debate on these issues has taken place as if the choice of interpretation were more a matter of the ideological preferences of the analyst than of actual research. Without underestimating the problems involved, I believe there are a number of ways in which the question can be empirically addressed. It is possible, in other words, to say something meaningful about the relative weight of consciousness, on the one hand, and repression (in fact, memory, or potential) on the other, in restraining acts of resistance.

The argument for false-consciousness, after all, depends on the symbolic alignment of elite and subordinate class values—that is, on the assumption that the peasantry (proletariat) actually accepts most of the elite vision of the social order. What does mystification mean, if not a group's assent to the social ideology that justifies its exploitation? To the extent that an exploited group's outlook is in substantial symbolic alignment with elite values, the case for mystification is strengthened; to the extent that it holds deviant or contradictory values, the case is weakened. A close study of the subculture of a subordinate group and its relation to dominant elite values should thus give us part of the answer we seek. The evidence will seldom be cut and dried, for any group's social outlook will contain a number of diverse and even contradictory currents. It is not the mere existence of deviant subcultural themes that is notable, for they are well-nigh universal, but rather the forms they may take, the values they embody, and the emotional attachment they inspire. Thus, even in the absence of resistance, we are not without resources to address the question of false-consciousness.

To relieve the somewhat abstract nature of the argument thus far, it may be helpful to illustrate the kind of evidence that might bear directly on this issue. Suppose, for example, that the "onstage" linguistic term for sharecropping or for tenancy is one that emphasizes its fairness and justice. Suppose, further, that the term used by tenants behind the backs of landlords to describe this rela-

27. But note the efforts of lower castes to raise their ritual status and, more recently, the tendency for *harijans* to leave Hinduism altogether and convert to Islam, which makes no caste distinctions among believers.

28. See, for example, Gerrit Huizer, *Peasant Mobilization and Land Reform in Indonesia* (The Hague: Institute of Social Studies, 1972).

tionship is quite different—cynical and mocking.[29] Is this not plausible evidence that the tenant's view of the relationship is largely demystified—that he does not accept the elite's definition of tenancy at face value? When Haji Ayub and Haji Kadir are called *Haji "Broom," Haji Kedikut,* or *Pak Ceti* behind their backs, is it not plausible evidence that their claim to land, to interest, to rents, and to respect is at least contested at the level of consciousness, if not at the level of "onstage" acts? What are we to make of lower-class religious sects (the Quakers in seventeenth-century England, Saminists in twentieth-century Java, to name only two of many) that abandon the use of honorifics to address their social betters and insist instead on low forms of address or on using words like "friend" or "brother" to describe everyone. Is this not telling evidence that the elite's libretto for the hierarchy of nobility and respect is, at the very least, not sung word for word by its subjects?

By reference to the culture that peasants fashion from their experience—their "offstage" comments and conversation, their proverbs, folksongs, and history, legends, jokes, language, ritual, and religion—it should be possible to determine to what degree, and in what ways, peasants actually accept the social order propagated by elites. Some elements of lower-class culture are of course more relevant to this issue than others. For any agrarian system, one can identify a set of key values that justify the right of an elite to the deference, land, taxes, and rent it claims. It is, in large part, an empirical matter whether such key values find support or opposition within the subculture of subordinate classes. If bandits and poachers are made into folkheroes, we can infer that transgressions of elite codes evoke a vicarious admiration. If the forms of outward deference are privately mocked, it may suggest that peasants are hardly in the thrall of a naturally ordained social order. If those who try to curry the personal favor of elites are shunned and ostracized by others of their class, we have evidence that there is a lower-class subculture with sanctioning power. Rejection of elite values, however, is seldom an across-the-board proposition, and only a close study of peasant values can define the major points of friction and correspondence. In this sense, points of friction become diagnostic only when they center on key values in the social order, grow, and harden.

THE EXPERIENCE AND CONSCIOUSNESS OF HUMAN AGENTS

It was with such issues in mind that I spent more than a year and a half in the village of Sedaka listening, asking questions, and trying to understand the issues that animated villagers during my stay among them. The result is, I hope, a close-to-the-ground, fine-grained account of class relations in a very small place (seventy families, 360 people) experiencing very large changes (the "green rev-

29. Tenancy in Central Luzon, the Philippines, is a striking case in point. Communication from Benedick Kerkvliet, University of Hawaii.

olution": in this case, the double-cropping of rice). Much of that account, though not all of it, is an account of what appears to be a losing class struggle against capitalist agricultural development and its human agents. It goes without saying that I have thought it important to listen carefully to the human agents I was studying, to their experience, to their categories, to their values, to their understanding of the situation. There are several reasons for building this kind of phenomenological approach into the study.

The first reason has to do with how social science can and ought to be conducted. It is fashionable in some of the more structuralist variants of neo-Marxism to assume that one can infer the nature of class relations in any nonsocialist Third World country directly from a few diagnostic features—the dominant mode of production, the mode and timing of insertion into the world economy, or the mode of surplus appropriation. This procedure entails a highly reductionist leap straight from one or a very few economic givens to the class situation that is presumed to follow from these givens. There are no human actors here, only mechanisms and puppets. To be sure, the economic givens are crucial; they define much, but not all, of the situation that human actors face; they place limits on the responses that are possible, imaginable. But those limits are wide and, within them, human actors fashion their own response, their own experience of class, their own history. As E. P. Thompson notes in his polemic against Althusser:

> nor is it [the epistemological refusal of experience] pardonable in a Marxist, since experience is a necessary middle term between social being and social consciousness: it is experience (often class experience) which gives a coloration to culture, to values, and to thought; it is by means of experience that the mode of production exerts a determining pressure upon other activities. . . . classes arise because men and women, in determinate productive relations, identify their antagonistic interests, and come to struggle, to think, and to value in class ways: thus the process of class formation is a process of self-making, although under conditions which are given.[30]

How else can a mode of production affect the nature of class relations except as it is mediated by human experience and interpretation? Only by capturing that experience in something like its fullness will we be able to say anything meaningful about how a given economic system influences those who constitute it and maintain it or supersede it. And, of course, if this is true for the peasantry or the proletariat, it is surely true for the bourgeoisie, the petite bourgeoisie, and even the lumpenproletariat.[31] To omit the experience of human agents from the analysis of class relations is to have theory swallow its own tail.

30. *The Poverty of Theory and Other Essays* (New York: Monthly Review Press, 1978), 98, 106–07.
31. It is also true for the regular pattern of human activities that we call institutions. For example—note well, structuralists—the state.

A second reason for putting the experience of human agents at the center of the analysis concerns the concept of class itself. It is all very well to identify a collection of individuals who all occupy a comparable position in relation to the means of production—a class-in-itself. But what if such objective, structural determinations find little echo in the consciousness and meaningful activity of those who are thus identified?[32] In place of simply assuming a one-to-one correspondence between "objective" class structure and consciousness, is it not far preferable to understand how those structures are apprehended by flesh-and-blood human actors? Class, after all, does not exhaust the total explanatory space of social actions. Nowhere is this more true than within the peasant village, where class may compete with kinship, neighborhood, faction, and ritual links as foci of human identity and solidarity. Beyond the village level, it may also compete with ethnicity, language group, religion, and region as a focus of loyalty. Class may be applicable to some situations but not to others; it may be reinforced or crosscut by other ties; it may be far more important for the experience of some than of others. Those who are tempted to dismiss all principles of human action that contend with class identity as "false-consciousness" and to wait for Althusser's "determination in the last instance" are likely to wait in vain. In the meantime, the messy reality of multiple identities will continue to be the experience out of which social relations are conducted. Neither peasants nor proletarians deduce their identities directly or solely from the mode of production, and the sooner we attend to the concrete experience of class as it is lived, the sooner we will appreciate both the obstacles to, and the possibilities for, class formation.

A further justification for a close analysis of class relations is that in the village, and not only there, classes travel under strange and deceptive banners. They are not apprehended as ghostly, abstract concepts but in the all-too-human form of specific individuals and groups, specific conflicts and struggles. Piven and Cloward capture the specificity of this experience for the working class:

> First, people experience deprivation and oppression within a concrete setting, not as the end product of large and abstract processes, and it is the concrete experience that molds their discontent into specific grievances against specific targets. Workers experience the factory, the speeding rhythm of the assembly line, the foremen, the spies, the guards, the owner, and the pay check. *They do not experience monopoly capitalism.*[33]

In the same fashion the Malay peasant experiences increasing land rents, stingy

32. See the persuasive argument along these lines by James Brow, "Some Problems in the Analysis of Agrarian Classes in South Asia," *Peasant Studies* 9, no. 1 (Fall 1981): 15–33.

33. Frances Fox Piven and Richard A. Cloward, *Poor People's Movements: Why They Succeed, How They Fail* (New York: Vintage, 1977), 20, emphasis added.

landlords, ruinous interest rates from moneylenders, combine-harvesters that replace him, and petty bureaucrats who treat him shabbily. He does not *experience* the cash nexus or the capitalist pyramid of finance that makes of those landlords, combine-harvester owners, moneylenders, and bureaucrats only the penultimate link in a complex process. Small wonder, then, that the language of class in the village should bear the birthmarks of its distinctive origin. Villagers do not call Pak Haji Kadir an agent of finance capital; they call him Kadir *Ceti* because it was through the Chettiar moneylending caste, which dominated rural credit from about 1910 until World War II, that the Malay peasant most forcibly experienced finance capital. The fact that the word *Chettiar* has similar connotations for millions of peasants in Vietnam and Burma as well is a tribute to the homogenization of experience which the capitalist penetration of Southeast Asia brought in its wake. Nor is it simply a question of recognizing a disguise and uncovering the *real* relationship that lies behind it. For the disguise, the metaphor, is part of the real relationship. The Malays historically experienced the moneylender as a moneylender *and* as a Chettiar—that is, as a foreigner and a non-Muslim. Similarly, the Malay typically experiences the shopkeeper and the rice buyer not only as a creditor and wholesaler but as a person of another race and another religion. Thus the concept of class as it is lived is nearly always an alloy containing base metals; its concrete properties, its uses, are those of the alloy and not of the pure metals it may contain. Either we take it as we find it or we abandon the empirical study of class altogether.

That the experienced concept of class should be found embedded in a particular history of social relations is hardly to be deplored. It is this rootedness of the experience that gives it its power and its meaning. When the experience is widely shared, the symbols that embody class relations can come to have an extraordinary evocative power. One can imagine, in this context, how individual grievances become collective grievances and how collective grievances may take on the character of a class-based myth tied, as always, to local experience. Thus, a particular peasant may be a tenant of a landlord whom he regards as particularly oppressive. He may grumble; he may even have fantasies about telling the landlord what he thinks of him or even darker thoughts of arson or homicide. If this is an isolated, personal grievance, the affair is likely to stop there—at fantasy. If, however, many tenants find themselves in the same boat, either because they share the same landlord or because their landlords treat them in comparable ways, there arises the basis for a collective grievance, collective fantasy, and even collective acts. Peasants are then likely to find themselves trading stories about bad landlords and, since some landlords are likely to be more notorious than others, they become the focus of elaborate stories, the repository of the collective grievances of much of the community against that kind of landlord in general. Thus, we have the legend of Haji Broom, which has become a kind of metaphorical shorthand for large-scale landlordism in the region. Thus, we have poems about Haji Kedikut, which are not so much stories about individuals as a symbol for an entire class of Haji landlords.

If there had ever been (and there has not) a large-scale movement of rebellion against landlords in Kedah, we can be certain that something of the spirit of those legends would have been reflected in action. The way was already symbolically prepared. But the central point to be emphasized is simply that the concept of class, if it is to be found at all, is to be found encoded in concrete, shared experience that reflects both the cultural material and historical givens of its carriers. In the West, the concept of *food* is expressed most often by *bread*. In most of Asia, it means *rice*.[34] The shorthand for *capitalist* in America may be *Rockefeller*, with all the historical connotations of that name; the shorthand for *bad landlord* in Sedaka is *Haji Broom,* with all the historical connotations of that name.

For all these reasons, the study of class relations in Sedaka, as elsewhere, must of necessity be as much a study of meaning and experience as it is of behavior considered narrowly. No other procedure is possible inasmuch as behavior is never self-explanatory. One need cite only the famous example of a rapid closing and opening of a single eyelid, used by Gilbert Ryle and elaborated on by Clifford Geertz, to illustrate the problem.[35] Is it a twitch or a wink? Mere observation of the physical act gives no clue. If it is a wink, what kind of wink is it: one of conspiracy, of ridicule, of seduction? Only a knowledge of the culture, the shared understandings, of the actor and his or her observers and confederates can begin to tell us; and even then we must allow for possible misunderstandings. It is one thing to know that landlords have raised cash rents for rice land; it is another to know what this behavior means for those affected. Perhaps, just perhaps, tenants regard the rise in rents as reasonable and long overdue. Perhaps they regard the rise as oppressive and intended to drive them off the land. Perhaps opinion is divided. Only an inquiry into the experience of tenants, the meaning they attach to the event, can offer us the possibility of an answer. I say "the possibility of an answer" because it may be in the interest of tenants

34. "Man does not live by bread alone." But "bread" may come to mean more than just food; it may mean the wherewithal for living or cash, as in "Can you loan me some bread, man?" In Malay society, the proverb *Jangan pecah periok nasi orang* (Don't break someone else's rice pot) means "don't threaten someone else's source of livelihood."

35. Clifford Geertz, *The Interpretation of Cultures* (New York: Basic, 1973), 6–9. An excellent summary of this intellectual position may be found in Richard J. Bernstein, *The Restructuring of Social and Political Theory* (Philadelphia: Univ. of Pennsylvania Press, 1978), 173–236. As Bernstein notes, "These intentional descriptions, meanings, and interpretations are not merely subjective states of mind which can be correlated with external behavior; they are constitutive of the activities and practices of our social and political lives" (229–30).

to misrepresent their opinion, and thus interpretation may be tricky. But without that information we are utterly at sea. A theft of grain, an apparent snub, an apparent gift—their import is inaccessible to us unless we can construct it from the meanings only human actors can provide. In this sense, we concentrate at least as much on the experience of behavior as on behavior itself, as much on history as carried in people's heads as on "the flow of events,"[36] as much on how class is perceived and understood as on "objective class relations."

The approach taken here certainly relies heavily on what is known as phenomenology or ethnomethodology.[37] But it is not confined to that approach, for it is only slightly more true that people speak for themselves than that behavior speaks for itself. Pure phenomenology has its own pitfalls. A good deal of behavior, including speech, is automatic and unreflective, based on understandings that are seldom if ever raised to the level of consciousness. A careful observer must provide an interpretation of such behavior that is more than just a repetition of the "commonsense" knowledge of participants. As an interpretation, it has to be judged by the standards of its logic, its economy, and its consistency with other known social facts. Human agents may also provide contradictory accounts of their own behavior, or they may wish to conceal their understanding from the observer or from one another. Hence, the same standards of interpretation apply, although the ground is admittedly treacherous. Beyond this, there simply are factors in any situation that shed light on the action of human agents, but of which they can scarcely be expected to be aware. An international credit crisis, changes in worldwide demand for food grains, a quiet factional struggle in the cabinet that affects agrarian policy, small changes in the genetic makeup of seed grain, for example, may each have a decided impact on local social relations whether or not they are known to the actors involved. Such knowledge is what an outside observer can often add to a description of the situation as a supplement to, *not a substitute for,* the description that human agents themselves provide. For however partial or even mistaken the experienced reality of the human agents, it is that experienced reality that provides the basis for their understanding and their action. Finally, there is no such thing as a complete account of experienced reality, no "full verbal transcript of the conscious experience."[38] The fullness of the transcript is limited both by the empirical and analytical interests of the transcriber—in this case, class relations broadly construed—and by the practical limits of time and space.

36. Clifford Geertz, "Blurred Genres: The Refiguration of Social Thought," *American Scholar* 49, no. 2 (Spring 1980): 175.

37. See, for example, Roy Turner, ed., *Ethnomethodology: Selected Readings* (Harmondsworth: Penguin, 1974).

38. John Dunn, "Practising History and Social Science on 'Realist' Assumptions," in *Action and Interpretation: Studies in the Philosophy of the Social Sciences,* ed. C. Hookway and P. Pettit (Cambridge: Cambridge Univ. Press, 1979), 160.

What is attempted here, then, is a plausible account of class relations in Sedaka that relies as much as possible on the evidence, experience, and descriptions of action which the participants have themselves provided. At numerous points I have supplemented that description with interpretations of my own, for I am well aware of how ideology, the rationalization of personal interest, day-to-day social tactics, or even politeness may affect a participant's account. But never, I hope, have I *replaced* their account with my own. Instead I have tried to validate my interpretation by showing how it "removes anomalies within, or adds information to, the best description which the participant is able to offer." For, as Dunn argues,

What we cannot properly do is to claim to *know* that we understand him or his action better than he does himself without access to the best description which he is able to offer. . . . The criterion of proof for the validity of a description or interpretation of an action is the economy and accuracy with which it handles the full text of the agent's description.

3 • The Landscape of Resistance

The setting within which the peasants of Sedaka today conduct their lives is, only in small part, their own creation. Perhaps a century ago, before British annexation, when land was still being cleared, when the cash economy and production for sale were but a minor facet of a basically subsistence economy, and when the intrusions of the state into village affairs were only sporadic, it might have been plausible to think of the pioneers of Sedaka as largely the creators of their small world. Even then of course they were scarcely autonomous.[1] The state was already mobilizing labor to dig drainage canals, thereby opening new paddy land and enlarging its revenue base. The trade in rice through Penang had already monetized the economy sufficiently to expose it to larger market forces. Beyond these social forces that shaped their world, there were, above all, the vagaries of a capricious nature that, year in and year out, determined how well they ate, or if they ate at all.

The shift has been a shift of degree, but massive enough to constitute a qualitative change. It is not so much that agriculture is no longer a gamble, but rather that the terms of the season-by-season wager are now decisively set by social forces that originate far outside the village sphere. Everything from the timing of water supply, and hence the schedule of transplanting and harvesting, to the cost of fertilizer and tractor services, the price of paddy, the cost of milling, the conditions of credit, and the cost of labor is so much an artifact of state policy and the larger economy that the sphere of local autonomy has shrunk appreciably.

A detailed account of the social history of Sedaka and of the outside forces that impinge on it is neither necessary nor plausible here. What is necessary, however, is a sketch of the major features of the landscape that forms the context of village class relations. The *background* of this landscape, the basic countours of the postcolonial state and of the economy, though definitely man-made, is for all practical purposes a given that is rarely, if ever, noticed by the petty actors who are the center of our attention. One cannot, after all, expect the fish to talk about the water; it is simply the medium in which they live and breathe. Most of the elaborate, commonsense knowledge that villagers have in great abundance is of course ultimately predicated on these gross features of their taken-for-granted landscape. In any different context, much of what they know would make little

1. For a picture of Kedah at the end of the nineteenth century, see Sharom Ahmat, "The Political Structure of the State of Kedah, 1879–1905," *Journal of Southeast Asian Studies* 1, no. 2 (September 1970): 115–28; and Zaharah Haji Mahmud, "Change in a Malay Sultanate: An Historical Geography of Kedah before 1939" (Master's thesis, University of Malaya, 1965).

sense. The characteristic features of this basic landscape create palpable limits to what, in the short run at least, is possible; they also create opportunities and exert a determinate pressure on the nature of class relations. Thus, it is the legally enforced system of private property in land that makes landlord-tenant relations both possible and common as a focus of class conflict. Thus, it is the practice of electoral competition, however severely circumscribed, that permits political conflict to be channeled and institutionalized in certain ways. Private property in land and elections, as social creations, are hardly immutable but, so long as they persist, they come to be assumed as "natural" facts like the clayey soils or monsoon rains in Sedaka.[2]

In what might be called the *middle ground* of this landscape stand the economic and social facts of, say, the past ten years. The most prominent of the landmarks here are the consequences of double-cropping for tenure, income, work, mobility, stratification, and social structure in the entire region, of which Sedaka is but a small fragment. Scarcely less prominent is the change in both the scope and nature of government activity. This middle ground is in sharper focus; it manifests itself more palpably in the daily lives of rice farmers; it represents the environment to which they have had to adjust; it is, finally, a subject about which peasants have very decided, if divergent, opinions. To sketch the contours of this middle ground is to establish the basic social and economic facts that are *then* subject to the interpretations that villagers give them. If, for example, the loss of wage labor income attributable to combine-harvesters is strongly deplored by many villagers, it would be helpful to know both how widespread this pattern is and what the typical losses are. The purpose of sketching this middle ground is not to let the facts speak for themselves (they never do), but rather to establish something of a baseline of experienced givens that form the point of departure for relations between classes.

The *foreground* of the landscape—the changes of the past decade as they have become manifest within the village of Sedaka—will be depicted in chapter 4. These two chapters constitute the setting for local experience and activity.

The array of facts presented have been chosen with two principles of selection in mind. First, I have judged that the massive transformation in techniques of production and production relations attendant on double-cropping were the central facts for class relations in Sedaka. Second, in selecting among those facts, I have also been guided by the concerns that seemed to preoccupy villagers themselves. If the levels of land rents or the loss of harvest work aroused great worry, I let that worry influence my selection of facts. No doubt I have left out some

2. It is in this sense, and only in this sense, that one may perhaps speak of "false-consciousness." Even in this realm, peasants are quite capable of imagining a different system of property or a political system without elections and of expressing an opinion on such issues. Speculations of this kind are, however, of little practical relevance to the context of daily social action.

pertinent, even vital facts. But it appeared preferable to be guided by their experience rather than my own, for it is from their experience that their reactions are shaped.

BACKGROUND: MALAYSIA AND THE PADDY SECTOR

If one had to be a peasant somewhere in Southeast Asia, there is little doubt that Malaysia would be the first choice by nearly any standard. Its advantages include an open, buoyant, capitalist economy with an abundance of natural resources, a relatively favorable population-to-land ratio, a political system that, if not democratic, does at least allow some political opposition, and a state that is less predatory than most of its neighbors. In terms of health services, education, water and electricity supply, transportation, flood control, and irrigation, it has almost surely done more for its population than any other Southeast Asian state.[3] Its rate of growth over the past twenty years has made it the envy of its neighbors and the darling of international lending agencies such as the World Bank and the Asian Development Bank. Gross national product per capita has grown at an average annual rate of 3.9 percent from 1960 to 1976, a rate far higher than the median for low-income countries or middle-income countries and higher also than the median for industrial nations.[4] Thus, despite rapid population growth (3 percent annually), Malaysia achieved a per capita gross national product of over US$1,100 by 1978, a figure that dwarfed, by a factor of 2, that of any major Southeast Asian country.[5]

If ever there was a case of export-led growth, it is Malaysia. In 1980 the country was the world's largest exporter of tropical hardwoods, tin, rubber, and palm oil, and it has been a net exporter of petroleum since 1975. One result of a consistently favorable balance of trade has been to swell government revenue nearly fourfold between 1966 and 1976, thereby enormously expanding the policy options and development expenditures of the state. By Southeast Asian standards at least the Malaysian treasury is literally awash with revenue. Another result has been to reinforce the dependence of the economy on the markets for its mostly primary export commodities. That dependence is now far more diversified than in the past when it rested on tin and rubber, but it is a marked dependence nontheless. As is so often the case, even the impressive growth of

3. For evidence along these lines see Jacob Meerman, *Public Expenditure in Malaysia: Who Benefits and Why,* A World Bank Research Publication (London: Oxford Univ. Press, 1979).

4. Kevin Young, Willem C. F. Bussink, and Parvez Hassan, *Malaysia's Growth and Equity in a Multiracial Society,* A World Bank Country Economic Report (Baltimore: Johns Hopkins Univ. Press, 1980), 24.

5. Far Eastern Economic Review, *Asia 1980 Yearbook* (Hong Kong: South China Morning Post, 1981), 10.

import-substitution industries has not lessened Malaysia's reliance on trade; such industrialization has depended heavily on imports of capital goods and inter-mediate goods (nearly three-fourths of total imports by value in 1974). Foreign domination of the economy has also persisted, albeit in modified form. Once entrenched, primarily in the plantation sector, foreign enterprises became prom-inent both in import substitution (for example, textiles, steel, motor vehicle assembly) and in export-goods industries (for example, electrical machinery, tran-sistors) in free-trade zones. As of 1974 more than 60 percent of the share capital of Malaysian corporations was held by foreigners.

In this context, the needs of smallholder agriculture in general and the paddy sector in particular have never been a top priority of either the colonial or the postcolonial state. As the main source of foreign exchange and government revenue, the plantation sector has always had its requirements for infrastructure, labor, land, and capital take precedence. Now, with a growing urban work force, the effort to minimize labor costs by keeping the domestic price of rice (the major staple) low has become even more compelling.

As elsewhere, the pattern of capitalist development, export-led growth, and encouragement of foreign investment has also resulted in a growing maldistri-bution of income. This has occurred despite a remarkable overall rate of growth and government programs directly aimed at redressing poverty. It is reflected in the growing disparity between average incomes in the traditional agricultural sector and the remainder of the economy from 1960 to 1970. While the gap was on the order of 1 to 2.5 in 1960, it grew to more than 1 to 3 in 1970.[6] It is reflected as well in the widening gulf between the incomes of those below the official poverty line and those above it. From 1960 to 1970, for example, the real incomes of the rural poor actually declined by as much as 0.4 percent per annum, while the incomes of the rest of the population grew at about 2.4 percent annually.[7] Over the next eight years (1970–78) the real incomes of the rural poor grew (2.4 percent annually), but at a rate less than half that of the rest of the population (5.2 percent). Not only have the disparities in income grown markedly over nearly two decades, but by 1978 the real incomes of the two major groups of rural poor—-paddy smallholders and rubber tappers—were not appreciably better than they had been in 1960. What we have, in effect, then is a pattern of overall capitalist growth that has generated greater inequities

6. Young et al., *Malaysia's Growth*, 31. The "traditional agricultural sector" here excludes the estate sector, which accounted for only 18 percent of the agricultural labor force in 1970. Three-fourths of agricultural employment is, by contrast, con-centrated in rubber and rice smallholdings.

7. Estimates taken from International Bank for Reconstruction and Develop-ment, *Malaysia: Selected Issues in Rural Poverty*, vol. 2, World Bank Report No. 2685-MA (Washington: World Bank, 1980), 3, 13–14. Figures given in the remainder of this paragraph are from the same source.

and from which the rural poor have benefited least.[8] The linkage between the extent of poverty and the pattern of growth in Malaysia is reflected in the anomaly that a substantially larger proportion of its rural population (44 percent) is below the nation's offical poverty line income than is the case in other countries with far lower per capita incomes.

Whatever policy attention the paddy sector has received has come about for three reasons. The first is the concern of the state to assure the steady domestic supply of rice.[9] When imported rice was cheap and abundant and when rubber and tin prices were buoyant, the colonial policy of using export earnings to buy rice from abroad seemed to make sense. From time to time, however, the assumptions on which the policy was based failed to hold. In 1931, for example, the slump in export prices called into question the colony's ability to pay for the rice it needed. For the first time, the government began to address the question of self-sufficiency in rice; Malay Reservation laws were passed to prevent land from passing out of Malay hands and out of paddy cultivation and in 1939 a guaranteed minimum paddy price was established. Despite these initiatives, Malaya continued to import, on average, half of the rice it consumed, for even at the depth of the Depression rubber tapping was more profitable than growing rice. A rice-provisioning crisis following World War II and then, in 1954, a paddy price slump that threatened producer incomes and prompted large demonstrations of farmers in Alor Setar gave renewed urgency to the issue of self-sufficiency. The result was a modest program of loans to help indebted farmers redeem their mortgaged land and a Padi Cultivators' Ordinance designed to control paddy rents and ensure security of tenure. This last has remained virtually a dead letter to this day. Such ineffective patchwork solutions were inevitable, inasmuch as the state was unwilling to raise greatly the farm-gate price for fear of what this would imply for the wages of the plantation and urban work force. Progress toward self-sufficiency would have to await the new inputs and double-cropping technology of the last two decades.

The second, and by far most important, stimulus for addressing the needs of the paddy sector has been the nature of political competition since independence. To put it crudely, the dominant political party since independence (the United Malay Nationalists' Organization, UMNO) is an exclusively Malay party that depends largely on Malay votes to keep it in power. Many of those votes must come from paddy farmers, who are overwhelmingly Malays. The electoral system

8. If one were to shift one's focus from income to amenities such as health services and education, the picture would be more encouraging. For it is in this area that government policies have made a substantial impact. It is also true of course that, without the government programs directed toward the rural poor, the income statistics would have been even more dismaying.

9. For a fine account of rice policy, see Otto Charles Doering, III, "Malaysian Rice Policy and the Muda Irrigation Project" (Ph.D. diss., Cornell University, 1973).

is, to be sure, hedged about by severe restrictions. There is virtually no municipal self-government, thereby ensuring that the largely Chinese towns will not fall into the hands of Chinese opposition parties. An internal security act allows the government to hobble the activities of both religious and left-wing opposition with preventive detention. Finally, a pattern of parliamentary constituencies of unequal population size makes the Malay vote far more influential than it would otherwise be. The electoral system has nevertheless played a vital role since 1957 in legitimizing the rule of the Malay political elite and of the National Front (Barisan Nasional), which it dominates.

The juxtaposition of a modified electoral regime with an open, export-oriented economy that has exacerbated inequities in income distribution provides a setting in which the Malay paddy farmer has become a vital political factor. Consider the following facts. First, the average per capita income of Malays in 1970 was roughly one-half that of Chinese, the other major ethnic community.[10] Taking only poor households, nearly three-quarters were Malay and over four-fifths were rural.[11] The incidence of poverty, moreover, is far higher among paddy farmers than any other major occupational group, and those paddy farmers are predominantly (84 percent) Malays. The regional distribution of this poverty is also noteworthy: It is concentrated in the northern states of the peninsula (Kedah, Perlis, Kelantan, and Trengganu), which produce most of the nation's paddy and which are most heavily Malay. Little wonder that the combination of a large, poor, rural Malay population, together with growing income disparities, has provided the most fertile ground for inroads by the major Malay opposition party, PAS (Partai Islam). Following the general elections of 1969, UMNO had every reason to be concerned about its political hegemony among Malays; PAS had won virtually as many Malay votes overall as UMNO, and in the 43 seats where there was a straight fight between the two PAS is estimated to have received more Malay votes than UMNO.[12] PAS has, at one time, controlled the state governments of Kelantan and Trengganu and in 1969 came within striking distance of winning in Kedah as well.

The third reason why the ruling party was forced to confront the problems of poverty and growing income disparities is that they became a threat not only to its electoral hegemony but also to the fragile peace of the civil society itself. The communal riots in Kuala Lumpur and in other cities following the 1969

10. Young et al., *Malaysia's Growth,* 104–05, and Meerman, *Public Expenditure,* 89. The figures in Meerman are in part derived from Sudhir Anand, *Inequality and Poverty in Malaysia: Measurement and Decomposition* (New York: Oxford Univ. Press, forthcoming).

11. Ibid., 90–91. The definition of poverty here is not the official poverty-line income but rather the lowest 40 percent of the income distribution.

12. UMNO won many such seats, of course, because of the non-Malay votes it received. K. J. Ratnam and R. S. Milne, "The 1969 Parliamentary Elections in West Malaysia," *Pacific Affairs* 43, no. 2 (Summer 1970): 219–20.

general elections were the most serious since independence and served notice that the pattern of growth to that point had not by any means purchased social peace. [13] Large demonstrations by rubber smallholders and tappers in Kedah and elsewhere in 1974 further reinforced the sense that policy changes were necessary. One major result of this concern, not to say panic, was what is now called the New Economic Policy. It was designed to eradicate poverty by the end of the century and restructure the economy so that race would be no longer identified with economic function.

The main threat to the political hegemony of the ruling party has thus been concentrated largely in the poor, Malay, paddy-growing states of the north, where race is very much identified with economic function. UMNO's effort to secure its political base in these areas is reflected in policies aimed at benefitting Malay rice producers. Virtually all of these policies can be regarded as "soft" options. What I mean by soft options is that there has been no attempt to restructure either the basic pattern of property relations or the rights attached to them. The redistribution of paddy or rubber holdings has never been actively considered, though the inequities in both sectors are founded on unequal access to productive land. Tenancy reform, a far more modest step, has been addressed, but the existing law has been effectively sabotaged by landlord resistance and the un-willingness of officials to enforce either registration of tenancy agreements or rental ceilings. Such hard options have been avoided because they have been both inconvenient and, in a sense, unnecessary. They are inconvenient (some would claim, impossible) because the source of UMNO's rural Malay support has always been among the influential large farmers and landlords—the class that would have most to lose in a redistribution of land or a reform of tenancy. They have proven unnecessary because the bonanza of overall growth and export earnings has provided the wherewithal for such a lavish treatment of the symp-toms of uneven development that the underlying malady could, for the time being at least, be safely ignored.

The fiscal and administrative resources devoted to soft options have been quite impressive. Rural development expenditures grew in real terms more than sixfold from independence (1957) to 1975. Much of it went to the provision of infra-structure and collective goods—roads, schools, clinics, piped water, electricity,

13. The riots, which constitute a significant political watershed, were, signifi-cantly, confined to cities on the west coast of the peninsula. It was particularly in such areas that Chinese and Malays were not only in proximity in large numbers but also felt themselves to be in economic competition. The countryside was impli-cated in these events in at least three ways: First, the large-scale migration of Malays from a stagnant rural economy was seen as a source of political volatility in the cities; second, poverty in the paddy, rubber, and fishing sectors seemed, by itself, to increase the risk of communal violence in rural areas; and third, rural poverty seemed certain to increase the appeal of the Malay opposition party, then called the PMIP (Pan-Malayan Islamic Party).

mosques, prayer houses, community halls—that have touched virtually every village in the country. Naturally the provision of most of these amenities was linked to electoral politics, and it is a rare UMNO candidate who does not constantly remind his constituents of what the party has given them in the past and what it plans to give them in the future. While such measures are hardly redistributive in intent, there is no doubt that they have materially improved the standard of living of all rural Malays, including the poor.

A further soft option pursued with great vigor has been the creation of government-sponsored resettlement schemes in the form of rubber and oil-palm estates.[14] Spending on such schemes since the mid-1960s has approached half of the total rural development expenditure and had accommodated over seventy thousand families by 1975.[15] Settler incomes in these schemes, especially oil-palm schemes, are far above average paddy farmer incomes, and it is the dream of nearly every young villager in Sedaka to be chosen in the sweepstakes. In fact, very few get to go and those who do are not by any means always the poorest, for settler selection is highly politicized.[16] There is little doubt, however, that the schemes have had some impact on reducing poverty not only for the actual settlers but also for those who remain behind, by at least marginally reducing the competition for land and work. Their effect is much like that of the industrial and construction boom in urban areas, which draws off (temporarily or permanently) a portion of the hard-pressed labor force in the countryside. The land schemes, however, are the ultimate in soft options; they are only possible in a nation that can afford to spend M$40,000 for each settler family and has an ample frontier of arable land.[17]

Beyond supplying collective amenities and providing some alternative employment, state policy toward the paddy sector has also aimed directly at increasing the productivity and incomes of rice growers. The centerpieces of this strategy are the Muda and Kemubu Irrigation Projects (in Kedah and Kelantan, respectively), which have allowed roughly eighty thousand families to double-crop rice on nearly 270,000 acres. Double cropping began in the early 1970s in both schemes and the overall results to date have been impressive. The combination of a second crop, fertilizers, and new seeds has pushed production to about 2.5 times its previous level. *Average* incomes, in real terms, have grown

14. Colin MacAndrews, *Land Settlement Policies in Malaysia and Indonesia: A Preliminary Analysis,* Occasional Paper Series, No. 52 (Singapore: Institute of Southeast Asian Studies, 1978), 7.

15. Ibid., 45, 47.

16. R. Thillainathan, "Public Policies and Programmes for Redressing Poverty in Malaysia: A Critical Review," in *Some Case Studies on Poverty in Malaysia: Essays Presented to Ungku Aziz,* ed. B. A. R. Mokhzani and Khoo Siew Mun (Kuala Lumpur: Persatuan Ekonomi Malaysia Press, 1977), 245–60.

17. Calculated from MacAndrews, *Land Settlement,* 46 (table 3) and 47 (table 5).

by more than half.[18] Despite these gains in output and income in two of Malaysia's poorest regions, the term *soft option* is still appropriate. The profits from this "green revolution" have gone disproportionately, as we shall see, to the large owners of the scarce factors of production: land and capital. The poorest farm households have benefited only marginally, and the distribution of income is now more skewed than it was previously. Direct government subsidies in the form of fertilizer and production loans offered through farmers' organizations were distributed on the basis of acreage farmed and thus compounded the advantages already enjoyed by large-scale commercial operators.[19] UMNO could hardly be expected to go against the interest of its main rural supporters, the rich farmers, who were in any case the source of most of the marketed paddy.

The impact of state intervention in paddy production on class relations was not by any means confined to its implications for income distribution. By the very logic of its policy, the state displaced both the private sector and to some degree even the weather as the crucial factor in farm incomes. Minimum farm-gate paddy prices had been set by the state since 1939, but after independence the price level became a hot political issue, sparking major demonstrations in 1954 and again in 1980. Production credit and fertilizer, once the nearly exclusive domain of the Chinese shopkeeper, became by 1970 a service offered through the farmers' associations to their members. Rice milling, also once a private sector preserve, has come to be increasingly dominated by large state mills and drying facilities. For those seeking outside work, which was previously available only through the private sector, the state is now a possible employer, whether through its settler schemes or through short-term employment, as during the 1978 drought. Finally, the very process of cultivation, once dependent on the onset of monsoon rains, is now for both seasons largely determined by the schedule of water release fixed in advance by the authorities. The state was once largely a bystander or mediator in these relations with nature and the private sector. It is now a direct participant, decision maker, allocator, and antagonist in nearly all vital aspects of paddy growing. Most of the buffers between the state and rice farmers have fallen away, thereby vastly increasing both the role of politics and the possibilities for direct confrontation between the ruling party and its peasantry.

All of the state policies thus far identified—collective amenities, settler

18. This estimate is for the largest scheme, Muda, as the income figures for Kemubu are a matter of current dispute.

19. In theory, the fertilizer subsidy implemented in 1979 was limited to 6 acres (or 8.5 relong) per farmer, but large farmers, with the tacit complicity of the farmers' organizations, quickly found ways around this restriction. Like the Padi Cultivators Act before it, the limitation remained a dead letter. Even in 1955, the Rice Committee made it clear that the loan fund it was providing to help redeem mortgaged lands was intended for commercial farmers, not for subsistence producers. See Doering, "Malaysian Rice Policy," 65–66.

schemes, irrigation, and double-cropping inputs—have played some role, however marginal, in the alleviation of poverty. At the same time, all of these policies have been at best neutral with respect to inequities in income and property or, in the case of settler schemes and double-cropping, have served to widen the gulf between the rich and the poor.[20] Thus they qualify as soft options. It is hardly worth noting that these inequities may have been unintended, for the state has continued to pursue them and has made no serious effort to undo their impact. Far from it. The ruling party has in fact recently embarked on a systematic policy that aims at creating what might be called a wealthy, Malay, "hothouse" bourgeoisie. This policy is pursued under the banner of increasing Malay participation in the modern sectors of the economy. Nearly M$1.5 billion in expenditures on commerce and industry under the third Malaysian Plan (1976–80) are devoted to the training and financing of Malay entrepreneurs or to direct government investment in corporations to be held in trust for Malays. Other dimensions of this policy include selling of private equity shares at concessionary rates to Malays, reserving a certain share of government construction and supply contracts for Malays, and making certain that licenses for certain trades are awarded preferentially to Malays. Whatever worthy rationales exist for this policy in theory, there is little doubt that in practice it has proven to be a bonanza for well-placed Malays and has provoked more than its share of scandals in a very short time.[21] It has also produced an instant Malay commercial class operating with special licenses, in protected markets, with guaranteed credit from public loan funds, selling goods or services—often to the state—at fixed prices with guaranteed profit. In the countryside, a good many rich farmers have taken advantage of the opportunities to obtain loans for taxis, small paddy mills, lorries, fish ponds, thereby becoming a new, "protected species" of petite bourgeoisie. As most of this recent class of state-sponsored capitalists is aligned with the ruling party and comes from the ranks of the already well-to-do, the nature of the traditional rural class cleavage based on land ownership has taken on a new dimension—one fraught with novel possibilites for political and economic conflict.

UMNO is a well-organized and well-financed political machine providing both individual and collective blandishments that reach into every Malay village. Following its impressive electoral victory in 1978, it controlled—alone or together with its non-Malay coalition partners in the National Front (Barison Nasional)—every state government on the peninsula and held over four-fifths of

20. It might however be argued that such collective amenities as health clinics and primary schools have actually been redistributive in the sense that the poor were previously the most deprived of these services and are now the major beneficiaries.

21. See the reference to the Bank Kerjasama Rakyat scandal and to the profit making on equity share sales to Malays in Far Eastern Economic Review, *Asia 1980 Yearbook,* 228, 237.

the federal parliamentary seats. In most rural areas UMNO represents a dominant faction of wealthy farmers—many of whom have branched out into other businesses—together with their kinsmen and retainers and supported by a host of petty officeholders in the area.

UMNO's main opposition among the Malay population (Partai Islam, or PAS) has managed to retain strong support among Malays[22] despite the fact that it cannot offer any of the material incentives that UMNO's control of the government provides. While it is not my purpose to examine party politics per se, the persistence of political opposition in PAS reflects a populist amalgam of class and ethnic and religious protest that merits brief comment. In the countryside, of course, PAS and UMNO may be seen partly as factions whose history predates parties. Thus many of the leaders of PAS are wealthy landlords and farmers much like their UMNO counterparts. Since the PAS leaders have rarely had access to government patronage, however, they are less likely to have the sideline businesses that require political connections. For the rank and file of PAS, as Clive Kessler has so brilliantly shown, the party has an appeal that combines class issues (touching on the income and economic security of Malay cultivators, fishermen, and rubber tappers), ethnic and religious issues (touching on respect for the rights and religious beliefs of the indigenous population), and, not least, a more general political opposition to a state and ruling party that are seen to have failed most of the Malay population in both respects.[23] PAS, unlike UMNO, seems to be rather informally organized. It relies heavily on popular religious teachers and their centers (*pondok*), which can be found throughout rural Malaysia and are distinct from the official religious establishment that is typically aligned with UMNO. The way in which, say, class and religious issues may be combined may be conveyed by noting the appeals made by a PAS speaker during a parliamentary by-election in Kedah (Bukit Raya) narrowly won by UMNO in 1980. The speaker noted the trivial profit farmers could expect for each gunny sack of paddy or for tapping rubber and then asked why UMNO gave out huge sums of money to build Chinese and Indian temples. "If the rubber price [per sheet] is M$2.00," he continued, "the government takes thirty cents ($.30) as its cess

22. For example, in at least four of the parliamentary constituencies in Kedah—those of Jerlun-Langkawi, Kuala Kedah, Ulu Muda, and Jerai (where Sedaka is located)—the UMNO winning margin in 1978 was so slim as to indicate that PAS had won a majority of Malay votes in those constituencies but had lost because the Chinese minority in each case threw its votes to UMNO. Despite the fact that PAS lost seats in this election, it got 38.5 percent of the total vote, just one percentage point less than it received in 1969 when it came near to capturing the state. See Ismail Kasim, *The Politics of Accommodation: An Analysis of the 1978 Malaysian General Election,* Research Notes and Discussion Paper, No. 10 (Singapore: Institute of Southeast Asian Studies, 1978), 73–74.

23. Clive S. Kessler, *Islam and Politics in a Malay State: Kelantan 1838–1969* (Ithaca: Cornell Univ. Press, 1978).

while the middleman takes seventy cents ($.70)." "The policy of the government is not based on Islam but on property only." Later in his speech he mentioned the large houses and Mercedes cars of government officials and the way in which they had abused the Koran for their own profit. "They'll be the first to enter hell!" he added. In this fashion a populist understanding of Islam that extends naturally to issues of income distribution, employment, and other class issues as well as to matters of piety and religious law provides an ideal medium of political protest. Nearly three decades of stubborn opposition suggest that the issues that underlie political opposition are a by-product of Malaysia's pattern of development and will, barring much heavier repression, continue to find institutional expression in one form or another.

MIDDLE GROUND: KEDAH AND THE MUDA IRRIGATION SCHEME

The Muda region, named after the Muda River, has been since at least the fourteenth century the major rice-producing area on the peninsula. Most of that cultivation takes place within the five hundred or so square miles of the Kedah/ Perlis alluvial plain, with its vast expanse of fertile, dense, marine-clay soil. (See Map 2) On an exceptionally clear day, from atop four-thousand-foot Gunung Jerai (Kedah Peak), which lies at its southern extremity, it is possible to take in the entire forty-mile-long rice plain bounded on the west by the Straits of Malacca and on the east by intruding foothills of the Central Range. The view is of one enormous rice paddy interrupted only by cross-hatching tree lines that indicate the typically linear villages of the region and, more rarely, by a larger urban agglomeration, such as the state capital of Alor Setar. Depending on the stage of rice cultivation during the main, monsoon-fed season, one may view what appears as a vast shallow lake of flooded paddy fields not much differentiated from the straits that border it, a sea of variegated greens, an expanse of golden ripening grain, or a great stretch of drab soil and stubble left after the harvest.

The political and social history of the Muda Plain has marked contemporary class relations in at least two significant ways. We must first keep in mind that we are dealing with a society composed largely of pioneers and newcomers—a frontier society—until well into this century. Despite the fact that paddy has been grown here since the fourteenth century, much of the Muda Plain was only recently cleared, drained, and brought under cultivation. What continuous settlement there had been was profoundly disrupted by the Siamese invasion of 1821, which reduced the population (through emigration) to roughly fifty thousand, or half its preinvasion level. [24] Kedah did not recover its former population until near the turn of the century, when a period of comparative peace and new drainage schemes stimulated a substantial immigration. It is in this period

24. R. D. Hill, *Rice in Malaysia: A Study in Historical Geography* (Kuala Lumpur: Oxford Univ. Press, 1977), 54.

MAP 1 • The Muda Irrigation Scheme Area in Peninsular Malaysia

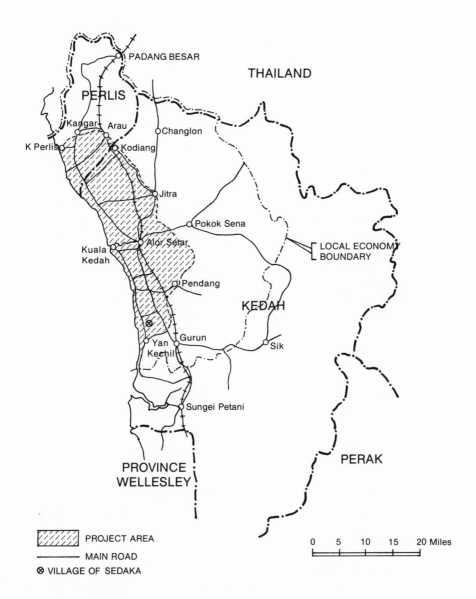

PADANG BESAR

THAILAND

PERLIS

Kangar Arau

K Perlis

Changlon

Kodiang

Jitra

Pokok Sena

LOCAL ECONOMY
BOUNDARY

Kuala
Kedah

Alor Setar

Pendang

KEDAH

⊗

Gurun

Yan
Kechil

Sik

Sungei Petani

PROVINCE
WELLESLEY

PERAK

///// PROJECT AREA
——— MAIN ROAD
⊗ VILLAGE OF SEDAKA

0   5   10   15   20 Miles

MAP 2 • Kedah and the Muda Scheme Area

(roughly 1880–1910) that many of the villages on the plain, including Sedaka, were settled and when paddy land definitively became a commodity that could be bought and sold. Initial grants of land for colonization and canal digging were usually given by the Sultan to favored aristocratic retainers, but they were quickly superseded and outnumbered by a "non-aristocratic, capitalist, 'commercial' land-owning group."[25] The importance of this frontier history is simply that class in rural Kedah is pretty much a straightforward affair of rich and poor, big and little, rather than being compounded by ancient feudal distinctions between lords and serfs, aristocrats and plebeians, as they are in those areas in Southeast Asia much longer settled and in close proximity to royal courts.[26]

The second notable feature of regional history, and indeed of Malay history generally, is that the state has not generally been an effective instrument for the exploitation of the peasantry. As Gullick concludes in his study of precolonial Malay states, "flight" was the peasant's most common reaction to oppression,[27] and owing to the mobile, frontier character of Malay society and the limited coercive power at the disposal of the court it was usually a successful, though painful, remedy. Attempts by the court to mobilize corvée labor (*Krah*) for the building of a road across the peninsula in 1864, for example, touched off a mass emigration to the south, and it appears that much, if not all, of the huge Wan Mat Saman Canal from Alor Setar, begun in 1885, had to be dug with paid Chinese labor despite the fact that its guiding spirit was the chief minister (Menteri Besar) of the Sultan. By the turn of the century at the latest, the growth of trade and of the Chinese population provided alternative sources of revenue that made it even less necessary to squeeze the Malay peasantry. Virtually all revenue collection in Kedah at this time was leased by auction to entrepreneurs who then endeavored to turn a profit by collecting more revenue than the rent for their monopoly or "farm." Opium and gambling farms were easily the most significant sources of state revenue, bringing in more than three times the revenue from duties on rice and paddy export.[28] It was the Chinese poor and

25. Ibid., 53.

26. Compare, for example, this situation with Kessler's fine analysis of politics in the east coast state of Kelantan, which shows how much of the strong opposition to the ruling party there derived not only from class issues but was compounded by a lively resentment against the aristocratic families in the state capital, who had come to dominate the colonial bureaucracy in their own interests. One can detect something of the sort in Kedah as well, but it is not nearly so pronounced. Kessler, *Islam and Politics.*

27. John M. Gullick, *Indigenous Political Systems of Western Malays,* London School of Economics Monographs on Social Anthropology, no. 17 (London: Athlone, 1958), 43. The limited extraction of the precolonial Malay state was due not to any lack of ambition or would-be rapacity, but rather to a lack of means to enforce its will.

28. Sharom Ahmat, "The Structure of the Economy of Kedah, 1879–1905," *Journal of the Malaysian Branch of the Royal Asiatic Society* 43, no. 2 (1970): 13.

not the Malay villagers who thus bore the brunt of colonial fiscal policy. Even after independence, as we shall see, the state, in fiscal terms at least, has rested rather lightly on the Malay peasantry. Here again, the rather unique pattern of development in Malaysia largely avoided the familiar and often brutal struggle in most agrarian kingdoms between a state voracious for corvée and taxes and a peasantry fighting to keep its subsistence intact. Even today the fiscal basis of the Malaysian state reposes on export-import taxes, excise taxes, concessions and loans, and commercial levies far more than on any direct appropriation from rice producers. It is not much of an exaggeration to say that the modern Malaysian state depends on paddy growers for food supply and political stability, but not for its financial wherewithal, which is extracted in ways that only marginally affect peasant incomes. Hostility, suspicion, and resentment toward the state are hardly absent, but these attitudes lack the long history of direct oppression that they have taken on elsewhere in Southeast Asia.

By 1970, the rural population in the Muda region had reached well over half a million, the vast majority of whom were Malays engaged almost exclusively in rice growing. The much smaller urban population (112,000) was scattered through nineteen townships in which Chinese and Malays were represented in nearly equal proportions. Well before double-cropping, Kedah politicians were fond of referring to their state as Malaysia's "rice bowl," inasmuch as it has by far the largest paddy acreage of any state in the country and has consistently been the major supplier to the domestic market.[29] Much of its commercial importance in the paddy sector is due to its traditionally high yields per acre and its comparatively large farm size, which have combined to produce a large marketable surplus above subsistence needs. Farm incomes, though low compared with those outside the paddy sector, were traditionally well above the norm for paddy farmers as a whole on the peninsula. To pursue a comment made earlier, if one had to be a paddy farmer somewhere in Malaysia, one could not do much better than on the Kedah Plain.

The rather favorable ecological and social conditions in the Muda area make it apparent that it has hardly been singled out as a promising site for the more dramatic forms of class conflict. Here one finds poverty but not great misery, inequalities but not stark polarization, burdensome rents and taxes but not crushing exactions. The last hundred years of Kedah's history are filled with the

---

29. *Jelapang padi Malaysia* (Malaysia's paddy granary). For the history of Malay Settlement and rice production in the area, readers are invited to consult Hill, *Rice in Malaysia*; K. K. Kim, *The Western Malay States, 1850–1873: The Effects of Commercial Development on Malay Politics* (Kuala Lumpur: Oxford Univ. Press, 1972); Sharom Ahmat, "The Political Structure of the State of Kedah, 1879–1905," *Journal of Southeast Asian Studies* 1, no. 2 (1970); R. Bonney, *Kedah, 1771–1821: The Search for Security and Independence* (Kuala Lumpur: Oxford Univ. Press, 1971); Zaharah Haji Mahmud, "Change in a Malay Sultanate."

peasant migrations and flight, land grabbing, and banditry of frontier society and more recently with protests and political opposition; but one looks in vain for the long history of peasant rebellion to be found elsewhere in Southeast Asia. One advantage of studying class conflict in such a setting is precisely that it is something of a hard case. If we encounter a rich domain of class-based resistance even in a region where a majority of the rural population is probably better off than it was a decade ago, then it is reasonable to suppose that the unwritten history of resistance in other rice-growing areas of Southeast Asia might be correspondingly richer.

Despite the blessings of good soil, a favorable climate, and relative prosperity, other aspects of the social structure and economy of the Kedah Plain were troubling. If the soil was suitable for paddy, it was not suitable for much else and the result was an increasing pattern of monoculture, with its attendant vulnerabilities. If the average farm size was substantial (4.0 acres, or 5.6 relong), most of the region's farmers worked smaller plots, which left them well below the poverty line and provoked an annual stream of migrants to towns and plantations where work was available during the off-season. If yields were above average, so was the rate of tenancy (35 percent), which meant that many farmers had only a tenuous hold on the means of their subsistence.[30] If nearly half of the paddy households owned the land they worked, their numbers had been steadily diminishing over the past six decades as the cycle of debt and crop failures pried the land from many hands.[31]

The Muda Irrigation Project, begun in 1966 and in full operation by 1973, was intended to solve some, if not all, of these problems. Basically, it consisted of two large dams, headworks, main and secondary canals, together with the institutional infrastructure to make possible the double-cropping of rice on some 260,000 acres. As elsewhere, the "green revolution" in Muda was coupled with the introduction of new fast-growing, high-yielding strains of rice, intensified fertilizer use, new technology and mechanization, credit facilities, and new milling and marketing channels. Nearly all the official principals involved—the

30. The data in this .paragraph are derived from the standard source on the agricultural economy of the Muda region before double-cropping, S. Selvadurai, *Padi Farming in West Malaysia,* Bulletin No. 27 (Kuala Lumpur: Ministry of Agriculture and Fisheries, 1972).

31. The inequities in landholding and hence the poverty of a large section of the Muda population, which the irrigation scheme was intended to address, were the historical deposit of initial land grabbing compounded by this cycle of debt. As early as 1913 the British Advisor to the Kedah, W. George Maxwell, observed that "The majority of the padi planters are at present in the hands of Chinese padi dealers." Unfederated Malay States, *Annual Report of the Advisor to the Kedah Government,* December 11, 1912, to November 30, 1913 (Alor Setar: Government Printer, 1914), 23. See also Federated Malay States, *Report of the Rice Cultivation Committee,* 1931, H. A. Tempany, Chairman (Kuala Lumpur: 1932), 40.

World Bank, the Malaysian government, and the officials of the scheme itself—were convinced by 1974 of its success. Double-cropping had been achieved in 92 percent of the project area, new varieties of rice had been nearly universally adopted, and the new impetus to production had placed self-sufficiency in rice within reach. The glowing report card issued by the World Bank, the major financial backer, was widely quoted.

> The project has resulted in an approximate doubling of average farm incomes, both for owners and tenants. . . . Paddy production which was 268,000 tons in 1965 increased to 678,000 tons in 1974 and is expected to reach 718,000 tons by 1980 . . . the rise in employment resulting from the project has been of great benefit to landless labourers and other unemployed groups. . . . The economic rate of return is now 18 percent compared with the 10 percent estimated at appraisal.[32]

From the vantage point of 1974, the project seemed a nearly unqualified success. A number of major studies documented that success in terms of production, technology, employment, and incomes.[33] From the vantage point of 1980, the evaluation of the project, especially in terms of employment and income, is far less clear-cut, although there is no doubt that without the project the Muda peasantry would be far worse off both relatively and absolutely.

What follows is essentially an attempt to establish the nature and degree of the major shifts in land tenure, employment, income, and institutions that have been brought about, directly or indirectly, by the "green revolution" in Muda. These changes can, and have been, documented. Once the basic contours have been sketched, they can serve as the raw material with which the human agents in this small drama must somehow come to grips.

Many of the dramatic changes in the Muda region since double-cropping began in 1970 are visually apparent to anyone familiar with rural Kedah earlier. Quite a few of these changes are attributable not to double-cropping but to the government's concerted political effort to supply amenities to rural Malays—mosques, prayer houses, electricity, roads, schools, clinics. Others stem more directly from the increases in average incomes that double-cropping has made possible. Once sleepy crossroads towns now bristle with new shops and crowded

32. International Bank of Reconstruction and Development, *Malaysia Loan 434-MA: Muda Irrigation Scheme Completion Report,* no. 795-MA (Washington, D.C.: June 1975), ii, quoted in S. Jegatheesan, *The Green Revolution and the Muda Irrigation Scheme,* MADA Monograph No. 30 (Alor Setar: Muda Agricultural Development Authority, March 1977), 3–4.

33. See, in addition to Jegatheesan, *Green Revolution,* Food and Agriculture Organization/World Bank Cooperative Program, *The Muda Study,* 2 vols. (Rome: FAO, 1975), and Clive Bell, Peter Hazell, and Roger Slade, *The Evaluation of Projects in Regional Perspective: A Case Study of the Muda Irrigation Project* (Baltimore: Johns Hopkins Univ. Press, forthcoming).

markets.[34] The roads themselves, once nearly deserted, are alive with lorries, buses, automobiles, taxis, and above all Honda 70 motorcycles—the functional equivalent of the Model T—now as common as bicycles.[35] Many houses that once had attap roofs and siding now have corrugated tin roofs and plank siding.[36] Within those houses are an increasing number of sewing machines, radios, television sets, store-brought furniture, and kerosene stoves.[37]

The visual transformation of the Muda region, striking though it may be, is surpassed by a series of changes that are far less apparent. They can in fact be described as beneficial absences, as catastrophic events that were once common and are now rare. Before double-cropping, for example, one-third of the farm households in the region rarely grew enough rice for the annual subsistence needs of the family. If they were unable to earn the cash necessary to purchase rice on the market, they were reduced to subsisting on tapioca, maize, and cassava (*ubi kayu*) at least until the next harvest was in. Following a crop disaster in the region—and there were many (1919, 1921, 1925, 1929, 1930, 1946, 1947, 1949, 1959, 1964)—most of the rural population found itself in the same boat. Double-cropping in this respect has been a great boon. Even smallholding tenants with a single relong (.71 acre) can now grow enough rice at least to feed a family, though they may be desperately short of cash. It is a rare peasant these days who does not eat rice twice a day.[38] The provision of irrigation water and the use of fertilizer not only raised yields somewhat but has also made those yields more reliable, season by season. The new agricultural regime is hardly invulnerable, as witnessed by the cancellation of the irrigated season in 1978

34. For quantitative details showing the scheme's effect on the regional economy, see Bell et al., *Evaluation of Projects*, chap. 7.

35. The number of motorcycles registered in Kedah and Perlis jumped from 14,292 in 1966 to 95,728 in 1976, an increase of more than sixfold. In the same period the number of private cars grew more than fourfold, buses nearly fourfold, and commercial vehicles nearly threefold. Economic Consultants Ltd., *Kedah-Perlis Development Study: Interim Report* (Alor Setar: December 15, 1977), 90.

36. See the statistics on housing materials and years of double-cropping in Food and Agriculture Organization/World Bank Cooperative Program, *Muda Study*, 1: 26, and 2: tables 19, 20.

37. Ibid., 2: table 21.

38. A strong case can be made, however, that this benefit has come at a considerable cost in nutritional diversity. Double-cropping has eliminated many of the vegetables that were previously planted between seasons. Small livestock such as ducks, geese, and chickens are also rarer now that off-season grazing is cut short and now that pesticides threaten waterfowl. Rice-paddy fish, once a poor man's staple, are both less plentiful and often contaminated with pesticides. For those who can afford to buy vegetables, fish, and occasionally meat from the market, the effect is negligible. For those of slender means, however, the effect is likely to be a diet that is at best monotonous and at worst nutritionally deficient and/or toxic.

due to a shortage of water, which gave Muda's peasantry a painful reminder of the old days. Nevertheless, the prospect of going without rice has been largely removed from the fears of even poor villagers.

The closely related scourge of malnutrition and its inevitable toll in human, especially children's, lives appears from sketchy data to have been sharply reduced, though not eliminated. Figures for the incidence of nutrition-related diseases and for infant and toddler mortality from such causes show a marked decline that correlates well with the progress of double-cropping.[39] Between 1970 and 1976 the rate of infant mortality in the Muda region was cut by nearly half, from a figure that was above the rates for the nation and for Kedah as a whole to a level below both. It is ironic testimony to "progress" on the rice plain that anemia and malnutrition, the seventh most common cause of death in 1970, had disappeared from the top ten by 1976, while motor vehicle accidents had moved from sixth to second place.

Another beneficial absence that can be largely attributed to double-cropping was the decline in out-migration during the off-season. Both temporary and permanent migration were systematic features of the regional economy before 1970. This was reflected in the fact that the population within Muda grew at only half the rate of natural increase, and the rates of out-migration seemed to be highest in the paddy districts.[40] It was, moreover, a rare smallholder or tenant family that did not have to send someone out, at least temporarily, to raid the cash economy between rice seasons. The beginning of double-cropping in Muda brought temporary relief and fostered a process that might be called "repeasantization." Many villagers, for the first time, were afforded the luxury of remaining at home the entire year. Small farms that were inadequate for subsistence with only a single crop now became viable enterprises. It was not just a matter of reaping two harvests from the same plot but also the opportunities for wage labor that two seasons provided. Adding to the good fortune of wage laborers were the restriction of Thai migrant laborers in 1969 and a tobacco boom in the poor, labor-exporting state of Kelantan, which reduced dramatically the competition for employment. As we shall see, however, this welcome respite was only temporary. Combine-harvesters had by 1978 eliminated much of the new work that irrigation had made possible and laborers from the land-poor classes in Muda were once again on the road.

39. Ajit Singh, "Laporan Kesihatan Kawasan Kedah-Perlis, 1970–1977" (Alor Setar: Jabatan Pengarah Perkhidmatan Perubatan dan Kesihatan, October 1978, mimeo). These figures are not decisive because only three districts are examined, one of which is the district of Kota Setar, the location of the major urban area in the region. The declines in nutritionally related mortality are far more striking for Kota Setar than for either Kubang Pasu or for Yan (the district in which Sedaka is located).

40. Economic Consultants Ltd. *Kedah-Perlis Development Study*, 17.

If the boon of staying at home was to prove brief, the effect of double-cropping on landholding appears far more durable. Two harvests, steadier yields, and paddy prices that no longer fluctuated wildly over the crop season served in most cases to break the cycle of indebtedness which, following a bad season, might mean the loss of land to creditors. Seasonal credit from shopkeepers and pawnbrokers is still the rule for much of the Muda peasantry, but such loans are typically cleared with each harvest and only rarely take the form of *jual janji,* which jeopardizes future ownership. The effect has been to stabilize the class of smallholders and to slow the process of proletarianization in the countryside.[41]

The changes noted thus far—in amenities, consumer goods, rice supply, nutrition, employment, and household solvency—might be appropriately termed the good news of the past decade in Muda. There is, however, other news too— news that can only be termed ambiguous, inasmuch as its evaluation depends a great deal on one's class position. Here again, the effort is to convey merely the basic documented facts, leaving the social interpretation to chapter 5. In dealing with the entire Muda region, resort to some statistical presentation should be helpful before we move to the village level ("foreground"), where such data acquire flesh and blood.

Land Ownership

The first fact that one would wish to know about any agrarian setting is how the ownership of the principal means of production—land—is distributed.[42] In Muda the land is distributed quite unequally (Gini coefficient of 0.538), although this is not a latifundia situation where a few massive holdings dominate most of the landscape. There is, furthermore, no evidence that the distribution

41. No precise figures are available but, as we shall see below, the statistics on the distribution of paddy-land ownership from 1966 to 1976 suggest the survival, if not the proliferation, of smallholding. Such holdings, however, are also produced by the fragmentation of ownership through inheritance.

42. Data in this section and in those immediately following are derived largely from the superb, detailed report by D. S. Gibbons, Lim Teck Ghee, G. B. Elliston, and Shukur Kassim, *Hak Milik Tanah di Kawasan Perairan Muda: Lapuran Akhir* (Land tenure in the Muda irrigatiaon area: Final report), Pt. 2, *Findings* (Pulau Pinang: Pusat Penyelidekan Dasar and Universiti Sains Malaysia, 1981). It will be cited henceforth as *USM-MADA Land Tenure Study.* It is based on a 1975–76 survey of all farms in the Muda region. Comparisons are drawn with previous sample surveys in the Muda region to reach conclusions about shifts in land tenure over time. For my purposes it has only two disadvantages: it provides no information beyond 1976, and the scope of the inquiry is limited to questions of land ownership, farm size, and tenure. Thus, for data since 1976 and for issues not covered in this study, I have had to rely on other sources that are less comprehensive. The care with which the basic data in this report were collected, checked, and interpreted make it a model for emulation elsewhere.

of paddy-land ownership has become any more unequal or concentrated since the initiation of double-cropping. The basic situation is summarized in table 3.1.[43] It must be kept in mind that the figures in table 3.1 cover only owners of paddy land and therefore exclude nearly 14,600 pure tenant and 8,000 landless labor households (37 percent of paddy sector households). Even then, the disparity is striking. Large holdings above 7 acres (10 relong) account for only 11 percent of the holdings but occupy 42 percent of the total paddy land. It is this strata of relatively well-to-do owners who, together with some large-scale tenants, from the core of the commercial farming class in Muda, selling perhaps three-quarters of all the paddy marketed in the region.[44] At the other end of the scale stand the great majority (61.8 percent) of owners with holdings below what is required for a poverty-line income. Fully 40 percent, in fact, own less than 1.42 acres (half the paddy land necessary for a subsistence-level income) and are insignificant as sellers of paddy.

TABLE 3.1 • Size Distribution of Paddy-Land Holdings, Muda Irrigation Scheme, 1975–1976

Size Class (Acres)	Holdings: Absolute Frequency (No. farm owners)	Holdings: Relative Frequency (%)	Area: Absolute Frequency (Acres)	Area: Relative Frequency (%)
0.01–2.83	27,898	61.8	32,198	21.7
2.84–7.09	12,198	27.1	54,028	36.3
7.1 and above	5,019	11.1	62,499	42.0
Totals	45,115	100.0	148,725	100.0

Along with double-cropping has come a roughly fivefold leap in paddy-land prices, far outdistancing the rise of the consumer price index or paddy incomes and fraught with implications for future social mobility. Before 1970 it was possible, though rare, for an industrious and thrifty tenant to buy a small plot of land, thereby improving his situation. With the prevailing land prices, it has become virtually impossible for anyone but the richest owners to expand their

43. USM-MADA Land Tenure Study, 145. The odd cutting points of the size categories arise from the fact that the original data were collected following local units (1 relong equals .71 acre) of land measurement. Thus 0.01 to 2.83 acres is equivalent to 0.01 to 3.9 relong; 2.84 to 7.09 acres is equivalent to 4.0 to 9.9 relong; and above 7.1 acres is equivalent to 10 relong and above.

44. No figures for the Muda area as a whole appear to be available, but this figure, derived from a careful study of selected districts, is likely to be close. See Masanabu Yamashita, Wong Hin Soon, and S. Jegatheesen, "MADA-TARC Cooperative Study, Pilot Project ACRBD 4, Muda Irrigation Scheme, Farm Management Studies" (May 1980, mimeo.), 5. Hereafter referred to as "MADA-TARC Farm Management Studies, 1980."

holdings. A traditional, if limited, avenue of upward mobility has been all but definitely closed.

Farm Size

The distribution of operated farm size is a good indication of access (whether by ownership or rental) to the primary factor of production. Comparative figures for before and after double-cropping are given in table 3.2.[45] Inequalities in actual farm size, while not as marked as in the case of ownership, are nonetheless apparent. Small farms, nearly half of Muda's households, cultivate a mere 17 percent of the paddy land, but large farms, only 14 percent of households, claim virtually 40 percent of the rice land. Between these two classes is a large middle peasantry cultivating modest farms. The most striking trend in the past decade is the growth in the proportion of small farms coupled with no appreciable change in their share of land resources, such that the mean small farm size has been driven down to a historic low of 1.4 acres.

TABLE 3.2 • Size Distribution of Farms, 1966 and 1975–76

Farm-Size Class (Acres)	1966			1975–1976		
	% Farms	% Area	Mean Farm Size (Acres)	% Farms	% Area	Mean Farm Size (Acres)
<2.83	38.1	17.3	1.8	46.7	17.0	1.4
2.84–7.09	46.4	44.9	3.8	38.9	43.2	4.5
>7.1	15.3	37.8	9.9	14.6	39.8	10.9

Tenure

It is above all in the social arrangements for cultivation that the most dramatic transformations have taken place. Land tenure in Muda is both complex and flexible: It is not uncommon, for example, to encounter farmers who farm some of their own land, rent out a small plot, rent in another, and even harvest others' land for wages occasionally. Nevertheless it is possible to identify three major tenure categories: owner-operators who farm their own land, pure tenants who rent all the paddy land they cultivate, and owner-tenants who farm land that is both rented and owned.[46] The precipitous decline in the proportion of pure tenants is the most striking feature of land tenure patterns since 1966, as shown in Table 3.3. There is some evidence that this trend was observable even before double-cropping, but there is no doubt that it has accelerated greatly since

45. *USM-MADA Land Tenure Study,* 167.
46. Ibid., 164.

TABLE 3.3 • Land Tenure in Muda, 1966 and 1975–1976

Tenurial Status of Farmers	1966			1975–1976		
	% Farmers	% Area	Mean Farm Size (Acres)	% Farmers	% Area	Mean Farm Size (Acres)
Owner-operators	44.5	39.5	3.6	56.1	45.3	3.2
Pure tenants	41.4	38.8	3.8	24.5	22.7	3.7
Owner-tenants	14.0	21.7	6.1	19.4	32.0	6.6

1970.[47] Pure tenants, who were in 1955 the dominant tenure category in Muda, had by 1976 become less than one-fourth of the farmers and cultivated less than one-fourth of the land. The evidence suggests that we are witnessing the not-so-gradual liquidation of Muda's pure tenant class. The overall picture from farm size and tenure data is one of gradual polarization—an increase in the proportion of small farms (mostly owner-operated) that produce a bare subsistence income, an across-the-board decline in tenancy, and a growing class of larger-scale commercial farms. This is very much in keeping with the results of the green revolution elsewhere in monsoon Asia.[48]

The explanation for these structural changes, which have produced a numerous, marginal, poverty-sharing class of small farmers at the bottom of the heap, a robust class of capitalist farmers at the top, and a still significant middle peasantry in between, is complex. Double-cropping, higher yields, and mechanization have made it increasingly profitable and feasible for landlords to resume cultivation. This would help account for the displacement of tenants and the growing share of owner-operators in both small and large farm categories. Demography has also played a role. Despite steady out-migration from Muda, the population grew by nearly 30 percent between 1957 and 1976. In the decade ending in 1980, Muda's population grew by more than 18 percent to 539,000. Given the nearly static area of paddy land over this period, population growth has encouraged owners to take back tenanted land for their children and to divide among their heirs land they previously farmed alone. This would also help account for the proliferation of small farms and the dismissal of tenants.

47. Ibid., 167, gives comparable figures for 1955 and for 1972–73 as well. It is not clear exactly what happened to these ex-tenants. Some have undoubtedly become landless laborers in the village, while others, particularly if young, have emigrated temporarily or permanently to urban areas for work. A small proportion have perhaps been tenants who have retired from active farming and who have then not been replaced.

48. See Keith Griffin, *The Political Economy of Agrarian Change: An Essay on the Green Revolution* (Cambridge, Mass.: Harvard Univ. Press, 1974), chap. 3. The one exception is that, while the green revolution has occasionally resulted in the near liquidation of small owner-operators, this class has more than held its own in Muda despite the fact that it is increasingly marginalized in economic terms.

There is every reason to believe that these trends, solidly documented until 1976, have continued and probably intensified since then. More important, changes in technology, costs of production, and rice prices since 1976 provide further incentives to displace small tenants. Combine-harvesters, by reducing supervision costs and by gathering the off-season harvest quickly, favor owner cultivation of larger farms. The provision of free fertilizer since the off-season of 1979 and a 30 percent increase in the farm-gate paddy price in late 1980 have also, given the "stickiness" of rents in Muda,[49] made self-cultivation more attractive than ever. What recent evidence is available supports this contention.[50]

Two other notable changes have taken place in the form of tenancy since 1966, both of which tend to favor large-scale tenants with capital—in particular, owner-tenants—at the expense of small-scale tenants. The first concerns when and how the rent is paid each season. In 1955 more than three-quarters of Muda's tenants paid their rents *after* the harvest was in and paid that rent in the form of a fixed quantity of paddy[51] or its cash equivalent. Cash rents (*sewa*

49. A majority of tenants in Muda are related to their landlord and rent land at prices below market rates. See the fine case study by Mohd. Shadli Abdullah, "The Relationship of the Kinship System to Land Tenure: A Case Study of Kampung Gelung Rambai, Kedah" (Master's thesis, Universiti Sains Malaysia, 1978), and the remarkable analysis of the same phenomenon elsewhere in Malaysia by Akimi Fujimoto, "Land Tenure, Rice Production, and Income Sharing among Malay Peasants: Study of Four Villages" (Ph.D. diss., Flinders University, Australia, 1980). Paradoxically, it is easier to withdraw the land from related tenants in order to farm it oneself—villagers accept that the owner and his children take precedence over more distant relatives—than to raise rents that kin must pay. This explains why landlords cannot simply take advantage of land hunger and higher returns from cultivation by extracting the full economic rent from tenants who are close relatives.

50. A recent restudy of a village near Alor Setar by Rosemary Barnard notes the importance of combine-harvesters in influencing landlords to rent out less land. "Recent Developments in Agricultural Employment in a Kedah Rice-Growing Village" (Paper presented at the Second Colloquium of the Asian Studies Association of Australia, James Cook University, August 29–31, 1979), 30. Increasing displacement of tenants is also noted by the head of the agricultural division of the Muda Agricultural Development Authority, Afifuddin Haji Omar, in "The Pivotal Role of an Integrated Institutional Reform in Socioeconomic Development of Rice Peasantry in Malaysia" (Paper presented at Conference on Development: The Peasantry and Development in the ASEAN Region, University Kebangsaan Malaysia, Bangi, May 26–29, 1980), 12.

51. For the statistics on paddy rents and cash rents from 1955 to 1976, see *USM-MADA Land Tenure Study*, 66. The term "paddy rent" (*sewa padi*) is always treated by studies as if it was actually paid in kind. It is my experience, however, that it has come to mean only that the rent is fixed in terms of the market price of a predetermined amount of paddy, which is usually given to the landlord in cash. It should also be noted that paddy rents were not crop-sharing arrangements, as the paddy rent was a fixed amount of grain, not a fixed share of the crop, which would have fluctuated with the harvest.

tunai) unrelated to an amount of paddy were rare, amounting to only 12 percent of all rental arrangements. By 1966 cash rents had become nearly as common as paddy rents, and by 1975 three-fourths of all tenancies were for cash rents, a reversal of the pattern twenty years earlier. While paddy rents may be paid out of the proceeds of the harvest and were therefore often negotiable depending on the size of the crop, cash rents require that the tenant raise the capital *before* the season opens and are not negotiable. At the moment the landlord moves to cash rent, the tenant is therefore subject to a one-time-only double rent, one for the past season and one for the coming season. No study has ever been made of the consequences of this shift, but there is no doubt that a good many poor tenants who were unable to raise the cash required were replaced by those who could.[52] Except for land rented from parents by children, most tenancy in Muda has now become pure rentier tenancy in which all the risks of cultivation are borne exclusively by the cultivator, who pays an invariable cash rent before the season opens.

A more momentous shift in tenancy relations is the increasing resort to *pajak*, or leasehold, tenancy in recent years. *Pajak* tenancy is the long-term rental of land over at least two seasons and may in fact extend to as many as ten or twelve seasons. The *entire* rent is paid in a lump sum and is in most cases covered by a written, notarized contract. As a form of tenancy, *pajak* has existed for a long time and was often a means by which farmers of modest means raised a substantial sum for such purposes as an important marriage, a new house, a pilgrimage to Mecca, or paying off an outstanding debt. The pressing need of the family renting out the land was usually reflected in rental rates that worked out to be well below the current market rents for seasonal tenancy. Now, however, *pajak* tenancy is increasingly at, or above,[53] market rents and is often resorted to by wealthy landowners seeking to raise cash for investment purposes.

For the landowner, leasehold rental has the advantage over *jual janji* that ownership of the land is retained even though use rights may be transferred for many years. For the small tenant, however, the effect is to price him out of the land rental market. A typical *pajak* contract (in 1979) involving, say, only 3 relong for six seasons (three years) would require raising anywhere from M\$2,700 to M\$4,000 in advance. As this represents two to three times the mean income of Muda peasants, it is far beyond the reach of the vast majority

52. The only figures I have are for Sedaka, where something like one in seven tenants may have been displaced, but it would be hazardous to project similar rates for all of Muda.

53. The authors of the *USM-MADA Land Tenure Study* found, to their surprise, that *pajak* rents worked out to M\$122.74 for the main season as compared with M\$112.49 for cash renting season by season. One interpretation they offer is that such leases "are highly commercial transactions struck up between landlords who are sensitive to market conditions of rent and well-to-do tenants (possibly including non-Malays who experience more difficulty in obtaining land and are anxious to obtain some degree of security of tenure)." P. 72.

of small farmers in the region. Leasehold tenants are increasingly drawn from the ranks of the wealthy Malay landowners and Chinese businessmen armed with capital and machinery (tractors, combine-harvesters) and looking for profitable investment opportunities. They are willing to pay premium rents and prefer to rent large tracts of paddy land. What is emerging, then, is a rich, fully commercial tenant class whose entry into the rental market serves to displace small, capital-poor tenants.

How much of the diminution of the tenant class before 1976 was due to the replacement of many small tenants by their capitalist competitors is impossible to estimate. What is clear, however, is that since 1976 there has been a marked acceleration of large-scale, long-term leasehold tenancy. Very few of the village studies conducted since then have failed to note its growing use or to express alarm at the likely consequences for the poor peasantry in the Muda region.[54]

Mechanization

Growing wet rice under traditional conditions can absorb an astounding amount of labor. Most of this labor is devoted to the four main stages of cultivation: land preparation, transplanting, reaping, and threshing. If hired labor is used, it is largely confined to these four operations, since other activities such as weeding or repairing bunds can be spread out conveniently and accomplished with family labor. Land-poor peasant households in Muda typically relied on just such wage labor opportunities to patch together their meager subsistence. The introduction of tractors for land preparation and combine-harvesters for reaping and threshing has thus effectively eliminated most of those opportunities;

---

54. Mohd. Shadli Abdullah, for example, found that in Gelung Rambal village nearly one-third of the tenancy agreements took the form of *pajak* leasehold, "Relationship of the Kinship System," 110. Diana Wong, in a subsequent study of the same village, writes that "An even more disturbing trend is the increasing shift to *pajak*." "A Padi Village in North Malaya" (1980, mimeo.), 18. Jon R. V. Daane, in his analysis of farmers' organizations, noted that *pajak* was increasingly used by even poor landlords to raise cash while avoiding the numerous claims of relatives who wished to rent land from them cheaply. See *Farmers and Farmers Organizations: A Study of Changing Resource Use Patterns in the Muda Area,* Preliminary Report No. 2 (August 1978, mimeo.). Afifuddin Haji Omar has also noted with alarm the tendency of syndicates that own combine-harvesters to lease in large plots at premium rents. "Pivotal Role," 12. In Province Wellesley, a highly commercialized rice-growing area to the south of Kedah, Fujimoto has found that 24 percent of all rental contracts are leasehold tenancies. "Land Tenure," 80. The only exception is Rosemary Barnard's restudy of Kampung Asam Riang, in which *pajak* seems to have disappeared in the past decade. "The Modernization of Agriculture in a Kedah Village, 1967–1968" (Paper presented at Second National Conference of the Asian Studies Association of Australia, University of New South Wales, Sydney, May 15–19, 1978, mimeo.), 19–20.

transplanting remains the only unmechanized farm operation that provides wage employment for poor households—and even it is now threatened.

Strictly speaking, the use of tractors for land preparation was neither a consequence of the green revolution nor a labor-replacing innovation. Most of the paddy land in Muda was ploughed by tractors before 1970, but speed in ploughing became vital if double-cropping was to take place. Thus, initially at least, tractors facilitated double-cropping, which in turn doubled the annual wage work in transplanting, reaping, and harvesting. Because tractors helped to create far more employment than they destroyed, their introduction caused no concern at the time.[55]

Combine-harvesters were a different matter. In 1975, virtually all the paddy in Muda was cut and threshed by hand. By 1980, huge Western-style combines costing nearly M$200,000 and owned by syndicates of businessmen were harvesting roughly 80 percent of the rice crop. If it is hard to imagine the visual impact on the peasantry of this mind-boggling technological leap from sickles and threshing tubs to clanking behemoths with thirty-two-foot cutting bars,[56] it is not so hard to calculate their impact on the distribution of rural income.

The consequences for income of combine-harvesting are especially applicable to households farming less than 2.8 acres (over 46 percent of Muda's families) and wage laborers (7 percent). The former depended on paddy wage labor for *at least* one-fourth of their net income, while the latter were often totally dependent on it. Calculations based on the share of cutting (usually women's work) and threshing (usually men's work) in total hired labor and the intensity of combine-harvester use suggest that the combines have cut paddy wage labor receipts by 44 percent.[57] For the poorest class of small farmers, this represents a 15 percent

55. It is instructive, however, to note the shift in income transfers that the use of tractors prompted. Before their use, large operators would often hire modest local farmers with water buffalo to plough (*menggembur*) and to harrow (*menyisir*) their land. The effect was mildly redistributive. With the use of tractors, the payments are typically made to outside businessmen and rich farmers who own this expensive item of capital.

56. Alas, it seems to have occurred to no one that an oral history of their appearance in the fields in 1975 would have been worth collecting.

57. Wages paid for transplanting, cutting, threshing, and in-field transportation comprise about 90 percent of the hired labor component in rice cultivation in Muda. Of that, cutting and threshing, which are carried out in one operation by the combines, comprise abut 55 percent. Combine-harvesters also eliminate a substantial amount of in-field transportation by transporting paddy directly to the bunds or to the roadside. This loss, however, is more or less compensated for by employment created in the bagging of rice. As of 1980, combines harvested about 80 percent of Muda's paddy land. Assuming that this figure is likely to remain the norm, I arrive at a net loss of hired labor income of 44 percent (80 percent of 55 percent). Farm income figures for 1974, before the combines were used, show that paddy wage labor

loss of net income in the case of tenants and an 11 percent loss in the case of owner-operators. For full-time wage laborers, of course, the results are catastrophic and it is hard to imagine how they can survive as a class in the new circumstances. Combine-harvesting has meant, then, a loss of nearly half the wages previously received for paddy work by the poorer strata of Muda's peasantry. The loss in the volume of work has by no means been compensated for by a rise in wage rates for the work still available.

The direct impact of combine-harvesting on wage income is obvious and dramatic, but in the long run the indirect consequences may prove more damaging. Mechanization, by promoting large-scale farming and leaseholding, has greatly reduced the opportunity for small-scale tenancy. It has also eliminated gleaning, shifted local hiring patterns, reduced transplanting wages, and transformed local social relations. These last changes, which are rarely captured in the aggregate regional statistics, are best deferred to our detailed discussion of Sedaka in the next chapter.

From Exploitation to Marginalization

The impact of double-cropping has thus far been considered as if it were largely a matter of access to land, work, and wages. It is well worth pausing briefly to suggest its implications for class relations as well. What the transformations brought about by Muda's green revolution have done is nearly to sever the bonds of economic interdependence betweeen agrarian classes. Prior to double-cropping and, to some extent, even until 1975, the land-rich class and the land-poor class of Muda were joined by an exchange of work and wages, cultivation and rents which, however exploitative, fused them together in the enterprise of rice farming. Rich landlords and farmers had more paddy fields than they could cultivate alone; they needed tenants, ploughing services, transplanters, reapers, and threshers. The land-poor and landless, having more labor than property, provided these services. Because of the labor peaks typical of rice cultivation, it was not uncommon for employers to help secure timely labor by modest gifts and loans or, in more general terms, to "cultivate" not only the land but also the poorer villagers whom they needed to make the land profitable.

With mechanization, tenancy became an expensive luxury. Those tenants who remained, aside from close kin, were typically paying fixed market rents with

---

income for small farm households (below 2.84 acres) was approximately M$350 per annum. A loss of 44 percent of that income would reduce it to M$196. For a tenant in this category, the loss in total net income is 15 percent; for an owner-operator, the loss is 11 percent. For a wage laborer the loss is far larger. As these classes comprise the more than half of Muda's population that lives below the official poverty line, the income consequences are grave. For a careful case study of the wage impact of combine-harvesting, see "MADA-TARC Farm Management Studies, 1980," 47–54.

no allowance for crop failures or were themselves large capitalist leaseholding tenants. More important, cultivation could now be undertaken largely independent of village labor. Except for transplanting and for those occasions when a plot that ripened early or lodged (was beaten flat by wind and/or rain) *had* to be harvested by hand, large farmers simply had little need to hire poor villagers. Thus, they had correspondingly little incentive to cultivate their goodwill. The linkage between classes has by no means totally disappeared, but there is little doubt that it is far more constricted than it was and that all indications point toward its eventual demise. If poor villagers were earlier tied to their richer employers by bonds of interdependence and exploitation, they now find themselves cut adrift and marginalized. If they are no longer exploited, if they are now "free," this is the freedom of the unemployed, the redundant.

Income

The effect of the Muda Irrigation Scheme on incomes and on the distribution of those incomes throughout the region is best examined in two phases: an initial phase from 1966 to 1974 and a subsequent phase from 1974 to 1979. The basic, summary figures are shown in table 3.4, covering five tenure categories of farmers that are most common in Muda. They are, as all averages must be, abstractions hiding an enormous variation of circumstances and conditions in order to create some measure of central tendency. Whenever judgments were necessary, they were made so as to avoid understating the income of small farmers.[58]

The initial impact of double-cropping in Muda was to raise incomes on a broad front in both nominal and real terms. This gain, however, was at the expense of a much worse distribution of that income.[59] Owner-tenants, the

58. For example, there is good reason to believe that gross paddy income may be overstated by as much as 20 percent because of differences between crop-cutting surveys and actual yields as well as reductions in sale price made for moisture content. "Other income" for most farmers is almost certainly overstated as well since the averages are inflated by a few farmers with steady off-farm salaries or wages. The picture given here is perhaps even more optimistic than a more complete account would allow.

59. Virtually all of the major studies in Muda concur with this conclusion. Thus the authors of the Food and Agriculture Organization/World Bank Cooperative Program report, *Muda Study*, write, "This increase in income at the farm level, however, has not been evenly distributed across the already unequal pattern of income distribution and has, therefore, served to worsen that distribution" 1:2. See also Afifuddin Haji Omar, "Peasants, Institutions, and Development: The Political Economy of Development in the Muda Region" (Ph.D. diss., Cornell University, 1977), 339–40, and Clive Bell, "Some Effects in the Barter Terms of Trade on a Small Regional Economy" (Washington, D.C.: Development Research Center, World Bank, July 1979, mimeo.), 32.

TABLE 3.4 • Family Income Comparisons for Different Tenure Groups and Farm-Size Categories in Muda, 1966, 1974, 1979

	All Farms									Small Farms					
	Average Tenant			Average Owner-Operator			Average Owner-Tenant			Average Small Owner			Average Small Tenant		
	1966	1974	1979	1966	1974	1979	1966	1974	1979	1966	1974	1979	1966	1974	1979
Average farm size (acres)		3.69			3.20			6.60			1.42			1.42	
Net annual income	1,408	3,469	2,917	1,379	3,732	3,548	1,886	6,405	5,801	1,021	2,209	2,097	958	1,855	1,606
Real income (1966 prices)	1,408	2,417	1,664	1,379	2,601	2,023	1,886	4,463	3,309	1,021	1,539	1,196	958	1,293	916
Income index by category (1966 = 100)	100	172	118	100	189	147	100	237	175	100	151	117	100	135	96

NOTE: A much expanded table from which this is derived, together with sources and explanation, may be found in appendix B.

wealthiest tenure category with by far the largest farm size, were the greatest gainers, improving their real income by 137 percent. The incomes of average tenants and average owner-operators grew by 72 and 89 percent respectively. By contrast, the gains of small tenants and owners (*nearly half of Muda's farm households*) were far more modest: 35 percent and 51 percent. Even the percentages are misleading here, given the different base incomes, for while the typical owner-tenant gained M$2,577 in real income, the average small tenant gained only M$335: a ratio of 8 to 1. Both the gains in income and their maldistribution, it should be added, were not due solely to the production effects of double-croppings. They were due as much to the doubling of farm-gate paddy prices in the worldwide economic crisis and inflation of 1973–74.[60]

The five-year period from late 1974 to 1979 was, by contrast, one of declining nominal and real income for *all* categories of farmers.[61] Losses for average tenants and small owners meant that, at the end of the period, they were less than 20 percent ahead of their 1966 real incomes. Small tenants suffered most dramatically, as their real incomes were, if anything, below what they had been thirteen years before. Only owner-tenants and owner-operators remained substantially ahead of their 1966 real incomes.

The causes of this retreat across a broad front may be traced to three factors. First, the earlier increase in production brought about by double-cropping had leveled off and yields remained stagnant throughout this period. Second, paddy prices after 1974 were steady for the next five years.[62] The cost of inputs to farmers, on the other hand, continued to rise as did the consumer price index (up 22 percent), thereby eroding the real incomes of all tenure categories. There

60. For a superb and meticulous analysis of the relative impact of production and prices in this period, see Jegatheesan, *Green Revolution,* 31–50.

61. As Jegatheesan notes, "Such estimates (i.e. yields, farm size, tenure, cost of production, paddy price) have always to be treated with care in the actual quantitative assessments of net income, but have as yet never been proven wrong in showing a continuing decline in average net farm incomes in Muda since 1975 owing to relatively static yields, a stable padi price, and rising production costs." "Monitoring and Evaluation in the Muda Irrigation Scheme, Malaysia"' (n.d., circa 1979, mimeo.), 39. Bell et al., *Evaluation of Projects,* on a related issue, have estimated the capital flow out of the Muda region following gains in production and reached pessimistic conclusions about the possibility for self-sustaining regional growth. "The conclusion that the project's effects were of a once-and-for-all kind seem to us virtually inescapable." Chap. 9, p. 35.

62. In 1981, after my research was completed, the government raised the paddy price by roughly one-third. The effect of this change by itself would have been to restore average real incomes to their 1974 level or slightly above. Income distribution would, however, have become even worse. The increase in the official support price was most certainly motivated in part by the farmers' demonstrations for a price hike held in January 1980 in Alor Setar.

is no doubt that declining farm incomes contributed to the January 1980 mass demonstration of paddy growers—the first in over fifteen years—in which thousands of peasants assembled in Alor Setar to demand an increase in paddy prices.

The worsening trend in income distribution from 1966 to 1979 is captured in table 3.5 in comparisons in the net income of small farmers over time as a proportion of the net income of other tenure categories. All the disparities, it is clear, were essentially generated in the first stage of double-cropping. Ironically, the second stage arrested (but did not reverse) these new inequities, although at the cost of lower real incomes all around. Small tenants who had half the income of owner-tenants in 1966 now have roughly one-quarter of their income. To put it more accurately, those tenants *who are lucky enough still to be tenants* have slid to about one-fourth the income of owner-tenants. Small owner-operators, even more numerous, had over half the income of owner-tenants thirteen years ago and now have roughly one-third that income. The declining position of Muda's small peasants is the result of their small farm size *and* of the direct and indirect effects of an irrigation scheme that disproportionately rewards the owners of scarce factors of production. They were poor to begin with; they remain poor; and they have grown relatively poorer. There is no need, on the basis of this data, to question the general assessment of the green revolution by Keith Griffin that "the changes which are at present occurring tend to increase relative inequality."[63]

TABLE 3.5 • Income Comparisons between Tenure Categories 1966, 1974, 1979

	1966	1974	1979
I. Net income of small tenant as proportion of income of:			
a. Average tenant	68	53	55
b. Average owner-tenant	51	29	28
II. Net income of small owner-operator as proportion of income of:			
a. Average owner	74	59	59
b. Average owner-tenant	54	34	36

The gulf separating the large, capitalist farmers who market most of the region's rice and the mass of small peasants is now nearly an abyss, with the added (and related) humiliation that the former need seldom even hire the latter to help grow their crops. Taking 1966 as a point of comparison, it is still the case that a majority of Muda's households are more prosperous than before. It is also the case that the distribution of income has worsened appreciably and that a substantial minority—perhaps 35–40 percent—have been left behind with very low incomes which, if they are not worse than a decade ago, are not appreciably better. Given the limited absorptive capacity of the wider economy,

63. Griffin, *Political Economy,* 73.

given the loss of wages to machines, and given the small plots cultivated by the poor strata, there is little likelihood that anything short of land reform could reverse their fortunes.[64]

Poverty

It is in the nature of large bureaucracies, of which the state is the outstanding example, to create a series of quantitative measures by which to define goals and to measure the extent to which they have been achieved. Thus it is that the human misery known as poverty is signified by numbers—a certain amount of cash per household, a certain number of calories ingested each day. While we shall have ample occasion later to explore the meaning of poverty—how it is experienced and understood—the gross numerical description of poverty does provide something of a baseline from which to begin.

The figures presented in table 3.6 are based on the official poverty-line income and show how the income of various tenure groups has changed since 1966 in relation to that standard.

The remarkable and sobering fact is that much of the gain made between 1966 and 1974 had been largely undone by 1979. Not even the initial boom in prices and production had raised small farmers, whether owners or tenants, above the poverty line, and by 1979 they were once again far below. Average tenants and owner-operators had improved their incomes appreciably but many, if not most, were still below poverty-line incomes. At a bare minimum there were 33,000 "officially" poor households in Muda in 1979.[65] These households

64. There is some dispute about how the poverty level has been established, with some claiming that it should be set lower for rural areas where the cost of living is lower. Without pretending to judge this issue, I believe it is clear that there may be strong political reasons for the government to set the poverty level reasonably high in order to justify certain programs aimed at attracting Malay votes. Quite aside from the question of what an appropriate poverty level might be, it should be added that, given the official level, the estimate of 30 percent is quite conservative. This is the conclusion reached by the most thorough recent study of poor households in the Muda region, in which households interviewed in 1972–73 were reinterviewed a decade later. The study confirms that half or more of Muda's population is still below the official poverty line and the "downstream" employment created by double-cropping has gone largely to wealthier households, not to those who need it most. See the excellent preliminary report by Sukur Kasim, "Evolution of Sources of Income in the Muda Irrigation Project (1972/73–1981/82)" (Paper presented at Conference on Off-Farm Employment in the Development of Rural Asia, Chengmai, Thailand, August 1983, mimeo.).

65. This very conservative figure is derived by adding the number of small farm households to that of nonfarming wage laborers. Of course a small percentage of small farm households are in fact above the poverty line. By the same token, however, a fair number of average tenants and owner-operators with farm sizes above 3 acres are below the poverty level.

TABLE 3.6 • Net Income of Various Tenure and Farm-Size Categories as Percentage of Rural Poverty-Line Income

	Average Tenant	Average Owner-Operator	Average Owner-Tenant	Average Small Owner	Average Small Tenant
1966	79	78	106	57	54
1974	134	145	248	86	72
1979	91	111	181	66	50

NOTE: Rural poverty-line incomes per household, per month, are as follows: 1966—M$148; 1974—M$215; 1979—M$267. If one were to make adjustments in these figures both for the actual yields and reductions in paddy prices due to moisture content, on the one hand, and for the new fertilizer and new support price (1981), on the other, small owners and tenants would remain, on average, well below the poverty line (72 percent and 52 percent, respectively), and average tenants and average owner-operators would be slightly above (109 percent and 126 percent). Only owner-tenants would be well above at 213 percent.

represent the intractable poverty problem of the region. They remain poor despite double-cropping, despite the fact that Muda is a privileged area in terms of soils, despite a dense network of institutions created to serve paddy farmers, despite government programs committed to eradicating poverty, despite recent increases in paddy price and fertilizer subsidies—in short, despite thirteen years of intensive agricultural development.

The fundamental problem, of course, lies in the inequities of landownership and farm size existing at the outset of the scheme. The gains from the new seeds, irrigation, and double-cropping are at best distributed in accordance with the control of productive assets. Small farmers simply did not have the land or capital that would have allowed them to raise their incomes dramatically. Long-term rentals, rising land prices, and the revocation of tenancies further limited their access to land. What they did have in abundance was labor. Before combine-harvesting, this asset was in large part responsible for raising their incomes. But the mechanization of harvesting together with rising production costs and consumer prices gradually eroded their modest gains.

Institutional Access

Along with the changes in production, farm size, tenure, and mechanization associated with the green revolution has come something of an institutional revolution as well. Nowhere is this more striking, as noted earlier, than in state control over water release and increasing participation in milling, marketing, credit provision, and fertilizer distribution. The main institutional vector of this transformation has been the Muda Agricultural Development Authority (MADA) and its twenty-seven local offices, each with its own Farmers' Association (*Persatuan Peladang*). The main function of these local offices has been to distribute credit to its membership for tractor rental costs, fertilizer, pesticides, and trans-planting. As many as 15,000 farmers (roughly 25 percent of the farm households) have benefited from these services. Far from remaining merely passive recipients of services, the Farmers' Associations, both individually and collectively, have become active and vociferous spokesmen for the interests of paddy farmers. They have come to constitute the functional equivalent of a paddy producer's lobby, which has consistently brought pressure to bear through annual resolutions, petitions, and delegations for changes in policy that would benefit their mem-bership. The competitive political atmosphere, especially in Kedah, contributes to their influence, and all but one or two of the local bodies are controlled effectively by members of the ruling party.

Nearly 40 percent of Muda's farmers have at one time or another joined a Farmers' Association, but this membership is by no means a cross-section of Muda's peasantry. Table 3.7 reveals just how skewed participation is. Farmers cultivating less than 2.84 acres (4 relong) comprise nearly half the farm popu-lation but only 12.4 percent of Farmers' Association members. At the other end

TABLE 3.7 • Relationship of Distribution of Farm Sizes, Farmers' Association Mem-bership, and Production Credit Recipients

Farm Size (Acres)	Percentage of Farms in Muda	Percentage of FA Members	Percentage of Credit Recipients
0.1–2.84	46.7	12.4	6.0
2.85–5.6	30.6	40.4	34.8
5.7–7.09	8.3	21.8	29.2
7.1 and above	14.5	25.4	30.3

of the scale, larger farmers planting 5.7 acres and above are only 23 percent of the farm population but make up fully 47 percent of the membership. The domination of these associations by well-to-do farmers is typical of most such bodies in the Third World.[66] It has come about not so much because of any systematic official policy but rather from the policies pursued by their elected leadership.[67]

66. As Norman Uphoff and Milton Esman note, "if such organizations become institutionalized, they would be as instruments of the large and middle farmers, while small farmers would be thrown back on traditional links of dependency on patrons or be compelled to rely wholly on their own meagre resources." *Local Or-ganization for Rural Development: Analysis of Asian Experience* (Ithaca: Rural Develop-ment Committee, Cornell University, 1974), 66.

67. Originally, membership and annual subscription fees were nominal (M$3), but as members began to subscribe to equity shares, new members were required to purchase a block of shares equivalent in value to the amount held by members of long standing. It is now rare for membership to cost less than M$30 and it often runs as high as M$100. For small farmers, whose production credit allowance, given their acreage, might be less than M$100, this provision is an effective bar to entry.

Credit distribution is even more skewed toward the well-to-do than membership. Large farmers operating more than 5.7 acres are less than 23 percent of the farm population, yet they constitute more than 60 percent of the credit recipients and of course a much higher share of the actual credit extended. Small farmers, who are nearly half Muda's population, constitute a mere 6 percent of those who get subsidized credit. Those who are most in need of credit on easy terms are denied access, while those who could borrow from banks or finance inputs from their own savings are provided for in abundance. Increasing rates of delinquency in repayment, moreover, indicate that many large farmers have managed to turn the loans into outright subsidies.[68] The accumulated bad debts have gone unprosecuted because the debtors, drawn largely from the ranks of local, ruling party stalwarts, are well-nigh untouchable. To this extent, MADA, the ruling party, and the Kedah state government are hostages to the interests of the relatively prosperous strata of farmers which the green revolution has helped create and solidify.

As the economic distance between rich and poor has grown, so has this privileged class's access to influence and credit. If the interests of paddy farmers are heard at all, they are increasingly the interests of larger farmers. On some questions, such as paddy support prices or fertilizer subsidies, this may make little difference, for the interests of rich and poor will largely coincide. But on many other issues—mechanization, agricultural wage policy, credit eligibility, land rents, land reform—their interests are sharply conflicting. The vise-like grip with which large operators now control the Farmers' Associations means both that the vital interests of Muda's poor are systematically excluded even from the policy agenda and that those who have already profited most from the green revolution will continue to have things their own way.[69]

These facts about agricultural "progress" are all too familiar from analyses of the green revolution elsewhere in Asia. As Keith Griffin has concluded:

Even were they to join, the annual deduction of at least M$15 for compulsory share purchase from their credit allowance makes joining less attractive than the familiar alternative of credit from shopkeepers. Compiled from *USM-MADA Land Tenure Study,* 68, and Zakaria Ismail, "Institutional Short-term Production Credit Programme in Muda Scheme," MADA Monograph No. 38 (Alor Setar: MADA, n.d., probably 1977), 24.

68. Ho Nai Kin has provided evidence of increasing delinquency up to 1977 in "Implementation and Supervision Problem of Institutional Padi Production Credit in MADA's Farmers' Association," MADA Monograph No. 35 (Alor Setar: MADA, 1978), app. 2. There is also evidence to suggest that delinquency is more characteristic of large farmers than small farmers. See Mohd. Noh Samik, "Delinquent Loanees" (Alor Setar: MADA, Bahagian Pertanian, n.d.).

69. For a convincing analysis of state agricultural policy in the Third World and its consequences for income distribution, power, and development, see Robert H. Bates, *Markets and States in Tropical Africa* (Berkeley: Univ. of California Press, 1981).

A major reason for this [the domination of larger farmers] was the bias of public policy which systematically channeled scarce resources to the larger and more prosperous farmers. Although policy aggravated inequality in the countryside, it had virtue, from the point of view of the government, of encouraging commercial agriculture and thereby augmenting the marketable surplus. Given the needs of urban areas for cheap and abundant wage goods . . . the best thing that could have happened, did happen: the "green revolution" strengthened those in the countryside who were the natural allies of the urban ruling groups and it enabled these ruling groups to perpetuate the status quo essentially unchanged.[70]

In Muda as well, the economic, political, and institutional facts combine to make it extremely unlikely that the great inequities now prevailing will even be addressed, let alone mitigated.

70. Griffin, *Political Economy,* 128.

4 • Sedaka, 1967–1979

THE VILLAGE

The foreground of the landscape we are viewing is formed by village-level "facts" as they have become evident in the past decade. Here the focus is even sharper, for they are "facts" that have been directly experienced—for example, changes in rental forms, mechanization, wages, land tenure, credit, charity. These facts are not simply the replication of the middle ground in the village context. This particular village is, as any other particular village would be, to some extent unique. Put another way, Sedaka has had its own special green revolution in keeping with its particular history, its particular cast of characters. It is this special, local variant of the green revolution that Sedaka's villagers have helped to fashion and to which they are responding.

The village of Sedaka falls within the administrative district of Yan, which straddles the southern frontier of the Muda Irrigation Scheme.[1] (See map 2) The small town of Yan itself, some eight miles to the south, houses the district office complex, including the local land office, police station, and a nearby clinic. It is to this town that villagers must go to execute and notarize land transactions of long-term rentals as well as to pawn gold jewelry at the licensed pawn shop. If Yan is the main focus of administrative life for Sedaka, the nearby town of Kepala Batas might be described as the main focus of commercial life. Villagers buy most of their food and provisions at its shops and at its twice-weekly rotating market on Wednesday and Sunday. It is also the center for credit and marketing, whether through the Chinese shopkeepers who extend loans and buy paddy or through the Farmers' Association and the local branch of the Paddy Marketing Authority (LPN), which has a large rice-drying facility on the outskirts of town

1. Sample data collected in 1982 indicate that the district of Yan, which was relatively poor by Muda region standards before double-cropping, appears to have benefited less in the past decade than other districts. In 1982 it had the highest proportion of poor households; more than 75 percent of Yan's households were below the official poverty level. Furthermore, only one of the other four districts studied had fared as badly in reducing the poverty rate. More of Yan's households, by far, described themselves as "hardup" (*susah*), despite the likelihood that real incomes for a majority of households in the district have improved somewhat. The fact that Yan is so heavily monocultural (paddy) that man/land ratios are comparatively high and that it is rather isolated from urban employment may help account for its relatively lackluster performance. For details see Sukur Kasim, "Evolution of Sources of Income in the Muda Irrigation Project (1972/73–1981/82)" (Paper presented at Conference on Off-Farm Equipment in the Development of Rural Asia, Chengmai, Thailand, August 1983, mimeo.). In this respect, Yan and Sedaka may be somewhat poorer than more representative districts within the Muda scheme.

near the village. Kepala Batas is also the site of the subdistrict (Mukim Sungai Daun) chief's (*penghulu*) office, at which minor administrative matters such as the registration or sale of water buffalo are handled, and of a once-a-week maternity clinic staffed by government nurses.

The seventy-four households of Sedaka are strung out along a nearly mile-long dirt path. (See map 3) This path leads from the all-weather road joining Yan to Kepala Batas and ending abruptly at the rice fields separating the village from the neighboring settlement to the east, Sungai Bujur. Like most villages on the Muda Plain established in this century, the pattern of settlement follows the linear plan of the drainage canals that originally brought the land into production. This ribbon of settlement is often contrasted with the pattern of nucleated or clustered villages, where social and ritual cohesion is said to be greater.[2] It is certainly true that villagers themselves are not quite sure where Sedaka ends and where Sungai Tongkang, the village along the main road, begins. Despite these vagaries of geography, the village is, as we shall see, far more than just a collection of households in close proximity. If its boundaries are ill defined, all but a few families are nevertheless quite unambiguously *of* Sedaka. If neighborhoods subdivide it, the prayer house (*surau*) as a focus for religious life and the large feasts to which all villagers are typically invited serve to ritually unify it. Administratively as well, it is usually treated as a distinct unit. When it is not, as in the case of the Farmer's Association until recently, villagers have lobbied to have Sedaka recognized as a separate branch. Above all, the moral existence of the village is recognized in discourse. When the collector of the Islamic tithe (*amil*) explains why he does not report villagers who fail to pay the full amount, he says, "We all live in the same village."[3] When a tenant tells me why he would not try to expand his farm by outbidding another local tenant, he says, "Everyday I see his face."[4] And when the rules are broken, as they occasionally are, the culprit is shamed in precisely the same terms.

Looking straight down the path, no houses are visible—just the solid archway of coconut palms, banana fronds, *nipah,* and the water hyacinths and grasses growing in the ditches alongside. Idris's store, facing the surfaced road leading north to Kepala Batas and south to Yan Kecil, is the first building in Sedaka. Idris takes advantage of his roadside location and the electricity it provides to sell drinks and cigarettes to the young men who gather there in the evenings and to offer the only popsicles available locally. A little farther along is a hinged timber spanning the path, which is fastened by chain and lock preventing trucks from entering. This village gate is, as we shall see, an object of some controversy.

2. Afifuddin in Haji Omar, "Irrigation Structures and Local Peasant Organisa-tions," MADA Monograph No. 32 (Alor Setar: MADA, 1977).

3. *Sama-sama duduk kampung.*

4. *Hari-hari tengok muka.*

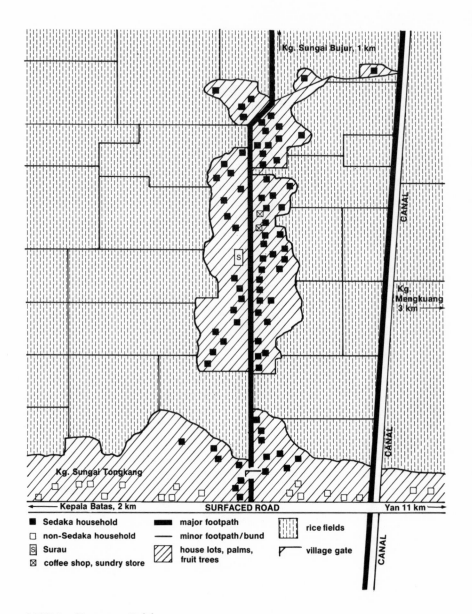

Kg. Sungai Bujur, 1 km

CANAL

Kg. Mengkuang 3 km

Kg. Sungai Tongkang

Kepala Batas, 2 km   SURFACED ROAD   Yan 11 km

CANAL

■	Sedaka household	▬▬	major footpath	▦	rice fields
□	non-Sedaka household	—	minor footpath/bund		
ⓈS	Surau	▨	house lots, palms, fruit trees	⌐	village gate
⊠	coffee shop, sundry store				

CANAL

MAP 3 • Kampung Sedaka

The key is held at the nearby house of Lebai Pendek, a wealthy, elderly cultivator who, together with his sons, Musa and Ariffin, is influential in the small group that controls village politics. Houses interspersed with paddy fields line the path for the next two hundred yards; the dwellings (see photos) of the well-to-do with zinc roofs and clapboard siding and those of most poor with attap roofing and siding made of bamboo split and beaten flat (*pelupoh*). Even the condition of the houses is an acrimonious political issue, which we shall explore, inasmuch as the local ruling party and its supporters are accused of having monopolized a government subsidy for house repair. Mansur, a landless laborer, and Taib, a poor smallholder, live in this stretch and their houses contrast sharply with the refurbished and repainted house of Shamsul, a ruling party stalwart who owns 6 relong (4.2 acres) and has a rare and coveted job at the government paddy-drying installation nearby.

Near the middle of the village stand the two most substantial houses in the village, each with high roofs, louvered shutters, and verandas. One belongs to Haji Kadir, the richest villager, and makes a stark contrast with the dilapidated houses of Hamzah and Razak just beside it. The other is the house of Haji Jaafar, the village headman (*ketua kempung*). As headman, Haji Jaafar is influential but rather retiring; his married son Daud, who lives with him, and the shopkeeper, Basir, are far more visibly active. Haji Jaafar prefers to emphasize his unifying role by giving an annual feast (*Kenduri*) to which the entire village is invited and by occasionally leading prayers at the village *surau* across the path (see photo). While there are many public gatherings in Sedaka, the *surau,* whose lower floor serves as a village meeting hall, classroom for religious teachers, and lecture hall for sermons and political speeches, is the only designated public space in the community.

The informal gathering places, however, the places where idle chatter and gossip are exchanged, are around the tables of the two small shops (see photo). Each shop carries a small inventory of daily items such as dried chillies, soap, matches, kerosene, tobacco, sweets, spices, tinned fish for last-minute purchase. After the day's work and during slack periods, men will gather to pass the time smoking and drinking homemade soft drinks, with the circle constantly changing as some arrive and others leave. Basir, the owner of the first store, is the acknowledged leader of the local ruling party (UMNO) branch and his shop thus serves as a gathering place for his allies. The same holds for Samat's store nearby, except that he and his father, Tok Mahmud, are staunch supporters of the opposition party and their clientele is drawn especially from its ranks. A few strongly partisan villagers will, on principle, never go to the "other" shop, but a majority claim that they go to both, being above such petty considerations.

The three best-known and most outspoken women live within shouting distance of the stores, farther along the path. All three are, as it were, honorary men in the sense that they have all had to assume male roles and responsibilities. Rokiah and Rosni are both heads of transplanting groups, which requires them to negotiate with farmers; Rosni is a widow, while Rokiah's husband is alive but judged rather feebleminded, and she has assumed control of the family. The third, the midwife Tok Sah Bidan, is a widow whose training and forty-odd years of midwifery give her a unique place in village life.

At the very end of the village path stand a number of houses of poor villagers, most of whom belong to the opposition. Many of the most pointed criticisms and opinions I heard were expressed by Pak Yah, a landless laborer, when he was talking with his equally poor brother-in-law, Mat "halus," and his friend Dullah. They and the other friends and relatives who occasionally joined them on the rough benches below Pak Yah's house could always be counted on for a perspective that broke sharply with that coming from the UMNO stalwarts at Basir's store or with that held by wealthy members (for example, Haji Kadir) of their own party.

In its pattern of settlement, its economy, its size, and its history, Sedaka is fairly typical of the rice-farming villages on the Kedah plain. But so are hundreds of other villages, and the choice of this particular village as a place to settle and conduct research merits a brief explanation. The first requirement I had was a village more or less exclusively devoted to rice cultivation. Sedaka fits this particular perfectly. Only two heads of household are salaried; one is a truck driver for the Farmers' Association, and the other examines paddy for moisture content at the local government purchasing complex. Both also farm in their spare time. There is in fact not a single household in the village that does not now or, in the case of aged couples, did not once grow rice. The advantage of rice mono-culture is not only that it is representative of most villages in Muda but also that the task of determining incomes and economic stratification is relatively straightforward. Villages on the fringes of the irrigation scheme, by contrast, have far more mixed economies, which may include fishing, rubber smallholding, and estate work. A paddy-farming community, on the other hand, is rather like a fishing village with only two catches a year.

Another requirement was by far the most restrictive: that the village be one that had been studied before 1971, when double-cropping was introduced, so that it would be possible to establish at least the basic changes in the local economy. Only three or four villages satisfied this condition. The first one I visited was Sedaka. Not only was the village headman, Haji Jaafar, hospitable to the idea of a strange family settling in his midst but it seemed possible, after a brief talk, that a part of Haji Kadir's large house might be rented out now that his own children had grown and left home. The ease with which such basic questions were resolved, together with the euphoria contributed by a remarkable sunset and the knowledge that the imposing beauty of Gunung Jerai (Kedah Peak) would always be visible to the south, were enough to settle the matter on the spot.[5]

5. I was not the first foreigner to settle in Sedaka. Dr. Kenzo Horii, a Japanese researcher, had lived there for two months in late 1966 and mid-1967, collecting

RICH AND POOR

Glaring inequalities were an integral feature of economic life in Sedaka before double-cropping. They remain so today. They are apparent from the most casual visual evidence of clothing, housing, food, furniture, kitchen or farm equipment, radios and, in a few cases now, television sets. They are, on closer inspection, produced and maintained by equally glaring disparities in the distribution of land ownership, of farm size, and hence of income.

Incomes in Sedaka were highly skewed in 1978–79. Despite the fact that there are no comparable figures for 1967, what we do know about land and farm-size distribution then suggests inequalities of a similar magnitude at the very least. The present situation can be seen from table 4.1, which reports net income for each household in the village, together with rice land owned and operated and the dominant occupation of the head of household. Families are ranked from poorest to richest on the basis of income per capita in the household. Readers may find it helpful to refer to this listing when they wish to identify the income, tenure status, major source of household income, party affiliation, and so forth of families who will appear and reappear throughout the text.

Using the standard government procedures to calculate per capita income— by which children and adults are counted equally—a total of forty households, or 54 percent, of village families would fall below the official poverty-line income of $572 per capita per year. A less stringent formula, employed in table 4.1, which counts infants below age six as only one-third of an adult equivalent and children aged six through twelve as two-thirds, places twenty-two households, or 30 percent, of Sedaka's families below the poverty line. It is for these twenty-two families and the eight or ten families who have incomes just above the poverty line that the problems of food and daily necessities take their most severe form. For these families, an illness of a working adult, a poor yield, a decline in harvest work, an increase in rents, or the withdrawal of a tenancy can easily spell disaster. Their income contrasts starkly with that of the best-off twenty-two families in the village. The poorest twenty-two households have an average net annual income of M$2,291 while the richest twenty-two households earn an average of M$6,044. The contrast is more pronounced if we consider per capita

---

basic economic data on landholding, tenure, and social organization. Although his stay was briefer than mine and his interests necessarily more limited, his research provided me with invaluable base-line data from which to draw inferences about the effects of double-cropping. Many of the historical comparisons that follow are based on the information he has generously supplied. The two most important published reports in English drawing on these data are Kanzo Horii, "The Land Tenure System of Malay Padi Farmers: A Case Study . . . in the State of Kedah," *Developing Economies* 10, no. 1 (1972): 45–73, and *Rice Economy and Land Tenure in West Malaysia: A Comparative Study of Eight Villages*. I.D.E. Occasional Papers Series No. 18 (Tokyo: Institute of Developing Economics, 1981).

TABLE 4.1 • Village Data by Households—Identified by Household Head and Ranked from Poorest to Richest according to Per Capita Annual Net Income

		Net Income Per Capita (Adjusted)	Net Household Income[a]	Paddy Area Owned[b] (Relong) 1979	Paddy Area Worked (Relong) 1979	Status by Major Source of Income	Political Party Affiliation[c]	Membership in Farmers' Association
1	Razak	186	747	.25	0	laborer	UMNO	No
2	Wahid	392	1,960	0	6	tenant	UMNO	No
3	Salleh	406	2,314	1.50	5.50	tenant	PAS	No
4	Taib	413	2,063	1.25	1.25	laborer	PAS	No
5	Sukur	421	2,108	.25	.25	laborer	PAS	No
6	Mat "halus"	426	1,960	0	0	laborer	PAS	No
7	Bakri bin Haji Wahab	453	2,992	0	4.00	tenant	UMNO	No
8	Hamzah	474	2,986	2	0	laborer	PAS	No
9	Mansur	479	1,580	0	0	laborer	UMNO	No
10	Karim	480	2,218	0	2	laborer	UMNO	No
11	Pak Yah	484	3,870	0	0	laborer	PAS	No
12	Mat Sarif	485	3,190	0	3	tenant	UMNO	No
13	Midon	497	1,640	0	0	laborer	PAS	No
14	Dullah	498	2,990	0	1.50	laborer	PAS	No
15	Hasnah	520	2,081	1.75	1.25	laborer	PAS	No
16	Tok Baba	526	2,366	10	4	owner	UMNO	No
17	Samad	539	3,236	0	8	tenant	UMNO	No
18	Rustam	544	3,429	1	2	owner	PAS	No
19	Sha'ari	548	1,260	0	.75	tenant	PAS	No
20	Salmah	560	1,120	1.25	1.25	laborer	PAS	No
21	Tok Zainah	562	1,124	2.50	1	owner	UMNO	No
22	Zin	566	3,170	.75	0	pensioner	PAS	No
23	Tok Radzi	583	3,846	0	5	tenant	PAS	No

24	Cik Puteh	614	2,826	2	4	owner	UMNO	No
25	Ishak	614	2,478	0	3	tenant	PAS	No
26	Rosni	662	3,507	0	4	tenant	PAS	No
27	Ariffin	670	2,680	0	3	tenant	UMNO	No
28	Samat	701	4,418	0	5	tenant	PAS	No
29	Nizam bin Haji Lah	712	1,424	0	3	tenant	PAS	No
30	Tok Jariah	716	1,145	1	1.50	owner	UMNO	No
31	Harun Din	717	2,152	0	.50	laborer	UMNO	No
32	Dzulkifli bin Haji Wahab	770	2,540	0	4	tenant	*pagar*	No
33	Mat Nasir	774	1,780	0	1.50	laborer	PAS	Yes
34	Mat Buyong	783	4,074	1	5	tenant	PAS	Yes
35	Lebai Hussein	784	6,272	3	6	owner	UMNO	No
36	Ali Abdul Rahman	803	1,846	0	2	tenant	UMNO	No
37	Tok Omar	806	3,226	0	4	tenant	UMNO	No
38	Hamid	828	3,810	9.75	0	landlord	UMNO	No
39	Onn	845	2,198	0	1	laborer	UMNO	No
40	Tok Ahmad	861	3,012	0	4	tenant	UMNO	No
41	Abdul Rahman	864	3,974	16.5	11.5	owner	UMNO	Yes
42	Fadzil	882	4,678	8.5	8	owner	UMNO	No
43	Cik Tun	938	1,876	1.5	3	owner	UMNO	Yes
44	Lazim	957	7,654	3	13.5	tenant	UMNO	No
45	Mustapha	973	2,540	3	4	owner	*pagar*	No
46	Tajuddin	994	3,579	0	4	tenant	UMNO	No
47	Mat Khir	1,020	5,710	0	2	tenant	UMNO	No
48	Tok Halim	1,060	1,060	6	0	landlord	UMNO	No
49	Abdul Rahim	1,083	2,490	0	3	tenant	UMNO	No
50	Cik Latifah	1,091	4,910	5	5	owner	UMNO	No
51	Jamil	1,096	6,138	6	6	owner	UMNO	Yes
52	Tok Sah Bidan	1,162	3,486	2.50	5.50	owner	UMNO	No
53	Zahid	1,169	2,688	1.50	3	owner	PAS	No

54	Ghani Lebai Mat	1,219	7,316	5.75	10	owner	UMNO	Yes
55	Kamil	1,246	6,230	0	15	tenant	*pagar*	Yes
56	Tok Mahmud	1,261	2,522	4	3	owner	PAS	No
57	Abu Hassan	1,343	6,180	3	6	salary	UMNO	Yes
58	Mat Isa	1,536	3,532	0	5	tenant	PAS	No
59	Tok Mah	1,542	5,094	7.5	8	owner	UMNO	No
60	Tok Kasim	1,569	4,708	5.5	6	owner	PAS	No
61	Tok Long	1,582	4,746	3	6	owner	UMNO	Yes
62	Haji Ngah	1,650	3,300	15	0	landlord	PAS	No
63	Shanon	1,769	5,308	4.5	5	owner	PAS	No
64	Basir	1,778	9,948	10	7	owner	UMNO	Yes
65	Ghazali	1,830	4,209	0	8.5	tenant	UMNO	No
66	Shamsul	1,845	7,380	6	8	salary	UMNO	Yes
67	Idris	2,061	6,184	7	6	owner	UMNO	Yes
68	Nor	2,137	7,692	11	11	owner	PAS	No
69	Yaakub	2,137	4,274	3	3	owner	UMNO	No
70	Haji Jaafar	2,154	6,412	15	6	owner	UMNO	Yes
71	Zaharuddin	2,226	5,120	0	5	tenant	UMNO	Yes
72	Amin	2,271	7,494	2.5	10	tenant	UMNO	Yes
73	Lebai Pendek	2,425	9,700	8	13	owner	UMNO	Yes
74	Haji Kadir	4,325	12,940	30	15	owner	PAS	No

[a]Net household income figures necessarily convey a level of precision that is unwarranted. Paddy income, the major component of income for most households, may be calculated with some precision. Income from wage labor and sideline jobs is somewhat less accurate, although efforts were made to double-check such figures. Thus, net household income figures should be considered fair approximations, accurate to within M$200 to M$300 in nearly all cases. Complete and accurate data might, therefore, change the rank ordering marginally.

[b]In a few cases (5) the household owns small amounts of orchard or rubber land. This landholding is not listed, but any income from it is included in the income data.

[c]In three cases, political affiliation is listed as *pagar* (the Malay word for "fence") indicating that the household head is affiliated with no party or both parties, or, in one case, that each spouse is affiliated with a different party. Party affiliations are typically known by all villagers and their independent assessments tally almost perfectly.

annual income within the household; here the richest twenty-two families receive nearly four times M$1,867, the per capita income of poor households (M$475).

The disparity in incomes is reflected, as one would expect, in the disparity of secure control over the key factor of production: land. Between them, the twenty-two poorest families in Sedaka own only 22.5 relong of land—an average of barely 1 relong (1 relong = .71 acres). Keeping in mind that the standard for a poverty-line income from paddy farming alone is a minimum of 4 relong, the poorest households own scarcely one-quarter of the land required to provide for their essential needs. The wealthiest twenty-two households, on the other hand, own a total of more than 142 relong, giving them an average owned holding of nearly 6.5 relong. The disparity in farm size, which includes land rented in, at the two poles of the village hierarchy is actually slightly less skewed only because the land owned by many richer families makes it unnecessary for them to rent in additional paddy acreage. Nevertheless, the poorest twenty-two families are able to rent in only enough land to give them an average farm size of less than two relong (1.89) while the richest families have an average farm size of 7.25 relong. Put another way, relatively well-to-do households actually manage to rent in almost as much additional paddy land as poor families, although they need it far less.

In fact, the figures on land ownership, seen from a slightly different per-spective, reveal far more glaring inequities. If we disregard for a moment the income figures in table 4.1 and simply count the households that own no paddy land whatever, thirty families (41 percent) fall in this category.[6] Thus nearly half the village lacks legal control over the major productive asset in rice farming. If we take the half (thirty-seven families) of Sedaka's households who own the least land, we find that they own a mere 7 relong between them. As the total rice land owned by all villagers is 235.5 relong, we have a situation in which half the village owns less than 3 percent of locally owned paddy land. The ten biggest village landowners, by contrast, represent only 14 percent of the house-holds but own outright 133.75 relong, or 47 percent of the rice land owned by villagers.

It is possible to compare the land ownership pattern in 1979 with the situation in 1967 and thereby assess the impact of double-cropping and new technology. There is essentially no change over the past thirteen years, that is, no change in a distribution of land ownership that was, at the outset, extremely skewed. Once account is taken of the increase in the village population from fifty-six to seventy-four households, even the marginal improvement in the proportion of land owned by land-poor households proves to be misleading. Thus, by 1979 the land-poor half of the village was comprised of nine more families than in

6. This finding places Sedaka close to the region-wide norm for the percentage of pure tenants and pure wage laborers in Muda's paddy sector, which is 37 percent. See chap. 3.

1967, and among them they owned a negligible 3 percent of the rice land. There are today more families (thirty) owning no paddy land in Sedaka than there were in 1967 (twenty-seven), despite the fact that the proportion of landless households has declined somewhat.

The relation between land ownership and income in this one-crop economy is obvious. Only four of the richest twenty-two families own no land. In all four cases the anomaly is accounted for by various combinations of small family size and outside wages and above all by the renting in of paddy land averaging more than 8 relong per household. For that half of the village with the lowest incomes, conversely, land ownership is conspicuous by its absence. Roughly 60 percent of these poor villagers own no land at all and only three families own more than 2 relong.

The distribution of ownership within the village in paddy land is unlikely to shift markedly in the near future. Higher and steadier yields, when coupled with the traditional Malay reluctance to part with land, has served to slow dramatically the process of land concentration through indebtedness. In the three decades before 1970, Haji Kadir (#74), now the largest landowner in the village, managed to purchase 25 relong in eight separate transactions from smallholders with insurmountable debts. Although he remains as avid for land as in the past, he has not added anything to his holdings since the beginning of double-cropping. Not only are the small landowners whose land he might covet less likely to find themselves in such dire straits, but the market for rental land is now so buoyant that a hard-pressed smallholder can clear his debts more easily by renting his land out for several seasons at a time (*pajak*) and retain title.

By the same token, the marked increase in paddy-land prices has also elim-

TABLE 4.2 • Distribution of Ownership of Paddy Land in Sedaka, 1967–1979

	1967	1979
Total No. of Village Households	56	74
Land-poor		
Percentage of total villager-owned paddy land held by land-poor half of village	1%	3%
—total area (relong)	1.25	7.00
—average owned per household (relong)	.04	.19
—no. of households	28	37
Land-rich		
Percentage of total villager-owned paddy land held by top 14% of village landowners	54%	57%
—total area (relong)	114.50	133.75
—average owned per household (relong)	14.3	13.3
—no. of households	8	10
Total paddy land owned by villagers (relong)	210.25	235.5

inated the possibility of upward mobility for all but the richest. Such upward mobility through land purchase was certainly not common, even before double-cropping, but five villagers who now own from 3 to 7 relong had managed to buy at least a portion of that land. Since 1970 not a single smallholder in this category has added to his holdings. And if this category is effectively barred from purchasing land, it follows that those with less than 3 relong of their own, which is to say most of the village households, do not even contemplate the possibility.

Since double-cropping began, only nine villagers have either bought or sold land. The pattern of these transactions reveals not only the diminished pace of land concentration but the fact that the process, if slowed, still moves in the same direction. The buyers are without exception well-to-do, and the sellers are predominantly poor. Four villagers have, since 1970, bought a total of 19.25 relong, much of it located outside the village. Daud, the son of the village headman, Haji Jaafar (#70), has with his father's help purchased 8 relong, including 3 relong from a villager. Nor (#68) has bought 8.25 relong with the help of his father (an outsider who already owns over 50 relong), all of it land at some distance from the village. Amin (#73) has from his own savings purchased 2.5 relong of local land from a wealthy landowning Haji in a neighboring village. Taken collectively, these three households illustrate which class in the village is still able to add to its holdings; they represent three of the six richest households in Sedaka. The one exception, Fadzil (#42), who bought 2.5 relong from another villager, is the exception that proves the rule. While he is not among the wealthiest ten villagers, he does own 8 relong, and his currently modest income is simply a reflection of the fact that he had to lease out much of his land to raise the capital for this purchase.

Five villagers have sold land. The two largest sales, for 5 and 10 relong respectively, were made by villagers who were admitted to government settlement schemes and were liquidating their local holdings.[7] All but 2.5 relong of this land was sold to wealthy outsiders for premium prices. A third sale, of 3 relong, illustrates the circumstances under which poor families may still have to part with their land. Mat "Halus" 's wife (#6) was co-heir, along with at least eight other brothers and sisters, of 3 relong. The heirs could not agree on a mutual division of paddy fields and after a year decided to sell the land and divide the proceeds. The land passed to Daud, son of Haji Jaafar, that is, from one of the poorest households to one of the richest. The two remaining sales were made by two poor widowed sisters, Hasnah (#15) and Salmah (#20), each of whom sold half a relong to a much wealthier brother living in a nearby village. Both sales were made under rather exceptional circumstances; normally neither sister would

---

7. It is far more common for those who leave for settlement schemes to retain their local land and rent it out.

have considered selling.[8] In all five cases, the paddy land sold has passed into the hands of the well-to-do or rich. Two of the sellers were well-off themselves, and their selling could reasonably be seen as investment decisions. For the others, however, the sales were a further step toward landlessness.

The inequities described in a pattern of land ownership can occasionally be mitigated by the actual pattern of tenure. That is, if those with the largest holdings rent out much of their paddy land to poorer farmers, the actual distribution of farm size may be more equitable than ownership statistics would imply. In the case of Sedaka, the actual distribution of cultivated acreage, though it is more equitable than ownership, is nevertheless highly skewed. The ten largest farms, for example, which constitute no more than 14 percent of village households, cultivate a total of 115.5 relong, or 36 percent of the total paddy land cultivated by villagers. The average size of their farms is 11.6 relong (8.2 acres). The half of the village (thirty-seven families) with the smallest farm sizes, by contrast, cultivates only 58.75 relong, or a mere 18 percent of the paddy land worked by villagers.[9] Their average farm size is only 1.6 relong, or slightly more than 1 acre. Here we have a replication of the general situation in the Muda region: much of the village's farm population does not have access to the productive resources that would allow them to achieve a reliable subsistence. While their small plots may provide many of them with their daily rice, they could not make ends meet without the cash they earn as wage laborers in the paddy fields or elsewhere.

As with the figures on land ownership, it is possible to contrast the distribution of farm size in 1979 with the situation in 1967, using Horii's data for the earlier period (table 4.3). The relative stability of the percentage distributions masks far more dramatic changes. The small farmers in Sedaka have quite literally lost ground. Their share of the total land farmed has diminished from nearly one-quarter to less than one-fifth; the total acreage they farm has declined by

8. The exceptional circumstances were that still another brother who lives on a government rubber estate elsewhere in Kedah and who inherited adjacent land, which he came to farm, simply took over these two small plots and farmed them himself. All entreaties failed and the two sisters, afraid to go to the police or courts, given their brother's reputation for violence, finally decided to sell their plots to another brother, since they had been unable to cultivate them for five seasons. The brother who bought the land was, as of 1981, still unable to farm it and had begun a costly law suit to enforce his title. The case illustrates the tenuous influence of the state and its agents in enforcing property law where anyone is willing to use violence to frustrate its working. According to villagers, however, it is quite an exceptional case.

9. I have included ten families who farm no land at all. While the usual practice in computing farm-size distributions is to include only those families who cultivate at least some land, the results of this procedure underestimate the extent of land hunger. Seven of the ten families in question would jump at the chance to rent in land if it were available; only three are retired cultivators who choose not to farm.

TABLE 4.3 • Distribution of Paddy Farm Size in Sedaka, 1967–1979

	1967	1979
Total No. of Village Households	56	74
*Small Farms**		
Percentage of total villager-farmed paddy land cultivated by		
that half of village with smallest farm sizes	24%	18%
—total area (relong)	85.0	58.75
—average farm size per household (relong)	3.0	1.6
—no. of households	28	37
Large Farms		
Percentage of total villager-farmed paddy land cultivated by		
that 14% of village with largest farm size	40%	36%
—total area (relong)	142.5	175.5
—average farm size per household (relong)	17.8	11.6
—no. of households	8	10
Total paddy land cultivated by villagers (relong)	357.75	323.25

*Includes, for 1979, 10 families with no farmland. See n. 9.

nearly one-third. Coupled with the growth in the population of the village, this has cut the average farm size for this hard-pressed sector of the village from 3 relong before double-cropping to only 1.6 relong in 1979. This change alone has been sufficient to more than negate the additional income that double-cropping could have provided.[10] It would appear from the figures that large-scale farmers have lost considerable ground as well, especially in terms of average farm size. Much of this loss, however, can be traced to a single farmer, Kamil (#55), who in 1967 rented in an amazing 38 relong, most of which has since been reclaimed by the outside landowner and distributed to his heirs.

The reasons for this basic structural change, which threatens the livelihood of the poorest villagers, are important and complex enough to merit extended analysis later; a few reasons have already been mentioned in the preceding chapter. Here it is sufficient to note that demography has played a role. Many rather poor families who have moved into the village have either no land to farm or, more typically, only a relong or two. The process of inheritance has also meant that

10. Double-cropping does not, other things equal, simply double income. The necessary inputs for double-cropping, including fertilizer, tractor preparation, and increased labor costs, drain away a portion of the new gains. In Kedah, it was initially estimated that the net return for rice land was raised by 60 percent because of irrigation. Thus 1.6 relong would, if double-cropped, be equivalent to 2.66 relong of single-cropped land. The decline by half in the average holding of small farmers in Sedaka has thus left them worse off in terms of farm income despite the fact that they harvest two crops a year.

many married sons and daughters are now farming several small plots their parents once operated as a single farm. Finally, the lure of higher profits has prompted landlords, especially outside landlords, to dismiss tenants in order to farm themselves or to rent out a single large plot on long term leasehold (*pajak*). Some of this is evident from the decline in total paddy land cultivated by villagers between 1967 and 1979.

VILLAGE COMPOSITION

Sedaka was not, in 1979, quite the same village it was in 1967. Some households had broken up or moved out. Still more households had established themselves. The total number of households had grown by 25 percent (from fifty-six to seventy), and the total village population had grown at roughly the same pace.[11] Simply by looking at such changes in detail we can learn a good deal not only about mobility in Malay society but also about how that mobility is linked to the vital issues of land, income, and kinship.

A more detailed analysis of changing village composition may be found in appendix A, but for my immediate purposes the following points merit special note. Of those leaving the village, the poor tended to leave as individuals— young men and women typically leaving to work in urban areas (as construction workers, manual laborers, factory workers, and domestic servants). Families that left Sedaka as families, on the other hand, tended to be well-off—buying land in a frontier area or being accepted as a "settler" on a government estate (*rancangan*). Fifteen new families have moved to Sedaka, and it is significant that they are among the poorest half of the village. As villagers put it, "People have children, but the land does not have children." There is no niche in the village economy that could accommodate most of the population increase already born.

LAND TENURE

Many of the major changes in the economic life of Sedaka are reflected in the basic data on overall land tenure shown in table 4.4. Detailed comparisons may be found in tables 1 and 2 of appendix C. The discussion here is confined to only the most striking findings.

The most obvious trend over the past dozen years has been an increase in both the number and proportion of marginally sized farms and a decline in the share of large farms. The number of households farming 3 relong or less has doubled from twelve to twenty-four. Five of those farms are less than a single

11. Expansion from fifty-six to seventy-four households would yield an increase of 32 percent, but my household figures include four "frontier" households that Horii chose not to consider as falling in Sedaka.

TABLE 4.4 • Frequency Distribution of Farm Holding in Sedaka, 1967–1979

Area Held* (Relong)	1967		1979	
	Households	Percentage of Total Households	Households	Percentage of Total Households
0–3	12	23%	24	35%
3 +−7	17	33%	25	36%
7 +−10	6	12%	7	10%
10 +−20	13	25%	12	17%
20 +−40	4	8%	1	1%

*"Held" includes both land operated and land owned but rented out. Thus a farmer who operates 15 relong and rents out another 15 relong falls in the 20 +−40 category. There is a small degree of double counting of plots that figure once as land owned by a village landlord and again if the land is cultivated by a local tenant. Since the great bulk of tenanted land in Sedaka is rented from outsiders, the double counting is not substantial.

relong, a size category that Horii could justifiably ignore altogether in 1967. Over the same period, the average size of these minuscule farms has declined to less than 2 relong, or 1.4 acres. The decline in small farm size is not a consequence of a stable class of smallholders squeezed onto less and less land; on the contrary, the proportion of village-held land that such small operators farm has actually grown nearly twofold from 7 to 13 percent. As a class, they have lost ground in part because they are so much more numerous and in part because the total paddy land farmed by villagers has diminished by nearly 10 percent (from 357.75 relong to 325 relong).

The compression of farm size among a growing number of poor cultivators has not been accompanied by a parallel expansion of farm size by larger-scale cultivators in the village. In fact, nearly the reverse has occurred. Before double-cropping there were seventeen farmers who owned and/or operated more than 10 relong; collectively they monopolized more than 57 percent of village-held land (206.5 relong). Today, when the village is more populous, there are only thirteen such households, and they farm only 37 percent of village-held land (123 relong). The average farm cultivated by this strata shrank in the same period from over 12 relong to 9.5 relong. Thus we find a situation in which the size of both small farms and large farms has diminished, but the number of small farmers has doubled while that of large-scale farmers has declined.

Looking at the average farm size for the village as a whole, the trend is comparable. The average paddy farm in 1967 was nearly 7 relong; now it is less than 5. This represents a farm size decline of 32 percent which, using the standard assumptions about the profits from double-cropping, means that over 90 percent of the potential profits have been eliminated merely by the striking reduction in farm size.[12]

Sedaka has been caught in something of a demographic and structural pincers movement. Its population of farm households has grown by nearly one-third while the paddy land it cultivates has diminished by nearly 10 percent. Even if the village had not lost farm land, population growth alone would have reduced the average farm size from nearly 7 relong to 5.2. The balance of the decrease in average farm size to its present level of 4.7 can be attributed to loss of nearly 33 relong of the farm land that villagers cultivated in 1967. How has this reduction come about? It has *not* come about, we can be certain, because village landowners have withdrawn land from village tenants. The amount of land that village landowners rent out to their fellow villagers, usually close kin, has remained stable over the last twelve years. All of the land withdrawn from village cultivation in this period has instead been withdrawn by *outside* landlords, many of them quite rich, who have chosen to farm the land themselves, give it to their grown children to farm, or rent it out on long-term lease (*pajak*) to other large-scale operators.

If we examine the distribution of tenure categories in 1967 and again in 1979, the pattern is one of relative stability. A partial exception is the emergence, for the first time, of five households of pure noncultivating landlords in the village. But two of these landlords rent out tiny plots because they are too poor even to finance a crop and see it through to the harvest. The rest are mostly old men who can no longer cultivate and, in one case, a man whose debts have temporarily forced him to rent out his land to meet his creditors' demands. The only other notable change has been a modest decrease in the proportion of village farmers who are pure tenants (from 44 to 35 percent). Far more striking, however, has been the decline in farm size for these pure tenants. They remain, as in 1967, by far the most numerous tenure category, but they had cultivated an average of 6.1 relong in 1967; by 1979, their average farm size had declined to 4.1 relong. If the three tenants who now cultivate more than 7 relong are removed, the average holding of the remaining tenants falls to 3.3 relong. As in the Muda region as a whole, the loss of land is largely confined to the class of pure tenants. Collectively, while their absolute numbers have grown from twenty-three to twenty-six, they have lost more than one-fifth of the land they cultivated before double-cropping. The farm size of the smaller class of pure owner-operators, by contrast, has remained small but stable over the same period.

12. The 1979 average farm size of 4.7 relong under double-cropping would represent the equivalent of 7.5 relong under single-cropping (see n. 10 above). The average farmer in Sedaka in 1967, however, had 6.9 relong to farm, or 92 percent of that figure.

CHANGES IN TENANCY

The erosion in the position of tenants has been closely related to important changes in the form of tenancy since the beginning of double-cropping. One key change, as noted earlier, was the virtual disappearance of what were called paddy rents (*sewa padi*) and their replacement by what are known as cash rents (*sewa tunai*).[13] In 1967, Horii found that just under half (48 percent) of the land rental contracts in Sedaka were cash denominated rather than tied to paddy.[14] By 1979, however, paddy-denominated rents were conspicuous by their absence, and over 90 percent of all tenancy contracts now provided for stipulated cash rents.

TABLE 4.5 • Classification of Tenancy Agreements in Sedaka by Timing of Rental Payment, 1967, 1979

	Preplanting Payment of Rent		Post-harvest Payment of Rent	
	%	(N)*	%	(N)*
1967	7	(3)	93	(43)
1979	42	(28)	58	(38)

*"N" represents the number of parcels rented in during a given year and is thus greater than the number of farmers renting in land because quite a few rent in more than a single parcel.

Before 1970, the payment of cash rent before planting season was quite rare, as shown in table 4.5. By 1979, however, prepayment of rent had become quite common and was approaching one-half of all tenancy agreements. Most of this shift occurred in the first two years of double-cropping, when the initial profits from the new irrigation scheme combined to give *most* tenants the means to pay, and hence landlords the possibility of requiring, rents in advance. For poorer tenants, the burden was considerable. Exactly how many villagers were unable to raise the cash and lost land in this fashion is, as we shall see, a matter of lively dispute—a dispute that basically follows class lines.[15]

13. See Horii, "Land Tenure System," 57, 58, who writes, "In connection with fixed rent in kind (*sewa padi*) it is important to note that the actual payment is made in cash received from the sale of the stated amount of padi. Tenants will sell the amount of padi determined in the agreement to merchants right after the harvest and use the money thus obtained to pay the landowner."

14. Ibid., 57.

15. It is not, of course, simply a matter of how good one's memory is for the facts, but a question of interpretation. One villager, typically well-to-do, may claim that the change of tenants was due to a personal dispute about other matters or that the previous tenant no longer wanted to farm the land. Another villager, typically poorer, may claim that the point at issue was precisely paying the rent in advance. For more discussion of how "social facts" are the subject of varying class-based interpretations, see chapter 5.

The second change in tenancy has eliminated the possibility of renegotiating rent after a poor harvest. The local term for negotiable rents is "living rent" (*sewa hidup*) to denote their flexibility, as opposed to "dead rent" (*sewa mati*), which is rigidly enforced. Non-negotiable rents include all tenancies in which rent must be paid before planting as well as a number of post-harvest-rent tenancies that are rigidly enforced. This is particularly the case with post-harvest rents between landlords and tenants who have no kinship tie.

TABLE 4.6 • Classification of Tenancy Agreements in Sedaka by Negotiability of Rents, 1967, 1979

	Rents May be Adjusted		Rents Not Negotiable	
	%	(N)	%	(N)
1967	72	(33)	28	(13)
1979	47	(31)	53	(35)

NOTE: For 1967, the figures are estimates based on Horii, who indicates that, in addition to leasehold tenancies, rentals between non-kin are rarely adjustable ("Land Tenure System," 60). Elsewhere, however, Horii also says that rent reduction is only possible in the case of paddy-denominated rents. I am confident that this last statement is partly in error, for even in 1979 cash-denominated rents between close kin were often negotiable. Accordingly, I have added non-kin rentals and leasehold tenancies together to approximate non-negotiable tenancies in 1969. The figures for 1979, by contrast, are based on direct inquiries I made about the possibility of adjustments in each case.

As table 4.6 shows, tenancies with inflexible rents were, before double-cropping, the exception, whereas by 1979 they had become common enough to constitute a majority of all tenancy agreements. A tenant paying average-to-high rents must harvest, depending on his production costs, anywhere from seven to eleven gunny sacks of paddy in order simply to break even.[16] Average yields in Sedaka are roughly thirteen to fourteen gunny sacks and occasionally drop as low as seven to eight. Under the older system of tenancy, the actual rent would typically be reduced to compensate, at least in part, for harvest losses. Now when the rice crop, which even with irrigation is still subject to the caprice of nature, is damaged, the tenant must absorb the entire loss and still come up with full rent in advance of the coming season. While the tenant will in almost every case continue to rent the land, the cost in a bad year is likely to be severe in terms of belt tightening, short-term migration to seek work, and new debts. The landlord-tenant relationship has in the meantime been transformed in such cases into a rigid, if unwritten, impersonal contract. The social bond once implicit in the adjustment of rents to reflect the actual situation of the tenant

16. See appendix C, table C3 and figure C3a for typical returns to village cultivators under various assumptions.

has given way to tenancies along commercial lines, in which no quarter is expected or given.

Despite the land hunger in Sedaka, which is reflected in declining farm size, the average level of paddy-land rents has not increased dramatically. They averaged M$71 per relong in 1967 and by 1979 had climbed to M$112, a rate of increase that was slightly below the increase in rice production costs generally. [17] For many tenants, especially those closely related to their landlord, land rents are no more burdensome a share of the harvest proceeds now than they were in 1967. But the fact that rent increases have been relatively modest by no means implies that landlords have suffered proportionally. The reverse is the case, for, with the onset of double-cropping, all landlords instantly received a *permanent* windfall doubling of their annual rental income, thanks to the irrigation scheme.

In Sedaka, as in the rest of Kedah, all but a very few tenancy agreements are oral contracts struck up informally between the two parties. This pattern is in violation of the Padi Cultivators' Ordinance of 1955 (reenacted in 1967), which provides for the registration of tenancy contracts and sets maximum rents (as a proportion of the average harvest) for each soil class. Needless to say, most rents in Sedaka exceed that ceiling today as they did in 1967. No serious effort has been made to enforce the act against what would surely be the stiff opposition of the landowning class, which forms the core of the ruling party in the countryside. For tenants renting from close relatives, the act is unnecessary, as they typically have fairly secure tenure and pay flexible, concessionary rents. For those who pay market rents, requesting registration would be an invitation to immediate dismissal and in any case would be pointless inasmuch as registration does not prevent the landlord from resuming cultivation himself or, in practice, from insisting on illegally high rents under the table.

Average rent levels are, however, quite misleading when what we have in Sedaka and in Kedah generally is a highly fragmented land rental market with rents that ran the gamut in 1979 from M$200 per relong to virtually zero. [18]

17. For 1967 I have combined the cash value of paddy-denominated rents with cash-denominated rents to arrive at an average.

18. The question of rent-free tenancies, nearly always between parents and their children, is not straightforward. Many quick surveys of land tenure using formal interview schedules seem to indicate that quite a lot of land is "rented" in this fashion. It is common for parents to claim that they charge no rent to their children and for children to say that they are charged no rent. This situation is in keeping with village-wide values concerning the relations that ought to obtain between parents and children. In practice, however, closer inquiry reveals that very few tenancies of this sort are actually free of rent. The one exception is the common practice of parents with sufficient land to rent a plot to a newly married son or daughter free of charge for the first year of their' marriage, as a wedding present to the new couple. Aside from this exception, children nearly always pay *something* for the land each

The major "fault lines" in the market for tenancies lie along the dimension of kinship, as table 4.7 clearly shows. The disparity in rent levels reflects a bifurcated tenancy system in which a substantial share (42 percent) of those who rent in land are the beneficiaries of concessionary terms from their parents or grandparents. Within this protected market, seasonal paddy-land rents are substantially below those prevailing outside. Rents between non-kin are, as would be expected, by far the highest, with rentals between more distant kin falling roughly midway between the two extremes. Despite the commercialization brought about by the green revolution, land tenure is still dominated by kinship tenancies, which form fully two-thirds of all land rentals, as they do in Muda as a whole, and which provide some shelter from the full effects of a thoroughly capitalist market for land. Concessionary kinship tenancies between close kin, however, represent only 40 percent of *land* farmed by tenants in Sedaka, since the average size of the plot rented from close kin is smaller than the plot rented to non-kin.

TABLE 4.7 • Rental Rates for Tenancies Classified by Degree of Kinship between Landlord and Tenant in Sedaka, 1979

	Close Kinship	Less Close Kinship	No Kinship
No. of cases	28	16	22
Percentage of all tenancy cases	42%	24%	33%
Average rent per relong, per season	M$98.82	M$117.61	M$131.80

Kinship is not the only social tie that mitigates the terms of tenancy. When landlord and tenant both live in the village, the rent is typically below what the market will bear. Thus the rent paid by an unrelated tenant to his landlord *outside* the village averages M$129 per relong a season, while rent to an unrelated

---

season whether in kind, if they live in the same household, or in cash. This payment is viewed by both parties as a gift and not rent, as the amount is often left to the discretion of the son or daughter. Even when no payment at all is made, it is usually the case that labor services in the household or farm or occasional gifts are given that are in part linked to the provision of land. For evidence of this practice elsewhere in Kedah, see Mohd. Shadli Abdullah, "The Relationship of the Kinship System to Land Tenure: A Case Study of Kampung Gelung Rambai" (Master's thesis, Universiti Sains Malaysia, Penang), 108, 134–35, and Diana Wong, "A Padi Village in North Malaysia" (1980, mimeo.).

landlord inside the village averages only M$105.[19] The economic impact of tenancy within Sedaka is also apparent in the timing of rent payments. Three-quarters of tenants who have some relation (but not a parent-child relation) to their landlord are permitted to pay after the harvest, while less than half of those renting from relatives outside the village are given this concession.[20] All this is palpable evidence, if one needed it, that the village is a community in modest but significant ways. Unfortunately, the land available under such terms is in no way equal to the land hunger and demographic pressures it confronts.

Outside the somewhat sheltered customary market for tenancy between kin and neighbors, the winds of a competitive market blow briskly. The average rent for land rented to non-kinsmen is one indication of this competition. Another indication is what might be termed the *Haji* landlord market for rents. As noted earlier, many members of the well-to-do Haji landowning class are highly commercial operators who in many cases have branched out into other related enterprises such as tractor rental, rice milling, and trucking. There are in fact nine villagers who rent land from Hajis to whom they are not closely related. The average rent for these nine tenancies is M$140 (per relong, per season), which is well above even the mean rent for all tenants who rent from outside landlords with whom they have no kinship relation. Though none of these Hajis operates on anything like the scale of Haji Broom, they are a key segment of a small but powerful landowning class operating on strict commercial principles.

Nowhere is the competition for land more apparent than in the dramatic transformation of long-term leasehold or *pajak* tenancy over the past decade. It was possible in 1967 to view leasehold tenancy as part and parcel of customary

19. Rent Levels for Tenancy in Sedaka by Kinship and Residence

	Close Kinship	Less Close Kinship	No Kinship
Tenant rents from local landowner	M$93.63 (11)	M$101.75 (4)	M$105.00 (3)
Tenant rents from outside landowner	M$99.19 (16)	M$125.00 (14)	M$129.05 (18)

20. Even the exceptions to the pattern are instructive. Only four of twenty-seven close kin pay rents before the season begins, and in three of these cases the parents who rent out the land are so poor that their children pay the rent in advance in order to help them out. The spirit of making a concession is still at work, but in these cases it is a concession made by tenants to their parents. Of non-kin tenants, only six of twenty-one are permitted to pay rents after the harvest, and here special circumstances are at work as well. In five cases the land has been rented to the same family for over twenty years, thus providing for a degree of familiarity and trust that is rare in most tenancy agreements between non-kin. The remaining anomalous case is one in which the land is so subject to flooding and harvest losses that no one would take the risk of renting it if the rent were not negotiable after the harvest.

tenure between relatives. Horii found three cases of leasehold tenancy in Sedaka, all of which were between relatives, and the average rent charged was well below the standard for cash rents at the time.[21] He concluded justifiably that such multiseason tenancies with rent paid in advance were not instances of a "landlord's hard-hearted demand for advance payment" of a large sum but rather "an expression of mutual aid between kin . . . a kind of subsistence credit system between related landowners and tenants."[22]

By 1979, leasehold tenancy had become a thoroughly commercial transaction reflecting the new profits available to some landowners and tenants under double-cropping. The number of cases of *pajak* tenancy had grown from three to seven; the amount of land involved had doubled from 10 to 20 relong and, most striking, the mean *pajak* rental, adjusted to a seasonal basis, worked out to M$142 per relong, well above even the mean rents between nonrelatives. If anything, the high rent is an understatement of current *pajak* rents, since a number of the existing agreements were struck well before 1979, when lower rents prevailed, and since one would also expect that lump-sum, long-term rents such as these would be discounted at something approaching the current rate of interest and result in lower, not higher, seasonal rents. The current levels of *pajak* rents are best indicated by the most recently concluded agreement, which allows the tenant (Tok Omar, #37) to cultivate 3 relong for two seasons in return for a rent of M$1,110—the equivalent of a seasonal rent per relong of $185.

If, as most observers agree, highly commercial *pajak* tenancies are becoming increasingly common in Muda as a whole as well as in Sedaka, the impact on access to land is ominous.[23] What leasehold tenancy along these lines implies, as we have noted earlier, is that it will no longer be predominantly the poor who rent in land but the wealthy commercial operators with the ready capital to bid for such tenancies. An example of the obstacles that confront even middle peasants who attempt to compete in this market is the case of Rokiah (the wife of Mat Buyong, #34) who was offered a lease of 2.5 relong for four seasons from her brother at a lump-sum rent of M$1,600. To raise this amount, all the gold jewelry in the house was pawned and $500 in loans were taken from two shopkeepers at the usual high interest. Now her brother has announced that he wants to tack another year (M$800) onto the lease, before the initial term has

21. Two of these three cases involved Chinese landlords who have written contracts, governed under the Padi Cultivators Act, with their tenants. In these two cases the element of trust is supplemented by the landlord's possible fear that, if the timing of the rent were changed, the tenant might question the illegally high rents currently being charged for these plots.

22. Horii, "Land Tenure System," 62.

23. See chap. 3, n. 50. It is possible, though there is no evidence on the subject, that a portion of the higher rents (when calculated seasonally) may be accounted for by leasehold land being, on average, more productive.

expired. Unless she scrambles to find the additional M$800, she risks losing the land to another tenant. Even Lazim, one of the largest farm operators in the village, was hard-pressed to raise the M$3000 *pajak* rent for the 4 relong he leased (for seven seasons) from Fadzil. Despite both the long-run attractiveness of the contract (on a per season basis the rent per relong was only M$107) and the fact that Fadzil allowed him to delay by one season the payment of a M$1,000 balance, much of the initial sum had to be borrowed from a nearby Chinese trader. It is thus no coincidence that not a single leasehold tenant in the village comes from among the poorest third of its households, while it is precisely these households that most desperately need land to farm. It is also indicative of the commercial nature of such leaseholds that they are now always written and notarized even when the parties are closely related.[24]

Four villagers have already lost land they previously rented when the owner insisted on shifting to a long-term lease and they were unable to come up with the necessary cash. Nearly 18 relong have passed out of village cultivation in this fashion. More worrisome still are the reports villagers receive almost daily at the market or from relatives about larger blocks of land passing into the hands of well-heeled, commercial tenants, many of whom they say are Chinese who already own tractors and in some cases shares in a combine-harvester syndicate. Thus a villager in nearby Sungai Bujur has rented 8 relong for fifteen seasons, at a rent of M$15,000, to a Chinese shopkeeper and tractor owner. On a somewhat more modest scale, Tok Kasim (#60) in Sedaka has leased out 4 relong for ten seasons in order to raise the M$6,000 down payment for a taxi his son now drives. The tenant is the Chinese tractor owner for whom Tok Kasim works as a broker, lining up ploughing jobs and collecting fees.[25] He says he would have liked to rent to a Malay but no one he knew had the cash when he needed it. Coupled with these reports is daily evidence of the competition for farming land by outside commercial entrepreneurs. Hardly a week passes according to Lebai Pendek (#73), a well-to-do landowner in Sedaka, that he is not asked by the Chinese shopkeepers with whom he trades if he would be willing to lease land to them.

It is not only that the initial capital outlay for any but the smallest leasehold tenancies is more than the annual net income of all but a few households in the village. Beyond this, the current rent levels for such leaseholds work out to

24. The tenant, of course, will insist on a written lease to protect his rights to cultivate for the specified number of seasons. There are a few stories circulating about leasehold tenants in the past who failed to insist on a written contract (*surat perjanjian*) and discovered one fine morning that their landlord had sold the land before the agreement had lapsed.

25. There are no reliable data available, locally or for the Muda region as a whole, that would indicate how significant the Chinese business class is in the leasehold market. Until there are, it is impossible to know whether local impressions are accurate or, if accurate, representative.

between M$180 and M$220 per relong per season, a level that would leave little or no profit if the harvest were mediocre. It is a risk that most local cultivators, assuming they had the capital, would be fearful of running. Only those who already own tractors and/or combine-harvesters, which reduce their production costs, and who farm enough land to spread their risks and absorb short-term losses can compete in this market. In effect, what appears to be happening is that the owners of capital—machinery, rice mills, cash reserves—are now moving directly into the production process and cultivating themselves. The landowners who give over their land to *pajak* tenants may be rich or poor, but the new tenants leasing this land are increasingly drawn from the ranks of the wealthiest Malay and Chinese rural entrepreneurs. Ownership may remain basically unchanged while the concentration of operation, a kind of usufruct monopoly, grows apace.[26]

CHANGES IN RICE PRODUCTION AND WAGES

The five years following the beginning of double-cropping in Sedaka until roughly 1977 is now the object of justified nostalgia for the poorer households of the village: work was not only plentiful, with two crops to transplant, cut, thresh, and carry from the fields, but the peaks of labor demand at planting and harvesting time so improved the bargaining position of laborers as to substantially raise their real wages. From the vantage point of, say, 1976, there was ample cause for optimism—nearly everyone had gained. Large farmers and landowners, of course, were the major beneficiaries of the increased yields and higher paddy prices, even if higher production costs ate away a portion of that gain. Smallholders who had been barely making do found for the first time that double-cropping afforded them a modest surplus and some relief from growing debts. Even the poorest villagers, with little or no land to farm, who relied heavily on wage labor to feed their families, could find enough local work throughout the two rice seasons to make ends meet without leaving the village each year in search of wages.

From the outside, it looked as if double-cropping had put the local peasantry

26. This usufruct monopoly seems to be taking another form as well: the selling of "green" rice in the fields to syndicates that own combine-harvesters. Under this practice, called *jual pokok padi* by villagers, the crop in the fields, after transplanting but before harvest, is sold at a discount. It is resorted to not only by cultivators in financial difficulties but by large-scale farmers who want cash before the harvest. In Mengkuang, directly to the south, it is said to be widespread, and there were at least six cases in Sedaka as well during my period there. As with *pajak,* the seller may be poor or rich, but the buyer is nearly without exception rich. In this connection, it should be added that there is no evidence that small farmers and small tenants with less capital have inferior yields to those of larger farmers, although of course they market a smaller proportion of their production.

on a sounder economic footing and provided a welcome breathing space from the pressures of demography, indebtedness, and labor migration. From the inside, the villagers of Sedaka responded with the classic signs of peasant optimism. They rebuilt their houses with sturdier materials; they celebrated marriages and other rites of passage more lavishly; they bought new bicycles or even small motorcycles; they treated themselves to small luxuries of food, clothing, furniture, and even jewelry; they traveled to visit relatives whom they had scarcely seen before. For the first time in their lives, the poorer households in the village found that the food, amenities, and ritual typical of the solid, middle peasantry before irrigation were within their grasp. Those who were already fairly well-to-do were in turn aspiring to styles of consumption, ritual, and investment that only the wealthiest might have considered possible a decade before. Small wonder that growing disparities in income were largely ignored in the general euphoria.

By 1978, and certainly by 1979, much of that euphoria had dissipated along with many of the material conditions that had underwritten it. But if the euphoria had been rather general, disillusionment was more selective, affecting especially the poor. Farm-gate prices had not changed since 1974, while production costs had mounted to erode incomes—an inconvenience for large farmers but a serious blow to small tenants and owners. A drought forced the complete cancellation of the irrigated crop in 1978, thus cutting farm incomes in half and depriving the poor of the wage incomes on which they had come to depend. At the same time, the very economic forces that had been responsible for the brief spurt of relative prosperity had begun to foster changes in tenure patterns and production techniques which served to undermine that prosperity, especially for those in the community who had benefited least. Large landlords, as we have seen, were encouraged by greater profits either to resume cultivation themselves or to rent out large blocks of land to well-heeled leasehold tenants who paid premium rents in advance. In either case, the pool of land available for rental by smallholders and modest tenants was reduced.

At about the same time, combine-harvesters began to make their appearance on the landscape. They were made possible in large part by the same economic forces that had earlier improved the incomes of village wage workers. Only in the context of relatively higher harvest labor costs and the possibility of harvesting virtually year round under double-cropping did the investment in large combine-harvesters become profitable.[27] The direct and indirect impact of machine harvesting has been enormous. The biggest losers have been almost ex-

27. These were not, of course, the only factors. Both the large increase in paddy prices in 1973–74 and the restriction of Thai harvest labor, coupled with the decline in migrant labor for Kelantan, were instrumental as well. The federal government, by lowering or eliminating import duties on harvesting machines, also lowered their capital cost to the syndicates that purchased them.

clusively the poorer households, who have seen their economic security and incomes driven back almost to the levels that prevailed before 1970. Reeling from the lost income when the off-season crop of 1978 was cancelled outright, they soon realized that the entry of combine-harvesters would prevent them from recouping their losses by hand-harvesting in 1979. They tightened their belts again. Feasts (*kenduri*) and marriages were foregone, postponed, or celebrated on a much smaller scale; the small luxuries they had permitted themselves all but disappeared; and by 1979 many of the poor were once again leaving for temporary work in the city in the familiar effort to make ends meet.

By examining the economic repercussions of these changes in Sedaka alone, it becomes possible to observe the larger changes described in the last chapter writ small. The local effects of this shift in production techniques also will reveal a variety of other, subsidiary consequences that are simply lost in any aggregate analysis of the Muda region as a whole. Here again we are concerned with the local "facts" and leave the all-important questions of their social meaning and the reaction to them for subsequent chapters.

The mechanization of rice cultivation naturally posed the most direct threat to the sector of the village that depended most heavily on agricultural wage labor as a source of income. The small class of pure wage laborers were most grievously affected. There are, however, only four such households in Sedaka; in Muda as a whole, the estimates of the proportion of pure wage labor households range anywhere from 7 to 10 percent. It is perhaps for this reason that so little attention has been devoted to the loss of wages brought about by mechanization. If the impact were confined to this class, such inattention might possibly be justified, given the buoyant labor market outside the rice economy. But the impact is far wider, embracing to some extent all those families historically dependent on farm labor for a portion of their income. The extent of this dependence in Sedaka during the main season of 1977–78 is striking, as can be seen in table 4.8.

TABLE 4.8 • Proportion of Total Net Income Derived from Paid Paddy-Field Labor* by Households in Sedaka: Main Season, 1977–1978

	100%	Over 50%	25%–49%	0–24%	0
No. of households	4	15	9	24	22
Percentage of total village households	5%	20%	12%	32%	30%

*Such labor includes, above all, transplanting, cutting, threshing, and in-field transportation. It also includes less common wage work: harrowing with water buffalo, pulling, bundling, and transporting of seedlings, repairing bunds, replanting (*sulam*) damaged areas after transplanting, weeding, and spreading fertilizer. It does not include transportation of bagged paddy once it is out of the field.

Fully one-quarter of the families in Sedaka should be considered predominantly wage laborers in the sense that over half their income derives from this source. All but two of these families are from among the poorest half of the village, and they typically have either so little land or such large families (or both) that only paddy wage labor allows them to keep their heads above water. Another nine households (12 percent) rely on such wages for more than one-quarter of their income, while a further twenty-four households receive at least some cash income from field labor. Thus more than two-thirds of Sedaka's families have some stake in agricultural labor; for more than one-third, that stake is substantial. Even these figures may understate the vital importance of field work for wages.[28] In fact, of the twenty-two households that have no income from wage labor, half are composed of retired or disabled members unfit for such work.

The first step in the mechanization of rice cultivation was the use of tractors for field preparation. Tractor hire was widespread well before double-cropping began but usually in conjunction with the use of water buffalo for breaking up clods of the clayey soil (*lanyak*), leveling (*menggiling*), and harrowing (*sisir, menyisir*). The importance of water buffalo in rice cultivation until as late as 1967 is reflected by Horii's finding that there were nearly as many water buffalo as households in Sedaka and that most of the villagers who did not own an animal leased one. Double-cropping, by putting a premium on speed in ploughing, favored the use of tractors for nearly all stages of field preparation. The added expense and the loss of income to owners and drivers of buffalo were considerable, but the peasants of Sedaka saw no reason to dwell on what, at the time, seemed like petty losses in the context of far more substantial gains.

The losses sustained by two of the poorer households in the village are fairly typical. Hamzah (#8), Razak's younger brother, used to earn as much as M$200 a year before double-cropping by cutting stalks and secondary growth (*merumput*)

---

28. First, when the rice yield is poor, many more villagers seek paddy wage work both inside and outside the village. The figures in table 4.8, however, reflect the importance of wage labor following a good season. Furthermore, combine-harvesters had already put in a modest appearance by 1977–78, thereby slightly cutting the wage-labor receipts of some households. Exchange labor (*derau*), which was a fairly common practice at this time for smallholders for both transplanting and cutting paddy, is also not calculated here since no cash changes hands. If it were counted, on the premise that it is labor that is in a sense "paid" in the amount by which it reduces production costs, the reliance on labor income would appear to be greater. I have also chosen not to include wage labor receipts by youngsters, which are typically kept as pocket-money and not given over to the household. Since such earnings, especially in poorer households, reduce expenses for the upkeep of children to some extent, they might arguably have been included in the figures, thus further increasing the importance of farm wages. Finally, the figures in the table were collected after the combine had already made inroads into wage work. Figures from 1973–74 would thus show more dependence on wage work.

in others' fields and by occasionally harrowing for wages with a leased water buffalo. By 1973, this work had all but evaporated. Samad (#17), who still owns a water buffalo, figured that he earned as much as M$500 a year by ploughing and harrowing over 20 relong for other farmers at a piece-rate of M$25 per relong. Now he is lucky to earn M$100 a year for such work and thinks he may soon sell his buffalo. It is nearly impossible to estimate the average losses suffered by the poorer households of Sedaka inasmuch as they were gradual and unevenly distributed. But an agroeconomic survey, which found that the labor input per unit of land per crop immediately following double-cropping in Muda fell by 17 percent, would probably not be far off the mark for income losses as well.[29] The tractors that now do almost all the field preparation in Sedaka are nearly all large, four-wheeled machines owned by wealthy entrepreneurs, both Malay and Chinese, living outside the village. Only four villagers own tractors. Three are owned by the three richest villagers (Haji Kadir, Lebai Pendek, and Amin), although the machines are two-wheeled pedestrian tractors used largely on the owners' paddy land. The ownership of water buffalo was, by contrast, much more evenly distributed throughout the village.[30]

If the mechanization of field preparation in Sedaka was generally applauded amidst the new wage-labor opportunities provided by double-cropping, the mechanization of paddy harvesting was far more divisive, not to say explosive. It is no exaggeration to say that the commercial combine-harvesters swept through the rice plain around the village. They first made their appearance during the irrigated season harvest in mid-1976, but only one or two outside

29. Clive Bell, Peter Hazell, and Roger Slade, *The Evaluation of Projects in Regional Perspective: A Case Study of the Muda Irrigation Project* (Baltimore: Johns Hopkins Univ. Press, forthcoming), chap. 2, p. 40. Labor input for land preparation alone fell by one-half between 1970 and 1973.

30. Today water buffalo have become almost more of a financial liability than a capital asset. Their number has fallen from forty-two to twenty-two over the past dozen years, reflecting not only their declining value but also the increased difficulty of feeding and breeding them. The costs for ploughing and harrowing that once circulated largely within the village sphere are now paid to the well-to-do, outside owners of this new factor of production. In the *mukim* of Sungai Daun, embracing Sedaka and many other villages, the number of water buffalo has fallen from 1,670 head in 1970 to 1,014 head in 1977, or nearly 40 percent. The current owners still use them for harrowing their own land and occasionally that of others, as well as for pulling seedlings or harvested paddy through flooded fields on a sled (*andur*). The labor time required to keep a water buffalo has also risen appreciably. Before double-cropping, the buffalo could be released to graze on the stubble and along the bunds and canals. Now, with two seasons, either fodder must be cut and brought to them or they must be carefully tethered lest they damage someone's crop. At least one animal in the past seven years was slashed and left to die by an (unknown) villager who presumably found it marauding in his field. Breeding is also more difficult now that open grazing is restricted.

landowners used them. By the irrigated season of 1979, five seasons later, they were harvesting fully 60 percent of Sedaka's paddy land. A year later they harvested more than 80 percent.

The first villagers to hire combine-harvesters were almost exclusively large operators of 6 relong or more. Given their farm size, they seldom had sufficient family labor to harvest their crop themselves or to exchange labor (*berderau*) with other neighbors. The costs of hired labor for harvesting their paddy had grown appreciably in real terms due to the prohibition of Thai laborers and the curtailing of migrants from Kelantan.[31] The new double-cropping regimen had also placed a premium on speed. The new high-yielding varieties shattered more easily when ripe; they were, in the irrigated season particularly, harvested under wet conditions that promoted spoilage; and, when the season had begun late, it was important to harvest quickly in order to ready the land for the next planting.

Small farmers and tenants were understandably more reluctant to hire the combine-harvesters. It had been both more feasible and more important for them to do part or all of the harvesting themselves: more feasible because they were typically "richer" in labor than in land and more important because the potential savings in the cash costs of cultivation were of greater significance for them.[32] They were also, of course, well aware that combine-harvesters could and did threaten the main sources of wage-labor earnings for the low-income families in the village. And yet, the matter was not quite so straightforward even for the small farmer. The harvest period was by far the most lucrative for the men and women of poor households; women working in small gangs could earn as much as M$7 a day cutting paddy, and strong men could, by threshing eight or nine gunny sacks, earn M$16–18 a day—*provided* they were available for work. Here was the rub. Each day that they harvested their own land or exchanged labor with their neighbors, they were foregoing the opportunity of earning high wages at the peak of harvest demand. Individually, it might make short-run sense to use the combine for their own small parcel, thus freeing themselves for many more days of wage labor on the land of others. Collectively, of course, it added up to a beggar-thy-neighbor policy in the long run as combine-harvesters replaced hand-harvesting on more and more of Sedaka's paddy land. For some,

31. The costs of cutting and threshing a relong of paddy had more than doubled from roughly M$28 in 1971 to M$60 in 1976. By contrast, the consumer price index had risen by only 44 percent. See S. Jegatheesan, "Progress and Problems of Rice Mechanization in Peninsular Malaysia," Working Paper No. 17 (Persidangan Padi Kebangsaan Malaysia [Malaysian National Conference on Paddy], Kuala Lumpur, February 26–28, 1980), 11.

32. Jagatheesan, ("Progress and Problems," 2), reports that for Muda as a whole, in 1975, farms below 2 relong in size relied on hired labor for only 39 percent of the total labor required for cultivation, while for farms above 15 relong hired labor formed nearly 90 percent of total labor required.

but not all, of the village's small farmers, the short-term logic prevailed, with the inevitable consequences.

The overall results can be seen by comparing the net losses in net household income between the irrigated season of 1977, when only 15 percent of the paddy land was machine harvested, and the irrigated season of 1979, when 60 percent of the crop was gathered by combine. Inasmuch as the figures in table 4.9 rely on recollections of earlier wage earnings, they must be regarded as rough approximations.[33]

TABLE 4.9 • Reported Losses of Net Household Income in Sedaka due to the Mechanization of Rice Harvesting: Irrigated Season, 1977, Compared with Irrigated Season, 1979

| | Proportion of Total Net Income Derived from Paid Paddy-Field Labor, 1977 | | | | |
	100%	Over 50%	25–49%	0–23%	0
No. of households	4	15	9	24	22
Percentage of net household income lost, 1979	31%	16%	8%	4%	0%
Approximate cash lost per household	M$550	M$269	M$258	M$156	M$0

The losses, as expected, fall heaviest on the poorest households in Sedaka. For the households of pure wage laborers, combine-harvesters represent an economic disaster. For an additional twenty-two families who rely on agricultural labor for more than one-fourth of their income, the consequences are severe and unambiguous given their generally low incomes. But for over half the village (forty-six families) the use of combine-harvesters is either a boon or, at worst, a mixed blessing. This fact helps explain both the general acceptance of combine-harvesting and the class basis of support and opposition to it, which we shall examine in the next chapter.

The pattern and variety of losses in the village is best reflected in a few concrete examples. Karim (#10) rents only 2 relong and counted on threshing wages for much of his cash income. Before the harvesters were widely used, he might earn as much as M$300 or M$400 a season by threshing paddy nonstop in Sedaka and nearby. Now he counts himself lucky if he can find enough threshing work to bring in M$100. As he details his losses, he adds, "If it

33. For example, a farmer might say that he earned anywhere from M$200 to M$250 threshing rice in 1977 and this season (1979) earned only M$100. His answer is really an order of magnitude and may reflect the earnings he typically expected before 1978. Despite the rough quality of these estimates, they are likely to be fairly accurate, given the striking ability of peasants to recall prices and wages over long periods of time.

weren't for the machines, I'd be working and sweating just like you."[34] The losses for the family are still larger, since Karim's wife has lost work cutting paddy as well. For some women who are heads of households, the combine-harvesters have spelled great hardship. Rosni (#26) is a forty-five-year-old widow with five children at home, famous for her hard work, and the head of a gang of women from poorer households who transplant and cut paddy. Although she rents in 4 relong, the rent is high, and she depends heavily on wage work to keep her large family going. Working with her eldest daughter cutting paddy, the two earned M$350 during the main season of 1978, but these earnings had dropped to a mere M$70 by the irrigated season of 1979. Even their transplanting earnings were down, because two of their past employers had chosen to broadcast seed directly. She is afraid that the belt tightening now required will mean that her thirteen-year-old son will have to drop out of secondary school. For households with no farming land, the consequences of combine-harvesting have been nearly catastrophic. Mat "halus" (#6), a poor landless laborer, could have expected to earn M$300 a season threshing paddy and his wife nearly the same amount cutting. Now their combined wages are only $200 a season. They have made up a portion of that loss by both planting rice[35] nearly ten miles north of Sedaka but fear that he or the whole family will have to move out of Kedah to find work. Pak Yah (#11), another landless laborer with an even larger family (nine children at home), is in the same boat. He and his wife, together with the four of their children who are of working age, could collectively earn as much as M$1400 in harvest labor. Their combined income from cutting and threshing paddy has now dropped to roughly M$800, and one of their sons has decided to strike out on his own and find work in the city.

The wage losses recounted here became even more serious by the 1980 main season, when another 20 percent of the village land was harvested by combines. Some work hand-cutting and threshing paddy is still available, but villagers must range farther afield to find it, and in any case it is only a small fraction of the work once available. Contrary to what one might expect, the piece-rates for hand harvesting—roughly M$40 a relong for cutting and M$2.50 per gunny

34. Here he is being somewhat sarcastic at my expense, as I had just finished helping to crush unripe padi with a large pestle (*antan*) to make a preharvest delicacy (*emping*), widely eaten in the village, and it was well-known how copiously I sweated when working. His words were: *Kalau mesin tak musuk, saya pun kerja, berpeloh macham Jim.* There is also in his remark an indication of the humiliation of idleness that we shall encounter later among other harvest laborers who have been displaced by the machine.

35. Normally, transplanting is exclusively women's work. But, as elsewhere, the gender-based division of work tends to break down for the very poorest families, with men transplanting and/or cutting paddy and women on occasion even threshing. In the past, poor migrant couples from Kelantan would routinely cut and thresh paddy without regard to any sexual division of labor.

sack for threshing—have risen at about the same rate as the wages for trans-planting in spite of competition from machines. But these piece-rates are de-ceiving, for they mask a diminishing return per unit of labor. Most of the paddy that is still hand harvested is planted in deep fields that are inaccessible to the machine or in which untimely winds or rain have caused widespread lodging of the plants. As a result, such hand labor is often done in water that is knee deep and where stalks cannot be easily cut or threshed. It may thus take nearly twice the usual time for women to cut a relong of paddy, and men who under good conditions might thresh four gunny sacks in a morning might be lucky if they manage two. As wages are still paid by the task rather than the hour, the effective wage rate has been substantially cut. As Mustafa (#45) complains, "These days they give poor people only the ditches to harvest."[36]

The impact of the combine-harvesters is by no means confined to the hand work they directly replace. For mechanization of the harvest has also set in motion a series of second-order consequences—new possibilities that, once grasped, have been nearly as devastating for the poor of the village. The first of these consequences is the virtual elimination of gleaning as a subsistence strategy of the poor. In 1978, before combine-harvesters were widely used, women and children from at least fourteen families regularly descended into the paddy fields, armed with mats (tikar mengkuang) and flails to collect the paddy grains that still clung to the threshed stalks. Such gleaning was more common in the main season when the ground was dry at harvest time than during the off-season when rain and mud made gleaning more difficult. A poor family might typically glean three or four gunny sacks of paddy in this fashion.[37] This represented a vital addition to the food supply of landless or near-landless households; it involved no cash outlay, and the work of gleaning occurred at a time when there were few other wage opportunities for women. For at least one family, gleaning was the main source of food supply. Mat "halus," his wife, and his daughter managed, by diligent gleaning for the better part of a month, to collect as much as fifteen sacks of paddy—enough to feed the family for much of the year. As one might expect, the gleaners in Sedaka came typically from the poorest fam-ilies; eleven of the fourteen families that gleaned were from among the half of the village households with the lowest incomes.

Now that combine-harvesting has all but eliminated gleaning, it is rare to see gleaners after the harvest except in those few plots that have been threshed by hand. Only Mat "halus" and his wife, spurred on by the food needs of their large family, have managed to recoup a portion of their losses. Observing that

36. La ni, alur sahaja bagi kat orang susah.

37. The imputed rate of pay for such work is quite high. Four mornings of gleaning will yield, on average, one gunny sack of paddy, which, valued at M$35, represents nearly M$9 per morning, or three times the then current standard rate of pay for a morning's labor.

combine-harvesters occasionally spill grain when they make sharp turns, stall, or jam, he and his wife have taken to following the machines and winnowing (*kirai*) the small deposits they leave.[38] This ingenious substitute for traditional gleaning can yield them as much as two gunny sacks a day when he is lucky, but the return is uncertain and irregular. Aside from this rather unique adaptation, gleaning has all but evaporated.

Once the greater part of harvesting work had been mechanized, the way was prepared for other, more subtle, changes in the pattern of the remaining wage work. Hired labor, generally speaking, had typically taken two forms. The first, which prevailed for the transplanting and cutting of paddy (locally defined as women's work), was a group, piece-work system in which the head (*ketua kumpulan share*) negotiated a price per relong with the farmer doing the hiring. The proceeds were then divided by the members of the labor gang. Threshing typically was by piece-work as well but was paid individually, or to a group of two working at the same tub, on the basis of the amount threshed. Other work done outside the busy planting and harvesting seasons—for example, repairing of bunds, weeding, replanting, digging pits to catch water during the dry season— was paid according to what is known as the *kupang* system: a fixed cash wage for a morning or day of work. Occurring at slack times in the paddy cycle, these wages were, and are, well below the effective wage rate for harvesting and transplanting.

Over the past two years, however, the *kupang* system has increasingly been used for the reaping of paddy that must still be done by hand. This shift is made possible precisely because combine-harvesting has displaced enough labor to strengthen substantially the bargaining position of the farmer doing the hiring. If he must have his paddy cut by hand, the farmer can now hire women by the morning. The effect is twofold. First, it is cheaper; the standard gang labor price for cutting a relong of paddy was in 1979 at least M$35, while under the *kupang* system the cost is M$30 or less. Second, it allows the hiring farmer to select laborers individually and to avoid having to negotiate with a group that is ready-made and led by women with something of an incipient trade-union ethos. By the main season harvest of 1980, nearly half the hand-reaped paddy in Sedaka was cut in this fashion. In some nearby villages, the *kupang* system has become standard practice for reaping. It is less commonly found in transplanting labor, but here too it appears to be making small inroads, and the savings to the farmers (losses to laborers) seem comparable.[39] For threshing,

38. He calls such deposits *tahi mesin,* or "machine droppings."

39. Haji Kadir, for example, planted 3 relong in this way during the main season in 1978–79. He thereby saved M$7 a relong over the prevailing gang-labor rate. There appear to be three reasons why the *kupang* system is less typically used for transplanting than for reaping. First, quality control is far more important in planting. Second, since planting is still done largely by hand and the labor surplus is not

kupang labor is even rarer but not unheard of. How widespread *kupang* payment will become for planting and threshing is difficult to foresee but already, in the case of reaping, it has served to lower wages somewhat and to weaken one of the few forms of informal labor organization in the village.

The stronger bargaining position now enjoyed by the farmer who employs labor is reflected in other aspects of the informal "labor contract" in the village. Until 1978, it had always been customary for the farmer hiring a transplanting group to feed them a full midday meal. By the off season of 1979, such meals were conspicuous by their absence. In some cases the employing farmers unilaterally scaled down what had been an ample fish curry or glutinous rice with prawns to dry bread and tea. In response, women began bringing their own food along. Other farmers offered the women two transplanting piece-rates: M$35 a relong without food or M$32 a relong with food. Inasmuch as M$35 had been the standard wage the season before and had included the meal, the new dispensation effectively lowered the cost of planting. Most groups preferred to forego the food, which had been in any case reduced to the barest essentials, and it now can be safely assumed that food for transplanters is past history.

In the days of single-cropping and during the halcyon period at the beginning of double-cropping it was common for farmers, especially large landowners, also to advance wages to transplanters and harvesters well before the work began. The advance might be in the form of rice or cash. This practice had advantages for both parties, for the farmer assured himself field labor during the peak season, while the worker, especially under single-cropping, received a welcome infusion of cash or rice at that point during the agricultural cycle when his family was most strapped financially and when his rice supply was nearly exhausted. The laborers, of course, paid a price for taking their pay early inasmuch as the wage was discounted by as much as 30 percent from the prevailing wage at harvest time. By 1979, when combine-harvesting had made significant inroads into the demand for harvest labor, almost all farmers had abandoned the practice, reasoning that, even if hand harvesting was necessary, laborers could easily be recruited on the spot.

---

so marked at this period, the farmer is less often in a position to dictate terms. The exceptions are farmers who plant much earlier or later than the rest and thus have abundant supplies of labor from which to select. Finally, and perhaps most decisive, the effective wage rate (return per hour) for transplanting is already lower than for reaping, and a shift to the *kupang* system would yield little or no savings. Transplanting now includes the pulling and bundling of seedlings as well and costs roughly M$35 per relong. Moving to the *kupang* system would still entail piece-rates for pulling and bundling (at 6 cents a bundle, with roughly 240 bundles per relong, or $14.40), and morning wages for ten women (at M$3 a head, or M$30), for a total of M$44.40. Only when family labor can be deployed to pull and bundle seedlings, as in Haji Kadir's case, would the *kupang* system appear to be advantageous.

Another custom, one closely related to the payment of advance wages, has also been discontinued or sharply curtailed since the appearance of combine-harvesters. This was the common practice of farmers making a small gift of paddy over and above wages to laborers who had helped with the harvest. The gift was made as a kind of "private Islamic tithe" (*zakat peribadi*) and, although the practice was never universal, it was widespread enough to become part of the anticipated wage for many harvest workers. For the farmer, such a gift served much the same purpose as an advance against wages; it was a kind of premium that increased the likelihood that he could recruit the necessary work force when his next crop was ready. The practice has not entirely disappeared, but it has become the exception to the rule. Of course, in the case of machine harvesting, the question of tithe gifts or prior wages is irrelevant, for there is no labor force save the machine operators, who are well-paid outsiders. But even in the cases of hand harvesting, the bagging of paddy, or the hauling of sacks, it is now extremely rare for the farmer to make any additional gift to workers.

In an indirect and somewhat perverse way, combine-harvesting has also contributed to the growth of broadcasting (*tabor kering*), a technique that now has made substantial inroads into the last major wage-labor opportunity in paddy growing: transplanting. Fields sown in this fashion have, unlike transplanted seedlings, no rows whatever, and the plants are far more likely to be of unequal height. For these reasons, they are more difficult to cut and thresh by hand— a difficulty that would be reflected normally in the costs of hand harvesting.[40] Neither the absence of rows or unevenness in growth, however, is an obstacle to the combine-harvesters, which charge a standard fee per relong regardless of how it has been sown. A farmer can now broadcast his seed, secure in the knowledge that he will not thereby simply raise the cost of gathering the crop.

The advantages of dry sowing are manifest. First and foremost, the cultivator saves the cash costs of transplanting as well as the time and labor devoted to raising, tending, uprooting and transplanting the seedlings to the main field. Cash savings at this point in the paddy cycle are particularly important, since transplanting costs must come from past savings while harvesting costs may be paid from the proceeds of the crop. Dry sowing also has special advantages in the Sedaka area, which is among the last areas to receive irrigation water. By broadcasting during the irrigated season, the farmer has a better chance of

40. This is especially the case when the crop must be gathered at the peak harvesting season. A few farmers who broadcast quite early and whose crop is ready before others may take advantage of harvesting before the peak labor season and employ otherwise idle women on the *kupang* system, thereby paying less for reaping than the contract system would have cost them. Normally, farmers avoid planting too early (or too late) as the earliest (or latest) ripening fields fall prey to pests such as rats and birds. In addition, early harvesters, unless their land lies along a road, cannot hire combine-harvesters, since the machines cannot enter the field without destroying the unripe crops of one or more surrounding cultivators.

harvesting in good time to have his fields cleared and prepared for the rain-fed main season. If erratic rains or poor drainage should ruin part or all of the broadcast crop, the farmer still has the alternative of reploughing and rebroadcasting or of buying surplus seedlings from neighbors and going back to transplanting.[41]

Since the irrigated season of 1979, the progress of broadcasting in Sedaka has been striking to all and disquieting to many. In the previous season, at least three large landowners in the neighboring village of Sungai Bujur, all of them Hajis incidentally, tried broadcasting in an effort to get their crop in early.[42] Two achieved better-than-average yields and their experience encouraged Abdul Rahman (#41), an owner of 16.5 relong, to try it himself on a portion of his land. His yield was not satisfying (eight gunny sacks per relong), but this was attributed more to his failure to tend the crop closely than to the technique itself. By the main season of 1979–80 seventeen households in Sedaka were broadcast sowing roughly 50 relong, or 15 percent of the acreage cultivated by villagers.

Four seasons later (main season 1981–82), nearly 40 percent of Sedaka's land was broadcast. A clear majority of those who broadcast are relatively well-to-do;[43] these are normally the villagers who first innovate and who are best able

41. Broadcasting has its drawbacks as well, and these together with its possible benefits are the subject of wide debate within the village. Debate centers on the yields that broadcasters may expect. Some say that broadcast yields are as high or higher than for transplanting, while others claim yields are lower. I have observed yields as low as six and eight gunny sacks per relong and as high as eighteen and twenty. One should remember, of course, that the savings in production costs that broadcasting makes possible mean that yields only slightly below those of transplanted fields will entail no net loss to the farmer. What is certain, however, is that the crop from dry-sown paddy is far more variable than for transplanted rice and thus involves greater risk. A few poor farmers have tried dry sowing, lost much of their crop, and are wary of attempting it again. Quite apart from the advantages and disadvantages of broadcasting, the option is not open to all villagers. Dry sowing requires fairly flat field conditions and good water control. Unless the farmer's land has direct access to an adjacent canal, it requires permission from and coordination with the farmers through whose fields the water must pass during the irrigated season. This permission may not be forthcoming. These technical and social structures place some limits on the possible growth of broadcasting.

42. The technique was not new; it was known to all but used only rarely before. The fact that the irrigated season of 1978 had been cancelled due to drought, that the next main season—owing to the dryness of the soil—was late and threatened to lap over into the subsequent irrigated season, and that combine-harvesting was now available undoubtedly encouraged the experiment.

43. In the main season of 1979–80, for example, eight of seventeen broadcasters were among Sedaka's wealthiest twenty-five families (per capita income), while only three were from among the poorest twenty-five.

to assume the risks of a variable yield. Even they were unlikely to broadcast more than half their land.[44]

What is more surprising is that a few of the poorest villagers have also resorted to dry sowing. In each such case, the decision to broadcast seems less of a calculated gamble than a response to the force of circumstances. Lacking the cash to pay transplanting costs *and* lacking the family labor either to exchange transplanting labor (*berderau*) or to transplant their own land, a few poor households have chosen to broadcast. For Bakri bin Haji Wahab (#7) who rents 4 relong from his father and whose wife has just given birth, broadcasting 3 relong was a means of conserving cash. For Wahid (#2), whose wife is ill and who felt he would earn more by leaving the village to do urban construction work at the time when the nursery is usually prepared, broadcasting half of his 6 rented relong both saved money and freed him for wage labor. Most of the poor in Sedaka, however, are reluctant to take such risks unless they are forced to, and broadcasting is likely, for the time being, to be confined largely to big operators. By the same token, it is precisely by transplanting the land of the larger farmers that poor women have earned most of their transplanting wages. As broadcasting gains ground, poor households lose ground. How general broadcasting will become is impossible to predict, but it appears to have the backing of the agricultural authorities in Muda.[45]

The second-order effects of combine-harvesting have thus been at least as massive as their direct impact. In addition to the virtual elimination of cutting and threshing, the combine-harvesters have made gleaning impossible. They have facilitated the shift to a new form of labor payment (*kupang*), which effectively lowers wages for what little work is left. They have favored the growth of broadcast planting, thereby reducing by nearly half the wages for transplanting. They have encouraged large landowners to dismiss small tenants in order to cultivate directly, and they have helped to create a commercial class of tenants with the cash and machinery to lease in large tracts for long periods at premium

44. There are other reasons for broadcasting as well. Nor, a well-to-do villager, farms six widely scattered plots; to establish six separate nurseries or transport mature seedlings from a single large nursery to the separate plots would have been time-consuming and/or expensive. Thus he had decided to broadcast much of his land. One or two others who have high land that must normally be planted later than the rest and is therefore subject to deprivations from rats find that broadcasting allows them to get the crop in earlier, keeping them in phase with surrounding fields.

45. Thus the Operation Manual for the MUDA II Project has a section entitled "Extension and Agricultural Support Services," which in part reads as follows: "He [that is, the specialist on rice agronomy] is responsible for the continuous improvement of all aspects in agricultural management practices, including better land preparation, better planting techniques, such as the possibility of direct seeding." Despite these straws in the wind, MADA had not, as of 1983, in fact adopted an "official" position on broadcast sowing.

rents. Most of these changes, though not all, have raised the incomes of the better-off households in Sedaka. All, without exception, have driven down the incomes of poor households.[46]

Taken collectively, however, we are not simply dealing with a quantitative growth in relative inequality but rather with a series of quantitative changes that amount to a qualitative change—where "degree" passes into "kind." It is enough to observe that a large farmer who broadcasts his seed and hires a combine-harvester when the crop is ripe need *never* employ a single poor villager for wages. A large landlord, for his part, need never rent land to his poor neighbors nor hire them to work on his fields. The traditional economic connection between rich and poor—that is, wage labor and tenancy—has been all but sundered. We have on one side an increasingly commercial class of large operators and on the other side a far more numerous class of what might only loosely be called "semiproletarians." The "looseness" is necessary because, although they continue to hold on to their small paddy fields, they are decidedly less and less an agrarian proletariat, since production is now conducted largely without them. If they are to be a proletariat at all it will be in the cities and plantations of Malaysia and not in the paddy fields where their services are no longer required.

In the meantime, a process of quasi proletarianization has already set in—a process that links many villagers not to rice production at all, but to the urban economy outside Sedaka and indeed outside Kedah. If the first stage of double-cropping allowed smallholders to stay at home, the second stage has proven to be a dramatic reversal. The steady exodus that was a permanent feature of agrarian Kedah after World War II has again become a hemorrhage. Eight heads of households, seven from among the poorer village households, have since 1978 regularly left the village to find temporary construction work in Kuala Lumpur, Penang, and other urban centers. Still more would have left if they were not, as they see it, too old for such work or were assured of finding jobs. Twelve married men have applied for resettlement schemes outside Kedah, although

46. I have neglected, in this account, another form of "mechanization" that is not related to combine-harvesting but that has reduced the incomes of poor households substantially. This is the general use of motorcycles to replace bicycles in the hauling of paddy in gunny sacks from the bund or granary to the main road, where it is picked up by trucks, or directly to the mill. This work, called *tarik* by villagers, was previously done by bicycles that both rich and poor generally possessed. Now the work, which often meant as much as M$100 or M$200 a season for poor families, is performed almost exclusively by motorcycles. The distribution of motorcycles, however, is very highly skewed. More than three-quarters of the twenty-eight motorcycles in Sedaka (1979) are owned by the wealthiest half of village households, and only one family among the poorest twenty-five households has one. Thus the proceeds from such lucrative labor, while remaining within the village, are now virtually the exclusive preserve of relatively well-off families.

their chances of success are slim.[47] Nearly thirty unmarried men and women have left—many temporarily, a few permanently—to seek work elsewhere. No doubt quite a few of them would have left eventually in any case, but the changes in local land tenure and employment since 1977 precipitated their early departure.

The proximate cause for the exodus was the outright cancellation of the 1978 irrigated season due to drought. Losing an entire crop and the wage labor it might have brought was enough to send many small farmers and laborers to the city temporarily. Those who stayed on in the village, accumulating debts, not only found that the next harvest was mediocre but that their harvest earnings had been substantially reduced by competition from combine-harvesters. Many of them left with their grown sons immediately after planting the subsequent crop, in the hope of recouping their losses and repaying debts to pawnbrokers and shopkeepers.

The result was probably the largest emigration of villagers seeking work in memory.[48] In a month or two of work most married men among them were able to save M$200 or more from their earnings to support their families back in Sedaka. Although it is something of an exaggeration, one small tenant who joined the exodus said that "the only ones remaining were those who were not up to the work."[49] In nearby villages the exodus has been, if anything, even more pronounced, and there is little doubt that, for those poor households and small farmers who remain in Sedaka, temporary wage-labor migration is becoming a way of life. So long as the urban economy provides this safety valve, it will be the only means by which Sedaka's marginal families can maintain a foothold in the community.

LOCAL INSTITUTIONS AND ECONOMIC POWER

The Farmers' Association

The enormous impact that double-cropping in Muda has had on tenure, incomes, and social relations has inevitably found expression in the character of local institutions. In Sedaka, this process can be seen most palpably in the brief history of the Farmers' Association, established by law in 1967 and designed originally to provide extension and credit facilities for paddy production for all farmers in the locality. It may never quite have lived up to its original promise,

47. Settlers must, in theory, be younger than forty-five years old, although in practice it is possible to bribe to have an identity card (*Kad pengenalan*) altered to show a later birth date.

48. The only possible exception was after a major drought and crop failure in 1954 in Kedah, when many able-bodied villagers left to find work on rubber estates and in the cities.

49. *Tinggal orang tak larat sahaja.*

but it has served other uses admirably. The local branch in nearby Kepala Batas theoretically serves over twenty villages and a population of some eighteen hundred families. Only six hundred families have ever become members. The vast majority of smallholders and tenants have never joined, judging the costs too great and the benefits too small. Local members of the Malay opposition political party (PAS), including many who are quite well-to-do, have never joined, judging—in most cases correctly—that the Farmers' Association was run by the state in the interests of the ruling party. The Kepala Batas branch has, like most others, thus become the creature of rich peasants affiliated with UMNO.

When farmers speak of the Farmers' Association they call it *MADA,* referring not to the Farmers' Association or its elected leadership, but to the government agency that directs its activities. Its main function, both as they view it and in practice, is the provision of production credit and fertilizer. Credit is allocated to members, on the basis of area farmed, to cover tractor costs (M$30 a relong for two passes in 1979) and fertilizer, which is supplied in kind.[50] When the 1978 irrigated season was cancelled, creating much hardship, MADA also served as the manager of a large program of drought relief (*bantuan kemarau*) consisting of generous wages paid to labor gangs for clearing draining and irrigation canals. MADA also makes small loans for such ventures as fish ponds and beef cattle raising as well as organizes occasional "study tours" at state expense to such far-flung places as Sumatra and Singapore. MADA is thus seen not so much as the seat of an autonomous Farmers' Association but as the font of credit and patronage distributed, above all, to its membership.

The principal beneficiaries of this largesse in Sedaka are the eighteen village members (sixteen families) listed in table 4.10. They stand out in several respects from the village as a whole. All but two are from among the richest half of the households in Sedaka. Twelve are from the richest twenty families. They farm an average of 8.3 relong apiece, far above the village mean, and, taken collectively, a total of 139.5 relong, or fully 43 percent of the total paddy land cultivated by villagers. Politically, all but two are members of the local branch of the ruling party.[51] In fact, all but three of the UMNO households among the richest twenty families have joined the Persatuan Peladang.[52] None of the seven

50. Since 1979 fertilizer has been supplied through MADA to all farmers, whether members or not, thereby further reducing the potential benefits of membership.

51. The two exceptions are Mat Buyong, an opposition PAS member who once paid dues to UMNO to hedge his bets and who has in any case not paid back his initial loan from MADA, and Kamil, who is a genuine fence-sitter considering moving to the UMNO camp.

52. Two of these anomalies are also easily explained. One, Tok Mah, is a widow who would not join what is nearly exclusively a men's organization and another, Ghazali, although a discreet UMNO member, is also the son-in-law of the wealthiest PAS landowner in the village and wishes to avoid a too open identification with the local UMNO elite.

TABLE 4.10 • Village Members of Farmers' Association, with Shares Owned, Land Claimed for Loan Purposes, Land Actually Farmed, Political Affiliation, and Income Rank, June 1979

Name of Household Head	No. of Shares Owned	Value of Shares (M$)	Cultivated Acreage Claimed for Loans	Actual Acreage Cultivated	Party Affiliation	Income Ranking
Lebai Pendek*	39	195	20	13	UMNO	73
Amin*	68	340	ineligible	10	UMNO	72
Zaharuddin	25	125	ineligible	5	UMNO	71
Haji Jaafar*	13	65	ineligible	6	UMNO	70
Idris	19	95	ineligible	6	UMNO	67
Shamsul*	5	25	10	8	UMNO	66
Basir*	42	210	20	7	UMNO	64
Tok Long*	15	75	10	6	UMNO	61
Abu Hassan*	5	25	14	6	UMNO	57
Kamil	27	135	16	15	UMNO	55
Ghani Lebai Mat*	35	175	15	10	UMNO	54
Jamil	5	25	5	6	UMNO	51
Lazim*	26	130	5	13.5	UMNO	44
Fadzil*	9	45	ineligible	8	UMNO	42
Lebai Hussein*	31	155	10	6	UMNO	35
Mat Buyong	14	70	ineligible	5	PAS	34
Daud bin Haji Jaafar*	51	255	30	7	UMNO	72**
Harun bin Haji Jaafar*	20	100	8	2	UMNO	72**
Total	449	$2,245		139.5		
Average	26	$ 130	13.6	8.3		

*indicates that the individuals or, in 3 cases, members of their immediate family, were members of the Executive Committee of UMNO in Sedaka.

**Sons of Haji Jaafar, thus three members of a single family.

PAS families has joined.[53] What we have here, then, is a Farmers' Association membership almost exclusively confined to the class of wealthy cultivators affiliated with the dominant party. So close is this linkage that the four elected leaders of the local unit of the Farmers' Association (Daud bin Haji Jaafar, son of #70, Basir, #64, Amin, #72, and Fadzil, #42) are precisely those who form the small cabal which, in practice, controls village politics. As for the poor of Sedaka, no matter which party they belong to, they are conspicuous by their almost complete absence from the Farmers' Association; only two have ventured to join.[54]

This small elite has profited substantially from its control over the Farmers' Association. In the matter of crop and production loans, the profiteering is most blatant. With four exceptions, the members of the Farmers' Association take loans for considerably more land than they actually farm (see table 4.10). They thus assure themselves an additional loan at subsidized rates and a surplus of fertilizer they can sell at a profit to nonmembers.[55] The salaried staff of MADA in Kepala Batas, where this petty but systematic loan fraud takes place, are well aware of what is happening. Their complicity in registering inflated acreage represents their effort to keep their present membership and to avoid antagonizing the rural leadership of the ruling party. Thus Daud bin Haji Jaafar, son of the village headman (#70), registers 30 relong and receives M$900 in cash when in fact he is entitled only to register 7 relong and borrow M$210; Basir (#64), shopkeeper and Sedaka's political kingpin, farms only 7 relong but takes loans for 20 relong, thus availing himself of working capital at subsidized interest rates.

It is only by the most charitable definition that these production credits could in fact be termed "loans." By June 1979 six of the eighteen members had, in effect, transformed these loans into outright grants by the simple expedient of not repaying them (the "ineligibles" of table 4.10). At least four others do not appear on the list of members, because they defaulted on their loans some time ago and no longer bother to pay dues. Of the remaining twelve members in more or less good standing in mid-1979, at least two—Basir (#64) and Ghani Lebai Mat (#54)—defaulted in the following season and became ineligible for further loans. Basir owes the Farmers' Association nearly M$2,000.

53. Four of these seven families are, in effect, one extended family: Haji Kadir, his father, his sister and her husband, and his daughter and her husband.

54. One of these exceptions is Mat Buyong, whose special situation is described in n. 51 above, while the other, Lebai Hussein, is the brother-in-law of the village headman, Haji Jaffar, while his son is treasurer of the local UMNO branch. Both are very close (ranks 34 and 35 respectively) to the middle of the village income distribution.

55. The free fertilizer given to all farmers beginning with the main season of 1979–80 eliminated this advantage as well as making loan repayments to MADA less attractive.

The Agricultural Officer who leads the local branch estimates that less than half the membership still qualifies for production credit. Delinquency has grown despite the easing of repayment schedules following the drought in 1978, which hurt even well-to-do cultivators. The reasons for default, however, have nothing to do with the capacity of the membership to pay. As a group, they come from that wealthy strata of the village that can most easily borrow from Chinese shopkeepers or, more likely, finance production costs from their own ample savings. Thus the sanction of being denied further credit from MADA is only a minor inconvenience for them, an inconvenience that is, moreover, far out-weighed by the attraction of simply appropriating as much as M$2,000 in a de facto grant. They know, with a political wisdom born of experience, that they will not be prosecuted, and they lightheartedly ignore the letters they periodically receive demanding repayment. As the local Agricultural Officer laments, "It's because politics is mixed in; if we take action, the courts will press hard [for repayment] and the political party wants the votes of the people."[56] The logic is impeccable but incomplete. Prosecuting for debt collection would not alienate the UMNO rank and file. It would, however, alienate precisely that class of large farmers who form the rural leadership of UMNO in the village.[57] A headlong pursuit of debtors would probably be the coup de grâce for the institution itself.

The partisan and class character of the Farmers' Association has never been in serious doubt. From the beginning, it has been run for and by that class of large cultivators and landowners affiliated to the ruling party. This acknowledged fact was, in itself, not much more than a minor irritant in village politics and class relations—the grating evidence that a small oligarchy enjoyed privileged access to credit from the Persatuan Peladang. In mid-1978, however, the partisan character of MADA and the Farmers' Association became more visibly and acrimoniously manifest in the course of administering a drought relief program. The drought, to the rare good fortune of many cultivators, coincided with the general election campaign in 1978, thus allowing the ruling party to kill two birds with one stone through its patronage. MADA, with its offices scattered throughout the rice plain, a professional administrative staff, and strong ties to UMNO, seemed the logical vehicle to distribute relief on a large scale. The results bore the distinctive marks of MADA's political and class character.

The drought relief was designed as a labor-intensive public works program. In practice, the wages were more intensive than the labor; many villagers received as much as M$80 for two days of canal clearing in a region where the typical

---

56. *Oleh Kerana politik campur kalau ambil tindakan, makamah nak tekan . . . dan parti politik mau suara rakyat.* For parallels from Africa, see Robert H. Bates, *Markets and States in Tropical Africa* (Berkeley: Univ. of California Press, 1981), chap. 7.

57. Not incidentally, it would also almost certainly further erode the membership base of the Farmers' Association, thereby weakening its already hollow claim to speak for all farmers in the Muda region.

wage for a day's labor was no more than M$10. The recruitment of laborers was preceded, in Sedaka, by a household-by-household survey conducted by Farmers' Association clerks inquiring about family size, income, and cultivated acreage, from which an index of eligibility was constructed based on need. Actual recruitment and supervision of work was handled by the elected head of the small agricultural unit (*Ketua yunit*), who was, in this case, an UMNO stalwart, Mat Tamin, from the adjoining village of Sungai Tongkang. Once the work was under way, the nearby MADA office was besieged by a storm of complaints as it became clear that the partisan affiliation of the needy mattered a great deal. Thus, for example, poor villagers known to favor PAS were lucky if they got to work once, while poor villagers linked to UMNO were hired an average of twice.[58] Complaints were not confined to PAS members alone as even small farmers favoring UMNO observed that wealthy members of their own party were taking full advantage of the opportunity to make easy money. The two sons of Haji Salim, an exceptionally wealthy farmer with 40 relong, lorries, and tractors, living just outside Sedaka, were each hired twice. Likewise, the son of the richest UMNO landowner in the village, Lebai Pendek (#73), was hired twice, while his other brother got the contract to build a chicken coop for the Farmers' Association as part of its relief program—netting him over M$500. Many PAS members applying for work were told that no more forms were available. In the scramble for jobs, charges flew thick and fast: the heads of work gangs were charged with listing fictitious workers and pocketing their pay, with extorting commissions from those they did hire, and with favoring their relatives and political allies. Villagers claimed that the unit chiefs who hired workers made anywhere from two to three thousand dollars each from the drought relief program. The residue of bitterness left by this manipulation of drought aid was largely responsible for the overwhelming defeat of Mat Tamin by Farmers' Association members of his own party when he stood for reelection a few months later. The younger brother of Basir, who lives near the village and serves as an Information Officer in the government, went so far as to claim that the scandals in administering drought relief were directly responsible for the poor UMNO showing in many Muda constituencies in the subsequent general election.

The Ruling Party in Sedaka

To speak of the membership of the Farmers' Association in Sedaka is to speak in the same breath of both the local leadership of UMNO and the "officials" of what passes as village government. Thus, thirteen of the eighteen current members of the Persatuan Peladang are now, or have been, elected by the local UMNO

---

58. Eight UMNO members among the poorest twenty villagers were hired an average of two times, while the twelve PAS members among the poorest twenty villagers were hired an average of 0.9 times.

branch to the Village Development Committee (Jawatankuasa Kemajuan Kampung, JKK).[59]

With the exception of only three families who may be described as "fence-sitters," the political affiliation of each family is common knowledge.[60] Forty-three families (58 percent) in the village are in the UMNO camp, while twenty-eight (38 percent) are with PAS. This count, however, masks a wide variation in how open and active this membership is. Beyond a small core of militants in each party, drawn in UMNO's case from among the most substantial villagers, there lies a rank-and-file membership whose affiliation is largely passive. Quite a few villagers, in fact, describe themselves openly as *Pak Turut* (followers) only, who have affiliated with UMNO to "be on the side of the majority" (*sebelah banyak*) and to qualify for petty patronage.

The benefits available to UMNO members are substantial. For wealthy villagers membership may mean the opportunity to receive a taxi license, a small business loan, a permit to operate a small rice mill or a lorry, or a local government job. At the district UMNO annual meeting in early 1979, a prominent party leader from Guar Cempedak openly complained about those who joined the fold simply to apply for a taxi license and then promptly ceased paying dues or attending meetings once it was granted. For rank-and-file members the benefits are more modest but no less vital. The dream of many young men to be accepted as a settler on a government land scheme is one likely to be realized only by those who have cast their lot with UMNO, as political criteria are openly used in the selection process. A number of small grants-in-aid to cover the cost of school uniforms and exercise books are available to poor village families from the principal of the nearby primary school. These grants are awarded on the basis of a list provided by the local UMNO leader, Basir, on which the names of children from poor PAS families rarely figure at all. Such patronage is, of course, supplemented by the distribution of loans and jobs conferred by the Farmers' Association, which works through the same interlocking village directorate.

By far the largest and most contentious distribution of patronage, however, occurred in late 1979, when the village was selected as a recipient of over M$20,000 in funds for a "village improvement scheme" (*Rancangan Pemulihan Kampung,* RPK). As with the drought relief scheme, a census was conducted of each village household to determine its income and needs, after which grants were made to families for such things as lumber, zinc roofing material, cement, septic tanks, and toilets. We shall examine this episode in some detail later, but it is worth noting here that the funds were distributed in a wholly partisan manner by the small "gang of four" who informally control UMNO and the Village Development Committee: Basir, Daud bin Haji Jaafar (son of the head-

59. See table 4.10.
60. The local Malay term for this is also *pagar,* or "fence."

man), Karim, and Fadzil. This was so true that by early 1980 it became possible to identify the political affiliation of virtually each household in the village in the course of a casual stroll down the path; no elaborate interviews were necessary. Houses with new roofs, new lumber in the walls, and/or a new outhouse were UMNO households and the remainder were PAS households.

The sociology of village UMNO is therefore a reasonably straightforward affair. It is dominated by a few well-off families who have taken full advantage of the benefits of their role—benefits that come almost entirely from government patronage of one kind or another. Much of the UMNO rank and file consists of families who are closely related to members of this petty oligarchy and/or who are often hired by them. Thus, ten of the sixteen poorest UMNO households have strong ties of blood, marriage, or employment to wealthier UMNO households which, while they may not explain party loyalty, at least serve to solidify it.[61] Village UMNO is only the ultimate link in a vast chain of kinship and patronage that extends on to the *mukim,* the district, and the state. Outside the village, the importance of kinship diminishes while the role of patronage is paramount. UMNO leaders at the district level are drawn disproportionately from among government clerks, schoolteachers, and wealthy farmers with business interests that depend on state loans or contracts. While the stakes are naturally greater at the apex of the party edifice than at the base, the cement that keeps the structure intact at each level is recognizably similar.

Despite the palpable advantages of UMNO membership, there are still many PAS members in the village, although, as an institution, the opposition can hardly be said to be thriving. A decade ago PAS members were a majority in Sedaka. Since then, however, the village headman, Haji Jaafar, and a few strategically placed families have switched sides, and the bulk of the new households moving in have joined UMNO. The drift toward the ruling party was brusquely reinforced following the 1978 general elections, when the Kedah state government conducted a purge of all village development committees (JKKs) to ensure that their membership was exclusively from UMNO. In some villages that were PAS-dominated, this entailed either abolishing the JKK or, more likely, appointing the one or two UMNO families in the hamlet to the JKK. In Sedaka it entailed throwing out the two members of PAS who had been elected to the JKK and who until then had helped preserve a facade of local nonpartisanship. Since then, PAS has led a shadowy local existence. With the exception of a death benefit society (Khairat Kematian), which pays funeral costs for many party

61. These ten are Wahid (#2), Mansur (#9), Mat Sarif (#12), Samad (#17), Tok Zainah (#21), Ariffin (#27), Harun Din (#31), Lebai Hussein (#35), Ali Abdul Rahman (#36), and Tok Omar (#37). Two of the remaining six—Razak (#1) and Bakri bin Haji Wahab (#7)—have recently switched from PAS to UMNO and make no bones about their desire to be considered for benefits such as school loans, short-term public works employment, etc.

members in return for a small annual premium, PAS in Sedaka has become largely an affair of demoralized grumbling, social avoidance, and character assassination. Open confrontation is rare, although a few shun Basir and boycott his store. PAS members now have their own joke about the JKK. They call it *jangan kacau kerja kami* which, freely translated, means "don't stick your nose into our business."[62]

With all the material incentives favoring membership in UMNO, it is the more surprising that such a large minority of Sedaka's households should have so far resisted such blandishments. (See table 4.11)

TABLE 4.11 • Political Affiliation of Households in Sedaka by Income Level, in Percentages

	Opposition Party (PAS)		Ruling Party (UMNO)		Fence-Sitters		Total	
	%	(N)	%	(N)	%	(N)	%	(N)
Poorest half of households	54%	(20)	43%	(16)	3%	(1)	100	(37)
Richest half of households	22%	(8)	73%	(27)	5%	(2)	100	(37)
Entire village	38%	(28)	58%	(43)	4%	(3)	100	(74)

The resistance is particularly marked among the poorest strata of the village, who are more than twice as likely to belong to the opposition as are their wealthier neighbors. That a majority of the village should have affiliated with UMNO requires little explanation, given the manifest advantages. Why a majority of the poorer villagers (and a minority of the rich) have chosen, against their material interests, to remain in the PAS camp, however, does require analysis. There appear to be several reasons. One is that the pattern of village partisanship has its roots in older, family-based factions that existed well before the formation of political parties. Thus, Haji Kadir, the richest man in the village, with his father and his two brothers in tow have constituted something of a minority faction in village politics for at least thirty years. But since all four of these households are quite well-to-do, it only helps to explain what might be termed the "leading" PAS faction and not the appeal of PAS to most of Sedaka's poor. For that explanation we must rely on a combination of family ties, special material interests, UMNO strategy, and, not least, the moral appeal of the opposition. Family ties are influential in at least four or five cases of sons whose fathers (often not residents) have been open and vociferous PAS supporters.

62. The pun here is more effective in Malay by the use of the word *kami*, rather than *kita*, for "we/us/our." *Kami* is used when the person(s) spoken to are explicitly excluded from the group referred to as "us."

But one finds nothing like the UMNO pattern. For in only seven of the twenty poorest PAS households can one find links of kinship or employment that might plausibly explain membership in the opposition. What is more striking is that there are at least five poorer PAS members whose partisan affiliation is, as it were, *not* compatible with their apparent economic interests—that is, PAS members who depend upon UMNO members for much of their wage labor.

Second, with the exception of the very poorest, many PAS supporters have long been dues-paying members of a PAS death benefit society. Were they to leave PAS, they would automatically forfeit the right to funeral costs, in which they have already made a substantial investment. In fact, the success with which PAS has tied this traditional form of social insurance to party membership has prompted recent efforts by UMNO to copy the formula.

Third, UMNO village strategy has not strongly encouraged substantial defections from PAS. The leadership of Sedaka's leading party has, it appears, adopted what game theorists have aptly called a "minimal winning coalition" policy. That is, having succeeded in controlling the village, they are not anxious to so enlarge their majority that the material advantages of UMNO membership would be further diluted and dispersed.

Fourth, while little is to be gained materially from aligning with the opposition, PAS has considerable moral appeal. This appeal stems only in small part from its claim to be more faithful to the tenets of Islam. PAS members, in this respect, are no more outwardly observant or orthodox as a group than members of the ruling party in Sedaka. What is involved, rather, seems to be a fusion of class issues, ethnic and religious sentiment, and a *populist* opposition to government policy and the inequalities it has fostered. Such a fusion is not surprising in view of the fact that PAS is the only open, institutional vehicle of opposition that is tolerated—if only barely—within the Malay community.[63] When poor PAS members talk about UMNO locally, they do not mean its rank and file, many of whom are as poor as they, but rather the wealthy families in Sedaka who run it and the coalition of government employees and rich landowners and businessmen with connections above them who control UMNO in the district. UMNO is, for them, nearly synonymous with "the haves" (*gologan berada*) and with "the government." Despite PAS's failure to win power in Kedah, it appeals to many poor farmers because it is "a religiously informed popular movement for the defense of peasant interests."[64] Members of PAS in Sedaka emphasize that it represents only one race and one religion, while UMNO, with its coalition partners, cannot just defend Malays and their religion. Issues of race and religion

63. Indicative of this was the widespread local disillusionment with PAS when, for a time, it joined the ruling coalition. There were few actual defections from the party, but members commented bitterly, *"Datuk Asri* (leader of PAS) *makan gagi kerajaan"* (Datuk Asri is taking [literally, "eating"] a government salary)."

64. Clive S. Kessler, *Islam and Politics in a Malay State: Kelantan 1838–1969* (Ithaca: Cornell Univ. Press, 1978).

are understood by most poor PAS members in a way that fuses them to issues of class relations and the needs of a smallholding peasantry that justifiably feels threatened. Thus, as we shall see, notions about exploitation, about rights to employment, land, and charity—all vital material issues—find expression through what are experienced as the norms of the Malay community and the requirements of Islam for pious conduct. To say that UMNO defends the well-off and has done little or nothing to help the poorer farmers is at the same time to say that it has violated both Malay and Islamic values. [65]

Finally, it would be a mistake to ignore the element of sheer pride and stubbornness that keeps PAS members from switching parties, despite the price they pay in foregone patronage. Having held out for so long, they now make a virtue of what UMNO leaders might call necessity and are unwilling to give up the public and private satisfaction of having followed a political path without material rewards for the sake of principle. This atmosphere is strong and reinforcing enough so that Taib, a poor man who told friends he was thinking of switching at the urging of his wife, has not taken the plunge because he says he fears the contempt for his opportunism that will come from his PAS friends. Recent episodes of blatant partisanship in the village, such as drought relief and the "village improvement scheme" have served, if anything, to increase the bitterness and resolve of PAS members.

Arrayed against PAS is a formidable coalition of well-to-do families who have come to monopolize UMNO affairs in the community. (See appendix C, table 4) The eleven villagers who are now, or have recently been, officers or members of the Village Development Committee farm an *average* of nearly 13 relong (close to three times the local average) and are, with a single exception, from among the wealthiest half of households. [66] The other link that fuses their politics is that all but two of the eleven are tied to the government by employment, licenses, or loans. [67] In one or two cases these ties antedated their political activity; for

65. Many of the conclusions Kessler reached in his study of Kelantan are applicable in Kedah as well. As he notes (ibid., 125), many of the leaders of PAS are drawn from the ranks of religious teachers, prayer leaders, and traditional headmen, many of whom feel threatened by the civil servants and licensed businessmen who appear to have taken over. There is, then, something of a displaced elite aspect to the PAS leadership. It is also the case, as Kessler asserts, that PAS represents a "revival and coalescence of the radical and Islamic variants of Malay nationalism (p. 126)."

66. The average is particularly inflated, because the son of Haji Salim, a very wealthy entrepreneur owning 45 relong and living, technically, just outside the village, is a member of the JKK.

67. The current chairman of UMNO, Shamsul, is an employee of the government rice mill; the treasurer, Taha bin Lebai Hussein, works part-time for the District Office; Abu Hassan, an Executive Committee member, is a lorry driver for the Farmers' Association. Yunus bin Haji Salim holds a government license to operate a market stall. Five others, including the deputy chairman, have sizable loans from the Farmers' Association.

the remainder, these ties represent the welcome fruits of having made an advantageous choice. What had initially, perhaps, been a mere political preference has become so cemented by the flow of material benefits as to make the choice all but irreversible.

The "inner circle" of four men, noted earlier, who control not only UMNO but also the local unit of the Farmers' Association and the Prayer House (*surau*) Committee, are connected by a dense network of kinship ties. Thus, for example, Basir is: the nephew of the village headman, whose son, in turn, is part of the inner circle; the uncle of another member and, beyond this, also the nephew of Haji Salim, who is head of the district-level party. Basir's grandfather was a subdistrict official (*penghulu*), and his brother is a full-time local employee of the Ministry of Information. He has parlayed his wealth, his family connections, and his considerable personal energy into a nearly unchallenged dominance of the local UMNO and the village unit of the Farmers' Association. He sits on the executive committees of the government primary school, the private religious school (Sekolah Arab), the mosque, the cooperative rice mill, and the nearby market, all located in nearby Kepala Batas. His preeminence is not only acknowledged by other members of the inner circle but his role has far eclipsed that of the nominal village headman, Haji Jaafar, who chooses to remain a respected bystander.

The UMNO leadership, then, is distinguished from its local competitor not only, or even primarily, by its wealth. The PAS leadership is also well-to-do, although it represents but a small minority of the "substantial" households.[68] What has come to distinguish Sedaka's UMNO leaders is their increasing reliance, as households, on various forms of state patronage and its privileged access to the institutions that distribute that patronage: the Farmers' Association, the subdistrict chief (*penghulu*), the primary school, the district office, and so forth. To be sure, their influence is not exclusively based upon patronage. Kinship relations continue to tie many of the leaders to one another and to a portion of the rank and file. Such family ties are further elaborated and extended by traditional village institutions such as a death benefit society (*khairat Kematian*), a "plate and bowl society" (*syarikat pinggan mangkuk*), which lends crockery for feasts, and rotating credit associations (*kut*)—all of which function basically along party lines.

What is largely missing from the village party today, however, is the social cohesion provided a decade ago by the enduring material ties of tenancy, employment, and charity. Before double-cropping, patronage was a largely village

68. Sedaka is, perhaps, rather special in this respect. A study of large landowners in the Muda area has shown that they are more or less evenly distributed among the two major Malay parties, UMNO and PAS. See the fine study by Mansor Haji Othman, "Hak Millik Tanah Padi dan Politik di Kedah" (Master's thesis, Universiti Sains Malaysia, 1978), chaps. 1–3.

affair in which the leading families in UMNO brought along, as a matter of course, those whom they hired, those to whom they rented land, and those (often the same people) to whom they made small loans and gifts. As we have seen, the economic opportunities presented by double-cropping have served to weaken, if not eliminate, this more traditional basis of leadership. Having become well-nigh redundant in village rice production, the village poor have become, in turn, more socially redundant as well. Put differently, if the rich peasants of Sedaka now spend less time and effort "cultivating" their poorer neighbors, it is precisely because their poor neighbors are no longer cultivating their fields.

The votes of the poor are still important, but they can no longer be secured quite so automatically through pre-existing economic and social ties. Politically, at least, the rich peasantry, which has always dominated Sedaka, is now composed increasingly of dependent brokers rather than patrons in their own right. They now operate largely with "borrowed" resources that emanate directly from the state. These resources may provide them with the wherewithal to reinforce their waning social domination of village life, but by the same token they have become far more vulnerable. Their fate is now largely out of their own hands. So long as Malaysian growth, state revenue, and a national leadership solicitous of its rural constituency continue to prevail, they are in no real danger. Should any or all of these assumptions, which now underwrite their position, cease to exist, however, they would find themselves in serious difficulty.

5 • History according to Winners and Losers

There is no quailing—even that forced on the helpless and injured—which does not have an ugly obverse: the withheld sting was gathering venom.

George Eliot, *Daniel Deronda*

CLASS-IFYING

For some very limited purposes, the laborious account of tenure, income, mechanization, and political power contained in the preceding chapter might suffice. It has at least the advantage of indicating how the "big battalions" of contemporary agrarian change—commercialization, capital, and irrigation—have reordered the relations of production in a very small place. To stop there, however, would merely add another small brick to an edifice that is the by now familiar and somewhat demoralizing story of the local effects of the green revolution.

As a social history—as human history—that account is inadequate. It is to real social history as the description of the technical features of an assembly line and a table of organization would be to a social history of the work force. To put this another way, the previous chapter did no more than sketch the determinate conditions with which the peasantry of Sedaka has had to come to grips.

If it is true that events are not self-explanatory, that they do not speak for themselves, it is also, alas, true that human subjects do not entirely speak for themselves. If they did, it would suffice merely to turn on the tape recorder and offer a complete transcript to the reader. This social-scientist-as-recorder technique has been tried with illuminating results, most notably by what might be called the "Oscar Lewis school of anthropology." Even Oscar Lewis, however, has found it necessary to arrange and edit the transcript and to add a preface or postscript. The necessity arises, I believe, for at least three reasons. First, the human subjects themselves often speak with a kind of linguistic shorthand—with similes and metaphors that they have no need to clarify to their neighbors but that would, without explanation, mystify an outsider. Thus, the fact that someone in Sedaka said of another villager that "he behaves like Razak" or that an American said of someone that he "struck out" when looking for a job, remain opaque until we know something about Razak and about baseball, respectively. Second, there are larger orders of meaning and coherence that human subjects "know" but have no need to verbalize in the taken-for-granted world of daily discourse. The standards for decorum at a funeral, the expectations about what gifts are appropriate for certain occasions might fall into this category. Such standards are, as it were, embedded in the pattern of activity and are only, if ever, specified when their performance becomes a bone of contention, that is, when they can no longer be taken for granted. Finally, the observer may find certain themes or values that appear to unify what might otherwise appear to be separate realms of practice, belief, or discourse. Ideals of "manhood" in some Mediterranean societies are a possible case in point.[1] Here, the observer is creating a synthesis or interpretation that is perhaps consistent with the record but is unlikely ever to be consciously thought or spoken by those who have created that record. Such interpretations are, as Geertz notes, "our own constructions of other people's [the human subjects in question] construction of what they and their compatriots are up to."[2]

The problem necessarily arises of how to evaluate these constructions; on what basis is one construction to be preferred over another? The conceptual ground is treacherous here and proof, in the strict sense of natural sciences, is unavailable. Nevertheless, some standards of evidence and inference are possible. Such constructions should be economical and, at the very least, consistent with the practices and beliefs they purport to illuminate. To the degree that they also make sense of what would otherwise be unrelated or anomalous data from the record of human action, they are to be preferred over competing constructions. One final standard by which interpretations might be judged is the object of considerable dispute; it is that our interpretation or characterization should, in principle, be found plausible by those whose actions are being interpreted. The problem here, of course, is not only that all human actors have interests that lead them to conceal or misrepresent their intentions, but that this standard must also contend both with Freudian doctrine that judges many motivations to be inaccessible to the actor and with the notion of "false-consciousness." Thus, while it may be unrealistic to insist that human actors confirm our construction of their actions, we can insist that our interpretations take account of the full range of self-descriptions they do offer.

The last ten years have been momentous for the villagers of Sedaka and for their compatriots on the Muda Plain. One would be hard-pressed to find another decade in which their material life and production relations changed so dramatically or in which older patterns of social and economic life came unstuck so radically.[3] These are the gross facts all villagers have had to grapple with, to

1. A healthy skepticism is surely called for when such claims are made. This is particularly the case when supposedly unifying themes are detached from their historical roots and appear to hover over a culture like some Hegelian spirit. This brand of "idealism" makes human actors into mere vectors or pawns of ideas that are, after all, human creations. Only when such ideas are linked firmly to the historical conditions that have favored their appearance and influence and that could, if altered, spell their weakening or disappearance do they merit being taken seriously at all.

2. Clifford Geertz, "Thick Description: Toward an Interpretive Theory of Culture," chap. 1 in *The Interpretation of Culture* (New York: Basic, 1973), 9.

3. The decade from 1940 to 1950, which includes the Japanese interregnum, is a plausible rival for this honor.

understand, and to interpret. It should not surprise us that their constructions of what has happened, its meaning, who is to blame, and what it all portends should vary greatly. There are significant variations by individual, by age, by status, and, not least, by property relations—that is to say, by class. Whose ox is being gored makes a striking difference. One cannot expect a landless laborer to look on combine-harvesters with quite the same equanimity or satisfaction as does the large-scale farmer. And yet their divergent experiences and interests form part of the same community of discourse. Their disparate and often contradictory understandings of events are intended to speak to, to appeal to, one another and are fashioned from the same cultural materials available to all.

What follows here and in the next chapter is thus an attempt to describe and analyze the beginnings of this new experience of class in Sedaka.

If, in the last chapter, I surveyed the impact of the green revolution with the eyes of an economic or social historian, in this chapter I propose to survey the same events through the partisan eyes of two sets of villagers—winners and losers. Depending on whom one talks to, there are at least two green revolutions at work here. Before plunging in however, it should be perfectly obvious that class is hardly the only social experience available to villagers. Factions, neighborhoods, and kinship ties, to mention only a few, create their own fracture lines, which do not often coincide neatly with class. Villagers are also united for some purposes with their local antagonists as members of the same ethnic group, the same religion, the same village, the same sector of the economy (paddy). Depending on the issue and context, these other experienced selves may be decisive. What is undeniable, though, is that property relations have become far more salient since double-cropping. But property relations are, as always, rather tangled and do not serve to divide the village neatly in two or three parts like some sharp sociological scalpel. Each aspect of the changes since 1972 defines a somewhat different collection of winners and losers; small landowners who would like to expand their farms by renting, for example, may share a distaste for leasehold tenancy with the poor while not sharing their aversion to the use of combine-harvesters. And yet, as we shall see, there is enough of a cumulative impact at the top and at the bottom of the village stratification to provide the existential basis for the generation of something like a class point of view.

The "poor" for the purposes of this analysis will generally mean the thirty-seven households with the lowest per capita income. The "rich," in turn, refers to those twenty-five households with the highest per capita incomes.[4] While per capita income is, by itself, a better measure of local class position than total

4. In practice, however, a disproportionate amount of the actual material comes from the poorer strata of "the poor" and from the richer strata of "the rich." This is the case, I think, both because the class interests of those at opposite ends of the class spectrum are less ambiguous and because I chose to devote more time listening to the poorest and the richest.

income or the amount of land owned, it nonetheless produced a few anomalies that ran square against local perceptions. In such cases, I followed local opinion, as it appeared in each case to be accurate in a larger sense than my numbers.[5] The divergent points of view examined below represent, then, what appeared to be the most salient differences in perspective between rich and poor. Apart from a "zone of agreement," only those views of double-cropping and its consequences that divided the rich and the poor and that were held by a substantial number of either group are discussed.

In a village deeply embedded in a larger economy, where a share of the local paddy land is owned by outsiders and where villagers seek work and land outside the community, class issues can hardly be confined to the local sphere alone. Most of these issues, however, have a clear local manifestation. Thus, for virtually every change in production relations that the poor have come to resent—for example, mechanization, rents in advance, decline in charity, shifts in wage rates—there are local, as well as outside, targets for their resentment. For a few matters—most notably leasehold tenancy—which are most definitely class issues, there are few local antagonists. Here the "winners" are largely outside the village, and most of the local population is largely in accord although, as we shall see, at quite different levels of enthusiasm.

SHIPS PASSING—AND SIGNALING—IN THE NIGHT

Two brief commentaries on the present state of affairs in Sedaka will serve to illustrate how the facts reported in the previous chapter can take on widely divergent meanings. I have chosen them to highlight a style of argument and for the contrast they provide. But they are neither the most divergent examples available nor the least. They are, in fact, fairly representative. Presented here with a minimum of interpretation, their meaning in the larger discourse between winners and losers will become apparent only later.

Pak Yah, a landless laborer with eight children, has always been hard-pressed to make ends meet. His situation is reflected not only in his house, which is a better maintained version of Razak's, but in his nickname. He is called *Yah*

5. For example, Hamid (#38) is in the middle of the income distribution, but nearly all villagers think of him as well-to-do since he owns nearly 10 relong and a tractor. It is his gambling, they say, that has forced him to lease out his land, thus making him appear temporarily poorer. Fadzil (#42) and Abdul Rahman (#41) are analogous cases, each being a substantial landowner; the former, however, has had to lease out some of his land to pay for a recent purchase of paddy land while the latter has had a string of crop failures. Both are considered among the well-to-do. Another anomalous case is Tok Mahmud (#56), who has always been a fairly poor man but is now a widower with only a single granddaughter at home. His per capita income is thus rather high, but villagers, taking a longer view of his life history, place him among the poor.

Botol (Yah-Bottle).[6] The reference is to the sound made by the bottle of cooking oil rattling in his bicycle basket as he pedals back and forth nearly every afternoon to his house near the far end of the village. It is at the same time a reference to his poverty, since he can seldom afford more than the 30¢ minimum purchase and must therefore buy oil daily. Unlike Razak, he is widely regarded as an honest and reliable worker. I have heard him complain bitterly before about the difficulty of finding work and about his futile efforts to rent in even a small piece of paddy land. On this occasion, however, he is angrier than usual about having been denied any of the funds recently distributed by local UMNO leaders as part of the Village Improvement Scheme (RPK). Spurred on by a couple of neighbors (Nor and Mat "halus"), who were also ignored at the handout, he launches into a more global assessment of the situation.

"The well-to-do are throwing those who are hard up aside." "The more we want to lift ourselves, the more we are pushed down, the more cruel [they are to us]." "They want to bury us."[7] As he says this last phrase, Pak Yah thrusts the heel of his hand toward the ground at his feet as if pushing something into the earth and adds, "We want to be higher." To illustrate what he means, he notes that in the past it was possible to get loans of rice from well-off villagers. But now, he claims, they sell their rice for cash and then claim they have no money.

This last charge, which I had heard several times before from other poor villagers, deserves some comment. The traditional medium for loans and advances was, fittingly, paddy or polished rice (*beras*), the basic food staple. Loans of cash were exceptionally rare, as they are today. The poor appear to believe that the sale of paddy for cash is, in part, an attempt by the wealthy to avoid being importuned for loans. Having sold most of their harvest, the rich can now claim that they have only enough paddy to feed their own family and that their cash is spent. This procedure has the added advantage of concealment, for while it is generally possible to know whether a man's granary is full, it is not possible to know whether he has any cash.[8]

6. Malay nicknames are typically formed by the last syllable of the given name: thus, Osman becomes "man"; Zakariah becomes "Ya"; Ahmad becomes "Mat." Appended to these nicknames is usually a reference to some personal characteristic of the individual or to his father or grandfather. Thus Mat Din is known, behind his back, as "Mat Kabur" (*kabur* is a coconut palm beetle that he is said to resemble); Mat Sarif is known as "Mat Rabit" (*rabit* means "torn" and is shorthand for his harelip); Jamil is known as Jamil Pak Ngah (Pak Ngah is a reference to his father, who as middle son was called Ngah, a shortening of *tengah* meaning "middle").

7. *Orang senang tauk orang susah ke-tefi. Lagi mau angkit, lagi dalam; lagi kejam. Nak bubuh dalam bumi.*

8. They can surely guess that a man is rich from the bounty of his harvest, but they are generally not in a position to know the debts that he may have had to pay off. Thus in one respect the widespread use of cash marks a shift to a village in

The refusal to give loans, Pak Yah adds, shows that "As they see it, those who are hardup are despicable." "They don't want us to speak up." "They don't want us to be clever." "[But] now the poor are acting up a bit [and when] the rich see that, they are even more angry."[9] The comment about "acting up" almost certainly refers to the open complaints that greeted the partisan distribution of government funds for house repairs.

He continues, "They say we are lazy, but we don't get the chance to continue school or to get government jobs [for example, government settlement schemes]." "They say we don't want to work, but it's hard to find work." Here, as elsewhere, Pak Yah and other poor villagers conduct what amounts to both sides of a debate, a dialogue, in which the accusations the rich make against them are first stated and then refuted. This debate is, moreover, cast in terms of rich and poor, although the immediate issue that has aroused Pak Yah's ire is one between UMNO members, by no means all of whom are rich, and PAS members, by no means all of whom are poor.

On an afternoon nearly a month later, I am listening to much the same group assembled below Pak Yah's house, and the anger at the partisan distribution of patronage is still rife. Their anger is focused particularly on what they regard as a fraudulent survey of households conducted before allocations were made. One of the questions the clerk asked was, quite literally, "Where do you shit?" Pak Yah's reply was to squat on the ground, flick his heel, and then to add that he even "had to shit on someone else's land." This expression is the standard, in village parlance, for real poverty.[10]

When the money was handed out, however, it was clear that the survey had been a mockery. As Pak Yah says, it was "thrown in the trash." He then does a short pantomime of a clerk checking a list of names with his index finger. "They say Pak Yah is well-to-do, even Dullah is well-to-do, even Sukur is well off."[11] Those assembled find this hilarious as they know that these three house-

---

which wealth is more easily hidden. Knowing how rich a family is, moreover, is no idle pastime in peasant villages; it is vital information that forms the basis of claims and obligations among neighbors. Zola might have been describing any peasant village when he wrote, "They went on endlessly, evaluating every inch of land, for they knew how much everybody in Rognes was worth, down to the value of the bed-linen." *The Earth,* trans. Douglas Parmee (Harmondsworth: Penguin, 1980), 194. The wealth of a paddy-growing family could in the past have been inferred from the amount of paddy stored in the granary. As the Malay proverb puts it: "If the granary is empty, so is the stomach" (*jelapang kosong, perut pun kosong*).

9. *Depa pandang, orang susah, hina! Cakap, tak mau, cerdik, tak mau. La ini, orang susah berlagak lebih; orang senang tengok, lagi marah.*

10. *Kena berak tanah orang.* This is almost precisely equivalent in meaning to the American slang expression that someone is so poor that "he doesn't have a pot to piss in."

11. *Depa kata Pak Yah, senang; Dullah pun, senang, Sukur pun, senang.*

holds, all PAS supporters and among the very poorest in the village, received nothing. Pak Yah continues his sketch: "They say Lebai Pendek is hard up, Shamsul is so hard up they have to give him house paint, Abu Hassan is hard up." These three men are, of course, from among the wealthiest UMNO supporters in the village, and all received assistance. The ridicule is so biting in large part because the village UMNO leadership wantonly disregarded its own facade of fair, impersonal procedures in order simply to reward themselves and their followers. Once again, however, the issue is cast in terms of rich and poor and the distortion of the facts by wealthy UMNO leaders.

If we listen briefly to other villagers, however, we hear a very different story. The occasion for this story was special. It was not, like most of my conversations with villagers, simply a casual encounter. When Haji Kadir, his brother-in-law Tok Kasim, and his son-in-law Ghazali sat down to talk with me one evening, it was clear that they had something to say which they had worked out together. The context in which they came was undoubtedly significant. I had spent much of the previous two weeks threshing paddy along with many of the poorer men in the village. [12] In the course of the work I had come to know quite a few heads of poor households whom I had known only slightly before. Their concerns about the loss of work to combine-harvesters and the decline of "charity" payments (*zakat peribadi*) previously given to threshers had found its way into the questions I had begun to ask other villagers. These three men appeared to be concerned that I was getting the wrong picture; they had come to set me straight. [13] All three were, as one might expect, well-off by village standards. Haji Kadir (*Pak Ceti*) is, of course, the richest man in the village; his son-in-law farms 8.5 relong, much of which he can expect to inherit; and his brother-in-law farms 6 relong, most of which he owns.

Haji Kadir begins with a rhetorical question: "Why is it," he asks, "that we call some people poor when they are really well-off, and others well-off when they are really poor?" He then proceeds to answer his own question with some

12. The rhythm of hand threshing normally requires that two men work at each threshing tub; while one is fetching a bundle of paddy stalks, the other is flailing the grain into the tub. Whenever I found that there were an odd number of threshers I would join the "odd man out" when invited. Although I was a good deal slower at threshing than most, my partner benefited since he collected the piece-rate (then M$2 per gunny sack) for the grain we both threshed.

13. It is of course true that my presence is the stimulus for their small "presentation." The argument they are making to me is not an argument they would bother making directly to Pak Yah. In this sense, what they say is artificial—an argument designed to impress and convince an outsider who might be powerful. What is notable, however, is that in making their case they must necessarily fall back on the values and standards embedded in village life and make more explicit—for someone quite ignorant—what could perhaps be conveyed among them by a mere gesture or phrase.

strategically chosen examples. "Like Kamil, he doesn't have any property, but he manages because he is resourceful."[14] "Or like Mat Khir, who has no land but is also resourceful." These two illustrations are both apt and selective. They are two of only five heads of household who own no paddy land and have no prospect of inheriting any but nonetheless have incomes that put them well above the median for the village. Kamil has, for decades, been the largest tenant in Sedaka and now farms 15 relong of productive paddy land, while Mat Khir rents in only two relong but has a stable and coveted job with a successful Chinese shopkeeper and paddy dealer in the nearby town. Both men are able to provide comfortably for their large families. They are striking exceptions to the general rule that landowning is the basis of wealth in the village. And yet, as Haji Kadir implies, their income is more precarious than that of a landowner and each must work unstintingly to achieve it.

Having cited two cases of families who are poor in property but nevertheless manage to do well by virtue of their resourcefulness, Haji Kadir takes up the opposite side of the coin. Here the examples he uses are Hamzah and his older brother, the ever-serviceable Razak. "They have property, they have land," says Haji Kadir, "as much as 2 or 3 relong, so much that they rent it out like big landlords." With the vigorous assent of his companions, Haji Kadir notes that, if Hamzah and Razak were clever and thought ahead, they could plant this land and harvest twenty to thirty gunny sacks of paddy a year, enough to feed their families. The fact that they do not is not because they are poor but because they are not "resourceful." Again, the illustrations are carefully selected. Only five of the poorest fourteen villagers own any paddy land at all, and Razak and Hamzah are among them. Strictly speaking, neither actually owns the land, inasmuch as they do not have the capital to pay the fees and Islamic inheritance tax (*faraid*) required to transfer ownership from their long-since-deceased father.[15] Nor is it clear that Hamzah would get title to the 2 relong his mother has let him rent out, as there are claims on the land by two additional sons who live outside the village. At the moment, Hamzah rents out his 2 relong as does Razak his .25 relong. Both claim that the loss of work during the drought-cancelled season, their large families, and their reduced wage-labor earnings make it impossible for them to finance a rice crop through till harvest. Hamzah actually planted a crop in the irrigated season of 1977 but claimed that he had to sell the standing paddy in the field before harvest to feed his family. But Haji Kadir and his friends obviously believe that it is improvidence, not poverty, that

14. "Resourceful" seems the best translation for *pandai pusing*, which literally means "clever at moving around." "To hustle," "to be diligent," or "to shift for oneself" also capture the spirit of this verb.

15. This process, known locally as *ambil kuasa* (to take legal title), costs roughly M$50 for legal fees plus 1 percent of the estimated market value of the land for the Moslem inheritance tax.

accounts for Hamzah and Razak becoming petty landlords. Who is correct is a matter of charged opinion that no resort to financial evidence alone could settle.

Tok Kasim and Haji Kadir then address themselves to the case of Hamzah in particular, taking it for granted that Razak's reputation speaks for itself. Although they stop short of calling Hamzah lazy, they do claim that he is "not very industrious."[16] "That's why," Tok Kasim says, "we don't much want to give him assistance or work all the time." "He has property; he's like us." When I ask who, then, is really poor in the village, they manage, after some discussion, to come up with three possible candidates—Pak Yah, Mansur, and Mat "halus," all of whom, they say, would be "finished" if they fell ill and could not work. The rest, they claim, are either not so badly off or are not resourceful.

Warming to the main theme after having been sidetracked momentarily by my question, Haji Kadir returns to the problem of those who ask for work and alms in bad faith. As an exhibit, he offers his nephew Hashim, from Yan. He regularly comes shortly before the harvest, Haji Kadir claims, to announce that he will help thresh and to ask for a portion of his wages in advance. When threshing time comes, however, he often goes to Megat Dewa in the neighboring state of Perlis where the wages and *zakat* gifts are better. Once, he adds, Hashim told him in the evening, after having been given an advance, to have the coffee ready early next morning as he would be coming to thresh. Early next morning Haji Kadir spied him walking along the canal to the south of Sedaka, but he turned off to work for someone else. He also suspects that the rice he and two other relatives had given Hashim before *Hari Raya* (Ramadan) was sold rather than eaten, and he once told Hashim that he should beg rice only from those for whom he threshes. Still, he continues, Hashim has come begging every year for the past decade like clockwork. When Haji Kadir offered to rent him nearly 2 relong he owns in Megat Dewa for a couple of years, Hashim declined. "He wasn't *that* interested," concluded Haji Kadir.[17]

Hashim is thus assimilated to the cases of Razak and Hamzah. None of them, by this account, are particularly interested in work; none are particularly resourceful, except perhaps when it comes to asking for alms or for wages in advance. Some, if not all of them, are pretty well-off after all. And certainly none of them, to judge by their conduct and resources, are worthy of the sympathy and help they have gotten.

The discourse, at a distance, between Pak Yah and Haji Kadir is as remarkable for what it ignores as for what it includes. The material facts of the present situation—wage rates, the loss of fieldwork, actual loans and charity given and received—are conspicuous by their relative absence. Perhaps this is merely because they are taken for granted as common knowledge. What is emphasized, however, are the social facts, the quality of human relations. Thus Pak Yah,

16. *Tak berapa rajin.*
17. *Dia tak beringat sampai la.*

when he talks about the refusal to give loans, focuses not on the material loss but on the attitude of the rich who regard the poor as "despicable." Thus Haji Kadir, when he speaks of being importuned for loans, is less openly concerned with what it costs him and more concerned with what he sees as the moral lapses of those who ask for help. Just as in the stories of Razak and Haji Broom, there is a text here on what decent and seemly social relations should be.

What is also striking is the attempt in these opinions to "place" people both in terms of their actual economic situation and in terms of social reputation. Pak Yah derides the village leadership for willfully distorting the "facts" of poverty and affluence to serve their own purposes. Haji Kadir devotes a great deal of effort to showing how it is that many of the poor are responsible for their own poverty and to distinguishing real destitution from feigned destitution. Why this struggle over the "facts" should be such a central feature of the dialogue between rich and poor in Sedaka will become clearer as we proceed.

TWO SUBJECTIVE CLASS HISTORIES
OF THE GREEN REVOLUTION

At the core of the social experience of class is the growth of a distinctive and shared understanding of history—an understanding that sets one class apart from others. Taken collectively, these perspectives amount to a shared worldview embodying both standards of justice and their application to events past and present. One could, for example, capture a great deal of the worldview of different classes in France from an examination of their outlook on the major watersheds of French history: the revolutions of 1789 and 1848, the Paris Commune, the Popular Front, Vichy, and May 1968. In the tiny world of Sedaka, the shifts in production relations associated with double-cropping define such a historical watershed. What makes these shifts decisive for class relations is simply the fact that their impact has marked out winners and losers largely along class lines. As a set of historical experiences they have provided both the basis and the occasion for muted struggles between rich and poor.

Despite the painful setbacks the poor have suffered in the past few years, there is no question of a class war developing on the Muda Plain now or in the foreseeable future. The prospect is rather one of continuing class struggle, sporadic resistance, and the war of words we have already witnessed. There are several reasons why escalation is unlikely. First, it is undeniable that nearly half the village is better off than they were before double-cropping. Whatever their residual dissatisfactions and fears, they can be counted, by and large, as winners. Second, those who have seen their fortunes reversed are rarely at the brink of a crisis that would threaten their livelihood or subsistence. The options they face of belt tightening, temporary and permanent migration, a marginal subsistence in the village are surely painful but are nothing like the draconian choices faced by their counterparts in Indonesia or India. Third, the social structure of Sedaka and of other villages in Kedah is not one of dramatic and sharp contrasts between a small monopolistic landlord class on the one hand and a great mass of undifferentiated poor peasants on the other. This is not Morelos in 1910. The stratification of Sedaka, while not a seamless web from top to bottom, is diverse enough to militate against the creation of a solid phalanx of victims. The presence of bystanders and neutrals tempers what might otherwise be a sharper conflict. Finally, the local conflict that does exist is further tempered by the fact that virtually all paddy cultivators share certain interests (for example, Malay political domination and a high support price for paddy) despite their class antagonisms. All of these factors make for "ordinary" forms of class struggle rather than a conflagration.

I turn, with these qualifications in mind, to a brief social history of Sedaka's green revolution by class. I shall ask how each of the major changes in production relations has been experienced and interpreted by the rich and by the poor—by winners and losers. From these interpretations, which can be seen as two, class counterpoints to the economic facts presented in the previous chapter, it should be possible to construct a picture of village class relations.

DOUBLE-CROPPING AND DOUBLE VISION

There are by now scores of studies of the consequences of double-cropping in Muda, many of them quite sophisticated. Reflecting the interests of international donors and the Malaysian state, they are virtually all concerned with production, incomes, and growth. In their entirety, it might seem they offer a more or less exhaustive account of the consequences of the green revolution in Kedah.

We should scarcely be surprised, however, if the overall assessment of double-cropping held by the actual participants in this drama differs significantly in tone and content from the official account. After all, the participants have their own narrow and homely concerns. Nor should it surprise us if the vantage point of the well-to-do should diverge sharply from that of the poor. If one asks villagers about the impact of double-cropping, what emerges is a core zone of general agreement that gives way to a zone of dispute as well as a zone of differences in perspective. It is in these last two zones that class is decisive.

Virtually everyone agrees that double-cropping has brought with it some beneficial changes. They note the rebuilding and patching of houses, the fact that only two of the richest villagers had motorcycles before 1972 while many of the wealthier households now have them, that the roads and bus service now allow them to visit Alor Setar and nearby relatives. But the big news that completely overshadows these welcome conveniences is the simple fact that, for the first time in living memory, virtually everyone has enough rice to eat throughout the year. Even well-off villagers rarely fail to mention this, for they can remember crop failures when even their supply gave out. For the poor, of course, the basic fear that has always plagued the peasantry has been all but banished. It is the first thing that comes to their minds: "Even the poor can hold out now, they can eat" (Dullah); "There's enough rice" (Sukur); "The rice is never used up." (Wahid). Their subsequent complaints about recent hardships must be seen against the backdrop of this cardinal achievement. And yet, one may look in vain through piles of official reports to find any recognition of the single result of double-cropping that dominates all others so far as the peasants are concerned.

Beyond this narrow but important zone of consensus, evaluations diverge. Neither the rich nor the poor of Sedaka are uniformly enthusiastic about the changes double-cropping has brought about. Given the recent setbacks the poor have experienced, their complaints are to be expected. The complaints of the larger farmers, however, are curious, since they have been the principal beneficiaries of this highly touted scheme. At first one is tempted to refer their grumbling to a universal human (at any rate, peasant) perverseness that only grudgingly admits to good fortune, but the nature of their complaints betrays an unmistakeable class perspective. They are resentful, above all, that it is no longer possible to buy land. Thus Haji Kadir says that things were "better before" irrigation when "we could save money and buy land at only M$1,000 a relong." Kamil, who rents 15 relong, grumbles that he is no better off now than he was ten years ago and that land is now out of reach. What is involved here is not only a nostalgia for the days when land went for M$1,000 a relong but also for the days when poor smallholders were forced by debts (*jual janji*) to forfeit their land to creditors. This is, in fact, how Haji Kadir and others made their small fortunes. Kamil senses that this avenue of mobility is now closed to him.

This does not exhaust their complaints. They grumble about the high cost of living, the difficulty and expenses of getting fieldhands when they need them, and the fact that even they often need loans. In more reflective moods, prosperous villagers occasionally regret the loss of leisure and the entertainment they once enjoyed between the harvest and the next planting—a time when most of their poorer neighbors were off looking for work. Now they are busy all year round. They miss especially the small feasts, games, and Islamic chanting that had graced the off-season before 1972.[18] Seldom is this lament terribly acute, for no one would be willing to forego a second crop of rice in order to recover these cultural amenities.

18. The feast they most often mention is the *kenduri berendul,* literally "cradle feast," celebrated for recently born infants, which includes a ceremonial haircutting and, for girls, circumcision. During my stay this was celebrated only twice. The games they mentioned included *main gasing,* or competitions with spinning tops, and *bersilat,* the Malay/Indonesian act of self-defense, both of which are very rarely seen today. The Islamic chanting from the Koran includes *berdikir* and *berzanji,* which are still occasionally performed, often by groups that are paid a fee, at feasts in the village. All of these activities are described as *hiboran,* or "entertainment."

When it comes to the effects of double-cropping on their own economic situation, the comments of the substantial farmers in the village are oddly out of keeping with the narrow facts of the matter. All these families have benefited substantially, to judge from their incomes and possessions. And yet, many of them acknowledge no improvement; they say things are about the same as before. If pressed, they may admit to some slight easing: "I'm a bit better off"; "We don't have to scrimp so"; "We can just get enough to eat."[19] When it comes to what irrigation has done for the village poor, though, these men are far more expansive. To hear them tell it, the poor have done very well. One of them says, "Since the change in seasons, even coolies (that is, landless laborers) are using motorcyles." Another, complaining of the cost of labor, insists that wage workers have become so comfortable that they can afford to be choosy. They often claim that nowadays the poor are as comfortable (*senang*) as the rich were before double-cropping. In effect, they greatly underplay their own gains and at the same time overdramatize the new prosperity of the poor—a pattern that we shall see repeated.

For villagers in more precarious circumstances, matters are more straightforward. After acknowledging that their basic food supply is secure, they generally go on to emphasize how their prospects have worsened. As Hamzah notes, "I work nonstop, [but] there's not a chance of becoming comfortable." He and others in the same boat contrast the substantial gains of the well-off with their own difficulty in providing their families with necessities such as fish, clothing, and school expenses. While the rich complain that they have no leisure, the poor have the mirror-image complaint: that they have no work. They can and do recite in minute detail who hired them and how much they earned in the past, comparing that income with the current lack of work. For them, unlike the rich, the watershed is not the beginning of double-cropping but the entry of combine-harvesters. Their sense of time, the significant dates in their lives, are necessarily different, as is their experience. A majority of them, it is true, are almost certainly no worse off than they were prior to the irrigation scheme. But their point of reference is now the first four or five years of double-cropping (1972–76) when work was plentiful and wages high. It is from that point that they measure their current hardships and it is perhaps only in the context of these hardships that the early years of irrigation have become "the good old days."

At the core of this reversal of fortunes, in their view, is not simply the impersonal working out of technological change, but the elimination of human dependencies. Karim, whom Haji Kadir once cited as a rare example of the hard-working poor, captures the perspective of many poor villagers. Before, he

19. *Sudah tambah sikit; tak kena layang macham dulu; boleh makan saja. Layang* means "to slice thinly," hence "to scrimp."

explains, "those who were hard up depended on people who were well-off."[20] He mentions, as did Pak Yah, wages paid in advance as an example and tells me that they are no longer given and instead poor villagers have only the Chinese pawnshop as a creditor of last resort. "They [the landowners]," he continues, "don't need us any more; if we don't come to thresh paddy, they can just call the machine." Mansur, another landless villager, covers much the same ground as he deplores the evaporation of postharvest *zakat peribadi* he once received from cultivators for whom he threshed but who no longer need his help. The village poor, then, not only realize precisely what they have lost in wages, in work, and in gifts but are quite well aware that they are no longer an integral part of rice production at all.[21]

FROM LIVING RENTS TO DEAD RENTS

Fixed cash rents payable before planting were not unknown before double-cropping, but it was only with the expanding cash economy after 1971 that they became the rule rather than the exception. We encounter once again a nearly intractable zone of disagreement about the facts when it comes to determining how many tenants actually lost part or all of their farms when the switch to prepaid rents was made. Estimates range from a maximum of about ten to a minimum of three or four. The higher figure is closer to the village consensus while the lower figure finds support among a handful of wealthy villagers. There seems no way to decide the matter. Razak, for example, had rented 5 relong under the traditional arrangements from his older brother (an outsider) until 1972, when his brother announced that he was taking it back to give to his own son to cultivate. Razak claims that his brother used this as an excuse to kick him off the land and gives as evidence the fact that two seasons later his brother rented the land out again to a new tenant, with the rent to be paid in advance. The story is plausible, in part, because dismissing a tenant to give the land to one's own child is one of the few ways of displacing a tenant that is seen as legitimate. For precisely that reason, it is often viewed as a ploy used by landlords who wish to act discreetly. But it is impossible to be certain of the facts in this case or in many others, where the landlord claims that the tenant simply decided to give up the land. In any event, the "damage estimate" attributed to the shift to *sewa tunai* is extensive if one listens to most villagers and relatively paltry if one listens to a few of the wealthiest.

For those who rent out land on any appreciable scale, the advantages of *sewa tunai* are obvious. As the rent is no longer denominated in paddy equivalents,

20. *Orang susah-lah bergantung kapada orang senang.*

21. This is, of course, especially true of the pure wage laborers in Sedaka, but it is also true of the more numerous marginal smallholders and tenants who have traditionally relied on fieldwork wages for a larger share of their income.

the landlord's return is not hostage to farm-gate prices. Should the paddy price increase, the cash rent can simply be raised the following season; should it decrease, the tenant absorbs the loss. Prepaid rents, of course, arrive five or six months earlier under the new arrangement, giving the landlord the use of the capital for that much longer. Above all, *sewa tunai* avoids disputes and confrontations on the threshing floor in the case of crop damage or failure. It was never an easy matter to determine the cause of a harvest shortfall, whether it was due to the negligence of the cultivator, in which case no remission was granted, or whether it was due to weather or pests, in which case a remission was ordinarily negotiated. The size of the remission was also a source of acrimonious exchanges that often left both sides feeling shortchanged. Now the landlord need never even look at his fields or listen to the dubious pleas of his tenants after a bad season. Only one option is open to a dissatisfied tenant: giving up the tenancy.

Those who adopt a landlord's perspective are naturally delighted. Kamil, himself a large tenant, but whose rents are very modest (M$120 per relong, per season), notes that "cheating" was common under the older, *sewa padi* system.[22] The cheating might take the form of surreptitious harvesting at night before the official harvest began, spiriting away some of the grain at the actual harvest if supervision was lax, shoddy threshing so as to leave much paddy on the stalks to be gleaned and kept later, and above all spurious claims of crop damage to cover any or all of these subterfuges and thereby reduce the rent. Tenants, to be sure, walked a fine line in pursuing these strategies which, if pushed too far too often, might lead to their dismissal. Under *sewa tunai,* however, all of these ploys are simply irrelevant. Haji Salim, a very large landowner and entrepreneur who lives just outside the village, makes it clear that prepaid cash rents provide an element of labor discipline. "These people [tenants] are scoundrels," he says.[23] Before *sewa tunai,* he adds, they could cultivate carelessly and then ask for a reduction in rent, claiming that worms or caterpillars had damaged the paddy. Now, however, "If they give the money first, they have to look after the crop carefully, they can't just play around. They have to take it a bit more seriously."[24]

The disadvantages of *sewa tunai* for tenants are as palpable as the advantages for landlords. Those who know most poignantly about the disadvantages are, of course, those who actually lost their tenancy when the shift was imposed. Even for the majority who managed to raise the cash in time, the costs were considerable. They typically took loans on their wives' gold jewelry (given to most

22. *Masa sewa padi, penyewa boleh tipu, senang-lah!* Kamil is referring here to actual sharecropping, which has long since disappeared from the usual meaning of *sewa padi.*

23. *Orang ini jahat.* This phrase might also be translated as "These people are playing tricks."

24. *Kalu bagi duit dahulu, depa kena jaga kuat, tak boleh main-main saja, kena ambil berat sikit.*

women by their parents upon marriage) and paid 2 percent a month to the pawnshop in Yan until it was redeemed, hopefully, after the harvest. If the paddy crop was good, this proved a minor inconvenience; if the crop was poor, however, it became a financial crisis.[25] The jewelry might be forfeit, the husband might have to leave the village to find work elsewhere, or debts might simply accumulate. As *sewa tunai* has become more prevalent, it has also exerted a subtle but unmistakable influence on other forms of tenancy. Those lucky enough to have tenancies in which the rent is payable after the harvest and thus, in principle, is negotiable are increasingly reluctant to avail themselves of this privilege for fear that the landlord will retaliate by moving to prepaid rents.[26]

The key objection from the tenants' perspective is simply that the rent is fixed and bears no relation to the paddy yields of a particular season, that is, to the tenant's ability to pay. As they say, "You can't take it into account, you can't bargain, you can't compromise, you can't do anything."[27] This is not simply a statement of fact delivered in an impersonal way. The phrase most often heard in connection with *sewa tunai*—often enough to have become almost a slogan—is, "If the paddy is ruined, that's your [the tenant's] lookout."[28] It is spoken with gestures and facial expressions to imitate a callous landlord announcing the facts of life to his tenant. It implies, of course, that the state of the paddy—and therefore of his tenant—most definitely *ought* to concern any self-respecting landlord.

What is involved here, as most villagers see it, is thus a shift in rents that mirrors a portentous shift in the quality of class relations. The attitude of landlords when rents were adjustable was described as magnanimous (*senang kira*).[29] This term is the opposite of *berkira,* or "stingy" and "calculating," which is normally the most devastating charge made against the rich, as we have seen. To be *senang kira* is to inhabit a social world in which an amicable reciprocity prevails and in which no one is trying to take undue advantage of others. It is a value as much breached as observed but is no less powerful for that reason. The contrast between how things were and how they are is apparent from Amin's description. "Before they said, 'If the harvest is bad, [we'll] reduce [the rent] a

25. Wahid is an illustration: he rents 6 relong and would ordinarily be expected to fall in the middle range of village incomes despite his large family. For the past two seasons, however, he has had quite poor yields of nine or ten gunny sacks per relong and fairly high rents that are not negotiable. As a result his earnings have been minimal and he is openly debating giving up two of his three rented plots and working much of the year in Penang.

26. This holds true for many tenancies in which the landlord is a close relative as well.

27. *Tak boleh rundingkan, tak boleh tawar-menawar, tak boleh tolak ansur, tak boleh apa-apa.*

28. *Padi rosak, hang punya pasal.*

29. *Senang kira* might be translated literally as "easygoing about calculating."

bit.' " "Then you could bargain, there was compassion." "Now they only care about the money." "They say, 'If you don't like this price, I'll find someone else.' " "It's done quite openly."[30]

The social construction of *sewa tunai* by a few large landlords is that it puts an end to a system that allowed tenants to avoid the consequences of their own carelessness by cheating their well-meaning landlords. The social construction of *sewa tunai* on the part of most others is that it puts an end to an arrangement in which the landlord showed a due regard for the circumstances and needs of his tenants.[31]

COMBINE-HARVESTERS

Mesin makan kerja ("the machine eats work")

Several villagers

We have examined in some detail the consequences of combine-harvesting that are amenable to statistical analysis. Many of the "facts" of the matter—the loss of direct harvest work, the loss of gleaning, the extent of lost income, the strata that have been most directly touched—are established with some assurance. Here I turn to the social construction of these facts by the inhabitants of Sedaka. At the crudest level, there are at least two social histories of the entry of combine-harvesters: one propagated by winners and one propagated by losers. The winners and losers, in this case, are not tenants and landlords but rather large-scale cultivators (whether owners or tenants) on the one hand and smaller-scale cultivators together with landless laborers on the other. In between lies a strata of modest farmers whose gains and losses are roughly offsetting and whose view is therefore ambivalent.[32] Size of farm is, of course, a fairly reliable indicator of income in Sedaka, so that winners and losers correspond closely to the rich and

30. *La, depa kata, kalau tak boleh padi, potong sikit. Dulu, boleh tolak ansur, ada timbang rasa. La 'ni, kira duit saja, kata, hang tak mau ini harga, aku cari orang lain. Terang-terang.* Amin, in village terms, is a wealthy man, but he also rents in 7.5 relong and thus has a tenant's perspective on this issue.

31. Ships are once again passing in the night and the distance between them has much to do with class. There is, as always, a reconstruction of history being undertaken here. Under *sewa padi,* there were some landlords who did not allow reductions after a bad harvest. Karim can remember a landlord who found after a bad harvest that the rent (this time paid in kind) was short by four *gantags* (a trivial amount). He came to collect it anyway, claiming that it had "been promised." The point is that, for tenants anyway, the older system has taken on a rosier hue now that they confront *sewa tunai.*

32. To these must also be added a few (five) small farmers who use the machine because it frees them quickly for wage work elsewhere and/or because they have little or no household labor that would allow them either to exchange labor (*berderau*) or harvest their own crop themselves.

the poor. Their respective social histories of the combines are an integral part of class conflict as it is in fact waged in the *kampung*.

Certain social facts about combine-harvesters are so apparent and indisputable that they are acknowledged by all concerned. These facts make up something of a zone of consensus. At the core of this consensus is the fact that the poor, who depended on harvest labor, have been hurt and that the well-to-do have benefited. How great the hurt, how substantial the benefit—the magnitudes—is another matter altogether, but the overall impact is not in dispute. As Abu Hassan, who has a steady job with the Farmers' Association and farms 6 relong notes, "Since the machine came in, those peasants who work for wages have just sat around."[33] Tok Kasim, also fairly well-to-do himself, adds, "It's certain that the poor have lost." Most often when talking of machine harvesting, the well-to-do are less reticent about acknowledging the losses of the poor than their own gains. For poorer villagers, it is typically the combine-harvester that brings to their lips the saying, "The rich get richer and the poor get poorer." In the process they often make it clear that the machines bring the rich pleasure as well as profit. Hamzah, a landless laborer, makes it clear just where the dividing line between pleasure and pain fell and which side he is on: "The *friends* who work for wages couldn't get enough [work] but those who don't earn wages were *happy*."[34] Even in the joint recognition of social facts, there is thus a special twist to the remarks of the poor, who are likely to link their losses to the profits of others, their pain to the pleasure of others.

When it comes to how efficient and profitable the machines are, we enter a zone of claims and counterclaims that divide the rich and poor. The claims of the well-off are essentially a series of assertions about the advantages of machine harvesting over hand harvesting. The large farmers note, above all, the speed with which the combine gathers and bags the crop. They believe that their harvest per relong is increased by anywhere from one to two gunny sacks of paddy over hand harvesting, and they note the savings in labor and cash over having to haul rice from the field to a nearby bund. This last operation often costs as much as one or two dollars a sack, thereby raising the cost of production appreciably.[35] Large cultivators such as Haji Jaafar, the village headman, contin-

33. Abu Hassan is to some degree showing off his school learning here by using *petani* for peasants. The term, common in official talk and newspapers, is not frequently used by villagers, who are likely to call themselves "villagers" (*orang kampung*). The term for combine-harvester in everyday use is simply *mesin* or *mesin padi*.

34. *Kawan yang ambil upah, tak jenuh, orang yang tak ambil upah, seronok.*

35. If the field is very wet the sacks are often hauled on wooden sleds (*andur*) pulled by water buffalo. Otherwise they are carried on men's backs to the narrow bunds to be transferred to bicycles and then, on larger bunds, to motorcycles or lorries. Piece-wages vary according to the distance and mode of transport. If the charge per gunny sack is M$1.50, the total cost per relong for an average yield (twenty-four gunny sacks) will amount to roughly 15 percent of production costs and between 12 and 13 percent of net profit for a tenant paying normal rents.

ually calculate the monetary advantages of machine harvesting as compared with hiring labor. Not counting the elements of speed and reduced spoilage, they estimate that they save anywhere from M$18 to $30 a relong—depending on the season, the location of the field, the yield, and so forth—by hiring the combine.

Machine use has at least two additional advantages, one of which is mentioned frequently while the other is, significantly, never noted openly by the well-to-do. Large farmers are pleased to be relieved of the management and supervision problems involved in recruiting harvest labor. This not only includes arranging for a group of reapers and threshers at the right time, when others may want them too, but also overseeing the threshing to make certain that it is thorough and providing meals and snacks for the work force. Hiring the combine-harvester not only saves labor and expense; it also eliminates a task that is complicated and liable to come unstuck at any moment.[36] The wage laborers in Sedaka point out another factor that they claim motivates the large farmers to mechanize. Machines, Karim pointedly notes, do not ask for wages in advance nor do they expect to receive Islamic charity (zakat peribadi) over and above their wages. This is a point on which the well-to-do are silent—perhaps because it would reflect a callous attitude toward time-honored customs now being breached. In any event, it is clear that most large cultivators have moved with alacrity from a harvesting system that enmeshed them in a series of customary social ties and obligations to their poorer neighbors to one in which only a single, impersonal contract with a machine broker is necessary. Others, particularly those who have most to lose, contest some if not all of these advantages and cite other drawbacks of machine use. The fact most often contested is that yields are greater with the combine. A low-keyed dispute that once took place between Mat "halus," a landless laborer, and Ghazali, a tenant on 9 relong, is fairly representative of many other such discussions. Mat "halus" claimed that the combine-harvester often missed rows close to the bund and flattened the paddy at the point where it entered the field. Furthermore, he said, the machine often jams and spills paddy when it is turning or when its bin is full. As the inventor of gleaning behind the machine, Mat "halus" is something of an expert in this area. Ghazali politely disagrees; he says he gets at least an extra gunny sack when he uses the combine and that, in any case, his neighbor's son, who hand threshed for him last season, spilled much paddy from the tub and left a great deal of grain on the stalks.

In other ways as well, the poor attempt to prove that, apart from the ethics involved, the use of combine-harvesters is not in the self-interest of cultivators. They claim, with some justice, that the huge machines create deep ruts, par-

---

36. Thus, hand harvesting is often described by large cultivators as renyah (troublesome, intricate) as compared with the machine, which requires only a single transaction.

ticularly during the irrigated season harvest when the fields are wet, which are difficult to smooth out before planting again. They cite the destruction of bunds as the machines pass from one plot to another and the inconvenience of having to coordinate planting times in order to ensure that the combine will have a route through cleared fields to any parcel that is not beside an access road. Large farmers are, with few exceptions, unmoved by this litany of disadvantages; they have made their decision and are satisfied with the results.

The richer peasants in Sedaka would, however, be loath to admit that they had in effect taken away a major part of the livelihood of poorer villagers merely because the machine was more convenient and saved them a few dollars. To do so would be to announce openly that their own marginal private advantage was paramount and to disavow openly any responsibility for the welfare of the rest of their community. Having acknowledged, as virtually all have, that the combine-harvester has meant economic hardship for the poor, the larger farmers are at pains to present a description of their behavior that justifies it in terms that their neighbors can understand if not accept. They endeavor to do this by asserting that there is a labor shortage and they have no choice but to use the combine-harvester if they are to harvest their paddy in good time. This is their second and more substantial line of social defense; practicality gives way to necessity. It is, as we shall see, a line of defense that is under constant sniper fire from the poor but is in no danger of being abandoned.

The concept of a labor shortage is tricky. At one level it simply means that some people are paying more for labor than they would like to pay. If labor were more abundant, its wage would decline. At another level—a more objective level—it could certainly be claimed that a labor shortage existed if paddy rotted in the fields for want of harvest workers. Not even the rich make this claim, for even before the combines came to the Muda region, but after double-cropping, the paddy crop was successfully gotten in. Their assertion instead is the more modest but no less insistent one that labor is short, hence too expensive, and that their crops are endangered if they rely on fieldhands. Thus Haji Jaafar, the village headman, and his brother Lazim, who farms 13.5 relong, explain that before combine-harvesting the village poor would often leave to thresh paddy elsewhere if the wages were higher than in Sedaka. The ripe paddy, they claim, was harvested late and was lighter than it should have been, thereby reducing the price it would fetch. "The cultivator lost," Lazim adds. Tok Kasim echoes these sentiments. He claims that at the last minute he would be short of both reapers and threshers, who did not show up, and would have to raise wages to recruit extra hands. Even then, he says, his crop was late. Mat Isa, a tenant on 5 relong who hires the combine, says he would prefer to hire workers from the *kampung* but he has no choice. He is especially concerned abut the irrigated season harvest, which will sprout (*padi tumbuh*) if not threshed promptly, and recalls that two seasons ago some of his paddy was ruined in this way. The government drying mill would only give him half price for it. He admits that villagers have lost work to the machine but adds that, if it were not for the combines, laborers would relax and not work fulltime because their earnings would be so high.

The facts of the matter are of less concern here than the argument that larger farmers are making on their own behalf. Like any public explanation of class behavior, it has a certain plausibility. Labor was tight in Muda at the peak harvest season even before double-cropping. Migrant labor from Thailand and Kelantan regularly supplemented the local work force. With irrigation, wages did initially rise nearly twofold, but between 1972 and 1974 the real wages of harvest workers actually declined.[37] And there is no evidence that crop damage due to labor shortages was a serious problem from 1972 until combines became available.[38] What the large-scale users of combines wish to assert is that their hands are tied, that if they do not hire machines they will lose part or all of their crop. Once accepted, this assertion justifies their behavior, for no one in Sedaka would blame a farmer for using combines if that was the only way to save his crop.

Those who depend heavily on field labor for their income see little merit in this claim. Rokiah, who works regularly as a transplanter and a reaper, says, "If they didn't want to hire the machine they could hire villagers; there are enough looking for work." Another woman, Rosni, a widow widely admired for her hard work, believes that those who hire the combine are "only interested in speed," implying, as do others, that large farmers are willing to sacrifice the welfare of the village poor for the sake of cutting their paddy two or three days early. It is clear to the wage workers in the village that the rich use the combine out of a desire for convenience and speed, not out of necessity.

If we scratch a bit deeper we find that, as the rich see it, the labor shortage in Sedaka is not just an impersonal statistic of too much work and not enough hands to do it. Instead, it is a question of whether the poor actually want to work. Haji Salim (three wives, tractor, lorry, and many relong of paddy fields) is a typical representative of this view. After conceding that "the poor just barely manage," that "they have no luxuries,"[39] he hastens to add that they will not do the work. "They're sluggards;[40] they don't want to work; they're well-off [so]

37. Clive Bell, Peter Hazell, and Roger Slade, *The Evaluation of Projects in Regional Perspective: A Case Study of the Muda Irrigation Project* (Baltimore: Johns Hopkins Univ. Press, forthcoming), chap. 2.

38. It is quite possible that some farmers did occasionally experience losses due to delays in harvesting the off-season crop. What is missing, however, is any indication that agricultural authorities thought this was a serious problem between 1972 and 1977. On the other hand, it is certainly plausible that, now that migration from Thailand has been sharply curtailed, a withdrawal of combine-harvesters would, today, result in serious crop losses.

39. *Orang susah bertahan saja, mewah tak ada.*

40. *Penyegan pun.*

they won't [work]." "Some of them didn't even have a broken-down bicycle in the old days; now they have a motorcycle."[41] Fadzil, an UMNO leader with 8.5 relong, shares this view. "Villagers don't come for work, they say they have a fever, that it's raining, [but] they're lazy, they go to eat cake in the coffee shops or quit early to go to the market for fish." "That's how our paddy is ruined." "They are more or less lazy; they have 2 or 3 relong themselves and don't much want to work." "But the machine is certain and fast." When this perspective is added to the assertion of a labor shortage, the combine users appear to be without blame altogether. They are not simply increasing their profits but are saving their paddy crops, which are threatened by the shiftlessness of local workers. No Victorian entrepreneur could have wished for a more satisfactory exoneration of his own behavior.

This outlook, it is worth noting, receives ample support and encouragement from the ranks of officialdom. Abdul Majid, the subdistrict chief (penghulu), claims that villagers do not want to work. "People say they are arrogant, they decline,[42] they won't even show up unless the wages are high." "If the wages are high, then only do they want [to work]." "Villagers are difficult."[43] The only difference between his view and that of Fadzil or Haji Salim is that he talks, from his exalted post, more globally of villagers in general (orang kampung), failing to make any distinctions. He concludes by comparing these intractable villagers with the combine-harvester, which he says is "fast, cheap, and doesn't have to be fed." At the annual meeting of the Farmers' Association membership from Sedaka and adjacent Sungai Tongkang—comprised almost exclusively of prosperous farmers—much the same sentiments were expressed. They were put bluntly and publicly by Ismail Arshad, the UMNO member of Parliament for this constituency and a member of a princely Kedah family. "People don't want to work for wages as they once did." "They work only in the morning and then pull out and go back home."[44] Basir, Sedaka's UMNO leader, concurs heartily. "People like that are hard to keep watch on; they climb up coconut trees [to escape work]; you can't believe them." The officials and their well-off supporters

41. *Setengah-setengah tak ada gerek buruk pun masa dulu, la' ni ada moto.* Haji Salim, it should be added, has some special reasons for defending himself. During the main season of 1979 he went to the central office of the Muda Scheme to request permission to import Thai transplanters, claiming he could not find help locally. More than a dozen Thai planters were brought, for which he is roundly criticized by the village poor, who believe that he simply wanted to find cheaper labor than he could get nearby and to have all his land planted simultanously so that it could later be harvested in a single combine pass.

42. *Orang kata sombong, tarik diri.*

43. *Orang kampung payah. Payah* might also be translated as "troublesome" or "fussy." Small children who are demanding and exasperating to their parents are typically described as *payah.*

44. *Kerja pagi saja, cabut, balek rumah.*

see eye-to-eye on this issue: on the one hand, there are wage workers who are, or have become, lazy, truculent, and untrustworthy; on the other hand, there is the perfect worker, a combine-harvester, which is economical, reliable, and fast.

The well-to-do in Sedaka, while granting the loss of wage work, are unlikely to dramatize the damage. As Hamid notes, there are not many in the *kampung* who depend on wages alone for their income. It is hardly surprising that those who have borne the brunt of mechanization should speak with less equanimity. When they recount the precipitous decline in their earnings over the past three years, a frantic tone is apt to enter their assessment. Rokiah speaks for most of them when she says, "People can't make any money if the machine comes and takes it all." "The rich get more profit and the poor lose." "You can't even lay your hands on ten cents." "It's no use looking for work; now there's nothing at all."[45] Hamzah puts the matter more succinctly: "We are being ruined." Mat "halus" rounds out this apocalyptic view: "[Since] the machine came in, what are the Malays going to eat?" "The machine can now take it all." It is not, of course, a question of starvation, as Mat "halus" 's rhetoric implies. It is instead a choice between a life of permanent penury in the village or the alternative, for the young, of permanent or semipermanent migration. The growing tendency for large farmers to broadcast some or all of their fields, thus eliminating transplanting, only serves to make the sense of foreboding that much more palpable.[46]

Just as substantial farmers see the "labor shortage" as a human problem rather than as a statistic, the poor see the introduction of combine-harvesters as a human problem rather than as machinery. If the rich think the poor are largely to blame for labor problems, the poor think the rich are largely to blame for mechanization. On the face of it, others might plausibly be held responsible for the combines: for example, the government, which has encouraged their use, and the syndicates of largely Chinese businessmen, who purchase and deploy them. The overwhelming consensus among the village poor, however, is that the cultivators who hire them are to blame. When I asked if MADA was at fault, Mat "halus" promply replied, "Not the government but *kampung* people; it is they who call and use the machines." "If they refused to use them, the machines wouldn't have come." "How could they even pay for the gas?" "It's as

45. "It's no use looking for work" is a translation of *Tak payah cari makan*, literally, "It's no use looking to eat." *Cari makan* is the universal phrase in Malay for "making a living" and thus covers both work and the goods, particularly food goods, which that work makes it possible to buy.

46. The social construction of broadcasting (*tabur kering*) follows much the same pattern by class as the dialogue about combines. Whether yields are higher or lower with broadcasting than with hand transplanting is a subject of constant discussion and dispute, with most of the large cultivators favoring it and most of the wage workers and small farmers opposing it. For many of the village poor it is the coup de grace to their livelihood; as Rokiah says, "If they braodcast, that will kill us (*mampus*)."

if the machines were asking for alms and we gave [them alms]." When Rokiah talks about the inroads the combine has made into her reaping wages, she says that people in Sedaka "had no compassion"[47] when they chose to use the combine. Comments along similar lines are frequently heard; thus, when Karim supposes that the rich prefer the combines because they thereby avoid paying advance wages and *zakat* to workers, he concludes, "Rich people don't bother themselves [about us]."[48] The calculus of blame, on this issue as on most others, finds a target quite close to home. It is not, I suspect, that poor villagers hold either the government or the syndicates blameless for their suffering. It is rather that large cultivators are, after all, within moral reach; they are a part of the community and therefore *ought* not to be indifferent to the consequences of their acts for their neighbors.

Much of the same calculus appears to be at work in the praise given to those cultivators who continued to hire local labor even after the combines became available. Altogether there are seven or eight farmers who are often singled out as examples of "compassion," as "good people."[49] The effect of this praise is to turn these men into positive symbolic examples, just as Haji Broom and Razak were used as negative examples. What is being said here is that, *if* other cultivators had due consideration for their fellow villagers, they would behave in the same way.

This modest propaganda offensive seems to have had little impact on the sensibilities of the rich unless, of course, one reads a certain defensiveness into their elaborate justification of combine-harvesting. The one exception is Tok Kasim, who is clearly at pains to justify his work as a combine broker—as someone who lines up a local harvesting schedule for his Chinese employer in return for a fee of M$5 per relong.[50] He is, in effect, the agent for the combine owner and is well aware of the contempt in which some of his poorer neighbors

---

47. *Tak ada timbang rasa.*

48. *Orang kaya tak ingat.* This might also be translated more literally as "Rich people don't remember (give a thought to) such matters."

49. Among them are Tajuddin, Bakri bin Haji Wahab, his brother Dzulkifli bin Haji Wahab, Tok Mahmud, Samat, Lebai Pendek, Abdul Rahman, Basir, and Kamil. Aside from Basir, whose political role might impel him to hire more labor than he might otherwise wish, there is nothing that distinguishes these cultivators from their neighbors except, perhaps, public-spiritedness. Even this list is somewhat controversial, since some suggest that X or Y actually employ villagers because their land is too waterlogged, etc., to take the machine.

50. As with tractors, combine brokers (*berokar*) are always Malays living in the village who then become personally responsible for seeing that the fees are paid to him. Any shortfall comes from his pocket. In this way, the machine owners make use of mutual obligations between Malays of the same village. It would be tempting to cheat the machine owner of his fee, but to cheat one's neighbor is another matter. Daud, the son of Haji Jaafar, is also a combine and tractor broker.

hold him. "They say I'm wrong,"[51] he declares, "but the landowner orders me to summon the machine." "If I didn't do it, someone else would." "I have to make a living too."[52] Tok Kasim is clearly squirming here; he simultaneously holds that he is "just following orders" and that someone has to do the job (why not he?). The signs of embarrassment seem obvious.[53]

There is in the village as a whole, but especially among the poor, a strong sense that the natural order of village economic relations has been turned topsy-turvy by combine-harvesting. The direction of wages has been reversed; they traditionally moved, as one might expect, from the rich to the poor. Now, lo and behold, they move in the opposite direction, for cultivators pay wages to tractor and combine owners who are far richer than themselves. Amin's comments capture the paradox:

> In the old days you had to seek the poor and pay them wages. Nowadays, you have to seek the rich and pay *them* wages. Before the Chinese [who owned or rented land] hired us; now we hire the Chinese. Even Pak Yah has to pay wages to rich people. Poor people go back home and sit quietly.

Agan and again the phrases, "Now the rich earn wages," or "Now the poor hire the rich" are repeated in wonderment, reflecting the irony of a situation that seems fundamentally out of joint. For the rich of the village, it is a noteworthy curiosity; for the poor, however, it is a bitter irony—work and income to which they were traditionally entitled now go to wealthy businessmen. Wage earners in Sedaka are pointing not to one but two ironies which, taken together, amount to an argument of sorts. The first is that it is now a "*machine* that takes all the money." The second is that the "money now leaves the village" and, in fact, the country (they mention Hong Kong, Japan, Australia) and is lost forever from the village sphere of circulation. The implication is that the hiring of fellow villagers should take priority over the hiring of outsiders—let alone machines—because the money remains a part of the local ritual cycle of religious feasts that benefit all.

A brief episode in local agricultural history perhaps best captures the relationship between the poor and combine-harvesting. During the off-season har-

---

51. *Karut.*

52. *Kita cari makan juga,* or, in its more common form, *sama-sama cari makan* (We all have to make a living) is the standard defense used to justify employment that others might imagine to be socially harmful.

53. Some villagers claim that another form of "squirming" is reflected in the fairly common practice of selling paddy in the field (*jual pokok padi*). In this way the landowner escapes censure by transferring the crop, prior to harvest, to someone else, often a machine owner. This, if true, has many parallels with the *tebasan* system in Java, where the object is not to avoid censure for use of combines but to avoid censure for hiring outsiders who harvest with sickles. In any event, there are a multitude of other reasons why a cultivator might wish to sell his standing crop.

1. The Muda Plain viewed from Gunung Jerai (Kedah Peak). Dark lines indicate linear villages. To left are Straits of Malacca.

2. Village path. Houses to left and right are obscured by foliage.

3. Paddy fields awaiting transplanting north of village. Gunung Jerai in background. Courtesy of Ray Friedman.

4. Transplanting group (*Kumpulan Share*) on break. Note newly transplanted plot rear left. Courtesy of Ray Friedman.

5. Hand threshing on small plot following irrigated season.

6. The combine-harvester. Workers are sewing shut the gunny sacks filled with harvested paddy.

7. Communal work group repairing village hall—at rear. The entire crew is composed of members of the ruling party, UMNO.

8. Brand-new outhouse constructed with grant from Village Improvement Scheme.

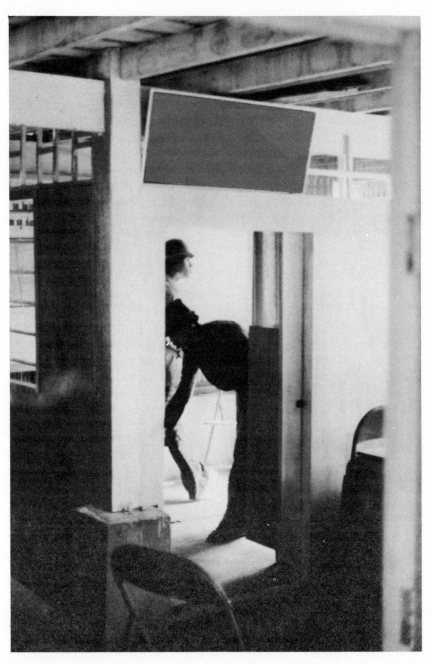

9. "Operations room" for Village Improvement Scheme in village hall.

10. House of well-to-do local farmer. Note clapboards, shutters, zinc roof, and veranda.

11. House of poor farmer. Courtesy of Ray Friedman.

12. Kitchen of poor household. Cooking is done on fire built on table, which is covered with sand for insulation. Courtesy of Ray Friedman.

13. Men of village beside *surau*/village hall after prayers marking the end of the fasting month.

14. House-moving crew to be thanked later with a meal prepared by owners.

15. Hauling paddy by Honda 70 to the main road. Courtesy of Ray Friedman.

16. A local Haji dressed for a visit to town. Courtesy of Ray Friedman.

17. Villager with his water buffalo preparing to haul sacks of threshed paddy on the *andur* (sled) at rear. Courtesy of Ray Friedman.

vest of 1979, which was both late and quite wet, word reached the village that a combine had become stuck in the paddy-field clay near Sungai Kering, some four miles to the south. Immediately, since the afternoon work was over, eight or ten villagers on bicycles and motorcycles went off to have a look. They returned an hour or so later to report that it was indeed stuck and that its operator's efforts to drive it out had only mired it more firmly. Beginning the following day—and for the next week and a half—the crowd of onlookers from Sedaka and surrounding villages grew. Within a few days the combine in Sungai Kering had become something of a pilgrimage site. All efforts to extract it had failed and each day a new strategy was tried—winches, tow trucks, cables attached to dump trucks fully loaded for extra traction, bulldozers—to no avail. Two owners from the syndicate were in daily attendance, visibly worried and angry, shouting and gesticulating to their workers as each new scheme was implemented and failed. Their spirits were not buoyed by the growing crowds, who were openly rooting against the combine and its owners and in favor of the gradually en-croaching Kedah mud. In fact, after a week, the line of sight from a hundred yards across the paddy fields offered only a view of the cab; time was definitely on the side of the Kedah mud. Meanwhile, local laborers were cutting and threshing around the stricken combine, now covered with mud and looking for all the world like the site of an archeological excavation.

Never in the course of my fieldwork had I seen a happier, more self-satisfied crowd.[54] The mood was definitely more and more festive as it appeared likely that the combine might actually be swallowed up. Talk centered on speculation about the fabulous sums that were daily being lost by the owners as the harvest proceeded and on the possibility that year-round flooding of the fields since 1972 and repeated machine use might make such events commonplace. At last the owners, despairing of other solutions, hired a gang of coolies who literally dug around the combine, creating a gentle ramp ahead of it, permitting it to be towed out.[55] The impromptu pilgrimage and festival abruptly ended, but it had provided a brief interlude of poetic justice.

What should also not be overlooked here is the way in which combine-harvesting has brought large cultivators and wage laborers into a more directly

54. One possible exception was the scene of another misfortune, when a local police officer from the station in Kepala Batas wrecked his new Volvo (purchased under a special car-loan plan for civil servants) after colliding with a lorry that had turned in front of him to deliver goods to a shop. The officer, a fairly new recruit, was infamous for extracting bribes from motorcyclists living nearby. Most motorcycle owners are in systematic contravention of the law, as they have not paid the necessary road tax or insurance fees to the state. They are thus easy game.

55. I was not there when the combine was finally freed, but it was widely believed that the combine owners had, in desperation, finally hired a Malay *bomoh* (specialist in traditional medicine and curing rituals), whose incantations were mainly respon-sible for releasing it from the clay.

antagonistic relationship. Any setback to the process of mechanization is a setback to big farmers and, at the same time, a boon to those who seek fieldwork. This is particularly noticeable during the irrigated season harvest period. In the past, a good crop for larger farmers was also a gain for fieldworkers; it meant more work and more pay. Now, however, a bad season for large farmers is a direct gain for wage laborers. The more paddy that has been lodged (*rebah*) by wind and rain, the deeper the water level in the fields, the less scope there is for combine-harvesting, leaving that much more employment for the poor. Due entirely to the combines, the poor thus find themselves for the first time actually looking forward to the kind of crop damage and flooding that serves their interests. Even the weather has become something of a class issue.

LOSING GROUND: ACCESS TO PADDY LAND

The proposition that it is becoming harder and harder to find paddy land to rent in is universally accepted in Sedaka and just as universally deplored. Old villagers can still recall when the father of Ghani Lebai Mat and a few others bought land in 20- and 30-relong lots from Tengku Jiwa for a nominal sum. Middle-aged peasants can recall a time, not long ago, when no one in the village was without land to farm, whether as a tenant or an owner. "Then," Abdul Rahman adds, "rents were figured with compassion,[56] the land was cheap, and there was a lot of it; a rich man couldn't farm more than 20 relong at most by himself." This phenomenon of "the good old days" is, of course, socially created for the explicit purpose of comparison with the current situation. "Now," says Abdul Rahman, completing the contrast, "one man can farm 50 or even 100 relong himself; he keeps all the money and he keeps all the rice." Tok Mahmud's comparison is different but complementary: "Now there are more people, rents are high, and landlords are using leasehold tenancy" (*pajak*). The two causes most often often cited for today's state of affairs (omitting population and *sewa tunai*) are, in ascending order of importance, the resumption of cultivation by large landowners and the growth of long-lease *pajak* rentals.

These are not issues on which there is much dispute within Sedaka.[57] After all, there is no landlord class worthy of the name in Sedaka. Most of the land rented out by villagers is to children or grandchildren on concessionary terms and in small parcels. The remainder is either inherited land that is too far away to farm conveniently or land that is leased out due only to the temporary financial embarrassment of the owner. Thus the widespread resentment over the shortage

56. *Senang berkira.*

57. There are, however, other villages such as Mengkuang, immediately to the south, in which there are substantial landlords residing in the village and either farming themselves or renting out *pajak,* large parcels of land. Here, some of the conflict to be described shortly would be internalized.

of paddy land available on reasonable terms is directed almost exclusively at the class of large landlords who live outside Sedaka. There is, however, a marked difference in the passion and intensity with which this issue is raised by villagers—a difference that depends very much on class. For the dozen or so well-to-do farmers who own and/or farm more than, say, 8 relong, the issue is not momentous. If they could rent in more land, some of them would welcome the opportunity, but it is not a matter of pressing concern. For the rest of the villagers, and particularly for the landless or nearly landless, by contrast, the issue is highly charged, inasmuch as it bears on whether or not they have a future at all in Sedaka.

A common way in which land is lost to poorer cultivators is when a landlord decides to resume cultivation in his own right, dismissing his tenants. Spurred by the profits of double-cropping and the ease of hiring the combine, many of Kedah's biggest landlords have taken back land once farmed by small tenants.[58] Haji Ani, the son of Haji Broom, has done precisely this with more than 100 relong in nearby Mengkuang. Another big landowner in Mengkuang, from a princely family living in Penang, has resumed cultivation of over 50 relong by employing a Chinese manager. Shamsul and Tok Ahmad in Sedaka were threatened with dispossession by their landlord, Haji Din, who claimed he wanted to farm the land himself or have his son farm it. By complaining at the district office they were able, luckily, to negotiate a compromise by which Haji Din resumed cultivating only half the land for the time being.[59] Landlords who take back large blocks of land in this fashion are generally hated for their avarice. Thus Tok Ahmad condemns Haji Din: "He doesn't care whether we eat or not; he wants to eat us up."[60] No such opprobrium attaches to petty landlords who

58. Wahid and others claim that the increasing resort to selling crops in the field (*jual pokok padi*) is a modified version of the same practice. In this case a landowner prepares the field, plants the crops, and then sells the standing crop to an entrepreneur, often a Chinese combine owner. The planter gets back his money quickly and avoids much of the risk associated with the harvest. This practice, common in Mengkuang, is somewhere between full cultivation and rental, but in any case the small tenant is excluded.

59. This was made possible by the fact that, unlike most tenancies, this one was of long duration and was actually registered under the Padi Act of 1955. This act regulates rents and dismissals, although most rents, even under registered tenancy, are well above the maximum provided for in the statute. The law allows for resumption of use of such plots by the landlord, but if a complaint is made the local land officer (usually the Assistant District Officer) is likely to seek a compromise or a delay. Such a delay, for example, explains why the aristocratic family mentioned above has resumed cultivation of only 50 relong of the more than 100 relong it owns in Mengkuang.

60. The supple use of the verb "to eat" (*makan*) here in the sense of consuming food and in the sense of exploitation is notable. *Boleh makan, tak makan, dia tak kira. Dia mau makan kita.*

resume cultivation, for it is understood that they too may be needy and will have to provide for their children's livelihood. The logic is rather that those who have more than enough for their own needs ought to rent the surplus to those who are poorer. If they refuse, they are called hard-hearted (*keras hati*) or greedy (*tamak, haloba*).

High rents and the resumption of cultivation by large landowners, while they excite much concern, are completely overshadowed by what appears to be a menacing trend to leasehold tenancy (*pajak*). Unlike traditional *pajak* arrangements under which smallholders in need of cash rented their small plots over several seasons for rents that worked out to be quite modest, the newer leaseholds involve larger plots and premium rents. Villagers keep their ears close to the ground and each reported leasehold rent in the area is typically the basis of morbid speculation. Thus a recent report that Mat Buyong's son in Sungai Tongkang had rented 3.5 relong for three seasons for a sum of M$2,000 was deplorable news, for the rent comes to more than M$190 per relong, per season. Most villagers thought that Mat Buyong's son was "daring to take on"[61] a lease at this price—that it would be a losing proposition.

It is not simply a question of the calculated rent that stirs such consternation, but the lump-sum capital that *pajak* requires. Nizam's landlord, Haji Zahir, who as we have seen extracted premium rents on a seasonal basis, announced in early 1979 that he wanted to switch to *pajak* for two seasons. Although the rent was no higher, it required Nizam to raise over M$1,000 immediately, which he managed to do only by scrambling to raise loans from his father and the pawnshop. Had he failed to raise the capital, the land would have passed to someone else. As Nizam says, "He wants to exploit us; he wants to take it all."[62] Others have not been this fortunate. Samad and Fadzil have each lost tenanted land when they were unable to come up with the capital for a longer lease on which the landowner insisted. In each case a wealthy villager, Ghani Lebai Mat, took the tenancy. Their anger is not so much directed at Ghani Lebai Mat as at the two outside landlords who would not compromise on the length or price of the lease. For young farmers seeking land, the *pajak* system is a formidable barrier. Mat Nasir, Rokiah's recently married son, for example, has been actively looking for a tenancy the past three years. Recently he heard of a possible leasehold on 4 relong for four seasons. The total cost was M$2,400 which, although it worked out to a modest rent of M$150 per relong, per season, was far beyond what Mat Nasir could raise. Despite the fact that the landlord was his wife's relation and might be expected to prefer him as a tenant, it was futile to pursue it without capital. As he bitterly observed, "Now they think only of their stomach first. Relatives are pushed aside."[63]

If the poorer villagers have most to lose in the move to *pajak* tenancy, the

61. *Berani ambil.*
62. *Dia mau tekan; dia mau makan semua.*
63. *Sekarang ini, depa mau perut dulu, adek-beradek tolak tepi.*

well-to-do are no less concerned. Their worries are reflected in their reaction to the most widely discussed leasehold contract struck during my stay in Sedaka. This contract was made between a very wealthy Malay landowner from Mengkuang, Haji Hassan (a grandson of Haji Broom), and his new tenant, the wealthiest Chinese shopkeeper in Kepala Batas, nicknamed *Cina Cerut*.[64] Fifty relong, an enormous expanse, was rented for eight seasons in return for a lump sum of M$88,000. The per relong, per season rent was itself unprecedented (M$220), but what was staggering was the fabulous sum involved—a sum well beyond the reach of even the wealthiest Malay landowners in the district. Together with stories of other large leasehold deals between very rich Malay landowners and Chinese tenants, most of whom were part-owners of combine syndicates, this episode created a sense of despair among rich villagers. While they might aspire to raising the capital for much smaller leaseholds, rents of anything like this magnitude (both in terms of the per relong cost *and* the capital required) would henceforth, they surmised, be monopolized by rich Chinese with their own machinery.[65] With these "auction" (*lelong*) rents, as Haji Nayan calls them, "Only the very rich can take [the land]; they [landowners] don't care about race, many [of the tenants] are Chinese." Rich and poor alike, then, have ample reason to worry about *pajak,* though their worries are not the same. For the rich, it means that an avenue of further accumulation is being choked off; for the poor—especially the tenants—it represents a threat to their precarious livelihood.[66]

The practice of leasehold tenancy reproduces in another form the topsy-turvy

64. So nicknamed because he always has a cigar (*cheroot*) stuck in his mouth.

65. At a rent of M$220 per relong, and ignoring the interest on the lump sum if it were borrowed, the net cash return would be only M$71 per relong, assuming an average yield of fourteen gunny sacks. Only someone with capital who is able to spread his risks across, say, 100 relong would be willing to accept such a small profit margin. If, on the other hand, one has access to tractors and combines at minimal cost (maintenance, fuel, and depreciation) the profits per relong are substantially higher. Although a good many wealthy Malays own tractors, only a handful in Kedah are members of a combine syndicate. Mechanization has thus had the double impact of raising the break-even rent for large tenants *and* increasing the optimum farm size.

66. Poor and modest peasants in the village who are leasehold tenants frequently complain bitterly about the practice of tacking on additional years at the whim of the landowner. A lease will be three or four seasons from expiration when the landowner suddenly shows up and announces that he wants rent for another so many seasons immediately. There follows a rush by the tenant to raise the required cash for fear of losing the land when the current contract runs out. When such sudden demands are condemned, it is usually in terms of the wealth of the landlord who, it is implied, has no business making such demands on tenants who are poorer than he. Thus Rokiah, who leases land from her younger brother (an outsider), who often comes to ask to extend the contract, notes that he has rubber land, a car, and three wives and denounces him as "very stingy" (*sangat berkira*).

social relations associated with the combine-harvester. Before, wealthy landlords rented to tenants who were poorer than themselves and that relationship was reflected in the traditional social ideology of tenancy. Now, however, landlords rent to a new breed of tenants who are as rich and, in many cases, richer than themselves. Few poor villagers fail to note with bitter irony that, today, harvesting and increasingly tenancy is becoming the preserve of the rich, not the poor. Sukur, a landless laborer speaks for most: "Before they rented land to the poor. Now you can't rent land at all. The rich rent to the rich and the poor live off (*tumpang*) the poor."

Who should be blamed for leasehold tenancy? The answer is not obvious. One might hold the Chinese responsible, as they are commonly seen as the successful bidders. One might hold the Malay landlords responsible. Or perhaps one might even hold the state responsible for allowing *pajak* tenancy.[67] In fact, the bitterest resentment is reserved for the Malay landlords, whose desire for the greatest profit has led them to ignore the needs of their relatives, their fellow villagers, and their race. When I occasionally asked directly who was to "blame" (*salah*) for a particular leasehold tenancy, the landlord or the (Chinese) tenant, I nearly always got the same answer. For example:

The landowner is to blame; he won't give [the land] to Malay people. (Rokiah)

The landowner, he wants only the money and he auctions the land, saying, "Who will bid most?" (Lazim)

They [landlords] won't rent land to their own race. (Razak)

Taib, one of the poorest men in the village, has discovered that his younger sister, who lives nearby and owns 1 relong, has leased it for ten seasons (M$500) to a Chinese shopkeeper. Mustapha, a young man looking to rent in land, is in the same boat; his mother has rented, *pajak,* her 2 relong for eight seasons to a Chinese tractor owner. While neither of them have any affection for the Chinese who have taken land which they would like to rent themselves, they are most dismayed by the failure of their own immediate family to consider their interests. As Mustapha says with an air of helplessness, "I can't even work my mother's land."

We have encountered this "logic of accusation" before in the view of combine-harvesters. It is not the strangers, the outsiders, who are most often singled out for censure. After all, they are beyond the moral reach of the community; they can only be expected to take advantage of opportunities that come their way. Relatives, fellow villagers, Malays, on the other hand, are seen as members of

67. One reason why the state might be held responsible is that the Paddy Act of 1967 in effect prohibits leasehold tenancy by limiting tenancy agreements to one year.

a community, who have obligations to one another beyond immediate material interests. Thus, it is possible to appeal to their sense of responsibility. Mat Nasir, for example, could say that he had appealed (*rayu*) to his relative to rent to him by the season rather than to lease land to a stranger. When that relative ignored his appeal, it was entirely appropriate that he should feel a sense of betrayal. Appeal and betrayal are concepts that are, quite simply, inapplicable beyond the frontiers of an imagined community. It makes no sense to appeal to a Chinese combine owner to forgo his profits to save Malay jobs or to feel betrayed when he pays no heed. For the large Malay landowner who hires the combine or leases out his land to a Chinese shopkeeper, however, matters are different. Something more can be expected from him; he is seen to have obligations to friends, neighbors, and relatives that can be betrayed. It is largely for this reason that many of the changes associated with the green revolution in Kedah have had a more profound impact on class relations among Malays than on relations between races.

RITUALS OF COMPASSION AND SOCIAL CONTROL

In Sedaka, as in any peasant society, there is a large variety of ritual ties that lie beyond immediate relations of production and serve both to create and to signify the existence of a community—one that is more than just an aggregation of producers. The particular ritual ties that involve gifts and exchanges between rich and poor are sensitive barometers of the vicissitudes of class relations. While they are not, by any means, connected to production relations in some crude mechanical fashion, they are nonetheless sensitive to changes in the realm of production. Using these gifts and exchanges as a valuable window on the transformation of class relations, it will become apparent that, as the poor have become increasingly marginal to the growing of paddy, so have they become increasingly marginal to the ritual life of the village. There have traditionally been three major forms of ritual gift giving joining the rich and poor in Sedaka. They include what villagers call the *zakat peribadi*, or "private" Muslim tithe, *sedekah*, or *derma* gifts, and *kenduri*, or ritual feasts to which other villagers are invited. All are either required or at least sanctioned by Muslim law as it is understood in the village. After a brief explanation of each form, I will examine how each has changed and how these changed have been experienced by classes in the village.

The *zakat peribadi* is to be distinguished from what most peasants call the *zakat raja*, the sultan's or government's *zakat*. The latter is the "official" *zakat*, owed by all but the very smallest cultivators, collected in paddy by an appointed local official (the *amil*, in this case Basir), and paid to Kedah's Department of Religious Affairs. Although the proceeds are devoted to specified works of Islamic charity, the tithe is generally resented—and widely evaded—by cultivators for its perceived inequities.[68] *Zakat peribadi,* which is actually a form of religious charity and not a tax as the term *zakat* implies, is viewed in a more favorable light because it is not compulsory and because the beneficiaries are local, often within Sedaka itself. A part of this *zakat peribadi* is actually collected by the *amil* at the same time the *zakat raja* is collected and is designated by the giver, according to his or her wishes, as a contribution to the mosque (*zakat mesjid*) in nearby Kepala Batas, to the village hall, which functions as prayer house, religious school room, and meeting place (*zakat madrasah*), and/or to the *imam* of the mosque. Private donations are also given personally to the mosque caretaker (Tok Siak) and to the popular religious teacher Lebai Sabrani, whose religious classes include many local children. Collectively, this portion of *zakat peribadi* might be termed gifts for religious services, and it comprises roughly two-thirds of all *zakat peribadi.* The remainder is given to other individuals, including especially poorer relatives, neighbors, friends, and wage workers who have helped with the planting and harvesting.[69]

It is this last category alone that might be called redistributive. We are by no means, however, dealing with vast quantities of paddy; the total *zakat peribadi* given out by villagers amounts to something like one hundred and ten gunny sacks or less than 2.5 percent of an average village harvest.[70] Of that amount, the potentially redistributive share is not more than forty gunny sacks, or less than 1 percent of the harvest. Even if we were to add the small voluntary

68. Evasion of the *zakat raja* merits a study in itself as an example of peasant resistance to the state. Here I can note only a few particulars. Of those seventeen small-scale cultivators whose harvest is sufficient to subject them to the *zakat raja* but is less than fifty gunny sacks, only three pay anything at all to the *amil.* Among middle and well-to-do peasants, no one, not even the *amil,* paid the full *zakat* due the state. For the entire village, the *zakat raja* actually paid is something on the order of 15 percent of what would be required if the regulations were adhered to strictly. Villagers complain that only paddy farmers are systematically taxed, whereas others who are richer (settlers on rubber and palm oil schemes, businessmen, non-cultivating landlords) are rarely taxed. They observe that none of the proceeds has ever found its way back to the village, and they suspect that much of it is siphoned off along the way to Alor Setar.

69. These categories often overlap. Thus a cultivator may give *zakat peribadi* to a brother or nephew whom he has employed as a wage laborer and who may also be a neighbor.

70. Nor is all of this distributed within the village, since gifts are often given to relatives and wage laborers living outside Sedaka. By the same token, however, a certain amount of *zakat peribadi* is also received by the poor of Sedaka from relatives and employers residing elsewhere. The figures cited here are necessarily approximate, as the amount of *zakat* given or received by any individual is frequently a matter of dispute, with the rich often exaggerating their generosity and the poor minimizing their receipts.

donations of milled paddy made to needy villagers just before Ramadan (a kind of *fitrah peribadi*), the total would not be appreciably greater.

The *zakat* is, of course, one of the five pillars of Islam—a sacred obligation. The religious and social reasoning behind it is best illustrated by the pamphlet distributed by the State Religious Council of Kedah.[71] After noting that Islam does not discourage the faithful from becoming rich, it asserts that the rich have an obligation to share a portion of their wealth with those who are poor and without property, and it quotes an injunction from the Koran: "And those who store up gold and silver and do not follow the path of Allah, let them know with the sharpest torment."[72] The purpose of the *zakat,* it continues, is not only to discourage stinginess (*sifat-sifat bakhil*) but to promote *social harmony* among the rich and the poor: "To cleanse those who receive *zakat* of jealousy and hatred toward the owners of property (*tuan-tuan harta*). To harmonize (*merapatkan*) the social relation between the haves (*golongan berada*) and the have-nots." The *zakat* is accepted by villagers in much the same spirit. They typically say that they give *zakat peribadi* in order to "cleanse [from sin] (*cuci*) their property."

The degree to which property is cleansed by voluntary *zakat* gifts varies enormously in the village. A few substantial property owners are quite generous with *zakat peribadi,* while others give almost nothing. Thus, Abdul Rahman gives over eight gunny sacks of paddy to relatives, workers, and religious officials, while Haji Kadir gives less than one sack. A small number of quite modest peasants give prodigiously, considering their means. Bakri bin Haji Wahab, a modest tenant on 4 relong, gives six gunny sacks—one each—to the families of those who have transplanted or harvested for him, and Rosni, a wage worker and tenant herself, gives away six gunny sacks divided between religious officials, poorer relatives, and a villager who worked for her (Pak Yah).[73] Others give nothing.

The amount of grain that poor villagers receive as *zakat* depends on their reputation, how good the paddy crop has been, and how much they have worked in a particular season. Thus Pak Yah and Mansur each received three or four gunny sacks of paddy after the irrigated season harvest of 1979, during which there was more manual work available than usual, owing to flooding. In each case, they received *zakat* only from those for whom they had threshed but not from all of them. Hamzah, the "*zakat* champ," does somewhat better, but a portion of the grain he is given is in recognition of his services as caretaker of the village prayer house (*surau*). Impoverished villagers who do not enjoy a good reputation fare much worse, even when they thresh regularly; Taib and Dullah

71. Badan Dakwah Islamiah, Pejabat Zakat Negeri Kedah, *Panduan Zakat* (Alor Setar: Majlis Ugama Negeri Kedah, n.d., probably about 1970).

72. Ibid., 5.

73. *Zakat* is essentially a transfer of grain among *men*. Thus, with rare exceptions, widows or divorced women who are poor wage workers receive no *zakat*.

are lucky to get more than a single gunny sack of paddy. What is notable here is that when the poor receive *zakat* it is almost entirely from their employers and its payment is rather carefully calculated according to the respectability of the recipient. It functions not only to "cleanse property" but also to promote labor control and social conformity.

Sedekah and *derma* are almost interchangeable as forms of alms or contributions. Unlike *zakat, sedekah* is not tied to the harvest, is not always paid in paddy, is as often requested by the needy as simply given unasked, and is almost exclusively given to the poor. *Derma* differs only in that it is more often a collection made house-to-house for a charitable purpose—commonly to help a poor family pay funeral expenses, as in the case of Razak's daughter.[74] Both *sedekah* and *derma* are seen as "good works" in the context of Islam for which the benefactor, if of pure heart, will be rewarded. In the village context, at least, such gifts are small—for example, enough milled rice (*beras*) for a few meals.

The third major form of what might be considered "charity" are the *kenduri,* or feasts that constitute the basis of much of the village's ritual life. Unlike *zakat* or *sedekah,* these are collective rituals marked by both prayer and a communal meal the sponsoring family provides to invited guests.[75] *Kenduris* may be held for a host of reasons, but the most common, roughly in order of frequency and importance, are: marriage feasts (*kenduri perkhawinan, kenduri bersanding, kenduri emas khawin*); feasts to pray for the dead, which often double as feasts to celebrate some good fortune such as a son passing his exams (*kenduri kesyukuran, kenduri arwah*); circumcision feasts (*kenduri berkhatan, kenduri masuk Jawi*); pregnancy feasts (*kenduri mandi tian*); cradle feasts (*kenduri berendul, kenduri buaian*); infant hair-cutting feasts (*kenduri cukur rambut*); house-moving feasts (*kenduri usung rumah*); new house feasts (*kenduri naik rumah baru*); and feasts for a fulfilled wish—often for a child of the sex desired (*kenduri berniat*). Both rich and poor sponsor *kenduri,* but the rich are naturally expected to sponsor them more often, more lavishly, and for a larger number of guests. Expenses, especially for sponsors of modest means, are met partly by donations in kind or cash by guests, although

---

74. Occasionally house-to-house collections are made by older Muslims from outside the village, who hope thereby to raise funds for the pilgrimage to Mecca. These donations are called *derma* as are donations to religious schools. Thus *derma* appears to have a more specifically religious connotation.

75. More rarely, as in a *keduri kekah* (haircutting ceremony, but in Sedaka, at least, seen as a religious feast in which three or seven families slaughter a larger animal and hold a feast to pray for the souls of their ancestors), *kenduri masuk Jawi* (circumcision ceremony), or *kenduri tolak bala* (feast, held in a field to ward off misfortune such as drought), several families will collaborate (*berpakat*) in a single feast. This last feast, held to have disappeared by many authorities and frowned upon by official Islam, was held twice in Sedaka during my stay, in each case because the rains were late.

poorer guests may avoid this by helping with the food preparation.[76] For the village poor, *kenduri* are virtually the only occasions when meat is eaten and, as Mansur says, the poor are "led" to feasts by the smell of meat cooking. Ritual feasts of this kind are the traditional means by which the well-to-do validate their status by conspicuous consumption in which their friends, neighbors, relatives, and often the entire village are invited to share.

When any form of charity is discussed by villagers, there is virtual unanimity for the view that, as a species of social relations, it has declined precipitously. Even the well-to-do farmers are in accord on this point, although many of them hasten to exclude themselves individually from the charge while pointing their finger at those who are even better-off. The village headman, Haji Jaafar, says the decline in charity began with double-cropping. Abdul Rahman, a substantial landowner who is renowned for his generosity, notes that even *zakat peribadi* is rarely given today and that *sedekah* hardly exists at all. The rich would rather, he says, sell their paddy and invest the cash in buying or renting in more land. Mat Isa, a fairly well-off tenant, gives voice to the general consensus when he claims, "The rich are arrogant (*sombong*); they don't take [the plight of] the poor seriously; [they're] cheap with *sedekah,* and [they're] reluctant to give it."[77] The village poor often put the facts bluntly. In the words of Rokiah, "The rich don't give anything to the poor."

For *kenduri,* there is also a consensus, albeit one with a slight wrinkle. Initially, the new profits of double-cropping in 1972 unleashed a memorable burst of feast giving that was unprecedented in Sedaka. Pak Haji Kadir, who then owned a battery-operated loudspeaker, can remember renting it out over seventy times in little over a year for *kenduri.* Nearly everyone, including small tenants and landless laborers, took advantage of their new-found prosperity to celebrate rituals they could not have afforded earlier. The *kenduri* of the poorer villagers were necessarily more modest, but even they were able, for a time at least, to emulate the ritual decencies that help to define citizenship in this small community.

After this short period of euphoria, both the frequency and scale of feasts has, by all accounts, been sharply reduced. Few villagers would find much to disagree with in Kamil's account of what has happened since then. "Before," he claims, "*kenduri* were big, even to the point of leasing out 10 relong for a few years [to cover expenses]." "Now," he says, "people are a bit more clever"; they figure

76. I have heard that in some villages *kenduri,* especially for marriages (*kenduri bersanding*), can turn a profit when many guests are invited from town who will contribute M$10 or more toward expenses. A cursory examination of the gifts (which are generally noted down in writing for later reciprocation when the guest in turn gives a feast) and expenses for *kenduri* suggests that this is unlikely in Sedaka. Paid entertainment of varous kinds is also provided at large *kenduri.*

77. *Orang kaya sombong; tak ambil berat orang susah. Sedekah berkira; susah bagi.*

out exactly how many people are coming, what they will contribute, and how much of the outlay will be recovered. "Then, people didn't look to make a profit; they didn't want a shabby *kenduri,* it had to be a cow, not chickens." In those days, people would ridicule a Haji who skimped on a feast, saying " 'Hey, Haji so-and-so is giving chicken *kenduri,*' and he would be shamed." "Today it happens all the time." Tok Kasim agrees, as he describes *kenduri* that lasted two nights and at which two cows were slaughtered.[78] Today, he says, they only last an afternoon and there is only chicken. The reason for the curtailing of ritual feasts by poor peasants is obvious; since at least 1976, their income has become more precarious. For richer peasants, the decline in the quality and number of *kenduri* is more a question of attitude than of resources. Most villagers would agree with Dullah's explanation that "The rich cut corners; they don't want to waste money."[79]

The affluent farmers in Sedaka are by no means tongue-tied when it comes to explaining why so little *zakat peribadi* or *sedekah* is given to the poor. They make, in effect, three arguments, any one of which would be sufficient to justify their position. The first is nearly a point of law, inasmuch as the nonhandicapped, working poor do not fall into any one of the eight categories of recipients who, according to Islamic regulations, are eligible to receive *zakat* gifts. Kamil takes the position that the government, since it established the state *zakat* system a decade or so ago, does not approve of *zakat peribadi* outside official channels. The implication is that private gifts of this kind are not only wrong but possibly illegal now.

A second argument, typically thrown in for good measure, is that there is virtually no one in the village who is truly in need of charity. Thus Haji Salim, the richest man in the immediate vicinity, asks rhetorically, "Why give *zakat* to those who are hard up? They have land, they grow paddy like us." Here, the appeal is to a kind of conceptual equality between all those who cultivate rice. We are, he implies, all on basically the same footing here and hence there is no need for *zakat* or *sedekah.* It is true, of course, that most of the poor in Sedaka do own or rent rice land, however lilliputian its size; that fact allows Haji Salim to make something of an abstraction of the difference between those who rent 1 relong and those who own 20. Another rich villager, Lebai Pendek, avails himself of the same argument and adds that, since those who thresh his

78. The shorthand ranking of *kenduri,* a nearly infallible guide to their sumptuousness, is by the kind and number of animals slaughtered for food. Thus, to say that the *kenduri* was an affair of twenty chickens is to describe what a modest feast it was. In order of declining prestige value, the meats in question are: water buffalo, cows, goats and sheep, chickens, and more rarely, fish, the everyday staple. The mythical granddaddy of *kenduri* in village lore is one held by the Sultan of Kedah at the marriage of his daughter; he is believed to have sold Penang and Province Wellesley to pay for it, and over two hundred water buffalo were eaten.

79. *Orang kaya pakai nipis; tak mau membazir duit.*

paddy are paid and usually have some land of their own, any further gifts would be "too much" (*terlampau*). If one accepts his logic, then it becomes pertinent to wonder why the practice of giving *zakat peribadi* to wage laborers was so widespread until at least 1975. The anomaly, I believe, is resolved by considering *zakat peribadi* as, in part, a system of labor control that was necessary when harvest labor was scarce but is no longer required now that combine-harvesters are easily available. Mat "halus," a landless laborer, captures what has occurred in precisely these terms: "The well-off gave out *zakat peribadi* so that they could call forth the work (*panggil kerja*). Poor people went everywhere. They called and we went. Now we go even without *zakat peribadi* because we need the work." It is certainly possible that wealthy villagers always considered the *zakat* given to harvest workers as an illegitimate imposition, perhaps even as a form of labor blackmail. The difference may be that now, thanks to the combine, they are able to make their opposition to *zakat peribadi* stick.

The third and last line of defense against *zakat* to harvest workers is one that is familiar by now—the claim that many, if not most, of the village poor are not fitting objects for charity. Thus Haji Salim asks, "Why should we give *zakat* without good reason to people who don't want to work?" He then illustrates the improvidence of the poor by saying that someone who got *zakat* last year sold the paddy to buy an expensive (M$35) pair of shoes. "He wears fancier [shoes] than the well-off."[80] Prosperous villagers invariably mention the ever serviceable Razak and other poor villagers whom they consider more or less disreputable (for example, Dullah, Midon, Taib, Mat "halus") to explain the decline in *zakat* and *sedakah*. The charges include lying (*bohong*), cheating (*tipu*), and laziness (*segan*). To the extent that this category begins to include most of the village poor the problem of charity is thus solved at one stroke. Giving help to such people, they imply, would only encourage such behavior. And here too we can see that the practice of *zakat peribadi* serves the purpose of social control as well as that of labor control. The rich put the poor on notice that only those who conform closely to their standard of correct conduct are eligible for their largesse. The only notable exception to this pattern is when death intervenes and even the poorest villager is accorded the minimal decencies.[81]

As for *kenduri*, there are still a few well-off villagers who have a reputation for not scrimping. Abdul Rahman and the headman, Haji Jaafar, in particular, rarely let a season go by without a sizable *kenduri* to which all the village is invited. Other substantial villagers typically admit, sometimes with a trace of embarrassment, that they have become more clever (*bijak, cerdik*) about feasts to

80. *Dia pakai lagi hebat dairpada orang senang.*
81. The other possible exception is before *Hari Raya Puasa* (the feast day to celebrate the end of the fasting month), when a spirit of greater generosity prevails comparable, perhaps, to the Christmas spirit in Christian countries.

avoid wasting their money. It is a rare landowner who, like Haji Nayan, rejects the custom altogether and says, "Stupid people give *kenduris.*"

The potential beneficiaries of *zakat* gifts, alms, and feasts have, as one would imagine, a quite different view. There is, of course, the lament for the loss of income they and their families have suffered; each of them can recount exactly what they have lost in grain and from whom. But that is by no means the whole story. There is also anger and bitterness made all the more galling by the fact that their losses have come at a time when prosperous villagers have been reaping the profits of double-cropping. The blame, as usual, is personalized; it is laid at the door of the rich, whose desire for further profit has led them to repudiate their obligations to their poorer neighbors. When the poor say, as they frequently do, that the rich are becoming stingier, it is above all the refusal of charity they have in mind. The account given by Sukur would be familiar to the other poor peasants in Sedaka. He remembers when *zakat peribadi* was given immediately after the threshing to all those who had worked. Now, he says, the paddy is all sold and loaded directly onto the trucks bound for the rice mill. The employer then has little grain—the traditional currency of charity—in storage and will contend that his cash has gone to pay off debts. This ploy allows him to plead poverty when in fact, Sukur explains, the rightful *zakat* (*zakat betul*) for 10 relong would be enough (fifteen gunny sacks) to take care of many village poor.

There is also the humiliation of asking for *sedekah,* and occasionally for *zakat,* and being refused—an experience that is far more common today. Hamzah, one of the more "reputable" poor, speaks with more feeling about this humiliation than about the gain he is denied. Before the harvest last season, when work was scarce and his family had nearly run out of rice and cash, he asked some of his usual employers for loans of rice as an advance on future wages. The results were meager. "I felt embarrassed asking friends [for help]. It's a pity; it reaches the point where I have to go everyday to ask. I'm ashamed."[82] When his mother died, he had to ask for help with funeral expenses. Rokiah, with few resources of her own, gave him M$150 immediately but Haji Kadir, the richest man in Sedaka, for whom he often worked, gave him nothing. "I went to ask Haji Kadir; he didn't give [anything]; I knew he wouldn't." As is usual in these cases, the refusal was not a blunt rejection but a cold shoulder—silence (*sengap*). Later in the year I listened to Hamzah grumble to a friend about being short-changed on wages by Haji Kadir. He had helped fill and sew gunny sacks with paddy disgorged from the combine-harvester, for which he expected a wage of 50¢ a gunny or M$25 for the fifty gunny sacks he had done. He was given only M$5. When I asked whether he complained (*merungut*), he explained, "Poor people can't [complain]. When I'm sick or need work, I may have to ask him again. I am angry in my heart." Here then is the bitterness, the swallowed bile,

82. *Berasa malu minta kawan. Sayang; sampai hari-hari pe minta. Malu.*

of a man who has decided to conduct himself according to the rules imposed by the rich—to be available, discreet, and deferential, unlike his brother Razak and unlike others of the poor who rarely ask for help.

Tok Mahmud, a semiretired widower living with his daughter, has experienced the same humiliations and is less reticent than Hamzah.[83] The only way these days to get rice from the rich, he claims, is to take money and pay for it. "We are even embarrassed to ask now. They say 'you grow rice, too.' They say, 'If you don't have enough to eat, you're lazy.' They never help." Like Pak Yah and others, he knows what the rich say about the poor. The village poor are caught in a situation where the old assumptions are no longer valid. Before, they could expect *zakat* from employers and ask for *sedekah,* or advance wages, with a reasonable expectation of receiving something. Now they may ask, but only at the potential price of a humiliating rebuff. A gift refused in this fashion is not simply grain foregone but, above all, a stark social signal that the relationship between the rich and poor, which the request assumed to be in force, has been unilaterally declared null and void. The rich have given notice that they are no longer responsible for the pressing needs of the village poor.

In the decline of the feast-giving cycle in Sedaka, the poor see the same symptoms of social withdrawal and selfishness by the well-to-do. No longer, says Mat "halus," are there feasts that last the whole night and at which three or four cows are eaten. Instead, the rich "think about money; they just want to invest their money."[84] "Before, rich people wanted to make a big name (*buat besar*). Now they do just a little bit; they're clever. Before they wanted to show off (*tunjuk-menunjuk*) and now they don't want to waste money." Where they might have spent M$2,000, he adds, they now spend only M$200. Sukur, putting himself in the shoes of the rich, performs what he imagines to be their calculations. "If a *kenduri* will cost $500, they ask, 'How many things can we buy for that?'" Instead of a *kenduri,* they decide to buy a television set. The rich, he concludes, "think only of this world." For others, like Taib, what is most grating is to be hired for work but not invited to his employers' feast. As he puts it, "If it's a question of work, the well-off have to go looking for the poor; if it's a feast they go look for a *lebai* or *haji* [someone who can lead chants and recite from the Koran], not poor people."

In this last comment by Sukur, we can capture the religious tone of his accusation. To think *beyond* this world is to think of Allah's judgment (*hukum Allah*) and thus to be generous and sympathetic to those who are less fortunate.

83. Tok Mahmud's 4 relong, 3 of which he farms, are now more than adequate for his modest household of two. Ten years ago, however, he was substantially poorer owing to his large family.

84. *Kira duit, mau pusing duit saja. Pusing* means literally "to turn or spin" and is used here in the sense of "turning over" money so that it is never idle, so that it is always multiplying.

This perspective is reflected in the prestige enjoyed by those few comfortable villagers (notably Abdul Rahman but also Haji Jaafar and Lebai Pendek) who continue to honor the *kenduri* tradition. Moreover, according to folk beliefs among the poor, the punishment for a failure of generosity is not confined to Allah's final judgment. Hamzah, with others, believes that generosity with feasts, *zakat,* and *sedekah* serves to protect rich people against such misfortunes as accidents and illnesses. This is why, he says, those who make the pilgrimage to Mecca always give a *kenduri* before setting out. When I wonder out loud how this applies to Haji Kadir, whose tightfistedness is renowned but who appears to enjoy robust health, Hamzah immediately reminds me of his wife's long stay in the hospital, her fall down the steps, and Haji Kadir's recurring back trouble. All of these misfortunes, he implies, are a sign of Allah's displeasure. It is hardly far-fetched to read into this interpretation an attempt, albeit feeble, by the poor to exert their own modest form of social control over the rich. Nor is it far-fetched to suggest that there is only a very short step between believing that the miserly rich will be punished in this world and the next and actually wishing on them the misfortunes and judgments which, by their conduct, they have called down on their own heads.

THE REMEMBERED VILLAGE

As we listen to the rich and poor of Sedaka attempting to make sense of the massive changes they have all experienced over the past decade, we find ourselves in the midst of an ideological struggle, however small in scale. It is a struggle over facts and their meaning, over what has happened and who is to blame, over how the present situation is to be defined and interpreted. Having lived through this history, every villager is entitled, indeed required, to become something of a historian—a historian with an axe to grind. The point of such histories is not to produce a balanced or neutral assessment of the decade but rather to advance a claim, to levy praise and blame, and to justify or condemn the existing state of affairs.

As in any history, assessing the present forcibly involves a reevaluation of what has gone before. Thus, the ideological struggle to define the present is a struggle to define the past as well. Nowhere is this more apparent than in the accounts given by poor villagers, who have had the least to be thankful for over the past decade and whose current prospects are bleak. They have collectively created a *remembered village* and a *remembered economy* that serve as an effective ideological backdrop against which to deplore the present.[85] They remember when rents

85. Lest this seems a particularly peasant form of consciousness, it is worth noting that Francis Hearn regards this imaginative appropriation of the past as a key element in the early solidarity of the English working class. *Domination, Legitimation, and Resistance: The Incorporation of the Nineteenth Century English Working Class* (Westport, Conn.: Greenwood, 1978), chap. 1.

were paid after the crop was in and reflected the actual harvest. They remember the time before mechanization, when large landowners sought them out as tenants and when rents were modest. They remember when harvest work was plentiful and larger farmers curried favor with them by giving advance wages, loans, and *zakat* gifts and throwing larger feasts to which they were always invited.

It is not that their memory is faulty. The older customs and practices to which they point did exist and worked to their advantage. Their memory is, however, quite selective. It focuses precisely on those beneficial aspects of tenure and labor relations that have been eroded or swept away over the last ten years. That they do not dwell upon other, less favorable, features of the old order is hardly surprising, for those features do not contribute to the argument they wish to make today. Their nostalgia, if one may call it that, is thus, like their memory, a highly selective affair. The central reason why the account of the village poor smacks of nostalgia is that so many of the innovations of the past decade have worked decisively against their material interests. They have ample cause to look back fondly at older arrangements. The well-to-do of Sedaka, as we have seen, are not above nostalgia themselves. But it is not so pronounced precisely because they have a far greater stake in the current arrangements, which are decisively in their favor.

Such reconstructions of the past in the service of present interests recall Hegel's dictum that "the owl of Minerva flies only at dusk." There is no doubt, for example, that the losses suffered by Sedaka's poor in the last few years have inspired them to cast a new and sympathetic eye on the older arrangements. Ten years ago these arrangements would not, in all probability, have elicited such praise; they were then part of the taken-for-granted practices that had governed rice production for some time. It is only against the background of the new threats posed by double-cropping that such routines have been elevated to the status of revered customs, rights, and entitlements. It is only now that the revalued past has become necessary to assess a menacing present.

The ideological work of the poor can be seen as an attempt to right a world that has been almost literally turned upside down by double-cropping. Everywhere they look they see dramatic reversals of the traditional production relations—all of which undermine both their sources of livelihood and their status in the village. Before, large landowners rented land out to poorer tenants; now they rent increasingly to wealthy entrepreneurs or farm their land themselves with machinery. Before, large farmers hired poorer neighbors to plough and harrow their fields with water buffalo; now they hire wealthy tractor owners to prepare their land. Before, larger farmers hired poorer neighbors to transplant their paddy; now many of them broadcast their own seed. Before, these same farmers hired the poor to reap and thresh their crop; now they hire wealthy combine owners for the same job. Before, well-to-do villagers had good reason to provide advance wages and give *zakat* payments to their work force; now, if they have a work force at all, they see no need to be as openhanded. Before, the village rich had good reason to build a reputation with lavish feasts; now many of them regard such large feasts as a waste of money. Taken together, these reversals call into question virtually every assumption that governed the social relations of production before double-cropping.

The new dispensation has also transformed the preexisting class structure of Sedaka and most other paddy villages on the Muda Plain. In that earlier class structure, rich peasants and larger landowners were joined to land-poor villagers in a symbiosis of dependency and exploitation. So long as land was reasonably plentiful and labor, at peak seasons, was reasonably scarce, there were limits to exploitation, although land concentration proceeded apace through moneylending and default. This symbiosis found expression in village ritual life—for example, *zakat peribadi, kenduri,* advance wages—and also in political life, where local party leaders, who were invariably well-to-do, could be relied upon to bring most of their dependent tenants and laborers into the fold. The middle peasantry was, by contrast, somewhat more autonomous, since they were less reliant on the rich for land to farm or for wages and they rarely hired workers, preferring to use (or exchange) household labor.

The new relations of production have broken most of the direct dependencies that characterized the earlier class system. Economically marginalized by mechanization and shifts in tenancy, poor villagers increasingly find themselves ritually marginalized as well. Kinship and indirect patronage (distributed by the state through local elites) still tie many of them to the ruling party, but their subordination is no longer embedded in village relations of production. Before double-cropping, one might describe them as poor, second-class, citizens of Sedaka. Now, they remain poor—though spared the extremes of malnutrition and hunger—and certainly second-class, but it is increasingly difficult to justify calling them citizens.

The question naturally arises, in this or in any other economic transformation in which a subordinate class has suffered a reversal in its fortunes, as to how such reversals are understood and interpreted. Later in my analysis I will want to examine the heavy consequences an answer to this question has for the larger issues of class consciousness, false-consciousness, resistance, and ideological hegemony. Here, however, it is sufficient only to note the general tenor of the answer as reflected in the discourse of the village poor.

There is no way in which the participants' interpretation of the impact of the green revolution in Kedah can be deduced from the crude economic facts. Such facts are compatible with any number of intepretations: they could be accepted as fatalistically as a drought or flood; they could be seen as the fulfillment of prophecy or of Allah's punishment for straying from the true faith; they could be seen as the malevolent effects of government policy or the result of the greed and resources of Chinese syndicates.

In fact, as we have seen, none of these interpretations figures very prominently, if at all, in the record. Instead, the poorer strata of Sedaka see the causes of their present distress as primarily *personal* (that is, a result of human agency), *local,* and largely confined to the Malay community. The increasing use of lease-hold tenancy and the dismissal of smaller tenants, for example, is seen as caused by the desire of large landowners (mostly Malays) to capture more of the profits of cultivation for themselves. The growth of labor-displacing combine hire is similarly viewed as a result of large farmers hoping to save the money and bother of hiring harvest hands. The reduction in local charity likewise reflects the new willingness of the rich to protect their wealth at the expense of their reputation. In each case, the logic of blame and condemnation is much the same as that applied to the class of landowning Hajis who were held responsible for the loss of mortgaged land. The more distant and impersonal causes that most assuredly play a role here are upstaged by a perspective that emphasizes moral lapses, selfishness, and the violation of social decencies. As the poor see it, the rich have callously chosen to ignore their obligations to their neighbors. How else are we to understand the tendency of the poor to focus at least as much on the disrespect and contempt they now confront as on the material losses they have suffered?

The poor are, of course, not the only ones in the village to make use of such logic. While wealthier farmers acknowledge the speed and profitability of com-bine-harvesters, they also insist that the poor have become unreliable, choosy, and indolent workers who are no longer entitled to their consideration. In this fashion, the rich, too, find a personal and moral rationale for the dramatic reversals in village social relations.

Neither the rich nor the poor, however, fail to see the broader and more impersonal forces that have shaped their circumstances. The poor, and many of the well-to-do, understand that the desire for accumulation and investment lies behind the new dispensation. Both understand the new possibilities that double-cropping and mechanization have made available. Every villager carries in his head an impressive personal and collective economic history replete with time series for fertilizer, seed, rents, paddy, rice, fish, consumer durable prices, wage rates, and crop yields that may, for older peasants, go back as much as half a century. As in any oral history of this kind, the dates are tied to events—"the Japanese period" (*masa Jepun*), "when my first child was born," "before double-cropping" (*se-belum dua kali padi*), and the focus is on the consequences of these figures—for example, income, access to land, the availability of work. The poor know exactly how much they have lost to the combines; the rich know exactly how much they have gained. Within the ambit of their local experience, they understand the workings of capitalism. Rich and poor alike see that Chinese entrepreneurs pay premium rents for land leases because they own farm ma-chinery and because they cannot let their capital lie idle. As they say: "the Chinese have to keep their money circulating (*pusing duit*)." They understand that the owners of the new means of production—tractors, combines, trucks—now capture the returns previously destined for water buffalo owners, harvest laborers, and porters, and that part of the profit now goes to overseas manufacturers. The poor fully understand that many of them have been proletarianized as they have lost their tenancies. Rokiah is not by any means the only one who has noted that "they want to make coolies of us," though she adds defiantly, "They can't do it." The poor also understand that they are being progressively marginalized; they talk about having no work, of being pushed aside (*tolak tepi*), of facing the prospect of leaving the village altogether.

If the poor dwell upon the local and personal causes of their distress, it is thus not because they are particularly "mystified" or ignorant of the larger context of agrarian capitalism in which they live. They do not, of course, use the abstract, desiccated terminology of social science—proletarianization, differentiation, accumulation, marginalization—to describe their situation. But their own folk descriptions of what is happening: being made into coolies, the rich getting richer and the poor becoming poorer, and being "pushed aside"—are adequate and, at the same time, far richer in emotive meaning than anything academic political-economy could possibly provide.

The choice—for it is a choice—to fasten on the more immediate sources of their difficulties contains elements of both convenience and strategy. It is convenient for the poor to blame those who are most immediately and directly responsible for their recent reverses. They observe their Malay landlord taking his land from them to farm himself or to rent out to a Chinese entrepreneur; they do not *directly* observe the concentration of capital in land use. They observe the large farmer who stops hiring his neighbors and calls in the combine-harvester; they do not *directly* observe the syndicates or government policies that have made this possible.

Their choice is also strategic because it focuses on precisely those human agents who are plausibly within their sphere of social action.[86] They have some hope of influencing their landlord or the larger farmer for whom they work; they do not have a prayer of influencing either the Chinese commercial farmer or the syndicates of machine owners. After all, those who rented them land or hired them in the past described their action as "helping them out" (*tolong*), thus implying a kind of noblesse oblige in keeping with village norms. It is only

---

86. In this context it is worth recalling Simmel's analysis of the differences in class conflict in early capitalism as opposed to what he calls "mature capitalism." In the latter, labor conditions are, he claims, seen as the product of "objective conditions" or "forms of production." "The personal bitterness of both general and local battles has greatly decreased. The entrepreneur is no longer a bloodsucker and damnable egoist." To the degree that it prevails, this larger, more "objective," view is likely to reduce conflict. Whether it is a more "objective" view, however, is questionable; the "personal" view, however narrow, has the merit of recognizing that processes like the market and technological innovations are social creations. See *Georg Simmel on Individuality and Social Forms,* ed. Donald N. Levine (Chicago: Univ. of Chicago Press, 1971), 88.

logical that rich villagers and landlords should now be hoisted on their own petard and accused of callous disregard, if not contempt, for those whom they once claimed to assist. The village poor thus choose to direct their anger primarily at those from whom they have some claim to consideration, however tenuous. In the context of the capitalist transformation of agriculture in Muda, their claims fall on increasingly deaf ears. Their victories—a few landlords who continue to rent to small tenants, a few who hire harvest hands when they can, a few who still observe the tradition of charity and large feasts—are meager and, in all probability, temporary. The sense of community and obligation on which their claims depend is a rapidly wasting asset. It is, however, virtually the only asset they have[87] in this rearguard action and one to which they would be expected to turn in preference to more quixotic goals.

87. Institutional factors are of course decisive here too. If there were a movement or political party that supported security of tenure, land reform, or full employment in rural areas, the realm of plausible action might be appreciably widened. As it is, neither UMNO nor PAS, each of which is dominated by rather well-to-do farmers and landlords, has addressed itself to the class issue on the Muda Plain.

6 • Stretching the Truth: Ideology at Work

Homo faber cannot be separated from *homo sapiens*. Each man, finally . . . carries on some form of intellectual activity . . . he participates in a particular conception of the world, has a conscious line of moral conduct, and therefore contributes to sustain a conception of the world or to modify it, that is, to bring into being modes of thought.

Antonio Gramsci, *Selections from the Prison Notebooks*

IDEOLOGICAL WORK IN DETERMINATE CONDITIONS

Double-cropping and mechanization in Sedaka have presented rich peasants and landlords with a host of unprecedented new opportunities for profit. These opportunities have, with few exceptions, been eagerly seized.

To exploit these new chances for capital accumulation, however, large farmers and landlords have stripped away many of the economic and social ties that previously bound them to poorer villagers. They have had to hire machines in place of village laborers, raise rents, dismiss tenants, and cut back their ceremonial and charitable obligations within the community. In doing so, they have found themselves operating in something of an ideological vacuum. What we observe in Sedaka and elsewhere on the Muda Plain is an emerging capitalist agrarian class which has been steadily shedding its ties to laborers and tenants but which acts in a largely precapitalist normative atmosphere that makes it extremely difficult to justify the actions it has taken. They are, in this sense, capitalists who are obliged to explain themselves—to justify their conduct publicly—without the benefit of the elaborated doctrines of a Malaysian Adam Smith, let alone a Bentham or a Malthus. This ideological handicap is, as we shall see, only partially circumvented by a rather tortured but creative attempt by rich farmers to bend the facts of the case to suit themselves.

The historically given, negotiated, moral context of village life is one in which, if only ideologically, the cards are stacked against the newer forms of capitalist behavior. This moral context consists of a set of expectations and preferences about relations between the well-to-do and the poor. By and large, these expectations are cast in the idioms of patronage, assistance, consideration, and helpfulness. They apply to employment, tenancy, charity, feast giving, and the conduct of daily social encounter. They imply that those who meet these expectations will be treated with respect, loyalty, and social recognition. What is involved, to put it crudely, is a kind of "politics of reputation" in which a good name is conferred in exchange for adherence to a certain code of conduct.[1]

Ironically, the moral context of class relations that rich farmers are now violating is a social artifact which they themselves had a major hand in creating at a time when it served their purposes. It was once in their interest to employ harvest laborers and to ensure their loyalty with advance wages, gifts (for example, *zakat peribadi* after harvest), and invitations to feasts. It was once in their interest to take on tenants to farm their surplus land and to adjust rents after a poor harvest in order to keep good cultivators. It was not only in their interest to behave in this fashion, but it was also in their interest to *describe* this behavior in ideological terms as assistance, help, kindness, and sympathy. They thus clothed their behavior—behavior that made eminent good sense when land was relatively plentiful and labor relatively scarce—in the language of patronage and liberality. No cynicism is implied here, only the universal tendency to put the best possible face on one's actions. Nor is anything necessarily implied about whether poorer villagers fully accepted this social construction of their behavior, although it is unlikely they would have challenged it publicly.

A word of qualification is in order about the social scope of this professed patronage and liberality. It applied with greatest force to the bilateral kinship group and to residents of the same village. Where close kin lived in the same village, the claim to consideration was particularly strong. The greater the distance from the core of this charmed circle, the more attenuated the claim to special consideration.

Within these limits, both the "ideology" and the practice of liberality are, today, more than just a fading historical memory. They exist, albeit in truncated form, in kinship tenure, lower rents for village tenants, surviving forms of charity, village feasts, and preferential hiring. Not even mechanization has completely eliminated the need for casual labor from time to time, for transplanters, or for a loyal political following. Thus, the rich farmers of Sedaka are not yet able to dispense entirely with the precapitalist normative context of village life.

They do, however, wish to limit radically the applicability of these values in which they once had a far greater vested interest. The full application of these values today would prevent them from stripping away the social obligations that stand between them and the profits of the green revolution. How they go about this "ideological work"—their strategy, its logic, its applications, and the resistance they encounter—is the subject of this chapter. I begin with the concept of exploitation as it is embedded in language and practice and then show how the rich and poor each manage to bend the facts so as to make these values serve partisan, class goals. Since these values are fashioned only through social conflict, I examine their practical use in three social conflicts: the attempt to raise land

---

1. See F. G. Bailey, *Gifts and Poison: The Politics of Reputation* (New York: Schocken, 1971).

rents or dismiss tenants, a dispute over the village "gate," and the charges and countercharges surrounding the distribution of government funds in the Village Improvement Scheme. Finally, I pause to explore the meaning of symbolic and ideological struggle in Sedaka.

THE VOCABULARY OF EXPLOITATION

Before examining how different classes of villagers maneuver to reinforce or alter the normative context of local conduct, it is essential to establish what that context is. The beliefs and practices surrounding class relations are by no means cut-and-dried, for like any set of norms they are the historical product of continuous struggle and negotiation. It is possible, however, to identify the broad outlines of what this process of struggle has yielded, and what now forms the normative environment of current discourse. This normative environment is perhaps best reflected in the vocabulary of exploitation as it is used in Sedaka.

As is so often the case, the terms and categories used by intellectuals and/or bureaucrats are an indifferent guide to the terms that humbler citizens use to describe the same situation. Thus, the loaded term *green revolution* (*revolusi hijau*) used in official papers and documents describing irrigated rice cultivation on the Muda Plain is rarely heard in the village; instead it is simply called "double-paddy-cropping" (*dua kali padi*). The same divergence of elite and "folk" categories of discourse is even more apparent in the case of exploitation.

There is a standard Malay verb (*tindas, menindas*), which may be accurately translated as "to exploit, to oppress, to crush, to rule unjustly." It is in common village use to cover such banal acts as the crushing of body lice between one's fingernails. Except for one or two younger villagers who were obviously showing off their school learning, however, it is not used to express the concept of exploitation.[2] Other words that carry much the same meaning—among them *tekan, kejam, peras, desak, sesak*—are occasionally heard in village conversations. Each conveys the sense of physical pressure—pressing, squeezing, pushing, choking—that makes it an appropriate vehicle for suggesting extortion and oppression. Thus, when Nizam bin Haji Lah's landlord, Haji Zahir, insisted on shifting to a higher rent and a two-year leasehold contract, Nizam told me, "He wants to squeeze (*tekan*), he wants to gobble up (*makan*) everything." And when local members of the opposition complain that only ruling party members have a chance of being accepted as settlers on government land schemes, Dullah adds, "The government really oppresses (*tekan sunggoh*) us; we can't stir (*bergerak*) at

---

2. The term *is* in use both in left-wing scholarship in the Malay language and occasionally in the speeches of opposition political leaders. The government, wary of the Marxist tone the word has acquired, uses it sparingly and then usually only to condemn Chinese middlemen, who are said to exploit Malay peasants, fishermen, and rubber tappers.

all." Some phrases that suggest exploitation carry this physical metaphor even further and imply that exploiters insist on their pound of flesh. Thus a poor villager refers to officials who "sit on soft chairs" and "beat on (*tutuh*) the backs of villagers." Another mentions landlords who "plough the backs (*menenggala atas belakang*) of villagers."[3]

There is, then, hardly any linguistic shortage when it comes to expressing the notion of exploitation. And yet the verb most consistently in favor—the one most often heard in daily conversation and the one with the richest connotation— is the verb "to eat" (*makan*). To get a salary is "to eat a salary (*makan gaji*), to collect interest is "to eat interest" (*makan bunga*), to take bribes is "to eat bribes" (*makan duit*), to betray one's friends is "to eat one's friends" (*makan kawan sindiri*), to drive someone hard is "to eat their bones" (*makan tulang*), to exploit another is "to eat their sweat" (*makan peluh orang*).[4] The most common formulation is simply, "He wants to eat us" (*Dia mau makan kita*). Here the peasantry's historical preoccupation with food and the accusation of what amounts to cannibalism are joined together in a powerful, suggestive metaphor.[5] As we have seen, moreover, the metaphor is used not only by the poor to describe what is done to them by the powerful but is used also by the rich to describe the demands for loans and charity pressed on them by the poor.

What is remarkable, though, is that the local vocabulary of exploitation is to be found less in this collection of verbs, taken together, than in the concepts of *stinginess* and *arrogance*. When a tenant rails against his landlord for raising the rent, he may or may not say privately that the landlord is extorting (*tekan*) from him or "eating" (*makan*) him. But he will almost certainly accuse the landlord of being stingy or greedy (*kedikut, kikir, bakhil, berkira, lokek, tamak, keras hati, tankai jering, haloba*) and, often, of being proud or arrogant (*sombong*). A poor villager whose request for a loan or charity from an employer has been spurned may not say privately that his employer is oppressing him, but he will rarely fail to complain that he is tightfisted and without shame. The terms in which these backstage accusations are cast constitute the core of "folk" concepts of exploitation in Sedaka. Taken collectively, they embody something close to an

3. *Gabus* (pronounced *gabuih* in Kedah dialect), "to rub or scour," is also used occasionally in this same sense.

4. The concept of blood sucking is also in popular use, and an oppressive landlord or moneylender may be called a "land leech" (*lintah darat*) or be accused of sucking blood (*isap darah*). The "land" in land leech is to distinguish the real thing, which is to be found in water or wet areas, from its human equivalent on dry land.

5. The same verb with the same connotation is encountered elsewhere historically in Southeast Asia. A district official in precolonial Burma, for example, was called a *myo-sa,* the "eater" of a district. The Thai equivalent is *kin muang.* The Malay official appointed by the Sultan to rule a district was known as the *Akan Pemakannya.* In most of these permutations, the use of the verb "to eat" also implies that the activity is an alternative to honest work.

ideology of class relations—an ideology which, moreover, is not exclusively the perspective of the village poor but is shared to a considerable extent by the rich as well.

The preoccupation with stinginess that characterizes Malay village society is already evident in the stories that make up the legend of Haji Ayub (Haji Broom). That he exploited his fellow Malays is hardly in doubt, but it is his surpassing stinginess that is the center of attention. We have seen in the previous chapter how frequently the accusation of stinginess rises to the lips of villagers. When Nizam bin Haji Lah complains of his landlord's oppression (*tekan*), he also explains that oppression by citing his stinginess (*berkira*) and heartlessness (*keras hati*). Rosni characterizes her landlord as very calculating or stingy (*sangat berkira*), and the fact of exploitation is left to be inferred from his conduct. Rokiah cannot expect any leniency from her landlord, who is her own brother, after a poor season and speaks bitterly of his heartlessness (*keras hati*) as well. When Taib laments the difficulty of renting in land these days he points, as do others, to the "greed" (*lokek*) of landowners as the cause. Yaakub, who depends on wage labor that has largely evaporated since the combines arrived, attributes their use to the fact that large farmers are "more stingy" (*lagi kedekut*) these days. Tok Kasim, when he notes that charity and large *kenduri* are much rarer now, adds, by way of explanation, that the rich are now stingier (*susah berkira la'ni*). Even the wealthy outside landowner Haji Nayan, noting that many dismissed tenants have had to emigrate, attributes their plight to landlords who have resumed cultivation by machine because they are now "more calculating" (*lagi susah kira*).

The perceived changes in the attitude of wealthy villagers and the manner in which they are condemned are not entirely new phenomena on the Muda Plain. In his study of credit in the nearby state of Perlis just before the initiation of irrigated double-cropping, Mokhzani reported:

> Whenever village conversation was steered to the subject of mutual help and the offer of cash loans as part of such help to fellow villagers, it rarely failed to raise statements bemoaning the decreasing cooperation between villagers and the increasing difficulty of raising friendly loans. Such statements were *always accompanied* with reference to the fact that people in the village are becoming *increasingly calulating* (*berkira*) in their approach to money matters. Villagers would then unfailingly hark back to what was termed as the "old days" when people were always ready to offer aid.[6]

6. Mokhzani bin Abdul Rahim, "Credit in a Malay Peasant Society" (Ph.D. diss., University of London, 1973), 255, emphasis added. See also Kessler's discussion of the popular condemnation of "rude materialism" and the use of the term *kira* in *Islam and Politics in a Malay State: Kelantan 1838–1969* (Ithaca: Cornell Univ. Press, 1978), 221.

In Sedaka itself, Kenzo Horii's 1967 study alluded more generally to "the weakening of the principle of mutual aid" and to the fact that "the land tenure system is approaching the stage where the class aspect of landowner-tenant relations is becoming manifest."[7] We may reasonably infer that the accusations of stinginess that we hear today are not uniquely the product of the green revolution but represent a more durable ethical tradition in response to the pressures of commercialization. What has occurred, surely, is that the impact of mechanization has greatly sharpened these complaints and swelled the back-stage chorus of accusations to a new level.

All of the accusations of stinginess contain, as we saw in the case of Haji Broom, a clear view—an ideology of sorts—of the relations that *should* obtain between the rich and the poor. In their dealings with the poor, most especially those who are kin and fellow villagers, the rich should be considerate (*timbang-rasa*), helpful (*tolong*), and unselfish (*senang kira*—the opposite of *berkira* or *susah kira*). Such behavior, as the poor see it, would involve providing employment, tenancies, loans, charity, and suitable feasts. The well-to-do who lived up to this standard of conduct would provide the standard of nonexploitive, proper conduct.

That these standards are embedded to a considerable degree in the very language of accusation receives odd confirmation from the sentences used to illustrate some of the key terms in standard Malay dictionaries.[8]

Word	Malay Illustrative Sentence (Translation)
Kedekut (stingy)	It is not easy to request alms from him, because he is a stingy (*kedekut*) person.
Bakhil (stingy)	That stingy (*bakhil*) rich person doesn't give alms to poor people.
Timbang rasa (sympathy, considerateness)	Assistance that shows sympathy (*timbang*) toward people who suffer hardship.
Miskin (poor)	He always contributes money to people who are poor (*miskin*).
Segan (unwilling, reluctant, shy, lazy)	He is reluctant to give assistance, even though he is a rich man.

In each case, "stinginess" is associated with the refusal of the rich, specifically, to help the poor; sympathy is associated with charity, and the poor are defined as fitting objects of that charity.

7. Kenzo Horii, "The Land Tenure System of Malay Padi Farmers: A Case Study . . . in the State of Kedah," *Developing Economies* 10, no. 1 (1972): 68.

8. Definitions for *kedekut, bakhil, miskin,* and *segan* are drawn from Awang Sudja, Hairul and Yusoff Khan, *Kamus Lengkap* (Petaling Jaya: Pustaka Zaman, 1977), 449, 55, 701, and 974. The definition for *timbang rasa* comes from Tenku Iskandar, *Kamus Dewan* (Kuala Lumpur: Dewan Bahasa dan Pustaka, 1970), 1255.

There is much evidence that the normative outlook identified here is not confined to the farmers of the Muda Plain but is rather a common characteristic of Malay peasant society in general.[9] That evidence comes from reports of field-work conducted over four decades in various parts of the Malay peninsula. Raymond Firth's classic study, *Malay Fishermen: Their Peasant Economy*, was based on fieldwork in the east coast state of Kelantan before the Japanese occupation. His discussion of wealth and charity would be very familiar to the villagers of Sedaka:

> On the whole, in this area men of wealth have accumulated their property by industry and saving. These two features, combined with the practice of charity *enjoined* on the rich, probably account to a considerable extent for the absence of any marked feeling of resentment towards the wealthy on the part of the poorer elements of the community . . . Where resentment and criticism do enter is when the rich man does not show himself generous, when "his liver is thin," when he does not practice charity to the poor, build wayside shelters or prayer houses, or entertain liberally.[10]

Much the same ethos was reported by M. G. Swift—this time in Jelebu, Negri Sembilan, during research in the mid-1950s.

> The relations of the rich with villagers not poor enough to be dependents are also not good. The strength of bitterness and jealousy are striking . . . The rich are the obvious source of material help, but since there are only a few of them in each village, they are continually subject to demands, while they do not have occasion to seek help themselves. The recipients accept the help they give *not with gratitude, but as a right, for the rich are their kin, or their neighbors, and they are wealthy*; a small gift is nothing to them. This one-sided relationship creates resentment, for the rich resent having to give all the time while their good nature is not sufficiently recognized. The recipient of help resents having to ask for it, and not receiving more.[11]

In the mid-1960s, S. Ali Husin conducted a comparative study of leadership in three villages, one of which was no more than twelve miles from Sedaka. His comments on wealth and status in all three communities reflect the findings of Firth and Swift.

9. For an argument that this ethos is relevant in many peasant contexts, see James C. Scott, *The Moral Economy of the Peasant: Subsistence and Rebellion in Southeast Asia* (New Haven: Yale Univ. Press, 1976), chaps. 1 and 6.

10. London: Routledge & Kegan Paul, 1971, reprint (first published 1946), 295, emphasis added.

11. *Malay Peasant Society in Jelebu*, London School of Economics, Monographs on Social Anthropology, No. 29 (New York: Humanities Press, 1965), 153, emphasis added.

Wealth, in itself, is not greatly respected, and is often skeptically regarded as the root of many evils that are detested by the villagers. A mean or squandering wealthy man is detested, but on the other hand, those who are generous with their money are often held in affection and respect. [12]

Finally, in a recent sociological study of a village in the state of Melaka (Malacca), Narifumi Maeda examined the practice of charity and the sanctions surrounding it. He concluded:

Unilateral gift-giving is supported by the ethos of Islam, and mutual help, which may be more strongly perceived as an insurance against future contingencies, by communal feeling. In the former case [zakat raja], recipients are anonymous under the category of poor and needy. In the latter, the helper and the helped have a specific relationship, for example, they are neighbors or relatives. Those who are in a position to help a particular individual are expected to do so in case of need. [13]

From these diverse studies it appears that quite similar expectations circumscribe the relations between rich and poor in the Malay village. The point here is not whether these expectations are consistently observed in practice but rather that they do exist and that, when they are violated, their violation calls forth the resentment and condemnation we have observed. The legitimacy of these expectations is triply guaranteed. First and foremost, they correspond with the customary values of Malay village life. They are, in addition, powerfully reinforced by a popular Islam that enjoins charity and compassion from the rich. Nor, finally, should we overlook the way in which two decades of electoral politics by the ruling Malay party (UMNO) has contributed to sustaining this normative legacy. The party has fashioned an electoral machine based largely on patronage politics within the Malay community and has counted on its largesse to gain for it the deference and loyalty to win elections. Its implicit model for state–peasant relations is remarkably like the ethos we have been examining.

The ethos described above is gradually losing its sanctioning power in Sedaka, but it is far from moribund *even among wealthier villagers.* It is invoked, in effect, whenever a large farmer describes the work, or *zakat peribadi,* he gives to a poorer villager as "help" (*tolong*). It is invoked in the shared ideology of Islam, which requires charity as a means of "cleansing" wealth and promoting social harmony. It is invoked, by implication, whenever a relative or neighbor is given

12. *Malay Peasant Society and Leadership* (Kuala Lumpur: Oxford Univ. Press, 1975), 76. In this context, see also the same author's *Kemiskinan dan Kelaporan Tanah di Kelantan* (Poverty and land hunger in Kelantan) (Petaling Jaya: Karangkraf Sdn. Berhad, 1978).

13. Masuo Kuchiba, Yoshihiro Tsubouchi, and Narifumi Maeda, eds., *Three Malay Villages: A Sociology of Paddy Growers in West Malaysia,* trans. Peter and Stephanie Hawkes (Honolulu: Univ. of Hawaii Press, 1979), 278–79.

a tenancy, whenever a loan is given before the feast of Ramadan, whenever rents are below their market value, whenever hand labor is used in preference to the combine, whenever a large marriage feast is given. Though under siege, all of these practices are still a part of the reality of contemporary village life. It is invoked as well whenever rich villagers criticize even wealthier outsiders for renting their land in huge parcels to big entrepreneurs rather than considering the needs of their own people.

Some quite remarkable and unique empirical findings, reported recently, shed further light on this ethos and its operation. Akimi Fujimoto examined four paddy villages in Malaysia (two in Province Wellesley, two in Kelantan) to determine whether rent levels, land prices, the amount of land rented out, and the wages and volume of agricultural labor in these communities can be explained entirely by neoclassical assumptions of maximizing net return.[14] He concluded in each case that actual practice did not coincide with these assumptions and that noneconomic income-sharing assumptions were necessary to explain sub-optimizing outcomes. Thus a good many landowners did in fact take on more tenants, charge lower rents, hire more laborers at higher wages than were compatible with maximizing their net return. They did so, it is clear, less from a spirit of liberality than as a response to the palpable pressures their neighbors and kin brought to bear upon them. The small redistribution that results is hardly sufficient to affect materially the existing inequalities; it does, however, indicate that the ethos has some impact on existing practices.

Both the ideology that enjoins a certain liberality by the well-to-do and its actual practice are realms of constant, if low-level, ideological conflict. This is to be expected, inasmuch as they have far-reaching implications for the distribution of land, work, and income as well as for the distribution of prestige, status, and subordination. Nowhere is this more apparent than in the use and interpretation given the verb *tolong* (to help, aid, assist), which is typically used to describe such liberality.

"Help" extended by one villager to another, when it is described as *tolong*, carries the implication of a mutuality that takes place among conceptual equals. It covers such common occurrences as the short-term loan of water buffalo or kitchen utensils, the last-minute request for a cooking ingredient from a neighbor, and the (now disappearing) mutual exchange of field labor for transplanting or harvesting (*derau*).[15] For my purposes, what is important about *tolong* is that it implies an equivalent (not identical) return favor by the recipient at some later time. To help, in this fashion, does not imply any subordination of the receiver to the giver. Even when the help is given by the manifestly well-to-do to a

---

14. Fujimoto, "Land Tenure, Rice Production, and Income Sharing among Malay Peasants: Study of Four Villages" (Ph.D. diss., Flinders University, Australia, 1980).

15. For such transactions the doubled term *tolong-menolong* is frequently used, thus emphasizing the reciprocity.

poorer neighbor or friend, the conceptual equality suggested by *tolong* is retained. A landless peasant who inquires about renting land from a large landowner is likely to ask if the landowner will "help" (*tolong*) him. Requests for temporary loans or advance wages take virtually the same linguistic form. In all these cases, a term implying reciprocity is appropriate in part because a return is built into the situation; the tenant will pay rents and cultivate, the borrower expects to repay, and the laborer will work for his or her advance wages. When it is a better-off villager who asks for services from a poorer person, *tolong* is also employed. The farmer who approaches his neighbor for help with transplanting, with repairing bunds, with cutting or threshing, will invariably ask if the neighbor can "help" him, even though the work will be paid.

The effect of the use of *tolong* in such exchanges is to emphasize the conceptually equal status of the parties involved, although the "facts" of the matter may be otherwise. It is to the advantage of richer villagers to use this formula because, as we have seen, they have a stake in minimizing the actual differences of property and income that exist. For the poor, the use of *tolong* is, quite literally, a face-saving formula that spares them the humiliation of being seen openly as inferiors or dependents. The exchange of "help" is thus to be sharply distinguished from relations of charity, which do indeed imply subordination and inferiority. To ask for alms (*minta sedekah*), which implies no reciprocal favor, is to place oneself in a permanent position of debt—and hence, subordination— to one's benefactor.[16] Razak is the only person in the village who has been systematically willing to go to this demeaning length to seek assistance.

Just who is helping whom and how much—who is the social creditor and who the debtor—in relations described as *tolong* is always a contested social fact. The matter is further complicated by the fact that shifts in land tenure and demography have upset the rules of the game. When harvest labor was scarce, before combines were available, it was at least plausible that the reapers and threshers were doing a favor by gathering in a farmer's crop in good time. This interpretation was reflected in the widespread practice of farmers giving *zakat peribadi* bonuses in paddy to those who had worked on the harvest. One purpose of the bonus was certainly to create a sense of gratitude and thereby socially obligate the wage laborer to the same promptness and diligence in the coming season. For their part, however, laborers came to view the *zakat* bonus not as a gift but as a right—as a part of the normal, anticipated pay for the harvest work. Much the same might be said of the tenant's relation to the landlord well before double-cropping. Then, villagers maintain, tenants were in short supply and land to farm was plentiful. Given his other opportunities, it was arguable that a good cultivator who accepted a tenancy was helping his landlord. Re-

16. Even here, however, folk Islam holds that the recipient of alms is in effect doing a favor for the almsgiver by providing him with the opportunity to perform an act of religious merit and thus to earn a reward (*pahala*) from God.

missions of rent after a crop shortfall might from the landowner's perspective have been seen as a favor or concession, while in the tenant's view they were a customary right built into the implicit contract.

Struggles of precisely this kind, I believe, are common whenever classes are in direct, personal contact. Members of the upper class wish to maximize the *discretionary* character of the benefits at their disposal, because it is precisely this aspect of their power that yields the greatest social control and, hence, conformity. For their part, members of the lower class strive to transform discretionary favors into rights to which they are automatically entitled to lay claim. Should they succeed, there is no longer a favor to be recognized with deference, no social subordination, no humiliation. The most likely outcome, of course, is a continuing struggle, expressed in language and gestures, over the meaning of such transactions in which no one view entirely prevails.[17]

Now, of course, the opportunities for wage labor and tenancy are sharply reduced. It is no longer so ambiguous who is doing the greatest favor for whom; both the tenant and the wage laborer count themselves fortunate to have land and work and acknowledge, by their *public* deference, their indebtedness. Landlords and farmers hiring labor can, and do, plausibly, contend that they are "helping" a tenant or a laborer merely by engaging him, even though the rents may be higher and inflexible and the work more sporadic and onerous. The meaning of "help" and its social weight is thus dependent, to some degree, on the need of the recipient, and this need is in turn an artifact of the near monopoly that larger farmers now enjoy over income-earning opportunities. The poor of Sedaka, as we have seen, privately resent the loss of status inherent in the new situation, but a due regard for their livelihood obliges them to steer a course of public prudence.

Despite the fact that the use of *tolong* preserves the facade of conceptual equality between villagers, it has always been clear that "help" is expected to flow predominantly in one direction—from the relatively well-off to the needy. This expectation is best seen in the astonished anger provoked when the norm is flagrantly violated. For five years Tok Ahmad and Shamsul had jointly rented nearly 10 relong of paddy land from Haji Din, a very wealthy outsider, at a high seasonal rent. When Haji Din announced that he expected his tenants to pay him, above and beyond the rent, a few sacks of paddy as *zakat,* they were indignant. As Tok Ahmad put it to me, "He came *himself* to ask. He wanted to eat *zakat* from us! How is that possible? It is as if we [are expected] to help

17. One of the best discussions of this process is to be found in Georg Simmel, "The Poor," pp. 150–78 in *Georg Simmel on Individuality and Social Forms,* ed. Donald N. Levine (Chicago: Univ. of Chicago Press, 1971). Another insightful analysis focusing on similar relations between staff and inmates in prisons may be found in Thomas Mathiesen, *The Defenses of the Weak: A Sociological Study of a Norwegian Correctional Institution* (London: Tavistock, 1965), 155–64.

(*tolong*) him!"[18] The force of Tok Ahmad's indignation depends on the listener's knowledge that both *zakat* and *tolong* should logically go from the richer to the poorer and *not* the other way around, as Haji Din had hoped. That he could make such a request directly is a further sign that he is without shame. Here, as elsewhere, social values are reinforced by religion. Islam, in this respect and in others, is not a reason for resignation and meekness but a set of values from which a condemnation of the rich may be fashioned. It would be difficult to find any disagreement with Tok Kasim's understanding that "The rich are enjoined to help (*di-suruh tolong*)" and that those who violate this injunction "are not afraid of God." It is certainly from the poorer villagers that one hears this norm most insistently evoked. But it is firmly embedded in the language of their better-off neighbors as well.

When, as is increasingly the case, the well-off farmers of Sedaka fail to help their needy relations and neighbors with work, loans, *zakat,* and smaller favors, they open themselves to two charges. The first is the familiar one of stinginess and tightfistedness. As Tok Kasim notes, "The rich were generous (*senang kira*) before. We could ask for help (*minta tolong*). Now it's hard to ask for their assistance. Now they 'watch the pennies' (*pakai nipis*)." Abu Hassan, speaking of Haji Kadir's unwillingness to rent out any land to him, also links the refusal to help with the accusation of stinginess. "Some time ago, those who had more land wanted to help (*tolong*) those without land. They were generous but now they're clever (*cerdik*), they really calculate (*kira sungguh*)."

The second charge is broader and quite revealing. It is the charge of being arrogant, proud, conceited—of placing oneself above and hence outside the village community. If the charge of stinginess implies the denial of generosity, of help, the charge of arrogance implies the denial of the conceptual equality of villagers. Accusations to the effect that someone is conceited (*sombong, bongak, bongkak*) are perhaps the most common and most damaging popular form of character assassination in Sedaka. They are most often, but not exclusively, directed at the well-to-do. The opposite characteristic, that of acting modestly (*merendahkan diri, malu*) is highly valued, and the best-respected local figure, Lebai Sabrani, is typically praised in precisely these terms. His religious learning and healing skills give him great prestige, but he has never put on airs.

At its simplest, the charge of arrogance can result from any denial of the common decencies of social intercourse that one villager expects of another. A villager who refuses or fails to return a greeting on the village path is open to the charge. Anyone who fails to invite certain of his neighbors to a feast runs a

18. *Dia datang sindiri minta. Dia mau makan zakat sama kita. Macham mana boleh? Macham kita tolong dia.* In effect, of course, Haji Din was after what is called tea money (*duit teh*), a premium for the privilege of continuing to rent, which he chose to exact in kind and to legitimize as *zakat.* Such requests, if made at all, would be expected to come indirectly in view of how morally offensive they are.

similar risk. Even someone who keeps to himself and avoids the lively banter that is the small change of village reciprocity may be accused. And, of course, anyone who, by the way he or she dresses, speaks, or walks, betrays an attempt at superiority will be singled out for being *sombong*.[19] Young men who stay in the village studying, usually in vain, for years to pass the High School Certificate Exam and find a government job, and who refuse to work in the fields, are often considered *sombong*. In all of these instances, what is involved is *not* the failure of villagers to recognize the existing differences in income, property, education, religious knowledge, or skills that are part and parcel of village life. Rather, it is a question of requiring that villagers *act* in a way that recognizes a common local citizenship and mutuality or, in other words, the conceptual equality of other villagers.[20]

Wealthy villagers are especially liable to the charge of being *sombong* for two reasons. First, it is they who are most likely to place themselves above others and who have the means of doing so with comparative impunity. Second, since they are more able to *help* their fellow villagers, their obligations of citizenship, as it were, are conceived to be that much greater. On the analogy that Sedaka is "one family"—an analogy frequently made by villagers in the context of pointing out the shortcomings of some—a wealthy man who turns a blind eye to the needs of his kin and neighbors is thereby placing himself above others and is seen as *sombong*. As Mokhzani points out in his study of rural credit, the well-off who refuse loans to their neighbors in an emergency will be called *sombong*.[21] The terms *stingy* and *arrogant* thus form a natural pair when applied to the rich. When Mat "halus" talks about how the attitude of the well-off has changed in the last decade, he says, "They're stingier, they're more arrogant" as if it amounted, in his mind, to the same thing. Mat Isa, referring to outside landowners in the same context, comments, "The rich are arrogant, as before;

---

19. As a case in point, two teenage women who lived in the village and attended the nearby *Sekolah Arab* took it into their heads to begin wearing the robe and head covering required for school as their normal dress, even when school was out. They were obviously attempting to show their piety by adopting self-consciously Islamic dress. It was interpreted by villagers, however, as an attempt to place themselves above others religiously. The two braved the resulting storm of quiet abuse and shunning for more than a week before succumbing and resuming the standard sarong without head covering when at home.

20. Of course, the accusation of arrogance is often directed at outsiders with whom villagers must deal as well. This includes, among others, district officials, clerks in the district office, staff of the Farmers' Association, clerks at the government rice mill (LPN), nurses and doctors at hospitals and clinics. The difference is that, with such outsiders, arrogance is expected and anything short of arrogance is a welcome exception. Within the village, by contrast, arrogance is an unwelcome exception.

21. Mokhazani, "Credit," 71.

they don't take the poor into account," as if their callousness was merely an expression of their conceit.

The view that the rich who turn a blind eye to their obligations are arrogant is naturally advanced most insistently by the local poor, for whom character assault is one of the few remaining social weapons. The view is hardly confined to them, however, and it is common to hear well-to-do villagers criticize in precisely the same terms large, outside landowners who resume cultivation or who lease huge plots to commercial tenants. But we miss much of the social import behind the charge of *sombong* by seeing it merely as an effort to call the rich to order by appealing to shared values. To avoid the accusation, a wealthy villager must not only attend to the most pressing needs of his kin and neighbors, but he must do so in a spirit of *tolong,* that is, in a manner that does not shame or humiliate the recipient. The benefactor must act in a fashion that preserves at least the form, if not the substance, of mutuality. To do otherwise will not exempt even the charitable rich from the accusation of being arrogant. *What is demanded, ironically, is patronage that is not patronizing.* Here it is as if the poor of the village want to have their cake and eat it too. They attempt, symbolically, not only to enjoin charity and assistance but simultaneously to negate the "social premium" the rich might expect to extract as compensation for their generosity.[22] They attempt, in other words, to protect their vital material interests while at the same time minimizing the public social stigma that systematic relations of one-sided charity usually bring in their wake.

The charge of arrogance is, however, a double-edged sword. If modest peasants in Sedaka make use of it to influence the rich, the rich for their part also make use of it, more successfully, to control socially the behavior of the poor. In the talk of wealthy farmers, arrogance is often imputed to the more aggressive, less deferential poor who violate their view of what constitutes seemly behavior. The accusation covers especially those villagers who demand help (*tolong*) or charity as a matter of right and who thus fail to evince the appropriate gratitude to their benefactors, whether by deference, small services, loyalty, or social support. It also covers wage laborers, men or women, who insist on settling the wage rate before they come to work. From the farmer's point of view, these matters should be left to his discretion and so should the timing of the payment for harvest work after he has sold his paddy. Laborers who violate these expectations (often because of bitter past experience) are seen as "uppity" (*sombong*). The poor who refuse work or, worse, accept and fail to appear, fall in the same category. Thus Lebai Hussein privately castigates a number of poor villagers who shun work but still expect *zakat* from farmers. He claims they are difficult (*payah*), uncooperative (*rukun tidak mau bikin*), and proud (*sombong*). Haji Kadir criticizes

22. I have appropriated this term from Brian Fegan's excellent dissertation, "Folk-Capitalism: Economizing Strategies of Wet Rice Farmers in a Philippine Village" (Ph.D. diss., Yale University, 1979), 317–25.

Mat Nasir, a landless laborer, in much the same terms for only wanting work at high wages when it suits him. "He's difficult, stingy, and proud; we [villagers] shouldn't be so calculating," he concludes.

It is a fairly simple matter to construct, from these accusations and others we have heard, something of a portrait of "the good poor" according to wealthy villagers. In fact, Shahnon provides a sketch of this "ideal type" in the course of praising a man who comes seasonally from his mother's village to work for him. This man, a distant relative, *always* comes when Shahnon needs him to thresh; he works carefully to thresh each sheaf thoroughly; he returns every day until the harvest is completed, he *never* asks what the wage is and when it will be paid but leaves that up to Shahnon; and he never asks for a *zakat* bonus, leaving that, as well, to Shahnon's discretion. For workers from Sedaka itself, the criteria are similar but more extensive. A good worker should not only take *any* work at *any* wage when an employer asks, but, unlike many of the poor, he should not be given to slandering the rich behind their backs. He should be deferential, that is, not *sombong* or *payah*.

That this composite sketch of "the good poor" is an "ideal type" of which any actual poor person is a pale reflection becomes evident if one classifies the village poor by their reputation among the well-to-do. The category of "good poor" is, then, nearly empty! Abdul Rahim, Hamzah, Mansur, and Pak Yah have the best reputations for being willing workers who defer to their employers; but even here, opinion is divided. A good many more poor villagers have an unambiguous reputation for being proud and choosy, including Mat Nasir, Dullah, Taib, Mat "halus," Rokiah, Rosni, Omar, Sukur, and, of course, Razak. As one might expect, the most deferential poor are not so highly thought of by their poor neighbors as by the rich. I have heard other wage laborers in the village disparage particularly Abdul Rahim and Mansur as "yes men" or slaves (*tukang suruh, hamba*) who simply do the bidding of their employers.

Here again, in the petty realm of pride and arrogance, we encounter a small ideological struggle over the social control of poor village workers. The traits of deference and loyal service that are necessary to qualify as one of the "good poor" in the eyes of the well-to-do are traits that are seen as demeaning by other wage workers. Inasmuch as the poor have few jobs or charity to offer one another, the struggle is an unequal one in which *public* behavior, at least, conforms largely with the expectations of the well-to-do.

BENDING THE FACTS: STRATIFICATION AND INCOME

The normative context is just that: a context and not a straightjacket. It provides the setting for conflict between winners and losers in Sedaka. The parties to this conflict are all *bricoleurs* with a given set of tools or a set of variations on themes that are, for the time being, largely given. Those themes include the normative expectations that those who are comparatively well-off should be generous to their less-well-off neighbors and kin, that such generosity should take nonde-meaning (*tolong*) forms, and that neither rich nor poor should conduct themselves in an arrogant or shameful manner. Just who is well-off, just how generous they should be, just what forms their generosity should take, just which forms of help are compatible with dignity, and just what behavior is arrogant and shame-ful are questions that form the substance of the drama.

Within these broad confines, both rich and poor have developed working strategies designed to make the normative principles serve their interests as much as possible.[23] The rich, whose interests are most directly threatened by these values, attempt to bend them so as to minimize their obligations and to place themselves in the most favorable light. Of course, at some level, they are in-creasingly able simply to impose themselves—to use machines, to forego taking on tenants and laborers, to trim back their ceremonial and charitable burdens. They are, however, concerned with justifying their behavior, not only to others but to themselves, for they too work within the same moral confines. For the village poor, somewhat less bending and squeezing of existing understandings is necessary, if only because these understandings already work, symbolically at least, to their advantage. They seek, more straightforwardly, to maximize the obligations due them under the existing rules.

The more or less constant ideological struggle that ensues is fought out, always inconclusively, on several terrains. One such terrain, the central one in some respects, is the terrain of stratification and income. Unless it is first known who is rich and who is poor and just *how* rich and poor they are, it is impossible to evaluate their conduct. Thus the first issue, the first terrain of conflict, is precisely over the facts that, once established, form the framework in which social ex-pectations are played out.

The resounding and insistent battle cry of Sedaka's wealthy families across this terrain is, "We are not rich." It is repeated and repeated in a bewildering, but consistent variety of forms—forms that go well beyond mere modesty. For example, the rich are never caught referring to themselves, individually or col-lectively, by the term "rich" (*kaya*). In fact, they only rarely use even the term *senang,* or "comfortable," which is most often applied to the modestly well-off in the village. To take what they say about their economic status purely at face value would lead to the conclusion that they were barely making ends meet.

23. For an interesting analysis of a French village in which the social ideology of patron and client are treated as symbolic weapons in a continuing conflict, see Alain Morel, "Power and Ideology in the Village Community of Picardy: Past and Present," pp. 107–25 in Robert Forster and Orest Ranum, eds., *Rural Society in France: Selec-tions from the Annales* (Baltimore: Johns Hopkins Univ. Press, 1977). As Morel notes, "These two ideologies, that of the 'deserving worker' and that of the patron-employer as 'father of the village,' are part of a consensus, a framework that permits both parties to develop their strategies, since each can count on certain predictable reac-tions." P. 118.

Thus, they typically describe themselves as having enough to eat (*boleh makan*) or just enough to eat (*boleh makan sahaja*). Cik Yah, a divorced woman fairly well-off considering her small household, describes herself as "just hanging on" (*tahan duduk*). Lebai Pendek, head of the second wealthiest family in the village, who farms 13 relong and owns a tractor, allows that he has just "a little paddy land" (*bendang sedikit sahaja*). If he is a large farmer, a man emphasizes how much of his land is rented in rather than owned. If he owns a sizable plot, he emphasizes how poor the land is and how many children he has.[24]

Wealthy villagers, in other respects as well, took great pains to emphasize that they were fundamentally no better off than the generality of their neighbors. Thus they lost no opportunity to point out that they, like everyone else, were farmers and that they, like everyone else, planted rice. This was, to be sure, largely true providing one was willing to equate the planting of 20 relong with the planting of half a relong and to ignore quite a few villagers with no land at all to plant. Here they took full advantage of the slender facts that still provide for the conceptual equality of all villagers so as to avoid standing out as privileged.

The local terms of stratification are not, however, symmetrical. While the rich portray themselves as barely managing, the poor describe them as "rich" (*kaya*) almost without exception. They take care never to do so within earshot, but only privately or in the company of other villagers of modest circumstances. The public stage is once again controlled by wealthy villagers but, offstage, the poor lose no time in calling a spade a spade. A few, like Bakar "halus," speak of the wealthy collectively as the "group"—or class—of "haves" (*golongan berada*).

---

24. Questions of wealth and income are of course inherently comparative, and to some extent the rich in Sedaka have a standard of comparison different from that of the poor. Compared, say, to really big outside landowners such as Haji Broom, to government clerks with a steady salary, or to Chinese storekeepers and traders, they are, indeed, not so comfortable. Although something of the kind is involved in their modesty, it is, as we shall see, neither the only nor even the main reason for their self-description. One might also imagine that much of this pattern was simply an effort to throw dust in the eyes of a naive outsider regarded with healthy suspicion. Yet the pattern continued long after wealthy villagers knew that I had become familiar with their actual economic circumstances, and it was sustained, especially in any situation in which other villagers were present.

A small number of wealthy villagers, notably Haji Jaafar and Haji Kadir, would, when talking privately with me, drop the pretense and occasionally boast of their holdings. This I took to be an effort to match or outdistance the stranger, who was paid, it seemed, a princely salary. Whenever the situation was public, however, the guarded financial modesty resumed. The occasional exception to the pattern of minimizing income and property is when the question of paddy yields is involved. Here a man's reputation as a good cultivator is at war with his desire to minimize his wealth, and the former occasionally wins out.

That the poor should call wealthy villagers "rich" is not merely a consequence of their standard of comparison, although the wealthiest in Sedaka are, as the poor see them, quite rich indeed. The poor, as we shall see, have a vested class interest in emphasizing, and exaggerating, the income and property of their wealthy neighbors.

If the rich consistently understate and downplay their economic comfort, the poor in Sedaka follow a parallel strategy of emphasizing their own poverty. They insist, "We are extremely poor." Thus they describe themselves to others, and especially to the rich, as "hardup" (*susah*) or "extremely hardup" (*sangat susah*). Instead of using the standard Malay word for "poor" (*miskin*), they avoid this Arab loanword, with its demeaning connotations of begging, and use *susah*. As part of a contrasting pair with *senang, susah* focuses on the quality of life—on how difficult it is to make ends meet—rather than on a fixed economic status. They avail themselves of every opportunity to reiterate that they have little or no land to farm, that they cannot find enough work, that they have to *buy* some of the rice which they eat, that the prospect of renting in more land at a rent that would leave them some profit has all but disappeared.

Well-to-do villagers emphatically reject this self-description of the poor as fraudulent. Haji Salim provides, in this context, what might be termed the gospel according to the rich:

> Before we had hard-up people—really hard-up people. So much so that they couldn't eat. Before 10 percent had to buy rice, but now no one has to buy rice. Before, the hard up were many and the comfortable, few. Now we still have some hard up, but they are not so many and not so hard up. When we want to call them [for work] we can't find enough. They have enough (*cukup banyak*) and with the new comforts (*kesenangan*), even if they don't work, they can get enough to eat and wear. [That's why] they are less diligent (*rajin*) about working.

The link here between an alleged labor shortage and the prosperity that must account for it is particularly important, for it is Haji Salim who is bitterly criticized by the poor for having gotten permission to bus in Thai laborers last season to transplant his rice. In one form or another, however, his views are echoed by nearly all the comfortable farmers of Sedaka. They seize on the fact that a few small tenants now hire combine-harvesters as evidence of both their prosperity and their laziness. Daud, the son of headman Haji Jaafar, thus notes that Rosni and Taib hired the machine once and calls them lazy, because "It's proper (*sepatutnya*) that those who farm only 2 or 3 relong should do their own work." "If they really needed money, they'd do the work themselves." Whenever a poor man is seen eating in a coffee shop, whenever poor men or women are seen in new clothes or shoes, whenever they buy anything but the cheapest fish, whenever they go off by bus to visit relatives, it is taken as further evidence that those who claim to be poor are dissimulating.

The constant debate about the facts of economic stratification was apparent to me from the outset of the research. In the first few months in Sedaka, I made a point of visiting each family to establish the basic "facts" of household farming and income. Given the pattern of local sociability, most of these conversations were joined by curious neighbors who happened to be around at the time. An interesting pattern emerged. If I asked, say, a poor man how much cash he and his wife had earned in planting, reaping, threshing, and other work, he would do some mental arithmetic and arrive at a set of figures, usually with his wife's help.[25] But the figure was often contested by one or more bystanders. If the man said, for example, that he had earned M$150 threshing, someone else might say, "No, it was a bit more; you must have threshed five days for so-and-so and another week for your uncle and Haji so-and-so in Sungai Bujur." "You must have earned at least M$200 threshing last season." Some time elapsed before I realized that it was invariably a relatively wealthy villager who disputed the poor man's estimate and that he invariably claimed the man had earned more.[26] A similar quarrel often swirled around how much *zakat peribadi* a poor man had received from wealthier households, with the well-to-do invariably asserting that the poor man had gotten one or two more sacks, or *naleh,* of paddy than he had claimed. Such disputes were rarely acrimonious and they were always inconclusive, with each party defending a different figure.

A mirror-image of this pattern, with one significant difference, developed when I spoke with well-off men about their income, yields, and rents. They too would arrive at a figure. In this case, however, the figure was *never* openly contested, as it was in the case of the poor. Instead, in the next few days, the matter might come up in a conversation with another small group, or I might be approached privately by someone who had been there. If the large farmer had

25. Women typically manage most of the cash resources of the Malay family. For a fine analysis of the historical pattern of gender-based economic roles in the Malay world, see Marie-André Couillard, "A Brief Exploration into the Nature of Men/Women Relations among Pre-Colonial Malayan People" (Paper presented at Second International Conference of the Canadian Council for Southeast Asian Studies, Singapore, June 1982).

26. The reader may reasonably wonder how it was possible, under these difficult circumstances, to establish the facts at all. It was not a simple matter, but the disputes were typically about income at the margin; depending on whose opinion one accepted, the difference was seldom more than 10 percent on either side of an average. Many of the facts could in fact be checked by direct observation, by asking those least likely to have a stake in dissimulating, or by actual records (in the case of owned land or of formal rental agreements for *pajak*) in order to establish an estimate in which some confidence could be placed. Data bearing on actual cultivation—expenses, yields, area farmed—were the easiest to establish by observation over two years, while income earned outside the village was hardest to pin down precisely, although I made a point of inquiring of outside employers and coworkers to cross-check quite a few figures.

claimed, say, a yield of thirteen gunny sacks per relong from 8 relong, they might disagree and put the yield at fifteen gunny sacks per relong and perhaps even point out that the man had an additional relong or two in another village, which he had failed to mention. The men offering the revised figures, I soon realized, were invariably from the poorer stratum of Sedaka, and they invariably offered figures that further elevated the income and wealth reported by better-off villagers. When it came to the *zakat peribadi* which the large farmer said he had given to laborers, the poor—often the laborer in question—would invariably insist that the *zakat* gifts were below what had been claimed.[27]

The fact that rich and poor peasants alike should make themselves out—to me *and* to each other—as somewhat poorer than they are is hardly of much interest. This is nothing more than the usual dissimulating pose of a class that is historically subject to onerous claims which it seeks to minimize. What is of note, however, is the clear pattern found both in each local class's view of the village stratification and in disputes about income. The economic gap between rich and poor is dramatically different depending on which point of view one adopts. As seen by the rich, the gap is quite small; they themselves are barely making do, while those who claim to be poor are actually doing quite nicely. Consistent with this perspective is their insistence, evident in their view of the impact of double-cropping detailed in the last chapter, that their gains have been modest and the gains of the poor, substantial. The view of Sedaka's stratification which they promote is one of a rather egalitarian setting where all plant rice, where neither real destitution nor real affluence exists, and where those who do have a bit more are generous to a fault. As seen by the poor, the economic gap is much greater; the rich are much better off than they let on and the poor are very poor indeed. The view of Sedaka's stratification that they in turn promote is one of great inequities, where a few privileged monopolize the land and income, where the poor live from hand to mouth and are without prospects, and where generosity is rare and insignificant.[28]

27. Again, the truth of such matters was not simple to determine, although the differences were small. As I remained through four crop seasons in the village, however, much of this information could be directly or indirectly ascertained. Thus, by observing actual *zakat peribadi* gifts, I could normally infer the most likely level for a previous season with a given yield and given paddy price. It was, in fact, in the matter of *zakat peribadi* that the claims of the well-to-do were most inflated, although the inflation declined as they realized I was increasingly familiar with village patterns.

28. In summarizing these opinions I have looked back over my fieldnotes to verify that these views were in fact held by a substantial majority of rich and poor, respectively. As many as eleven of the poorest thirty-seven households could not be counted as part of the consensus among the poor; among these eleven, seven household heads did not actually disagree but were reserved or silent on many of these issues. Among the wealthiest fifteen households, only four were substantially out of line with the general view.

The class issues at stake in these divergent interpretations of economic reality are by now obvious. These interpretations are provoked by the fact that the "rules of the game," which impose certain standards of liberality on the rich, are largely accepted by most participants. What is not given, what is not fixed, however, and what can therefore be manipulated within limits is the *position* of a particular family or household within this pattern of established obligations. The "haves" of Sedaka minimize the inequalities because, by doing so, they also minimize their obligations to provide work, rice, and land to their poorer neighbors. If their neighbors are not poor and they themselves are not rich, then the question of their obligations does not even arise. As an afterthought, in effect, they add that the small differences that may exist have come about for reasons (laziness, stupidity, improvidence) that disqualify the few poor in the village from any special consideration. The "have-nots" of Sedaka, in contrast, exaggerate the inequalities because, by doing so, they also maximize the obligations the rich ought to have toward them under the existing values. Once these huge inequities are accepted as social fact, then it follows that the stingy and self-centered behavior of the village rich is in flagrant violation of a shared normative code. What we observe, in brief, is not some trivial difference of opinion over the facts, but rather the confrontation of two social constructions of the facts, each designed and employed to promote the interests of a different class.[29]

RATIONALIZING EXPLOITATION

It is manifestly clear that most of the changes in land tenure, rents, and employment in the past decade have either violated or sharply limited the applicability of earlier understandings. The question I would like to consider here is how these changes have been put across ideologically, how they have been represented. How have different classes inside and outside Sedaka asserted their claims and pressed them in the face of resistance? To examine this issue at close range is to watch ideology at work where it really counts—in the rationalization of exploitation and in the resistance to that rationalization.

Here we are concerned with appearances, with the mask that the exercise of economic or political power typically wears. Things in this domain are rarely what they seem; we should expect disguises, whether they are self-conscious or not. There is nothing either surprising or mysterious in this process. The executive who fires some of his work force is likely to say that he "had to let them go." This description of his action not only implies that he had no choice in the matter but that those he "let go" were being done a favor, rather like dogs on

29. What might be termed the "middle" peasantry—roughly the twenty households directly below the richest twenty households—is difficult to classify in these terms. Their view of the village stratification is ambiguous or mixed; if there is any tendency at all, it is to see things rather more the way the richer villagers see them.

a leash who had finally been released. Those who are the beneficiaries of this magnanimous act are likely to take a different view; their metaphors are usually more colorful: "I got the sack," "I was axed." The victim may be excused if he fails to share the executioner's perspective. Whatever term the Vietnamese peasantry used to describe what was done to them by U.S. forces, one may be sure that it was not "pacification."[30]

The disguises, however, are diagnostic. This is particularly the case where two parties are in a continuing relationship that is partly antagonistic and partly collaborative. Here the mutual claims and counterclaims are likely to be phrased in language that each party has reason to believe the other will consider relevant and legitimate. Thus, someone asking his employer for a raise is more likely to cite his diligent work, his loyalty, and his contribution to his employer's enterprise in support of his claim than, say, his desire for a new automobile or an expensive vacation. And the employer wishing to deny the raise is more likely to cite stagnant profits, equity among employees, and the fact that the present salary is comparatively generous than, say, the employer's desire to increase his own profit or to invest in a new business. What is of interest here is not the true value of such claims but the way in which they help us define what appears to each party to be a mutually acceptable terrain of discourse.

In this context, it occurred to me to wonder what happened when a landlord decided to raise the rent, change the form of tenure, or actually dismiss a tenant. How was such a decision presented, justified, and rationalized to the tenant? In what terms did the tenant resist the claim? Such cases are diagnostic, because they typically involve what would seem in principle to be a serious breach of shared values. With few exceptions, someone who is relatively well-off is, in such encounters, attempting to extract more rent from a poorer person or to deny him or her access to the means of production. How could such a demand possibly be rationalized if it flew in the face of the injunction that wealthy peasants should, within their means, assist their less fortunate neighbors and relatives? To answer this question, I collected as many accounts as I could of what actually was said in such confrontations.

Raising the rent has always been a delicate matter, and yet it has of course happened with great regularity since the 1960s. Before that, when land prices and paddy prices varied little, both tenure and rent levels were comparatively stable, and this stability was in part due to social pressure. As the Rice Production Committee report noted in 1953, arbitrary rent increases were rare, "since public opinion would make itself felt against any landlord who insisted on higher rent, or who sought to eject a tenant who was cultivating with normal

30. For a brilliant analysis of the social function of euphemisms by powerful groups, see Murray Edelman, "The Political Language of the Helping Professions," *Politics and Society* 4, no. 3 (Fall 1974).

diligence and care."[31] Even today, there is unanimous agreement in Sedaka that if the rent *is* raised, the landlord is bound by custom to give the current tenant the option of accepting before he offers the land to anyone else. I know of only a single case in the village where this custom was perhaps violated.[32]

Just how ticklish a matter it is to raise a tenant's rent depends, of course, on a variety of other factors. We are never dealing with an abstract landlord and his abstract tenant confronting one another in an abstract situation. Some of the crucial factors that color the social view of the transaction are the price of paddy,[33] the closeness of the kinship tie between landlord and tenant, the number of years the tenant has been farming the land, and the relative wealth of the owner vis-à-vis the cultivator. Generally speaking, a rent increase is easiest to put across when the price of paddy has risen sharply (increasing the tenant's return under fixed cash rents), when the landlord and tenant are unrelated, when the tenant is a short-term renter, and when the landlord, as occasionally happens, is manifestly poorer than the tenant. A higher rent is hardest to justify when, in contrast, the reverse of all these conditions applies.

The case of Rosni and her landlord, Abu Saman (an outsider), falls toward the "ticklish" end of the spectrum. When Abu Saman moved to raise the rent a year ago, the price of paddy had not changed since the last rent increase in 1974 to M$600 (or $150 for each of 4 relong per season). Rosni's own return, due to increasing production costs, had been declining. While there was only a rather distant kinship tie between her late husband and the landlord, she and her husband had rented the land from the landlord's grandfather and had farmed it for more than twenty years. Rosni is not well-off; she has no land aside from these 4 relong and has managed only by dint of prodigious wage labor transplanting and reaping to raise her seven children since she was widowed nine years ago. Abu Saman, in contrast, is a rich man with more than 25 relong of paddy land and a profitable shop.

Under the circumstances it is not surprising that Abu Saman avoided broaching the subject directly. He chose instead to "let it be known" (*cara sembunyi*

31. Government of Malaya, *Report of the Rice Production Committee, 1953* (Kuala Lumpur: 1953), vol. 1, pp. 45–46.

32. Lebai Hussein and his son Taha claim that Tok Mah gave the 3 relong they had been farming to Pak Yah without giving them a chance to accept a higher rent. In her defense, Tok Mah claims that she had told them of her intention of raising the rent and took their grumbling as a refusal. The truth of the matter will perhaps never be known but, for my purposes, what is instructive is that Tok Mah recognizes the custom by claiming that she *had* given them the right of first refusal and that they had refused.

33. The rental increases that occurred following the sharp 1973 increase in farm-gate paddy prices were generally accepted as legitimate, providing they were modest. The reasoning was that the new profits could be divided equitably between the landowner and the tenant.

tau) through mutual friends that he wanted to raise the rent to M$700 a season for the 4 relong and that he now wanted to rent in advance for two seasons. Abdul Rahman, who was listening in when Rosni noted her landlord's round-about tactics, explained for my benefit why he did this: "He didn't want to come himself; he was embarrassed (*malu*) and reluctant (*segan*), because he's related to (*adek-beradek dengan*) Rosni."[34] His interpretation is plausible because this indirect approach is a common practice in ticklish situations when a con-frontation or a humiliating rebuff is possible. It is used as a means of conveying criticism[35] and of broaching the delicate matter of marriage negotiations. If the criticism misfires or the marriage proposal is turned down, it allows the initiator to beat a dignified retreat or even disown the initiative. Abu Saman's use of an intermediary is a strong, though not definitive, sign that he knew his demand ran counter to what was considered legitimate. When Rosni sent no reply back through the same channels, Abu Saman had little choice but to come and push his demand directly.

After the required pleasantries, coffee, and cakes, Abu Saman got to the point of his visit. He needed more rent because, he claimed, "I am also in bad shape" (*saya pun teruk*). His wife was ill and he had large doctor and hospital bills; he had borrowed money against other land he owned and had to pay this debt or lose the land. From Rosni's point of view, his sad tale was a completely bad-faith performance, of which not a word could be believed. But, of course, she did not challenge his story openly and replied in terms of her own situation: last season's crop had been bad, her oldest daughter was pregnant and could not earn anything transplanting, the children needed school uniforms, and she had little cash to last her until the harvest was in. For our purposes, what is significant is that Abu Saman's case for the rent increase is based entirely on *need*. Whether that case has any merit or not—most likely it does not—Abu Saman, in effect, makes himself out to be as poor or poorer than Rosni. By doing so, he affirms in effect the normative straitjacket within which he must operate. The only way to justify extracting a higher rent is to portray himself

34. The tactic of *sembunyi-tau* is used to broach delicate matters even between parties who are closely related and see one another constantly. Thus, when Haji Kadir decided that he would like his son-in-law Ghazali to pay his rent before the season rather than after the harvest, he had his wife tell her sister-in-law, who in turn told Ghazali's wife. Next season, the rent appeared in advance without a word ever having passed directly between the two principals. Had the rent not appeared, Haji Kadir would have had a choice between simply dropping the matter and making a direct suggestion.

35. Criticism of my frequent social missteps early in my stay was invariably conveyed in this way. Thus, when I unthinkingly would occasionally whistle a tune in the house, Haji Kadir, my co-resident landlord, chose to inform me through his brother-in-law Shahnon that whistling in the house was dangerous, as it was believed to entice snakes into the dwelling.

as the party in greatest need—the party most in need of help (*tolong*) and compassion. The same logic prevails here as in the question of stratification and income; a working strategy is followed that pays symbolic homage to the shared value of the rich helping the poor, but the facts are turned upside down to the advantage of the landlord. Abu Saman, however, plays his trump card toward the end of the exchange by mentioning that someone else has asked about the land. He needs to say no more. The meeting ends inconclusively, but within a week Rosni sends her son with the higher rent, but for only a single season, not two seasons. By accepting the cash and by his subsequent silence, it appears that Abu Saman has accepted this tacitly negotiated compromise.

The case of Tok Ahmad and Shamsul, who jointly rent 6 relong from another outside landlord, Haji Din, also lies toward the ticklish end of the spectrum. They too have rented this land for a long time, nearly thirty years, and Tok Ahmad is distantly related to the landlord. Tok Ahmad, who farms 4 of the 6 relong, is a middle peasant by Sedaka standards but has no land other than what he rents from Haji Din, while Shamsul is relatively well-off due to his salary as an examiner of paddy for moisture content at the nearby government rice mill. Both, however, are far poorer than Haji Din, who is a retired paddy dealer owning at least 20 relong and two tractors. Unlike Abu Saman, Haji Din did not attempt a roundabout method of raising the rent but came directly.[36] His argument, when he came to insist on M$180 a season per relong rather than M$150, differed only in particulars, not in substance, from Abu Saman's claim. He also pleaded that he was hard up (*teruk*) and elaborated by saying how expensive materials had become for the planned addition to his house, by emphasizing that he had fourteen children and grandchildren in his house who had to be clothed and fed, and by talking of the debts he owed on a small piece of orchard land. In a word, he claimed poverty. His plight left Tok Ahmad and Shamsul unmoved. Privately, they said he was lying (*dia membobong*)—this is, after all, the man who tried to extract *zakat* from them, and they know how wealthy he is. In his presence, however, they pleaded poverty as well: the paddy price had not improved; fertilizer and tractor costs were going up; after the harvest was in they had only eating rice left (*tinggal makanan sahaja*). The dialogue is already familiar. It is all but forced on the participants by a set of prevailing values that legitimate the claim to concessions by the poorer party. While the claim in the case of Tok Shaway and Shamsul is at least plausible, Haji Din's posturing is almost pure theater, as there is no other way, within existing values, of justifying his claim.

Lest his story fail to win his tenants' sympathy, Haji Din availed himself of the ultimate threat. He mentioned that his grandson was clamoring for land to

36. The fact that, since 1955, this particular tenancy had been covered by a written contract extending for at least two seasons at a time (*pajak*) perhaps precluded the informal approach, since a new agreement would in any case have to be filed.

farm. The threat was not an idle one, for Haji Din had taken back 4 of the 10 relong Tok Ahmad and Shamsul had earlier farmed. Faced with this warning, it did not take long for the tenants to settle reluctantly on the landlord's terms.

Additional accounts of a comparable kind could be multiplied indefinitely. Sukur notes that landlords have to say (*kena kata*) that they do not have any money, that they are hard up, when they come to ask for more rent. He captures the belief that such performances are a mandatory routine by adding that this is also the "tune" (*lagu*) that Haji Kadir used when denying loans or advance wages. The outcome is rarely in doubt, of course, since the tenant is always afraid of losing the land. "You have to take it (*terpaksa ambil*) or else he'll change [tenants]." "If you lose the land, it's finished, and you're back to hoeing for wages." Wahid says that his landlord always claims he "doesn't have enough money" (*duit tidak cukup*) when he wants more rent, although both the landlord and his wife are salaried schoolteachers who have bought much rubber and rice land with their savings. Ghani Lebai Mat's cousin, from whom he rents, invariably claims that he is hard-pressed (*sesak*) financially when he wants more rent, despite the fact that he is very comfortable. Lazim rents land from his brother, who has a fat salary but uses the same ploy of being hard-pressed (*sesak*) to justify higher rents. The claim, in his case and others, is typically backed by details designed to justify a higher levy.

Aside from personal reverses—debts, illness, a son's improvidence, poor crops—the landlord is likely to note anything that has reduced his own return, such as land taxes and inflation, and to mention any improvement in the tenant's return from higher paddy prices or a new fertilizer subsidy. The logic here is one of appealing to changes in the relative return of owner and tenant. If the current rent is clearly below the average rent for the area, the landlord will point that out too. In such a case, the landlord can argue that he has been *too* generous in the past. A fair amount of time is then usually devoted to disagreements over what *is* the average rent, how good the land in question is, how large the harvests have been, and how much profit the tenant has received after rents and expenses. As with questions of income, the landlord exaggerates the quality of the land and the tenant's profits, while the cultivator loses no opportunity to denigrate the field and understate his harvest and profits. These details, taken collectively, are footnotes to a discourse intended to establish the relative need of each party, which in turn is the fulcrum on which shared notions of mutual obligation rest.

The standard scenario for these encounters is perhaps most remarkable for the homage it pays, in however distorted and even cynical a form, to precapitalist niceties. It is extremely rare for a landlord to forgo the ritual and present the tenant with an unvarnished take-it-or-leave-it proposition. Haji Nayan claims that such crude (*kasar*) approaches do occur in which the owner simply says, "This year I'm raising the rent to M$175; if you don't want the land, I'll give it to someone else." Given the shortage of land and work, of course, it is precisely this coercive choice the tenant normally faces; knuckle under or lose the land.

And yet the symbolic amenities are almost always observed, since the normative atmosphere requires it. As Mat Sarif says, "The landlord has to (*terpaksa*) say he is hard up (*susah*). How else could he raise the rent?" This is so, he continues, even though "he really (*sebenarnya*) wants to buy even more land." It is, of course, not for me to say anything meaningful about the actual sincerity of the landlord's performance. The fact that its sincerity is doubted by most of its intended audience, however, is an important social fact. What is, in addition, very clear is that the landlord has little in the way of raw material and props—values, customs, or ideology—that would allow him to strike a convincing pose.

When the landlord wishes to make other changes in tenure conditions that are disadvantageous to the tenant, the logic is identical. Thus when Haji Zahir (an outside landlord) announced that he wanted Nizam and his father to pay the rent in advance (*pajak*) for two seasons on 8 relong, he told a tale of financial woe worthy of a poor man at the end of his luck. Nizam and his father believe, with good reason, that Haji Zahir merely wants the lump sum to lend out to someone else in order to gain the use of the debtor's land. When Samat's landlord decided to collect rents before the season began rather than after the harvest, he used his penury as the excuse. The landlord, Samat commented, "read (*bacha*) [his lines] as usual," implying that this was the routine performance that could be expected in the circumstances.

The same social logic can be seen in action whenever a landlord wishes to dismiss a tenant. This, of course, is a far more threatening possibility than an increase in rents or a switch to leasehold (*pajak*) tenancy, as it often spells ruin for the small cultivator. In terms of shared values, there is scarcely any way in which a rich landlord can rationalize taking the means of subsistence from a poor tenant. The qualifier "scarcely" is used purposely here, because the landlord's position is not ethically hopeless. One possibility for the landlord is to claim that he needs the land to provide for his son or son-in-law. Everyone recognizes and accepts that one's obligations to children should take precedence over any obligation to poorer but more distant relatives, let alone non-kin. A good many verbal tenancy contracts are, in fact, struck in just these terms: a landlord agrees to rent out the land with the understanding that he will reclaim part or all of it when his children marry or begin to farm. Thus, when Haji Din took back 4 relong from Tok Ahmad and Shamsul in 1975, he gave the only acceptable excuse. One of his sons, he said, had lost his tenancy and needed this to farm. Knowing his reputation, neither Tok Ahmad nor Shamsul took his explanation at face value and, since they had a rare written tenancy contract, they went to the District Office to lodge a complaint. The Assistant District Officer who deals with land matters forced a compromise in which Haji Din took back only 4 of the 10 relong he wanted. The next season, the ex-tenants' suspicions were confirmed as Haji Din's son never appeared, and the cultivation was done by a hired laborer. The following season the land was sold to a wealthy Malay paddy trader.

The experience of Taib, after his dispossession a landless laborer, followed much the same script. The landowner announced that his son was going to be married at the end of the main season and would need the land that Taib rented in order to provide for his new family. As the landlord had at least 15 relong of paddy land, much of it closer to his own village, Taib thought he was lying. The usual protestations, in this case quite accurate, that the loss of the land would be a disaster, got Taib nowhere. During the following season, his landlord's son actually did cultivate the land, occasionally hiring Taib to spread fertilizer and harrow. But sure enough, the second season after his dismissal, Taib discovered that the land had been leased for ten seasons to a Chinese shopkeeper and tractor owner. He surmises that this is what his landlord had in mind all along, but he was too embarrassed (*malu*) to reveal his deception immediately. Other land-lords have been less concerned with appearances; in any event, hardly a tenancy has been lost in Sedaka in which the landlord's duty to his children has not been invoked. [37]

In a few cases, of course, the landlord's justification is not mere rhetoric. Some landlords have no other way of providing for their children; some do fall on hard times and have little choice but to resume cultivation. Often, however, the landlord's goal is further accumulation of land or other productive assets or else a new house or a sumptuous wedding feast. As the land is his and his right to dispose of it as he pleases is protected, with few qualifications, by the force of law, he need not give any justification at all for his action. Nevertheless, he typically appeals to the only shared values that might possibly justify his behavior in the eyes of its victims by dramatizing his hardships or the needs of his children. His appeal, whether based on fact or not, serves to confirm and consolidate the existing symbolic order. The landlord's performance, like that of Dickens's Mr. Wegg, places him securely "with that very numerous class of impostors, who are quite as determined to keep up appearances to themselves as to their neighbors."[38] The tenant, for his part, contributes to the same

37. This is the case even when other reasonably legitimate grounds exist for dismissing a tenant. Razak's other brother (not Hamzah), who lives outside the village, once rented land to Razak. Villagers claim, plausibly, that Razak seldom actually paid the agreed rent for the land. Although the brother would have been justified, in terms of local values, if he had taken back the land for that reason alone, he also told Razak that he had to take the land for his son. So strong is the obligation to provide sons or sons-in-law with land whenever possible that parents are criticized when they fail to do it, and not a few sons fail to pay rents regularly knowing that it will be difficult for parents, even if poor, to revoke their tenancy. Parents, for their part, rarely transfer the land legally long before their death, since the question of inheritance is one of the few material sanctions they have to ensure that they are adequately provided for in their old age.

38. Charles Dickens, *Our Mutual Friend* (Harmondsworth: Penguin, 1971), 97.

symbolic edifice with his tale of ruin and woe, although in this case appearances are far less deceiving.

The greater economic power of the landlord usually ensures that the outcome of the drama is known in advance. But not always; this is not *pure* theater. Occasionally, the landlord appears, at least, to concede something. Perhaps he takes back only a portion of the land he originally insisted on; perhaps, as in Rosni's case, he accepts a higher rent while giving way on the issue of advance payment; perhaps he settles on a rent slightly lower than his initial demand. I have, of course, no way of telling whether the original demand was a bluff intended to produce the final settlement, which may now appear as a concession due to his generosity. Kamil claims, for example, that his landlord, Haji Azaudin, who had wanted to sell the 5 relong Kamil rents from him, changed his plans when he (Kamil) could not raise the M$18,000 to purchase them. He chose instead to sell another rented parcel, where the tenant did have the cash for purchase. On this basis, Kamil calls him a good (*bagus*) landlord. Tenants are generally quite cynical and thus not easily impressionable, but there are a *few* landlords who consistently go easy (*senang kira*) on their tenants—charging lower than normal rents, collecting after the harvest, and making allowances following a poor harvest. Such landlords, by their liberality, help keep the symbolic edifice I have described intact; they help to animate the amateur theatrics that even the tight-fisted landlord feels obliged to stage when he puts the screws to his tenant.

IDEOLOGICAL CONFLICT: THE VILLAGE GATE

If the richer farmers of Sedaka operate under some disadvantages, those disadvantages are more a matter of ideology than of action. There is, however, a small but significant exception to this pattern. It concerns virtually the only *collective* and *public* recognition that the village has an obligation to protect the livelihood of its members. As a rare and formal impediment to capitalist relations of production, it is little wonder that it would have come under attack. The attack was, as it happens, beaten back for the time being. The victory for older values was a small one, but the struggle was diagnostic for the issues we have been considering.

What the stakes were is perhaps best expressed in the crude lettering that adorns a wooden, swinging gate that bars the entrance to the main village path: "LORI PADI, LORI LAIN, DAN KUBOTA TIDAK BOLEH—JKKK." Translated, it says simply that "Paddy trucks, other trucks, and tractors cannot [enter]" and the warning is "signed" by the Village Development Committee. The gate is a single timber about six feet high, which spans the path and is secured by a locked chain. It does not impede the passage of pedestrians, bicycles, motorcycles, small "walk-behind" tractors, or even automobiles, but it does effectively bar entry to trucks or large tractors. The key is kept at the house of

Lebai Pendek just to the left of the gate, and the driver of any large vehicle must stop and ask that it be opened. Many, but not all, of the neighboring villages have similar gates, and this one has been here for at least the past fifteen years.[39]

The purpose of the gate is twofold. First, it is meant to restrict traffic along the dirt path, which during much of the year is muddy and slippery and therefore easily rutted. During the wettest months, a heavily loaded truck will be required to stop and unload its freight—for example, firewood, bricks, lumber, zinc roofing, furniture—which will then be carried by foot or cycle. At other times a fee of M$3 is collected for opening the gate and the truck is allowed to pass. The purpose of the fee was to create a small fund that was used annually to buy additional fill (*tanah merah*) to repair the damage done to the path in the previous monsoon.[40] A second and, for my concerns, critical purpose of the gate was to prevent paddy dealers' trucks from entering the village at all and thereby encroaching on the wages paid largely to villagers for hauling gunny sacks of paddy out to the main road. If the rice was to be sold or milled, as was usually the case, in nearby Kepala Batas, and if no large number of gunny sacks was involved, it made sense to pay villagers to haul it, a sack at a time, directly to the mill or buyer. The potential earnings for a villager were significant. It is not uncommon for a young man to earn as much as M$150 during a normal harvest and now, with double-cropping, such earnings were doubled.

The gate, then, was a *collectively enforced* example of *tolong*, a protected monopoly of work reserved for villagers alone.[41] When it was first established, it was of particular advantage to poor villagers, since the gunny sacks were transported

39. No one seems to remember exactly when it was erected, but most agree that it was the gradual improvement of the road near the village and the attendant growth of lorry traffic that explain its construction. Thus it is not as if villagers decided to protect this opportunity for wage work only in early 1960; it is rather that no real threat to bicycle hauling had existed until that time. Villagers also agree that their initial concern was that farmers who cultivated land near the village but did not live there would be the first to avail themselves of trucks to haul paddy.

40. *Tanah merah,* literally "red earth," is not available in the immediate vicinity. Local soils of marine clay, while they harden to the consistency of concrete during the dry season, are not suitable for roads because they become extremely viscous and slippery when wet. It is common to use *tanah merah* not only for roads and heavily trafficked paths but also to build up the elevation of the compound around and under the house.

41. There is some evidence that similar customs are observed outside Kedah as well. Fujimoto, for example, reports that in the Province Wellesley village of Guar Tok Said, "There was an agreement among the villagers that a rice dealer's lorry should be parked outside the village, at the time of the sale of *padi,* so that sacks of rice must be carried to the lorry, thus providing jobs especially to young boys in the village. . . . The road was narrow and it was difficult for a lorry to enter the village, but it was certainly possible." "Land Tenure," 196.

by bicycle, which even the poorest villager had. Now that motorcycles are more common, the principal beneficiaries have changed too, as we shall see. The gate itself was a fitting symbol for what it represented. It said that, in this small respect at least, Sedaka was a *closed economy*, that the hauling (*tanggung, tarik*) of paddy was open only to villagers, that the local monopoly on such work would not be lifted to accommodate the commercial paddy buyers and millers (mostly Chinese) who might provide the service more cheaply. Economically, of course, the gate represented a subsidy the larger farmers in the village paid to those of their neighbors who hauled paddy. The amount of the subsidy varied with the distance of the farmer's rice fields from the gate and with the size of his harvest. He would, with or without the gate, have to pay hauling fees (per gunny sack) from the field to the main village path. But once the bagged paddy had reached the village path, he had to pay the haulers for each sack they took to the head of the village track where the paddy could then be loaded onto a truck, if he wished, or to pay the village haulers themselves to continue on into town. If there had been no gate—if the paddy dealer's truck could come directly to that point on the village path closest to his paddy field—a farmer might save as much as M$2 a gunny sack. For a large farmer, of say 8 relong, the savings for two seasons might be as much as M$500. Farmers of 2 relong or less were little affected, since they were likely to keep most of their paddy at home and, when they did sell or mill some paddy, they could transport it themselves, a sack at a time.

In late March 1980, toward the end of a late harvest season, the gate was opened briefly to admit two paddy dealers' trucks, thus stirring up a bitter controversy, the effects of which still reverberate in Sedaka. It was opened initially by Fadzil, a middle-aged farmer who owns 8.5 relong and has for some time been a member of the UMNO committee (JKK) that runs village affairs. Fadzil is not much liked, even by his factional allies; he is reputed to be one of the two or three most careless cultivators, with consistently low yields, and spoiled (*sayang manja*) from an early age as the favorite adopted son of the late Tok Halim. Despite his air of superiority (*sombong*), his literacy and skills as a public speaker are valued by Bashir and others on the JKK. His position on the JKK is notable here because, as everyone in Sedaka knows, he spoke and voted for keeping the ban on paddy trucks a few years back when the issue was raised.

Fadzil's story is that, after his harvest was bagged and lying in the fields, he approached Lebai Pendek's son, Musa, who is a member of a small group that hauls paddy. Musa told him that the price per gunny sack would be M$1.80. Fadzil was furious, not only because he thought the rate was far too high but also because the rate is often left to the discretion of the farmer. But he did not negotiate further, simply saying that M$1.80 seemed too much. His reasoning was that the existence of the gate had allowed these young men to "extort" (*tekan*) from the farmers. The previous year, he noted, the fee was only M$1.20 and there was no justification for it to jump to M$1.80. The price of consumer goods (*harga barang*) had not gone up much, nor had the price of paddy.[42] This was not all. He added that the road itself had been improved recently by the addition of fill, making the transport by motorcycle much easier, especially now, late in the dry season (*musim kemarau*), when it was not slippery. Since it was the tail end of the harvest and there was not much paddy left to be hauled, the piece-rate should have declined.

Had the paddy been hauled that afternoon, the matter might have ended with no more than Fadzil's grumbling. But the haulers did not show up. Fadzil went again to see Musa, who promised that the paddy would be hauled early the next day. By noon the following day Fadzil's fifty sacks of paddy were still stacked in the middle of the field, and Musa sent word that it would be hauled that afternoon. By 3 P.M. nothing had happened; Fadzil was, he said, concerned that sacks might be stolen that night, and he was also scanning the horizon for the storm clouds that might soak his paddy. He briefly considered approaching another group of paddy haulers but thought better of it. Musa and his friends were all from UMNO families, politically aligned with Fadzil and the JKK, while the other group (*puak lain*) were from the PAS faction of the village. To have PAS men haul the paddy of an UMNO stalwart such as Fadzil would have been a serious breach of factional loyalties.

At this point, Fadzil apparently decided to attack the issue of the gate head on. He claims that he went to talk with Bashir, who while not the village headman is acknowledged as UMNO leader, to explain the situation and ask that the gate be opened. Here the stories diverge somewhat. Bashir denies that he was ever approached about opening the gate, while Fadzil claims that Bashir told him to open it. At any rate, Fadzil then went to Kepala Batas to contact his Chinese paddy dealer, who sent a truck to the village, led by Fadzil on his motorcycle. Reaching the gate, Fadzil dismounted and got the key from Lebai Pendek's wife, claiming that he had Bashir's permission to open it. By 5 P.M. the Chinese driver and his two Malay laborers had loaded Fadzil's crop aboard the truck and had left to deliver it to the dealer in town.

Meanwhile, word spread quickly, and many angry men were soon assembled in Bashir's village shop, a gathering place for the UMNO faction in Sedaka. Their tone was unmistakable. A few had already torn down the gate itself, as if to magnify Fadzil's crime. What he had done, they said, was "wrong" and "dishonest" (*karut*). He had done it, moreover, "as if he were in charge," as if "he wanted to take over" (*dia mau jadi kuasa*). Others spoke of violence. "He should be shot" (*kena peluru*), "He should be shot straight away" (*kena tembak terus*). The members of the UMNO paddy-hauling group (*golongan moto-tarik*) were, not surprisingly, the most inflammatory, but the anger was general.

---

42. The reasoning here is significant, as it manifests a belief that the piece-rate should be tied to the cost of living—to need—and that any increase in the cultivator's profits, as reflected in the farm-gate price, should be shared with laborers.

The most active members of PAS lost no time in responding. As they gathered at "their own store," Samat's, only two doors down from Bashir's, they shared with great glee the unseemly spectacle of an open battle among members of the UMNO ruling group. Some realized that, once one person had disregarded the gate, others could too (*mula se-orang, habis*) and that, if the rule was to be broken, it was important that members of the PAS faction establish their right to bring in paddy trucks too. Accordingly, Nizam bin Haji Lah, whose antipathy for Bashir was legendary (he neither spoke to Bashir nor traded at his store) and who still had bagged paddy in his field, left to call in a truck to fetch his own rice. Within a half hour after Fadzil's truck had left, Nizam's truck had entered and parked in front of Samat's store. The Chinese driver, to judge from the fear written on his face, would rather have been anywhere else; he would not get down from the cab. Before loading could begin, Bashir himself came to talk to the driver. And while he did not directly order the driver to leave, he made it clear that it would be better if the driver allowed the village to settle this matter before any more paddy trucks were loaded. Seizing this golden opportunity, the driver sped away empty, not even pausing to explain his hasty retreat to Nizam.

Basir had good reason to try to defuse a potentially violent conflict. He certainly was aware of what had happened in nearby villages when large farmers tried to circumvent the fees for transporting paddy to the main road. In Dulang Kechil a farmer had tried to use his own tractor to haul his harvest to the road in order to save the local piece-rate charges. The young men whose wages were at stake stopped his tractor, removed the battery, and threatened to slash his tires unless he abandoned the attempt. Under the circumstances, he relented. In Mengkuang a few years before a Chinese landowner brought trucks right into his large field during the dry season to haul rice directly to the mill. Alerted to the threat, a large number of villagers managed to fell two large coconut trees across the road, after the first loaded truck had left, to prevent the others from leaving. The other trucks were finally unloaded and the sacks of paddy taken one by one to the main road after a large crowd shouting threats of violence persuaded the landowner that discretion was the better part of valor. With this in mind, Bashir undoubtedly realized that the situation might easily take a violent turn, one that was as likely to involve fighting among UMNO members as between UMNO and PAS members.

Bashir's dilemma was a difficult one. There were other large farmers, including himself, who would have been only too pleased to see the gate demolished. Other villages had already done it. But he faced determined opposition from his own immediate political following, many of whom were his relatives. Amin, his cousin, Daud and Khalid, the two sons of headman Haji Jaafar, Musa and Sahil, the sons of Lebai Pendek, as well as Taha, the son of Lebai Hussein, were the very core of Bashir's "kitchen-cabinet" and, at the same time, the core of the UMNO paddy-hauling group. All of them represented influential families whose support he needed.

That evening Bashir brought together a group of five (Lebai Pendek, Taha bin Lebai Hussein, Amin, Daud Haji Jaafar, and Fadzil) to discuss the issue. The group was perhaps designed especially to isolate Fadzil. Bashir's position was that Musa had demanded too much for hauling the paddy but that Fadzil ought to have negotiated a lower piece-rate rather than taken matters into his own hands by opening the gate: "Such an important issue cannot be decided by one person." Fadzil, realizing that the group would go against him, tried to justify his action but stopped short of explicitly implicating Bashir in the opening of the gate. He added, significantly, that he knew that others thought that he had not been considerate (*tak timbang rasa*) nor compassionate (*tak bersimpati*) but that he believed that "we are free (*kita bebas*) [to open the gate]." "Other villages have taken down their gates and we will be forced (*terpaksa*) to do the same." This is the closest he came to asserting boldly the priority of his economic freedom of action over the village's right to protect its diminishing sources of wage income. Lebai Pendek and the three members of the UMNO hauling group all argued that the work should be given to villagers, not outsiders, and that the trucks would damage the road. Bashir finally spoke for closing the gate but was concerned that, if they called a general meeting on the issue, richer UMNO peasants who typically attend such gatherings might actually vote to let the paddy trucks in.

The following afternoon a small meeting was held in the room beneath the *surau* that doubles as a village hall (*dewan*) and classroom. Attending were about fifteen villagers, all from UMNO families, and two outsiders: Akil, a clerk at the government rice mill (LPN) and an official of both the Farmers' Association and the District UMNO executive, and Gaafar, the retired subdistrict official (*penghulu*) from Dulang. The meeting was conducted by Akil, not Bashir, in what appeared to be an attempt to portray the decisions shortly to be announced as those of higher officials. Lest the official character of the occasion be misunderstood, Akil flashed a *typed* report for all to note.[43] He began by referring to the events of the day before without mentioning names and then gave Fadzil a chance to speak. Knowing what was required, Fadzil made a roundabout apology for his hasty action but also pointed out that many villagers were angry because those who hauled paddy and thus benefited from the gate had, "in return [for the favor], gouged us (*makan kita balek*)"—so much so, he added, that he was almost driven to hire the other group of haulers (*cari puak lain*). Akil then proceeded to read his report, which consisted entirely of the reasons for maintaining the gate. First, the road would be badly damaged, especially during the wet season, if paddy trucks were admitted. Second, the men in the village "who depend on hauling wages would lose them" and third, the farmers

---

43. This report, Basir later confided, had been worked out that morning between himself, Daud bin Haji Jaafar, and Akil.

will instead "turn to different races" who own the trucks.[44] He added that many villagers were angry at the JKK for squabbling among themselves and that the current subdistrict chief, Abdul Majid, would be discontented (*tidak puas hati*) if Sedaka took down its gate and then came running to him next year for government money to fix up the road. The meeting concluded with a brief talk by Gaafar, a locally respected elder statesman, about Islam, solving things peacefully, helping others, and not acting selfishly. No vote was taken; the matter was closed and two days later a new gate was in place. Fadzil was conspicuously absent from the small work party that erected it.[45]

As word got around about the decision, it became clear that members of the opposition (PAS) faction had not been called (*panggil*) to the meeting. They were livid, objecting not so much to the outcome as to the manner in which the ruling faction had conducted this affair. Everyone should have been called to the meeting, they said, and everyone should be treated equally (*sama-rata*). Here they took full advantage of the conceptual equality of all villagers to make their point. Instead, the meeting was confidential (*sulit*) and the matter was decided by a small group that "chooses itself" (*depa angkat sindiri*) and that, in any case, is composed mostly of relatives. All this talk, which took place out of earshot of UMNO members, was phrased very much in "we–they" (*kita-depa*) terms.[46] Bashir in particular came in for ridicule for his lack of education, his arrogance (*sombong*), and his inability to prevent such quarrels within his own faction. Sukur, a strong PAS man, pointed out that the high-handed manner in which Bashir and his friends ran things was the reason why only a few UMNO members showed up to repair and grade the road when the government delivered new fill. In the old days, when PAS and UMNO members were both in the JKK, he said, everyone would help. Even the truck fees, he and the others agreed, now disappeared ("who knows where") and no receipt was ever given.

The preservation of the village gate was certainly a modest victory for the closed economy—for the principle that the village's first obligation is to protect its own sources of wages and income. The winners were the villagers who hauled paddy to the main road and the losers were both the large farmers who could save substantially by loading directly onto the trucks and the truck owners

44. *Orang yang bergantung kepada upah tarik padi sudah hilang. Lari ka-bangsa asing.*

45. A few adjustments in the gate's operation were discussed. Lebai Pendek would continue to hold the key and would get 20 percent of the fees from the trucks permitted to enter. Shamsul and Tok Ahmad, whose fields were immediately inside the gate, would be exempted from the rule.

46. Factional feeling was at a high pitch during this period, not only because of the gate issue but because of the highly partisan distribution of benefits from the Village Improvement Scheme (*Ranchangan Pemulihan Kampung*, RPK), which had just concluded. The RPK episode is described and analyzed below.

(typically the Chinese paddy dealers and millers).[47] The gate continues to represent a small but significant impediment to fully "rationalized" capitalist relations of production. The smallness of the impediment, however, merits emphasis. Changes in tenancy and the mechanization of the harvest have already swept away far more opportunities for work and income than this quaint, isolated vestige of older values could ever hope to replace. Even this small victory was a qualified one. The palpable threat posed by the opening of the gate once, and the possibility that it might later be opened for good, had their intended, chilling effect. Piece-rates for paddy hauling within the village the following season were no higher and in many cases lower than they had been earlier. Gaafar's homely lecture about the evils of selfishness was directed as much at the men who hauled papddy as at Fadzil. If they did not heed his warning, they ran the risk of killing the goose that laid the golden eggs.

It would be a grave misreading of this minor victory for local rights to interpret it as in any sense a victory for Sedaka's poor. The fact is that even this petty aspect of rice farming has been thoroughly mechanized over the past decade. With few exceptions, all the paddy now hauled along the village path is taken by motorcycles, not bicycles. And the ownership of motorcycles (mostly Honda 70s) is, as one might expect, highly correlated with income. The pertinent statistics are that nineteen of the richest twenty-five households own a motorcycle, while only two of the poorest twenty-five households own one. Even the figure of two motorcycles for the poorest families is something of an exaggeration. They are so frequently repossessed for failure to pay the installment loan or not operating because the owner cannot afford spare sparts that their existence is an episodic affair. Nearly half the middle peasants own a motorcycle. Thus, the beneficiaries of the gate are to be found exclusively among the middle and, especially, the rich households. This helps to explain why the gate was reestablished. Its constituency has shifted over the past few years from the poor and middle peasants, who all had bicycles, to the privileged, whose profits have allowed them to make a down payment on a motorcycle. Although there is no way of knowing, it is unlikely that the gate would exist today if paddy were still hauled by bicycle. Ironically, the gate that once protected the earnings of the poor has been successfully defended precisely because it now largely benefits those who have gained most from the green revolution. The poor, in fact, hardly

47. A single well-to-do family can contain both winners and losers. Thus Lebai Pendek is a large farmer but also has two sons who earn money hauling paddy with their motorcycles. Fadzil's position is more comprehensible when one realizes that he is a large farmer without any children who haul paddy. Middle peasant households stand to gain less from the reduction in transport costs simply because they market less paddy, but they may still oppose the gate, especially if they have no one in the family who can haul paddy.

figure in this issue at all; they neither haul paddy for others nor sell enough themselves to care one way or the other.[48]

IDEOLOGICAL CONFLICT: THE VILLAGE IMPROVEMENT SCHEME

The most divisive and acrimonious issue to convulse Sedaka during my stay there was the highly partisan distribution of building materials under the government's Village Improvement Scheme (*Ranchangan Pemulihan Kampung,* RPK). It was a topic of daily conversation for months; it greatly exacerbated the political divisions in the village; it came near to provoking violence on several occasions; and its social repercussions are still being felt. Unlike the gate episode, which it preceded by five months, the RPK was manifestly a partisan political issue. But, like the question of the gate, it erupted into an ideological struggle in which many of the same principles were at stake. As it developed, the actual allocation of assistance violated both of the principles which, we have shown, animate much of the moral discourse in Sedaka: the conceptual equality of all villagers and the obligation of the well-to-do toward their poorer neighbors. The ruling elite in the village achieved its immediate purpose but found itself hard put to justify its actions to its own faction, let alone the rest of the village. Inasmuch as the village poor are heavily overrepresented in PAS, the issue of partisanship took on distinctly class overtones.

Examining this episode in some detail, it will become apparent that there is an interesting parallel here with changes in the relations of production. In that domain, the large farmers and landlords have been able more or less to have their own way. Justifying what they have imposed, however, has required them to distort the facts, to plead necessity, to engage in bad-faith performances of little credibility. In parceling out the benefits of the Village Improvement Scheme, as well, the leading village families have been able to do as they pleased. Here again, however, they have been driven to a series of distortions, feigned necessities, and rather lame face-saving gestures. The problem, of course, is that the shared values of the local society provide no justification *either* for the single-minded pursuit of profit at the expense of one's neighbors or for the crude denial of benefits to an entire category of villagers. Not that profit making and political favoritism are new experiences in Sedaka. It is rather that the *new* opportunities for each are unprecedented and that these opportunities have vastly outstripped the available means for defending and legitimating their pursuit.

The Village Improvement Scheme (hereafter RPK) was the brainchild, credible rumor has it, of Dr. Mahathir Mohamed, the current prime minister, when he

---

48. Strictly speaking, the poor continue to haul paddy, particularly after the off-season when the fields are wet, from the field itself to a path that will accommodate a motorcycle. This hauling is necessary, however, regardless of whether the gate exists or not.

was still deputy prime minister. It was conceived as an instrument of political patronage in which a number of villages would be selected on the basis of need *and* political loyalty to receive a lump sum that would then be devoted to vaguely specified "development" purposes.[49] By October 1979, the scheme was under way throughout Kedah. A dozen lucky villages were designated in and around the Yan area after what must have been protracted negotiations between UMNO officials and the District Office.[50] They were all allegedly "backward villages" (*kampung mundur*). But "backwardness" was not enough; a village had also to be an UMNO stronghold.

Sedaka, having fulfilled both criteria, received M$35,000. The JKK as a whole was never assembled to discuss how the allocation was to be distributed. Instead, Haji Salim, a district UMNO official and large landowner living just outside the village, together with Bashir, Fadzil, Amin, and Daud bin Haji Jaafar met with the subdistrict chief, Abdul Majid, to make plans. As in other villages, the lump sum was allocated to different uses: M$15,000 for truckloads of fill to improve the road and for outdoor toilet materials; M$20,000 for materials to improve dwellings, including lumber, zinc roofing, paint, and concrete pilings. The households slated to receive assistance would, as the administrative regulations provided, be selected on the basis of a house-by-house survey which, in this case, would be conducted by Taha, a clerk at the District Office and the son of a local UMNO stalwart, Lebai Hussein. Amidst a general air of anticipation (and foreboding as well), the survey was in fact conducted. The questions, as noted in the previous chapter, were exclusively related to need: income, landownership, farming acreage, present housing materials, sanitary facilities, number of children, farm animals, and small livestock. Taha explained that assistance would be given not in cash but in the form of slips of authorization that would entitle villagers to materials, up to a certain sum, at any one of three nearby suppliers of building materials. A corner of the village hall (*dewan*) was partitioned off to create a small office with table and chairs and a sign reading: "Operations Room for Village Improvement Assistance, Kampung Sedaka."

It was quickly apparent that the worst suspicions of PAS members in the village had been fully realized. The survey had been a deception. This was not a program to "improve" the lot of poor villagers but rather a program to improve the lot exclusively of UMNO villagers. Even poverty, it turned out, was not

49. Gibbons and De Koninck have shown empirically that, in Muda, loyal villagers and loyal farmers, that is, those aligned with UMNO, are systematically favored as beneficiaries of government assistance. D. S. Gibbons, Rodolphe de Koninck, and Ibrahim Hassan, *Agricultural Modernization, Poverty, and Inequality: The Distributional Impact of the Green Revolution in Regions of Malaysia and Indonesia* (Farnborough: Saxon House, 1980), chap. 7.

50. Other villages, besides Sedaka, included Sungai Kering, Bedong, Setiti Batu, Dulang Besar, Peropuk, Sinkir Genting, Raga, Kampung Kubang Pasu, and Selankuh.

required, since virtually every UMNO member, no matter how rich, participated in the division of loaves and fishes. Forty-four households participated, getting at least a grant of M$200 for an outdoor toilet and, in three cases, as much as M$1,000 for housing materials and a toilet. There was a modest degree of equity *among* UMNO households. UMNO households that were poor according to the official tally got an average grant of M$672; UMNO households with middle incomes received an average of M$486; and the richest UMNO households' average was M$388. The averages hide a great deal of variation within each category, which seems to be related to how closely and actively the household in question was tied to the UMNO leadership. Since so many (sixteen of twenty-five) of the poorest villagers are from opposition families, this partisan allocation of the loot could hardly be redistributive. Thus, 71 percent of rich and middle peasant families were in the charmed circle, while only 36 percent of the poorest households got anything at all. In the midst of these inequities, the members of the JKK did not forget themselves. Although three-quarters of the JKK members are from the wealthiest twenty-five families, they nevertheless managed, officially, to award themselves an average of M$579. Unofficially, as we shall see, they may have done even better.

Even the apparent anomalies in the pattern of assistance reveal a finely tuned partisanship. Only two opposition households got any assistance, and they were, not by coincidence, Hamzah (M$1,000) and Rokiah (M$200), the only two PAS households who had hedged their bets by also paying dues to UMNO. Rokiah had the further advantage of being a good friend of Taha, who had done the survey. Hamzah had the further advantage of being the caretaker of the *dewan* and prayer house and of working often for UMNO landowners. Two of the three village fence-sitters, Kamil and Dzulkifli bin Haji Wahab, received help,[51] while the latter's much poorer brother, Bakri bin Haji Wahab, who had remained in PAS, got nothing.

Within a matter of days, the air was thick with charges and countercharges, which were by no means confined to those who had been excluded altogether. Nearly all of them were directed at the JKK and Bashir in particular. They were accused of misappropriation, bribe taking, corruption, kickbacks, diversion of funds, favoritism, and dishonesty—all activities for which the Malay language has amply provided.[52] The charges alone might fill a book, but a few examples will convey the flavor. Bashir and the JKK were widely accused of having made a deal with the Chinese lumber yards to receive kickbacks in return for allowing

---

51. The third fence-sitter, Mustapha, is Kamil's son-in-law; since he was staying with his wife in his father-in-law's house while preparing to move his wife and young child to his parent's village, he was seen as ineligible on those two counts. If that were not enough, he is also known to sympathize strongly with PAS.

52. Some of the terms most commonly used include *makan rasuah, tumbuk rusuk, penyelewengan, berselinkuh, suap, cari kepentingan diri, tipu, pileh-kasih.*

the dealer to overcharge and supply low-grade materials. That's why, said Mat "halus," much of the lumber came in short lengths, split, and had the consistency of cork (*gabus*). Members of the JKK were believed to have gotten more than their "official" allotment. Thus Bashir, who claimed to have gotten only a toilet, was said to have gotten a large supply of lumber which, for appearance's sake, he had stored under Fadzil's house. Shamsul, who officially got only M$200, was rumored to have gotten at least M$800 in materials and paint. Many poor UMNO members made invidious comparisons between what they had received and what wealthier UMNO leaders had received. Karim says he was entitled to M$600-worth of materials and got only M$400, while Fadzil, far richer, got M$750. Rokiah, ignoring the fact that she is a fair-weather UMNO member, complained about her small allocation, which was no more than that of her wealthier neighbor, Ghazali. Mansur protested to Bashir that he, a poor man with no land, had gotten less than others who owned as much as 8 relong. In each case, the complaints were based on relative need, in keeping with the logic of local charity.

Not even the three hundred truckloads of fill brought in to raise and widen the village road were free of acrimony. Some of the fill was sold cheaply to individuals to spread around their house lots. Bashir claims that this was done as a means of rewarding those who had come to help spread and grade it. No, claim others; those who worked on the road, all UMNO members, had gotten two or three hundred dollars as wages. The new fill, it turned out, never quite reached the far end of the village. Some eighty yards short of that, just before Tok Radzi's house, a few loads of fill were simply dumped and left. Bashir explained that there was simply not enough in the budget to complete the work and that those who lived at the far end would have to spread what was left themselves. The PAS faction has a simpler explanation. It just so happens that five of the mere seven families who live beyond the dumped fill are strong PAS members—the strongest geographical concentration of opposition families in the village. Since the fill had been spread largely by bulldozer for the rest of the village, and since it was not nearly enough for the job, these families refused to come spread it themselves. To do so would have been humiliating (*malu*), they said. In a few days much of it was gone—spread in Lebai Hussein's compound, which now looks, they say, "like the garden of a Sultan."

The ideological contours of the struggle over the Village Improvement Scheme are best appreciated if we begin with the realization that the party split between PAS and UMNO has never been entirely legitimate. It is not that the notion of aligning with PAS or UMNO violates any sense of village decorum. In fact, as is abundantly clear, virtually every household in Sedaka has long since chosen sides politically. What does exist, however, is a widely shared feeling that politics should be kept in its place, that partisan strife should not be allowed to disrupt the ritual unity and neighborly relations that villages believe should prevail in the community. While such pious hopes have surely not prevented partisan feelings from intruding upon local social relations, they have almost certainly exercised a restraining influence on the more blatant forms of party conflict.

Before the RPK created a new and deeper fissure, nearly everyone thought that the partisanship stirred up by earlier elections had diminished somewhat (*sudah lega sedikit*). The late 1960s and early 1970s were seen as the worst period of factionalism, when neighbors occasionally refused to speak with one another and close relatives found themselves on opposite sides of the fence. For my purposes, what is instructive is that these days were always spoken of with a tone of embarrassment and shame. Villagers blamed themselves for having been taken in by the candidates and their entourages, who were in turn blamed for having promoted a fiercely partisan spirit. The entire period and the incidents that marred it were seen as something of a disgrace and compared to the state of affairs in village households where parents and children or spouses are constantly bickering, shouting, and fighting. The relative improvement that villagers typically note was no doubt due in some measure to the entry of PAS into the government coalition in 1974. The local partisan alignment of households was little changed, for it had roots in familial alliances that existed well before independence, but its public manifestation was definitely muted. When PAS later bolted the government coalition, shortly before my arrival in the village in 1978, local party strife did not immediately resume its former vigor.[53]

What the villagers found most unseemly about the earlier excesses of partisanship was their affront to traditional ritual decencies. Thus Tok Kasim, himself a strong PAS member, illustrates how severe (*teruk*) things had become in those days by telling about a marriage *kenduri* in Sedaka in which the next-door neighbors, because they belonged to the other party, were either not invited or chose not to come. As the *kenduri* began, he emphasized, guests were arriving and food was being cooked directly below the window of the neighbors. The sense of embarrassment was finally so great that the neighbors simply left the village for the day and returned only after the *kenduri* was over. It was the fact that "neighbors in the same village" should quarrel that so offended him. "If the village society is ruined," he concluded, "there will be no peace."[54]

Tok Kasim's story, in one variation or another, together with the values it embodies, is a constant refrain. Everyone has stories to tell about Sedaka or neighboring villages "when the quarreling was at its worst" (*masa teruk berbalah*) and, without exception, they involve ritual feasts in which neighbors or relatives

---

53. For many local PAS members, the decision of Datuk Asri and the other leaders of PAS to enter the ruling coalition was an act of betrayal. Their sense of having been sold out was so strong that when he later returned to opposition they were skeptical. It did not change their membership in PAS, which was firmly rooted in local realities, but did shake their confidence. As many put it, "He took government wages" (*Sudah makan gaji kerajaan*).

54. *Kalau masyarakat kampung rosak, tak jadi aman.*

were excluded or refused to come. As Rokiah laments, it went so far that neighbors might not even come when there was a death, that even relatives would boycott (*boikot*) a *kenduri*.[55] Explicitly or implicitly the refrain distinguishes between the values of community (*masyarakat*) and party (*parti*), with the former invariably accorded priority. Lebai Pendek, an UMNO leader, thus thinks that "the villagers have become a bit smarter." "They know [now] that the community is different; before, they mixed up community with politics."[56] When Mansur, a landless member of UMNO, explains why he goes to all *kenduris*, regardless of which party the host belongs to, he says simply, "I only take the community into account."[57] In fact, it is difficult in Sedaka even to raise with anyone the question of party affiliation without provoking a disclaimer that, when it comes to marriages, sickness, funerals, or even helping to move a house (*usung rumah*), "party makes no difference at all." Even those whose political passions have occasionally led them to break this rule pay it constant lip service, thereby reinforcing its status as an ideal.

In this context it becomes easier to understand the basis of the principal objections raised against the allocation of RPK assistance. The loudest cries came, naturally, from PAS members, but many of the UMNO faithful objected too, and not just those who felt individually shortchanged. There were essentially three ways in which the money might have been divided. First, it might have been given preferentially to the poor of the village, thus satisfying the norm that help should be extended to those most in need, regardless of party loyalty. Originating in the older agrarian order and applying to both individual and communal obligations, this principle might plausibly be extended to government assistance as well. A second possibility might have been to divide the money among all villagers, disregarding both their need and their politics. This would have satisfied the norm that all villagers are, at some level, conceptually equal. The third possibility, and the one adopted, was to distribute the aid along strictly partisan lines. This surely was the most satisfactory option for the local UMNO leadership, but it was at the same time the least defensible in moral terms. For however firmly rooted partisan loyalties may have become in practice within Sedaka, they carry little moral weight and certainly not enough to begin to legitimate the JKK's actions. As in the case of double-cropping, so also in the realm of politics. The new opportunities for "profit-making" activity have far outpaced the normative means available to justify taking full advantage of them.

55. As one might expect, the worst case of partisanship that villagers can imagine is when kin of different parties refuse to come to one another's funerals. It is as if the solidarity surrounding funeral rites is the ultimate repository of both village and religious values; once this is breached something irretrievable has been lost. See a similar lament from Kelantan in Kessler, *Islam and Politics*, 154.

56. *Depa tau masyarakat lain dulu campur sekali masyarakat dengan politik.*

57. *Kira masyarakat saja.*

The first salvo of condemnations thus took the form of pointing to the glaring inequities of party patronage. Here were some of the wealthiest men in the village—Lebai Pendek, Shamsul, and Amin—serving themselves while most of the poorest villagers got nothing. Pak Yah (Yah Botol) was mentioned most often as the outstanding example of a demonstrably poor man who ought to have been helped. Was his house not in disrepair (*buruk*) for lack of funds? This was, after all, a program designed to help people fix up their houses! Pak Yah was also a strategic example because of his reputation as an honest, hard-working laborer and, moreover, one who frequently worked for UMNO leader Bashir. If anyone deserved help, he did. On the basis of this case alone, many villagers said the allocation was "not fair" (*tak adil*), "not proper" (*tak patut*), "not right" (*tak betul*). Quite a few UMNO members who benefited nevertheless declared that the poor should have been helped first. Kamil, for example, said that "[only] when the strata (*lapisan*) of the worst-off was helped, should those who were less badly off be taken." Mansur, who as a poor UMNO member got M$750 in materials, agrees: "We should help the condition of the poor no matter what party; first come the poor, those who have less than 2 relong."

Much as UMNO members were pleased with their good fortune, they felt an acute embarrassment before their PAS neighbors, with whom they had maintained cordial relations. As the new lumber was delivered and work began, they felt the envy and resentment of adjacent families, a resentment that was often reinforced by stony silences along the village path. Many felt the need to apologize for their stroke of luck to their PAS friends by agreeing that the JKK had been unfair but saying that they could not do anything about it. A few salved their consciences and repaired their friendships by selling some of their wood cheaply to PAS neighbors. Others actually hired a poorer PAS friend to help with the repair or construction.[58] There were, in other words, sporadic private efforts partly to undo the JKK's actions by redistributing the benefits to needy PAS families.

Denunciations of the RPK for its failure to help the poorest villagers were all the more appropriate because the survey that preceded the distribution had been conducted ostensibly to establish which families were most in need of aid. It was the contrast between the appearance of an impartial survey and its flagrant violation in practice that allowed PAS members—but not only them—to claim plausibly that the JKK had defied the wishes of the government. Much of the village believed that the government intended the money to go to the poor, regardless of party, and stories abounded about villages where the grants were given first to the neediest. Yaakub, for example, claimed that in Merbuk and Jenun, where he had relatives, *all* the poorest families had gotten the largest grants. Mansur said that, in nearby Sungai Kering, nearly everyone had received

58. Negotiations about such matters were delicate, since most PAS members were too proud to accept such secondhand assistance.

help.[59] As if to reinforce the belief in the treachery of the JKK, a parallel story circulated about the village of Setiti Batu, where a petty official had supposedly done a fair survey and the lumber had started to arrive. When the UMNO JKK there saw what was happening, they trooped en masse to the local Kedah member of Parliament and had the official transferred. Wood already stacked by the houses of PAS members was removed, they said, amid fistfights, and real-located to UMNO families. The pretense of a survey had been such a gratuitous insult that one of the poorest PAS members, Mat "halus," went to see Subdistrict Chief Abdul Majid to tell him that, if Taha ever returned to do another survey, he would "hit him and kill him" (*saya tumbuk mampus*).

In a more realistic mood, many PAS villagers realized that a distribution of funds by need alone, though in accord with local values, might have been utopian under the circumstances. Surely all UMNO members would have insisted on getting a share of the spoils. Why not then, they argued, give everyone an equal amount? The angry Mat "halus" said, "Even if they gave it out equally, that's all right. If each person got $300, all right. But we got nothing." The principle of equal shares to all was echoed by many others, especially those rank-and-file UMNO members who were offended by purely partisan criteria. Jamil, a fairly well-off UMNO member, also thought that equal awards would have been best: "In terms of village society (*kira masyarakat*), it would have to be done equally (*kena buat sama-rata*)." Abu Hassan, although nominally a member of the JKK, believed that "equal shares are fair."[60] PAS members were quick to point out that the government used one standard for collecting taxes and, in this case, another standard for distributing assistance. This contradiction was best captured by Ishak, when he said, "When they take the land tax and the irrigation tax, they don't go by party, but when they give out lumber and toilets, then they go by party." Here too, there were stories circulating about other villages, other JKKs, which had given something to everyone in the village.

The argument for treating all equally was reinforced by rumors about dis-agreements among the UMNO group that had met at Haji Salim's house to decide how the RPK money should be used. Lebai Sabrani, the greatly respected religious teacher from Sungai Tongkang and Tok Mudin, who is in charge of circumcision ceremonies, had apparently argued for giving something to everyone or at least including very poor PAS members like Pak Yah. Later, when I spoke with Lebai Sabrani alone, he said it was true. He had suggested dividing it all equally but, he said, Haji Salim and Bashir had objected by pointing out that, if all the PAS members got something, they would say, "See, we are in the

---

59. In the five or six villages about which I was able to gather reliable information, it appears that the distribution was also largely along partisan lines. Mansur's com-ment is nonetheless true, for Sungai Kering is known to be something like 90 percent in the UMNO camp.

60. *Cara rata lagi patut.*

opposition and we still get the assistance." That, Haji Salim said, would not do, and his position carried. Lebai Sabrani is reluctant to broadcast his dissent, but knowledge of it contributed a good deal to the indignation of PAS members. They could now point to the views of the most respected religious figure in UMNO itself as confirmation that they had been treated unfairly. Haji Salim and Bashir then became the principal villains of the piece. PAS members reported that Haji Salim had openly said in the market coffee shop that "PAS people won't get even one house pillar" and that Bashir had shown Taha a secret (*sulit*) list of PAS families who were on no account to be given anything.

The talk was angry and even violent. Dullah said, "They're making war [on us]; we're going to make war back." But with the exception of Mat "halus"'s threatening remark about Taha, most of it was safely confined to small groups of friends and allies. They made their anger known by snubbing members of the JKK in the coffee shops and along the village path. Open confrontations were avoided, and the JKK learned indirectly, through the "grapevine" (*cara sembunyi tau*), most of what they knew about the charges made against them. The absence of direct challenges had its origins in both pride and fear. Rosni is a striking example of the former. When I asked her if she had complained (*merungut*) to Bashir or Amin, for whom her transplanting group often works, she explained that she would be embarrassed (*malu*) to ask.[61] They both had told her, she added, that she should join UMNO, so she would be included. She did not. Besides, she had fixed up her own house by herself without their wood. "If they gave me the assistance, I would take it, but I won't beg (*minta*) or make trouble (*kacau*)." Others, however much they complained privately, were careful not to provoke an open confrontation with Bashir for the harm he might do them later. Ghazali, an UMNO member who married into a strong PAS family, may have been upset enough to contribute to a formal letter of complaint, but he said nothing directly to Bashir. Why? "I don't want to break my connection (*pecah perhubungan*) with Bashir; so I was silent."

The protest against the JKK, however, was not just confined to private character assassination and shared indignation about the injustice done. At an informal gathering in Samat's village shop, a number of PAS members urged that they all go as a crowd to the District Office to complain.[62] They had learned earlier that a group from Sungai Kering had already gone to the District Office in Yan Besar to protest the manner in which the survey was being conducted there. But there was not much enthusiasm for setting off. As Ghazali said, "It was just talk, they weren't brave enough to go." Apparently Mat "halus" was the only one angry and/or brave enough to protest in person, but he went to

---

61. She added, incidentally, that they had been avoiding her recently, presumably because they would be hard put to justify their behavior to her.

62. As reported secondhand to me, one of them said, "Let's go in a crowd to meet the D.O." (*Mari kita pergi ramai jumpa D.O.*).

the nearby *penghulu's* office, not the District Office. Finally, a number agreed to write a letter of formal protest and send copies to Kedah's chief minister (*Menteri Besar*), the District Officer, and the National Bureau of Investigation (*Biro Sisiatan Nasional,* BSN), which deals with charges of corruption. The letter was drafted that night and signed by Mat Isa, Bakri bin Haji Wahab, Mat Nasi— all PAS members—and by Ghazali, an UMNO member actually on the JKK, at least nominally. The letter respectfully complained about the unfair survey and allocation, blamed the JKK for the state of affairs, said village harmony was being destroyed, and asked that someone be sent to put things right.[63] It appears that similar letters were pouring in from many of the other villages selected to get RPK grants.

Nothing came of this protest, although people say that someone from the BSN came to the village a couple of weeks later to talk with Bashir. Bashir denies it. He is, of course, aware that letters have been sent but adds, with a self-assured smile, "They have no effect" (*tak ada kesan*). Haji Salim also tells me that he knows letters have been written condemning him and threatening to take him and the JKK to court. "If they don't like it, then they should win the next elections and give to their own people."

One night, shortly after it became clear that only UMNO members would be helped, the sign for the RPK in the village *dewan* was painted completely over in black. The police were called the next day and made a cursory search for black paint brushes or cans under a few houses to no avail. The perpetrator(s) were never found.

For the most part, the open protest was limited to what those who were excluded were able to insinuate by shunning members of the JKK when they passed and by a kind of "ritual boycott." The power of such "understatements" in a small village such as Sedaka is not trivial. Bashir bore the brunt of the public disdain. It happened that his daughter was to be married the following month, and he made a point of having every family called to the *bersanding* ceremony. At least ten families stayed away altogether from the feast, although most of them would have gone had it not been for this episode.[64] A few of the poorer PAS men, such as Pak Yah and Mat "halus," who occasionally worked for Bashir, felt obliged to put in an appearance but, to register their disapproval, remained only very briefly (*sa'at saja*). Haji Kadir came only to eat a snack of sticky rice (*menyerok pulut saja*) and then left. A few, like Mansur, who would normally have helped with the cooking, came only as guests. There were a host of nuanced ways of insinuating degrees of contempt, and nearly all were em-

63. I did not actually see the letter, as no copies were kept, but was told by all four men of its contents. They were particularly proud of having had the courage to sign it with their names and identity card numbers.

64. Among them, the families of Sukur, Rosni, Ishak, Samat Tok Mahmud, Tok Kasim, Osman Haji Ismail, and Nor.

ployed. Even those PAS members who went as usual found a way to make their appearance into a political statement. They explained to UMNO friends that it was not their side that had started this, it was not they who were trying to "split" (*pecah*) the village. By doing so, they took the high road as the defenders of village values and placed themselves in a position of moral superiority to the UMNO leadership.

Bashir was not the only one to experience the new chill in neighborly relations. Cik Tun had used her new lumber to repair and extend a small house her son had used in front of the older, family house. Now she wanted to move the new house around to the side of the old one and attach it. The operation would require at least seventy people, who would simply pick it up and move it into place. Accordingly, she arranged a house-moving feast (*kenduri usung rumah*), invited all her neighbors, and prepared a large meal for the work force. Only thirty or forty men appeared. Most of the PAS families at her end of the village pointedly stayed away;[65] they were understandably reluctant to help move a house built with lumber and zinc roofing they had been denied. As more than one said to me, "If UMNO built her house, well, UMNO would just have to move her house too." Despite shouts, grunts, and repeated efforts, the house could simply not be moved with the available manpower. To avoid prolonging what was already an acute embarrassment, Bashir sent out five or six UMNO men on motorcycles to fetch another twenty or thirty men. Within an hour they had finally scoured up enough additional help so that the house could finally be lifted and moved to its new location. But most of the new faces had not come from Sedaka, and the absent PAS members took great pleasure in retelling, among themselves, this small humiliation for the JKK and Cik Tun.[66]

As he surveyed the social debris of complaints, wounded feelings, boycotts, and seething anger that the Village Improvement Scheme had left in its wake, Bashir confided to me that it had been a political disaster. Half the UMNO members were angry with him because they thought they had been short-changed. Some were boycotting his store, among them the influential midwife Tok Sah Bidan and her friends. "A shopkeeper," he reminded me, "has to stay on the good side of everyone" (*kena baik dengan semua*). All in all, he concluded, his "influence" (*pengaruh*) among villagers had fallen, even though he had given away "thousands" of dollars to them. Far from making UMNO stronger, the whole exercise had left it weaker.

In the course of presiding over the distribution of spoils, Bashir and other

65. Those who were conspicuously absent included Pak Yah, Dullah, Mat "halus," Bakri bin Haji Wahab, Dzulkifli bin Haji Wahab, Shahnon, and Mat Isa. Samat and Taib, however, went.

66. The number of people one can assemble for such an occasion is an important reflection on the prestige and friendship network of the host family. In this case, however, the sparse turnout was more a reflection on the JKK than on Cik Tun.

members of the JKK were implicitly or explicitly called upon to justify their actions. How was it possible to explain this strictly partisan treatment of the village? How could the glaring fact that even the poorest PAS members had been passed over while wealthy UMNO members were rewarded be explained, let alone legitimated? The justifications that were attempted, with indifferent success, depended a great deal on the audience to which they were addressed. For the village as a whole, including PAS members, one explanation was given; for UMNO members, another; and for a small inner circle of confidants, still a third.

The justification publicly offered to PAS friends by Bashir and most of the JKK was, significantly, no real justification at all. It was instead the time-honored refuge of petty officials everywhere, namely, that they were simply following instructions from above, doing what they were told. As always in such cases, the explanation was an attempt to distance themselves morally from the blame that attached to their actions. As always, it also implied that their hands were tied; they had no choice in the matter. Thus Bashir explained to those in his shop shortly after the program was announced that everything had been decided "from above" (daripada atas). "Above" in this case, he said, was the District Officer and the Executive Committee of UMNO in this constituency, Bahagian Jerai. The government had "studied" the matter and had "ordered" (suruh) the JKK to give the aid only to UMNO members. It was "they who wanted to split the village."[67] Fadzil adopted the same stance at the coffee shop in town when he knew PAS members were at the next table. "It's the higher-ups," he said, "it's their (saluran) way of doing things." "We didn't know; it's their decision." This lame effort to pass on the responsibility for the RPK is notable for two reasons. The first is that it is, almost certainly, a convenient lie. Lebai Sabrani and others with strong UMNO credentials have made it clear that the decisions were taken at Haji Salim's house, with most of Bashir's "kitchen cabinet" present. And it is also clear that the RPK was distributed equally to all families in at least a few villages. The second notable aspect of this attempt to avoid blame is simply that it amounts to a clear admission that, at least for the village as a whole, the favoritism of the RPK cannot be justified or legitimized. That being the case, the only strategy left was to shift the onus to other shoulders.

Another level of justification emerged when the audience was composed exclusively of UMNO beneficiaries of the largesse, even those who were uneasy with the frankly partisan atmosphere. Here was at least an attempt at legitimation, albeit for only one set of listeners. Against the claims of the most needy or the claims of all households in the village was placed a homely metaphor from family life. The village was, in effect, divided into our children and their children, good children and bad children, "real" children and stepchildren. As

67. *Depa yang mau pecah kampung.*

Bashir so often put it to his allies, "We must give to our own children (*anak sindiri*) first, and if there is still more left, then only can we give to our stepchildren (*anak tiri*)." The theme is echoed with only minor variations by core members of the JKK. Amin: "We have to give property to our children first." Fadzil: "We must help our own children. How can we give to other people's children (*anak orang*)?" Haji Salim develops this theme further, perhaps along the lines he used when he tried to convince Lebai Sabrani and others that only UMNO families should benefit.

> The UMNO government gives first and foremost to those people who support (*sokong*) them. There's not enough for everyone, so all of them can't get it. The rebellious children (*anak derhaka*) who oppose (*lawan*) the father must wait; they are headstrong (*nafsu*) and stubborn (*keras kepala*). When there are many children, we must give more to the children who listen to us, not to those who don't follow. When our own children are [made] comfortable, only then can we give to the stepchildren.

This notion of a justifiable favoritism within the family was, I suspect, designed as much to reassure the members of the JKK as to provide a plausible rationale to the wider UMNO membership.[68] Poor UMNO members, for example, could willingly accept the stepchild analogy and still justifiably wonder why there were so many anomalies in the distribution within their own party, with quite a few well-to-do UMNO activists receiving more than poor party members. Even here, however, we can detect a kind of hedging that gives something away to other village values. The claim of our *own* children, or the *loyal* children, is paramount but *not* exclusive, and it is implied that all children, even stepchildren, have a claim as well to the "parents'" largesse. This last was emphasized frequently by Bashir, who expected that there would be a second stage to the RPK later in which even PAS members would be permitted to share.

Among the more committed and partisan members of the JKK, a rather more cynical atmosphere prevailed—an atmosphere not for public consumption even by the generality of UMNO members. Here the talk of retribution and punishment of the PAS faction was openly voiced. Speaking with Amin and me late one evening in the privacy of his house, Bashir adopted a frankly partisan tone, which I imagine was usually reserved for the inner circles of UMNO. Those who are in PAS, he said, will never change; "Even if you cut off their heads they wouldn't change." So why give them anything? Even if we gave assistance to them, he continued, they would still complain, just as they did about the free fertilizer subsidy, saying they did not get their share or that it

---

68. Once or twice the argument was made that, even if PAS members were helped, they would not return the kindness (*balas budi*) or ever say "thank you." Here the principle of reciprocity was invoked and joined to the metaphor of the ungrateful or rebellious child.

was mixed with sand. That is their "rule" (*undang-undang*), "always complain." When I interjected that even some UMNO members seemed to think that everyone, or at least the poor, should have been helped, he replied, "This is not village social relations. Politics is a little different. The world is like that."[69] This was the closest Bashir came to recognizing openly that what village values required and what politics required were different and that, in this case, the former would just have to be ignored.

Finally, if one were to step outside the village altogether, even the semblance of homage to local norms tended to evaporate. In the course of a conversation with the *penghulu* Abdul Majid after hours in his office in Sungai Tongkang, I delicately raised the question of complaints about the RPK. His reply was as unvarnished as were his opinions about villagers replaced by combine-harvesters. In no uncertain terms, he made it clear that the RPK is, in effect, intended to starve out the "recalcitrants" (*pembangkang*). "Sooner or later they've got to weaken; the rich may be able to hold out, but the poor won't be able to last."[70] Freed by his outsider status from any need to adopt a social mask or to prettify the facts, Abdul Majid can speak without guile.

The smaller and more partisan the audience, the more powerful and untouchable the speaker (Haji Salim and especially Abdul Majid), the less tongue-tied the explanations become. The largest landowners and the secure officials can, if they wish, dispense with the need to explain themselves or justify their action to those beneath them whose vital interests are at stake. Within Sedaka, however, the niceties are largely preserved and an effort is made, however lame, to justify the new opportunities for profit and patronage. The normative raw material at their disposal, alas, is not quite up to the task. The winners are more or less obliged to distort the facts, to give patently bad-faith performances, to claim that their hands are tied, and to make do with whatever scraps of moral justification they can cobble together on short notice. Their behavior may serve a higher, or at least different, rationality, but in village terms, in terms of the moral givens of Malay rural society, it is not convincing.

ARGUMENT AS RESISTANCE

Taken collectively, the arguments that the village poor have been making have a striking coherence to them. They single out the most damaging economic and social consequences of double-cropping and mechanization. They assert a wide array of "facts" about income, combine-harvesting, land-tenure shifts, and employment to bolster their case. They promote the view that the well-off, by reason of custom, neighborliness, kinship, and race, are called upon to provide

69. *Ini bukan masyarakat, politik lain sikit, dunia macham itu.*

70. *Lama-lama depa kena lembut. Orang kaya boleh tahan, tetapi, orang susah tak boleh tahan.*

work, land, loans, and charity when possible. Referring to these claims, they condemn those whose callousness and concern for profit has led them to violate what the poor consider their legitimate expectations. These themes, and the assertion of rights which they imply, are much in evidence in the disputes over the gate and the Village Improvement Scheme. In the first case, the owners of motorcycles—themselves comfortable families—successfully availed themselves of the logic that once defended the village poor. In the second case, the moral logic of tradition yielded to the logic of faction but at substantial symbolic cost and only because the co-optation of the UMNO poor secured their complicity or silence. Such attempts, partly successful, to preserve and promote a particular worldview, a style of normative discourse, constitutes a form of resistance that is much more than purely symbolic.

At a minimum, the worldview of the poor represents something of a symbolic barrier to another latent form of discourse that would openly legitimize the current practices of most well-off farmers. The latent form of discourse would be the straightforward language of narrow economic interests, profit maximization, accumulation, and property rights—in short, the language of capitalism. As it is, such language has no moral standing in village life. This symbolic disadvantage under which the wealthy labor has, in fact, material consequences. The values promoted most vigorously by the poor, and given tacit recognition even in the discourse of the rich, confer reputation, status, and prestige on those who observe them. Conversely, they make those who systematically violate them the object of character assassination. Forced to choose, in effect, between their reputation in the village and the full profits of double-cropping, many of the wealthy steer a course that does not completely repudiate those norms. The choice is not, after all, a single choice, but one that must be made day in and day out in a host of small transactions. Thus, there are seven farmers in the village, four well-off, who are praised for not using the combine-harvester on part or all of their land, at least after the irrigated season. A few rent out to neighbors or relatives small plots of land, seldom more than a single relong, that they might otherwise farm themselves. Abdul Rahman is particularly notable for occasionally renting a relong or two to poorer friends and charging modest rents. Land rented within the village, as this and other studies have shown, is provided at lower rents than land rented to outsiders. Some comfortable villagers, among them Lebai Pendek, Haji Jaafar, and Bashir, are often praised for the frequency with which they hold feasts to which all villagers are invited.[71] At least ten villagers, not all of them wealthy, are known to be rather more generous with *zakat* to laborers and to give wages in advance. None of these facts should obscure the overall tendency for wealthy villagers, and especially

71. In Basir's case this praise is tempered with a realization by villagers that his dual role as shopkeeper and political leader requires him to make a greater effort than others—an effort that, in large part, is seen to be self-interested.

outside landlords, to pursue profit at the expense of their reputation. What they do suggest, however, is that the sanction of local opinion and custom continues to exert a small but perceptible influence on conduct. The desire to be thought well of, or at least not despised, is a material force in the village made possible only by the symbolic mobilization of the poor around certain customary values.[72] Put another way, the delaying of the complete transition to capitalist relations of production is in itself an important and humane accomplishment. It is often the only accomplishment within reach of a beleaguered peasantry.[73]

The values the poor are defending are all, without exception, very much tied to their material interests as a class. We would, however, mistake the full nature of the struggle here if we were to limit ourselves to its material effects alone. So long as men and women continue to justify their conduct by reference to values, the struggle for the symbolic high ground between groups and classes will remain an integral part of any conflict over power. In this context, the conclusions of E. P. Thompson, in his discussion of eighteenth-century plebian culture and protest, are applicable, with a few adjustments, to Sedaka.

> The gentry had three major sources of control—a system of influence and preferment which could scarcely contain the unpreferred poor; the majesty and terror of law; and the symbolism of their hegemony. There was, at times, a delicate social equilibrium, in which the rulers were forced to make concessions. Hence the contest for symbolic authority may be seen, not as a way of acting out ulterior "real" contests, but as a real contest in its own right. Plebian protest, on occasion, had no further objective than to challenge the gentry's hegemonic assurance, strip power of its symbolic mystifications, or even just to blaspheme.[74]

If we understand that the "protest" in Sedaka is rarely openly manifested and that the "symbolic hegemony" of the wealthy class is far more tenuous, we are still in the presence of a "contest for symbolic authority." By rewarding, if only symbolically, those whose conduct is more nearly in accord with their values and by slandering those whose conduct most blatantly transgresses their values, the village poor undercut the moral authority of their enemies by allocating virtually

72. That social pressure, of course, is not purely symbolic, since the labor of villagers is still necessary for some phases of paddy cultivation. Beyond that, as we shall see, the social pressure is reinforced by threats of violence and theft as well.

73. This effort to delay capitalist relations of production is often and, I believe, mistakenly used to demonstrate the superior historical role of the proletariat. See Georg Lukacs, *History and Class Consciousness: Studies in Marxist Dialectics*, trans. Rodney Livingstone (Cambridge: MIT Press, 1971), 59. For a critique of this position, see my "Hegemony and the Peasantry," *Politics and Society* 7, no. 3 (1977): 267–96, and chap. 8 below.

74. "Eighteenth-Century English Society: Class Struggle without Class," *Social History* 3, no. 2 (May 1978): 158–59.

the only resources over which they have some control: reputation and social prestige. In the process, they help unite most of those disadvantaged by double-cropping behind a particular version of the facts, behind a particular set of claims, behind a particular worldview—or perhaps "villageview" would be a more appropriate term. This symbolic barrier is hardly insurmountable, but it is nonetheless a real obstacle to the designs of the rich.[75]

The symbolic resistance of the poorer villagers is as important for what it rejects as for what it asserts. It rejects, nearly wholesale, the characterizations the rich give to themselves and their actions. Haji Kadir may be called *Pak Haji* to his face, but he is called *Pak Ceti* behind his back. Rich farmers may explain their use of the combine-harvester by their inability to find local labor on time, but this account is rejected by those most affected, who see it as an avaricious desire for quick profits. Landlords may plead poverty when raising the rent, but the poor "know" it is a ruse and mock the performance. The list could be extended indefinitely but the point is clear; at virtually every turn the self-characterizations and justifications of the rich are contested and subverted.

Above all, the symbolic resistance of the poor rejects the categories the rich attempt to impose upon them. They know that the large farmers increasingly see them as lazy, unreliable, dishonest, and grasping. They know that, behind their backs, they are blamed as the authors of their own victimization and that, in daily social encounters, they are increasingly treated with little consideration or, worse, ignored. Much of what they have to say among themselves is a decisive rejection of the attempt to relegate them to a permanently inferior economic and ritual status and a decisive assertion of their citizenship rights in this small community.

To understand what is at stake here, we must begin with a far broader and more penetrating appreciation of the meaning of poverty in this context. I fear that I may have thus far contributed to a narrow view both by emphasizing the economic losses of mechanization and tenure shifts and by continually referring to "the poor" of Sedaka.

Poverty is far more than a simple matter of not enough calories or cash. This is particularly the case in Sedaka, where no one is in imminent danger of actually starving. For most of the village poor, poverty represents a far greater threat to their modest standing in the community. It is possible in any peasant community

75. Kessler, in his study of the social basis of PAS opposition in Kelantan, puts the matter persuasively by emphasizing the fusion of symbolic and material action: "It [this study] has also dispensed with the equally forced distinction between instrumental and symbolic political actions and goals, between material and ideal factors. Local issues are but national issues in a particular guise, concrete and immediately apprehendable, and the articulation of responses to them, in the distinctive dialects of particular contexts, is far from unreal. . . . Symbols and symbolic action are viable only when they relate to real issues and popular experience of them. . . . They have a real basis and also real consequences." *Islam and Politics*, 244.

to identify a set of minimal cultural decencies that serve to define what full citizenship in that local society means. These minimal cultural decencies may include certain essential ritual observances for marriages and funerals, the ability to reciprocate certain gifts and favors, minimal obligations to parents, children, relatives, and neighbors, and so on. Barrington Moore, Jr., places such cultural requirements at the core of his analysis of popular conceptions of justice:

> If we confine our attention to the lower classes, who of course have less favorable property rights . . . , we find very frequently the notion that every individual ought to have "enough" property rights to play a "decent" role in the society. Both "enough" and "decent" are defined in traditional terms. A peasant should have enough land to support a household and enable its head to play a respectable role in the village community . . . Whenever an increase in commercial relationships has threatened this type of independence, it has produced an angry sense of injustice. . . . It is important to realize that there is much more to this anger than straightforward material interest. Such people are morally outraged because they feel that their whole way of life is under unfair attack.[76]

All of these decencies, as Moore indicates, assume a certain level of material resources necessary to underwrite them. To fall below this level is not merely to be that much poorer materially; it is to fall short of what is locally defined as a fully human existence. It is as much a socially devastating loss of standing as it is a loss of income.

In Sedaka, the cultural and ritual standing of many poor peasants was seriously compromised even before double-cropping. For example, the village has more than its share of poor women who have married late or not at all. Men sometimes refer to them as "unmarketable maidens" (anak dara tak laku), but they will also add that their parents can promise no farming land to the groom. During the feast of Ramadan (Hari Raya Puasa), a good many men from poor households remain at home rather than visit wealthier neighbors. A few will admit that they are absent because they are "embarrassed" (malu), since they "cannot afford to reciprocate" (tak boleh membalas) the sweets and cakes that are expected for this major Muslim feast day.[77] The feasts that the village poor do manage to

76. *Injustice: The Social Bases of Obedience and Revolt* (White Plains: M. E. Sharpe, 1978).

77. Perhaps the comparable humiliation for poor Christian Americans is the inability to provide their children with the presents that have come virtually to define what Christmas means. The sacrifices they will make, including mortgaging their own future, to achieve the minimal decencies are no less than what poor Malays will make to provide an acceptable *Hari Raya* fare. Along these same lines, it is frequently said that conversion to Protestantism in Central and South America appeals particularly to the poor, who are unable to finance the ritual cycle that has become associated with Catholicism. By doing so, they make a virtue of necessity and dignify their nonparticipation.

celebrate are often abbreviated versions with less than the standard ritual, entertainment, and food. Their shabbiness is typically seized upon by the better-off as a mark of the host's inability to acquit himself honorably. The poor find it difficult or impossible to contribute food for the *moreh* [evening meals after prayer] during the fasting month. They actually avoid promising a feast in their prayers for recovery from an illness or in their prayers for a child of a certain sex (usually male) during a pregnancy, because they know they will be unable to fulfill that sacred vow. *Kenduri* that are frequently held by wealthier villagers—for example, *kenduri berendul* (or *buaian*) for a young child, *kenduri cukur kepala* (or *rambut*) also for a young child, *kenduri* to thank Allah for some good fortune or to pray for ancestors—are rarely celebrated by the poor. Aside from the obligatory ceremonies for the dead, there are at least seven families who have held no feasts whatever for the past six years. All are among the poorest twenty families in the community. Their loss of status in a culture where feast giving is perhaps the main coin of exchange is severe.[78] The poor are largely excluded, by their penury, from both the death-benefit associations and the groups that buy and share the crockery necessary for any substantial feast. It is extremely rare for a poor peasant family to be able to send any of their children beyond primary school, given the expenses involved. Their children, as we have seen, are far more likely to leave early and permanently, since there is no paddy land to hold them in the village.

It is in this larger context alone that poverty as it is experienced in Sedaka takes on its full meaning. Those with little or no land of their own have always been relegated to a rather marginal ritual position. But as long as tenancies and work were available they managed, if only barely, to achieve the minimal ritual decencies. The burst of feast giving during the first four years of double-cropping when work was plentiful is an indication of the pent-up ritual deficit that was being remedied. In this brief boom, the poor were able to assert a claim to status and ritual dignity formerly available only to middle and rich peasants. Now, with machine-harvesting, broadcasting, and the loss of tenancies, the resources to back those claims are either gone or receding fast.

The cultural and material consequences of double-cropping are, of course, inseparable here. The modest ritual status to which the poor could lay claim was predicated not only on their earnings but also on the fact that they remained essential to the process of paddy cultivation and hence essential to the large farmers who grew most of that paddy. If they were treated with some consideration, if they were invited to *kenduri,* if they were given small gifts of *zakat* after the harvest, if their requests for loans or advance wages were heeded, it

---

78. Quite a few of them who have no farming land—either rented or owned—are thereby excluded both from the practice of exchanging labor and from feasts such as *kenduri tolak bala* designed to pray for rain or ward off specifically agricultural disasters.

was largely because their labor was required. While there is no mechanical relationship between the role of the poor in production (the "base" in Marxist terms) and their role in cultural life (superstructure), it is undeniable that, as the need for their labor has plummeted, they have experienced a corresponding loss in the respect and recognition accorded them. Thus, when the poor speak among themselves, they emphasize far more their loss of standing and recognition than the loss of income per se. How else are we to understand the many comments about the humiliation of idleness at harvest time when, before, they would have been out working? How else are we to understand the bitter comments about not being invited to *kenduri*, about not being greeted on the village path, about not even being *seen*, about being treated rudely or "pushed aside" (*tolak tepi*)? The loss of the simple human considerations to which they feel entitled is at least as infuriating as the drop in their household income. Much of the local furor over the Village Improvement Scheme, and even the gate opening, can be seen in these terms. In each case, what is being resisted by appeal to custom is the attempt to revoke the claim of one group of villagers to what are considered the normal rights of local citizenship.

Amidst the attention typically devoted by left-wing scholars to the economic privations of low wage rates, unemployment, poor housing, and inadequate nutrition among workers and peasants, more homely matters of ritual decencies and personal respect are frequently lost sight of altogether. And yet, for the victims themselves, these issues appear to be central. One of the major resentments among the historically turbulent rural workers of Andalusia, for example, is the "upper-class practice of social self-removal" called *separación*. As Gilmore observes:

> They denounce *separación* because they feel it is a reflection of arrogance and contempt. . . . The bitterness of the working-class response stems partly from a deeply felt moral postulate: the poor people of the community feel that to ignore a man is actively to disparage and insult him, purposefully to treat him as something less than a man.[79]

Closer to our own terrain, Wan Zawawi Ibrahim's fine study of Malay plantation workers recently recruited from east coast villages deals at length with the

79. David Gilmore, "Patronage and Class Conflict in Southern Spain," *Man* (N.S.) 12 (1978): 449. In his detailed history of the German working-class movement from 1848 to 1920, Barrington Moore emphasizes how frequently the demand for what he calls "decent human treatment" appears in the accounts of workers themselves. Writing of the workers councils after the First World War, he concludes:

The source of the workers' anger was essentially a combination of two things: certain material deprivations and what they themselves called lack of decent human treatment. Lack of decent human treatment offended their sense of fairness. In their terms it apparently meant the failure to treat the worker as a human being in the course of ordinary routine contacts, such as excessive gruffness, failure to use polite forms, and the like.

reaction to what the author terms "status exploitation."[80] Thus, an older Malay worker who would expect to be addressed respectfully as *Pak Cik* was summoned by the Malay overseer with a rude, "Hey, you come here" (*Hai, mu mari sini*) and was deeply insulted at having been treated "like trash in the middle of the road." Many of the complaints of the ex-peasant work force focused as much on such inconsiderate, rude treatment as on the standard issues of pay and working conditions.

If we are to appreciate the full dimensions of the ideological struggle in Sedaka we must at the same time appreciate the full dimensions of the threat they face. That threat has at least three facets: it is the palpable threat of permanent poverty; it is the no less palpable loss of a meaningful and respected productive role in the community; and it is the related loss of a great part of both the social recognition and cultural dignity that define full membership in this village. To call such matters *bread-and-butter* issues is largely to miss their significance. When the poor symbolically undermine the self-awarded status of the rich by inventing nicknames, by malicious gossip, by boycotting their feasts, by blaming their greed and stinginess for the current state of affairs, they are simultaneously asserting their own claim to status. Even when, as frequently happens, a poor family holds a feast they can ill afford, it is a small but significant sign of their determination not to accept the cultural marginalization their scant means imply. It is in this sense, especially, that the war of words, the ideological struggle in Sedaka, is a key part of "everyday resistance." The refusal to accept the definition of the situation as seen from above and the refusal to condone their own social and ritual marginalization, while not sufficient, are surely necessary for any further resistance.

80. Wan Zawawi Ibrahim, *A Malay Proletariat: The Emergence of Class Relations on a Malay Plantation* (Ph.D. diss., Monash University, 1978), 398 et seq.

7 • Beyond the War of Words: Cautious Resistance and Calculated Conformity

> Whatever happens Schweik mustn't turn into a cunning, underhanded Saboteur, he is merely an opportunist exploiting the tiny openings left him.
>
> Bertolt Brecht, *Journal,* May 27, 1943

> The damned impertinence of these politicians, priests, literary men, and what-not who lecture the working class socialist for his "materialism"! All that the working man demands is what these others would consider the undispensable minimum without which human life cannot be lived at all. . . .
> How right the working classes are in their "materialism"! How right they are to realize that the belly comes before the soul, not in the scale of values but in point of time.
>
> George Orwell, "Looking Back
> on the Spanish War" (1943)

From the account thus far, one might justifiably assume that the struggle between rich and poor was largely confined to a war of words. That assumption would not be entirely wrong, but it would be misleading. For the poor and wealthy peasants of Sedaka are not merely having an *argument*; they are also having a fight. Under the circumstances, the fight is less a pitched battle than a low-grade, hit-and-run, guerrilla action. The kind of "fight" to be described and analyzed in this chapter is, I believe, the typical, "garden variety" resistance that characterizes much of the peasantry and other subordinate classes through much of their unfortunate history. More specifically, however, we are dealing here with the undramatic but ubiquitous struggle against the effects of state-fostered capitalist development in the countryside: the loss of access to the means of production (proletarianization), the loss of work (marginalization) and income, and the loss of what little status and few claims the poor could assert before double-cropping. Most readings of the history of capitalist development, or simply a glance at the current odds in this context, would conclude that this struggle is a lost cause. It may well be just that. If so, the poor peasantry of Sedaka finds itself in distinguished and numerous historical company.

After considering the major reasons why open collective protest is rare, I examine the actual patterns of resistance to changes in production relations: arson, sabotage, boycotts, disguised strikes, theft, and imposed mutuality among the poor. I then assess the role of coercion—of what might be called "everyday forms of repression"—in producing such disguised forms of struggle amidst overt compliance. Finally, I take a step backward to explore, in more general terms, the definition of resistance and the reasons why many of the actions considered here might justifiably be termed resistance.

OBSTACLES TO OPEN, COLLECTIVE RESISTANCE

An observer need not look long and hard to find examples of further resistance in Sedaka. In fact, they abound. They are, however, forms of resistance that reflect the conditions and constraints under which they are generated. If they are open, they are rarely collective, and, if they are collective, they are rarely open. The encounters seldom amount to more than "incidents," the results are usually inconclusive, and the perpetrators move under cover of darkness or anonymity, melting back into the "civilian" population for protective cover.

To appreciate why resistance should assume such guises, it is helpful to pause briefly to consider a few of the major "givens" that determine the range of available options. This will anticipate somewhat the material that follows, and a few of the issues raised only schematically here will be developed at greater length later in this chapter and the next.

Perhaps the most important "given" that structures the options open to Sedaka's poor is simply the nature of the changes they have experienced. Some varieties of change, other things equal, are more explosive than others—more likely to provoke open, collective defiance. In this category I might place those massive and sudden changes that decisively destroy nearly all the routines of daily life and, at the same time, threaten the livelihood of much of the population. Here in Sedaka, however, the changes that constitute the green revolution have been experienced as a series of piecemeal shifts in tenure and technique. As painful as the changes were, they tended to come gradually and to affect only a small minority of villagers at any one time. The shift from rents collected after the harvest (*sewa padi*) to fixed rents paid before planting (*sewa tunai*), for example, affected only tenants and was pushed through over several seasons, so that only a few tenants found themselves simultaneously in jeopardy. Furthermore, most of them were able to hang on to their tenancy even if it meant an additional burden of debt. If we could imagine a single, large landlord insisting on *sewa tunai* from all the village tenants in the same season, the response might have been very different. The loss of tenancies that resulted when landlords decided to resume cultivation themselves or to lease (*pajak*) their land to wealthy commercial operators followed a similar pattern. Much the same can be said for the raising of rents and for the substitution of broadcasting for transplanting. The screws were turned piecemeal and at varying speeds, so that the victims were never more than a handful at a time. In this case as in others, each landlord or farmer insisting on the change represented a *particular* situation confronting one or, at most, a few individuals.

The only exception to this pattern was the introduction of combine-harvesting and, as we shall see, it provoked the nearest thing to open, collective defiance. Even in this case, however, the impact was not instantaneous, nor was it without a certain ambiguity for many in the village. For the first two or three seasons the economic impact on the poor was noticeable but not devastating. Middle peasants were genuinely torn between the advantage of getting their crop in quickly and the loss of wage earning for themselves or their children. A few of the smallest farmers, as I have noted, succumbed to the temptation to use the combine in order to hasten their exit for contract labor in the city. At no single moment did combine-harvesting represent a collective threat to the livelihood of a solid majority of villagers.

Another striking characteristic of the agricultural transformation in Kedah— one that serves very powerfully to defuse class conflict—is the fact that it removes the poor from the productive process rather than directly exploits them. One after another, the large farmers and landlords in the Muda Scheme have *eliminated* terrains of potential struggle over the distribution of the harvest and profits from paddy growing. In place of the struggle over piece-rates for cutting and thresh-ing, there is now only a single payment to the machine broker. In place of negotiations over transplanting costs, there is the option of broadcasting the seed and avoiding the conflict altogether. In place of tense and contentious disputes over the timing and level of rents, there is the alternative of hiring the machines and farming oneself or leasing to an outsider for a lump sum. Even the shift to *sewa tunai* eliminates the tales of woe and ruin that previously dominated the post-harvest claims for rent adjustment. The changes themselves, of course— dismissing a tenant, switching to the machines, moving to fixed rents before planting—are not so simple to put across. But once they have been put across, the ex-tenant or ex-wage laborer simply ceases to be relevant; there is no further season-by-season struggle. Once the connection and the struggle in the realm of production have been severed, it is a simple matter also to sever the connec-tion—and the struggle—in the realm of ritual, charity, and even sociability. This aspect of the green revolution, by itself, goes a long way toward accounting for the relative absence, here and elsewhere, of mass violence. If the profits of the green revolution had depended on squeezing more from the tenants, rather than dismissing them, or extracting more work for less pay from laborers, the consequences for class conflict would surely have been far more dramatic. As it is, the profits from double-cropping depend much less on exploiting the poor directly than on ignoring and replacing them.[1] Class conflict, like any conflict, is played out on a site—the threshing floor, the assembly line, the place where piece-rates or rents are settled—where vital interests are at stake. What double-cropping in Muda has achieved is a gradual bulldozing of the sites where class conflict has historically occurred.

1. As a recently sacked factory worker once remarked ruefully to me, "The only thing worse than being exploited is *not* being exploited."

A second obstacle to open protest is already implicit in the piecemeal impact of double-cropping. The impact of each of the changes we have discussed is mediated by the very complex and overlapping class structure of Sedaka. There are well-off tenants and very poor tenants; there are landlords who are (or whose children are) also tenants and laborers; there are smallholders who need wage work to survive but also hire the combines. Thus each of the important shifts in tenure and production creates not only victims and beneficiaries but also a substantial strata whose interests are not so easily discerned. Sedaka is not Morelos, where a poor and largely undifferentiated peasantry confronted a common enemy in the sugar plantation. It is in fact only in comparatively rare circumstances that the class structure of the countryside was such as to produce either a decisive single cleavage or a nearly uniform response to external pressure. The very complexity of the class structure in Sedaka militates against collective opinion and, hence, collective action on most issues.

The obstacles to collective action presented by the local class structure are compounded by other cleavages and alliances that cut across class. These are the familiar links of kinship, friendship, faction, patronage, and ritual ties that muddy the "class waters" in virtually *any* small community. Nearly without exception, they operate to the advantage of the richer farmers by creating a relationship of dependence that restrains the prudent poor man or woman from acting in class terms. Thus Mansur, a poor landless laborer, is related to Shamsul, one of the richest men in the village, and can expect occasional free meals at his house as well as casual work now and then. While this does not prevent Mansur from privately complaining about the loss of work and the tightfisted rich in general, it does help explain his UMNO membership and his deferential profile in village politics. Mat "halus" is extremely poor, rather outspoken privately on class issues, and a member of PAS. But he rents a single relong from his father-in-law, Abdul Rahman, a fairly wealthy UMNO landowner, and takes care not to embarrass him by making trouble in the village. Other examples might be cited, but the point is clear. A small minority of the village poor are hedged in by links of kinship and/or petty economic dependencies they are reluctant to jeopardize. If they disagree with their relative, landlord, or employer, they are likely to do so with circumspection. It would be a mistake to overemphasize such ties, for they are certainly rarer and more fragile than they once were, and many of the poor are not constrained in this way at all. They do, nevertheless, neutralize a fraction of the poor.[2]

2. It goes virtually without saying that the meager possibilities for joint action among the village poor all but evaporate once we leave the community. Even the values that the poor use to justify their claim to work, land, and charity are meant to apply largely within the village itself. While kinship links join most of the poor to relatives elsewhere, these are links of family and not of class. If there were a national or even regional political vehicle that gave effective voice to the class interests of the poor on such issues as land reform, mechanization, and employment, it would undoubtedly find a large following. But Partai Islam (PAS) is not that vehicle,

A third obstacle to open resistance is, perhaps, not so much an obstacle as a viable alternative. As Moore reminds us in quite another context, "throughout the centuries one of the common man's most frequent and effective responses to oppression [has been] *flight*."[3] Nowhere has this option been more historically significant than in Southeast Asia in general and Malaya in particular. So long as there was a land frontier and so long as control over manpower rather than land was the basis of surplus extraction, the possibility of what one writer has awkwardly called "avoidance protest" has *always* proved more attractive than the risk of open confrontation.[4] Much to the consternation of their indigenous leaders as well as their colonial rulers, the rural Malay population has always been exceptionally mobile—moving to another petty chiefdom, leaving one plot of land to make a new clearing and homestead in the forest, switching crops and often occupations in the process—and has classically "voted with its feet." Because of its particular demography and social organization, it would not be an exaggeration to say that "exit" rather than "voice" had come to characterize the traditional and preferred response to oppression in Malay society.[5] Fortunately for the contemporary losers in the green revolution, this traditional option is still available to many.

For half a century at the very least, a substantial portion of the population increase in Kedah's rice bowl has been moving away. They have contributed, as pioneers, to the opening up of new paddy areas in Perak, Perlis, Pahang, Johor, and the inland districts of Kedah itself. Virtually every poor family in the village has, at one time or another, applied for acceptance to government-sponsored settlement schemes (*ranchangan*), where incomes from rubber and especially oil palm are routinely more than can be wrested from even a substantial paddy farm. Only a few have been selected, and they are typically not from among the poorest villagers. Still, the slim chance of becoming a sponsored settler (*peneroka*) is a factor in preventing more open expressions of local conflict. For the children of modest and poor villagers, the option of factory work and domestic service (for women) and full-time urban contract labor (for men) are available. For the

---

dominated as it is by large landowners, and the socialist party (Partai Rakyat), for reasons of repression and communalism, has never established a real foothold in Kedah.

3. Barrington Moore, Jr., *Injustice: The Social Bases of Obedience and Revolt* (White Plains: M. E. Sharpe, 1978), 125.

4. For an illuminating discussion of this pattern in the region generally, see Michael Adas, "From Avoidance to Confrontation: Peasant Protest in Precolonial and Colonial Southeast Asia," *Comparative Studies in Society and History* 23, no. 2 (April 1981): 217–47.

5. The terms "exit" and "voice" are taken from the analysis in Albert O. Hirschman, *Exit, Voice, and Loyalty: Responses to Decline in Firms, Organizations and States* (Cambridge, Mass.: Harvard Univ. Press, 1970).

poor families who largely choose to remain, short-term contract labor in the cities offers a means to a viable, if unsatisfactory, livelihood. This last, and most common, resort not only reduces the economic pressure on poor families but also removes the head of household from active participation in village affairs for much of the year. Such semiproletarians still reside largely in the village and may even farm a small plot of paddy land, but they play an increasingly marginal role in the local issues that might provoke class conflict. A major slump in off-farm employment would, of course, change this picture dramatically by making local work and access to land that much more salient.[6] For the time being, however, the ability to raid the cash economy to make good the local subsistence deficit continues to provide a less risky alternative to local conflict.

Lest one gain the impression from the foregoing that the obstacles to class conflict in Sedaka are entirely a matter of the complex local stratification, the piecemeal character of changes in production relations, and the alternative sources of income, I hasten to add that repression and the fear of repression are very much involved as well. The chilling role of repression as it is experienced by poor villagers will become all too apparent in the accounts that follow. Here it is sufficient simply to note that the efforts to halt or impede the growth of combine-harvesting occurred in a climate of fear generated by local elites, by the police, by the "Special-Branch" internal security forces, by a pattern of political arrests and intimidation. There is good reason to believe that the local campaign against the combine would have assumed a more open and defiant course had it not been for the justifiable fears generated by coercion.

The fifth and final obstacle to open resistance makes sense only against a background of expected repression. This obstacle is simply the day-to-day imperative of earning a living—of household survival—which Marx appropriately termed "the dull compulsion of economic relations."[7] Lacking any realistic possibility, for the time being, of directly and collectively redressing their situation, the village poor have little choice but to adjust, as best they can, to the circumstances they confront daily. Tenants may bitterly resent the rent they must pay for their small plot, but they must pay it or lose the land; the near landless may deplore the loss of wage work, but they must scramble for the few opportunities available; they may harbor deep animosities toward the clique that dominates village politics, but they must act with circumspection if they wish to benefit from any of the small advantages that clique can confer.

At least two aspects of this grudging, pragmatic adaptation to the realities

6. Malaysia's strong foreign-exchange position and its diversified exports make it less vulnerable than many other Third World economies, but it is nevertheless vulnerable to any deep and prolonged slump. Shortfalls in private investment and in export earnings and the resulting need to trim public spending over the past two years (1981–82) have made this vulnerability increasingly apparent.

7. Karl Marx, *Capital*, vol. 1 (Harmondsworth: Penguin, 1970): 737.

merit emphasis. The first is that it does not rule out certain forms of resistance, although it surely sets limits that only the foolhardy would transgress. The second is that it is above all pragmatic; it does not imply normative consent to those realities. To understand this is simply to grasp what is, in all likelihood, the situation for most subordinate classes historically. They struggle under conditions that are largely not of their own making, and their pressing material needs necessitate something of a daily accommodation to those conditions. Dissident intellectuals from the middle or upper classes may occasionally have the luxury of focusing exclusively on the prospects for long-term structural change, but the peasantry or the working class are granted no holiday from the mundane pressures of making a living. If we observe, as we shall, a good deal of "conforming" behavior in daily social life in Sedaka, we have no reason to assume that it derives from some symbolic hegemony or normative consensus engineered by elites or by the state. The duress of the quotidian is quite sufficient. Durkheim and Weber recognized, as did Marx, "that human beings are forced to behave in certain directions regardless of their own preferences and inclinations."[8] Durkheim's view of the daily constraints on the industrial working class could be applied with even greater emphasis to the peasantry:

> This tension in social relations is due, in part, to the fact that the working classes are not really satisfied with the conditions under which they live, but very often accept them only as constrained and forced, since they have not the means to change them.[9]

In the long run, and in certain circumstances, the peasantry and the working class *do* have "the means to change" fundamentally their situation. But in the short run—today, tomorrow, and the day after—they face a situation that very sharply restricts their real options.[10] The few opportunities for land and work remaining to Sedaka's poor depend today, as always, on the sufferance of the wealthy. If much of the day-to-day public behavior of the poor reflects that fact,

8. Nicholas Abercrombie, Stephen Hill, and Bryan S. Turner, *The Dominant Ideology Thesis* (London: Allen & Unwin, 1980), 46. In their analysis of feudalism, early capitalism, and late capitalism these three authors present a persuasive case that the concept of "the dominant ideology" or "hegemony," as expounded by such well-known contemporary Marxist scholars as Althusser, Poulantzas, Miliband, and Habermas, are neither logically convincing nor empirically persuasive. I will return to the issue of "hegemony" and "false-consciousness" in the next chapter.

9. Emile Durkheim, *The Division of Labour in Society* (New York: Free Press, 1964), 356, quoted in Abercrombie et al., *Dominant Ideology Thesis,* 43.

10. For two studies which, in different contexts, emphasize both repression and "the compulsion of economic relations," see Juan Martinez Alier, *Labourers and Landowners in Southern Spain,* St. Anthony's College, Oxford, Publications, No. 4 (London: Allen & Unwin, 1971), and John Gaventa, *Power and Powerlessness: Quiescence and Rebellion in an Appalachian Valley* (Urbana: Univ. of Illinois Press, 1980).

it can be explained by nothing more than a healthy and expedient regard for survival. "Going for broke" can have little appeal in a context in which the final word of this expression must be taken quite literally.

THE EFFORT TO STOP THE COMBINE-HARVESTER

The introduction of combine-harvesting, as the most sudden and devastating of the changes associated with double-cropping, also stirred the most active resistance. This resistance went well beyond the arguments about its efficiency, the complaints over lost wages, and the slander directed against those who hired it, which I have already described. Throughout the rice bowl of Kedah there were efforts physically to obstruct its entry into the fields, incidents of arson and sabotage, and widespread attempts to organize "strikes" of transplanters against those who first hired the machine. All of these actions ultimately failed to prevent the mechanization of the paddy harvest, although they undoubtedly delayed it somewhat. A close examination of the forms of resistance and the responses of large farmers can teach us a great deal about both the possibilities and limits that help structure this resistance.

Combines were, of course, not the first machines that had threatened the livelihood of poorer villagers in Muda. As we have seen in the preceding chapter, the use of tractors and trucks to haul paddy directly from the field to town had earlier sparked spirited and successful resistance in some villages. The threat posed by combines, however, was of a far greater magnitude. Sporadic resistance began as early as 1970, when the first small experimental machines, adapted from a Japanese prototype, were used in field trials near the town of Jitra. Officials of the Muda Agricultural Development Authority, who conducted the trials, recalled several incidents of sabotage, all of which they chose to call "vandalism."[11] Batteries were removed from the machines and thrown in irrigation ditches; carburetors and other vital parts such as distributors and air filters were smashed; sand and mud were put into the gas tank; and various objects (stones, wire, nails) were thrown into the augers. Two aspects of this sabotage deserve particular emphasis. First, it was clear that the goal of the saboteurs was not simple theft, for nothing was actually stolen. Second, all of the sabotage was carried out at night by individuals or small groups acting anonymously. They were, furthermore, shielded by their fellow villagers who, if they knew who was involved, claimed total ignorance when the police came to investigate. As a result, no prosecutions were ever made. The practice of posting a night watchman to guard the combine dates from these early trials.

Starting in 1976, when combine-harvesting began with a vengeance, peasant

---

11. The term *sabotage* is precise descriptively as we shall see, originating as it does with the wrecking of machinery by nineteenth-century French workers who threw their wooden shoes (*sabots*) into the works.

acts of vengeance likewise spread throughout the paddy-growing region. Poorer villagers in Sedaka can remember several incidents, which they recount with something akin to glee. Tok Mahmud, for example, told me that he knew exactly how to jam a combine's auger—where to put the barbed wire or nails— because he had friends (*kawan*) who had done it. He declined to elaborate because, he said, if he talked openly his friends might be arrested (*tangkap*). Sukur described a more dramatic incident, two seasons before I arrived, near Tokai, just a few miles south of Sedaka, where a combine was set on fire. A number of poor people (*orang susah*), he said, surrounded the Malay night watch-man and asked him who owned the machine (*Jentera siapa?*). When he replied that it belonged to a Chinese syndicate, they ordered him to climb down and then poured kerosene over the engine and cab and set it alight. Two Malay young men were arrested the next day but were quickly released for lack of evidence. Villagers report several other incidents of trees being felled across the combine's path into one village or another and of wire being jammed into the auger, particularly near Selangkuh.

I made no effort to assemble a complete inventory of reported incidents, although it was a rare peasant who could not recall one or two. No one, however, could recall any such incident in Sedaka itself. This may merely reflect an understandable reluctance to call attention to themselves. And at no time did the overall volume of sabotage reach anything like the level of machine breaking that accompanied the introduction of mechanical threshers into England in the 1830s. [12]

At the same time that individuals and small groups of men were attacking the machines, there were the beginnings of a quiet but more collective effort by women to bring pressure to bear on the farmers who hired the machines. Men and women—often from the same family—had, of course, each lost work to the combine, but it was only the women who still had any real bargaining

---

12. For the now classic study of this movement, see E. J. Hobsbawn and George Rude, *Captain Swing* (New York: Pantheon, 1968). Without attempting an inevitably strained comparison, I note that the rural Luddites of the early nineteenth century had several advantages over the peasantry of Kedah when it came to mobilizing against threshing machines. They were far more fully proletarianized and dependent on wage labor; they could look to a set of traditional legal protections that reinforced their claim to a living wage; and they faced a repressive apparatus that was less firmly planted in the countryside. They too, of course, were overcome, but only by a military force that by the standards of the time was unprecedented. The resistance in Kedah was much more sporadic and abbreviated, although the saboteurs shared with their English counterparts a preference for the anonymity that acting under cover of darkness provided. By 1979, public warnings by officials and more rigorous guarding of the machines themselves had reduced the incidence of this form of resistance to negligible proportions.

power. They were, for the time being, still in control of transplanting.[13] The group of women (*kumpulan share*, from the English) who reaped a farmer's land were typically the same group that had earlier transplanted the same field. They were losing roughly half their seasonal earnings, and they understandably resented transplanting a crop for a farmer who would use the combine at harvest time. Thus, in Sedaka and, it appears, throughout much of the Muda region, such women resolved to organize a boycott (*boikot*) that would deny transplanting services to their employers who hired the combine.

Three of the five "share groups" in Sedaka evidently made some attempts to enforce such a boycott. Those groups of anywhere from six to nine women were led by Rosni (a widow), Rokiah (the wife of Mat Buyong), and Miriam (the wife of Mat Isa). The remaining two groups, led by the wives of Tajuddin and Ariffin, appear not to have been involved, but neither group would agree to plant paddy for a farmer who was being boycotted by one of the other three gangs. Why the groups of Rosni, Rokiah, and Miriam took the initiative is not entirely clear. They are composed of women from families that are, on average, slightly poorer than those in the remaining two groups, but only slightly. The first two are, as well, largely from PAS households, but this may be as much due to kinship and neighborhood as to factionalism per se, and in any case they were frequently boycotting farmers from their own political faction. If we rely on local explanations for the pattern of resistance, the consensus is that Rosni and Rokiah depend heavily on wage labor to support their families and are at the same time "courageous" (*berani*).[14]

The forms the boycott took were very much in keeping with the kinds of cautious resistance I have so far described. At no time was there ever an open confrontation between a farmer who used the combine and his transplanters. Instead, the anonymous and indirect approach of *cara sembunyi tau* with which we are familiar was employed. The women "let it be known" through intermediaries that the group was dissatisfied (*tak puas hati*) with the loss of harvest work and would be reluctant (*segan*) to transplant the fields of those who had hired the combine the previous season. They also let it be known that, when and if a combine broke down in the course of the harvest, a farmer who wanted then to get his crop in by hand could not count on his old workers to bail him out.

13. Broadcasting (*tabor kering*) only began to pose a serious threat to hand transplanting by 1979 or 1980.

14. Rosni, as we have noted, is a widow, while Rokiah's husband is considered rather weak-minded, so that Rokiah is normally seen as the head of her household, making all the basic decisions. Such women, especially if they are past child-bearing age, are treated virtually as "honorary" males and are exempt from many of the customary requirements of modesty and deference expected of women in Malay society.

When it came time at the beginning of the irrigated season of 1977 to make good on this threat, circumspection again prevailed. None of the three groups refused outright to transplant paddy for those who had harvested with the combine in the previous season. Rather, they delayed; the head of the share group would tell the offending farmer that they were busy and could not get to his land just yet. Only a dozen or so farmers had used the combine the previous season, so the share groups had a good deal of work to occupy them just transplanting the crops of those who had not mechanized. [15] The transplanters thus kept their options open; they avoided a direct refusal to transplant, which would have provoked an open break. Fully abreast of the rumors of a boycott, the farmers who had been put off became increasingly anxious as their nursery paddy was passing its prime and as they feared their crop might not be fully mature before the scheduled date for shutting off the supply of water. Their state of mind was not improved by the sight of their neighbors' newly transplanted fields next to their own vacant plots.

After more than two weeks of this war of nerves—the seeming boycott that never fully announced itself—six farmers "let it be known" that they were arranging for outside laborers to come and transplant their crops. By most accounts, these six were Haji Kadir, Haji Salim, Tok Kasim, Lazim, Kamil, and Cik Mah, who between them cultivate nearly 100 relong. They claimed in their defense that they had pressed for a firm commitment for a transplanting date from their local share group and, only after being put off again, had they moved. At this point, the boycott collapsed. Each of the three share groups was faced with defections, as women feared that the transplanting work would be permanently lost to outsiders. They hastily sent word that they would begin transplanting the land in question within the next few days. Three of the six farmers canceled their arrangements with the outside gangs, while the other three went ahead either because they felt it was too late to cancel or because they wished to teach the women a lesson. Transplanters came from the town of Yan (just outside the irrigation scheme) and from Singkir and Merbuk, farther away. Haji Salim, using his considerable political influence, arranged with MADA to bring in a gang of Thai transplanters—a practice he has continued and for which he is bitterly resented.

The brief and abortive attempt to stop the combine by collective action was

15. Not all farmers in Sedaka that season could be neatly classified either as combine hirers or share-group hirers, since at least four farmers had used the combine for one plot and hand labor for another. In two cases, these were decisions based on the ripeness of the crops in each field when the combine was available or the inability of the machine to harvest a given plot (because it was on soft, waterlogged land or because it was surrounded by plots or unripe paddy). In the remaining two cases, the decision was almost certainly an attempt by the farmer to hedge his bets and avoid the threatened boycott.

the subject of demoralized or self-satisfied postmortems, depending on which side of the fence one happened to be. Aside from the pleasure or disappointment expressed, the postmortems, for once, converged on the inevitability of the outcome. Those with most to lose from mechanization realized that the women could not really move beyond talk and threats. Thus, Wahid said that the rumored boycott was "just talk and they planted anyway." "What could they do?" he asked, throwing up his hands. Tok Mahmud echoed this assessment: "Other people took the work; once the work is gone they couldn't do anything." "People are clever," Sukur added, "If you don't want to transplant, they'll take the work and money." It is for this reason, Samad claimed, that the women were careful not to burn their bridges and only talked of a boycott well out of earshot (*kot jauh saja*) of large farmers. Finally, in the same vein, Hamzah summed up the long odds against the women:

> Whether you complain or don't complain, it's no use. You can't do any-thing; you can't win. If you say anything, they won't hire you to plant even. The women will even have to cut paddy for a farmer if the combine breaks down. If you're hard up, you have to take the work. If you refuse (*tolak*), if you don't do it, others will. Only those who are well-off (*senang*) can refuse.

We could ask for no clearer exposition of the "dull compulsion of economic relations." The well-to-do were not only aware of this "dull compulsion" but were counting on it. As Mat Isa noted, "They didn't *do* anything; it was only idle talk (*mulut saja*)."[16] Tok Kasim, whose stake in mechanization was higher because he was a machine broker as well as a farmer, realized the boycott would never be carried out, since "the poor have to work anyway; they can't hold out (*tahan*)." And Lebai Hussein said that, although they were "angry," the women could only talk about (*sembang-sembang saja*) a boycott, since they needed the money. He concluded with a Malay saying that precisely captured the difficulties the women faced: "Angry with their rice, they throw it out for the chickens to eat."[17] The closest English equivalent is "cutting off your nose to spite your face."

If we step back a few paces from our single village perspective, a wider and more melancholy pattern appears. The share groups of women in Sedaka were, in this same period, occasionally hired to transplant paddy fields as much as thirty miles away. Rosni told me that once a woman from Setiti Batu, where their share groups was planting, had told her that the farmer for whom they were working had not been able to recruit local transplanters because he had

16. He then concluded by saying *padi tumpah,* which, literally, means "spilled paddy," but its idiomatic sense would perhaps best be expressed by the English "just chaff " (as opposed to wheat).

17. *Marah sama nasi, tauk, bagi ayam makan.*

harvested last season with the combine. When she learned this, Rosni told the woman that she was "sick at heart" (*sakit hati*) but that the work was nearly finished anyway.[18] It is only too likely that there were similar cases as well. Thus, from this wider perspective, the poorer women of Sedaka were inadvertently serving as "strike-breakers" in other Muda villages. And women from these villages, or others like them, were undoubtedly coming to break the boycott in Sedaka. What we have here is a nearly classic example of the crippling effect of class action by peasants when it is confined, as it typically is, to one or a few villages in a much wider labor market.[19]

Similar attempts at a labor boycott occurred throughout much of the Muda region. An official at the state headquarters of MADA confided to me that he suspected most of the landlords, like Haji Salim, who applied there for permission to import Thai transplanters were actually attempting to get around a local labor boycott. Inasmuch as they were invariably quite large-scale farmers, they were the ones most likely to have hired the combine at the first opportunity. Talk of a boycott was certainly very common. Thus Rosemary Barnard writes of a village near the state capital of Alor Setar in which (in 1978) there was "talk of combining forces to attempt to block combine harvesters next season."[20] In Sedaka itself I frequently heard the names of villages that had, it was claimed, kept the combine harvesters off their fields. Lebai Pendek said that the village of Gelam Dua to the north still harvested all its local fields by hand. Kubang Jerai and other villages in the Bukit Raya district, a PAS stronghold, were often mentioned as places where the boycott and machine breaking had prevented the combines from coming. Mansur said that in Kangkong, to the north, the poor were "better organized" (*lagi teratur*) and hand harvesting was still the rule.[21]

18. The fact that the paddy field they were planting belonged to the brother of one of the women in the share group further complicated matters.

19. This serves as a salutary reminder of the limitations of local or village studies that treat only local fragments of class which stretch over wider areas and whose members are unknown personally to one another. A more accurate view of class would in fact include not only a spatial dimension but a temporal one as well, as the class of tenants as a concept must include those who have ever had this status in the past as well as those who are tenants today. The spatial dimension of class by itself may, in this context, seem to argue for the role of an elite or intelligentsia to coordinate and unify its fragmented action. As we shall see later, this conclusion is not necessarily warranted.

20. Rosemary Barnard, "The Modernization of Agriculture in a Kedah Village, 1967–1978" (Paper presented at Second National Conference of the Asian Studies Association of Australia, University of New South Wales, Sydney, May 15–19, 1978), 33.

21. The salaried head of the MADA branch office in Kepala Batas explicitly emphasized this when he explained to me why the attempted boycott had "no effect" (*tak ada kesan*) and added that the improvement in surfaced roads now permitted large farmers to bring in labor from much farther away.

In nearby Mengkuang, the police had to be called to prevent a near riot when a large landowner had, at the last minute, attempted to send his assembled harvest laborers home upon discovering that a nearby combine could be hired immediately.

The village most often mentioned in this connection, however, was Permatang Buluh, about twelve miles to the north. In this *kampung,* many said, combines were still not used because the poor had banded together so successfully. The harvest workers and transplanters of Sedaka spoke of this community with something approaching awe, so I made a point of visiting Permatang Buluh to see for myself. My companion that day was Amin, who had an uncle living there. The uncle, who himself farmed over 10 relong, reported that he and most others now used combines and that the boycott had failed. It was only when I walked through the paddy fields unaccompanied that I heard a slightly different account from a small tenant. He said that the "poor" in Permatang Buluh had, in fact, prevented the combine from harvesting paddy for three seasons, until 1978. When I asked how they had done it, he replied that the large farmers had been "afraid." And when I asked why they were afraid, he simply said *golok putih-putih,* which might be translated as "the machetes were gleaming (or very sharp)." Perhaps sensing that he had already volunteered too much to a stranger, he declined to elaborate, but it was clear from his remark that the threat of violence was a factor. Two other characteristics of Permatang Buluh may help account for its relative success in delaying mechanization. It appeared that the village had more than the usual proportion of landless and smallholders who depended heavily on wages. The headman of the village was also unusual in a way that might have facilitated solidarity among the poor. Although he was born, like most headmen, into a well-to-do household, his father had lost nearly all his land through gambling debts and thus the present headman was himself a part-time harvest worker. Even with those particular "advantages" the success of the Permatang Buluh had been short-lived.

When the would-be boycotters and machine breakers of Sedaka spoke about their own experience or about the relative success of others, what one heard was not just a litany of discouragement and despair. There was also more than just a glimmer of what might have been (or might be) if the poor had acted with more unity and force. Thus Samad saw Permatang Buluh as something of an inspiration: "If we had done the same thing here, the machines wouldn't have come. It would have been good (*bagus*) if we had, but we weren't organized (*tak teratur*)."[22] Rokiah herself spoke with disdain of the share groups in Sedaka compared with Permatang Buluh: "Here they didn't want [to carry it through]." "If they had all agreed, if they had struck, [the machines] would not have been brave enough to come in."[23] Mansur, one of the few pure landless laborers in

22. *Teratur* might in this context be translated also as "disciplined."

23. *Kalau berpakat, kalau mogok, tak berani masuk.* The term *mogok* is the standard Malay word for "strike."

the village, echoed these sentiments precisely. "People here weren't unified; they were afraid and only followed [the rich]; if they were stronger, then they could lift themselves up." The same assessment of present disunity together with a faint promise of greater solidarity is evident when talk turned to the possibility that there will one day be transplanting machines that will replace the women. Bakri bin Haji Wahab said that if such machines came the women would then charge a dollar for uprooting each small bundle (*cap*) of seedlings from the nursery bed. "It could become a war," he added.[24] Then Ishak more realistically pointed out that if the women charged M$1 for each bundle then others would agree to do it for 90 cents, others for 80 cents or 70 cents and that "would be the end of it."

As the large farmers see it, the attempted boycott was "all talk"—virtually a "nonevent." There is something to this view, inasmuch as the boycott was never openly declared and collapsed without fanfare. The use of delays and barely plausible excuses meant that the intention to boycott itself could be disavowed. As the losers see it, however, it was an effort in the right direction that fell short. They are under no illusions about their own weak position or the obstacles in their path, but they do look to the modest successes elsewhere as something of a goad and inspiration.

"ROUTINE" RESISTANCE

The attempt to halt combine-harvesting, while hardly the stuff of high drama, was at least out of the ordinary—a new, if largely futile, initiative. It took place against a rarely noticed background of routine resistance over wages, tenancy, rents, and the distribution of paddy that is a permanent feature of life in Sedaka and in any stratified agrarian setting. A close examination of this realm of struggle exposes an implicit form of local trade unionism that is reinforced both by mutuality among the poor and by a considerable amount of theft and violence against property. Very little of this activity, as we shall see, poses a fundamental threat to the basic structure of agrarian inequalities, either materially or symbolically. What it does represent, however, is a constant process of testing and renegotiation of production relations between classes. On both sides—landlord–tenant, farmer–wage laborer—there is a never-ending attempt to seize each small advantage and press it home, to probe the limits of the existing relationships, to see precisely what can be gotten away with at the margin, and to include this margin as a part of an accepted, or at least tolerated, territorial claim. Over the past decade the flow of this frontier battle has, of course, rather consistently favored the fortunes of the large farmers and landlords. They have not only swallowed large pieces of the territory defended by wage workers and tenants, but in doing so they have thereby reduced (through marginalization) the perim-

24. *Boleh jadi perang.*

eter along which the struggle continues. Even along this reduced perimeter, however, there is constant pressure exerted by those who hope to regain at least a small patch of what they have grudgingly lost. The resisters require little explicit coordination to conduct this struggle, for the simple imperative of making a tolerable living is enough to make them dig in their heels.

My goal here is only to convey something of the dimensions and conduct of this routine resistance, not its full extent, for that could fill a volume in itself. Inasmuch as a great deal of this resistance concerns the disposition of the proceeds of paddy farming, the best place to begin is in the paddy field itself, with threshing.

Trade Unionism without Trade Unions

Threshers, unlike reapers, are hired and paid by the farmer as individuals. They work in pairs at a single threshing tub and then divide the piece-rate earnings at the end of the day. In 1979, the average piece-rate per gunny sack was M$2. The piece-work organization of the work produces a conflict of interest between the thresher and the farmer whose paddy is being threshed. The farmer naturally wants *all* the rice from his field and, for that reason, prefers to have the threshers beat each bundle of cut paddy until virtually all the grains are in the tub. The thresher, in contrast, is interested in the cash he can earn for a day's work.[25] Depending on the ripeness of the paddy, roughly 80–90 percent of the grains are dislodged in the first two or three strokes. To dislodge most of the remaining paddy may require as many as six or seven strokes. The tub fills up faster, and the thresher earns more for the day's work, if he beats each sheaf only two or three times and moves quickly to the next sheaf.[26] If he were to work in this fashion, he might thresh as many as ten gunny sacks (M$20) in a day, compared with, say, M$10 or M$12 if he were to thresh each sheaf thoroughly. The difference is vital when one recalls that, for poor men, threshing is the best-paid work of the season, and there is a premium on making the most of it while it lasts. Nor does the conflict of interest between the thresher's wages and the farmer's paddy end here. A thresher can, in fact, recover the paddy he has left on the stalks if there is someone in his family who gleans. The more paddy poor men leave lying beside the threshing tubs, the more paddy the women in

25. This is especially the case if the season is a busy one and other threshing jobs are available when the current one is finished. Frequently threshing work is in fact morning work rather than day-long work, since the job is so physically demanding that the day begins at dawn and ends early in the afternoon. If the moon is bright, threshing is occasionally done in the evening to take advantage of the cool temperatures.

26. There is also, to be sure, an element of competition among the threshers as well if we see each pair competing to thresh as much as possible of the paddy in a given field.

their household can collect once the harvest is over. This provides them with a further incentive to leave some behind.

Expectations have of course developed concerning how many times each sheaf of paddy, depending on the variety and its ripeness, should be beaten. But these expectations require constant pressure and constant supervision to enforce. The first few times I threshed, I wondered why the farmer, even if he was relatively poor, did not thresh himself. After all, I reasoned, he could save as much as M$20 in wages he was paying to others. When I asked a farmer (Mat Isa) at the end of the day, he said that if he did not watch the threshers he would lose half his paddy. This was surely an exaggeration, but it explains why most small farmers supervise their threshers rather than work themselves. As the laborers work, the farmer circulates slowly and makes his presence felt. And when he is at the far corner of the field, when the matting inserted high around the tub to catch flying grains blocks his view, or when he is busy preparing a snack, the number of times each sheaf is beaten diminishes appreciably. The advantage to be gained is marginal and limited, since the farmer—or, as he is called in Malay, "paddy owner" (*tuan padi*)—will notice how fast the tub fills, may casually check the threshed sheaves, and in any event can always decide not to invite the worker back the following season.[27] It has, I was told, occasionally happened that a thresher whose work has displeased the farmer is told he will not be needed the next day, but this is extremely rare. The farmer also avoids, whenever possible, hiring a thresher who has many gleaners in his household. Thus Mat "halus," whose entire family does a prodigious amount of gleaning, is seldom if ever invited to thresh in Sedaka. Other poor men will occasionally send their wives or daughters to glean fields they have threshed, but they are careful not to make a practice of it lest they jeopardize their employment.

Now that there is considerably less threshing work available, the margin for such routine resistance has narrowed. It has not, however, disappeared entirely. The actual number of times a sheaf of paddy is beaten is still a compromise between what the farmer would like and what he is able to enforce—a compromise determined not only by the overall balance of power but by a daily, unremitting struggle in the paddy fields.

Another focus of routine resistance is the determination of the rates of pay for transplanting, reaping, and threshing. The scope for movement is relatively

---

27. When a close relative of the farmer is threshing, a certain amount of this behavior is overlooked, and the relative, if poor, may take full advantage of the leeway. A number of farmers have told me that they thus *prefer* to hire non-kinsmen (or, for that matter, to have non-kin tenants), since it is then easier to insist on careful work. Kinsmen who are threshing, they add, make it that much easier for the other threshers to emulate their performance. Since it is difficult to deny relatives gleaning rights on one's land, that is another reason to avoid hiring them for threshing whenever possible.

small, since something like a going rate based on labor market conditions is established in the course of each season. But there is some variation and room for maneuver both early in the particular phase before the rates have settled or when a temporary labor shortage develops. The share groups of women and the men who thresh are incredibly alert to news that *any* farmer is paying even fractionally more than the rate for the previous season. As Rosni noted, "once someone gets it [a higher wage], the others will have to follow."[28] What in fact is the going rate for given tasks is the object of heated debate nearly every season, with the head of the share group quoting the highest rate she has heard of (or can plausibly invent) and the employer quoting the lowest in the same fashion. The workers are restrained by the possibility of losing the job to others and the farmer is restrained by his concern for having his crop transplanted or harvested in good time. So far as the laborers are concerned, the Chinese who farm in the area play a beneficial role in this negotiating process inasmuch as they are the most likely to break ranks and pay more.[29] It is fairly common to hear complaints by large farmers about how their workers lie and cheat (*bohong, tipu*), when it comes to quoting the going-rate. They keep their ears to the ground as well and attempt, whenever possible, to dispute a report of higher wages or to explain it away by reference to special conditions (for example, deep water, or lodging, in the case of reaping and threshing) that do not apply to their own fields. The advantage to be gained through these contesting representations of the labor market may seem trivial but, for those at the margin, the possibility of a marginal gain is never trivial. What appears in Muda statistics as the seasonal "labor market"—the average price for transplanting, reaping, and threshing— is, at the village level, the outcome of constant maneuvering.

The inroads made by mechanization now mean that much of the paddy gathered by hand comes from low-lying fields that are waterlogged or from fields where wind and rain has caused the heavy panicles to lodge. Such special conditions call, in principle, for special wages; precisely what those special wages should be is an arena of struggle. They way in which this struggle is conducted reveals the same elements of "strike" behavior and circumspection that we encountered in the resistance to combine harvesting. In the case of reaping, for example, the head of a share group, such as Rosni, will typically look over the field in advance. Should the water be particularly deep or the paddy lodged (or both) she will rarely ask the farmer directly for a higher price per relong. Instead she will "let it be known" (*cara sembunyi tau*) that the reaping will take much longer than usual and that the rate should be considerably more than the standard (1979 main season) of M\$35. The farmer may "reply" in several ways: he may

28. *Satu kali dapat, lain kena turut.*

29. Whether this is due to their greater and more diversified wealth, or, more likely, to their desire as outsiders to be absolutely certain of labor when they require it is uncertain, but they are looked to as the pace setters for wage rates.

"let it be known" that he is willing to consider a higher rate depending on how the work goes, he may remain silent, or he may let it be known that he thinks the standard wage is enough in this case. Unless the farmer's rate is clearly out of line and alternative work is available, however, the women will show up for work. Should the field conditions be as bad or worse than anticipated, they are likely to grumble openly as they cut the paddy, passing comments such as "Your paddy is hard [work]; [we're] losing [money]."[30] This is a clear signal to the farmer that he is in danger of losing his work force, and he often responds by indicating that he will raise the wage somewhat, though he rarely specifies by how much. If, on the other hand, he believes their claim unwarranted, he may simply remain silent, which is interpreted as a sign of refusal. In this case, the women are faced with a difficult choice; they can continue to work and grumble or they can walk off the job.

The decision to walk off is not taken lightly, because the farmer may well switch to a different share group next season and because any loss of precious harvest income is a sacrifice. If the farmer has a generally good reputation for paying fair wages in the past, the women will probably continue to work while making their dissatisfaction known.[31] But if the farmer has a reputation for stinginess, the women will strike, as they do once or twice a year. The "strike" is not announced, but everyone understands what is happening. Rather than leaving the fields directly, the women are more likely not to return after the midday meal or on the following morning. The farmer will then typically send someone to the share group leader to propose a modest increase in pay to end the strike. More rarely, the farmer may refuse to budge and, if he does, he must recruit outside labor, since no village share group will agree to take the place of another, once the work has begun.

Disputes over reaping wages have become increasingly common as more farmers have turned to broadcasting. A paddy field that has been broadcast-planted is a good deal harder to reap, owing to both the absence of orderly rows and to the much greater variation in the height of the mature stalks. Women have asked for, and gotten, wages as high as M$60 a relong for reaping such fields, especially during the irrigated season when the fields are wet at harvest time.[32] They are also conscious that high reaping wages are a fitting retribution for those farmers who do not hire transplanters. As Rosni said privately when her

---

30. *Hang punya padi susah, rugi.*

31. The women's attitude is perhaps best captured by the English expression, "Fool me once, shame on you; fool me twice, shame on me."

32. Members of the share group frequently point out that both transplanting and reaping have become more time-consuming since double-cropping because the density of plants per relong has increased appreciably. If transplanting and reaping fees are higher than they were in 1969, the women claim that this only reflects inflation and the additional work required.

group had asked for M$50 per relong to reap Abdul Rahman's broadcast field, "If he takes away our transplanting, we'll get it back reaping." The farmers' riposte to higher reaping costs is to move, when possible, to the *kupang* system of paying a flat rate (M$3 or M$3.50) to individuals for a morning's work. This is an option only if the farmer's fields are out of phase with others, so that there is a surplus of idle labor at the time. Even then, however, many women in the share groups will refuse to transplant or reap for *kupang* wages, as they understand that is another way of reducing their wage and breaking their rudimentary organization. It is too early to say whether large farmers will succeed in establishing the *kupang* system as the norm for transplanting and reaping. What is clear, however, is that the resistance of poor women to *kupang* work is, thus far, a major factor impeding its adoption.

Conflict over piece-rates for threshing follow much the same pattern as for reaping. Under normal circumstances, those who are threshing paddy can expect to thresh about four gunny sacks in a long morning; at the standard pay of M$2 per sack prevailing in the 1978–79 main season, the laborer would receive at least M$8. But if the paddy is wet or immature and the water deep, it may take an entire morning just to thresh one or two sacks. Open grumbling will inevitably begin, and the farmer understands that an adjustment is called for.[33] He is under great pressure to make some concession, for any further delay in gathering and drying his crop will inevitably lead to its spoiling. Again, as with reaping, direct demands are rarely presented, but the farmer is made to understand the implicit threat. If he makes, or promises, an adequate adjustment—as is typically the case—the work continues in an improved atmosphere. If he fails to raise the piece-rate, he may provoke a strike. Unlike the share groups, however, which strike as a unit, threshers walk out as individuals, although pressure is brought to bear on those who would remain to join in the walkout. The irrigated season harvest of 1979 was an exceptional opportunity for village threshers in this respect, since heavy rains had caused widespread lodging at the last moment, and a good part of the harvest had to be gathered by hand or not at all. Farmers were desperate to save their paddy, and two such walkouts by threshers helped to establish a wage of M$3 per sack as the minimum. In each case *all* the threshers agreed among themselves not to return the following morning and sent word that they were sick or had been called away

33. Compare this with the description of Russian harvest workers' more explosive reaction to standard piece-rates when the crop had been beaten down by hail, thus requiring much longer to reap. The greater violence of the labor gangs in this case seems particularly attributable to the fact that they were outsiders and strangers. Timothy Mixter, "Of Grandfather Beaters and Fat-Heeled Pacifists: Perceptions of Agricultural Labor and Hiring-Market Disturbances in Saratov, 1872–1905," *Russian History/Histoire Russe* 7, Pts. I & II (1980): 139–68.

to other, more pressing, work. Their unanimity helped to shield them against the possibility that the farmer would never invite them back to thresh in subsequent seasons. Neither of the two farmers attempted to hire other villagers for the work, as they knew none would come.[34] One (Zaharuddin) thought of recruiting outsiders from his in-laws' village but quickly thought better of it when he learned they could not come for three days, during which he would lose most of his already cut crop to the moisture. The threshers had thus seized a rather unique opportunity to press their claims. They and the reapers, however, continued to operate with circumspection, avoiding an open confrontation and strikes whenever possible, since they knew that their future earnings depended on retaining a measure of goodwill between them and their employers. Within these decorous limits they nevertheless carried on a struggle to protect their interests as wage earners.[35]

Imposed Mutuality

It would be apparent that even the modest forms of resistance mounted in Sedaka depend for their effect upon a certain degree of mutuality among the poor. That is, the first, and minimal, requirement of class solidarity is a negative one: that the poor at least refrain from undercutting one another and thereby further magnifying the considerable economic power of their employers and landlords. "Otherwise," as Marx notes, "they are on hostile terms with each other as competitors"[36]—surviving at one another's expense. The mutuality that exists can be seen in the refusal of other share groups or threshers to act as strikebreakers in the village. It exists, as we shall see, in the vital realm of tenancy, where those seeking land are unwilling to undercut their own neighbors. No extravagant claims can be made for this sanctioned self-restraint, inasmuch as it operates only within the confines of the village itself, and even in this context its operation is narrowly circumscribed.[37] It does, however, prevent the most

34. In this context, it is notable that there is only one man in the village, the "adopted" son of Haji Salim, Abdul Rahim, who could be considered a "tied" laborer working almost exclusively for one wealthy man. His position is regarded with disdain by other poor villagers, who call him a "slave" (*hamba*), in part because he must accept whatever terms his employer imposes.

35. There is some indication that the threshers were less exacting when they were dealing with a relatively poor farmer who enjoyed a reputation as a good man and more exacting when they were dealing with the rich and stingy.

36. Karl Marx, *Pre-Capitalist Economic Formations,* trans. Jack Cohen, with an Introduction by E. J. Hobsbawm (London: London & Wishart, 1964), 133.

37. Thus, for example, while a share group will not agree to replace its "striking" colleagues, it will accept work the following season from a large farmer who wishes to hire a new group to replace those who gave him trouble the previous season.

damaging excesses of competition between the poor for the few opportunities available.[38]

Such minimal solidarity depends, here as elsewhere, not just on a seemly regard for one's fellows, but on the sanctions that the poor can bring to bear to keep one another in line. Since the temptation to break ranks is always alluring to members of a class that has chronic difficulty making ends meet, these sanctions must be powerful enough to prevent an ever immanent Hobbesian struggle among the poor. The modest level of restraint that has been achieved makes ample use of social sanctions such as gossip, character assassination, and public shunning. There is no surer way for poor men or women to call scorn upon themselves than to work at a lower wage than the prevailing rate or to take a job that "belongs" by custom to others. Nor is it merely a question of reputation, for the offender will find that he or she is shunned in labor exchange (derau), not included in share groups, not told about possibilities of finding work, denied the petty jobs that the poor can occasionally offer, and not invited to join "rotating credit associations" (kut) in their neighborhood. Each of these material sanctions, taken separately, is fairly trivial, but collectively they represent a potential loss of some magnitude. Nor is the threat of violence entirely absent from these sanctions, as we shall see. Thus, the poor man who is tempted to break ranks must measure very carefully his short-term gain against the losses his angry neighbors may be able to impose. By their opinion and by their sanctions, the poor have erected a set of customary prohibitions that symbolize the acceptable limits of self-seeking.

These limits are best illustrated by examining the values that apply to the never-ending search for land by would-be tenants. Since access to land is so vital to the well-being of the poor, they are under constant temptation to pry land away from other poor families by agreeing to a higher rent. And yet, the sanctions against behaving in this way are such that it happens very rarely. I often had occasion to ask poorer villagers why there were not more attempts to bid away land from local tenants by offering more for the privilege. Their replies are illuminating in their uniformity. They make clear that to do so would be an offense against another tenant. Thus, Yaakub said that such attempts are rare

38. What prevails in Sedaka is a variant of what Alier has called "union" in Southern Spain. As he describes it, "Labourers use the word *union* when trying to explain the existence of norms which make obligatory—or at least commendable— ways of behaving which aim at maintaining or increasing wages, or at reducing unemployment. These ways of behaving are, on many occasions opposed to the individual workers interest, and they may even entail some risk or sacrifice." While such norms are occasionally violated, they appear to work best in small villages. Thus a laborer told Alier, "It is very rare to work for less than the prevailing wage, in this village, because it is small and people know each other. They do not do it; they would be badly looked upon." Alier, *Labourers and Landowners in Southern Spain,* 122, 136.

because they would go against local "social opinion" (*pandang masyarakat*). Karim, who is always looking for land to rent, said that he would not try to bid away land, since he would feel "embarrassed before his friend(s)" (*malu sama kawan*). "In our society (*masyarakat kita*), you can't do that," he added. Sukur and Jamil each used the identical phrase in explaining why such behavior was contemptible: "You can't cut (*potong*) your friends." When Hamzah explained why it was not done, he focused on his sense of the decorum that should prevail among the poor: "Our friends wouldn't agree to it; it wouldn't be seemly (*tak elok*) to scramble (*berebut*) like that." Even wealthier villagers recognize the force of these norms and are wary of breaking them. Amin thus noted that a landlord who promoted such a bidding war or a poor man who tried to displace another tenant in this way would "not be respected (*tak hormati*). We are all friends; we are one village; he would feel guilty (*hati-nya tak ada baik*)."

There are intimations by some villagers that the sanctions that restrain such self-seeeking may go well beyond the matters of shame, reputation, and customary rules. Samad made it clear that any tenant who lost his land in this fashion would be "very angry and might do anything." Mat "halus" was a bit less cryptic when speaking of the offended tenant: "You can't do that, he would be angry, he would look for his machete (*cari golok*)."

The comments of Rokiah and Samat are especially noteworthy in this respect, not because they add very much to what has already been reported, but because they provide the one unambiguous case in which the injunction against competition among tenants was broken. Samat explained that it was rare for a poor man to try to outbid the current tenant because, if he did, "he would be accursed (*jahanam*) as far as we were concerned: you and I are finished [we would say]." Rokiah's opinion was just as forceful: "Someone who steals land like that would be despised (*dengki*)." As it happens, Rokiah has had a chance to act on her convictions. Until 1975, both Rokiah and Samat rented adjacent paddy fields from the same outside landlord: 4 relong were rented to Rokiah and a single relong to Samat. On the strength of the fact that his mother-in-law had once owned all this land, Samat went to see the landlord before the 1975 off season began and, by offering M$20 more in rent, persuaded him to transfer an additional relong from Rokiah to him. Since that day, no one in Rokiah's family has spoken to anyone in Samat's family or to his father, Tok Mahmud. It goes without saying that, although she is known to favor PAS, neither she nor anyone in her family has set foot in Samat's small store, which is a recognized PAS gathering place. In fact, some villagers claim, although Rokiah denies it, that she has been responsible for an informal boycott of Samat's store by others, which may explain why it was on the verge of failure during my stay.[39] When Rokiah's daughter was married in 1980, Samat and Tok Mahmud told me that they were

39. The shop finally failed and was closed the year after I left, when Samat could no longer get supplies on credit, because of his outstanding debts.

the only two families in the village who had not been invited. Rokiah claimed that she had, in fact, invited them but that they were too embarrassed to put in an appearance. One sure way of finding out whether a given norm exists is to observe what happens when it is violated. In this case, the episode involving Rokiah and Samat is the exception that proves the rule.[40]

To return to the rule for a moment, it should be made explicit that it does not prevent some forms of competition between tenants. Thus, if a landlord wants to raise the rent paid by his customary tenant to a point where the tenant is unwilling to continue, it is then permissible for others to ask for it under the new terms. It is also permissible—but frowned upon—for a would-be tenant to approach a landlord for land if the tenant he might displace is neither a fellow villager nor a relative. Once again, as with the boycott of the combines, the restrictions of mutuality break down outside the community, and their effect is partly undone by extra-village competition. What is not countenanced within the village, however, is for a poor man to take the initiative and attempt to "steal" a tenancy by proposing a higher rent.[41]

What practical effect does the restraint the poor impose upon one another have? To the extent that the market for tenancies is still a rather localized affair, it is likely, along with kinship tenure, to impede slightly the landlord's efforts to extract the maximum possible rent. A good many agroeconomic studies of the Muda region have, in fact, remarked that rent levels in general, even for non-kinship tenancies, are somewhat lower than a purely economic analysis would predict. The difference, while it is not large, is at least in part attributable to the small degree of local mutuality the poor have managed to create. When it

40. The rule in question is one of a larger category of rules that dominated classes typically develop to limit their exploitation. As Barrington Moore has noted, "A challenge to the moral authority of precedent, to *accustomed ways of behaving that subordinates have created to protect their own interests, vis-à-vis superiors* as well as the integrity of their own social group, will generally produce a reaction of moral outrage. (That is also true when the challenge comes from a member of the subordinate group itself, as in the case of the worker who is a rate-buster and exceeds informally set norms of output)." *Injustice,* 30–31. Samat is, in this case, the agrarian equivalent of a "rate-buster" who has breached one of those petty but vital rules the poor have fashioned to afford themselves some protection.

41. The episode related in the previous chapter in which Tok Mah switched the tenancy for 3 relong from Lebai Hussein and his son Taha to Pak Yah is an ambiguous one. It appears that Pak Yah approached Tok Mah for the land only *after* she had said that Lebai Hussein no longer wanted to rent it at her proposed new rent. Lebai Hussein and Taha made it clear that they did not hold Pak Yah at fault but rather their landlady, who chose to interpret their initial grumbling over the new rent as an outright refusal. The norm is every bit as strong as the norm that tenants should not try to undercut one another, and it is the former, not the latter, that was apparently violated in this instance.

comes to wage rates for transplanting, reaping, and threshing, or the volume of such employment, the impact of this mutuality is probably less pronounced, for the labor market is more regionalized than the market for tenancies. The very localism of the mutuality is thus a more severe handicap in this sphere. Nevertheless, in small but significant ways, the mutuality of the poor represents a form of daily resistance that prevents, or at least delays, the worst consequences of the full "rationalization" of production relations in the countryside.

Self-Help and/or Enforcement

Thus far I have dealt largely with attempts at collective action—with "sanctions" that the poor bring to bear on their landlords and employers, as well as on themselves, to prevent a "dog-eat-dog" competition. There is, however, another realm of resistance that is more shadowy and individual; it includes a large variety of thefts and the murder of livestock. Inquiry into this realm is a necessarily delicate affair, inasmuch as the silence of most of the participants is compounded by an understandable desire on the part of the inquirer to avoid danger. Without ever pursuing this matter actively, a pattern of facts nevertheless emerged from casual listening over two years which suggested that such activities had implications for class relations and resistance.

Rural theft by itself is unremarkable; it is a nearly permanent feature of agrarian life whenever and wherever the state and its agents are insufficient to control it. When such theft takes on the dimensions of a struggle in which property rights are contested, however, it becomes essential to any careful analysis of class relations. Such was certainly the case for parts of England, where poaching was the most common—and the most popular—crime for at least two centuries, and in France, where Zola claimed without undue exaggeration that "Every peasant had a poacher hidden inside him."[42] Here the political and class meaning of poaching was perfectly evident, since the peasantry had never fully accepted the property rights of those who claimed ownership of the forests, streams, "wastes," and commons that had previously been the joint property of the community. Poaching was not simply a necessary subsistence option but an enactment of what was seen to be a natural right.[43]

42. Emile Zola, *The Earth*, trans. Douglas Parmee (Harmondsworth: Penguin, 1980), 317. For additional literary evidence from rural France, see Honoré de Balzac, *Les Paysans* (Paris: Pleiades, 1949). For English material, see Douglas Hay, "Poaching and the Game Laws on Cannock Chase," in *Albion's Fatal Tree: Crime and Society in Eighteenth-Century England,* by Douglas Hay, Peter Linebaugh, John G. Rule, E. P. Thompson, and Cal Winslow (New York: Pantheon, 1975), 189–253.

43. Marx is said to have told Engels that "it was the study of the law on the theft of wood and the situation of the Mosell peasantry that led him to pass from a purely political viewpoint to the study of economy and from that to socialism." Peter Linebaugh, "Karl Marx, The Theft of Wood, and Working Class Composition: A Contribution to the Current Debate," *Crime and Social Justice* 6 (Fall–Winter, 1976): 5–16.

Theft was far more common in Kedah before 1950 than it is today. Older residents of Sedaka can recall a time not so very long ago when the rustling of water buffalo was such a common occurrence that every man slept with a rope tied to his wrist that led through the floor to his water buffalo's nose beneath to alert him in case rustlers approached. They can also remember the names and exploits of the most famous rural bandits, such as Awang Poh, Saleh Tui, and Nayan, who acquired reputations as "social bandits," robbing from the rich and giving to the poor.[44] At that time, settlements were smaller and more scattered, and much uncleared brush and forest remained. This frontier quality of many Kedah districts, the weakness of rural police units, and the poverty and mobility of the peasantry all provided a hospitable environment for banditry and rustling.

Today neither the physical terrain nor the freedom from pursuit provide anything like a favorable setting for bandits with any large ambitions. All the land around Sedaka is flat and cultivated and the police in Kepala Batas and in Yan are far more numerous, mobile, and well armed. Nor is there the class provocation of a mere one or two huge landowners, who have monopolized virtually all of the land, facing a uniformly poor and united peasantry. The sort of theft one finds now in Sedaka reflects all these conditions; it is carried out anonymously under cover of darkness; it appears to be the work of individuals or, at most, pairs; it is what the police records would call "petty larceny."

All kinds of things disappear regularly in Sedaka. Fruit regularly disappears from trees and around the houses of wealthier farmers, and few expect to harvest more than half of their small crop of mangoes, papayas, fallen coconuts, or bananas. Those who have the palms whose leaves are required for making mats, baskets, or the traditional attap roofing regularly complain that fronds frequently disappear. Those who keep small livestock, such as chickens, ducks, or geese, complain that both the eggs and the fowl themselves are regularly pilfered. During the dry season, when drinking water is sporadically delivered in government tank trucks, the villagers must leave their plastic or metal water cans (*tong ayer*) near the main road to take advantage of unpredictable delivery. These containers, typically worth roughly M$5, are often stolen. On a somewhat larger scale there are occasional thefts of bicycles, water buffalo, and even motorcycles (three thefts in the last two years).

These petty, and not so petty, thefts have a pattern that is inscribed in the very social structure of the village. The targets are, with the possible exception of bicycles, the wealthier inhabitants of Sedaka. This is hardly surprising in view of the fact that it is the relatively well-to-do who are most likely to have the large house lot with fruit trees and palms, who have the largest number of water

44. See Cheah Boon Kheng's excellent account of Nayan and Saleh Tui in "Social Banditry and Rural Crime in Kedah, 1910–1929: Historical and Folk Perceptions" (Paper presented to Conference of International Association of Historians of Asia, Kuala Lumpur, 1980).

containers, who have the feed for small livestock, who are most likely to own a water buffalo or a motorcycle. The perpetrators, it is generally agreed, are to be found among Sedaka's poorer inhabitants. This pattern is not in itself proof that such thefts are conceived by the poor as a means of resistance or some form of "social banditry." Evidence on this score was simply unobtainable. What is significant, however, is that the class character of theft is built into the very property relations prevailing in Sedaka. The rich, by and large, possess what is worth taking, while the poor have the greatest incentive to take it. One is reminded of the reply of the American bank robber, "Slick" Willie Sutton, when he was asked why he robbed banks: "Because that's where the money is."

Apart from the disappearance of water buffalo and motorcycles, the other forms of pilfering we have encountered are deplored by well-off villagers, but they are more of a nuisance than a serious threat. Their concern is focused on the main product of this single-crop economy: paddy. For the would-be thief the advantages of stealing paddy are self-evident. It is all about him, it is easily taken in small quantities, and, once taken, it is virtually untraceable.

The amount of paddy stolen over a single season, while not large as a proportion of the total harvest, is alarming to large farmers and, what is more, they believe that it is growing. No firm statistics are, of course, available, but I made an effort to record all the losses of paddy reported to me during the 1979–80 main season. By far the largest category of thefts was whole gunny sacks of threshed paddy left in the fields overnight during the harvest. These are listed in the accompanying table. To this total one must add paddy that was spirited away in other ways. At least four gunny sacks of paddy drying on mats in the sun disappeared, two of which were taken from Abu Hassan. Haji Jaafar and Kamil each lost a gunny sack that was stored beneath their respective houses. Something like the same quantity of paddy was reported stolen from rice barns

Reported Thefts of Threshed Paddy by the Sack in Main Season, 1979–80

Farmer	Reported Losses (no. of gunny sacks)
Shahnon	1
Haji Kadir	1
Samat	1
Abu Hassan	2
Ghani Lebai Mat	1
Amin	2
Tok Long	2
Idris	1
Lebai Pendek	2
Fadzil	1
Total	14

Approximate cash value = M$532.

(*jelapang*) in the course of the season.[45] A small amount of paddy was reported taken on the stalk from the fields. How much is difficult to say, but the quantity is not substantial; villagers point out that the sound of threshing and the disposal of the straw would present a problem for the thief, while the rich claim that thieves are too lazy actually to put themselves to the trouble of threshing.[46] Finally, a thorough accounting of paddy thefts would have to include some estimate of the grain that threshers are said to stuff in their pockets and inside their shirts at the end of the day's work. Such pilfering is winked at by most farmers, and I have made no attempt to calculate how much paddy is appropriated in this way.

Certain facts about the pattern of theft are worth noting. The first is that, with the exception of Samat and Fadzil, who are only modestly well-off, all of the victims are among the wealthiest third of Sedaka's households. This may indicate nothing more than the obvious fact that such households are likely to have more paddy lying in the field at harvest time and that smallholders, who can ill afford the loss, take pains to get threshed paddy to their house quickly. It is certainly true that large farmers with plots far from their houses that cannot be threshed (and hence stored) in a single day are the most prone to such losses. But here again the observation made earlier still applies; the pattern of theft is an artifact of the distribution of wealth—in this case indicated by farm size. No one doubts either that poor men, *local* poor men at that, are responsible for the vast majority of the paddy thefts.

The total amount of paddy stolen, perhaps twenty to twenty-five gunny sacks, is less than one hundredth of the paddy harvested in a season by all village farmers. By this measure, the losses are fairly trivial and are borne largely by those who produce a substantial surplus.[47] If, however, we measure its significance by what it may add to the food supply of a few of the poorest families in the village, then it may be quite significant. It is of some interest that these

45. This is a crude estimate. Such paddy is stolen by prying apart the boards of the granary or by making a hole through which paddy can be collected. Although many farmers mark the level of paddy inside the *jelapang* periodically, it is difficult to know precisely how much has been taken. As a rule, only well-off farmers have such rice barns; the poor keep their paddy in a corner of the house. One such attempted theft was thwarted when Ishak was awakened by noise beneath his house and rushed down to find two abandoned pairs of slippers and two filled gunny sacks.

46. A majority of the six or seven cases of this description that reached my ears were thefts from Chinese landowners or tenants who lived outside the village. The problem of concealment and secret threshing would not be so severe in such thefts.

47. The 1978–79 main-season losses to theft were, from all reports, considerably greater than the thefts for the season examined here. The reason for this, they suspect, is that the previous irrigated season had been canceled by drought and the poor families in the village were more destitute than they had been since the beginning of double-cropping.

twenty to twenty-five gunny sacks of paddy are more than half the quantity of grain given voluntarily by farmers as *zakat peribadi* after the harvest. The comparison is apt precisely because I twice heard poor men refer smilingly to paddy thefts (*curian padi*) as "*zakat peribadi* that one takes on his own" (*zakat peribadi, angkat sindiri*). This evidence is certainly not conclusive, but it is likely that some of the poor, at any rate, consider such acts as not so much theft as the appropriation of what they feel entitled to by earlier custom—a kind of forcible poor tax to replace the gifts and wages they no longer receive. In this connection, two other items of circumstantial evidence are relevant. Only one of the farmers who lost paddy (Samat) was among those ever praised by the poor for their reluctance to hire the combine. All the others have used the machine whenever possible. There is also some indication that paddy thefts may be used as a sanction by disgruntled laborers. Thus, Sukur once told me that farmers were careful to hire the threshers they had customarily invited, since anyone who was omitted might, in his anger, steal paddy from the fields. If, indeed, the theft of paddy has a certain element of popular justice to it, the scope for such resistance has been considerably narrowed by the use of combines, which make it possible to gather and store (or sell) a farmer's entire crop in a single day. Combines thus not only eliminate hand reaping, hand threshing, in-field transport, and gleaning; they also eliminate theft.

The attitude of wealthy farmers toward such thefts is a combination of anger, as one might expect, and fear. Haji Kadir, for example, was furious enough over his loss to consider spending the following night in the fields guarding his paddy with his shotgun.[48] He did not follow through, because he reasoned that the mere rumor that he might lie in wait would be sufficient to deter any thief. The element of fear can be gauged, in part, by the fact that no police report of a paddy theft has ever been made in Sedaka.[49] Wealthy farmers explained to me that, if they made such a report and named a suspect, word would get around quickly, and they feared that they would then become a target for more thefts. Haji Kadir, in fact, once spied someone stealing a gunny sack at night from a neighbor's field. Not only did he fail to intervene to stop the theft, but he would not even inform his neighbor, though he was certain about the identity of the thief. When I asked him why, he replied that the thief had seen him too, would know he was the informer, and would steal his paddy next. In an earlier season, Mat Sarif lost two gunny sacks but told me that he did not *want* to know who

48. He is the only person in the village who owns a firearm. The use of firearms in Malaysia has been rigorously controlled since at least the time of the "Emergency" in the 1950s. When purchasing new ammunition, for example, the owner must produce all the expended cartridges to prove that ammunition has not been given to a third party.

49. Such reports have been made elsewhere, but in each of the three cases I learned about the thefts were of three gunny sacks and more.

did it. Old and quite frail, he added simply, "I'm afraid of being killed (*takut mampus*)." For a handful of the more daring village poor, it would appear that something of a small balance of terror has been struck that permits such limited pilfering to continue.[50]

There is, however, a more subtle means of naming the suspect that amounts to a traditional form of "letting it be known" (*cara sembunyi tau*). This consists of consulting one of the medicine men (*bomoh*) in the district who have acquired a reputation for finding lost property or identifying the thief.[51] After learning the particulars, the *bomoh* will use incantations (*jampi*) and conjure up the face of the thief in water prepared especially for the occasion. Not surprisingly, the visage thus called forth is typically seen to be that of the man whom the client had all along suspected. In the case of stolen paddy, the purpose is not so much to recover the paddy as to identify the thief. The farmer, when he returns to the village, will tell his friends that the *bomoh* saw someone who looked like so-and-so. News will spread and the suspected thief will learn that he is being watched, without a direct accusation, let alone a police report, ever having been made. Thus Haji Kadir said that the *bomoh* had, in his case, seen Taib and another unidentified man in the water. If, indeed, Taib was the culprit, Haji Kadir hoped that this roundabout accusation would prevent any subsequent thefts from that quarter. On at least two occasions, however, villagers recall that some or all of the paddy taken has mysteriously reappeared after a *bomoh* has been consulted. The kind of circumspection employed by those few farmers who actually resort to the *bomoh* is another indication that an open confrontation is considered dangerous.

The larger farmers in the village *think* they know who is to blame for most thefts. Three names are most frequently mentioned, always in guarded way that implies secrecy: Taib, Midon, and Dullah. The last of these three is the only "certified" thief in the village, having spent two months in prison for the theft of paddy from a household in nearby Sungai Bujur. Five or six years ago, it

---

50. Compare this with Georges Lefebvre's description of the sanctions of *mauvais gré* (ill will), by which poorer peasants *enforced* a continuation of a communal view of property. They evidently "began with warnings (grave dug in the front yard, bullet on the doorstep, unlit torch in the thatch, then if necessary resorted to more violent expressions of 'ill will' (animals crippled, crops devastated, barn burned) with the aim of driving off tenants who had consented to rent increases." Those familiar with Irish agrarian history will be struck by the parallels. David Hunt, "Charting the Peasant Route in the French Revolution" (November 1982, mimeo.). Hunt is discussing Lefebvre's *Les Paysans du nord pendant la révolution française* (Paris: F. Rieder, 1972), 93ff.

51. In the classic Malay folktale called *Pak Belalang,* the *bomoh* has turned this trade into a lucrative racket. His sons steal villagers' water buffalo and tether them in the forest, and then Pak Belalang is paid by the anxious owners for his ability to discern where they are located.

appears that he had stolen two gunny sacks of paddy from beneath a farmer's house and was returning for the third when the farmer called on his neighbors for help and grabbed him. In this case the police were called and Dullah was convicted. Neither of the other two have ever been caught red-handed but they know they are under suspicion. Razak himself was once in the same category, but because of his bad health villagers say he is no longer up to the arduous work of hauling full gunny sacks from the fields. All four men are, as we have seen, "charter" members of the "undeserving," "disreputable" poor, so far as the rich farmers are concerned. They pay heavily for their reputation in terms of a kind of social and economic embargo: no one wants to rent them land; they are rarely invited to *kenduri,* they are seldom hired, they are never given loans, and they are typically denied any *zakat peribadi.* It is ironic, of course, that, if the suspicions of the rich are correct, they appear to be helping themselves clandestinely to the *zakat peribadi* they are openly denied.[52]

There is one final dimension to what may be termed clandestine and anonymous resistance in Sedaka. It finds expression in the killing of small and, more rarely, large livestock by the poor. Most of the village's ragtag collection of chickens, ducks, geese, goats, water buffalo, and three beef cattle are owned by well-to-do households. They pose a considerable nuisance to the poor in many ways. Although barriers and chicken wire are often used to bar them, they frequently forage into the nursery beds, paddy fields, and small gardens of the poor, doing considerable damage. The poor are, of course, not the only ones affected (the livestock have, as yet, no class loyalties themselves), but they are the ones most deeply angered. Their anger does not merely stem from the fact that they can least afford the loss; it grows from something that might be called a "moral economy of diet." What is at stake can be captured from Hamzah's complaints about Haji Kadir's chickens next door, which he frequently finds in his kitchen pecking rice through the small holes in the bags of rice stacked there. As Hamzah puts it, "His meat is eating my rice." Once we recall that Hamzah's family and many other poor families eat meat only when they are invited to a *kenduri,* the injustice is palpable. After a warning or two the recourse of the poor man is to kill the animal, as happens with some regularity. The fact that the animal is killed, not stolen, is an indication that this is a protest and not a theft.[53] Two of Haji Kadir's goats broke down the fence around Rokiah's small vegetable garden on the canal bund behind her house and ate everything except the watermelon. Her anger was put in nearly the same terms

52. Recall in this context that the poor will occasionally refer to paddy thefts as *zakat* "which one takes oneself " and that Fadzil, among the better-off villagers, has recognized the possible connection between the decline of charity and theft.

53. Chickens are stolen as well but not in cases like this. When they are stolen they must be sold, for the smell of chicken cooking in a poor man's compound would be a dead giveaway.

as Hamzah's: "Pak Haji's meat is eating my vegetables." One or two goats and quite a few chickens (more rarely ducks and geese) are found slashed or beaten to death annually.[54] Six years ago, Tok Long's water buffalo was found slashed with a *parang* and dying in a poor man's paddy field after having broken its tether. The "murderer" was never identified, but that particular water buffalo had been infamous for breaking loose and grazing in the ripening paddy. Double-cropping has, in this context, made matters appreciably worse by eliminating the long, dry off-season when livestock could roam the stubble without fear of damage. The fairly regular killing of livestock is, like the theft of grain, a petty affair that hardly touches the overall structure of property relations and power. But both of these acts of token resistance are among the few, relatively safe, methods of resistance open to peasants seeking to protect their hold on the means of subsistence.[55]

Prototype Resistance

My concern with the forms of resistance available to the poor has excluded any consideration of a host of conflicts and strategies that have little or no direct bearing on local class relations. Thus, for example, I have not dealt with the many disputes over water rights or with the ways in which land may be appropriated by moving boundary markers or by gradually shifting the bunds in one's field to add another row of paddy at the neighbor's expense. Nor have I examined the resistance of the village as a whole to the Islamic tithe or to other government initiatives affecting all paddy farmers. The resistance of the rich would itself make for a fascinating inquiry that could fill volumes. While I have described some aspects of their resistance as it relates to wages, employment, and tenure, it takes many other forms that contribute to their domination of both local institutions and the local economy.[56] Whatever place resistance in this larger sense might justifiably occupy in a full account of social relations in Sedaka, it is marginal to my main objective.

The diverse forms of resistance by the poor that I have examined bear certain

54. Not having been slaughtered by bleeding (*sembelih*) in the proper way, such animals cannot be eaten by Muslims even if they are discovered immediately after death.

55. For a fascinating analysis of rural crime and disorder on a much larger, but still uncoordinated, scale, see Neil B. Weissman, "Rural Crime in Tsarist Russia: The Question of Hooliganism, 1905–1914," *Slavic Review* 37, no. 2 (1978): 228–40.

56. The way in which the rich farmers are able to turn government policies and programs—loan programs, the state fertilizer subsidy, development subsidies, school admissions, settlement scheme applications, small-business subsidies, licenses for rice mills and taxis, government employment—to their advantage would constitute the core of any such analysis.

distinguishing marks. Whether it is a matter of resistance to combine-harvesting, wage negotiations, the effort to prevent ruinous competition among the poor, theft, or the murder of livestock, the relative absence of any open confrontation between classes is striking. Where resistance is collective, it is carefully circumspect; where it is an individual or small group attack on property, it is anonymous and usually nocturnal.[57] By its calculated prudence and secrecy it preserves, for the most part, the onstage theater of power that dominates public life in Sedaka. Any intention to storm the stage can be disavowed and options are consciously kept open. Deference and conformity, though rarely cringing, continue to be the public posture of the poor. For all that, however, one can clearly make out backstage a continuous testing of limits. At the very least, one can say that there is much more here than simply consent, resignation, and deference.

Resistance in Sedaka has virtually nothing that one expects to find in the typical history of rural conflict. There are no riots, no demonstrations, no arson, no organized social banditry, no open violence. The resistance I have discovered is not linked to any larger outside political movements, ideologies, or revolutionary cadres, although it is clear that similar struggles have been occurring in virtually every village in the region. The sorts of activities found here require little coordination, let alone political organization, though they might benefit from it. They are, in short, forms of struggle that are almost entirely indigenous to the village sphere. Providing that we are careful about the use of the term, these activities might appropriately be called *primitive* resistance, or perhaps *ur* resistance. The use of *primitive* does not imply, as Hobsbawm does, that they are somehow backward and destined to give way to more sophisticated ideologies and tactics.[58] It implies only that such forms of resistance are the nearly permanent, continuous, daily strategies of subordinate rural classes under difficult conditions. At times of crisis or momentous political change, they may be complemented by other forms of struggle that are more opportune. They are unlikely, however, to disappear altogether so long as the rural social structure remains exploitive and inequitable. They are the stubborn bedrock upon which other forms of resistance may grow, and they are likely to persist after such other forms have failed or produced, in turn, a new pattern of inequity.

57. For some interesting parallels, see Thompson, "The Crime of Anonymity," in *Albion's Fatal Tree,* by Hay et al., 255–344.

58. See E. J. Hobsbawm's *Primitive Rebels: Studies in Archaic Forms of Social Movement in the 19th and 20th Centuries* (New York: Norton, 1965). Hobsbawm's otherwise illuminating account is, I believe, burdened unduly with a unilinear theory of lower-class history which anticipates that every primitive form of resistance will in due course be superseded by a more progressive form until a mature Marxist-Leninist vision is reached.

"ROUTINE" REPRESSION

Just as the forms of resistance in Sedaka are "routine," so also are the forms of repression. One searches in vain for the more depressing excesses of coercion found in much of the rest of Southeast Asia: mass arrests, liquidations, martial law, and paramilitary units with license to abduct and kill. The Malay peasantry, unlike the Indonesian peasantry, does not live with the fearful memory of recent massacres that might intimidate them to utter silence.[59] In the place of such large-scale brutality and morbid fear, there is instead the steady pressure of everyday repression backed by occasional arrests, warnings, diligent police work, legal restrictions, and an Internal Security Act that allows for indefinite preventive detention and proscribes much political activity.

It is no simple matter to determine exactly how influential such repression is in constraining the forms of resistance we have thus far observed. If the repression were to lighten or if it were to disappear altogether, it might be possible to judge, retrospectively, what its effect had been. Similarly, if the alternatives to resistance—for example, short-term wage work in the cities—were suddenly to evaporate, it might become possible to gauge whether the existing level of repression was sufficient to contain a more hard-pressed peasantry. In the absence of any such natural experiments, judgment must remain quite speculative. What we can show, however, is that the element of fear is present in the minds of many villagers and that it structures their view of the options open to them.

An atmosphere of intimidation infects especially, but not exclusively, those villagers who are closely identified with the opposition party, PAS. Shortly after the 1978 elections, all PAS members were systematically dismissed from every village committee (JKK) in the state. This step not only set the stage for the denial of government benefits to all PAS members but also indicated that, henceforth, the opposition would have no legitimate role in community politics. In mid-1979 the Religious Affairs Office of Kedah took the further step of forbidding at least eight prominent PAS religious teachers, including Ustaz Fawzi from nearby Yan, from delivering sermons in any mosque or village *madrasah* in the state. The general atmosphere was such that many PAS meetings in the district were held secretly from 1978 to 1980. Opposition members in Sedaka itself experienced this general intimidation as an ever-present possibility of arrest at the whim of Bashir or other UMNO leaders. Thus a strong PAS member, Nizam bin Haji Lah, explains that he never goes to Bashir's store to buy anything because he is afraid that Bashir will claim he stole something and have him arrested. He and other PAS members who haul paddy by motorcycle are always concerned that Bashir will arrange to have the police stop them on the road and fine them for their unpaid road tax and insurance. Shahnon claims that he is

59. See, for example, Ann Stoler, "The Limits of Class Consciousness in North Sumatra" (Mimeo. 1979).

"silent" (*sengap*) politically because the JKK could have any member of PAS arrested if they wished and that the police would take the word of the JKK over that of any PAS farmer. When someone painted over the Village Improvement Scheme sign board in the *madrasah,* the police were called the next morning and questioned several PAS members. No arrests were made, but the visit had precisely the chilling effect the JKK desired. Tok Mahmud, as noted earlier, is afraid to tell me what he knows about machine breaking for fear of the police. To the particular fear of the JKK and the police in Sedaka must be added the general suspicion that even the most seemingly innocuous activities of the state arouse among the peasantry. This was evident when a petty official of the Information Department came to the village in February 1980 to prepare the way for the coming decennial census. Most of his talk was devoted to scolding villagers for their false replies in the past and to reassuring them, in vain, that the census had nothing to do with taxes and that they should not be afraid or run away. Thus, quite apart from specific fears, the classic peasant mistrust of the state operates to reinforce an atmosphere of apprehension.

An object lesson in the limits of permissible protest was provided by the government's reaction to a large demonstration held in the state capital of Alor Setar on January 23, 1980. The origins and details of the protest need not detain us long, for the purpose of this brief account is to focus on the fear created in its aftermath. The ostensible issue sparking the demonstration was a demand for an increase in the farm-gate price of paddy and opposition to a recently introduced *cupon* scheme whereby M$2 of the price per *pikul* of paddy would be retained and saved for the seller. Although the forced savings would yield a profit (not "interest," which is forbidden) and could be redeemed after six months, the scheme was almost universally unpopular. It appeared to many that the producer price had thereby been lowered by M$2, and it was unclear whether the majority of growers who sold their paddy to Chinese middlemen would recover the "savings" at all.[60] The fact that the chief minister of Kedah had campaigned on a promise of raising the paddy price and that the UMNO-dominated Farmers' Associations had themselves opposed the *cupon* system added a certain legitimacy to the discontent. At any rate, a crowd of roughly ten thousand gathered in front of the state office building on January 23 to protest the *cupon* system and to demand a M$10 increase in the paddy price.[61] When the chief minister finally

60. As of that date, only 11 percent of the paddy produced in Kedah was sold directly to the state grain agency (LPN). Most of the rest was sold to private dealers and much of that was sold not for cash but to pay off accumulated debts at the shop of the paddy dealer.

61. This summary description is based on accounts of villagers in Sedaka, four of whom attended the demonstration (*pertunjukan perasaan*), officials of MADA near Alor Setar, and newspaper accounts in *Utusan Malaysia, Berita Harian, The Star,* and the *Straits Times* for the period.

appeared, he was shouted down, and the police and riot control troops (the Federal Reserve Unit—FRU—and Police Field Force) moved in to disperse and arrest demonstrators, some of whom fled in vain to the state mosque across the street. It was, by all accounts, the largest demonstration by paddy cultivators held in Kedah since at least 1954, when thousands of farmers demonstrated for government relief after a disastrous season.

Over ninety people were arrested on the spot and held. The chief minister immediately claimed that the demonstration was "provoked by certain groups of a militant persuasion"[62] and noted ominously that the Bolshevik, French, and Iranian revolutions had all "used" the peasantry.[63] In the weeks following the demonstration more arrests and charges were made. Seven PAS officials in Kedah, including a state assemblyman, were arrested and detained. Three hundred special police officers were brought into Kedah to help with the investigation. The chief minister charged that "the PAS strategy of creating terror and fear is similar to that adopted by the communists and that the entire leadership of Kedah PAS must take responsibility for . . . organizing the demonstration."[64] A shadowy underground organization sharing the same initials as PAS (Pertu-buhan Angkatan Sabilullah) and implying a "holy war" was identified as the center of the conspiracy.

The effects of the police roundups were felt immediately in Sedaka. As men in nearby villages were taken in to be questioned, the word spread rapidly. Three men in neighboring Kepala Batas and one from Sungai Bujur were picked up, questioned, and released on bail. Well-known PAS members from Mengkuang, Guar Cempedak, Kampung Jawa, and villages in the Pendang and Bukit Raya areas suffered a similar fate. Most of them had not even attended the demon-stration. As news of continued arrests poured in, an understandable fear began to grip local PAS members, three of whom had actually gone to the demon-stration.[65] Taib, a PAS member, interpreted the government response as an attempt "to smash us to pieces" (*pukul jahanam kita*) and said that he wanted to get a sickle to defend himself.[66] Another PAS member, Sukur, spoke of "spies" (*mata-mata gelap*) in the village who might call the police and make false ac-cusations. "It's as if you didn't steal but they say you did; they can do anything, it is tyranny (*aniaya*)." As it happened, no one in Sedaka was detained or arrested. But police from the Special Branch came twice to speak with Bashir

62. "Curfew Sekitar Alor Setar," *Berita Harian,* Jan. 24, 1980, p. 1.

63. "Tunjuk perasaan issue padi bukan politik," *Utusan Malaysia,* Feb. 7, 1980, bahagian kedua, p. 4.

64. "MB: PAS out to create fear, terror," *Straits Times,* Mar. 20, 1981, p. 1.

65. Mustapha, Bakri bin Haji Wahab, and Mehat (son of Haji Kadir) had gone, as well as Ghazali, an UMNO member.

66. The choice of the sickle (*sabit*) is deliberate since it also means "the crescent moon," a symbol of PAS.

and with the headman, Haji Jaafar. The visits had their intended effect, as I suspect they did in countless other villages on the rice plain. Many PAS members knew that a word from Bashir or the JKK could spell arrest and feared they would be victimized. As Mustapha noted, "Of course we're afraid; they want to crush (*menindas*) PAS."

The kinds of resistance and the kinds of compliance we find in Sedaka cannot be understood without reference to this larger context of real and anticipated coercion. Routine repression does its work unobtrusively: an arrest here, a visit from the Special Branch there, an indirect warning from the head of the JKK are all that is normally needed to create boundary markers that no wary peasant would deliberately breach. The very existence of fairly stable boundaries of permissible dissent, however, makes this more a situation of fear than of terror, where there is no margin of safety. What is at least clear is that these boundaries—created, shifted, and occasionally reinforced by historical experience—serve to inhibit certain forms of open protest and defiance. Those who have benefited least from double-cropping have every reason to believe in "the law of anticipated reactions" and to avoid placing themselves in jeopardy. When they say, as they have, that "whether you complain or not it will come to nothing," they are referring not only to the local economic power of the large farmers but, beyond that, to the coercive power of the state and its local agents. The resignation this implies is "not an indigenous product of culture, but of the power situation in which the non-elite find themselves."[67]

It is against this background of larger constraints on resistance that the relative effectiveness of the "dull compulsion of economic relations" must be understood. Wealthy farmers can still provide or withhold, at will, wage work in the paddy fields, *zakat peribadi,* government assistance (for example, employment, loans, subsidies), recommendations for settlement schemes, aid to school children, loans, short-term credit (for example, at Bashir's shop), and can stand guarantor for credit in a crisis.[68] It is little wonder that quite a few poor households should not wish openly to offend those who control these strategic assets. But this potentially co-opting "benevolence" is inextricably linked with malevolence. The

67. John Gaventa, *Power and Powerlessness,* 145. Gaventa provides an interesting analysis of how the miasma of repression and control can become "self-sustaining," but in my view he never adequately addresses the issue of "false-consciousness." For a specifically Malaysian view that the quiescence among Malay peasants is rooted in culture and not in "circumstances," see Chandra Muzaffar, *Protector? An Analysis of the Concept and Practice of Loyalty in Leader-Led Relationships within Malay Society* (Pulau Pinang: Aliran, 1979).

68. When Hamzah's mother died, for example, he had no credit with which to purchase the necessary materials for the funeral. Basir agreed to vouch (*sanggup*) for him at the shops where the shroud material, the canvas for the bottom of the casket, and food for mourners were purchased. Much, but not all, of the debt was covered by subsequent contributions.

tenant who pays reasonable rents could have them raised or have his tenancy revoked; the poor family whose daughter is on the school aid list could be stricken from it; the man employed for casual labor could be replaced by someone else; the "troublesome" poor man who is tolerated could be charged with theft. The occasional benevolence of the wealthy farmers thus is not so very different from a protection racket. And, to the extent that it works, it works precisely because the larger coercive context of rural class relations all but excludes the kinds of direct resistance that might materially change the situation of the poor. That is, the coercive context creates and maintains the setting of relative powerlessness within which "the dull compulsion of economic relations" can then extract its daily toll. [69]

ROUTINE COMPLIANCE AND RESISTANCE THAT COVERS ITS TRACKS

The economic and political power of the wealthy farmers in Sedaka requires a certain minimum of public compliance on the part of any prudent poor man or woman. For those who now leave regularly for work elsewhere and depend little on help or wages within the village, that compliance can be minimal. But for those whose livelihood is more decisively tied to the village economy, the pressure for compliance is more pervasive. There is every reason for such men and women to conform to the stereotype of the "respectable poor" for the advantages that such a reputation can bring. The place, then, to look for the symbolic "taxes" that this agrarian system can extract is particularly among those who most closely approximate the stereotype. Even here we will find routines of deference and compliance which, while perhaps not entirely cynical, are certainly calculating.

We have had an opportunity to hear Pak Yah's views of the UMNO leadership ("They want to bury us") and of the attitude of the village rich ("As they see it, those who are hard up are despicable") when he is among friends. Pak Yah, however, is not always in such secure company. Much of the wage labor he manages to find comes from Bashir, the leader of those who "want to bury us." In his relations with Bashir, he is the very model of the deferential worker: reliable, never questioning the wages, never refusing any work. Even at the

69. Perry Anderson, in a discussion of the relationship between consent and coercion, has resorted to an analogy that is appropriate here. Paper currency, he writes, is backed by gold and circulates because of that backing, but in normal times the gold is invisible. Only in a crisis does paper currency collapse and give way to a rush to gold. Consent, like paper money, prevails ordinarily, but it prevails because it is "constituted by a silent, absent force which gives . . . [it] currency: the monopoly of legitimate violence by the State. . . . Deprived of this, the system of cultural control would be instantly fragile, since limits of possible action against it would disappear." "The Antinomies of Antonio Gramsci," *New Left Review* 100 (1976): 43.

height of his anger over being excluded from the RPK subsidy, he did not dare boycott Bashir's daughter's wedding, although his appearance was a brief one. A due regard for his livelihood requires a public comportment that is not in keeping with his private views.

The public behavior of Hamzah, another "reputable" poor man, is, if anything, a more delicate affair. He works fairly regularly for Haji Kadir *and* for Bashir, although they are political enemies. Perhaps because, as a next-door neighbor, I got to know him quite well, he was disarmingly frank about why he, unlike most PAS members, received RPK assistance through Bashir and the JKK. He said he was favored because he was poor, because he worked for Bashir and never complained, because he looked after the *madrasah,* and because he did not "pay any attention" (*tak peduli*) to political parties. He added that he bought goods from both stores in the village and went to everyone's *kenduri* when invited. Hamzah then actually went on to tick off the benefits that his tact and circumspection had secured for him. Before the last Ramadan when he was sick and could not work, he got twenty *gantangs* of rice, while Razak, his brother, got only five or six; he was given more *zakat peribadi* than most others; he had a line of credit up to M$60 at Bashir's store; he got scarce jobs when others could not find work; and when he was sick at home recently many villagers stopped by and offered to help. Listening to him one had the impression of hearing an accountant self-consciously adding up the profits of his investment in deference and pleased with the results for the fiscal year. He is aware that Bashir and the others know he leans toward PAS, but he adds that he is not an active PAS member because "If I were a strong PAS member, UMNO people would not want to hire me." Thus Hamzah's comportment is a delicately balanced tightrope walk designed to bring him and his family safely through the inevitable economic crises. This does not mean that he does not experience anger and indignation, only that he is careful to control it for his own good. Here it is worth recalling again what he had to say when I asked him if he had complained when Haji Kadir underpaid him for filling gunny sacks with paddy from the machine: "Poor people can't [complain]; when I'm sick or need work, I may have to ask him again." "I am angry in my heart." There is no false-consciousness here but just the necessary daily pose of a poor man. Hamzah has no difficulty recognizing when he has been exploited or shabbily treated; his effort and his achievement, in one sense, have been to swallow his anger lest it endanger his livelihood.[70]

---

70. Robert Coles makes much the same point about American blacks when he writes, "Until now nonviolent action has come naturally to Negroes because the only alternative has been to turn their suffering on themselves, converting it to sullen despair. Negroes are not now *becoming* angry. At some levels of the mind, that are out of both the white man's sight and often enough his own, the Negro has always *been* angry." *Children of Crisis: A Study of Courage and Fear* (Boston: Little Brown, 1967), 322, emphasis in original.

One could claim for Hamzah's deference what has been claimed for the deference of the English rural poor in the eighteenth century:

> And the deference was often without the least illusion; it could be seen from below as being one part necessary self-preservation, one part calculated extraction of whatever could be extracted. Seen in this way, the poor imposed upon the rich some of the duties and functions of paternalism just as much as deference was in turn imposed upon them.[71]

The needs of the poor may also drive them actively to cultivate a rich farmer. Thus when Hamzah fell ill and could no longer work for Haji Kadir, Taib began to appear regularly at Haji Kadir's house in the evening to chat. When I casually asked Shahnon why Taib, who had never come before, was always dropping in, he explained that Taib was coming to "chat up"[72] and to flatter (jek) Haji Kadir in the hope of being given work. The strategy was successful, although it must have required a certain amount of willpower on Taib's part, given the comments I had heard him make about Haji Kadir in other contexts.[73]

The element of self-protecting compliance is most apparent in the choice of party made by a good many poor villagers. Mansur, another "good" poor man, is a member of UMNO, as is the man for whom he often works, Shamsul. When Mansur explains why, as a comparative newcomer to the village, he joined UMNO, he does not conceal the straightforward calculation of possible benefits:

> I keep in mind that I am a poor man. I figure this way: If I enter UMNO I can latch on to work from a rich man. I can take wage work from him. If I enter on the side of the poor, they can't call me for work. I have to look after my own household. Because of that I'm friendly with everyone.[74]

One could scarcely imagine a less sentimental account of the logic behind a choice of parties; it is also a formula for switching parties, if the logic of advantage were reversed.

Two recent political "conversions" will help to illustrate the calculations that

71. Thompson, "Eighteenth-Century English Society," 163. For contemporary evidence, see Howard Newby, "Agricultural Workers in the Class Structure," *Sociological Review* 20, no. 3 (1971): 413–39. Much the same argument is made in great detail for American slavery in Eugene D. Genovese, *Roll, Jordan, Roll: The World the Slaves Made* (New York: Pantheon, 1974), especially Book One.

72. The verb *sembang* can be a transitive verb meaning "to chat up someone."

73. The success was totally unexpected on my part, since Haji Kadir had clearly implied that Taib had been responsible for thefts of his rice. It crossed my mind that Taib was applying his own version of a protection racket here, but there is no way to verify that possibility.

74. *Saya ingat, saya orang susah. Saya kira lagu ini: Kalau musuk Kati {UMNO}, boleh menumpang kerja orang kaya, boleh ambil upah sama dia. Kalau masuk sebelah susah, depa tak boleh panggil kerja. Saya punya rumah, kena jaga. Pasal itu saya berkawan semua.*

often lie behind UMNO membership. Dzulkifli bin Haji Wahab comes from a strong PAS family in another village but decided, in 1979, to convert to UMNO. When I asked why he shifted, he replied that "It was a little better in UMNO; there is development," by which he means government subsidies. "PAS," he adds, "can't do anything." In his case, he was rewarded by a small grant (M$200) from the RPK program, while his brother Bakri next door, who remains in PAS, got nothing. Karim is another recent "turncoat." He explains to me that if he stayed in PAS "it would be hard to ask for assistance (*bantuan*)" and "difficult to go see the primary school principal" [about a special subsidy from school funds for his children]. He left PAS, he said, because "there were no services (*jasa*)" while UMNO provides "many services." And yet, Karim may be playing a double game, since Sukur and Haji Kadir claim that Karim still votes for PAS, although he has paid his UMNO dues. "He's clever," Haji Kadir concludes, "he really follows us." Whether or not this is the case is unclear, and Karim is not about to clear up the confusion. What is certain, however, is that it is quite plausible to anyone in Sedaka that a poor man, especially, might wish to dis- simulate about his party affiliation in order to claim the benefits that nominal membership in the government party can provide. Rokiah and Hamzah have already done so to their advantage.

Much the same logic of power and benefits prevail when ordinary UMNO members say they merely want to be on "the majority side" or that they "want benefits" by joining UMNO. Quite a few imply that the safest course is to be with the government party—a reasoning that combines the promise of benefits with a certain element of fear. Thus Abdul Rahman explained his UMNO membership by saying "I notice [who has] the power (*kuasa*) every day I live under the hand of the Raja." Not more than six or seven villagers, most of them members of the JKK, even bother to refer to *any* public-spirited reasons for siding with UMNO.

The pressures for deference, compliance, and political conformity in Sedaka are palpable and self-evident to all concerned. In view of the rewards of com- pliance, it is little wonder that quite a few villagers have chosen to live up to the stereotype of the "reputable poor." What is perhaps more surprising is that so many others have held themselves rather aloof and distant, remaining in PAS, rarely currying favor with the JKK or rich farmers and, in some cases, becoming examples of the "disreputable" poor. Even for those who comply, however, the compliance is routine in the sense that it is calculating and without illusions.

In this respect, there is a striking analogy between routine compliance and routine resistance. If routine compliance is conducted with a calculating eye to the structure of power and rewards in the village, so is routine resistance. If routine compliance avoids unnecessary risks, so does routine resistance. Nearly all the resistance we have encountered in Sedaka is the kind of resistance that rather effectively "covers its own tracks." A snub on the village path can be excused later by haste or inattention. What appears to be a boycott of transplanting can be rationalized as a delay or difficulties in assembling the work force. And, of course, acts of theft, sabotage, and vandalism have no authors at all. Thus, while there is a fair amount of resistance in Sedaka, there are virtually no publicly announced resisters or troublemakers.

Even the more purely symbolic resistance—malicious gossip, character assassination, nicknames, rumors—we have examined follows the same pattern.[75] Gossip, after all, is almost by definition a story told about an absent third party; once launched, it becomes an anonymous tale with no author but many retailers. Although it is by no means a respecter of persons, malicious gossip *is* a respecter of the larger normative order within which it operates. Behind every piece of gossip that is not merely news is an implicit statement of a rule or norm that has been broken. It is in fact only the violation of expected behavior that makes an event worth gossiping about. The rule or norm in question is often only formulated or brought to consciousness by the violation itself. Deviance, in this sense, defines what is normal. Thus, no one may pay attention to the prevailing code of dress until it is breached and thereby provokes a statement of what is proper.[76] Rules of grammar, only implicitly known, pass unnoticed until a speaker or writer makes an obvious misstep. Much of the gossip and character assassination that are relevant to class relations in Sedaka are an appeal by the poor to norms of tenancy, generosity, charity, employment, and feasts that were taken for granted before double-cropping. At the same time that a reputation is slandered by gossip, a rule that was once generally accepted is being affirmed and promoted. Gossip is never "disinterested"; it is a partisan effort (by class, faction, family) to advance its claims and interests against those of others. But this manipulation of the rules can only be successful to the extent that an appeal is made to standards of conduct that are generally accepted. Gossip thus accomplishes its malicious work as an admittedly weak social sanction by remaining more or less *within* the established normative framework. In this respect the use of gossip by the poor also manifests a kind of prudence and respect, however manipulative, of its own.

As a form of resistance, then, gossip is a kind of democratic "voice" in conditions where power and possible repression make open acts of disrespect dangerous. The rich, of course, are far freer to show openly their contempt for the "undeserving poor." For the poor, however, gossip achieves the expression of opinion, of contempt, of disapproval while minimizing the risks of identification and reprisal. Malicious gossip symbolically chips away at the reputations of the rich in Sedaka in the same fashion that anonymous thefts in the night materially chip away at the property of the rich. The overall impact on the structure of power of this nibbling away is not very appreciable. But it is one of the few

75. I am indebted here to the discussion of gossip in John Beard Haviland, *Gossip, Reputation, and Knowledge in Zinacantan* (Chicago: Univ. of Chicago Press, 1977).

76. Ibid., 160.

means available to a subordinate class to clothe the practice of resistance with the safe disguise of outward compliance.

There is no doubt that the caution and anonymity of resistance in Sedaka yields control of the "public stage" to the village elite. By steering clear of any direct and open attack—symbolic or material—the elite-controlled pattern of *public* interaction continues to prevail. One may appreciate the importance of the domination of onstage behavior merely by imagining the tumult that would certainly have ensued if those who attempted an unannounced boycott had openly and publicly committed themselves to that course of action or if those who privately denounced the abuses of the Village Improvement Scheme had openly denounced the JKK at a village meeting. That the poor chose not to burn their bridges is altogether understandable, but their prudence preserves a surface decorum that serves the symbolic interests of the wealthy. Appearances *are* important[77] and, as Bourdieu has aptly noted, "The concessions of *politeness* always contain *political* concessions."[78]

The symbolic "dues" that the poor thus pay to the officially constituted village order is, however, not simply a reaction of fear and self-preservation. When, for example, poor men approach richer villagers with an eye to securing land to rent, work, a loan, or charity, they typically proceed very indirectly, so that the question is actually posed only after a favorable reply is virtually assured. If the response is likely to be negative, the line of inquiry is quietly dropped. In this way, the possibility of a decisive and humiliating rebuff is avoided. What is *also* avoided, however, is the opening that a direct question would provide for the wealthy party to repudiate the legitimacy of the request itself. Since the poor, as we have seen, find themselves defending the justice of older principles of assistance (*tolong*), it is in their interest to avoid creating situations in which these principles could be publicly and finally renounced.[79]

77. The decisive rupture of appearances can, in many contexts, amount to a declaration of war. Three brief examples from other settings are instructive. One of the most effective and inflammatory techniques used by opponents of Indira Ghandhi in the last general elections before her death was for thousands of her opponents in an audience silently to turn their backs to her when she began to address the crowd. In Java, during the 1965 massacres of alleged communists, it is reported that peasant women occasionally lined the roads as trucks carrying soldiers and their squads of civilian supporters passed and, in a gesture of total contempt, lifted their *sarongs* to display their backsides. Not a few of them paid for their gesture with their lives. In Lodz, Poland, following the declaration of martial law and the outlawing of Solidarity, thousands of angry citizens showed their contempt for the government television news broadcast by placing their television in the window, with the screen facing outside, at precisely 7:30 P.M. when the official news began.

78. Pierre Bourdieu, *Outline of a Theory of Practice*, trans. Richard Nice (Cambridge: Cambridge Univ. Press, 1977).

79. See, for example, Erving Goffman, *Interaction Ritual: Essays on Face-to-Face Behavior* (Garden City: Anchor Books, Doubleday, 1967), 30, 106–07.

On a wider view, of course, all those forms of resistance such as gossip and character assassination which involve an appeal to shared normative standards are steadily losing their sanctioning power. The shift in the relations of paddy production that has eroded the value of poor households as suppliers of tenants and laborers has, at the same time, made their opinions count for less. More and more of the rich can now safely ignore what poor villagers think of them, as they are increasingly beyond the reach of social sanctions no longer reinforced by economic power. In this respect, the "politics of reputation" has lost much of its force as a weapon of the poor. It is almost as if part of the social arsenal of the poor consisted of outmoded weapons which, however useful they may have been before double-cropping, are now less suitable to the unfavorable new terrain on which they are fighting.

CONFORMITY AND THE PARTIAL TRANSCRIPT

The poor of Sedaka nearly always adopt a protective disguise in their relations with more powerful villagers or outsiders. This disguise is apparent both in their conformity *and* in their resistance. Thus, Hamzah conceals his anger when he is underpaid by Haji Kadir but, in the privacy of his home, vents his anger at being unfairly treated. Thus, Pak Yah goes dutifully to Bashir's feast though he is seething with anger at having been excluded from the Village Improvement subsidy. An attempted boycott of machine users is presented as a delay in transplanting, which can be abandoned and disavowed. What amounts to a strike over threshing wages is conducted as if the workers had either been taken ill or had suddenly remembered prior commitments. The "full transcript" of class relations in Sedaka is simply not ascertainable from the public interaction between rich and poor, powerful and weak. To move beyond the domain in which poses and dissimulation prevail, it has in fact been necessary to talk to the poor alone or in small groups where they are among friends. Only then does one encounter that part of the full transcript that would, if openly declared in other contexts, jeopardize their livelihood.

That the poor should dissemble in the face of power is hardly an occasion for surprise. Dissimulation is the characteristic and necessary pose of subordinate classes everywhere most of the time—a fact that makes those rare and threatening moments when the pose is abandoned all the more remarkable. No close account of the life of subordinate classes can fail to distinguish between what is said "backstage" and what may be safely declared openly. One of the more remarkable oral histories ever collected, that of the French tenant farmer 'Old Tiennon,' who lived from 1823 until the beginning of the twentieth century, is literally filled with accounts of swallowed bile.[80] Throughout his daily encounters with land-

80. Emile Guillaumin, *The Life of a Simple Man,* ed. Eugene Weber, rev. trans. Margaret Crosland (Hanover, New Hampshire: University Press of New England, 1983).

lords, overseers, officials, and powerful gentry, he was careful to adopt a public mask of deference and compliance and keep his dangerous opinions to himself:

> When he [the landlord who had dismissed his father] crossed from Le Craux, going to Meillers, he would stop and speak to me and I forced myself to appear amiable, in spite of the contempt I felt for him.[81]

Old Tiennon knew at first hand the perils of candor from his own father's rashness:

> My father, who usually undertook the grooming and such duties, never failed to tell the master how annoying it was to have to stay at home when there was so much to be done elsewhere. *He was absolutely ignorant of the art of dissimulation, so necessary in life.*[82]

It is probably just this necessary "art of dissimulation" that has been largely responsible for much of the conservative historiography of the peasantry. As the sources are almost invariably created by classes above the peasantry, they are likely, quite apart from ideological intent, to see only that cautious and deferential aspect the peasantry adopts in the presence of power. What they may describe on this basis is not false, but it is at best a partial and misleading truth that takes a necessary pose for the whole reality. When that happens, we get a picture of rural society that is distorted in the way that E. P. Thompson described for eighteenth-century England:

> On the surface all is consensus, deference, accommodation; the dependents petition abjectly for favor; every hind is touching his forelock; not a word against the illustrious House of Hanover or the Glorious Constitution breaks the agreeable waters of illusion. Then, from an anonymous or obscure level, there leaps to view for a moment violent Jacobite or levelling abuse. We should take neither the obeisances nor the imprecations as indications of final truth; both could flow from the same mind, as circumstance and calculation of advantage allowed.[83]

Even so close an observer as Zola was led in this fashion to a view of the peasantry as a class that oscillated between abject, unquestioning deference and violent outrage. What is missing is the *massive* middle ground, in which conformity is often a self-conscious strategy and resistance is a carefully hedged affair that avoids all-or-nothing confrontations. Had Zola taken a closer look at deference, he might have noticed what has become almost the leitmotif of modern studies of slavery: the gap between the beliefs and values that might find expression in the safety of the slave quarters and the typically prudent conduct of these same

81. Ibid., 83. See also 38, 62, 64, 102, 140, 153 for other instances.
82. Ibid., 48, emphasis added.
83. Thompson, "The Crime of Anonymity," 307.

men and women in the face of power.[84] It is just such vital considerations that have led one perceptive sociologist to reject all those conceptions of deference that treat it as if it were an attribute or attitude of persons and to insist that it be seen as "the *form of social interaction* which occurs in situations involving the exercise of traditional authority."[85]

The fact is that power-laden situations are nearly always inauthentic; the exercise of power nearly always drives a portion of the full transcript underground. Allowing always for the exceptional moments of uncontrolled anger or desperation, the *normal* tendency will be for the dependent individual to reveal only that part of his or her full transcript in encounters with the powerful that it is both safe and appropriate to reveal. What is safe and appropriate is of course defined rather unilaterally by the powerful. The greater the disparity in power between the two parties, the greater the proportion of the full transcript that is likely to be concealed.[86]

Thus it might be possible to think of a continuum of situations ranging from the free dialogue between equals that is close to what Habermas has called the "ideal speech situation"[87] all the way to the concentration camp in which most of the victims' transcript is driven underground, leaving only a virtual parody of stereotyped, stilted deference born of mortal fear. In fact, in the most extreme situations of Caligulan terror, where there are no rules of what is permissible,

84. See, for example, Lawrence W. Levine, *Black Culture and Black Consciousness* (New York: Oxford Univ. Press, 1977); Genovese, *Roll, Jordan, Roll*; and Gerald W. Mullin, *Flight and Rebellion: Slave Resistance in Eighteenth-Century Virginia* (New York: Oxford Univ. Press, 1972).

85. Howard Newby, "The Deferential Dialectic," *Comparative Studies in Society and History* 17, no. 2 (April 1975): 146.

86. Some qualifications should be noted here. In situations where power is balanced but each party can do considerable damage to the other, much of the full transcript will also be concealed. Superpowers, each of which can destroy the other, play their cards very close to the vest. Thus, unhindered communication may be most likely between two actors who are not only equal in power but who cannot appreciably affect each other with their power. The rule is also less applicable to situations where the exercise of power is firmly institutionalized and law regarding. In such cases the weaker party may not be so constrained to conceal those parts of his transcript that fall clearly outside the defined domain of power. Finally, one may also wish to exclude from this rule situations of normally benevolent power such as a parent-child relationship. The secure knowledge that the parent will act in the child's interest may permit the child to reveal his or her full transcript without fear of victimization. In the case of unrequited love, however, the weaker party is led to conceal those parts of his or her transcript that are unlikely to win the love of the prized person.

87. See Jurgen Habermas, *Knowledge and Human Interests*, trans. Jeremy J. Shapiro (Boston: Beacon, 1971), and "Towards a Theory of Communicative Competence," *Inquiry* 13 (1970): 360–75.

the *entire* transcript may be concealed, leaving only paralysis. Ranged in between these extremes are a host of more common conditions in which subordinate classes typically find themselves: the boss and the worker, the landlord and the tenant, the lord and the serf, the master and the slave. In each case, the weaker party is unlikely to speak his or her mind; a part of the full transcript will be withheld in favor of a "performance" that is in keeping with the expectations of the powerholder.[88]

If we wish to recover more than just the performance, we must move backstage where the mask can be lifted, at least in part. In the case of slaves this means moving from the "big house" to the slave quarters; in the case of the working class it may mean moving from the choreographed encounters between rich and poor to the relative privacy of the house or the company of a few close companions. It is in these "non-mask" situations where some of what is habitually censored finally leaps to view. Much of this material, as we have seen, is in direct and stark contradiction to what takes place in the arena of power relations: Haji Kadir becomes Pak Ceti. The relationship between this non-mask, or backstage, transcript and the center stage transcript bears very directly on the issue of false-consciousness. Much of the ethnographic material supporting the notion of "mystification" and "ideological hegemony" is, I suspect, simply the result of assuming that the transcript from power-laden situations is the full transcript. Short of total institutions such as the concentration camp, however, most subordinate classes can repair occasionally to a social setting that is not so confining. To the extent that the transcript found here is markedly different from or else negates what is found in the context of power relations, the case for false-consciousness is weakened.[89]

88. How much of the full transcript is withheld cannot be simply deduced from the labeling of the power relationship. Different forms of slavery or serfdom, for example, are likely to vary considerably in this respect. Within a given form of subordination, moreover, a particular individual, say a blacksmith-slave with scarce and valuable skills, may enjoy a greater relative autonomy. In addition, most forms of subordination may permit a good deal of unconstrained communication in areas that are defined as neutral to the power relationship. Finally, in a more speculative vein, it would seem that, where the power situation drives most of the transcript of subordinates underground, the culture may often provide authorized ritual occasions when it is possible to break the rules. The Roman Saturnalia, the court jester, the Christian tradition of Carnival, the Hindu Feast of Holi are all rituals that allow subordinates, momentarily, to turn the tables. See, along these lines, James C. Scott, "Protest and Profanation: Agrarian Revolt and the Little Tradition," *Theory and Society* 4, no. 1 (1977): 1–38, and 4, no. 2 (1977): 211–46.

89. To the extent that the backstage transcript confirms and reinforces the onstage behavior, of course, the case for ideological hegemony is strengthened. The real interest, however, lies in the detailed analysis of the relationship between the two transcripts, which are likely to be neither perfectly identical nor perfectly contradic-

The public transcript of the powerful is likely to be rather more in accord with their total transcript than is the case with the weak. After all, they are freer, by virtue of their power, to speak their mind with relative impunity. Razak can be safely and publicly insulted in a way that Haji Kadir or Bashir cannot be. And yet the powerful are also somewhat constrained both by a due regard for their reputation—a commodity of declining but real value—and by the desire to uphold the "theater" of power. Thus they will excoriate many of the village poor in the privacy of their own homes but rarely to their face. This is also not surprising; the transcript of the factory manager speaking with his workers is different from the transcript when he is in the safety of his own club; the transcript of the slave owner dealing with his slaves is different from his unguarded remarks to other slaveholders over dinner. It is only when we compare the "unedited" transcript of elites with the unedited transcript of subordinate classes that we uncover the extent of mutual dissimulation that prevails in the context of power relations. In the usual day-to-day conduct of class relations, these unedited transcripts are never in direct contact. Only at rare moments of historical crisis are these transcripts and the actions they imply brought into a direct confrontation. When they are, it is often assumed that there has come into being a new consciousness, a new anger, a new ideology that has transformed class relations. It is far more likely, however, that this new "consciousness" was already there in the unedited transcript and it is the situation that has changed in a way that allows or requires one or both parties to act on that basis.

Both the rich and poor in Sedaka are, of course, aware that what takes place in the domain of power relations is not the whole story. They suspect and often know that a good portion of village discourse takes place behind their backs. Their knowledge is not, however, symmetrical. Here, at least, the poor have a slight advantage—if we can call it that—in the realm of information. They know a good deal about what the rich think of them, as we have seen from their comments. Their greater knowledge is due not only to the fact that the village elite is able to speak more freely, and disparagingly, of them but also to the fact that it is simply more important and vital for the poor to keep their ear to the ground. The rich, by contrast, know less about the unedited transcript of the poor because the poor are more discreet and because the rich can more easily afford not to listen. Knowing less, they are free to suspect the worst. What they do know is that they cannot easily penetrate behind the pose of dissimulation, though they sense that behind the public routines of deference and respect lie contempt and anger. They are in precisely the situation of the

---

tory. I do not, in this analysis, mean for a moment to imply that the anthropologist-outsider is privy to the entire concealed transcript of various villagers. While outsider status confers some advantages, it surely blocks access to other information. I was, for example, always aware that most villagers were rather reluctant to talk about healing and magical practices that they imagined I might regard as superstitions.

lord as described in Hegel's dialectic of lord and bondsman.[90] The very exercise of power precludes the village elite from ever knowing what poorer villagers really think, thereby vitiating the value to the elite of their ritual compliance and deference. It is perhaps for this reason that the most dominant elites have historically so often credited their underclasses with all manner of malevolent powers and intentions emanating from the desire for revenge.[91] The situation in Sedaka is not so extreme, but its form is qualitatively similar. The village elites suspect the worst from the poor in terms of anonymous thefts, slander, ingratitude, and dissimulating. Their fear, however, has a real basis in the nature of local power relations.[92]

WHAT IS RESISTANCE?

We have encountered a bewildering array of resistance and compliance within Sedaka. It is no simple matter to determine just where compliance ends and resistance begins, as the circumstances lead many of the poor to clothe their resistance in the public language of conformity. If one takes the dictionary definition of the verb *to resist*—"to exert oneself so as to withstand or counteract the force or effect of . . ."—how is one to categorize the subtle mixture of outward compliance and tentative resistance involved in the attempted boycott of combine-using farmers? So far as the public record is concerned, it never happened and yet, at another level, it was a labor strike, albeit one that failed. There are still other problems. Can individual acts such as theft or the murder of livestock be considered resistance even though they involve no collective action

90. See, for example, chapter 2 of George Kelly, *Hegel's Retreat from Eleusis* (Princeton: Princeton Univ. Press, 1979); Hans-Georg Gadamer, *Hegel's Dialectic* (New Haven: Yale Univ. Press), 54–74; and G. W. F. Hegel, *Phenomenology of the Spirit,* trans. A. V. Miller, with analysis and foreword by J. N. Findlay (Oxford: Clarendon, 1977), 111–19, 520–23.

91. It is at least plausible that there is something of a guilty conscience at work here that knows the poor must resent their marginalization from the village's economic and social life. This interpretation is very much in keeping with I. M. Lewis's analysis of possession by spirits among women and low-status men in a variety of cultures. In the context of a low-caste cult among the Nayar in India, he concludes, "Thus as so often elsewhere, from an objective viewpoint, these spirits can be seen to function as a sort of 'conscience of the rich.' . . . Their malevolent power reflects the feelings of envy and resentment which people of high caste assume the less fortunate lower castes must harbour in relation to their superiors." *Ecstatic Religions: An Anthropological Study of Spirit Possession and Shamanism* (Harmondsworth: Penguin, 1971), 115.

92. For an interesting account of this process as applied to both class and gender relations, see also Elizabeth Janeway, *The Powers of the Weak* (New York: Morrow Quill Paperbacks, 1981), chaps. 9–10.

and do not openly challenge the basic structure of property and domination? Can largely symbolic acts such as boycotting feasts or defaming reputations be called resistance, although they appear to make little or no dent in the distribution of resources? Behind each of these queries is the prior question, "What is resistance?" More accurately stated—since definitions are analytical tools and not ends in themselves—what, for my purposes, can usefully be considered acts of resistance?

At a first approximation, I might claim that class resistance includes *any* act(s) by member(s) of a subordinate class that is or are *intended* either to mitigate or deny claims (for example, rents, taxes, prestige) made on that class by superordinate classes (for example, landlords, large farmers, the state) or to advance its own claims (for example, work, land, charity, respect) vis-à-vis those superordinate classes. While this definition, as we shall see, is not without problems, it does have several advantages. It focuses on the material basis of class relations and class struggle. It allows for both individual and collective acts of resistance. It does not exclude those forms of ideological resistance that challenge the dominant definition of the situation and assert different standards of justice and equity. Finally, it focuses on intentions rather than consequences, recognizing that many acts of resistance may fail to achieve their intended result.

Where there is strong evidence for the intention behind the act, the case for resistance is correspondingly strengthened. Thus it is reasonably clear that the women in the share groups intended to deny machine users transplanting services and thereby force them to revert to hand harvesting. The mutuality among the poor that prevents them competing for tenancies is also clearly intended to prevent a scramble that would eventually harm all tenants. In each case, the intentions are not inferred directly from the action but rather from the explanations the participants give for their behavior. For "speech acts," such as character assassination or malicious gossip directed against wealthy villagers, the act and the intention are fused into one whole; the condemnations of the stingy rich have inscribed within them the intention to recall them to a different standard of conduct or, failing that, to destroy their social standing and influence.

The insistence that acts of resistance must be *shown* to be intended, however, creates enormous difficulties for a whole realm of peasant activity which, in Sedaka and elsewhere, has often been considered resistance. Take, for example, the question of theft or pilferage. What are we to call the poor man in Sedaka who "appropriates" a gunny sack of paddy from a rich man's field: a thief, *tout court,* or a resister as well? What are we to call the act of a thresher who takes care to leave plenty of paddy on the stalks for his wife and children who will glean tomorrow: an act of petty pilfering or an act of resistance? There are two problems here. The first is the practical problem of obtaining evidence of the intentions behind the act, of what it means for the actor. The very nature of the enterprise is such that the actor is unlikely to admit to the action itself, let alone explain what he had in mind. That some poor men in Sedaka considered such thefts to be a kind of self-help *zakat* gift may count as circumstantial evidence that such thieves see themselves as taking what is theirs by right, but it is hardly decisive. Thus, while it may be possible to uncover a set of beliefs shared by a class that legitimize theft or pilfering, it will rarely be possible to uncover the beliefs of the actor in question. The "transcript" of petty thieves, especially those not yet apprehended, is notoriously hard to come by.

The second problem concerns broader issues of definition and analysis. We tend to think of resistance as actions that involve at least some short-run individual or collective sacrifice in order to bring about a longer-range, beneficial goal. The immediate losses of a strike, a boycott, or even the refusal to compete with other members of one's class for land or work are obvious cases in point. When it comes to acts like theft, however, we encounter a combination of immediate individual gain and what *may* be resistance. How are we to judge which of the two purposes is uppermost or decisive? What is at stake is not a petty definitional matter but rather the interpretation of a whole range of actions that seem to me to lie historically at the core of everyday class relations. The English poacher in the eighteenth century *may* have been resisting gentry's claim to property in wild game, but he was just as surely interested in rabbit stew. The slaves in the antebellum U.S. South who secretly butchered their master's hog may have been asserting their right to a decent subsistence, but they were just as surely indulging their fondness for roast pork. The Southeast Asian peasant who hid his rice and possessions from the tax collector may have been protesting high taxes, but he was just as surely seeing to it that his family would have enough rice until the next harvest. The peasant conscript who deserted the army may have been a war resister, but he was just as surely saving his own skin by fleeing the front. Which of these inextricably fused motives are we to take as paramount? Even if we were *able* to ask the actors in question, and even if they could reply candidly, it is not at all clear that they would be able to make a clear determination. Students of slavery, who have looked into this matter most closely, if only because such forms of self-help were frequently the only option open to slaves, have tended to discount such actions as "real" resistance for three reasons. All three figure in Gerald Mullin's analysis of slave "rebelliousness":

> In addressing these observable differences in slave behavior, scholars usually ask whether a particular rebellious style represented resistance to slavery's abuses or *real* resistance to slavery itself. When slave behavior is examined in light of its political context, the most menial workers, the field slaves, fare badly. Speaking generally, their "laziness," boondoggling, and pilferage represented a *limited,* perhaps *self-indulgent* type of rebelliousness. Their reactions to unexpected abuses or to sudden changes in plantation routine were at most only *token* acts against slavery. But the plantation slaves' *organized* and *systematic* schemes to obstruct the plantation's workings—

their *persistent* acts of attrition against crops and stores, and *cooperative* nighttime robberies that sustained the blackmarkets—were more "political" in their *consequences* and represented resistance to slavery itself.[93]

Although Eugene Genovese's position on this issue differs in some important particulars, he too insists on distinguishing between prepolitical forms of resistance and more significant resistance to the regime of slavery. The distinction for him, as the following quotation indicates, lies in both the realm of consequences *and* the realm of intentions:

> Strictly speaking, only insurrection represented political action, which some choose to define as the only genuine resistance since it alone directly challenged the power of the regime. From that point of view, those activities which others call "day-to-day resistance to slavery"—stealing, lying, dissembling, shirking, murder, infanticide, suicide, arson—qualify at best as prepolitical and at worst as apolitical. . . . But "day-to-day resistance to slavery" generally implied accommodation and made no sense except on the assumption of an accepted status quo the norms of which, as perceived or defined by the slaves, had been violated.[94]

Combining these overlapping perspectives, the result is something of a dichotomy between *real* resistance, on the one hand, and token, incidental, or even epiphenomenal activities, on the other. *Real* resistance, it is argued, is (a) organized, systematic, and cooperative, (b) principled or selfless, (c) has revolutionary consequences, and/or (d) embodies ideas or intentions that negate the basis of domination itself. Token, incidental, or epiphenomenal activities, by contrast, are (a) unorganized, unsystematic, and individual, (b) opportunistic and self-indulgent, (c) have no revolutionary consequences, and/or (d) imply, in their intention or meaning, an accommodation with the system of domination. These distinctions are important for any analysis that has as its objective the attempt to delineate the various forms of resistance and to show how they are related to one another and to the form of domination in which they occur. My quarrel is with the contention that the latter forms are ultimately trivial or inconsequential, while only the former can be said to constitute real resistance. This position, in my view, fundamentally misconstrues the very basis of the economic and political struggle conducted daily by subordinate classes—not only slaves, but peasants and workers as well—in repressive settings. It is based on an ironic combination of both Leninist and bourgeois assumptions of what constitutes political action. The first three of the paired comparisons will be addressed here while the final, and vital issue, of whether intentions are accom-

93. Mullin, *Flight and Rebellion*, 35, emphasis added.
94. Genovese, *Roll, Jordan, Roll*, 598.

modationist or revolutionary will be touched on only briefly and examined in more detail in the next chapter.

Let us begin with the question of actions that are "self-indulgent," individual, and unorganized. Embedded in the logic of Genovese and, especially, of Mullins, is the assumption that such acts intrinsically lack revolutionary *consequences*. This *may* often be the case, but it is also the case that there is hardly a modern revolution that can be successfully explained without reference to precisely such acts when they take place on a massive scale. Take, for example, the matter of desertion from the army and the role it has played in revolutions.

The Russian Revolution is a striking case in point. Growing desertions from the largely peasant rank and file of the army in the summer of 1917 were a major and indispensable part of the revolutionary process in at least two respects. First, they were responsible for the collapse of the main institution of repression of the tsarist state, inherited by the Provisional Government—an institution that had earlier, in 1905, put down another revolutionary upheaval. Second, the deserters contributed directly to the revolutionary process in the countryside by participating in the seizures of land throughout the core provinces of European Russia. And it is abundantly clear that the hemorrhage in the tsarist forces was largely "self-indulgent," "unorganized," and "individual," although thousands and thousands of individuals threw down their arms and headed home.[95] The June attack into Austria had been crushed with huge losses of troops and officers; the ration of bread had been reduced and "fast days" inaugurated at the front; the soldiers knew, moreover, that if they stayed at the front they might miss the chance to gain from the land seizures breaking out in the countryside.[96] Desertion offered the peasant conscripts the chance of saving their skins and of returning home where bread and, now, land were available. The risks were minimal since discipline in the army had dissolved. One can hardly imagine a set of more "self-indulgent" goals. But it was just such self-indulgent ends, acted on

95. See Allan Wildman, "The February Revolution in the Russian Army," *Soviet Studies* 22, no. 1 (July 1970): 3–23; Marc Ferro, "The Russian Soldier in 1917: Undisciplined, Patriotic, and Revolutionary," *Slavic Review* 30, no. 3 (September 1971): 483–512; Barrington Moore, Jr., *Injustice*, 364, and Theda Skocpol, *States and Social Revolutions* (Cambridge: Cambridge Univ. Press, 1979), 135–38. There is a consensus that Bolshevik propaganda at the front was not instrumental in provoking these desertions.

96. One may wish to call the land seizures and sacking of gentry property a revolutionary act, and it was certainly revolutionary in its consequences in 1917. But it was a largely spontaneous affair out of the control of any party, and it is extremely unlikely that those seizing the land self-consciously saw themselves as bringing about a revolutionary government, let alone a Bolshevik one. See Skocpol, *States*, 135, 138.

by unorganized masses of "self-demobilized" peasant soldiers that made the revolution possible.[97]

The disintegration of the Russian army is but one of many instances where the aggregation of a host of petty, self-interested acts of insubordination or desertion, with no revolutionary intent, have created a revolutionary situation. The dissolution of the Nationalist armies of Chiang Kai-shek in 1948 and of Saigon's army in 1975 could no doubt be analyzed along similar lines. And long before the final debacle, acts of insubordination and noncompliance in each army—in the U.S. Army serving in Vietnam as well, it should be added—had set sharp limits on what the counterrevolutionary forces could expect and require of their own rank and file.[98] Resistance of this kind is of course not a monopoly of the counterrevolution, as George Washington and Emiliano Zapata, among others, discovered. We can imagine that the eminently personal logic of Pedro Martinez, a sometime soldier with the Zapatista forces, was not markedly different from that of the tsarist troops leaving the front.

> That's where [battle of Tizapan] I finally had it. The battle was something awful: The shooting was tremendous! It was a completely bloody battle, three days and three nights. But I took it for one day and then I left. I quit the army . . . I said to myself, "It's time now I got back to my wife, to my little children. I'm getting out." . . . I said to myself, "No, my family comes first and they are starving. Now I'm leaving."[99]

The refreshing candor of Pedro Martinez serves to remind us that there is no necessary relationship between the banality of the act of self-preservation and of family obligations, on the one hand, and the banality of the consequences of such acts, on the other.

While the consequences of peasant self-serving are essential to any larger analysis of class relations or of the state, I do not wish to argue that resistance

97. E. H. Carr, *The Bolshevik Revolution: 1917–1923*, vol. 1 (Harmondsworth: Penguin, 1966), 103. If we wished to extend this account of Russian peasant "self-demobilization" back into history, we might plausibly include the massive and persistent flight of serfs to the frontier in the eighteenth century. The effort to retain the serfs and their labor was perhaps the key to domestic statecraft throughout this period. Jerome Blum reminds us that "There were more laws about runaways and their recovery than any other subject—a fact that in itself bears witness to the proportions of peasant flight." *Lord and Peasant in Russia: From the 9th to the 19th Century* (Princeton: Princeton Univ. Press, 1961), 553.

98. The initial successes of Solidarity in Poland can in a similar fashion be attributed largely to the fact that the unpopular regime could not count on its own army actively to suppress the rebellious civilian population and was instead forced to rely on the hated paramilitary police, the *Zomos*.

99. Oscar Lewis, *Pedro Martinez: A Mexican Peasant and His Family* (New York: Vintage, 1964), 102.

should be defined with reference to its consequences alone. Such a view runs into formidable difficulties, if for no reason other than the "law of unintended consequences." Many acts that almost any reasonable observer would call acts of resistance may backfire and produce the very opposite of what was intended. The terrorism of revolutionary movements that *explicitly* aim at crippling the state may instead usher in a more terrible and permanent dictatorship. The effective strike of peasant laborers *explicitly* intended to raise wages and increase employment may instead prompt a wholesale mechanization of production, thereby eliminating jobs.[100]

The problem with existing concepts of resistance is therefore not that they must inevitably deal with intentions and meaning as well as with consequences. Rather, the problem lies in what is a misleading, sterile, and sociologically naive insistence upon distinguishing "self-indulgent," individual acts, on the one hand, from presumably "principled," selfless, collective actions, on the other, and excluding the former from the category of *real* resistance. To insist on such distinctions as a means of comparing forms of resistance and their consequences is one thing, but to use them as the basic criteria to determine what constitutes resistance is to miss the very wellsprings of peasant politics.

It is no coincidence that the cries of "bread," "land," and "no taxes" that so often lie at the core of peasant rebellion are all joined to the basic material survival needs of the peasant household. Nor should it be anything more than a commonplace that everyday peasant politics and everday peasant resistance (and also, of course, everyday compliance) flows from these same fundamental material needs. We need assume no more than an understandable desire on the part of the peasant household to survive—to ensure its physical safety, to ensure its food supply, to ensure its necessary cash income—to identify the source of its resistance to the claims of press gangs, tax collectors, landlords, and employers.

To ignore the self-interested element in peasant resistance is to ignore the determinate context not only of peasant politics, but of most lower-class politics. It is precisely the fusion of self-interest and resistance that is the vital force animating the resistance of peasants and proletarians. When a peasant hides part of his crop to avoid paying taxes, he is both filling his stomach and depriving the state of grain.[101] When a peasant soldier deserts the army because the food is bad and his crops at home are ripe, he is both looking after himself and

100. More farfetched, but still possible, is the opposite situation, where an act that we would not, by any stretch of the imagination, wish to call an act of resistance (for example, a completely inadvertent setting on fire of an aristocrat's crop land or a hunting accident in which a peasant kills the provincial governor) may set off a chain of events that weakens the class domination of rural elites. Any definition of resistance thus requires at least some reference to the intentions of the actors.

101. Again, such resistance is not the monopoly of lower classes. Tax evasion and the so-called black economy in advanced capitalist countries are also forms of resistance, albeit pursued with most vigor and success by middle and upper classes.

denying the state cannon fodder. When such acts are rare and isolated, they are of little interest; but when they become a consistent pattern (even though un-coordinated, let alone organized) we are dealing with resistance. The intrinsic nature and, in one sense, the "beauty" of much peasant resistance is that it often confers immediate and concrete advantages, while at the same time denying resources to the appropriating classes, *and* that it requires little or no manifest organization. The stubbornness and force of such resistance flow directly from the fact that it is so firmly rooted in the shared material struggle experienced by a class.

To require of lower-class resistance that it somehow be "principled" or "self-less" is not only utopian and a slander on the moral status of fundamental material needs; it is, more fundamentally, a misconstruction of the basis of class struggle, which is, first and foremost, a struggle over the appropriation of work, produc-tion, property, and taxes. "Bread-and-butter" issues are the essence of lower-class politics and resistance. Consumption, from this perspective, is both the goal and the result of resistance and counterresistance. As Utsa Patnaik has noted, "Consumption is nothing but the historically 'necessary labor,' the share of net output allowed to be retained by the petty producers as the outcome of their struggle with the surplus-appropriating classes."[102] This is then the self-inter-ested core of routine class struggle: the often defensive effort to mitigate or defeat appropriation.[103] Petty thefts of grain or pilfering on the threshing floor may seem like trivial "coping" mechanisms from one vantage point, but, from a broader view of class relations, how the harvest is actually divided belongs at the center.

A further advantage of a concept of resistance that begins with self-interested material needs is that it is far more in keeping with how "class" is first expe-rienced by the historical actors themselves. Here I subscribe wholeheartedly to the judgment reached by E. P. Thompson on the basis of his own fine analysis of working-class history:

In my view, far too much theoretical attention (much of it plainly

102. Utsa Patnaik, "Neo-Populism and Marxism: The Chayanovian View of the Agrarian Question and Its Fundamental Fallacy," *Journal of Peasant Studies* 6, no. 4 (July 1979): 398–99.

103. In a factory or in "state farms" the "self-interested core of class struggle" may involve the reappropriation of time for one's own use in forms that appear quite trivial. Thus, Alf Ludke and Shelby Cullam argue that "horse-play" in the German factory and other examples of "the articulation and assertion of individual needs" ought to be seen as "political behavior." They add that the resistance to discipline and hierarchy found expression not only on the factory floor but in resistance to the socialist party itself "corresponding to a massive dis-interest in any sort of formal and state-centered politics." "Cash, Coffee-Breaks, Horse-Play: Eigensinn and Poli-tics among Factory Workers in Late 19th and Early 20th Century," Davis Center Seminar, Princeton University, April 2, 1982, mimeo.

ahistorical) has been paid to 'class' and far too little to 'class-struggle.'
Indeed, class struggle is the prior, as well as the more universal, concept.
To put it bluntly, classes do not exist as separate entities, look around, find
an enemy class, and then start to struggle. On the contrary, people find
themselves in a society structured in determined ways (crucial, but not
exclusively, in productive relations), they experience exploitation (or the
need to maintain power over those whom they exploit), they identify points
of antagonistic interest, they commence to struggle around these issues and
in the process of struggling they discover themselves as classes, they come
to know this discovery as class-consciousness. Class and class-consciousness
are always the *last,* not the first, stage in the real historical process.[104]

It is impossible, of course, to divorce the material basis of the struggle from the
struggle over values—the ideological struggle. To resist a claim or an appropriation is to resist, as well, the justification and rationale behind that particular
claim. In Sedaka, this ideological resistance is generally kept from public view,
but it forms a vital part of the normative subculture among the poor.

The inclination to dismiss "individual" acts of resistance as insignificant and
to reserve the term "resistance" for collective or organized action is as misguided
as the emphasis on "principled" action. The privileged status accorded organized
movements, I suspect, flows from either of two political orientations: the one,
essentially Leninist, which regards the only viable class action as one led by a
vanguard party serving as a "general staff," the other more straightforwardly
derived from a familiarity and preference for open, institutionalized politics as
conducted in capitalist democracies. In either case, however, there is a misap-
prehension of the social and political circumstances of peasant resistance.

The individual and often anonymous quality of much peasant resistance is of
course eminently suited to the sociology of the class from which it arises. Being
a class of "low classlessness" scattered in small communities and generally lacking
the institutional means to act collectively, it is likely to employ those means of
resistance that are local and require little coordination. Under special historical
circumstances of overwhelming material deprivation, the legal protection of open
political action, or a breakdown in the institutions of repression (more rarely, all
three), the peasantry can and has become an organized, political, mass movement. Such circumstances are, however, extremely rare and usually short-lived—
even if they contribute to a revolution. In most places at most times this political
option has simply been precluded. The penchant for forms of resistance that are
individual and unobtrusive are not only what a Marxist might expect from petty
commodity producers and rural laborers, but have certain advantages. Unlike
hierarchical formal organizations, there is no center, no leadership, no identifiable

104. "Eighteenth-Century English Society," 149.

structure that can be co-opted or neutralized. What is lacking in terms of central coordination may be compensated for by flexibility and persistence. These forms of resistance will win no set-piece battles, but they are admirably adapted to long-run campaigns of attrition.

If we were to confine our search for peasant resistance to formally organized activity, we would search largely in vain, for in Malaysia as in many other Third World countries, such organizations are either absent or the creations of officials and rural elites. We would simply miss much of what is happening. The history of Malay peasant resistance to the state, for example, has yet to be written. When, and if, it is written, however, it will not be a history in which open rebellion or formal organizations play a significant role. The account of resistance in the precolonial era would perhaps be dominated by flight and avoidance of corvée labor and a host of tolls and taxes. Resistance to colonial rule was marked far less by open confrontations than by willful and massive noncompliance with its most threatening aspects, for example, the persistent underreporting of land-holdings and crop yields to minimize taxes, the relentless disregard for all regulations designed to restrict smallholders' rubber planting and marketing, the unabated pioneer settlement of new land despite a host of laws forbidding it. Much of this continues today. There is ample evidence for this resistance in the archives,[105] but, inasmuch as its goal was to evade the state and the legal order, not to attack them, it has received far less historical attention than the quite rare and small revolts that had far less impact on the course of colonial rule. Even in advanced capitalist nations, the "movements" of the poor take place largely outside the sphere of formal political activity.[106] It follows that, if

105. Tax evasion is evident from the steady reports of land tax arrears from Kedah and from indications of systematic misreporting of yields. Thus, Unfederated Malay States, *Annual Report of the Advisor to the Kedah Government, 1921* (Alor Setar: Government Printer, 1922), 38, notes, "The padi planter regards with suspicion the collection of statistics as a possible basis for further taxation and minimizes his harvest." The *Report* for May 1930 to May 1931 puts the underreporting between 15 and 18 percent (p. 8), in some districts at nearly 50 percent (p. 55). For evasion of the rubber restriction schemes from 1913 until World War II, see Lim Teck Ghee, *Peasants and Their Agricultural Economy in Colonial Malaya, 1874–1941* (Kuala Lumpur: Oxford Univ. Press, 1977), and Donald M. Nonini, Paul Diener, and Eugene E. Robkin, "Ecology and Evolution: Population, Primitive Accumulation, and the Malay Peasantry" (Typescript, 1979).

106. "Whatever the intellectual sources of error, the effect of equating movements with movement organizations—and thus requiring that protests have a leader, a constitution, a legislative program, or at least a banner before they are recognized as such—is to divert attention from many forms of political unrest and to consign them by definition to the more shadowy realms of social problems and deviant behavior. As a result such events as massive school truancy or rising worker absenteeism or mounting applications for public welfare or spreading rent defaults rarely attract the attention of political analysts. Having decided by definitional fiat that

a persuasive case can be made for such forms of political activity among the poor in highly industrialized, urban economies with high rates of literacy and a relatively open political system, the case would be far stronger for the peasantry in agrarian economy where open political activity is sharply restricted. Formal political activity may be the norm for the elites, the intelligentsia, and the middle classes which, in the Third World as well as in the West, have a near monopoly of institutional skills and access. But it would be naive to expect that peasant resistance can or will normally take the same form.

Nor should we forget that the forms of peasant resistance are not just a product of the social ecology of the peasantry. The parameters of resistance are also set, in part, by the institutions of repression. To the extent that such institutions do their work effectively, they may all but preclude any forms of resistance other than the individual, the informal, and the clandestine.[107] Thus, it is perfectly legitimate—even important—to distinguish between various levels and forms of resistance: formal–informal, individual–collective, public–anonymous, those that challenge the system of domination—those that aim at marginal gains. But it should be made crystal clear that what we may actually be measuring in this enterprise is the level of repression that structures the available options. Depending on the circumstances they confront, peasants may oscillate from organized electoral activity to violent confrontations to silent and anonymous acts of foot dragging and theft. This oscillation may in some cases be due to changes in the social organization of the peasantry, but it is as likely, if not more likely, to be due to changes in the level of repression. More than one peasantry has been brutally reduced from open, radical political activity at one moment to stubborn and sporadic acts of petty resistance at the next. If we allow ourselves to call only the former "resistance," we simply allow the structure of domination to define for us what is resistance and what is not resistance.

Many of the forms of resistance I have been examining may be individual actions, but this is not to say that they are uncoordinated.[108] Here again, a

---

nothing political has occurred, nothing has to be explained, at least not in terms of political protest." Frances Fox Piven and Richard A. Cloward, *Poor People's Movements: Why They Succeed, How They Fail* (New York: Vintage, 1977), 5.

107. See in this context the fine article by William M. Reddy, "The Textile Trade and the Language of the Crowd of Rouen 1752–1871," *Past and Present* 74 (February 1977): 62–89. Reddy argues that it was precisely the *lack* of organization in crowd behavior that was enabling and that the crowd came to value and use spontaneity in the knowledge that it was the most effective and least costly means of protest. The cultural understandings were so well developed that any just grievance could, he says, bring together a crowd without any planning or organization, let alone formal leadership.

108. In his interpretation of nineteenth-century working-class history, Francis Hearn finds in just such informal structures of ritual and community the heart and

concept of coordination derived from formal and bureaucratic settings is of little assistance in understanding actions in small communities with dense informal networks and rich, and historically deep, subcultures of resistance to outside claims.[109] It is, for example, no exaggeration to say that much of the folk culture of the peasant "little tradition" amounts to a legitimation, or even a *celebration,* of precisely the kinds of evasive and cunning forms of resistance I have examined. In Malay society this tradition is captured in the *Sang Kancil,* or mouse deer tales familiar to all peasants. The mouse deer is the stereotypical "trickster" figure: a small and weak but agile creature who survives and triumphs over far more powerful beasts by his wits, his deceit, and his cunning. It takes no literary legerdemain to recognize *Sang Kancil* as a popular metaphor for the necessary survival skills of the peasantry. They have of course their cultural equivalents in the popular traditions of other historically subordinate groups— Til Eulenspiegel and Brer Rabbit, to name only two. At the very least, they encourage the kind of resistance celebrated in this South Carolina slave saying: "De bukrah (white) hab scheme, en de nigger hab trick, en ebery time the bukrah scheme once, the nigger trick twice."[110]

In this and in other ways (for example, tales of bandits, peasant heroes, religious myths) the peasant subculture helps to underwrite dissimulation, poaching, theft, tax evasion, avoidance of conscription, and so on. While folk culture is not coordination in the formal sense, it often achieves a "climate of opinion" which, in other more institutionalized societies, would require a public relations campaign.[111] The striking thing about peasant society is the extent to which a whole range of complex activities—from labor exchange to house moving to wedding preparations to feasts—are coordinated by networks of understanding and practice. It is the same with boycotts, wage "negotiations," the refusal of tenants to compete with one another, or the conspiracy of silence surrounding

---

soul of direct action by the working class. Their erosion by midcentury was the key, he believes, to the "domestication" of the working class. "In all societies, formal organizations which significantly threaten the stability of the existing arrangements are, if not directly banned, subject to legal sanctions which restrict the scope of their activity. . . . For this reason the informal, often opaque, structures and institutions of the viable community are indispensable to sustained collective action." *Domination, Legitimation, and Resistance: The Interpretation of the 19th Century English Working Class,* Contributions in Labor History, No. 3 (Westport: Greenwood, 1978).

109. For an extended argument along these lines, see Scott, "Protest and Profanation," and "Hegemony and the Peasantry," *Politics and Society* 7, no. 3 (1977): 267–96.

110. Levine, *Black Culture and Black Consciousness,* 81.

111. For a suggestive and detailed analysis of how folk beliefs and ritual may be mobilized to serve political and social class objectives, see the fine discussion in Maurice Agulhon, *La République au village: Les populations du Var de la Révolution à la Seconde République* (Paris: Plon, 1970).

thefts. No formal organizations are created because none are required; and yet a form of coordination is achieved that alerts us that what is happening is not just individual action.

In light of these considerations, then, let us return briefly to the question of intention. For many forms of peasant resistance, we have every reason to expect that actors will remain mute about their intentions. Their safety may depend on silence and anonymity; the kind of resistance itself may depend for its effectiveness on the appearance of conformity; their intentions may be so embedded in the peasant subculture *and* in the routine, taken-for-granted struggle to provide for the subsistence and survival of the household as to remain inarticulate. The fish do not talk about the water.

In one sense, of course, their intentions are inscribed in the acts themselves. A peasant soldier who deserts the army is in effect "saying" by his act that the purposes of this institution and the risks and hardships it entails will not prevail over his family or personal needs. A harvest laborer who steals paddy from his employer is "saying" that his need for rice takes precedence over the formal property rights of his boss.

When it comes to those social settings where the material interests of appropriating classes are directly in conflict with the peasantry (rents, wages, employment, taxes, conscription, the division of the harvest), we can, I think, infer something of intentions from the nature of the actions themselves. This is especially the case when there is a systematic pattern of actions that mitigate or deny a claim on the peasant surplus. Evidence about intentions is, of course, always welcome, but we should not expect too much. For this reason, the definition of resistance given earlier places particular emphasis on the effort to thwart material and symbolic claims from dominant classes. The goal, after all, of the great bulk of peasant resistance is not directly to overthrow or transform a system of domination but rather to survive—today, this week, this season— within it. The usual goal of peasants, as Hobsbawm has so aptly put it, is *"working the system to their minimum disadvantage."*[112] Their persistent attempts to "nibble away" may backfire, they may marginally alleviate exploitation, they may force a renegotiation of the limits of appropriation, they may change the course of subsequent development, and they may more rarely help bring the system down. These are possible consequences. Their intention, by contrast, is nearly always survival and persistence. The pursuit of that end may, depending on circumstances, require either the petty resistance we have seen or more dramatic actions of self-defense. In any event, most of their efforts will be seen by appropriating classes as truculence, deceit, shirking, pilfering, arrogance—in short, all the labels intended to denigrate the many faces of resistance.

It should be apparent that resistance is not simply whatever peasants do to

112. Eric Hobsbawm, "Peasants and Politics," *Journal of Peasant Studies* 1, no. 1 (1973): 7.

maintain themselves and their households. Much of what they do, as we have seen, is to be understood as compliance, however grudgingly. Survival as petty commodity producers or laborers may impel some to save themselves at the expense of their fellows. The poor landless laborer who steals paddy from another poor man or who outbids him for a tenancy is surviving, but he is surely not resisting in the sense defined here. One of the key questions that must be asked about any system of domination is the extent to which it succeeds in reducing subordinate classes to purely "beggar-thy-neighbor" strategies for survival. Certain combinations of atomization, terror, repression, and pressing material needs can indeed achieve the ultimate dream of domination: to have the dominated exploit each other.

Allowing that only those survival strategies that deny or mitigate claims from appropriating classes can be called resistance, we are nevertheless left with a vast range of actions to consider. Their variety conceals a basic continuity. That continuity lies in the history of the persistent efforts of relatively autonomous petty commodity producers to defend their fundamental material and physical interests and to reproduce themselves. At different times and places they have defended themselves against the corvée, taxes, and conscription of the traditional agrarian state, against the colonial state, against the inroads of capitalism (for example, rents, interest, proletarianization, mechanization), against the modern capitalist state, and, it must be added, against many purportedly socialist states as well. The revolution, when and if it does come, may eliminate many of the worst evils of the ancient regime, but it is rarely if ever the end of peasant resistance. For the radical elites who capture the state are likely to have different goals in mind than their erstwhile peasant supporters. They may envisage a collectivized agriculture, while the peasantry clings to its smallholdings; they may want a centralized political structure, while the peasantry is wedded to local autonomy; they may want to tax the countryside in order to industrialize; and they will almost certainly wish to strengthen the state vis-à-vis civil society. It therefore becomes possible to an astute observer like Goran Hyden to find remarkable parallels between the earlier resistance of the Tanzanian peasantry to colonialism and capitalism and its current resistance to the institutions and policies of the *socialist* state of Tanzania.[113] He provides a gripping account of how the "peasant mode of production"—by foot dragging, by privatizing work and land that have been appropriated by the state, by evasion, by flight, and

---

113. Goran Hyden, *Beyond Ujamaa in Tanzania* (London: Heinemann, 1980). Also relevant is Issa Shivji, *Class Struggles in Tanzania* (London: Heinemann, 1976). For a similar account of Algeria's state-created agricultural organization and attempts to evade it, see Peter Knauss, "Algeria's Agrarian Revolution: Peasant Control or Control of Peasants," *African Studies Review* 20, no. 3 (1977): 65–78. As one member of a state cooperative said, "Before we were khames [tenants] of the great landowner. . . . Now we are the khames of the State. . . . All workers know it."

by "raiding" government programs for its own purposes—has thwarted the plans of the state. In Vietnam also, after the revolution was consummated in the south as well as in the north, everyday forms of peasant resistance have continued. The surreptitious expansion of private plots, the withdrawal of labor from state enterprises for household production, the failure to deliver grain and livestock to the state, the "appropriation" of state credits and resources by households and work teams, and the steady growth of the black market attest to the tenacity of petty commodity production under socialist state forms.[114] The stubborn, persistent, and irreducible forms of resistance I have been examining may thus represent the truly durable weapons of the weak both before and *after* the revolution.

114. See, for example, the forthcoming articles by Christine White and Adam Fforde in *Journal of Peasant Studies*.

8 • Hegemony and Consciousness: Everyday Forms of Ideological Struggle

And as to the causes of social change, I look at it in this way—ideas are a sort of parliament, but there's a commonwealth outside, and a good deal of commonwealth is working at change without knowing what the parliament is doing.

George Eliot, *Daniel Deronda*

No one who looks even slightly beneath the fairly placid official surface of class relations in Sedaka would find it easy to argue that the poor are much mystified about their situation. Their account of the green revolution and its social consequences is widely divergent from that of the rich. Seemingly straightforward social facts about who is rich and who is poor—and how rich and how poor—are contested in this community. The poor, when they may do so with relative safety, display an impressive capacity to penetrate behind the pieties and rationales of the rich farmers and to understand the larger realities of capital accumulation, proletarianization, and marginalization. They emphasize and manipulate those values that will serve their material and symbolic interests as a class. They reject the denigrating characterizations the rich deploy against them. And within the narrow limits created by the fear of repression and the "dull compulsion of economic relations," they act to defend their interests by boycotts, quiet strikes, theft, and malicious gossip.

In this final chapter, I hope to bring these rather homely insights from Sedaka in touch with the larger issues of the social experience of class and the typical contexts of class struggle. It should be possible also to say something meaningful about class-consciousness, mystification, and ideological hegemony. The objective is a deeper appreciation of everyday forms of symbolic resistance and the way in which they articulate with everyday acts of material resistance. Just as peasants—Zola and many others notwithstanding—do not simply vacillate between blind submission and homicidal rage, neither do they move directly from ideological complicity to strident class-consciousness. If, behind the facade of behavioral conformity imposed by elites, we find innumerable, anonymous acts of resistance, so also do we find, behind the facade of symbolic and ritual compliance, innumerable acts of ideological resistance. The two forms of resistance are, of course, inextricably joined. Examining these issues in more analytical detail, though it requires us to step back a few paces from Sedaka, should allow us to clarify the debate about the extent to which dominant classes are able to impose their own vision of a just social order, not only on the behavior of subordinate classes, but on their consciousness as well. Before addressing these larger issues, however, it will be helpful first to clarify the nature of the ideological struggle in Sedaka.

THE MATERIAL BASE AND NORMATIVE SUPERSTRUCTURE IN SEDAKA

There is no doubt whatever that the ideological conflict now under way in Sedaka is a reaction to the massive transformation of production relations made possible by double-cropping and mechanization backed by the state. It is these exogenous changes in the material base that have allowed large landowners and farmers to change the tenure system, raise rents, dismiss tenants, replace wage workers with machinery, and either to lease out large plots for long periods or to resume cultivation themselves. This shift in the balance of economic power has also allowed rich farmers to eliminate or curtail a host of social practices that were part and parcel of the earlier scheme of production relations: feast giving, Islamic charity, loans and advance wages, and even much of the social recognition and respect previously accorded to poorer villagers. What has occurred, in short, is that those facets of earlier relations of production that are no longer underwritten by the material interests of wealthy farmers are being abandoned piecemeal or wholesale.

These transformations of the material base and their economic and social consequences for class relations have worked themselves out within the context of a given, normative environment. Two general facts about this normative environment are worth noting. First, it is not some Parsonian value consensus in which actors conform to a normative order that is somehow outside and above themselves but rather a normative environment of conflict and divergent interpretations. Well before double-cropping, for example, large farmers regarded *zakat peribadi* given to harvest workers as a favor or gift, while the workers themselves came to regard it as a payment to which they were entitled as a matter of right. Second, this normative environment was itself, in part, a product of the material conditions of production prior to double-cropping and mechanization. We are not therefore dealing with purely mental constructs outside day-to-day practical activity but rather with values that were firmly anchored in a host of commonplace material practices.[1] The main point for my purposes is that the peasants of Sedaka do not simply react to objective conditions per se but rather to the interpretation they place on those conditions as mediated by values embedded in concrete practices.

In this connection, it is important to sketch briefly both the material practices associated with rice production and the normative understandings of them that

---

1. See, for example, Nicholas Abercrombie, *Class Structure and Knowledge* (Oxford: Blackwell, 1980), 68.

prevailed before double-cropping. As for the practices themselves, one can satisfactorily account for them almost entirely in terms of the concrete material interests of the actors involved. These material interests were, in turn, largely an artifact of the striking inequity in the distribution of the means of production (rice land) prior to double-cropping. For substantial farmers, the key production problem was the timely and reliable mobilization of a labor force for the major operations of transplanting, reaping, and threshing. The constraints of a rainfed production schedule produce striking peaks of labor demand which, even with migrant workers, required readily available local help in the inevitable rush to get the paddy planted and harvested. Thus it made eminent good sense for large farmers to develop a loyal work force by means of material and symbolic acts of social consideration and friendship. In the first few years of double-cropping, when migrant workers were no longer easily available but combines had not yet appeared, this strategy became even more imperative. The same process was apparent in the relations between landlords and their tenants. When it was easy to rent in land, the landlord had a vested interest in making occasional concessions in order to retain a good cultivator. To these more strictly economic motives must be joined the incentives for village elites, especially since independence, to build loyal political followings as a precondition of their preferential access to the benefits available from local state and party institutions.

For those who needed land and work—or both—a similar, but even more compelling calculus prevailed. For them, living from hand to mouth, often having to leave after the harvest to find work elsewhere, the prospect of a steady tenancy or reliable field work each season was important. The contingent but inevitable crises of crop failure, a death or illness in the family, or a sudden ritual expense meant that the possibility of loans, charity, or emergency assistance was not just a convenience but a virtual necessity for the household.[2] If they accommodated themselves publicly to these social relations of production while continually striving to redefine them to their advantage, their behavior made good sense as well.

But it is not sufficient merely to understand the obviously self-interested basis of these social relations of production. What is critical for my purpose—that is, the analysis of ideological conflict—is to grasp the nature of the normative filter through which these self-interested actions must pass and how and why they are socially transformed by this passage. Why, in other words, is economic power "euphemized" in this fashion and what are the consequences of its eu-

2. As we have seen, this class was also capable of recognizing and bitterly resenting the way in which rich landowners could take advantage of such loans through *jual janji*, taking over title to more land and thereby reinforcing the basis for economic dependency.

phemization?[3] From one perspective what the wealthy did was to transmute a portion of their disproportionate economic means into forms of status, prestige, and social control by means of acts they *passed off* as voluntary acts of generosity or charity. This social control was, of course, again convertible into labor services—and hence again into material wealth. Are we, as Bourdieu asks in a similar context, to see in this simply a clever sleight-of-hand, "a disguised form of purchase of labor power or a covert exaction of corvées?" He answers:

> By all means, as long as the analysis holds together what holds together in practice, the *double reality* of intrinsically *equivocal, ambiguous* conduct . . . the complete reality of this appropriation of services lies in the fact that it *can only* take place in the disguise of the *thiwizi* [a ritual of disinterested gift giving], the voluntary assistance which is also a corvée and is thus a voluntary corvée and forced assistance.[4]

The euphemization of economic power is necessary both where direct physical coercion is not possible and where the pure indirect domination of the capitalist market is not yet sufficient to ensure appropriation by itself.[5] In such settings, appropriation must take place through a socially recognized form of domination. Such domination is not simply imposed by force but must assume a form that gains social compliance. If it is to work at all, it requires that the weaker party—if only publicly—acquiesce in the euphemism.

Three consequences of this euphemization of economic control are central to

3. The term is Pierre Bourdieu's (*Outline of a Theory of Practice,* trans. Richard Nice [Cambridge: Cambridge Univ. Press, 1977], 191). The analysis in this and the next paragraph relies very heavily on Bourdieu's subtle analysis of precapitalist forms of domination.

4. Ibid., 179, emphasis in original. Bourdieu also elaborates that "Gentle, hidden exploitation is the form taken by man's exploitation by man whenever overt, brutal exploitation is impossible. It is as false to identify this essentially *dual* economy with its official reality (generosity, mutual aid, etc.), i.e. the form which exploitation has to adopt in order to take place, as it is to reduce it to its objective reality, seeing mutual aid as corvée, the khammes [client, bondsman] as a sort of slave, and so on. The gift, generosity, conspicuous distribution—the extreme case of which is potlatch—are operations of social alchemy which may be observed whenever the direct application of overt physical or economic violence is negatively sanctioned, and which tend to bring about the transmutation of economic capital into symbolic capital." Ibid., 192.

5. In this respect, the Marxist position that feudal domination is direct, undisguised appropriation, whereas capitalist domination works through the mystified form of commodity fetishism in which the worker "appears" to sell his labor as a commodity is in error. The "gift" as a disguised appropriation can be seen as the functional equivalent of commodity fetishism under capitalism. This is not, however—as will be apparent later—an argument on behalf of false-consciousness.

my analysis. The first is simply that, if it is achieved at all, it is not achieved without costs. The cultivation of people, no less than the cultivation of paddy land, demands time, effort, and resources. The large farmer who wanted to ensure his labor supply and his political following had to handcraft his social authority link by link by means of strategic gifts, charity, loans, sociability, feasts, and other concrete and symbolic services.[6]

A second, and closely related, consequence is that the euphemization of economic domination could be achieved only by virtue of a degree of socialization of the profits of cultivation. I use the word *socialization* cautiously, as there has of course never been any socialization of the ownership of the means of production. Instead what occurred was a modest and strategic socialization of a portion of the crop itself and the proceeds from it, which took the form of gifts in emergencies, *zakat* after the harvest, feasts, liberality, and so forth. This limited socialization of wealth—carried on, to be sure, between private individuals—was the only way in which wealth could be successfully converted into social credit and labor services. Here we have something of a rural analogue of what Marx called the contradiction between private appropriation and socialized production, except that in this case it is a contradiction between private appropriation and the *social use* of property. When we look closely at the charges the poor make against the rich, they are almost without exception arguments for the social use of property. Thus, the charges about the decline of feast giving, the disappearance of post-harvest *zakat,* the refusal of alms (*sedekah*), and hence the more global charge of stinginess and tightfistedness are directly related to the social use of property. Even the major issues of production relations—combine-harvester use, the resort to leasehold tenancy (*pajak*), accelerated rent collection, and the abuses of the Village Improvement Scheme—can be viewed as appeals to past practices, both customary and specifically Islamic, in which the property and influence of the rich were condoned only if they also served to provide land, work, and income to the rest of the community. This is perhaps also why the ideological struggle is largely confined to the Malay community, the only unit within which the social use of property was actively sanctioned. Such claims are now tenaciously defended precisely because they are grounded in both the symbolic and material practices of a shared, if contested, tradition.

A third aspect of the euphemization of property relations is that it is *always* the focus of symbolic manipulation, struggle, and conflict. We must not view these patterns as *merely* a ploy, a mystification, as dust thrown in the eyes of subordinate classes. While the symbolic conduct of the rich is certainly self-

6. One may plausibly argue, I think, that the total of these services—in terms of their cost—was no more than what a free market wage and tenancy market would have required to achieve the same purpose. The point, however, is not that these traditional forms of appropriation are less onerous but rather that they were necessary under the circumstances.

interested, the very definition of what constitutes self-interest is the outcome of a class struggle. Thus, we fail to apprehend the full significance of the occasional gift or *zakat* not only when we see it as the elites intend it to be seen—as disinterested liberality—but also when we treat it simply as a cynical disguise for appropriation. A more complete view requires us to grasp the double symbolic manipulation of the euphemization itself. As E. P. Thompson has observed in a related context:

> Even "liberality" and "charity" may be seen as calculated acts of class appeasement in times of dearth and calculated extortions (under threat of riot) by the crowd: what is (from above) an "act of giving" is (from below) an "act of getting."[7]

For a moment, let us try to ground this insight in a particular example from Sedaka with which we are familiar: the relationship between Hamzah and his frequent employer, Haji Kadir. Hamzah knows that Haji Kadir is in a position to provide him with, say, work or a loan against future wages. He also knows that Haji Kadir and others like him have typically described such actions in terms of help (*tolong*) or assistance (*bantuan*). Hamzah then *uses* this knowledge to pursue his concrete ends; he approaches Haji Kadir, using all the appropriate linguistic forms of deference and politeness, and requests his "help" and "assistance."[8] In other words, he appeals to the self-interested description that Haji Kadir would give to his own acts to place them in the most advantageous light. We know enough about Hamzah to gather that this is more or less what actually goes through his mind. If he wins he achieves his desired objective (work or a loan) and in the process he contributes willy-nilly to the public legitimacy of the principles to which he strategically appealed. Just who is manipulating whom in this petty enterprise is no simple matter to decide. It is best seen, perhaps, as a reciprocal manipulation of the symbols of euphemization.

I shall return to this issue later, but at this stage it is sufficient to note that the key symbols animating class relations in Sedaka—generosity, stinginess, arrogance, humility, help, assistance, wealth and poverty—do not constitute a set of given rules or principles that actors simply follow. They are instead the normative raw material that is created, maintained, changed, and above all manipulated by daily human activity. The argument I am making here about the norms surrounding the relations between rich and poor is very much like

---

7. E. P. Thompson, "Eighteenth-Century English Society: Class Struggle without Class," *Social History* 3, no. 2 (May 1978): 150.

8. In practice, he is likely to feel his way toward a request by hinting of the work that might be done or noting his own financial straits in order to ascertain in advance whether a request has a good chance of success. If a refusal seems likely, he will go no further, since an outright "no" would jeopardize the possibility of asking again in the future.

the distinction Bourdieu makes between "kinship systems" seen as "a closed, coherent set of purely logical relationships" that are obeyed and "kinship" as a practical activity of real social actors:

> In short, the logical relations of kinship to which the structuralist tradition ascribes a more or less complete autonomy with respect to economic determinants, and correlatively a near-perfect internal coherence, exist in practice only through and for the official and unofficial uses made of them by agents whose attachment to keeping them in working order and to making them work intensively—hence, through constant use, ever more easily—rises with the degree to which they actually or potentially fulfill functions indispensable to them or, *to put it less ambiguously, the extent to which they do or can satisfy vital material and symbolic interests.*[9]

As with kinship then, the objective of a social analysis of the ideology of class relations is not somehow to tease out a consensus of agreed-upon rules but rather to understand how divergent constructions of those rules and their application are related to class interests. Thus, it is hardly surprising to find that the poor in Sedaka work incessantly at maintaining, strengthening, and sanctioning a particular view of who is rich, who is poor, and how they should behave toward one another. Their view of what counts as decent conduct, their gossip, their account of the "facts," their use of nicknames, their view of what Islam requires, their strikes and boycotts, their selective appeals to customary practices are all bent toward a normative outlook that serves their material and symbolic interests. Since, as it happens, the transformation of production relations has worked largely to their disadvantage, they find themselves defending a large array of earlier practices.

The well-to-do villagers, for their part, also make use of the plasticity in any normative discourse to present themselves, their claims, and their interests in the best possible light. Their problem, as we have seen, however, is slightly different. They are unable simply to renounce the older practices and the normative assumptions lying behind them, but they are also unwilling to forgo the profit that respecting them would require. Thus they are largely driven to a construction of the "facts" that allows them to claim that the older practices are inapplicable. They assert, as we have seen, that the differences in income are negligible, that everyone here cultivates paddy on roughly the same footing, and that the conduct of those who are manifestly poor morally disqualifies them from any sympathetic consideration.

Two aspects of the ideological position of the rich deserve particular note. First, although it is rarely challenged in public, we know from unguarded derisive commentary by the poor that they hardly find it convincing—let alone hegemonic. Second, and equally important, the fact that the wealthy never

9. Bourdieu, *Outline,* 37–38.

explicitly deny the *principle* that the rich should be considerate of the needs of the poor—disputing rather the facts and their applicability to a particular case—means ironically that they themselves inadvertently "contribute to the—entirely official—survival of the rule."[10]

From a larger perspective, the ideological difficulties of the wealthy farmers in Sedaka stem from the fact that their economic behavior is increasingly based on the logic of the new market opportunities, while their social authority has been based on traditional forms of domination. They face, therefore, the classic ideological contradiction of the transition to more capitalist forms of production.[11] To the degree that the new production relations have prevailed, there is a corresponding decline in the social use of property and hence in the social authority of the propertied class.

The net result of the process has been that the large farmers and landlords affiliated with the ruling UMNO party have been losing their social grip on the poor. In the past, UMNO's political control of the countryside was predicated squarely on the social control that wealthier families could exercise over smallholders by virtue of relations of economic dependence, particularly tenancy and employment. It was enough for UMNO to attach to itself a large share of the wealthier villagers; their economic dependents were brought along as a matter of course. As the "organic" dependence of production relations has come unraveled, as profit has been steadily detached from social control over poorer villagers, these economic networks of local authority have become far more tenuous. They have not disappeared altogether but have become less numerous and less reliable. Those economic relations of dependence that remain, moreover, are now often organized more strictly by impersonal market forces—for example, *kupang* labor, leasehold tenancy, full and inflexible economic rents—so as to yield far less in terms of systematic social subordination.

It is worth recalling in this context that the inequitable distribution of paddy land in the Muda region has never in itself been legitimate. Most of the sizable landholdings in the area were, after all, acquired by *jual-janji* and other sharp dealings that took advantage of the periodic destitution of smallholders. As the stories about Haji Broom amply illustrate, the extent to which the privileged

10. Ibid., 40–41.

11. Raymond Williams, *The Country and the City* (New York: Oxford Univ. Press, 1973), 182. Their situation is not unlike that of English landowners in the early nineteenth century as described by Raymond Williams:

> Yet there was always a contradiction in English agrarian capitalism: its economics were those of a market order; its politics were those of a self-styled aristocracy and squirearchy, exacting quite different and "traditional" disciplines and controls.

Although there is hardly an aristocracy in Sedaka, it is nevertheless clear that mechanization, leasehold tenancy, and their consequences for the ties of subordination and dependency are incompatible with "traditional disciplines and controls."

position of rich landowners ever carried social authority (as opposed to control) with it was based only on the extent to which their property served the practical needs of poor villagers for tenancies, work, and assistance.[12] The connection I am emphasizing between social control and the social use of property is perhaps best captured in the example of self-styled charity—*zakat peribadi, fitrah* gifts, occasional loans, and alms. Such acts serve both to symbolize and to reaffirm the existing social hierarchy. Because they are so eminently divisible and discretionary, they are also used to single out the "deserving" poor for preferential treatment and thereby reinforce—at least publicly—their compliance with the norms of subordination.[13] Once the strategic rationale behind such charity loses its economic and political force, a major element of social control is also lost. Thus many villagers have effectively been "turned loose" to fend for themselves, and it is this that wealthy farmers are at pains to justify. The results of this "freedom" are as economically painful for the poor as they are financially rewarding for the rich. But they also undermine the basis of social domination by the propertied class.

This is not to imply that the large farmers of the village have lost their control of local affairs, let alone that they face an insurgent peasantry. What has occurred, however, is that the basis of their domination has been transformed. Their control, which was once embedded in the primary dependencies of production relations, is now based far more on law, property, coercion, market forces, and political patronage. They have themselves become much more dependent upon the state for their credit and inputs, for their supply of patronage resources, and for the ultimate force that guarantees their continued control over scarce land and capital. The rewarding ties that now inextricably bind much of this class to the state mean, of course, that its members have become increasingly vulnerable to any events (for example, a prolonged recession or a major political change) that might jeopardize their access and influence. It is ironic but entirely logical that this class has been so securely wedded to the state at precisely the

12. Poor villagers undoubtedly viewed such rationalizations with skepticism. The point is, however, that in any structure of organized inequality, the only possible justification for privilege must reside in its social function. When, as in Sedaka, the practical and self-interested actions of the rich that reinforce this rationale are largely abandoned, and only the rhetoric remains, the social authority of the propertied class is bound to suffer.

13. See, for example, Howard Newby, "The Deferential Dialectic, *Comparative Studies in Society and History* 17, no. 2 (April 1975): 161–64, and Brian Harrison, "Philanthropy and the Victorians," *Victorian Studies* 9, no. 4 (June 1966): 353–74. In another penetrating analysis of agrarian "patronage" by landowners, Ronald Herring suggests that the resources devoted to such activities be termed a "legitimacy fund." "Landlordism as a Social System: Quiescence and Protest in Kerala" (Paper presented to Annual Meeting of the Association for Asian Studies, San Francisco, March 23–27, 1983).

moment when its own autonomous control over subordinate classes is fast erod-ing. Lacking the economic control that grew from the earlier relations of pro-duction, lacking even an ideological position that is convincingly embedded in actual practices, this elite will now sink or swim depending on the resources for patronage, profit, and control the state can put at its disposal.

If the poorest strata of the rural population in Muda is no longer an integral part of paddy production, if they are no longer necessary to the process of surplus appropriation, one may reasonably wonder why wealthy farmers even bother to justify their new pattern of behavior at all. Why rationalize an agrarian system to those who are mostly irrelevant to it? Two observations are germane here. The first is that the justifications offered for the new behavior of rich farmers are in fact rather cursory, makeshift, and transparent. They are at any rate hardly convincing to those who have been disadvantaged. The second is that wealthy farmers are themselves the product of the earlier agrarian system and the nor-mative ideas that underpinned it; we should hardly be surprised if they choose to understand and explain the new arrangements in terms of the categories with which they are most familiar.

It might be supposed, however, that if ideological hegemony is increasingly unnecessary as a part of day-to-day production relations in rice farming, it has nevertheless been historically important for surplus appropriation by the state itself. Even this supposition would, I believe, be largely mistaken for any period after, say, 1900 in the paddy sector. The remarkable thing about the colonial and independent states of peninsular Malaya is how little they have depended on systematic appropriations from paddy cultivators. Taxes on paddy land have typically been minimal, and the local producer's price has often been above the world market price. State revenue in Kedah, even in the earlier colonial period, was derived largely from sources that impinged little on rural incomes. In 1918 and 1919, for example, the "tax farming" of the opium and gambling mono-polies provided the major sources of provincial revenue.[14] What the state has wanted, and continues to want, from the peasantry of the Muda Plain is a surplus of marketable rice at reasonable prices with which to feed the work force in mines, on plantations, and now in the urban areas. The vast majority of smallholders in Muda are, and have been, basically irrelevant even to this ob-jective. We need only recall that the great bulk (roughly three-fourths) of the paddy marketed in Muda is sold by a small minority (11 percent) of cultivators, who farm more than 10 relong. The surplus can, of course, now be produced largely without the labor power of the poor. And this labor power is not required elsewhere. Recent estimates show that the natural increase of the existing labor force now on plantations and in the cities will be more than sufficient for the

14. See, for example, Unfederated Malay States, Annual Report of the Advisor to the Kedah Government for each year. The pattern extends well back into the period of Thai control at the very least.

manpower needs of these sectors for the foreseeable future.[15] The plain fact is that the poorest two-thirds of the rural population in Muda is now basically irrelevant to the process of production or appropriation, whether by wealthy farmers or by the state itself.

If we wish, therefore, to understand the reasons for the continuing ideological efforts made by local elites and by the state to justify their domination, we will look in vain to production relations in the paddy sector. We must instead look to the realm of politics. In such a diversified, open, export economy, the revenue of the state is drawn mostly from export and import duties, the corporate income tax, licenses, concessions, excise taxes, and loans. If the conservative Malay elite is to continue benefiting from the privileges and opportunities the economy and the state provide, it must, as a basic precondition, maintain its political domination over that state. Given the semicompetitive election system that currently prevails, this objective requires the political support of the bulk of the Malay electorate.[16] The largest Malay-majority states of Kedah and Kelantan, which also happen to be the main paddy-growing regions, are necessary for that support. It is in this context that one can understand the very considerable efforts in the field of development programs, grants, clinics, schools, loans, and infrastructure that the state has undertaken with an acute eye to maximizing political support. One might even say that it is now the state and the ruling party that have taken over the task of euphemizing domination by means of their discretionary subsidies to rural areas. This euphemization is accomplished of course through the mediation of the wealthy, landowning, local UMNO elites. In any event, the political control of the paddy-growing peasantry is not an end in itself nor a means by which to justify a pattern of direct appropriation. Political control is an essential precondition for appropriation, which takes place elsewhere.

RETHINKING THE CONCEPT OF HEGEMONY

Our examination of class relations in Sedaka suggests rather forcefully that the concept of hegemony—of ideological domination—merits a fundamental rethinking. Such a rethinking, as I hope to show, is required not only in the context of the seventy families that have preoccupied us in this account, but for subordinate classes in general.

15. This is the import of the *Kedah Perlis Development Study: Interim Report,* by Economic Consultants Ltd. (Alor Setar: 1977), although the consultants expect an outmigration pattern similar to past experience to continue unabated. Even during the colonial period the need for urban workers and plantation labor was met largely by migrants from China and India rather than from the Malay population.

16. I do not doubt for a moment that, if this political domination were seriously threatened at the polls, the already hedged-about electoral system would be quickly dismantled, as it was following the riots of 1969.

The concept of hegemony, as it is used here, comes to us, of course, from the work of the remarkable Italian militant and scholar, Antonio Gramsci.[17] Since his prison writings became widely known, the concept has been employed in one fashion or another by a large number of influential, revisionist, Marxist scholars, including Althusser, Miliband, Poulantzas, Habermas, and Marcuse. The ultimate source in Marx and Engels's own writings from which this analytical tradition arises is the well-known passage from *The German Ideology* cited at length below:

> The ideas of the ruling class are in every epoch the ruling ideas: i.e. the class which is the ruling material force of society, is at the same time its ruling intellectual force. The class which has the means of material production at its disposal, has control at the same time over the means of mental production, so that thereby, generally speaking, the ideas of those who lack the means of mental production are subject to it. The ruling ideas are nothing more than the ideal expression of the dominant material relationships, the dominant material relationships grasped as ideas; hence of the relationships which make the one class the ruling one, therefore, the ideas of its dominance. The individuals composing the ruling class possess, among other things, consciousness, and therefore think. Insofar, therefore, as they rule as a class and determine the extent and compass of an epoch, it is evident that they do this in its whole range, hence among other things, rule also as thinkers, as producers of ideas, and regulate the production and distribution of the idea of their age: thus their ideas are the ruling ideas of the epoch.[18]

Hegemony is simply the name Gramsci gave to this process of ideological domination. The central idea behind it is the claim that the ruling class dominates not only the means of physical production but the means of symbolic production as well. Its control over the material forces of production is replicated, at the level of ideas, in its control over the ideological "sectors" of society—culture, religion, education, and the media—in a manner that allows it to disseminate those values that reinforce its position. What Gramsci did, in brief, was to explain the institutional basis of false-consciousness.

For my purposes, the critical implication of hegemony is that class rule is

17. Antoni Gramsci, *Selections from the Prison Notebooks,* ed. and trans. Quinten Hoare and Geoffrey Nowell Smith (London: Lawrence & Wishart, 1971). Ironically, Anderson writes that "hegemony" was first used by the Bolsheviks to refer to the domination the proletariat must establish over the peasantry to defeat the enemies of the revolution. As such it implies political control but not necessarily consent. Perry Anderson, "The Antinomies of Antonio Gramsci," *New Left Review* 100 (1976): 6.

18. Karl Marx and Friedrich Engels, *The German Ideology* (London: Lawrence & Wishart, 1965), 61.

effected not so much by sanctions and coercion as by the consent and passive compliance of subordinate classes. Hegemony, of course, may be used to refer to the entire complex of social domination. The term is used here, however, in its symbolic or idealist sense, since that is precisely where Gramsci's major contribution to Marxist thought lies. It is in fact the pervasiveness of ideological hegemony that normally suffices to ensure social peace and to relegate the coercive apparatus of the state to the background. Only "in anticipation of moments of crisis and command, when spontaneous consent has failed, is force openly resorted to."[19]

Exactly how voluntary and complete this hegemony is likely to be is not entirely clear, even on a close reading of Gramsci.[20] At times he appears to imply that hegemony involves an active belief in the legitimacy and superiority of the ruling group; at other times he implies that the acceptance is a more passive act in which the main features of the social order are merely accepted as given. Gramsci does, however, draw a sharp distinction between thought and action.[21] The concrete action of workers who defend their material interests may, for example, *suggest* a radical consciousness but, at the level of ideas—the level at which hegemony operates—that incipient radical consciousness is undermined by the substratum of values and perceptions socially determined from above. This blockage implies, as Femia notes, that "left to their own devices then, the masses in Western countries are powerless to overcome their intellectual and moral subordination. . . . The long and arduous process of demystification requires an external agency."[22] The function of the revolutionary party, then, is to provide the working class with the conceptual apparatus and "critical consciousness" it cannot produce on its own. Only such a party will be capable of breaking the hegemony of the bourgeoisie and replacing it with its own hegemony; this new hegemony is not, Gramsci insists, a consequence of revolution, but rather a precondition of an authentic revolution.[23]

Gramsci and other twentieth-century Marxists have, of course, developed their analysis of ideological domination in large part to explain why the material contradictions of capitalism as depicted in *Capital* have thus far failed to produce socialist revolution in the industrialized democracies. It was the manifest durability of capitalism that directed their attention forcibly to ideology and "superstructure." This attention was welcome and instructive in a number of ways.

19. Gramsci, *Selections,* 12.

20. See the excellent discussion by Joseph Femia, "Hegemony and Consciousness in the Thought of Antonio Gramsci," *Political Studies* 23, no. 1 (March 1975).

21. Gramsci, *Selections,* 326–27, 419.

22. Femia, "Hegemony," 35.

23. Gramsci, *Selections,* 57, 207. This implies, among other things, that the revolutionary party will somehow be able to create its own separate institutions, which will resist incorporation by the ruling class prior to the revolution. It was never clear how Gramsci tought this could occur.

First, it avoided the pitfall of the more extreme forms of economic determinism and accorded the realm of ideology, broadly conceived, a certain degree of autonomy. The very terms *hegemony* and *false-consciousness* are, after all, a clear admission that culture, values, and ideology cannot be directly read off objective, material conditions.[24] But in making long overdue room for the analysis of ideological domination per se, many of Gramsci's successors have, it seems to me, substituted a kind of ideological determinism for the material determinism they sought to avoid. Curiously enough, Gramsci's own work is less open to this charge than the more purely theoretical elaborations of those who have followed in this tradition (for example, Miliband and Althusser).[25]

I hope to show in what follows that the notion of hegemony and its related concepts of false-consciousness, mystification, and ideological state apparatuses not only fail to make sense of class relations in Sedaka, but also are just as likely to mislead us seriously in understanding class conflict in most situations.[26] The gist of the argument to be developed at some length is summarized very briefly below and will serve to order the subsequent discussion:

First, the concept of hegemony ignores the extent to which most subordinate classes are able, on the basis of their daily material experience, to penetrate and demystify the prevailing ideology.

Second, theories of hegemony frequently confound what is inevitable with what is just, an error that subordinate classes rarely, if ever, make. This conclusion stems from a surface examination of public action in power-laden situations that overlooks both the "hidden transcript" and the necessity of routine and pragmatic submission to the "compulsion of economic relations" as well as the realities of coercion.

Third, a hegemonic ideology must, by definition, represent an idealization, which therefore inevitably creates the contradictions that permit it to be criticized *in its own terms.* The ideological source of mass radicalism is, in this sense, to be sought as much *within* a prevailing ideological order as outside it.

Fourth, a historical examination of the rank and file of nearly any manifestly revolutionary mass movement will show that the objectives sought are usually

24. See, for example, Philip Carl Salzman, "Culture as Enhabilments," in *The Structure of Folk Models,* ed. Ladislav Holy and Milan Stuchlik, ASA Monograph No. 20 (New York: Academic, 1981), 233–56.

25. It is perhaps not entirely surprising that intellectuals further removed from political combat and from the working class itself have fastened on analysis that ascribes a nearly coercive influence to the product of their own class, that is, ideology!

26. I am indebted for parts of the following analysis to the excellent general critique of hegemony in its various guises by Nicholas Abercrombie, Stephen Hill, and Bryan S. Turner, *The Dominant Ideology Thesis* (London: Allen & Unwin, 1980), as well as to the more polemical—and entertaining—broadside against Althusser in E. P. Thompson's *The Poverty of Theory and Other Essays* (New York: Monthly Review Press, 1978), 1–210.

limited and even reformist in tone, although the means adopted to achieve them may be revolutionary. Thus, "trade union consciousness" is not, as Lenin claimed, the major obstacle to revolution, but rather the only plausible basis for it.

Fifth, historically, the breaking of the norms and values of a dominant ideology is typically the work of the bearers of a new mode of production—for example, capitalists—and *not* of subordinate classes such as peasants and workers. Thus, subordinate classes are often seen as backward looking, inasmuch as they are defending their own interpretation of an earlier dominant ideology against new and painful arrangements imposed by elites and/or the state.

Penetration[27]

If there were a dominant, hegemonic ideology in Sedaka, it would make its presence known in several ways. At a minimum, it would require that the beliefs and values of the agrarian elite penetrate and dominate the worldview of the poor so as to elicit their consent and approval of an agrarian order which, materially, does not serve their objective interests. Its function would be to conceal or misrepresent the real conflicts of class interests that we have examined and to make of the poor, in effect, coconspirators in their own victimization.

We have surely heard enough from the poorer farmers in Sedaka to reject, out of hand, such a summary characterization of their ideological situation. If there is any penetration to be accounted for here, it is less the penetration of elite beliefs among the poor than the capacity of the poor to pierce, in almost every particular, the self-serving picture presented by wealthy farmers, landlords, and outside officials. It is true, of course, that the rights and claims the poor assert are essentially those prevailing before double-cropping. Perhaps, in this sense, they can be seen as appealing to a (pre-)existing hegemonic order. I shall return to this issue later, but here I should note at once that such an appeal is in their material interest and that the rich subscribe, in their own way, to the same values, although their economic behavior is now predicated along more nearly capitalist lines. Ironically, it is the wealthy of Sedaka who fail to subscribe to the ideology that would best explain how they behave and provide a plausible rationale for that behavior.

There is every good reason to suppose that the effective penetration of "official" realities by Sedaka's poor is not unique or rare but, in fact, commonplace. To view the peasantry of Sedaka as particularly insightful is grossly to overestimate

27. The term *penetration* as used here is borrowed from two sources: Anthony Giddens, *Central Problems in Social Theory: Action, Structure, and Contradiction in Social Analysis* (Berkeley: Univ. of California Press, 1979), and Paul Willis, *Learning to Labour* (Westmead: Saxon House, 1977). I am indebted particularly to Willis's study of working-class school culture, which is a remarkable combination of careful ethnography and subtle ideological analysis grounded securely in class experience.

the power, weight, and cohesiveness of any dominant ideology. Here I subscribe fully to Paul Willis's trenchant critique of Althusser:

> Structuralist theories of reproduction present the dominant ideology (under which culture is subsumed) as impenetrable. Everything fits too neatly. Ideology always pre-exists and preempts any authentic criticism. There are no cracks in the billiard ball smoothness of process. All specific contradictions are smoothed away in the universal reproductive functions of ideology. . . . on the contrary, and in my view more optimistically . . . there are deep disfunctions and desperate tensions within social and cultural reproduction. Social agents are not passive bearers of ideology, but active appropriators who reproduce existing structures only through struggle, contestation, and a partial penetration of those structures.[28]

The penetration of official platitudes by any subordinate class is to be expected both because those platitudes are unlikely to be as cohesive or uniform as is often imagined *and* because they are subject to different interpretations depending on the social position of the actors. Such divergent understandings are, in turn, rooted in daily experience. The platitudes are not received as disembodied symbolic messages but are given meaning only in the context of a continuing struggle to defend material interests.[29]

The process by which any system of political or religious beliefs emanating from above is reinterpreted, blended with pre-existing beliefs, penetrated, and transformed is characteristic of any stratified society. In this sense, one can speak in an agrarian society of "folk" socialism, "folk" nationalism, and "folk" communism just as one speaks of folk religion. If the form of Christianity believed in and practiced in the slave quarters is quite distinctive from the form of Christianity believed in and taught by the masters, we should not be surprised if tenants have an understanding of paternalism that is not at all like the one

---

28. Willis, *Learning to Labour,* 175. Giddens writes that one of his "leading theorems" is that "every social actor knows a great deal about the conditions of reproduction of the society of which he or she is a member." *Central Problems,* 5 and see also 72.

29. The failure to link ideology with actual class experience is often responsible for unwarranted conclusions. As Abercrombie et al., *Dominant Ideology Thesis,* 141, analyzing the research of others, concludes, "Workers will often agree with dominant elements, especially when these are couched as abstract principles or refer to general situations, which is normally the case in interview surveys using standardized questionnaires, but will then accept deviant values when they themselves are directly involved or when these are expressed in concrete terms which correspond to everyday reality." They go on to note that the "confusion" in working-class ideology is no more than one may find among dominant groups. P. 144.

held by their landlords.[30] The principles by which these belief systems originating outside the peasantry are transformed are varied, but it is clear that, in large part, they are reinterpreted in line with the material and symbolic interests of the class receiving them. Deviant interpretations—ideological heterodoxy—are hardly astonishing when they arise among subordinate classes which, by definition, have the least stake in the official description of reality.[31]

One may perhaps take this logic one step further and contend, as some have, that the normative incorporation of subordinate classes is simply "not a necessary requirement of social order."[32] Abercrombie and his collaborators, in their general critique of "the dominant ideology thesis," make a persuasive case that neither capitalism nor feudalism has been successful in achieving the internalization of the dominant ideology by subordinate classes. They explain this failure by the weakness of the mechanisms of socialization (another name for the strength of resistance?) and by the effectiveness of other forms of coercion, including the constraints that produce what we have earlier called "routine compliance." From this perspective, the function of the dominant ideology may be largely to secure the cohesion of dominant classes, while the conformity of subordinate classes rests instead primarily on their knowledge that any other course is impractical, dangerous, or both.

If this logic is applicable to the working class in advanced capitalist nations, as is claimed, then it is surely more forcefully applicable to the working class of early capitalism and to the peasantry of the Third World. This is so because the institutional bases of hegemony—for example, schools, media—are simply thicker on the ground in late capitalism and presumably therefore more effective.[33] By contrast, the early working class was, by most accounts, virtually

30. For slave society, see Eugene D. Genovese, *Roll, Jordan Roll: The World the Slaves Made* (New York: Pantheon, 1974). For the process in general, see my "Hegemony and the Peasantry," *Politics and Society* 7, no. 3 (1977), and "Protest and Profanation: Agrarian Revolt and the Little Tradition," *Theory and Society* 4, nos. 1 and 2 (1977). For other works that bear directly on this theme, see R. C. Cobb, *The Police and the People: French Popular Protest, 1789–1820* (Oxford: Clarendon, 1970); McKim Marriott, "Little Communities in an Indigenous Civilization," in *Village India,* ed. McKim Marriott (Chicago: Univ. of Chicago Press, 1955); and Christopher Hill, *The World Turned Upside Down* (New York: Viking, 1972).

31. "In general, the fewer the rewards a society offers to a particular group . . . the more autonomous that group will prove to be with reference to the norms of the society." Lee Rainwater, "Crucible of Identity: The Negro Lower Class Family," *Daedalus* 95 (1966): 212, cited in Lawrence W. Levine, *Black Culture and Black Consciousness* (New York: Oxford Univ. Press, 1977), 283.

32. Abercrombie et al., *Dominant Ideology Thesis,* 50.

33. Religion is perhaps an exception, but here we have only to look at the way both the early working class and the peasantry create their own sects and religious understandings outside official orthodoxy, including revolutionary millennial beliefs.

outside the institutional framework of capitalism in nearly every respect except their work. As Engels observed in his study of the nineteenth-century English working class:

> The workers speak other dialects, have other thoughts and ideals, other customs and moral principles, a different religion and other politics than those of the bourgeoisie. Thus they are two radically dissimilar nations as unlike as difference of race could make them.[34]

The peasantry, if anything, is even further removed from the institutional circuits of symbolic power. Living outside the cities where the agencies of hegemony are quartered, operating largely within an oral tradition that somewhat insulates it from printed media, being an old class (unlike the proletariat) with its own cultural traditions and patterns of resistance, and having its own shadow institutions (for example, informal religious schools, rituals, and festivals), the peasantry is simply less accessible to hegemonic practice. When we add to this the fact that the material and symbolic interests of poor peasants are likely to make them skeptical of a dominant ideology that rationalizes their material deprivation and low status, we can appreciate why they might resist "symbolic incorporation."

The fact that the penetration of official reality by the poor is so apparent in the case of Sedaka is reason to wonder how it could escape notice in any other comparable situation. It could, however, be overlooked if one observed only the public encounters between rich and poor ("the partial transcript") and ignored entirely the insinuations beneath the surface, the discussion outside the context of power relations, and the anonymous, quiet acts of routine practical resistance that occur daily.[35] For it is in the immediate interest of most poor villagers to uphold the official realities in nearly all power-laden contexts. The partial transcript, taken alone, therefore would create the impression of mystification. But we would commit the error of not realizing that mystification and impression management are as much a pose of the powerless as ideological domination by

---

For example, see the fascinating discussion of "peripheral spirits" and forms of possession that characterize women and also men of low status in many societies in I. M. Lewis, *Ecstatic Religion: An Anthropological Study of Spirit Possession and Shamanism* (Harmondsworth: Penguin, 1971).

34. Friedrich Engels, *The Condition of the Working Class in England* (Moscow: Progress Publishers, 1973), 162–63. The cultural gulf was noted by conservatives as well, for example by Disraeli in *Sybil: or the Two Nations,* which Engels cites approvingly.

35. Giddens, writing of the working class, notes, "To mistake pragmatic, ironic (for example, working to rule), humorous, distanced participation in the routines of alienated labour for normative consensus, was one of the great errors of the orthodox academic sociology of the 1950's and 60's." *Central Problems,* 148.

the rich. Gramsci is, I believe, misled when he claims that the radicalism of subordinate classes is to be found more in their acts than in their beliefs. It is more nearly the reverse. The realm of behavior—particularly in power-laden situations—is precisely where dominated classes are most constrained. And it is at the level of beliefs and interpretations—where they can safely be ventured—that subordinate classes are least trammeled. The rich in Sedaka can usually insist on conforming public behavior and get it; they can neither insist on private ideological conformity, nor do they need it.[36]

Inevitability, Naturalization, and Justice

There is another more sophisticated and influential argument for mystification and false-consciousness that does not depend upon the presumed ability of dominant classes to impose their own beliefs on subordinate classes. If the idea of hegemony implies something that is done to lower orders by those above them, this second position implies that mystification is something that subordinate classes do, in part at least to themselves, given the force of circumstances. Briefly put, the argument is that a system of social domination often appears to be inevitable. Once it is considered inevitable, the logic goes, it is apt to be considered natural even by those who are disadvantaged by it, and there is a tendency to consider whatever is natural also to be just or legitimate. The most limited statement of this position, one that omits the last step and carefully avoids equating natural with legitimate, is found in Richard Hoggart's fine analysis of English working-class culture:

> When people feel that they cannot do much about the main elements of their situation, feel it not necessarily with despair or disappointment or resentment, but simply as a fact of life, they adopt attitudes toward that situation which allow them to have a liveable life under its shadow, a life without a constant and pressing sense of the larger situation. The attitudes remove the main elements in the situation to the *realm of natural laws,* the given and now, the almost implacable material from which a living has to be carved. Such attitudes, at their least adored, a fatalism or plain accepting, are generally below the tragic level; they have too much of the conscript's lack of choice about them.[37]

Barrington Moore, who is more generally concerned with historical patterns of systematic subordination, does not hesitate to take the final step of associating inevitability with justice and legitimacy:

36. Juan Martinez Alier's analysis of Andalusian agricultural laborers is quite detailed and convincing on this score. *Labourers and Landowners in Southern Spain,* St. Anthony's College, Oxford, Publications, No. 4 (London: Allen & Unwin, 1971), chap. 1.
37. *The Uses of Literacy* (London: Chatto & Windus, 1954), 77–78, emphasis added.

In varying degrees and in different ways all these people felt that their sufferings were unavoidable. For some victims such suffering appeared to a degree inevitable and legitimate. People are evidently inclined to grant legitimacy to anything that is or seems inevitable no matter how painful it may be. Otherwise the pain might be intolerable.[38]

Piven and Cloward echo Moore's assessment in their study of poor people's movements in the United States:

However hard their lot may be, people usually remain quiescent, conforming to the accustomed patterns of daily life in their community, and believing those patterns to be both inevitable and just.[39]

What is described appears to be akin to the "naturalization" of the inescapable—a reification of the "dull compulsion of economic relations" that is here to stay.[40] Thus, Bourdieu writes of certain beliefs as being "unthinkable" and of the inclination of social "agents" "to make a virtue of necessity," that is, "to refuse what is anyway refused and to love the inevitable."[41]

Except for very rare and special circumstances to which I shall return later, I believe all of these closely related arguments for mystification to be either misleading or wrong—or both. First, they provide no convincing logic for the process by which the inevitable becomes just. Second, they ignore the great variety of ways in which the notion of inevitability itself can be, and is, negated by the historical practice of subordinate classes. I shall take up each issue in turn.

38. *The Social Bases of Obedience and Revolt* (White Plains: M. E. Sharpe, 1978), 458–59. Elsewhere Moore notes, "What is or appears to be unavoidable must also somehow be just." Ibid., 64. As usual, Moore is so scrupulous about disconfirming evidence that his bold position is somewhat qualified in his case studies. The addition of "some" and "to a degree" in the second sentence of the citation is a more accurate reflection of his position than the final sentence. It is worth noting that the only reason he gives for the transformation of the inevitable into the "just" is similar to Hoggart's, namely, the desire of victims to somehow escape the constant psychological pain of living in an intolerable situation that must nevertheless be endured.

39. Frances Fox Piven and Richard A. Cloward, *Poor People's Movements: Why They Succeed, How They Fail* (New York: Vintage, 1977), 6.

40. One might expect these conclusions from scholars of a conservative bent except for the fact that the problem itself requires a prior recognition of situations that could be described as exploitive. I have quoted from these writers especially because they could all be described as left-wing scholars working on socialist issues, broadly defined. This general process is very much what Bourdieu had in mind when he wrote that "every established order tends to produce . . . the naturalization of its own arbitrariness"—an effect produced in part by "a sense of limits" and a "sense of reality." Bourdieu, *Outline*, 164.

41. Ibid., 77.

The inherent plausibility of the argument for this particular form of false-consciousness rests on the plain fact that the larger contours of the stratification system within which most subordinate classes have lived out their lives must surely have seemed inevitable and hence natural. It is unlikely, the reasoning goes, that the untouchables in nineteenth-century India, the serfs in thirteenth-century France, or perhaps even the tenants in Sedaka today could seriously entertain the possibility of raising their basic status, let alone of living in a world without castes, lords, or landords. And even if they could, they would be unlikely to devote much time or thought to possibilities that appear to be entirely excluded as practical goals. This argument, as I understand it, asks us to believe that, for subordinate classes, the larger structure of domination is typically experienced in the same way a peasant might experience the weather. If we accept this analogy for the sake of argument, it is not at all clear why the weather, which is surely inevitable, unavoidable, and even fated should, on this basis alone, be considered either just or legitimate. It is far more plausible to assume that the concepts of justice or legitimacy are simply irrelevant to something that is inescapably *there,* like the weather. There is no logical warrant for equating justice and inevitability virtually as a matter of definition; in the absence of further evidence, whatever is inevitable is simply that and no more. In fact, the analogy with the weather is instructive at another level. The inevitability of the weather has not prevented every group of traditional cultivators from personifying this natural force or from developing rituals to influence its course or, when their efforts have failed, from cursing their fate. Thus, far from removing it to the realm of the inevitable, the peasantry has historically considered even the weather to be amenable to human manipulation. If there is any "mystification" of natural laws in traditional societies, it is in the direction of bringing them under human control, not the reverse.[42]

I shall return to the critique of inevitability later, but first it is worthwhile to consider why inevitability should be so frequently confounded with legitimacy. *Appearances,* of course, nearly always seem to confirm the legitimacy of the inevitable. No matter how conscious members of a subordinate class may be of having gotten a raw deal, the daily pressure of making a living and the risks of open defiance are usually enough to skew the ethnographic record systematically in the direction of compliance, if not acceptance, of the inevitable. Here again, however, resignation to what seems inevitable is not the same as according it legitimacy, although it may serve just as efficiently to produce daily compliance. A certain tone of resignation is entirely likely in the face of a situation that cannot, in the short run, be materially altered. When the poor in Sedaka talk about combine-harvesters and say, "It doesn't matter whether you protest or not,

---

42. See, for example, Maurice Godelier, "Fetishism, Religion and Marx's General Theories Concerning Ideology," in his *Perspectives in Marxist Anthropology,* trans. Robert Brain, Cambridge Studies in Social Anthropology, No. 18 (Cambridge: Cambridge Univ. Press, 1977), 169–85.

nothing comes of it," they are merely expressing a realistic, pragmatic, view of the situation as they experience it. They have tried to stop the combines and have failed. They certainly must adapt to the consequences, but this hardly implies approval. In this respect their situation is no different from that of most subordinate classes most of the time. Except for those comparatively rare moments when a political opening or a revolutionary situation creates new possibilities or revives old aspirations, an attitude of pragmatic resignation is likely to prevail.[43]

Compliance can of course flow either from grudging resignation or from active ideological support. What we should not do, however, is to infer ideological support even from the most apparently faithful compliance. To prove the case for ideological support—for hegemony—one would have to supply *independent* evidence that the values of the subordinate class are in fact largely in accord with those of the dominant elite. Such evidence, to be credible, would have to come from social contexts in which members of the subordinate class were least constrained by power relations.

There is another reason why the ethnographic record, even where it is collected with a view to minimizing the constraints of power, may be skewed in the direction of apparent acceptance. This is because the record is invariably oriented toward the quotidian and rarely contains much discussion of options that seem out of reach.[44] The smallholders in Sedaka, for example, do not talk about land reform. When I raised the subject with them, however, they were almost uni-

43. Thus Abercrombie, Hill, and Turner, in their analysis of the "quiescence" of the English working class in the decades just after 1850, find no evidence of effective indoctrination or normative approval, but rather a "factual" acceptance of "the economic order of capitalism and its class based social organization." *Dominant Ideology Thesis,* 122). John Gaventa, in his study of Appalachian coal miners, also finds an attitude of resignation and even demoralization. But this attitude, far from being evidence of ideological hegemony or approval, "is not irrational. . . . It has been instilled historically through repeated experiences of failure." *Power and Powerlessness: Quiescence and Rebellion in an Appalachian Valley* (Urbana: Univ. of Illinois Press, 1980), 254. Finally, Alier's detailed analysis of Andalusian farm workers carefully distinguishes compliance from legitimacy. "Andalusian labourers choose conduct which is compatible with the maintenance of *latifundismo* and the social structure based upon it; but they also have values which *would* result in conduct incompatible with its maintenance. If they do not adopt these forms of conduct, it is because of controls, which are not social sanctions derived from the agro-town's value system, but rather political controls exercised from the provincial capital and from Madrid, and because they remember with fear the period after 1936." *Labourers and Landowners in Southern Spain,* 314–15.

44. It is just such attention to the quotidian that gives rise to the notion that traditional social structures are accepted as a matter of fatalism—in Malay, *rezeki.* There is surely no doubt that, as a practical matter, adaptation to circumstances that cannot be changed, at least in the short run, imposes itself coercively. To conclude that this is the end of the matter, however, is not warranted, as we shall see below.

formly enthusiastic, as one might expect, often suggesting that 10 relong of paddy land was sufficient to provide the well-off with a comfortable living. But it was not a subject that ever arose spontaneously, since it was purely academic; it had never been broached by either of the political parties with which they are familiar nor by agricultural officials. Their attention was, instead, more realistically focused on the possibility of securing a reasonable tenancy within the existing system of landownership.[45] However desirable, it is simply not a realistic goal under present circumstances.

From a much more modest view of what hegemony is all about, it might be said that the main function of a system of domination is to accomplish precisely this: to define what is realistic and what is not realistic and to drive certain goals and aspirations into the realm of the impossible, the realm of idle dreams, of wishful thinking. There is surely a good deal to be said for this limited construction of hegemony, since it recognizes the vital impact of power on the definition of what is practical. If we adopt this more plausible notion of hegemony, however, at least two qualifications are in order. First, we are no longer speaking of justice and legitimacy, but only of the more or less rational understanding of what is achievable in a given situation. Second, and more important, this view is decidedly static, as it systematically excludes from our analysis just *how* the realm of the possible might, in new circumstances, be expanded.[46] While it is true that the poor in Sedaka do not now consider land reform a real option, it is also true that their view of current inequities, their resentment of large landowners, and their off-the-record bitterness all suggest powerfully that they might well become enthusiastic supporters of land reform *if* it were to become a historical option. What is nothing more than idle speculation today may become a realistic goal tomorrow, and we will best infer the possible response of the peasantry not from what they now consider possible but rather from their overall evaluation of the social order within which they live.[47] One would not expect, for example, to find French peasants talking, in 1788, about the chateaux they would be sacking in 1789 or Russian peasants discussing, in 1916, the land seizures they would be carrying out the following year. What one could have found in all likelihood, however, were attitudes about the aristocracy and land rights that were entirely consistent with their later actions.

45. I recognize that no social context is entirely free from power relations. The opinions expressed by the powerless are often constrained as well by the opinions of their peers. There is no "true" transcript in the sense of a transcript that is entirely unconstrained. What I am comparing here are relative degrees of constraint.

46. Andalusian workers, similarly, do not often speak of *reparto,* or land distribution, although it was at one time long ago a real option and is still considered the only just solution to inequity.

47. Here I bracket temporarily the fact that it is often the action of subordinate classes that may be influential in creating new possibilities, including often those not foreseen by the actors themselves.

Having shown how pragmatic resignation and the relative absence of currently implausible objectives from class discourse might mimic the effects of hegemony, it remains to consider one final argument for linking inevitability to hegemony. This is the case that Barrington Moore makes on the basis of accounts from Nazi concentration camps and, to a lesser extent, accounts of the Hindu caste system. He contends that there *are* situations in which oppression is exercised so totally and so pervasively that the poses so often necessary to the powerless— flattery, deference, and so forth—represent the whole reality, the whole transcript, of subordinate groups. Noting that "it is very difficult to act a mask or a role continually without acquiring the character that goes with the role," he asks, in effect, what happens when the mask must be worn at all times.[48] The question of legitimacy and justice, he implies, hardly arises at all, since the realm of necessity exhausts the whole of human conduct. At this extreme it is possible to show, as Moore does, that *some* victims do indeed come to identify with the oppressor and to copy both his behavior and his values.[49] But the very extremity of the measures required to achieve this end make it, for my purpose, precisely the exception that proves the rule. As the most total of institutions, the Nazi concentration camp systematically set about destroying every vestige of independent social life. The victims, before they were murdered, were stripped of all possessions and family, worked to the extremes of exhaustion, underfed to

48. Another way of phrasing this issue is to focus on the unavoidable duality— or multiplicity—of subordinate class consciousness. Much of the daily struggle to make a living, as we have seen in the case of Hamzah and others, necessarily involves appeals to the normative system of the dominant class—flattery, deference, obsequious polite forms of address, and so forth. There will almost invariably be other offstage values as well that may contradict such poses. And yet, we are not entirely justified in treating the former as merely insincere poses and the latter as the truth. In situations where the exercise of power is quite pervasive, the offstage discourse may be confined to the nooks and crannies of social life, thereby making the formulas for action imposed by elites hegemonic in practice. Arnold Strickon, writing of an Argentine agro-town, notes that the gauchos have two sets of stratification terms: one is cast entirely in patron–client terms, the other is class based. The first, however, dominates daily life in the local context; it is both explanatory *and* strategic for lower-class action. The second is more appropriate to the rare occasions of provincial and national elections. An observer might plausibly conclude that traditional, clientelist consciousness dominated, but this conclusion would merely amount to the observation that the situational context relevant to that style of action was dominant. If the situational context relevant to class discourse were to become more frequent, so would class terminology and action. What one would be observing then would be not so much a change in consciousness per se as a shift in the relative frequency of situational contexts relevant to one style of action as opposed to another. "Folk Models of Stratification, Political Ideology, and Socio-cultural Systems," *Sociological Review Monographs,* No. 11 (1967), 93–117.

49. Moore, *Injustice,* 464.

the point of starvation, brutalized both systematically *and* capriciously, while their waking life was minutely controlled by the guards. No effort was spared to destroy all networks of informal solidarity and thoroughly to atomize the prisoners. Virtually the only autonomous choice left was that of suicide. What is remarkable is not that such extremity produces a certain "identification with the oppressor" but rather that only "*some* concentration camp inmates came to accept the moral authority of their oppressors."[50]

One might, in this context, compare different forms of oppression by the degree to which they allow their victims some semblance of an autonomous social existence. By this criterion, the concentration camp would lie at one extreme, followed perhaps by mental asylums and civilian and military prisons. Here one might plausibly expect that atomization and nearly total control might achieve a perverse moral authority.[51] The fact is, however, that all of the "routine" and historically common patterns of social subordination and exploitation— slavery, serfdom, sharecropping, or even wage labor—are unlike the concentration camp in that their "victims" retain considerable autonomy to construct a life and a culture not entirely controlled by the dominant class.[52] In other words there are, for each of these groups, situations in which the mask of obsequiousness, deference, and symbolic compliance *may* be lifted. This realm of relatively "safe" discourse, however narrow, is a necessary condition for the development of symbolic resistance—a social space in which the definitions and performances imposed by domination do not prevail.[53] This social space is, moreover, defined not only by the absence of vertical power relations but by the presence of sanctions and influence exercised by others who find themselves in the same boat.[54] Thus,

50. In his analysis, Moore (*Injustice,* 64) relies heavily on Bruno Bettelheim, *The Informed Heart: Autonomy in a Mass Age* (Glencoe, Ill.: Free Press, 1960). For an account of how various forms of moral and organized resistance can grow in only slightly less draconian conditions, see Emmanuel Rigelblum, *Notes From the Warsaw Ghetto,* trans. Jacob Sloan (New York: Schocken, 1974).

51. Especially, perhaps, in mental institutions and civilian prisons where there is at least an ideology claiming that they are operated for the ultimate benefit of their inmates. Even here, however, control is not total and resistance is evident. See, for example, Erving Goffman, *Asylums* (New York: Anchor Books, Doubleday, 1961), and Jack Henry Abbot, *In the Belly of the Beast* (New York: Vintage, 1982).

52. Such autonomy, it is often pointed out, is not simply a failure of control but is necessary to the very functioning of the institution.

53. The dominant class may make efforts to infiltrate this social space with spies. The effect of such spies may be less the information they carry back than the way in which the fear of spies itself may neutralize a possible realm of autonomous discourse.

54. The monoclass village under the domination of a single outside landlord thus has marked advantages for class mobilization that are not confined to the fact that the material situation of all villagers is more or less the same. They also have a realm of autonomous discourse that is coterminous with the village itself.

when Pak Yah gathers on his steps with a few other laborers and smallholders who belong to PAS, the discourse is not only different from what one would hear if Basir or Haji Kadir were present, but its content is influenced by the social fact that the men gathered are both poor and opposed to UMNO. This influence is stronger by virtue of the fact that these men also depend on one another for a wide array of petty favors and exchanges; there are power relations here too, although they are more nearly reciprocal and balanced. If the exercise of domination depends upon a social context for its creation and maintenance, so does the exercise of resistance.[55]

It is, of course, theoretically possible for the discourse found even in "non-mask" situations to conform in most or all particulars with the dominant ideology. But whenever we are dealing with any of the large-scale structures of social subordination, which invariably imply both the appropriation of labor and the assignment of inferior, if not degrading, status to its subjects, this is unlikely. Thus, there is some evidence that the untouchable castes in India, when they may do so safely, reject much of the stigmatized identity assigned to them by the caste system.[56] The work of Genovese and others reveals that, in the slave quarters of the antebellum South, one encountered a set of values very different from those that officially prevailed.[57] There was a religious emphasis on liberation and equality drawn from Old Testament texts, a profane view both of the masters and of slavery, justifications for resistance in the form of theft, pilfering, flight, and shirking. Not all of these attitudes were incompatible, as Genovese notes, with the continuation of slavery as a system, but they were decidedly different from the dominant ideology. The subculture created in the slave quarter was normally hidden from the master's view. It might, however, occasionally intrude onto the public stage when strong drink temporarily overcame the slaves' normal caution. As Mullin notes in his study of slavery in nineteenth-century Virginia:

> While drunkenness tends to leave most people either quiet and withdrawn, or out-going and loud-spoken, acculturating slaves when drunk and addressing their masters—with no exceptions—were always "bold," "obstinate," "daring," "impudent," or "turbulent."[58]

Except for those rare instances when the curtain is momentarily parted, the

55. We know enough from ingenious psychological experiments to conclude that resistance to domination increases markedly once there is the slightest possibility of social support for it from peers. See Stanley Milgram, *Obedience to Authority: An Experimental View* (New York: Harper & Row, 1974), 116–21.

56. Joan P. Mencher, "On Being an Untouchable in India: A Materialist Perspective," in *Beyond the Myths of Culture: Essays in Cultural Materialism,* ed. Eric B. Ross (New York: Academic, 1980), 261–94.

57. Genovese, *Roll, Jordan, Roll.*

58. Gerald W. Mullin, *Flight and Rebellion: Slave Resistance in Eighteenth-Century Virginia* (New York: Oxford Univ. Press, 1972), 100.

relatively uncensored subculture of subordinate classes must be sought in those locales, behind the scenes, where it is created—in all those social situations outside the immediate surveillance of the dominant class. Given its shadowy but palpable existence in informal discourse, this subculture is unlikely to be a systematic refutation of the dominant ideology. One does not expect *Das Kapital* to come from working-class pubs, although one may get something quite close to the labor theory of value! Unless the curtains are parted by open revolt, political freedoms, or a revolution that allows the subculture to take on a public, institutionalized life, it will remain elusive and masked. What is certain, however, is that, while domination may be inevitable as a social fact, it is unlikely also to be hegemonic as an ideology within that small social sphere where the powerless may speak freely.

My argument to this point has focused on the danger of equating the possible fact of inevitability with the norms of justice and legitimacy, even though the ethnographic record may encourage it. I have also stressed the importance, in anything short of total institutions, of an autonomous sphere in which the values of elites may be contested despite their practical inevitability. Completing this critique requires that I also reexamine the concept of inevitability itself, a term I have thus far taken for granted. The question is not whether or not a given structure of domination is inevitable at a factual level, since no historically contingent state of affairs is inevitable in that sense. The question is rather the extent to which a system of domination can be made to appear inevitable to those who live in it and under it.

The first problem is to specify exactly what it is that is "inevitable." If it is taken to mean a pattern of domination in all its historical particulars, then it is clear that no system is inevitable to its subjects in this sense. To imagine that long-established systems such as feudalism or slavery were, even in their heyday, so inevitable that those who lived within them were not constantly trying— and succeeding—to modify their contours is to ascribe an unwarranted "thing-ness" to any social order.

If, however, by "inevitable" we mean the central features of a mode of domination, not just its details, then the argument for perceived inevitability becomes far more plausible. From one perspective, the argument is in fact both self-evident and coercive. How would it be possible for a thirteenth-century French serf or an eighteenth-century Indian untouchable, neither of whom we may assume had any experience of any social order other than the one into which he was born, to conceive of anything else than what he knew, namely, feudalism or the caste system? It is but a short logical step to claim that these cognitive limitations rule out, in principle, any possible revolutionary consciousness. If the fish do not talk about the water, how can we expect them to talk about the air? Such reasoning seems to lie behind Jean-Paul Sartre's position:

For it is necessary to reverse the common opinion and acknowledge that it is not the harshness of a situation or the sufferings it imposes which lead people to conceive of another state of affairs in which things would be better for everybody. It is on the day when we are able to conceive of another state of affairs, that a new light is cast on our trouble and our suffering and we *decide* that they are unbearable.[59]

This position is, I believe, quite wrong. On my reading of the evidence it is in fact more plausible to contend that *so far as the realm of ideology is concerned, no social order seems inevitable,* even in this larger sense, to all of its subjects. The fact that serfs, slaves, or untouchables have no direct knowledge or experience of other social orders is, I believe, no obstacle to their creating what would have to qualify as "revolutionary" thought. To argue along these lines is not so much to refute Sartre as it is to show that the imaginative capacity of subordinate groups to reverse and/or negate dominant ideologies is so widespread—if not universal—that it might be considered part and parcel of their standard cultural and religious equipment. Here again we may stand Gramsci on his head; subordinate classes—especially the peasantry—are likely to be more radical at the level of ideology than at the level of behavior, where they are more effectively constrained by the daily exercise of power.

The argument against inevitability may be made at two levels. As I have made this case at much greater length elsewhere, I shall confine myself to a summary exposition.[60] The first point to be made is that, even if one accepts that the serf, the slave, and the untouchable will have trouble imagining social arrangements other than feudalism, slavery, or caste, they will certainly not find it difficult to imagine reversing the distribution of status and rewards within that social order. In a great many societies, such a simple feat of the imagination is not just an abstract exercise: It is historically embedded in existing ritual practice. To mention but a few, the Feast of Krishna (*Holi*) in large parts of India, Carnival in Western and Latin American Roman Catholic societies, Saturnalia in Roman society, the variant of the water festival in Buddhist Southeast Asia, Dionysian cults in antiquity—all involve to a considerable extent a reversal of status, the breaking of routine codes of deference, and the profanation of the existing social order. In some forms, these rituals of reversal may be seen as a sanctioned and contained ritual effort to relieve temporarily the tension unavoidably produced by a rigid hierarchy. To stop here, however, would ignore both the degree to which such rituals often get out of hand and the strenuous attempts made by dominant elites to eliminate or restrict them. The centuries-long campaign of Roman Catholic authorities to eliminate the pagan aspects of carnival—burlesques of the mass, hedonism—and to replace them with the passion plays and more orthodox ritual is a striking example.

59. Jean-Paul Sartre, *Being and Nothingness* (London: Methuen, 1957), 434–35, quoted in Bourdieu, *Outline,* 74.

60. "Protest and Profanation," 224–42.

If it requires no great leap of the imagination to reverse the existing social order, then it should come as no surprise that it can as easily be negated. This is precisely what is involved in nearly all of the millennial religious ideologies that have formed the normative underpinning of a host of large-scale peasant revolts throughout history. Such movements are often closely linked to the reversals discussed earlier, but they are not so easily dismissed as empty rituals, given their practical consequences for political control. The radical vision contained in millennial and utopian ideologies can best be understood as a negation of the existing pattern of exploitation and status degradation as it is experienced. At the risk of overgeneralizing, one can say that this reflexive symbolism often implies a society of brotherhood in which there will be no rich or poor and no distinctions of rank (save those between believers and nonbelievers). Property is typically, though not always, to be held in common and shared. Unjust claims to taxes, rents, and tribute are to be nullified. The envisioned utopia may also include a self-yielding and abundant nature as well as a radically transformed human nature in which greed, envy, and hatred will disappear. While the earthly utopia is an anticipation of the future, it often harks back to a mythic Eden from which mankind has fallen away. It is no exaggeration to see in such historically common ideologies a revolutionary appropriation of religious symbolism in the service of class interests.

Millennial and utopian thought typically make their appearance in the archives only when they take the form of sects or movements that pose a threat to the state. In this respect, the written record is as negligent of ordinary forms of symbolic resistance as it is of everyday material resistance. The prophetic tradition that underlies such sects may remain dormant and peripheral for long periods. But, as Marc Bloch observed, the tradition is both continuous and deeply rooted in popular culture. Citing peasant revolts in France from 821 through "the blazing summer of 1789," which Taine had described as "spontaneous anarchy," Bloch writes:

> But there was nothing novel about this "anarchy." What appeared a newly-minted outrage in the eyes of the ill-instructed philosopher was little more than the recurrence of a traditional phenomenon which had long been endemic. The forms rebellion took (and they were nearly always the same) were also traditional: mystical fantasies: a powerful preoccupation with the primitive egalitarianism of the Gospels, which took hold of humble minds well before the Reformation.[61]

The circumstances under which these beliefs triggered mass action had, to modern eyes, all the marks of revolutionary crises. Thus, in Europe and elsewhere, famines, plagues, wars, invasions, crushing new taxes, subsistence crises, or

61. Marc Bloch, *French Rural History: An Essay on Its Basic Characteristics,* trans. Janet Sondheimer (Berkeley: Univ. of California Press, 1970), 169.

periods when "traditional social bands were being weakened or shattered and the gap between rich and poor was becoming a chasm"[62] might form the backdrop against which millennial expectations become mobilizing myths. The deroutinization of daily life, in which the normal categories with which social reality is apprehended no longer apply, appears to be as important as material deprivation in creating the social soil for millennial activity.

It has occasionally been assumed that millenarianism is a particular product of the prophetic and apocalyptic tradition of the Judeo-Christian world. And yet we find parallel religious traditions in both the Buddhist and Islamic regions of Southeast Asia, as well as in the largely Christian Philippines. In Burma, for example, a belief in the return of a just king (*Setkya min*) who will return to set things aright exists side by side with a belief in a Buddha-Deliverer (*Buddha yaza*) who will usher in a Buddhist millennium. In Islamic Indonesia, we encounter both a traditional belief in a returning monarch-savior (*ratu adil*) and a traditional belief in an Islamic conqueror who will sweep away the heathen and restore justice. The belief in a returning just king, similar to that of the tsar-deliverer in Russia, represents a striking example of how an erstwhile conservative myth of divine kingship can, in the hands of the peasantry, be turned into a revolutionary myth by a kind of symbolic jujitsu. While kingship per se is symbolically maintained, both the actual king and the social order he represents are negated. It goes without saying that these religious traditions in Southeast Asia have also formed the ideological basis for countless rebellions.[63]

The paradox of millennial beliefs is of course that they typically envision the most radical change in the distribution of power, status, and wealth—not to mention human nature—while at the same time being very much leadership centered. At the center of virtually all such movements is a leader, a prophet, a just king, a savior, who will set things right. Compared to everyday forms of resistance that avoid direct symbolic confrontations in the interest of concrete, piecemeal gains, millennial beliefs are all-or-nothing affairs[64] which, once activated, aim at changing the society root and branch. As such they are inherently extralocal and depend on a shared collective history, with its antiestablishment symbols and myths.

62. Norman Cohn, *The Pursuit of the Millennium* (London: Seecker & Warburg, 1957), 32.

63. For examples from Burma and Indonesia, see E. Sarkisyanz, *Buddhist Backgrounds of the Burmese Revolution* (The Hague: Martinus Nijhoff, 1965), and Sartono Kartodirdjo, *Protest Movements in Rural Java: A Study of Agrarian Unrest in the 19th and Early 20th Centuries* (Singapore: Institute of Southeast Asian Studies, 1973).

64. Not a few millennial sects have historically settled into the social fabric as more or less permanent, district communities that aim either to live their own lives in relative isolation from the rest of society or to transform the world merely by their example of piety, etc. A peaceful outcome seems to depend at least as much on how the sect is treated by the state as on its initial beliefs.

In Sedaka itself, one can hardly speak of a lively millennial tradition. There is evidence, however, that religious prophecies are far from entirely dormant. Four or five villagers spoke to me of predictions made by religious men (*orang alim*) who teach at the various informal religious schools (*pondok*) in the region. Such prophesies were typically vague and predicted much bloodshed, the punishment of the wicked, natural disturbances (earthquakes, flood) as well as often naming the Islamic year in which all this would come to pass. Occasionally, prophesies circulate in the form of "flying letters" (*surat layang*) of anonymous authorship—letters purportedly written at some sacred Islamic site in the Middle East under the inspiration of a vision or dream. (One such *surat layang* came into my hands and is reproduced in translation in appendix E.) In 1969, after racial riots had erupted in several Malaysian cities, a climate of fearful anticipation swept much of Kedah. Local religious figures, politicians, and those versed in the traditional Malay art of self-defense (*silat*) joined a group called the Red Sash Society (Pertubohan Selendang Merah), a body with shadowy connections to UMNO politicians in the national capital. Its purpose was to defend the race and the religion. To this end, an "oathing" ceremony was held for at least forty men from Sedaka and Sungai Tongkang in the house of Haji Salim, now a prominent UMNO official in the district. Someone claiming to have been sent from Kuala Lumpur conducted an initiation, using chants (*jampi*), anointment with lime juice and water, and a demonstration of how the red sash worn by members would render them invulnerable to wounds from a machete (*golok*). In the end, the unrest did not spread to Kedah and the group never went into action.

The point of this brief account of prophesy and religious mobilization in Sedaka is not to claim that such exceptional events preoccupy villagers. They do not. It is rather to suggest only that prophesy and religious mobilization are a part, however dormant in relatively ordinary times, of the cultural equipment of the Malay peasantry. In 1979 a shadowy organization (*Nasrul Haq*) which, it was said, had thirty thousand members in Kedah was banned. The government claimed that it had political connections as well as teaching *silat* (self-defense) and that its "un-Islamic" promotion of magical chants, trances, and female participation as well as unorthodox dress made it a threat to public order. A mystical cult named *Auratis mailiyyah,* which developed in the poor Kedah district of Sik and about which far less is known, was outlawed by an Islamic (*Syariah*) court at about the same time.[65] For Malaysia as a whole, Stockwell has documented the reappearance of millennial and ecstatic Islamic cults during virtually every episode of historical crisis.[66] Had I attended more carefully to it,

65. Judith Nagata, *The Reflowering of Islam: Modern Religious Radicals and Their Roots* (Vancouver: Univ. of British Columbia Press, forthcoming), chaps. 3, 6.

66. A. J. Stockwell, *British Policy and Malay Politics during the Malayan Union Experiment, 1945–48,* Malaysian Branch of the Royal Asiatic Society, Monograph No. 8 (Kuala Lumpur: Art Printing Works, 1979), 151–61.

I am certain that I would have uncovered more *surat layang* and local prophesies.[67] Under exceptional circumstances it is entirely possible that such marginal phenomena could move quickly to the center of the political stage.[68]

My concern here has been exclusively directed to the issue of whether or not a subordinate class, having no experience or knowledge of other social systems, can conceive of the domination under which they live as anything other than completely inevitable. The historical fact is that they can and do. All three of the claims examined in this section have proved to be untenable. There is no basis for supposing that subordinate classes equate the inevitable with the just, although the necessity of pragmatic resignation may often make it seem so. There is no basis for imagining that *any* of the common historical patterns of domination so completely control the social life of subordinate classes as to rule out the creation of partly autonomous and resistant subcultures. Finally, there is no reason to assume that the lower orders are so encompassed by an existing system of domination that they cannot either imagine its revolutionary negation or act on that negation.

Conflict within Hegemony

For the sake of argument, I have thus far taken for granted what I believe to be the core assumption of the case for hegemony and false-consciousness. Put bluntly, the assumption is that, to the extent dominant classes can persuade subordinate classes to adopt their self-serving view of existing social relations, the result will be ideological consensus and harmony that will in turn block the perception of conflicting interests, let alone class conflict. Hegemony is, after all, fundamentally about the misrepresentation of "objective" interests. Once this assumption is granted, we find ourselves inquiring if and how subordinate classes can penetrate, neutralize, and negate that hegemony. But is the initial premise credible? I believe it is not credible for at least three reasons, one of which is theoretical or conceptual and two of which are empirical. The theoretical problem requires our prior attention, as it stems from what I take to be a misunderstanding of the nature of any purported hegemonic ideology.

This misunderstanding can best be grasped by recalling the basic feature of

67. Rarely a month goes by without a newspaper account of the prosecution of a religious teacher accused of propagating false doctrines. In 1979 one such teacher, a Cambodian Muslim, led an attack of his disciples on a police station in the state of Pahang.

68. The belief in invulnerability, produced both by magic and by the aid of divine sanction, is a standard feature of most millennial practices. It also illustrates a final, key element of the negation of inevitability. The effect of millennial ideology is not only to negate the social order itself but also to negate the very power that serves to keep that social order in place. Of course, the conquest of inevitability at the level of religious ideology is, alas, not the same as its conquest in practice, as the fate of the vast majority who have joined such rebellions tragically attests.

ideological struggle in Sedaka: the fact that it takes place almost entirely *within* the normative framework of the older agrarian system. The struggle is, in other words, within what most observers would call an existing hegemony.[69] Small-holders, petty tenants, and landless laborers are continually using the values and rationale of that earlier social order to press their claims and disparage the claims of their opponents. They make abundant use of the values of help (*tolong*) or assistance that rich villagers have typically used to describe their own behavior. They stigmatize the rich as stingy and hardhearted, thereby turning the values of generosity and liberality against those who justified their property and privilege in just such terms. They insist, albeit in vain, on their right to employment and to tenancies, which the large landowners once claimed to bestow upon them out of a sense of helpfulness. In each respect, the claims of the poor derive their normative force and strategic value from the fact that lip service is still being paid to them by the locally dominant elite. There is virtually no radical questioning of property rights or of the state and its local officials, whose policies are designed to further capitalist agriculture. Almost everything said by the poor fits easily within the *professed* values—within the hegemony—of local elites. And if the ends sought by the village poor are modest, so are the means used to accomplish them. The modesty of means, however, is less a consequence of small ambitions than of other givens—the presence of economic alternatives, the fact of "dull compulsion," and the knowledge of probable repression.

Short of the deroutinizing crises that are said to touch off millennial expectations, such modest claims may be found at the core of most class conflict. Nor are such small demands incompatible with more violent and even revolutionary action when conditions permit. There is, in other words, no necessary symmetry between modesty of ends and modesty of means. The claims can be said to arise from the inevitable gap between the promises that any hegemony necessarily makes and the equally inevitable failure of the social order to fulfill some or all of these promises. Properly understood, any hegemonic ideology provides, within itself, the raw material for contradictions and conflict.

To appreciate why this is so, we need only turn to the implications of the passage from *The German Ideology* quoted at length earlier. "The ruling ideas [that is, the hegemonic ideology] are nothing more than the *ideal expression* of the dominant material relationships." Gramsci understood, far better than many of his successors, precisely what was involved in idealizing the dominant material relationships:

Undoubtedly, the fact of hegemony presupposes that account be taken of

69. There is a problem with the term *hegemony* itself since it often implies that a hegemonic ideology is the sole creation of an elite, whereas in fact it is always the creation of prior struggle and compromises that are continually being tested and modified. See, in this connection, the illuminating discussion of "counterpoints" in W. F. Wertheim, *Evolution or Revolution* (London: Pelican Books, 1973).

the interests and the tendencies of the groups over which hegemony is to be exercised, and that a certain compromise equilibrium should be formed—in other words, that the leading group should make sacrifices of an economic-corporate kind. But there is also no doubt that such sacrifices and such a compromise cannot touch the essential; for though hegemony is ethical-political, it must also be economic.[70]

Thus, a hegemonic ideology requires, by definition, that what are in fact particular interests be reformulated and presented as general interests. If it is to become an effective instrument of consent, it must meet two criteria. First, it must claim that the system of privilege, status, and property it defends operates in the interest not only of elites but also of subordinate groups whose compliance or support is being elicited. To do this it must, in effect, make implicit promises of benefits for subordinate groups that will serve as the stake which they too have in the prevailing social order.[71] Second, as Gramsci realized, the dominant class must make good on at least a portion of these promises if it is to have the slightest hope of gaining compliance. That is, hegemony is not just a symbolic bone tossed to subordinate groups; it requires some actual sacrifices or restraint by the dominant groups.

The dominant ideology that developed before double-cropping in Kedah and that still, by and large, prevails as a normative framework may be understood in just these terms. The large farmers rationalized their social status, their property, and their privileges by emphasizing the benefits they provided for the rest of the village—tenancies, wage labor, charity, loans, feasts, *zakat*. This rationalization was embedded in concrete material practices and entailed a modest socialization of their profit in the interest of continued domination. For the issue at hand, it matters not that this rationalization and the practices associated with

70. Gramsci, *Selections,* 161.

71. Writing of the state in particular, later in the same essay, Gramsci makes a similar observation about dominant ideologies:

[The winning party brings] about a unison of economic and political aims, but also, intellectual and moral unity, posing all the questions around which the struggle rages not on a corporate but on a "universal" plane, and thus creating the hegemony of fundamental social group over a series of subordinate groups. . . . In other words, the dominant group is coordinated concretely with the general interests of the subordinate groups, and the life of the State is conceived of as a continuous process of formation and superseding of unstable equilibria . . . between the interests of the fundamental group and those of the subordinate groups—equilibria in which the interests of the dominant group prevail, but only up to a certain point, i.e. stopping short of narrowly corporate economic interest.

Selections, 181–82. Thus a key function of the dominant ideology is to discipline elites so that their short-run interests do not jeopardize the stability of the social order as a whole.

338 · HEGEMONY AND CONSCIOUSNESS

it were a product of struggle or that they did not infringe on the fundamental interests of the agrarian elite. The crucial point is rather that the very process of attempting to legitimate a social order by idealizing it *always* provides its subjects with the means, the symbolic tools, the very ideas for a critique that operates entirely within the hegemony. For most purposes, then, it is not at all necessary for subordinate classes to set foot outside the confines of the ruling ideals in order to formulate a critique of power. The most common form of class struggle arises from the failure of a dominant ideology to live up to the implicit promises it necessarily makes. The dominant ideology can be turned against its privileged beneficiaries not only because subordinate groups develop their own interpretations, understandings, and readings of its ambiguous terms, but also because of the promises that the dominant classes must make to propagate it in the first place.[72]

In this context, what we find in Sedaka is an eroding dominant ideology that never quite delivered the goods and that now no longer even serves the interests of the larger cultivators. It is therefore a vanishing and even retrograde tradition that has become the ideological weapon by which the rich may be further delegitimated. The irony, of course, is that the ideological weapon the poor now find so serviceable was earlier fashioned and handed to them by the same rich cultivators and landlords. A "shared" ideology is by no means a guarantee of consent or harmony.[73]

The structure of ideological conflict in Sedaka is far from unusual. In his searching analysis of slavery in the United States, for example, Genovese has shown how its legal codes and its ideology of paternalism—both violated with impunity in practice—came to be used by the slaves themselves to assert their claims for subsistence, humane treatment, and the preservation of the slave family. As in Sedaka, a large part of the critique of ruling group practice could be read directly from the text of ruling group ideology.[74] Much the same analysis

72. See, in this context, Gidden's discussion of the struggle by the working class to universalize what are originally the "sectional" interests of the bourgeoisie. *Central Problems,* 193ff.

73. Once again, the concept of hegemony is, to my mind, not sufficiently reflexive here, since both the "compromise" and the "corporate sacrifices" are as much won by resistance and struggle as given or imposed by an elite. The struggle of subordinate classes, in other words, helps determine what kind of compromise will make consent possible.

74. See, for example, Frank Parkin, *Class Inequality and Political Order* (New York: Praeger, 1971), 72–102. Willis (in *Learning to Labour,* 110) would go much further and claim that if in fact the dominant class were successful in inculcating the dominant ideology it would find itself with far more working-class anger and dissent. In particular, he argues that if English working-class children believed what was taught them at school—that is, that doing well in school and following its rules would result in social mobility in a working life where competence and skill are

could almost certainly be made of the critique of "real existing socialism" in Poland that found expression in the Solidarity movement.[75] How is it possible to understand what amounted to the revolt of most of civil society against the state in Poland except against the background of a self-proclaimed socialist system that *ideologically* insisted that it operated on behalf of proletarian interests?[76] Polish workers daily confronted evidence that flew in the face of official ideology (hardly a hegemony in this case)—entrenched privilege and corruption, declining standards of living for workers, special shops for party officials, repression of worker protests, and so forth. This is not to say that neither slaves nor Polish workers were able to imagine a social order run along quite different lines. It is only to claim that, in each case, the ideology formulated by the ruling class to justify its own rule provided much of the symbolic raw material from which the most damning critique could be derived and sustained.

Similar logic might be applied to the routine forms of working-class disaffection in advanced capitalist nations. Although the work force in such countries has easier ideological access to radical alternatives, much of its critique of the social order appears to rest on premises that are also, broadly speaking, drawn from the ruling ideology itself.[77] Without straying beyond the prevailing ideology, workers may contrast the meritocratic ethos with the reality of "connections," favoritism, and unequal access to superior education; they may contrast the democratic ideology of "one man, one vote" with the reality of corporate influence on the media and elections; they may contrast the bountiful promise of capitalism with periodic recessions and unemployment. The solutions proposed by radical parties and intellectuals may, and frequently do, lie outside the dominant ideology. But for my purposes, it is clear that a radical critique of *existing* arrangements may arise in virtually any subordinate class that takes the dominant ideology to heart and, at the same time, penetrates in daily life the realities that betray or ignore the implicit promises of that ideology. On closer inspection,

---

rewarded—they would feel far more cruelly deceived later. Thus, he argues implicitly that social stability and compliance requires that the ideology of the school fail to impress itself on working-class youngsters. Indeed, those working-class youngsters who pose the greatest problem for school authorities enter the work force thoroughly cynical but without aspirations that could possibly be betrayed. *Learning to Labour* is, in my opinion, the finest study available of hegemony in any setting.

75. The term "real existing socialism" is taken from Rudolf Bahro, *The Alternative in Eastern Europe*, trans. David Fernbach (London: Verso, 1981).

76. See the forthcoming book on Solidarity by Roman Laba. For a socialist critique—within the hegemony—of working life in Hungary, see the remarkable account by Miklós Haraszti, *A Worker in a Worker's State*, trans. Michael Wright (New York: Universe Books, 1978).

77. On this point see, for example, Abercrombie et al., *Dominant Ideology Thesis*, 17; Richard Hoggart, *Uses of Literacy*, and Charles Sabel, *Work and Politics: The Division of Labor in Industry* (Cambridge: Cambridge Univ. Press, 1982).

then, the ideologies of slavery, communism, liberal democracy, and even "agrarian paternalism" à la Sedaka may turn out to be a provocation and incitement rather than the general anesthesia which a hegemonic ideology is presumed to be.[78]

The implicit promises embodied in any would-be hegemonic ideology may seem, even to many of its subjects, to be nothing more than a cynical "protection" racket. From whom was the feudal lord protecting the serf, if not from other marauding lords like himself? How can the slaveholder be said to provide a "service" of subsistence when it is the slaves who feed both themselves and him? Such hypocrisies are, however, "the tribute vice pays to virtue" and they have *real* consequences.[79] In Sedaka, it is tactically sound for the poor to make their case in terms of older agrarian norms. They are not only the moral categories in which villagers actually think; they also allow the poor to appropriate, as it were, the ideological resources of the well-off and turn them to good advantage. Finally, by remaining prudently within the accepted and familiar categories of moral discourse, the poor minimize the risks of a more dramatic confrontation.

Trade Union Consciousness and Revolution

> Common sense is not a single unique conception, identical in time and space. . . . Its most fundamental characteristic is that it is a conception which, even in the brain of one individual, is fragmentary, incoherent and inconsequential, in conformity with the social and cultural position of those masses whose philosophy it is.
>
> None the less the starting point must always be that common sense which is the spontaneous philosophy of the multitude and which *has to be made ideologically coherent.*[80]

For Gramsci and for many other Marxist scholars, the primary obstacle to radical

78. In his fine study of inmates in a Norwegian prison, Thomas Mathiesen stresses that, while in practice there is little peer solidarity, there is a widespread attitude of "censoriousness." By this he means a readiness to seize on the norms propagated by the prison officials themselves and accuse them of violating their own standards at every turn. In this case, the progressive (paternalistic?) ideology of prison officials provided effective raw material to serve prisoners' interests. The inmates constantly pushed for "mechanical" equality, automatic rights, seniority rules, and stated minimum requirements along trade union lines, while prison officials strove to maintain discretionary controls just as management would. *The Defenses of the Weak: A Sociological Study of a Norwegian Correctional Institution* (London: Tavistock, 1965).

79. Moore, *Injustice,* 508 and 84. See also James C. Scott, *The Moral Economy of the Peasant: Subsistence and Rebellion in Southeast Asia* (New Haven: Yale Univ. Press, 1976), chap. 6. It is of interest in this context that Russian Orthodox priests in tsarist Russia were occasionally beaten when the crops, which were under their ritual protection, failed.

80. Gramsci, *Selections,* 419, 421, emphasis added.

change is to be found at the level of ideas. For reasons of "intellectual subordination,"[81] Gramsci argued, the working class gets most of its ideas secondhand from dominant groups and, by itself, is therefore not able to rise above an "incoherent" and "fragmentary" conception of its situation. The result, at best, is a kind of "trade union consciousness" focusing on limited and concrete benefits rather than the "revolutionary consciousness" that might make radical change possible. It is this ideological shortcoming of the proletariat, of course, that defines the intellectual role of the vanguard party.

A number of assumptions lie behind this position, each of which requires examination. The first is that dominant classes *do*, in fact, share a well-defined and coherent ideology. I will not examine this claim here, but it is worth suggesting that such ideological coherence may be quite rare—perhaps even among intellectuals whose stock in trade is the formulation of systems of thought. To what standard of coherence the consciousness of the working class is being compared, in other words, is not entirely clear. A second, and more nearly explicit, assumption is that revolutionary action can follow only from a thoroughly radical (Marxist?) consciousness that is not only diametrically opposed to the dominant ideology but that envisions an entirely new social order that will take its place. This assumption is certainly true, but tautological, if we define revolutionary action solely in terms of the consciousness of the actors. If, however, we do not adopt this sleight of hand, is it correct to assume that a less than revolutionary consciousness will inevitably lead to accommodations with the dominant class—to reformism and/or "trade union" politics?

What I wish to argue briefly here is that there is no necessary relationship between the small and limited demands typical of a "reformist" consciousness and the kinds of actions taken to achieve these demands. One may go still further and assert with some assurance that the rank-and-file actors in most, if not all, revolutionary situations are in fact fighting for rather mundane, if vital, objectives that could in principle—but often not in practice—be accommodated within the prevailing social order. The typical revolutionary crisis is, in other words, brought about by small but essential demands that are experienced by large numbers of people simultaneously and, because they are thwarted, can be achieved only by revolutionary action. The making of a revolutionary crisis, to be sure, depends on a host of factors outside my immediate concern, but the one factor it does *not* require is revolutionary ambitions among the rank and file. In this sense there is no fit between ends and means. At one level, this is no more than commonsense; the demands of subordinate classes spring from their daily experience and the material they face. The only reason why this commonplace merits restatement is that so many theoretical discussions appear to assume otherwise and to impose quite fanciful ideological requirements on working-class

81. Ibid., 327.

consciousness. Those requirements have, to my knowledge, never been met by any real working class.

Let us turn briefly to two revolutionary situations and examine the issue of working-class consciousness in each context. The groundwork has been laid by Barrington Moore's analysis of German workers in the Ruhr after World War I who participated in what he terms "the closest approximation to a spontaneous proletarian revolution that has taken place in a modern industrial state"[82] and of the Russian proletariat on the eve of the Bolshevik revolution.

For Germany, Moore has uncovered some remarkable evidence from open-ended surveys of proletarian values conducted around 1912 that allows him to address this issue. Although support for the Social Democratic Party was common, the hopes and aspirations of workers were largely personal rather than public or political. Among the most common wishes were those for better wages, enough to eat, decent humane treatment, and, more farfetched, a house of one's own with some land. These were the modest aspirations of a working class that was already quite radical in its actions and would become more so. Those who had joined the socialists were a minority, and the vast majority of them were, it appears, absolutely innocent of socialist theory. Even in the case of coal miners, who, prior to 1914, were the most militant sector of the working class, "there is not the slightest hint that they were the carriers of revolutionary sentiments."[83]

> Over and over again the evidence reveals that the mass of workers was not revolutionary. They did not want to overturn the existing social order and replace it with something else, least of all one where ordinary workers would be in charge. They were however, very angry. They were backed into a corner and fought in self-defense . . .
>
> Yet even if one grants all those points, from the standpoint of political consequences they do not really matter. Revolutionary objectives are generally imposed by leaders on an angry mass that serves to dynamite the old order when other conditions make it possible. Indeed, I would hazard a guess that in any of the great revolutions that have succeeded, the mass of the followers has not consciously willed an overturn of the social order . . .
>
> To the extent that angry little people want something new, it generally amounts to their perception of the old order minus the disagreeable and oppressive features that affect them.[84]

To call the issues behind the near revolution in Germany "bread-and-butter" issues and petty questions of decent treatment is, as Moore notes, to miss their

82. Moore, *Injustice*, 351. Recent events in Poland offer another competing case for such honor.

83. Ibid., 340.

84. Ibid., 351–52.

significance.[85] They were not only materially vital to a working class with its back to the wall, but they were reinforced by the anger arising from their felt legitimacy. In fact, it is fair to say that the tenacious pursuit of such small goals was in part generated *because* they appeared to lie within the normative framework of the existing order. The claims of the German working class in this period were not much more ambitious or far-reaching than those of Sedaka's poor. The reason why a revolutionary situation prevailed in the former case but not in the latter is due to many other factors; it does not, however, have anything to do with the presence or absence of revolutionary class consciousness per se.

The evidence for working-class demands in Russia immediately before the October revolution—and after the February revolution—comes from the autonomous demands of factory committees formed all over European Russia.[86] Once again they reflect exactly what Lenin would have termed a reformist, trade union consciousness. The most popular demand was for an eight-hour day. Other demands included an end to piecework, a minimum wage, raises, and severance pay in case of dismissal. In the workplace the laborers insisted on politeness from management, on an end to arbitrary fines deducted from their pay, cooking and toilet facilities, and tools supplied by the factory, not the workers. Their most radical demand was apparently for the abolition of child labor and discrimination by sex, but they fully supported differential pay based on skills and experience. These were hardly the kinds of demands that, of themselves, suggested a revolution.[87] As Moore summarizes them, "the whole thrust of these demands . . . was to improve working conditions, not to change them. . . . Once again we see that the workers' idea of a good society . . . is the present order with its most disagreeable features softened or eliminated."[88]

Further examples might be added to the weight of evidence here—for example, from the demands of the peasantry in Morelos during the Mexican Revolution

85. Ibid., 273. See also E. P. Thompson, *The Making of the English Working Class* (New York: Vintage, 1966), 168.

86. Moore, *Injustice,* 369.

87. As for the Russian peasantry, their actions were, of course, quite radical, seizing land and burning the homes of the gentry and officials. Their goals, however, were quite modest and parochial. According to one assessment:

> While the various elites argued constitutional and policy questions in the capital, the peasants were forming their own political order in the countryside. . . . They repudiated the national level, and their alternative was something quite different from simply a new version of the modern centralized state. . . . Petrograd may well have constituted the center of the national political state, but the peasants were boycotting the play and writing the script for their own production.

John H. Kress, "The Political Consciousness of the Russian Peasantry," *Soviet Studies* 31, no. 4 (October 1979): 576.

88. Moore, *Injustice,* 370.

and from the *cahiers de doleances* during the French Revolution.[89] The point of introducing evidence from the working class is precisely that, for Marxist theory, it is among this class and no other that a revolutionary consciousness is considered possible. Even here, however, we find not only that it is largely absent, but that petty reformist demands are quite compatible with revolutionary action. A revolutionary vanguard party may be necessary for revolution to occur, but its necessity does not arise from the need for ideological instruction and consciousness raising among subordinate classes.[90] Revolutionary conflict, so far as the rank and file is concerned, is normally generated within the confines of the existing hegemony. It is often only the means employed that are out of the ordinary. This observation is at least as applicable to peasant movements as to proletarian.

As Hobsbawm quite correctly observes, "Revolution may be made *de facto* by peasants who do not deny the legitimacy of the existing power structure, law, the state, or even the landlords."[91] The peasantry of Morelos, as a case in point, set out merely to recover communal lands the sugar haciendas had taken from them, not to destroy the hacienda system, let alone transform the Mexican state. Their dogged persistence in recovering their land, however, helped bring about both of these larger consequences. Just as small and uncoordinated acts of petty resistance may aggregate to a point where they jeopardize state structures, so may petty, reformist, "ideological" goals aggregate to a point where their attainment implies a revolution.

It is, of course, still possible to assert that outside leadership in some form—

89. Assembled just before the revolution, the *cahiers* were essentially lists of complaints and demands from every department. As they were written by local elites, they were not quite mass opinion, though for that reason one might judge the *cahiers* to represent something closer to the eventual program of the bourgeois revolution. In fact, virtually all of the *cahiers* focused on local grievances; the vast majority assumed the continuation of feudalism and demanded adjustments (for example, restrictions on lords' hunting rights, uniform weights and measures, rights to woodland, a limitation on curé salaries). No *cahier* outside Paris even hinted at popular sovereignty, and most argued their claims by reference to custom. As one historian concludes, "it follows that the revolutionary state of mind expressed in the Declaration of the Rights of Man and the decrees of 1789–91 was a product and not a cause of the crisis that began in 1787." George V. Taylor, "Revolutionary and Non-Revolutionary Content in the Cahiers of 1789: An Interim Report," *French Historical Studies* 7, no. 4 (Fall 1972): 501.

90. Here the debate between Luxemburg and Lenin is relevant, but neither appreciated, I believe, the possibly radical consequences of modest working-class—or peasant—demands. See Kathy E. Ferguson, "Class-Consciousness and the Marxist Dialectic: The Elusive Synthesis," *Review of Politics* 42, no. 4 (October 1980): 504–32.

91. Eric Hobsbawm, "Peasants and Politics," *Journal of Peasant Studies* 1, no. 1 (October 1973): 12.

for example, a political party, an intelligentsia—may be necessary to transform a host of insurrections into a revolution that will seize power and transform the state. I do not address this particular issue here except to note that, if this argument is admitted, it is largely a matter of taste as to whether one sees subordinate classes as helpless without a radical intelligentsia or the radical intelligentsia as helpless without an insurgent mass. What is definitely being asserted, however, is that neither "revolutionary consciousness" nor an elaborate ideology, as those terms are ordinarily understood, is necessary to create the revolutionary crisis of which such leaders might conceivably then take advantage.

Who Shatters the Hegemony?

> To sum up provisionally, spontaneous conceptions among pre-factory work-ers, factory workers, and modern revolutionary peasants have been mainly backward-looking. They have been attempts to revive a social contract that had been violated, most frequently they were efforts to remedy specific and concrete grievances in their particular occupation.[92]

Is it possible to speak of a social contract that is being violated in Sedaka? I believe it is possible, providing the social contract is understood as a set of practices and the norms associated with them, providing we recognize that the interpretation of this contract varies markedly by class, and providing we realize that the poor have in large part created and recognized their version of the contract only in the context of its violation. This violation has been mediated almost exclusively by the larger farmers, seeking to improve their returns, al-though the opportunity to create new relations of production was provided by the state-built irrigation scheme. These budding capitalists have dismissed ten-ants, raised the rent, switched to leasehold, and called in the machinery. It is they who have steadily abrogated the customs of *zakat,* charity, loans, and large feasts. It is they who have thus all but eliminated the modest "socialization" of paddy profits, which once served their interest. It is they who have increasingly monopolized the supply of state subsidies and inputs as well as the political institutions of village life.

The rich of Sedaka thus find themselves in an anomalous, though powerful, position. The precondition of their new wealth has been the systematic disman-tling of the practices that previously rationalized their wealth, status, and lead-ership. Their economic domination has come at the cost of their social standing *and* of their social control of their poorer neighbors—the cost implied by their having broken their own hegemony. The poor, by contrast, find themselves with an ideologically serviceable past; they have a vital stake in defending both the norms and practices of the earlier agrarian order. It is useful, in this context, to distinguish two sorts of tradition: one that is taken for granted—what Bourdieu

92. Moore, *Injustice,* 476.

calls *doxa*—and is thus not perceived as tradition but is simply what is done and another that is the imaginative reconstruction of the past in the service of current interests.[93] It is this latter form of tradition that the poor are both creating and defending. It is not, of course, constructed out of whole cloth. If it were, it would have little ideological value. It is instead a recognizable but partisan facsimile of earlier values and practices drawn up to legitimize essential class interests.

If the ideological situation in Sedaka is at all characteristic of early capitalism, as I believe it is, then the usual argument about dominant ideologies will have to be fundamentally recast. Gramsci and many others assume that the key task for any subordinate class is to create a counterhegemony that will ultimately be capable of transforming the society.[94] This position may have some merit for mature capitalist societies, where an elaborated ideology may already be in place. But it ignores the central fact that it has been *capitalism* that has historically transformed societies and broken apart existing relations of production. Even a casual glance at the record will show that capitalist development continually requires the violation of the previous "social contract" which in most cases it had earlier helped to create and sustain. The demystification of an existing hegemony is thus accomplished at least as much by the inevitable disregard for custom inherent in capitalism as by the "penetration" of subordinate classes themselves. The history of capitalism could, in fact, be written along just such lines. The enclosures, the introduction of agricultural machinery, the invention of the factory system, the use of steam power, the development of the assembly line, and today the computer revolution and robots have all had massive material and social consequences that undermined previous understandings about work, equity, security, obligation, and rights.

The conflict in Sedaka can be grasped only against this background of the transforming power of capitalism—its tendency to undermine radically the past and the present. Raymond Williams vividly captures the process:

> Since it has become dominant in one area after another, it has been un-controllably disturbing and restless, reaching local stabilities only almost at once to move away from them, leaving every kind of social and technical debris, disrupting human continuities and settlements, moving on with brash confidence to its always novel enterprises.[95]

This is also what Brecht must have had in mind when he claimed that it was not socialism, but capitalism, that was revolutionary.

The backward-looking character of much subordinate class ideology and pro-

93. See also Bourdieu, *Outline,* 164–71.
94. Gramsci, *Selections,* 178, 334.
95. *Problems in Materialism and Culture: Selected Essays* (London: New Left Books, 1980), 259.

test is perfectly understandable in this context. It is the revolutionary character of capitalism that casts them in a defensive role. If they defend a version of the older hegemony, it is because those arrangements look good by comparison with the current prospects and because it has a certain legitimacy rooted in earlier practice. The defense and elaboration of a social contract that has been abrogated by capitalist development is perhaps the most constant ideological theme of the peasant and the early capitalist worker[96]—from the Levellers and Diggers of the English Revolution to the craftsmen and weavers threatened with extinction to the "Captain Swing" rebels fighting the use of threshing machines. The same defense of beleaguered traditional rights is found at the core of popular intellectual attacks on capitalism by figures as ideologically diverse as Cobbett, Paine, and Carlyle.[97]

In Sedaka, as in nineteenth-century England, the attack is directed less against capitalism per se than against capitalists. The violation of hard-won earlier arrangements appears to its victims as a heartless and willful choice of concrete individuals and not as the impersonal working out of some larger systematic logic. As in the case of Andalusian laborers, described by Alier, the victims see malevolence when nothing more than economic rationality is involved:

> My point is that there is and has been unemployment, and that labourers have attributed, and still do attribute unemployment to the unwillingness of landowners to give them work. As we have seen, there is some substance to this view, even though it is not as much a matter of bad will on the part of the landowners as of decisions which are economically rational from the point of view of the individual enterprise.[98]

At another level, however, the personalization of the causes of distress is not a misperception at all. The choices made by the large farmers in Sedaka or Andalusia—though they may be constrained by economic logic—are *also,* manifestly, the result of conscious individual choice. In seeing that things might be otherwise, those who personalize the issue also perceive the larger fact that even capitalistic logic is a social creation and not a thing. What is certain, moreover, is that the personalization evident in charges of stinginess, greed, and hardheartedness, whether in the novels of Dickens or in the mouths of Sedaka's poor, are far more generative of anger and possible action than if the causes were seen as impersonal and inevitable. If personalization is partly a myth, then it is a powerful, politically enabling myth.

The conquest of this sense of inevitability is essential to the development

96. The creation of the modern state has many of the same rupturing effects on local arrangements and might be examined in the same fashion.

97. See, for example, Thompson's analysis of Cobbett in *The Making of the English Working Class,* 761.

98. Alier, *Labourers and Landowners in Southern Spain,* 93–94.

of politically effective moral outrage. For this to happen, people must perceive and define their situation as the consequence of human injustice: a situation they need not, cannot, and ought not to endure. By itself of course such a perception . . . is no guarantee of political or social changes to come. But without some very considerable surge of moral anger such changes do not occur.[99]

The personalization I observed in Sedaka is to a large degree the natural consequence of the capitalist transformation experienced there. For the victims as well as the beneficiaries of the large abstractions we choose to call capitalism, imperialism, or the green revolution, the experience itself arrives in quite personal, concrete, localized, mediated form.

Let us suppose for a moment that poor peasants in Sedaka had instead chosen to emphasize the larger causes of their difficulties. They are not, as we have seen, unaware of these larger issues. But what if they had, as an intellectual critic (or supporter) of Malaysian development might have, focused on such matters as the accumulation of wealth, the growth of capital-intensive agriculture, and the policies of the state, which favor the interests of rich farmers to ensure the provision of cheap wage goods to the enclaves of urban industry? Can one imagine a rural protest movement with banners proclaiming "stop agrarian capitalism" or "down with the cash nexus"? Of course not. Such undeniable facts are far too abstract and remote; they fail completely to capture the texture of local experience. Were they in fact the center of attention, one imagines that the smallholders and landless laborers of the village might simply stand aside in recognition of the apparently inextricable forces that will shape their future. To see the causes of distress instead as personal, as evil, as a failure of identifiable people in their own community to behave in a seemly way may well be a partial view, but it is not a wrong view. And not incidentally, it is quite possibly the only view that could, and does, serve as the basis for day-to-day resistance.

Resistance in Sedaka begins as, I suspect, all historical resistance by subordinate classes begins: close to the ground, rooted firmly in the homely but meaningful realities of daily experience. The *enemies* are not impersonal historical forces but real people. That is, they are seen as actors responsible for their own actions and not as bearers of abstractions. The *values* resisters are defending are equally near at hand and familiar. Their point of departure is the practices and norms that have proven effective in the past and appear to offer some promise of reducing or reversing the losses they suffer. The *goals* of resistance are as modest as its values. The poor strive to gain work, land, and income; they are not aiming at large historical abstractions such as socialism, let alone Marxist-Leninism. The *means* typically employed to achieve these ends—barring the rare crises that might precipitate larger dreams—are both prudent and realistic.

99. Moore, *Injustice,* 459.

When flight is available—to the frontier, to the cities—it is seized. When outright confrontation with landlords or the state seems futile, it is avoided. In the enormous zone between these two polar strategies lie all the forms of daily resistance, both symbolic and material, that we have examined.

Such resistance, conceived and conducted with no revolutionary end in mind, can, and occasionally does, contribute to revolutionary outcomes. The end in such cases is ironically likely to appear to the peasantry or the working class not as an end at all, but rather as the necessary means to their modest goals. Even when such slogans as "socialism" take hold among subordinate classes, they are likely to mean something radically different to the rank and file than to the radical intelligentsia. What Orwell had to say about the English working class in the 1930s is almost surely true for lower classes in general:

> The first thing that must strike any outside observer is that socialism in its developed form is a theory confined entirely to the middle class.
>
> For it must be remembered that a working man . . . is seldom or never a socialist in the complete logically consistent sense. . . . To the ordinary working man, the sort you would meet in any pub on Saturday night, socialism does not mean much more than better wages and shorter hours and nobody bossing you about. To the more revolutionary type who is a hunger-marcher and is blacklisted by employers, the word is a sort of rallying cry against the forces of oppression, a vague threat of future violence. . . . But I have yet to meet a working miner, steelworker, cotton-weaver, docker, navvy, or whatever who was "ideologically" sound.
>
> One of the analogies between Communism and Roman Catholicism is that only the educated are completely orthodox. [100]

The observation is of course nothing more than the intellectual division of labor one might expect in any class-based movement between workers or peasants whose struggle must grow directly from the realities of material life and an intelligentsia whose sights are set on a more distant horizon. The division of labor in this case, as in others, is not only a complimentarity but carries within it the possibility of conflict as well.

It is true, as Lukacs has argued, that the peasantry as a class is unlikely to envision a new plan for the total organization of society:

> The outlook of other classes (petty bourgeois or peasants) is ambiguous or sterile because their existence is not based exclusively on their role in the capitalist system of production but is indissolubly linked with the vestiges of feudal society. Their aim, therefore, is not to advance capitalism or to transcend it, but to reverse its action or at least to prevent it from devel-

100. George Orwell, *The Road to Wigan Pier* (London: Left Book Club, 1937), 173, 176–77.

oping fully. Their class interest concentrates on *symptoms* of development and not on development itself.[101]

What he might have added, however, is that the working class itself, for different reasons perhaps, is in the same boat. That class too, if Moore, E. P. Thompson, Orwell, and Luxemburg are at all correct, deals with the "symptoms" of development as they are manifested in daily life. There is no point in aspiring in vain for a proletariat or peasantry that will somehow detach itself from its insistence on the mundane objectives that will make for a tolerable material life and a modicum of dignity. There is, on the contrary, every point in seeing precisely these ends and their dogged pursuit through thick and thin as the central hope for a more humane social order—as the core of the critique, in symbol and in action, of any and all social orders erected above peasants and workers by those who claim to serve their interests.

The reader will detect, correctly, a certain pessimism about the prospects for revolutionary change that will systematically and reliably respect the insistence on small decencies that are at the core of peasant or working-class consciousness. If the revolution cannot even deliver the petty amenities and minor humanities that animate the struggle of its subjects, then there is not much to be said for whatever else it may accomplish. This pessimism is, alas, not so much a prejudice as, I think, a realistic assessment of the fate of workers and peasants in most revolutionary states—a fate that makes melancholy reading when set against the revolutionary promise.[102] If revolution were a rare event before the creation of such states, it now seems all but foreclosed. All the more reason, then, to respect, if not celebrate, the weapons of the weak. All the more reason to see in the tenacity of self-preservation—in ridicule, in truculence, in irony, in petty acts of noncompliance, in foot dragging, in dissimulation, in resistant mutuality, in the disbelief in elite homilies, in the steady, grinding efforts to hold one's own against overwhelming odds—a spirit and practice that prevents the worst and promises something better.

101. Georg Lukacs, *History and Class Consciousness: Studies in Marxist Dialectics*, trans. Rodney Livingstone (Cambridge: MIT Press, 1971), 59, emphasis in original.

102. To quote Orwell one last time: "For a left-wing party in power, its most serious antagonist is always its own past propaganda." Sonia Orwell and Ian Angus, eds., *The Collected Essays, Journalism, and Letters of George Orwell*, vol. 1 (New York: Harcourt, Brace, 1968), 515.

Appendix A • A Note on Village Population, 1967–1979

Despite the growth of Sedaka's population, the first point to note is that it has grown much less than the rate of natural increase would suggest. Had the rate of household formation kept pace with natural increase, there would have been something on the order of eighty-three households by 1979, nearly twice the actual increase. This finding is neither new nor surprising.[1] Population has been leaking away from the rice plain of Kedah for some time,[2] owing both to the extended boom in the national and urban economy and to the fact that, even with double-cropping, the prospects for the children of tenants and smallholders are hardly encouraging. Their departure has slowed the process of involution in the local economy but has hardly reversed it.

Aside from the departure of young people, which simply reduces the size of an existing household, there were fourteen households present in 1967 that are absent today. Six families simply died out.[3] Eight households left the village. Four of these bought paddy land elsewhere, renting or selling locally owned land in the process. All but one of these four families purchased land in Seberang Perak, one of the last "paddy frontier" areas where suitable land can be bought at reasonable prices and cleared for cultivation. This form of mobility required capital; one such family owned 10 relong in Sedaka, another owned 6 relong, and still another had rented in at least 15 relong. Only one household, which owned 2 relong, was anything less than a family of substance. The four remaining families had the good fortune to be accepted as settlers on government plantation schemes (*ranchangan*). Attracted by the assurance of high incomes, they left and in three cases were able to arrange for one or more of their brothers to be taken in as well. Again, these families were not by any means poor in the village context. One owned a shop and small rice mill, two others owned nearly 5 relong apiece, and the last owned only 1 relong but was said by villagers to have been fairly well-off. In fact, of the eleven individuals who applied successfuly for

1. This assumes, of course, that the average size of a household did not increase. Since all evidence indicates that household size, even in rural areas, has been declining, this is a safe assumption.

2. S. Jegatheesan, *Land Tenure in the Muda Irrigation Scheme*, MADA Monograph No. 29 (Alor Setar: MADA, 1976), 26, notes that the rural population in Muda grew at an annual rate of only 1.54 percent from 1957 to 1970, while the national rate of population increase was 3.1 percent for the same period.

3. In two of these cases the surviving widow or widower has moved to a nearby *pondok* in Yan. The *pondok* in this and many other cases is both a center for religious teaching and a kind of Islamic retirement home at which old people prepare themselves spiritually for death.

settlement schemes, nearly two-thirds were from the top half of the village income distribution.[4]

Paradoxically, such settlement schemes are intended to benefit the rural poor, but, like so many government programs, accomplish quite the reverse. The reasons for this are not obscure. Incomes on the schemes are high enough to attract the sons of even the wealthiest villagers. Application requires at least two trips, usually all the way to Pahang, and a number of documents that typically require bribes. The cost involved is substantial. Even when they make the effort, however, poor applicants have a lower success rate for at least two reasons.[5] First, they are less likely to meet the literacy standards required, as their parents are likely to have withdrawn them from primary school at an early age. Second, they are less likely to have the political connections that can often mean the difference between success and failure.

Both rich and poor quit the village, but their manner of leaving is decidedly different. The poor tend to leave as individuals—the sons and, more rarely, daughters, of families whose local prospects are bleak. With the rare exception of those with secondary education, they leave for such urban jobs as manual labor and construction work or, in the case of young women, domestic service or factory work. The well-to-do, when they leave at all, often go as families to land they have bought or to a settlement scheme plot. In other words, the poor leave to join the ranks of the proletariat and the rich leave as a propertied, if petite, bourgeoisie.

In the course of the past dozen years, a total of twenty-eight new families have established themselves in Sedaka. Thirteen reflect the natural process of new family formation: six are the sons of villagers who have married and set up separate households; seven are daughters of villagers whose husbands have moved in and established new households. Another ten families moved in because the husband's or, more rarely, the wife's father owned land in the village (though he did not reside there), which the couple could rent. Thus, in twenty-three cases, the combination of kinship and available land (whether rented or inherited) explains the appearance of new households in Sedaka. The kinship tie, in this context, is decisive *only* because it provides access to farming land. There are no hard-and-fast rules in Malay society governing whether a new family should live near the husband's or wife's parents, and it is a safe bet that in nearly all twenty-

4. In cases where a son or co-resident younger brother in the same household was accepted to a *ranchangan* and left, the household remained in both the 1967 and 1979 censuses. For this reason, the number of individuals going to *ranchangan* was greater than the number of families that dropped out of the 1979 census. In two cases, also, individuals who were accepted chose not to take up the opportunity.

5. Such is the attraction of the *ranchangan* that at least twelve villagers applied during my eighteen-month stay. Half the applicants were from among the poorer families and had risked considerable capital (typically M$200) in order to apply.

three instances the choice was made according to which side could provide the most paddy land. Of the remaining five families, two are pure wage laborers with only a house lot in the village, and three are special cases.[6]

The economic status of these new households offers something of a window on the past decade. Despite the fact that nearly all established households in Sedaka because it was economically advantageous to do so, their incomes place a majority of them among the poorest half of the village. Far more significant, however, is the average farm size among this group.[7] The land they now rent from their parents is likely, with a few notable exceptions, to represent the maximum acreage they will eventually inherit; in many cases they will inherit less.[8] Thus, the present size of farms for this group of active rice growers is a fair indication of their future farm size as well. The average farm size for this group in 1979 was 3.5 relong, nearly 1 relong below the village average. If, however, we eliminate the five privileged farmers among the twenty-eight who now farm more than 6 relong, the average farm size for the remaining twenty-three is a meager 2.6 relong, well below the minimum 4 relong required for a subsistence income.

The situation of these twenty-three families illustrates the long-term demographic dilemma of village agriculture. Put in more anthropological terms, one writer has called this the problem of the "establishment fund," which is the "cost of setting up a household with access to a means of living comparable to that of the previous generation."[9] For an agrarian society, such access means above all access to land. Given the disappearance of the rice frontier and high

6. Of the special cases, one is a pensioner from the national railways who was born in Sedaka and has chosen to retire there; another is a storekeeper who has set up shop next to the main road; and the third is a widow who has moved from her old house to a smaller house where she lives with her niece, who is still schooling.

7. Landownership for this group is significantly below the village average but that is to be expected, since few are of an age when they could expect to inherit land. The usual practice is that land is not actually transferred until the father is deceased; when a farmer retires from active cultivation he is thus likely to rent land to his children.

8. A farmer with a good deal of land may occasionally rent more land to a son than that son will inherit. This is likely to happen when other sons are not yet of farming age or have taken work that does not permit them to cultivate. When the land is eventually inherited, these underage and noncultivating sons will typically receive a full share of property. Of the new households, there were only four farmers who could expect to inherit more land than they were now farming, and the amount of additional land involved was less than 6 relong.

9. Brian Fegan, "The Establishment Fund of Peasants and Population Increase in Central Luzon: Changing Class Structures" (Paper presented at Second Conference of the Asian Studies Association of Australia, University of New South Wales, Sydney, May 15–19, 1978).

birth rates, each new generation finds itself pressing against a resource base that is largely fixed. To be sure, double-cropping and a buoyant urban economy provide a welcome breathing space. What space they provide, however, is largely undercut by the fact that well over half the population now farms plots that are already less than adequate as well as by the impact of structural changes that have reduced both wage work and the land available for rental. The stark reality is that there is simply no viable niche in the village economy for the greater part of the next generation.

Appendix B • Farm Income Comparisons for Different Tenure and Farm Size Categories, Muda, 1966, 1974, 1979

	Average Tenant			Average Owner-Operator			Average Owner/Tenant[g]			Average Small Owner			Average Small Tenant		
Year	1966	1974	1979	1966	1974	1979	1966	1974	1979	1966	1974	1979	1966	1974	1979
Average paddy area (acres)[a]	3.76	3.69	3.69	3.55	3.20	3.20	6.11	6.60	6.60	1.78	1.42	1.42	1.78	1.42	1.42
Average family size[b]	5.58	5.58	5.58	5.58	5.58	5.58	5.58	5.58	5.58	4.94	4.94	4.94	4.94	4.94	4.94
Gross paddy income (M$)[c]	1365	5384	5564	1289	4670	4826	2219	9631	9952	643	2072	2141	643	2072	2141
Production costs[d]	383	2837	3603	269	1660	2018	570	4246	5306	98	694	853	161	1048	1344
Net paddy income[e]	982	2547	1961	1020	3110	2808	1649	5385	4646	545	1378	1288	482	1024	797
Other income[f]	426	922	956	359	722	740	237	1020	1155	476	831	809	476	831	809
Total net annual income (current prices)	1408	3469	2917	1379	3732	3548	1886	6405	5801	1021	2209	2097	958	1855	1606
Real income: 1974, 1979 figures corrected for changes in consumer price index (1966 base)	1408	2417	1664	1379	2601	2023	1886	4463	3309	1021	1539	1196	958	1293	916
Real M$ gain over 1966		1009	256		1222	644		2577	1423		518	175		335	(42)
Percentage gain over 1966 (real) M$		72	18		89	47		137	75		51	17		35	(4)
Monthly net income per household (nominal dollars)	117	289	243	115	311	296	157	534	483	85	184	175	80	155	134
Official poverty-line index—rural (M$ per month per household)	215	215	267	215	215	267	215	215	267	215	215	267	215	215	267

[a]Average paddy area for 1966 is derived from *Farm Economy Survey of the Muda River Project, 1966* (Ministry of Agriculture, 1967), table II. The 1974 figures are from the 1975 *USM-MADA Land Tenure Study*, 153; 1979 paddy areas are assumed to be the same as for 1975 since no newer figures are available. Thus from 1966 to 1975 the paddy area for each category of farm changes to reflect the actual area under cultivation. One acre equals 1.4 relong.

[b]Family size is adjusted from 1966 to 1974 for small farms to reflect data reported by the *USM-MADA Land Tenure Survey.*

[c]It is assumed that all paddy harvested is sold, to arrive at a cash equivalent for the total crop.

[d]Unpaid family labor on the farm is not imputed as a part of production costs. Though not strictly a production cost, the Islamic *zakat* tax is included here, but the percentage of gross yield paid is reduced from figures typically used in line with recent field research findings. For tenants, rent is calculated as part of production costs.

[e]There is good reason to believe that this figure is overstated. Yields are based on crop-cutting surveys that systematically overstate yields by about 10 percent. Furthermore, paddy sales receipts do not adjust for the reduction that is made for moisture content, etc., and that averaged 14.5 percent for both seasons of 1977 and 17.5 percent for 1979. A more realistic gross paddy income figure would therefore have to be reduced by over 20 percent. Net paddy income would be reduced by a greater percentage—one that grows larger as the proportion of production costs to gross paddy income expands.

[f]Includes home production for consumption and sale, wages received for wage labor on other paddy farms, and other income in the form of wages, salaries, remittances, gifts, etc. There is reason to believe that "other income" is exaggerated, especially for small farms, since, typically, a small percentage of this category receives regular wages from public or private sector jobs that are then averaged for the entire category. The median for such income would be far lower and would, perhaps, reduce this income as a whole by as much as 20 to 30 percent.

[g]Assume one-half paddy area owned, one-half rented.

Appendix C • Data on Land Tenure Changes, Net Returns, and Political Office

TABLE C1 • Land Tenure in Sedaka, 1967

(1 relong = .71 acre)

Area held (relong)		Landlord	Landlord/ Owner-Operator[a]	Owner-Operator/ Landlord	Tenant/ Landlord	Owner-Operator/ Tenant/ Landlord	Owner-Operator	Owner-Operator/ Tenant	Tenant/ Owner-Operator	Tenant	Total
.01–3	No. of households	—	—	—	—	—	3	—	—	9	12
	Area operated	—	—	—	—	—	5.25	—	—	21.5	26.75
	Area rented out	—	—	—	—	—	—	—	—	—	—
3+–7	No. of households	—	1	1	1	—	3	1	1	10	17
	Area operated	—	2	—	5	—	11.75	7	7	46.5	79.25
	Area rented out	—	3	—	2	—	—	—	—	—	5
7+–10	No. of households	—	1	1	1	—	1	1	1	1	6
	Area operated	—	4	5	—	—	8	8	9.25	10	44.25
	Area rented out	—	5.5	3	—	—	—	—	—	—	8.5
10+–20	No. of households	—	2	2	1	3	—	1	2	2	13
	Area operated	—	8	16	8	28.5	—	11	26	25.5	123
	Area rented out	—	23	6.5	5	14.5	—	—	—	—	49
20+–40	No. of households	—	1	—	—	—	—	1	1	1	4
	Area operated	—	1	—	—	—	—	23	21.5	38	83.5
	Area rented out	—	20.5	—	—	—	—	—	—	—	20.5
Total	No. of households	—	5	3	2	3	7	4	5	23	52[b]
	Area operated	—	15	21	13	28.5	25	49	63.75	142.5	357.75
	Area rented out	—	52	9.5	7	14.5	—	—	—	—	83
Average	Area operated	—	3	7	6.5	9.5	3.6	12.3	12.8	6.2	6.9[c]
	Area rented out	—	10.4	3.2	3.5	4.8	—	—	—	6.2	6.4[d]

Source: Kenzo Horii, "The Land Tenure System of Malay Padi Farmers: A Case Study . . . in the State of Kedah," *Developing Economies* 10, no. 1 (1972): 55. A few obvious errors in summary figures have been corrected.

[a] In each of the mixed categories, the classification is determined on the basis of how the majority of the land farmed is held. Thus landlord/owner-operators rent out a majority of their land, while owner-operator/landlords own and operate the major share of their land.

[b] Total households exclude 4 nonfarming households and thus are 52 rather than 56.

[c] Total relong operated (357.75) divided by households (52).

[d] Horii's published figure for this observation is 3.6. I could find no basis for this figure from the observations in the table. I have accordingly divided the total acreage rented out (83 relong) by the total number of households that rent out land (13) to arrive at 6.4.

TABLE C2 • Land Tenure in Sedaka, 1979

(1 relong = .71 acre)

Area held (relong)		Landlord	Landlord/Owner-Operator[a]	Owner-Operator/Landlord	Tenant/Landlord	Owner-Operator/Tenant/Landlord	Owner-Operator	Owner-Operator/Tenant	Tenant/Owner-Operator	Tenant	Total
.01–1	No. of households	2	—	—	—	—	1	—	—	2	5
	Area operated	—	—	—	—	—	.25	—	—	1.75	2
	Area rented out	.36	—	—	—	—	—	—	—	—	.36
1+–3	No. of households	—	1	—	—	1	4	3	—	10	19
	Area operated	—	1	—	—	2	7	7.5	—	24	41.5
	Area rented out	—	1.5	—	—	.5	—	—	—	—	2
3+–7	No. of households	1	1	1	—	1	2	6	2	11	25
	Area operated	—	2	3	—	5	11	31.5	10.5	50	113
	Area rented out	6	3	1	—	2	—	—	—	—	12
7+–10	No. of households	1	1	1	—	—	—	1	1	2	7
	Area operated	—	4	7	—	—	—	8	10	16.5	45.5
	Area rented out	9.75	6	3	—	—	—	—	—	—	18.75
10+–20	No. of households	1	1	1	—	6	1	—	1	1	12
	Area operated	—	6	11.5	—	51	11	—	13.5	15	108
	Area rented out	15	9	5	—	28.25	—	—	—	—	57.25
20+–40	No. of households	—	—	1	—	—	—	—	—	—	1
	Area operated	—	—	15	—	—	—	—	—	—	15
	Area rented out	—	—	15	—	—	—	—	—	—	15
Total	No. of households	5	4	4	—	8	8	10	4	26	69[b]
	Area operated	—	13	36.5	—	58	29.25	47	34	107.25	325
	Area rented out	31.11	19.5	24	—	30.75	—	—	—	—	105.36
Average	Area operated	—	3.25	9.1	—	7.25	3.7	4.7	8.5	4.1	4.7[c]
	Area rented out	6.2	4.9	6	—	3.8	—	—	—	—	5[d]

[a]See note a in table C1.

[b]Total households exclude 4 nonfarming families (wage laborers) and 1 pensioner and thus are 69 rather than 74.

[c]Total relong operated (325) divided by housholds (69). If we excluded the 5 pure landlords from this calculation, the figure would be 5.1.

[d]Total relong rented out (105.36) divided by total number of households that rent out land (21).

TABLE C3 · Net Returns per Relong for Various Classes of Cultivators in Sedaka, Depending on Size of Yield, 1979

Yield in Gunny Sacks[a]	6		8		10		12		14		16		18	
Categories of Cultivators	Production[b] Costs	Net Cash[c] Return	Production Costs	Net Cash Return	Production Costs	Net Cash Return	Production Costs	Net Cash Return	Production Costs	Net Cash Return	Production Costs	Net Cash Return	Production Costs	Net Cash Return
A. Low production costs[d] with no rent (owner)	76	133	82	197	88	261	94	325	100	389	106	453	112	517
B. High production costs[e] with no rent (owner)	171	39	178	102	185	165	192	228	199	291	206	354	213	417
C. Low production costs with concessionary rent (M$100) (tenant)	176	33	182	97	188	161	194	225	200	289	206	353	212	417
D. High production costs with concessionary rent (M$100) (tenant)	271	(61)	278	2	285	65	292	128	299	191	306	254	313	317
E. Low production costs with economic rent (M$160) (tenant)	236	(26)	242	37	248	101	254	165	260	229	266	293	272	357
F. High production costs with economic rent (M$160) (tenant)	331	(121)	338	(58)	345	5	352	68	359	131	366	194	373	257
G. Low production costs with high rent (M$180) (tenant)	256	(46)	262	17	268	81	274	145	280	209	286	273	292	337
H. High production costs with high rent (M$180) (tenant)	351	(141)	358	(78)	365	(15)	372	48	379	111	386	174	393	237

[a] Gunny sacks are used as the unit of output because that is the form in which farmers state their own yields.

[b] Production costs include all inputs plus rental charges, if any. They include hired labor only; unpaid family labor is excluded.

[c] Based on 1979 farm-gate paddy prices for standard gunny sack weight, assuming entire harvest marketed.

[d] Low production costs assume that the cultivating family transplants and reaps the crop using family and/or exchange (derau) labor rather than hired labor. They also assume that the field is ploughed by tractor only once, that somewhat less fertilizer is applied, and that transportation costs are small.

[e] High production costs assume that hired labor is used for transplanting and reaping, that the field is ploughed twice, that somewhat more fertilizer is applied, and that transportation costs are at the higher range of the scale.

Explanation of Categories

A. Occurs only for smallholders with less than 3 relong who have abundant supplies of family labor. B. Occurs in the case of *many* larger-scale landowners and/or those with little available family labor. C. As in A, except that farmer is a tenant renting (usually from a parent or parents-in-law) at concessionary rent. D. As in B, except that farmer is a tenant at concessionary rent. E. As in A, except that farmer is a tenant at standard non-kin rent for *new* tenancies. F. As in B, except that farmer is a tenant at standard non-kin rent for *new* tenancies. G. As in A, except that farmer is a tenant at highest local rents. H. As in B, except that farmer is a tenant at highest local rents.

FIGURE C3a • Net Returns per Relong for Various Classes of Cultivators in Sedaka, Depending on Size of Yield, 1979

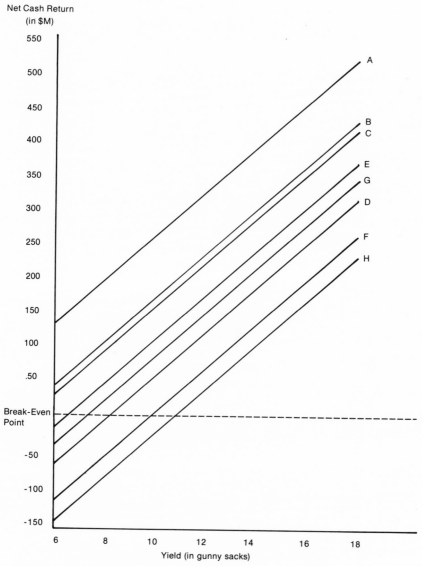

Note: See table C3 for actual figures and for a key to the classes of cultivators

Note: See table C3 for actual figures and for a key to the classes of cultivators whose returns are described.

TABLE C4 • Officers and Members of the Village Development Committee (JKK) of UMNO in Sedaka, with Income Rank of Family, 1979

Name	Office in UMNO	Income Rank of Family
Shamsul	Head	66
Fadzil	Ass't Head	42
Taha Lebai Hussein	Treasurer	35
Basir	Exco member	64
Ghazali	Exco member	65
Amin	Exco member	72
Yunus bin Haji Salim	Exco member	*
Sofiah, wife of Tok Long	Exco member	61
Daud bin Haji Jaafar	Exco member	70
Sahil bin Lebai Pendak	Exco member	73
Abu Hassan	Exco member	57

*Son of extremely rich landowner (45 relong, two lorries, small rice mill) residing at edge of village. His father is the elected head of the UMNO committee for the federal parliamentary constituency (Jerai) that includes Sedaka.

Appendix D • Glossary of Local Terms

Bang—To hear about, to overhear, to eavesdrop.

Belaga—To fight, to oppose.

Cam—To notice.

Dangau—Shed, covered lean-to, hut for crop watching.

Depa—They.

Derau (n)—An exchange labor group for planting or cutting paddy and, more rarely, threshing, in which equivalent amounts of labor are traded, with no money changing hands. The verb form is *berderau*.

Duit—Money, in standard Malay, but in Kedah it can also mean cents, as opposed to dollars.

Gagah—Brave, strong, in standard Malay, but in local usage, as in *boleh gagah*, it means "to get by," "to manage," "to struggle through."

Gerek—Bicycle.

Habak—To tell, to let know (*bagi tau*).

Habis—Finished, used up, literally, but it can be used to make a superlative when joined to an adjective. Thus *habis teruk* means "the very worst."

Hang—You, used colloquially in place of *awak*.

Jak—To flatter or to praise, usually insincerely, from the English verb "to jack up."

Jelapang—Small barn in which paddy is stored.

Kat—To (a person), as in "give [it] to him" (*bagi kat dia*). Colloquial for *kepada*.

Keleh—To notice, to recognize.

Kerja kupang—To work for a fixed wage for a given time period (usually a morning).

Kot 'ni—Here, in this area, close by.

Kumpulan share—Share group, from the English, meaning a small gang of laborers (usually women) who contract to transplant or cut paddy for a negotiated price per relong, which is then divided among the workers.

Kut—Rotating credit association.

La 'ni—Nowadays, these days (*la ini*).

Main kut—To participate in a rotating credit association.

Menyorok—To eat a snack, small breakfast.

Se-kupang—Ten cents, from the name of an old coin.

Tak dan—Not to have time (to do something).

Timbun—Fat.

Tok—Term of respect for grandparents of both genders, and used as a term of respect for the aged in general.

Tok sah—No use. Don't bother, as in *tok sah pe* (no use going).

Appendix E • Translation of *Surat Layang*

NOTE: *This copy of a* surat layang *circulated in the region of Sedaka in March 1979. Its form is similar to other such letters. They are distributed in the same way as chain letters in the West.*

In the name of Allah, most
gracious and merciful.

[This letter has been copied sentence
for sentence from a letter coming
anonymously without changing its contents].

This letter, in the form of a will, from the holy land of Mecca is sent to all Muslims by Syed Ahmad. It was brought to Indonesia by Haji Malek, a member of [sect] *Hara Baham Balanganum.* Syed Ahmad, having fallen asleep at the grave of the Prophet Muhamad [blessings from Allah and peace be upon him], was spoken to by the Prophet in his sleep.

"I will no longer bestow blessings upon Muslims nor protect them from God's punishment because many of them have committed grave sins such as adultery, drinking; who do not bother to pay the *zakat*; who always make their own selfish interest the object of worship; who are conceited. Syed Ahmad, I command you to remind all those who call themselves Muslims. Have undivided faith in Allah, the all pure, and be patient in confronting difficulties, and do not let the faithful betray Allah."

Signs of the Day of Judgement (*kiamat*)

1. In 1971, there were many cases of
   housewives leaving their houses without
   telling their husbands.
2. In 1972, two stars were seen as big as hens.
3. In 1980, the earth will be in darkness
   for three days and three nights;
   the sun will rise in the west and set
   in the north, and from that moment
   Allah will no longer accept repentance.

Oath of Syed ahmad

I swear to Allah if I have lied about my dream, I will be cast out of the Muslim faith, and whoever does not believe in my dream will become an unbeliever and, when the day of judgement comes soon, will be put in hell.

Attention 1. To whoever calls himself a Muslim; this letter should be sent to Muslims in other areas. Read it carefully because this letter is a will and oath in the name of Allah from Syed Ahmad to all those of the Muslim faith.

Saudi Arabia

2. While reading the Koran at the grave of the Prophet Muhamad, Syed Ahmad fell asleep and had this dream. 80,000 Muslims have passed away but, of that total,

not even one was of the true faith. Housewives do not listen to the advice of their husbands. Rich men do not have sympathy for the poor. Many do not pay the *zakat,* do not wish to do good works. This is why Syed Ahmad is sending out this testament to the faithful in order that they follow the right path because the Day of Judgement is coming suddenly. A star will rise in the sky and the door of repentence will be closed. All writings will decline and the sun will move closer [to the earth].

On reading a letter such as this whoever is poor will become rich. All wishes will be answered if thirty copies of this are printed and circulated. In two weeks, whoever has followed these instructions will be rewarded with good life. In Bombay there was a man who copied this will and made a profit in his business. On the other hand, whoever says this testament is false, his male son will die. Whoever, having read this will and having understood it, and who does not tell other people, will confront all sorts of difficulties in life. But whoever copies and circulates this letter will receive great profit.

It is only Allah who knows all
It is only Allah whom we can worship
It is only Allah who can protect and guide us.

Bibliography

Abercrombie, Nicholas. 1980. *Class Structure and Knowledge*. Oxford: Blackwell.

Abercrombie, Nicholas, Stephen Hill, and Bryan S. Turner. 1980. *The Dominant Ideology Thesis*. London: Allen & Unwin.

Adas, Michael. 1981. "From Avoidance to Confrontation: Peasant Protest in Precolonial and Colonial Southeast Asia." *Comparative Studies in Society and History* 23 (2): 217–47.

Afifuddin Haji Omar. 1977. *Irrigation Structures and Local Peasant Organisation*, MADA Monograph No. 32. Alor Setar: MADA.

———. 1978. *Peasants, Institutions, and Development in Malaysia: The Political Economy of Development in the Muda Region*. MADA Monograph No. 36. Alor Setar: MADA.

———. 1980. "The Pivotal Role of an Integrated Institutional Reform in Socioeconomic Development of Rice Peasantry in Malaysia." Paper presented at Conference on Development: The Peasantry and Development in the ASEAN Region, Universiti Kebangsaan Malaysia, Bangi.

Ahmad Mahdzan bin Ayob. 1980. "Choice of Technology in Rice Harvesting in the Muda Irrigation Scheme, Malaysia." Ph.D. diss. University of Florida.

Alavi, Hamza. 1972. "The State in Post-colonial Societies: Pakistan and Bangladesh." *New Left Review* 74: 59–81.

Alier, Juan Martinez. 1971. *Labourers and Landowners in Southern Spain*. St. Anthony's College, Oxford, Publications, No. 4, London: Allen & Unwin.

Anand, S. Forthcoming. *The Size Distribution of Income in Malaysia*. Washington, D.C.: World Bank.

Ayoob, M. 1981. *The Politics of Islamic Reassertion*. London: Croom Helm.

Badan Dakwah Islamiah, Pejabat Zakat Negeri Kedah. N.d., probably about 1970. *Panduan Zakat*. Alor Setar: Majlis Ugama Negeri Kedah.

Bahro, Rudolf. 1981. *The Alternative in Eastern Europe*. Trans. David Fernbach. London: Verso.

Bailey, Connor, 1976. "Broker, Mediator, Patron and Kinsman." Athens, Ohio: Ohio University Center for International Studies.

Bailey, F. G. 1971. *Gifts and Poison: The Politics of Reputation*. New York: Schocken.

Balzac, Honoré de. 1949. *Les Paysans*. Paris: Pleiades.

Banks, David. 1972. "Changing Kinship in North Malaya." *American Anthropologist* 74 (2): 1254–75.

Barnard, Rosemary. 1973. "The Role of Capital and Credit in a Malay Rice-Producing Village." *Pacific Viewpoint* 14 (2): 113–36.

———. 1978. "The Modernization of Agriculture in a Kedah Village, 1967–1978." Paper presented at Second National Conference of the Asian Studies Association of Australia, University of New South Wales, Sydney, May 15–19.

Bell, Clive. 1979. "Some Effects in the Barter Terms of Trade on a Small Regional Economy." Washington, D.C.: Development Research Center, World Bank. Mimeo.

Bell, Clive, Peter Hazell and Roger Slade. Forthcoming. *The Evaluation of Projects in Regional Perspective: A Case Study of the Muda Irrigation Project.* Baltimore: Johns Hopkins Univ. Press.

Berwick, E. J. H. 1956. *Census of Padi Planters in Kedah, 1955.* Alor Setar: Department of Agriculture, Government of Malaysia.

Bloch, Marc. 1970. *French Rural History: An Essay on Its Basic Characteristics.* Trans. Janet Sondheimer. Berkeley: Univ. of California Press.

Bonney, R. 1971. *Kedah, 1771–1821: The Search for Security and Independence.* Kuala Lumpur: Oxford Univ. Press.

Bourdieu, Pierre. 1977. *Outline of a Theory of Practice.* Trans. Richard Nice. Cambridge Univ. Press.

Brow, James. 1981. "Some Problems in the Analysis of Agrarian Classes in South Asia." *Peasant Studies* 9 (1): 15–33.

Caldwell, M., and M. Amin. 1977. *Malaya: The Making of a Neo-Colony.* London: Spokesman.

Carr, E. H. 1966. *The Bolshevik Revolution: 1917–1923.* Vol. 1. Harmondsworth: Penguin.

Cheah Boon Kheng. 1981. "Social Banditry and Rural Crime in North Kedah, 1909–22." *Journal of the Malaysian Branch of the Royal Asiatic Society* 54 (2): 98–130.

———. 1980. "Social Banditry and Rural Crime in Kedah, 1910–1929: Historical and Folk Perceptions." Paper presented to Conference of International Association of Historians of Asia, Kuala Lumpur.

Cobb, R. C. 1970. *The Police and the People: French Popular Protest, 1789–1820.* Oxford: Clarendon.

Cohn, Norman. 1957. *The Pursuit of the Millennium.* London: Seecker and Warburg.

Corner, Lorraine. 1979. "The Impact of Rural Out-Migration Labour: Supply and Cultivation Techniques in a Double-Cropped Padi Area." Typescript.

———. 1980. "Mobility in the Context of Traditional Family and Social Relationships: Linkages, Reciprocity and Flow of Remittances." Typescript.

———. 1982. "The Impact of Rural Outmigration on Labour Utilization of Padi Households in Muda." Paper presented at Second International Conference of the Canadian Council for Southeast Asian Studies, Singapore.

Couillard, Marie-André. 1982. "A Brief Exploration into the Nature of Men/Women Relations among Pre-Colonial Malayan People." Paper presented at Second International Conference of the Canadian Council for Southeast Asian Studies, Singapore, June.

Daane, John R. V. 1978. "Farmers and Farmers' Organizations: A Study of Changing Resource Use Patterns in the Muda Area." Preliminary Report No. 2. Mimeo.

Daane, John R. V., and Gert Kalshoven. 1979. "Rural Organizations and Rural Development in West Malaysia." Mimeo.

De Koninck, Rodolphe. 1979. "The Integration of the Peasantry: Examples from Malaysia and Indonesia." *Pacific Affairs* 52: 265–93.

Department of Statistics, Government of Malaysia. 1973. *Household Expenditure Survey.* Kuala Lumpur.

Dickens, Charles. 1971. *Our Mutual Friend.* Harmondsworth: Penguin.

Disraeli, Benjamin. 1950. *Sybil: Or the Two Nations*. Oxford: Oxford Univ. Press.

Djamour, J. 1959. *Malay Kinship and Marriage in Singapore*. London: Athlone Press, Univ. of London.

Dobby, E. H. G. 1951. "The North Kedah Plain: A Study in the Environment of Pioneering for Rice Cultivation." *Economic Geography* 27: 287–315.

Doering, Otto Charles, III. 1973. "Malaysian Rice Policy and the Muda Irrigation Project." Ph.D. diss., Cornell Univ.

Donohue, J. J., and J. L. Esposito. 1982. *Islam in Transition: Muslim Perspectives*. New York: Oxford Univ. Press.

Dumont, Louis. 1970. *Homo Hierarchicus*. London: Weidenfeld & Nicholson.

Dunn, John. 1979. "Practising History and Social Science on 'Realist' Assumptions." In *Action and Interpretation: Studies in the Philosophy of the Social Sciences*, edited by C. Hookway and P. Pettit. Cambridge: Cambridge Univ. Press.

Durkheim, Emile. 1964. *The Division of Labour in Society*. New York: Free Press.

Economic Consultants Ltd. 1977. *Kedah-Perlis Development Study: Interim Report*. Alor Setar.

Edelman, Murray. 1974. "The Political Language of the Helping Professions." *Politics and Society* 4 (3): 295–310.

Elwert-Kretschmar, K. 1983. "Zur sozialen und ökonomischen Organisation von Haushalten im ländlichen Westmalaysia." Diplom Thesis, Universität Bielefeld.

Engels, Friedrich. 1973. *The Condition of the Working Class in England*. Moscow: Progress Publishers.

Far Eastern Economic Review. 1981. *Asia 1980 Yearbook*. Hong Kong: South China Morning Post.

Fatimah, H. 1980. "Differentiation of the Peasantry: A Study of the Rural Communities in West Malaysia." *Journal of Contemporary Asia* 10 (4): 400–22.

Fatimah, M. A. 1978. "The Effectiveness of the Government Policy Measures Relating to Padi and Rice Industry." Ph.D. diss., University of Newcastle-upon-Tyne.

Fegan, Brian. 1979. "Folk-Capitalism: Economizing Strategies of Wet Rice Farmers in a Philippine Village." Ph.D. diss., Yale University.

———. 1978. "The Establishment Fund of Peasants and Population Increase in Central Luzon: Changing Class Structures." Paper presented at Second Conference of the Asian Studies Association of Australia, University of New South Wales, Sydney, May 15–19.

Femia, Joseph. 1975. "Hegemony and Consciousness in the Thought of Antonio Gramsci." *Political Studies* 23 (1).

Ferro, Marc. 1971. "The Russian Soldier in 1917: Undisciplined, Patriotic, and Revolutionary." *Slavic Review* 30 (3): 483–512.

Firth, R. 1981. "Spiritual Aroma: Religion and Politics." *American Antropologist* 83: 582–601.

Firth, R., and B. D. Yamey, eds. 1964. *Capital, Saving and Credit in Peasant Societies*. London: Allen & Unwin.

Food and Agriculture Organization/World Bank Cooperative Program. 1975. *The Muda Study*. 2 vols. Rome: FAO.

Fredericks, L. J., G. Kalshoven, and J. R. V. Daane. 1980. "The Role of Farmers'

Organizations in Two Paddy Farming Areas in West Malaysia." Bulletin Nr. 40. Wageningen: Afdelingen voor Sociale Wetenschappen aan de Landbou-whogeschool.

Fujimoto, Akimi. 1980. "Land Tenure, Rice Production, and Income Sharing among Malay Peasants: Study of Four Villages." Ph.D. diss. Flinders University, Australia.

Fukui, H., and Y. Takaya. 1978. "Some Ecological Observations on Rice-Growing. in Malaysia." *Southeast Asian Studies* 16 (2): 189–97.

Funston, J. N. 1980. *Malay Politics in Malaysia: A Study of PAS and UMNO.* Kuala Lumpur: Heinemann.

Gaventa, John. 1980. *Power and Powerlessness: Quiescence and Rebellion in an Appalachian Valley.* Urbana: Univ. of Illinois Press.

Geertz, Clifford. 1973. "Thick Description: Toward an Interpretive Theory of Culture." Chap. 1 in *The Interpretation of Culture.* New York: Basic.

———. 1980. "Blurred Genres: The Refiguration of Social Thought." *American Scholar* 49 (2): 165–79.

Genovese, Eugene D. 1974. *Roll, Jordan, Roll: The World the Slaves Made.* New York: Pantheon.

Gibbons, D. S. 1983. "Paddy Poverty and Public Policy." Mimeo.

Gibbons, D. S., Rodolphe de Koninck, and Ibrahim Hassan. 1980. *Agricultural Modernization, Poverty and Inequality: The Distributional Impact of the Green Revolution in Regions of Malaysia and Indonesia.* Farnsborough: Saxon House.

Gibbons, D. S., Lim Teck Ghee, G. B. Elliston, and Shukur Kassim. 1981. *Hak Milik Tanah di Kawasan Perairan Muda: Lapuran Akhir* (Land tenure in the Muda irrigation area: Final report). Part 2, *Findings.* Pulau Pinang: Pusat Penyelidekan Dasar and Universiti Sains Malaysia.

Giddens, Anthony. 1979. *Central Problems in Social Theory: Action, Structure, and Contradiction in Social Analysis.* Berkeley: Univ. of California Press.

Gilmore, David. 1978. "Patronage and Class Conflict in Southern Spain." *Man* (n.s.) 12: 446–58.

Goffman, Erving. 1956. "The Nature of Deference and Demeanor." *American Anthropologist* 58 (June).

———. 1967. *Interaction Ritual: Essays on Face-to-Face Behavior.* Garden City: Anchor Books, Doubleday.

Goldman, R., and L. Squire. 1977. "Technical Change, Labour Use and Income Distribution in the Muda Irrigation Project." Development Discussion Paper No. 35. Cambridge: Harvard Institute for International Development.

Gramsci, Antonio. 1971. *Selections from the Prison Notebooks.* Ed. and trans. Quinten Hoare and Geoffrey Nowell Smith. London: Lawrence & Wishart.

Griffin, Keith. 1974. *The Political Economy of Agrarian Change: An Essay on the Green Revolution.* Cambridge, Mass.: Harvard Univ. Press.

Guillaumin, Emile. 1983. *The Life of a Simple Man.* Ed. Eugene Weber, rev. trans. Margaret Crosland. Hanover, New Hampshire: University Press of New England.

Habermas, Jurgen. 1971. *Knowledge and Human Interests.* Trans. Jeremy J. Shapiro. Boston: Beacon.

———. 1970. "Towards a Theory of Communicative Competence." *Inquiry* 13: 360–75.

Haraszti, Miklós. 1978. *A Worker in a Worker's State.* Trans. Michael Wright. New York: Universe Books.

Harrison, Brian. 1966. "Philanthropy and the Victorians." *Victorian Studies* 9 (4): 353–74.

Haviland, John Beard. 1977. *Gossip, Reputation, and Knowledge in Zinacantan.* Chicago: Univ. of Chicago Press.

Hay, Douglas. 1975. "Poaching and the Game Laws on Cannock Chase." In *Albion's Fatal Tree: Crime and Society in Eighteenth-Century England,* by Douglas Hay, Peter Linebaugh, John G. Rule, E. P. Thompson, and Cal Winslow. New York: Pantheon.

Hegel, G. W. F. 1977. *Phenomenology of the Spirit.* Trans. A. V. Miller, with analysis and foreword by J. N. Findlay. Oxford: Clarendon.

Herring, Ronald. 1983. "Landlordism as a Social System: Quiescence and Protest in Kerala." Paper presented to Annual Meeting of the Association for Asian Studies, San Francisco, March 23–27.

Hill, Christopher. 1972. *The World Turned Upside Down.* New York: Viking.

Hill, R. D. 1977. *Rice in Malaysia: A Study in Historical Geography.* Kuala Lumpur: Oxford Univ. Press.

Hirschman, Albert O. 1970. *Exit, Voice, and Loyalty: Responses to Decline in Firms, Organizations and States.* Cambridge: Harvard Univ. Press.

Hobsbawm, Eric. 1965. *Primitive Rebels: Studies in Archaic Forms of Social Movement in the 19th and 20th Centuries.* New York: Norton.

———. 1973. "Peasants and Politics." *Journal of Peasant Studies* 1 (1): 3–22.

Hobsbawm E. J., and George Rude. 1968. *Captain Swing.* New York: Pantheon.

Hoggart, Richard. 1954. *The Uses of Literacy.* London: Chatto & Windus.

Ho Nai Kin. 1978. *Implementation and Supervision Problem of Institutional Padi Production Credit in MADA's Farmers' Association.* MADA Monograph No. 35. Alor Setar: MADA.

Horii, Kenzo. 1972. "The Land Tenure System of Malay Padi Farmers: A Case Study . . . in the State of Kedah." *Developing Economies* 10 (1): 45–73.

Huizer, Gerrit. 1972. *Peasant Mobilization and Land Reform in Indonesia.* The Hague: Institute of Social Studies.

Husin, Syed Ali. 1975. *Malay Peasant Society and Leadership.* Kuala Lumpur: Oxford Univ. Press.

———. 1978. *Kemiskinan dan Kelaporan Tanah di Kelantan* (Poverty and land hunger in Kelantan). Petaling Jaya: Karangkraf Sdn. Berhad.

Hyden, Goran. *Beyond Ujama in Tanzania.* London: Heinemann.

Ikmal Said. 1980. "Capitalist Encroachment in Padi Production in West Malaysia." Paper presented at Conference on Development: The Peasantry and Development in the ASEAN Region, Universiti Kebangsaan Malaysia, Bangi.

International Bank for Reconstruction and Development. 1975. *Malaysia Loan 434-MA: Muda Irrigation Scheme Completion Report,* No. 795-MA. Washington, D.C.

———. 1980. *Malaysia: Selected Issues in Rural Poverty.* Vol. 2. World Bank Report No. 2685-MA. Washington, D.C.

Ishak Shari and Jomo K. Sundaram. 1980. "Malaysia's 'Green Revolution' in Rice Farming: Capital Accumulation and Technological Change in Peasant Society." Paper presented at Conference on Development: The Peasantry and Development in the ASEAN Region, Universiti Kebangsaan Malaysia, Bangi.

Janeway, Elizabeth. 1981. *The Powers of the Weak*. New York: Morrow Quill Paperbacks.

Jegatheesan, S. 1976. *Land Tenure in the Muda Irrigation Scheme*. MADA Monograph No. 29. Alor Setor: MADA.

———. 1977. *The Green Revolution and the Muda Irrigation Scheme*. MADA Monograph No. 30. Alor Setar: MADA.

———. 1980. "Progress and Problems of Rice Mechanization in Peninsular Malaysia." Working Paper No. 17, Persidangan Padi Kebangsaan Malaysia (Malaysian national conference on paddy), Kuala Lumpur, February 26–28.

Kartodirdjo, Sartono. 1973. *Protest Movements in Rural Java: A Study of Agrarian Unrest in the 19th and Early 20th Centuries*. Singapore: Institute of Southeast Asian Studies.

Kessler, Clive S. 1972. "Islam, Society and Political Behaviour: Some Implications of the Malay Case." *British Journal of Sociology* 23: 33–50.

———. 1974. "The Politics of Islamic Egalitarianism." *Humaniora Islamica* 2: 237–52.

———. 1978. *Islam and Politics in a Malay State: Kelantan 1838–1969*. Ithaca: Cornell Univ. Press.

Kim, K. K. 1972. *The Western Malay States, 1880–1873: The Effects of Commercial Development on Malay Politics*. Kuala Lumpur: Oxford Univ. Press.

Kuchiba, Masuo. 1980. "Kin Groupings in a Kedah Malay Village." Paper presented at Third National Conference of the Asian Studies Association of Australia, Brisbane.

Kuchiba, Masuo, and L. Bauzon, eds. 1979. *A Comparative Study of Paddy-Growing Communities in Southeast Asia and Japan*. Kyoto: Ryukoko University.

Kuchiba, Masuo, Yoshihiro Tsubouchi, and Narifumi Maeda, eds. 1979. *Three Malay Villages: A Sociology of Paddy Growers in West Malaysia*. Trans. Peter and Stephanie Hawkes. Honolulu: Univ. of Hawaii Press.

Lai, K. C. 1978. "Income Distribution among Farm Households in the Muda Irrigation Scheme: A Development Perspective." *Kajian Ekonomi Malaysia* 15 (1): 38–57.

Levine, Lawrence W. 1977. *Black Culture and Black Consciousness*. New York: Oxford Univ. Press.

Lewis, I. M. 1971. *Ecstatic Religions: An Anthropological Study of Spirit Possession and Shamanism*. Harmondsworth: Penguin.

Lewis, Oscar. 1964. *Pedro Martinez: A Mexican Peasant and His Family*. New York: Vintage.

Lim Joo-Jock. 1954. "Tradition and Peasant Agriculture in Malaya." *Malayan Journal of Tropical Geography* 3: 44–57.

Lim Mah Hui. 1980. "Ethnic and Class Relations in Malaysia." *Journal of Contemporary Asia* 10: 130–54.

Lim Teck Ghee. 1977. *Peasants and Their Agricultural Economy in Colonial Malaya, 1874–1941*. Kuala Lumpur: Oxford Univ. Press.

Lim Teck Ghee, D. S. Gibbons, and Shukur Kassim. 1980. "Accumulation of Padi Land in the Muda Region: Some Findings and Thoughts on their Implications for the Peasantry and Development." Paper presented at Conference on Development: The Peasantry and Development in the ASEAN Region, Universiti Kebangsaan Malaysia, Bangi.

Lukacs, Georg. 1971. *History and Class Consciousness: Studies in Marxist Dialectics.* Trans. Rodney Livingstone. Cambridge: MIT Press.

Lyons, M. L. 1979. "The Dakwah Movement in Malaysia." *Review of Indonesian Malaysian Affairs* 13: 34–45.

MacAndrews, Colin. 1978. *Land Settlement Policies in Malaysia and Indonesia: A Preliminary Analysis.* Occasional Papers Series, No. 52. Singapore: Institute of Southeast Asian Studies.

Maeda, N. 1975. "Family Circle, Community and Nation in Malaysia." *Current Anthropology* 16: 163–66.

Malaysia, Government of. 1954. *Report of the Rice Production Committee, 1953.* Vol. 1. Kuala Lumpur.

Mansor Haji Othman. 1978. "Hak Milik Tanah Padi dan Politik di Kedah." Master's thesis, School of Comparative Social Science, Universiti Sains Malaysia.

Marriott, McKim. 1955. "Little Communities in an Indigenous Civilization." In *Village India,* edited by McKim Marriott. Chicago: Univ. of Chicago Press.

Marx, Karl. 1970. *Capital.* Vol. 1. Harmondsworth: Penguin.

Massard, J. L. 1983. "Kinship and Exchange Practices in a Malay Village." Paper presented at Seminar on Cognitive Forms of Social Organization in Southeast Asia, Amsterdam.

Meerman, Jacob. 1979. *Public Expenditure in Malaysia: Who Benefits and Why.* A World Bank Research Publication. London: Oxford Univ. Press.

Mencher, Joan P. 1980. "On Being an Untouchable in India: A Materialist Perspective." In *Beyond the Myths of Culture: Essays in Cultural Materialism,* edited by Eric B. Ross. New York: Academic.

Milgram, Stanley, 1974. *Obedience to Authority: An Experimental View.* New York: Harper & Row.

Ministry of Agriculture and Fisheries, Government of Malaysia. 1973. *Implementation of Padi Cultivators Act, 1967.* Kuala Lumpur.

Mochtar, Tamin. 1980. "Rural Credit: Past Record, Present and Future." Paper presented at Seminar on Economics, Development and the Consumer, Consumers' Association of Penang. Penang.

Mohamed Abu Bakar. 1981. "Islamic Revivalism and the Political Process in Malaysia." *Asian Survey* 21: 1040–59.

Mohd. Noh Samik. "Delinquent Loanees." MADA, Bahagian Pertanian.

Mohd. Shadli Abdullah. 1978. "The Relationship of the Kinship System to Land Tenure: A Case Study of Kampung Gelung Rambai. Master's thesis, Universiti Sains Malaysia, Penang.

Mokhtar Mohamed. 1974. *Sistem Pondok dan pendidikan Islam zaman pembangunan: satu tinjauan ke atas Pondok di Pendang, Kedah* (Pondok system and Islamic education in the development area: An examination of the Pondok at Pendang, Kedah). Thesis, Universiti Kebangsaan Malaysia, Bangi.

Mokhzani bin Abdul Rahim. 1973. "Credit in a Malay Peasant Society," Ph.D. diss., University of London.

Moore, Barrington, Jr. 1966. *Social Origins of Dictatorship and Democracy.* Boston: Beacon.

———. 1978. *Injustice: The Social Bases of Obedience and Revolt.* White Plains: M. E. Sharpe.

Mullin, Gerald W. 1972. *Flight and Rebellion: Slave Resistance in Eighteenth-Century Virginia.* New York: Oxford Univ. Press.

Muzaffar, Chandra. 1979. *Protector? An Analysis of the Concept and Practice of Loyalty in Leader-Led Relationships within Malay Society.* Pulau Pinang: Aliran.

Nagata, Judith. 1974. "What is a Malay? Situational Selection of Ethnic Identity in a Plural Society." *American Ethnologist* 1 (2): 331–50.

———. 1975. *Pluralism in Malaysia: Myth and Reality.* Leiden: Brill.

———. 1976. "Kinship and Social Mobility among the Malays." *Man* (n.s.) 11: 400–09.

———. 1979. *Malaysian Mosaic: Perspectives from a Poly-ethnic Society.* Vancouver: Univ. of British Columbia Press.

———. 1980. "The New Fundamentalism: Islam in Contemporary Malaysia." *Asian Thought and Society* 5: 128–41.

———. 1980. "Religious Ideology and Social Change: The Islamic Revival in Malaysia," *Pacific Affairs* 53: 405–39.

———. 1982. "Islamic Revival and the Problem of Legitimacy among Rural Religious Elites in Malaysia." *Man* (n.s.) 17: 42–57.

Newby, Howard. 1972. "Agricultural Workers in the Class Structure." *Sociological Review* 20 (3): 413–39.

———. 1975. "The Deferential Dialectic." *Comparative Studies in Society and History* 17 (2): 139–64.

Nonini, Donald M., Paul Diener, Eugene E. Robkin. 1979. "Ecology and Evolution: Population, Primitive Accumulation, and the Malay Peasantry." Typescript.

Ouchi, T., et al. 1977. *Farmer and Village in West Malaysia.* Tokyo: Univ. of Tokyo Press.

Orwell, George. 1937. *The Road to Wigan Pier.* London: Left Book Club.

Paige, Jeffrey M. 1975. *Agrarian Revolution: Social Movements and Expert Agriculture in the Underdeveloped World.* New York: Free Press.

Parkin, Frank. 1971. *Class Inequality and Political Order.* New York: Praeger.

Patnaik, Utsa. 1979. "Neo-Populism and Marxism: The Chayanovian View of the Agrarian Question and Its Fundamental Fallacy." *Journal of Peasant Studies* 6 (4): 375–420.

Piven, Frances Fox, and Richard A. Cloward. 1977. *Poor People's Movements: Why They Succeed, How They Fail.* New York: Vintage.

Popkin, Samuel L. 1979. *The Rational Peasant.* Berkeley: Univ. of California Press.

Purcall, J. T. 1971. *Rice Economy: A Case Study of Four Villages in West Malaysia.* Kuala Lumpur: Univ. of Malaya Press.

Radin, Soenarno. 1960. "Malay Nationalism, 1900–1945." *Journal of South East Asian History* 1: 1–28.

Rainwater, Lee. 1966. "Crucible of Identity: The Negro Lower Class Family." *Daedalus* 95: 172–216.

Roff, W. R. 1967. *The Origins of Malay Nationalism.* New Haven: Yale Univ. Press.
———, ed. 1974. *Kelantan: Religion, Society and Politics in a Malay State.* Kuala Lumpur: Oxford Univ. Press.

Rude, George. 1964. *The Crowd in History, 1730–1848.* New York: Wiley.

Sabel, Charles. 1982. *Work and Politics: The Division of Labor in Industry.* Cambridge: Cambridge Univ. Press.

Said, Edward. 1981. *Covering Islam: How the Media and the Experts Determine How We See the Rest of the World.* New York: Pantheon.

Salzman, Philip Carl. 1981. "Culture as Enhabilments." In *The Structure of Folk Models,* edited by Ladislav Holy and Milan Stuchlik. ASA Monograph No. 20. New York: Academic.

Sarkisyanz, E. 1965. *Buddhist Backgrounds of the Burmese Revolution.* The Hague: Martinus Nijhoff.

Scott, James C. 1976. *The Moral Economy of the Peasant: Subsistence and Rebellion in Southeast Asia.* New Haven: Yale Univ. Press.
———. 1977. "Hegemony and the Peasantry." *Politics and Society* 7 (3): 267–96.
———. 1977. "Protest and Profanation: Agrarian Revolt and the Little Tradition." *Theory and Society* 4 (1): 1–38, and 4 (2): 211–46.
———. 1979. "Revolution in the Revolution: Peasants and Commisars." *Theory and Society* 7 (1): 97–134.

Selvadurai, S. 1972. *Padi Farming in West Malaysia.* Bulletin No. 27. Kuala Lumpur: Ministry of Agriculture and Fisheries.

Shamsul, Amri Baharuddin. 1979. "The Development of Underdevelopment of the Malaysian Peasantry." *Journal of Contemporary Asia* 9: 434–54.
———. 1981. "Malay Village Politics: Some Past Observations and Recent Findings." Paper presented at Fourth National Conference of the Asian Studies Association of Australia, Melbourne.
———. 1981. "Politics of Poverty Eradication: Local Level Implementation of Development Programmes in Malaysia." Paper presented at Fifty-second ANZAAS Congress, Section 25, Anthropology. Macquarie University, North Ryde, New South Wales, Australia.

Sharil Talib. 1979. "Malay Society in the Nineteenth Century: Programme for Southeast Asian Studies." Universiti Malaya. Mimeo.

Sharom Ahmat. 1970. "The Structure of the Economy of Kedah, 1879–1905." *Journal of the Malaysian Branch of the Royal Asiatic Society* 43 (2): 1–24.
———. 1970. "The Political Structure of the State of Kedah, 1879–1905." *Journal of Southeast Asian Studies* 1 (2): 115–28.

Shukur Kassim et al. 1983. "Study of Strategy, Impact and Future Development of Integrated Rural Development Projects." 2 vols. Report prepared for the Ministry of Agriculture by the Centre for Policy Research, Universiti Sains Malaysia. Penang.

Singh, Ajit. 1978. "Laporan Kesihatan Kawasan Kedah-Perlis, 1970–1977." Alor Setar: Jabatan Pengarah Perkhidmatan Perubatan dan Kesihatan.

Skocpol, Theda. 1979. *States and Social Revolutions.* Cambridge: Cambridge Univ. Press.

Snodgrass, D. 1981. *Inequality and Economic Development in Malaysia.* Kuala Lumpur: Oxford Univ. Press.

Solzhenitsyn, A. 1968. *The First Circle.* Trans. Thomas P. Whitney. New York: Bantam.

Stenson, M. R. 1976. "Class and Race in Malaysia." *Bulletin of Concerned Asian Scholars* 8: 45–54.

Stoler, Ann. 1979. "The Limits of Class Consciousness in North Sumatra." Mimeo.

Sundaram, Jomo Kwame. 1977. "Class Formation in Malaysia." Ph.D. diss., Harvard University.

Swift, M. G. 1964. "Capital, Saving and Credit in a Malay Peasant Economy." In *Capital, Saving, and Credit in Peasant Societies,* edited by R. Firth and B. D. Yamey, 133–56. London: Allen & Unwin.

———. 1965. *Malay Peasant Society in Jelebu.* London School of Economics Monograph on Social Anthropology, No. 29. New York: Humanities Press.

Thillainathan, R. 1977. "Public Policies and Programmes for Redressing Poverty in Malaysia: A Criticial Review." In *Some Case Studies on Poverty in Malaysia: Essays Presented to Ungku Aziz,* edited by B. A. R. Mokhzani and Khoo Siew Mun. Kuala Lumpur: Persatuan Ekonomi: Malaysia Press.

Thompson, E. P. 1966. *The Making of the English Working Class.* New York: Vintage.

———. 1975. "The Crime of Anonymity." In *Albion's Fatal Tree* by Douglas Hay et al. New York: Pantheon.

———. 1978. "Eighteenth-Century English Society: Class Struggle without Class." *Social History* 3 (2).

———. 1978. *The Poverty of Theory and Other Essays.* New York: Monthly Review Press.

Thomson, A. M. 1954. *Report to the Government of the Federation of Malaya on the Marketing of Rice.* Rome: Food and Agriculture Organization.

Turner, Roy, ed. 1974. *Ethnomethodology: Selected Readings.* Harmondsworth: Penguin.

Unfederated Malay States. 1907–1956. *Annual Reports of the Advisor to the Kedah Government.* Alor Setar: Government Printer.

Uphoff, Norman, and Milton Esman. 1974. *Local Organization for Rural Development: Analysis of Asian Experience.* Ithaca: Rural Development Committee, Cornell University.

Wan Zawawi, Ibrahim. 1978. "A Malay Proletariat: The Emergence of Class Relations on a Malay Plantation." Ph.D. diss., Monash University.

Wharton, C. R. 1962. "Marketing, Merchandising and Moneylending: A Note on Middleman Monopsony in Malaya." *Malayan Economic Review* 7 (2): 24–44.

Wildman, Allan. 1970. "The February Revolution in the Russian Army." *Soviet Studies* 22 (1): 3–23.

Williams, Raymond. 1973. *The Country and the City.* New York: Oxford Univ. Press.

Willis, Paul. 1977. *Learning to Labour.* Westmead: Saxon House.

Wilson, T. B. 1955. "The Inheritance and Fragmentation of Malay Padi Lands in Krian, Perak." *Malayan Agricultural Journal* 38 (2): 78–109.

Windstedt, R. O. 1936. "Notes on the History of Kedah." *Journal of the Malay Branch of the Royal Asiatic Society* 14: 155–89.

Wolf, Eric R. 1969. *Peasant Wars of the Twentieth Century.* New York: Harper & Row.

———. 1975. *Agrarian Revolution: Social Movements and Export Agriculture in the Underdeveloped World.* New York: Free Press.

Wong Hin Soon. 1980. "Field Problems in Post-Production Handling of Padi." Working Paper No. 19. Persidangan Padi Kebangsaan Malaysia (Malaysian national conference on paddy), Kuala Lumpur, February 26–28.

Yamashita, Masanabu, Wong Hin Soon, and S. Jegatheesan. 1980. "MADA-TARC Cooperative Study, Pilot Project ACRBD 4, Muda Irrigation Scheme, Farm Management Studies." Mimeo.

Young, Kevin, William C. F. Bussink, and Parvez Hassan. 1980. *Malaysia's Growth and Equity in a Multiracial Society.* A World Bank Country Economic Report. Baltimore: Johns Hopkins Univ. Press.

Zakariah Ismail. 1980. "Economic and Social Aspects of Padi Production: Some Recent Trends." Paper presented at Seminar on Economics, Development and the Consumer, Consumers' Association of Penang. Penang.

Zola, Emile. 1980. *The Earth.* Trans. Douglas Parmee. Harmondsworth: Penguin.

Index

Abdul Majid, 5, 159, 218, 221, 226, 233

Abdul Rahim, 93, 198, 261*n*

Abdul Rahman, 22, 93, 122, 141*n*, 161*n*, 164, 171, 173, 175, 207, 234, 244, 260, 281

Abercrombie, Nicholas, 247*n*, 319*n*, 320

Abu Hassan, 21, 94, 127, 135*n*, 144, 155, 195, 227, 267, 360

Abu Saman, 206–08

Accumulation, 181–82, 234–35; of capital, 181, 184; of land, 14–17, 96–97, 149

Accusation: language of, 186–89; logic of, 160–62, 168–69, 181–83

Afifuddin Haji Omar, 72*n*, 74*n*

Agricultural labor, 51*n*, 113 and *n*, 306; gender-based division of, 117*n*, 119. *See also* Wage labor, paddy

Agriculture, 51; capitalist, 27, 42, 44, 71, 80, 110, 167 and *n*, 181–83, 184, 234–35, 241, 349; commercialization of, 71, 74, 85, 106, 107, 123–24, 181–82, 189; plantation sector, 32, 51, 55, 124, 313. *See also* Double-cropping; Green Revolution; Rice cultivation

Ahmad, Tok, 93, 165, 194–95, 208–09, 210

Akil, 217–18

Ali Abdul Rahman, 93, 132*n*

Alier, Juan Martinez, 262*n*, 322*n*, 325*n*, 347

Ali Husin, 190

Alor Setar, 52, 62, 80, 170*n*, 275

Althusser, Louis, 42, 43, 247*n*, 315, 317, 319

Amin, 4, 5, 7, 94, 97, 114, 153–54 and *n*, 162, 228, 254, 263, 267; in village politics, 127, 128, 216–17, 221, 226, 232, 360

Andalusia, rural labor of, 239, 322*n*, 325*n*, 326*n*, 347

Anderson, Perry, 278*n*, 315*n*

Ani, Haji, 13, 16, 20, 165

Ariffin, 5, 89, 93, 132*n*, 250

Arrests, political, 246, 274, 276

Arrogance, charge of, 187, 199; against the poor, 197–98, 301; against the rich, 195–97, 239

Arson, 29, 248, 249; absent in Sedaka, 273

Asian Development Bank, 50

Ayub, Haji (Haji Broom), 13–19, 21, 22–26, 188, 200*n*, 311

Azaudin, Haji, 212

Bakar "halus," 200

Bakri bin Haji Wahab, 92, 123, 132*n*, 161*n*, 171, 222, 229, 230*n*, 255, 281

Barnard, Rosemary, 72*n*, 74*n*, 253

Basir, 2, 4, 7, 11–12, 19, 89, 90, 94, 128, 131, 136, 159, 161*n*, 226, 234, 274, 277 and *n*, 278–79; in village politics, 127, 128, 131, 136, 169, 214–18, 221, 222–23, 227–33, 276–77, 360

Behavior, 38, 46; onstage vs. backstage, 284–89. *See also* Compliance and conformity; Resistance

Bell, Clive, 79*n*

Bernstein, Richard J., 45*n*

Blacks, American, 33–34, 279*n*, 329, 338

Blame, assignment of, in Sedaka: to local neighbors, 160–62, 168–69, 182; to Malays, not Chinese, 168–69, 181–83

Bloch, Marc, 332

Blum, Jerome, 294*n*

Bourdieu, Pierre, 283, 307 and *n*, 310, 323*n*, 345

Boycotts, 290, 291; farm labor, 250–55